AN ATLAS
of
ADVANCED
SURGICAL
TECHNIQUES

EDWARD J. BEATTIE, Jr., M.D.

Chief, Thoracic Service, Chairman, Department of Surgery, and Chief Medical Officer, Memorial Hospital for Cancer and Allied Diseases, New York; Member, Sloan-Kettering Institute; Professor of Surgery, Cornell University Medical College

STEVEN G. ECONOMOU, M.D.

Attending Surgeon, Presbyterian-St. Luke's Hospital, Chicago; Clinical Associate Professor of Surgery, University of Illinois College of Medicine

Illustrations by
JOANN GOLDIN

W. B. SAUNDERS COMPANY
Philadelphia, London, Toronto, 1968

W. B. Saunders Company: West Washington Square
Philadelphia, Pa. 19105

12 Dyott Street
London W.C.1

1835 Yonge Street
Toronto 7, Ontario

An Atlas of Advanced Surgical Techniques

*Dedicated
to our wives,*

*Joan
and
Kathryn*

PREFACE

The title originally proposed for this atlas was "Difficult Surgery." It soon became obvious that even minor surgery is difficult surgery for one who is inadequately trained or is well trained but has not adequately prepared himself or the patient for the operation. From our experience with the education of surgical residents, we have felt the need for a convenient surgical atlas describing difficult but primarily advanced surgical techniques. The need seems even greater for those well established operations done less frequently and for recently developed techniques in which it is difficult to separate experimentation from sound, established principles.

It is valuable that surgical trainees see operations done in a variety of ways. It may also be confusing. This atlas strives to present clearly techniques which have proved most effective in the experience of the authors. In no sense does this presentation imply that other techniques are inferior. Modifications of techniques are best learned after standard techniques are well learned.

It is important to stress principles. To the nonsurgeon, surgery appears to be only a technique. A surgical atlas would seem to substantiate this opinion. An operation should represent a small portion of the care given the patient by a surgeon. Furthermore, this atlas does not suggest that the operative procedures presented should be attempted by any but a properly qualified surgeon.

Modern techniques have tended to make surgery statistically safer, but one patient is never a statistic. The patient and his family are apprehensive, for all surgery is dangerous. Our responsibility as surgeons is to decide whether surgery is indicated. This decision can be properly made only by the well-trained, honest surgeon, who must know not only the risk of operation in the patient under consideration but also know accurately the risk of not performing surgery in this patient. The surgeon must know how to prepare the patient for surgery and how to recognize when the optimum time for surgery has arrived. There is normally a considerable difference in risk between "elective" and "emergent" surgery. The surgeon must know how to perform the proper operation when the true disease is exposed at the operating table. No matter how sophisticated the preoperative diagnostic work-up may be, the "moment of truth" is when the pathologic situation is laid bare. Finally, the surgeon must know how to care for the patient postoperatively, how to avoid complications, and how to handle complications if they occur.

A great responsibility of the surgeon is to explain accurately to the patient and his family why he feels surgery is indicated, thus providing a proper basis for "informed consent." The surgeon must gain the confidence of the patient and his family and should allay their undue apprehension without minimizing the necessary risks involved. When the patient or his family ask specific questions about the operation, its risks or its complications, the surgeon should give clear, accurate answers in proper perspective. It is just as important to do necessary operations as it is to avoid unnecessary operations. Unfortunately, the course of action in the practice of surgery is not always obvious. Problems tend to be more readily solved in retrospect. It is for this reason that the regular review of past cases is such an essential part of surgery. Because of the difficulty and inherent danger of his art, the surgeon strives to be a scientist, constantly seeking self-improvement in both knowledge and art.

Whenever a body cavity is opened surgically, except in the instance of abscess drainage, an exploration is indicated. Exploration should be done, and it should be complete. In abdominal explorations the status of the abdominal arteries and veins is apt not to be checked. In the thorax, exploration of the heart and great vessels is often omitted in pulmonary surgery just as exploration of the lung and mediastinum may be omitted during cardiac surgery. There probably are advantages in using appropriate check lists as has been suggested by Moore. Whatever system he uses, the surgeon is responsible for gaining all the information he can when the surgical exposure has been completed.

This volume presumes that a surgeon knows the basic principles of surgery: The operative area, whether skin, bowel or other, should be cleansed. Surgeons should protect their own skin and not permit the growth of pathogenic resident bacteria. The patient should be in homeostasis and in the best possible condition. The skin should be covered during the operation and kept covered until the fascia is closed. This practice tends to confine infections to subcutaneous spaces. Tissue should be kept moist and handled delicately. Sharp dissection is less traumatic than blunt dissection. Hemostasis should be precise. The kind of suture is less important than the way it is used. Dead spaces should be avoided. Cavities should usually be drained. One should seek the cause of all postoperative fevers rather than assume they are due to the operation. Antibiotics should be used as indicated rather than prophylactically. The blood volume should be maintained at normal levels. Dressings should be comfortable. Complications should be anticipated. The surgeon by an alert, compassionate and confident manner should sustain his patient.

EDWARD J. BEATTIE, JR.
STEVEN G. ECONOMOU

ACKNOWLEDGMENTS

Conception of the idea to prepare an Atlas is associated with many pleasant plans and thoughts. Executing these plans becomes another matter, however, as one quickly realizes the immense effort involved and the need and value of advice from numerous colleagues. We were fortunate to have ready access to the talent of colleagues and wish to thank those people who provided it so freely. We especially wish to thank the following who, because of special interests and effort, provided most valuable assistance with specific procedures:

Dr. Frederic A. dePeyster, Attending Surgeon, Department of General Surgery, Presbyterian-St. Luke's Hospital, Chicago: Abdominoperineal Resection and Total Colectomy.

Dr. L. Penfield Faber, Assistant Attending Surgeon, Section of Thoracic Surgery, Presbyterian-St. Luke's Hospital, Chicago: Lung Series.

Dr. Stanton A. Friedberg, Attending Surgeon and Chairman, Department of Otolaryngology and Broncho-esophagology, Presbyterian-St. Luke's Hospital, Chicago: Radical Laryngectomy.

Dr. Hushang Javid, Attending Surgeon, Section of Cardio-Vascular Surgery, Presbyterian-St. Luke's Hospital, Chicago: Carotid Endarterectomy.

Dr. Charles F. McKiel, Jr., Associate Attending Surgeon, Department of Urology, Presbyterian-St. Luke's Hospital, Chicago: Urinary Diversion.

Dr. Hassan Najafi, Assistant Attending Surgeon, Section of Cardio-Vascular Surgery, Presbyterian-St. Luke's Hospital, Chicago: Portal Hypertension.

Dr. Denes Orban, Assistant Attending Surgeon, Division of Obstetrics and Gynecology, Presbyterian-St. Luke's Hospital, Chicago: Radical Abdominal Hysterectomy and Pelvic Lymphadenectomy.

Dr. Harry W. Southwick, Associate Attending Surgeon, Department of General Surgery, Presbyterian-St. Luke's Hospital, Chicago: Forequarter Amputation and Hindquarter Amputation.

Dr. E. Wilson Staub, Attending Surgeon, Moore Memorial Hospital, Pinehurst, North Carolina: Abdominal Aortic Aneurysm.

Dr. Jerome A. Urban, Associate Attending Surgeon, Memorial Center for Cancer and Allied Diseases, New York: Radical Mastectomy—Extended.

Dr. Willet F. Whitmore, Chief, Urologic Service and Attending Surgeon, Memorial Center for Cancer and Allied Diseases, New York: Radical Nephrectomy.

The illustrations are the heart of this book. It is one thing for a surgeon to know how to perform a difficult operation and quite another for an artist to visualize and draw it in its proper components and sequence. This depiction is even more difficult with advanced surgical techniques such as those shown in this Atlas. Most of these operations involve complicated anatomical dissections which many times encompass several areas, and in which anatomical applications to the surgery at hand must be made cohesive and understandable. There are relatively few other drawings of such operations available to serve as guides. The operations shown tend not to be so numerous that one can observe a considerable number of them performed in close sequence, which would permit the many facets to be easily assembled. In essence, to compile these illustrations presented numerous problems that probably have been responsible for discouraging such an earlier venture by others. The keen perception and sketching of complex operations as they took place in surgical suites charged with urgent activity, the refinement of these drawings with true fidelity into a meaningful whole, and the final renditions with imaginative flair into plates of artistic merit and scientific accuracy make it clear that the considerable talents of Mrs. JoAnn Goldin were indispensable to this endeavor. For this we are deeply grateful.

THE AUTHORS

TABLE OF CONTENTS

ILIOINGUINAL LYMPH NODE DISSECTION (RADICAL GROIN DISSECTION)

HINDQUARTER AMPUTATION

AN ATLAS
of
ADVANCED
SURGICAL
TECHNIQUES

MAXILLECTOMY

Involvement by cancer is the most common indication for excision of the maxilla, one of the largest bones of the face. The maxillectomy may be necessary for a cancer originating extrinsically and growing up into the maxillary sinus such as a palatal cancer, or for a cancer originating from within the maxillary sinus and growing in various directions. Most primary cancers involving the maxilla are of the squamous cell variety. (Benign or malignant tumors of minor salivary gland origin and odontogenic tumors occur less commonly.) A wide variety of other primary as well as metastatic cancers may be found here; among metastatic cancers, those of renal origin are apparently the most common.

Cancer of the maxillary sinus may first present with fleeting pain and be misinterpreted as sinusitis or neuralgia. When cancers are situated on the floor of the sinus, the pain may evolve from dental nerve root involvement, making it necessary that dentists be cognizant of this possibility. Instead of pain, hypesthesia may be experienced with destruction of a nerve, most notably the infraorbital nerve. Maxillary sinusitis from an infection may be superimposed on cancer; this may lead the unwary otolaryngologist to persist with treatment of the sinusitis and to miss the primary disease. Similarly, unilateral bloody nasal discharge may not be regarded seriously. The tumors may course upward and through the thin infraorbital plate to produce unilateral exophthalmos; they may also give rise to severe epistaxis by growing medially through and into the lateral nasal cavity. Those tumors growing inferiorly will produce a downward bulge of the palate or swelling of the gingiva.

There is variable difficulty in confirming the diagnosis of maxillary tumors. Those invading the maxilla from the outside are easiest to diagnose by virtue of accessibility. A sublabial maxillary antrostomy may be needed to reach a lesion arising within the sinus unless the lesion has come to the surface, in which case only a biopsy need be taken for confirmation of the diagnosis. X-rays of the maxillary sinuses are diagnostically valuable, especially if bone destruction can be demonstrated. Laminagrams are particularly helpful in determining which area has been destroyed and to what extent. Lateral laminagrams are best for determination of the extent of any sphenoidal involvement in posteriorly placed tumors. Laminagraphy is a prognostic aid in that those lesions demonstrated to be in the ethmoidal, sphenoidal and pterygomaxillary areas are the most difficult to cure by operation and may well be treated by maxillary fenestration and irradiation. Bone destruction may, on occasion, be seen with benign tumors, so this finding is not necessarily pathognomonic of cancer. Cytologic examination of maxillary sinus washings is helpful if cancer cells can be demonstrated, but negative findings do not rule out the diagnosis. Placement of water-soluble contrast media into the maxillary sinus aids in accurate delineation of the intracavitary extent of the tumor.

In all presumed maxillary cancers considered nonresectable and for which radiotherapy is planned, a Caldwell-Luc maxillary antrostomy is necessary and serves two purposes: tissue can be obtained for microscopic confirmation of the diagnosis, and there is also established a portal for drainage of destroyed and secondarily infected maxillary contents. The Caldwell-Luc antrostomy can be used even for resectable lesions to obtain tissue for microscopic diagnosis, and this antral opening can be excised with the specimen during the maxillectomy. Tumors about to penetrate the medial maxillary wall or the hard palate can have tissue for diagnosis excised through these areas, again with the provision that these areas be included in the surgical specimen.

The maxilla is pyramidal in shape, with the base facing medially. It helps to form the boundaries of three cavities: the medial cavity, the lateral wall and floor of the nose; the upper, the floor of the orbit; and the lower, the roof of the mouth. Thus, although the maxilla is located superficially, it cannot easily be removed en bloc without destroying the integrity of one or more of the adjoining cavities. The Weber-Fergusson incision is used most commonly because it provides the exposure necessary for a wide resection. There is as yet no unanimity of opinion on the degree to which surgery and radiotherapy should complement or supplement each other.

Because they are so well ensconced, it is virtually impossible to excise en bloc the ethmoid and sphenoid sinuses. Most surely, patients with such involvement, those with cancer of the pterygomaxillary area and those who have undergone inadequate surgical excision should receive postoperative radiotherapy.

References

Baker, R.: Carcinoma of maxillary sinus. Arch. Oto-laryng. 84:201, 1965.
Frazell, E. L.: The surgical treatment of cancer of the paranasal sinuses. Laryngoscope 65:557, 1955.
Rossi, G., Demichelis, G., and Cherubini, E.: Primary malignant tumors of the maxillary sinus—A clinical study. Acta oto-laryng. Suppl. 181.

Maxillectomy

A   This view of the skull shows some of the landmarks that will be utilized in performing this operation. The heavy dashed line indicates where bone will be cut on the anterior surface. Notice that the hard palate is cut just lateral to the septum and continues backward in this plane to the soft palate. On the right side of the face the incision is in line with the pterygomaxillary fissure so that as the maxilla is brought forward later the pterygoid plate remains. If consistent with an adequate operation, a substantial portion of the zygomatic bone should be retained so that the cheek contour is not altered significantly. One can see at this point why it is necessary to disengage some of the anterior fibers of the masseter muscle from this anterior portion of the zygomatic bone to gain the necessary exposure. Although it is sometimes necessary to separate the tip of the coronoid process for better exposure, one can usually gain the needed exposure without this maneuver.

B   A substantial portion of the upper part of the masseter muscle and the ramus of the mandible have been removed for a better view of the deeper anatomy pertinent to this operation. The temporal muscle is not shown; it originates in the temporal fossa and passes under the zygomatic arch to insert at the coronoid process and the anterior portion of the mandible, both of which have been removed here for better visualization of the underlying structures. The internal pterygoid muscle will require division of those fibers which originate at the maxillary tuberosity. The external pterygoid muscle is disturbed only in the area of the lateral pterygoid plate, which is one of its points of origin. Obviously, if the lateral pterygoid plate is also to be removed, the external pterygoid muscle must be divided.

Most of the blood supply to the maxilla comes from the internal maxillary artery, which is the larger of the two terminal branches of the external carotid artery. Notice how it arises behind the neck of the mandible and makes its way anteriorly. Here it is shown superficial to the internal pterygoid muscle although it frequently runs deep to it. If location and size of tumor or previous radiotherapy leads one to anticipate excessive bleeding, the technique described herein can easily be used to locate and ligate the internal maxillary artery early in the operation and thus lessen bleeding considerably. It is not reasonable to ligate the external carotid artery for the same benefit. A small portion of the blood supply to the maxilla comes from the ethmoidal branches of the internal carotid artery.

C
C₁   Digital control of the upper lip steadies it for the incision which must be made cleanly and also provides temporary hemostasis. The circumoral artery should be clamped accurately and tied with 4-0 chromic catgut so that a minimum of foreign or devitalized tissue remains in this area. The incision is centrally placed, although some prefer to make it central up to the vermilion border and then to deviate laterally to the ridge of the columella before proceeding upward again. At some point both upper central incisor teeth must be extracted; occasionally, only the one on the operative side need be removed.

D   The incision continues in the nasolabial fold and progresses above the nares and to the lateral aspect of the nose where a natural crease is lacking. The superior labial artery will be encountered and will require division. The angular artery is also often, and sometimes recurrently, in the line of incision. The incision is carried to the inner aspect of the lower lid, and care is taken not to damage the lacrimal sac. The incision is then extended laterally. This lateral incision must be made close to the inferior tarsus even though this is more difficult than placing it in the crease commonly seen over the infraorbital ridge. With the latter placement, the loose areolar tissue between the incision and the tarsus will often become edematous postoperatively, sometimes chronically, with an unfavorable "baggy-eyed" look unilaterally. A bland ointment should be placed under the eyelids before beginning the operation and the lids kept closed with a lightly placed single stitch.

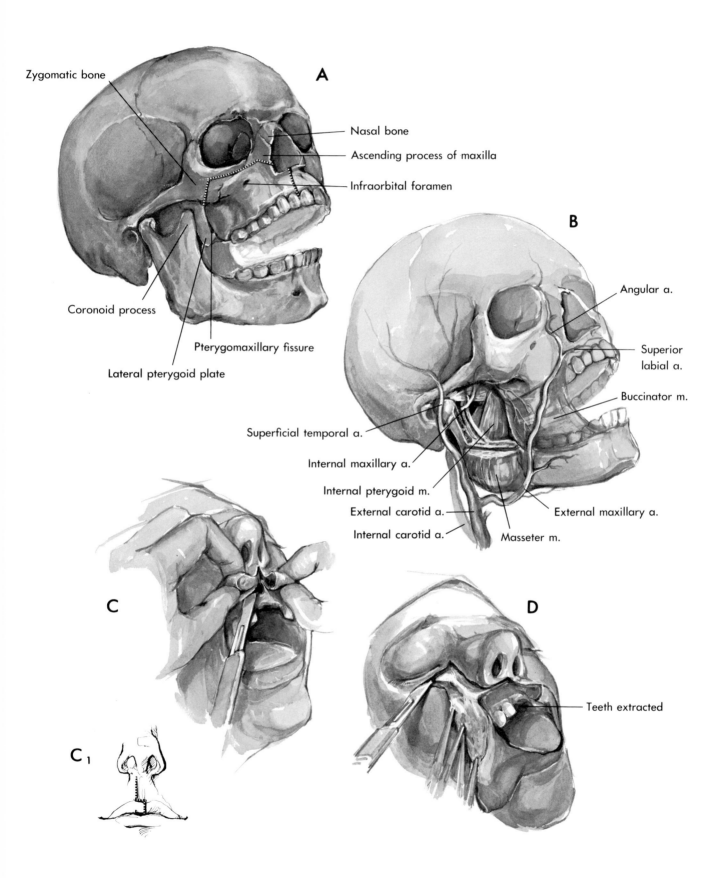

Zygomatic bone

A

Nasal bone

Ascending process of maxilla

Infraorbital foramen

Coronoid process

Pterygomaxillary fissure

Lateral pterygoid plate

B

Angular a.

Superior labial a.

Buccinator m.

Superficial temporal a.

Internal maxillary a.

Internal pterygoid m.

External carotid a.

Internal carotid a.

External maxillary a.

Masseter m.

C

C₁

D

Teeth extracted

E The full thickness of the cheek is dissected off the anterior portion of the maxilla. If the cancer has involved the anterior maxillary wall, the flap is made thinner because of the likelihood that there will be more scarring and more difficulty in preventing depression of the cheek when final healing has occurred. The flap is dissected along the buccogingival sulcus as far posteriorly as the pterygomaxillary fissure. The anterosuperior fibers of the masseter muscle are removed from the zygoma. The infraorbital nerve will require division, as will the infraorbital artery, a branch of the internal carotid artery. If a Caldwell-Luc procedure has been performed for diagnosis or incidental to preoperative radiotherapy, the incision in the buccogingival sulcus should encompass this antral opening. We, however, do not follow the practice of some in doing an anteromaxillary fenestration to assess the extent of involvement. In practice the posterior recesses, which are the areas most difficult to evaluate and which one wishes to encompass if involved, cannot be evaluated any better through a window than by the preoperative studies, unless one makes an excessively large opening, which is likely to violate the physical integrity of the cancer.

F Work on the bone during this operation may be done largely with only osteotomes or Gigli saws with but incidental use of bone-cutting forceps, rongeurs, rasps and motor-driven saws, burrs and drills. This is largely a matter of preference but there is advantage to specific tools. If there is cracking of the bone with the osteotome applied as shown, its direction can be changed so that it will cut upward and on the same plane as the bone. It would make its first bone purchase at the lateralmost aspect of the pyriform aperture. The nose will require more medial displacement than shown here. The eggshell consistency of the bone along the infraorbital ridge makes it liable to cracking without regard to a true line of cutting. If one wishes also to excise some of the infraorbital plate, the appropriate divisions of the infraorbital ridge are made with a fine bone-cutting forceps.

G
G₁ Prior to division of the palate, the palatal mucosa along the proposed line of incision should be infiltrated with 1:1000 solution of adrenaline to reduce oozing; otherwise, an excessive amount of cauterization may be necessary. The osteotome is driven backward to the soft palate and as it wedges its way it sometimes loosens the specimen slightly. Since the brisk bleeding really begins at this point, it is well to restate that the aim of this operation is to excise the tumor widely, to keep the specimen of the contained cancer intact and to do this with a minimal loss of blood. As the bleeding cannot really be stopped with the usual clamping and will have to be sucked away to provide reasonable visibility, one must know how to proceed with deliberate but controlled speed in removing the specimen so that the bleeding can then be controlled with hemostats and pressure.

It is this necessity for speed from this point on that the use of Gigli saws helps to overcome. This requires placement of both the Gigli saws prior to commencement of the sawing. At point 1 a wedge is removed from the zygomatic bone up toward the infraorbital ridge. A similar piece is removed from the ascending process of the maxilla at point 2. A medium-sized ligature carrier is used to pass a silk ligature through the apices of the two wedges, and the ligature used to pull through the Gigli saw. It should be passed behind the lateral pterygoid plate if one intends to do a more radical excision or wishes to avoid having to disengage this bone later. This, of course, means that the exposure initially would require that the external pterygoid muscle and the coronoid process be divided. This technique removes somewhat more of the ascending process of the maxilla. Points 3 and 4 show the starting points for the second Gigli saw, which is used to divide the hard palate. A small sharp hemostat is used to go immediately behind the hard palate through point 4, and point 3 is at the lower and lateralmost aspect of the pyriform aperture.

H As the incision reaches the posterior portion of the hard palate it is directed laterally toward the maxillary tuberosity, from which protuberance it is necessary to separate some of the fibers of the internal pterygoid muscle.

I The dashed line in this drawing indicates the pterygomaxillary fissure. An osteotome is used to wedge the maxillary tuberosity. Some of the pertinent anatomic landmarks

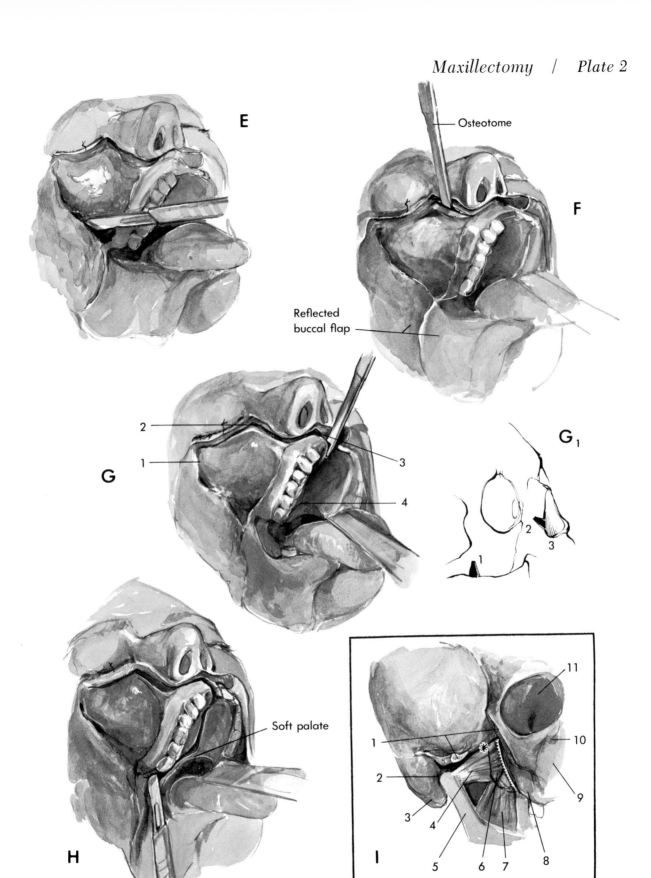

E

F

Osteotome

Reflected
buccal flap

G

2

1

3

4

G₁

2

3

1

H

Soft palate

I

11

1

10

2

3

4

9

5   6   7   8

are identified: (1) point of removal of zygomatic bone for better demonstration of underlying structures, (2) temporomandibular joint, (3) mastoid process, (4) external pterygoid muscle, (5) ramus of mandible, (6) lateral pterygoid plate, (7) internal pterygoid muscle, (8) maxillary tuberosity, (9) anterior wall of maxilla, (10) infraorbital foramen, and (11) orbit.

The coronoid process is not in place. If the lateral pterygoid plate is also to be excised, the Gigli saw engages at the point marked with an asterisk (*). One can see, as is mentioned in Figure G, that this requires more exposure and dissection laterally but at the same time offers a better chance to ligate the internal maxillary artery.

Maxillectomy *(continued)*

J   A large bone-cutting forceps is used to section the zygoma up to the lateral aspect of the infraorbital ridge. This and the previous step are done in concert. The specimen is being displaced and rotated medially. Some rocking motion is usually required to free the specimen.

K   As the specimen is removed, bleeding is evident from many sites, the major one being the internal maxillary artery. If this artery is seen and can be clamped quickly, so much the better; otherwise, the wound should be packed to allow for spontaneous cessation of bleeding from most of the smaller vessels. The pressure can be kept in one area while another is made dry by clamp, transfixion ligature or electrocoagulation. The latter is especially valuable along the palatal incision. The operation thus far has not removed the ethmoidal or sphenoidal mucosa or sometimes even all the mucosa of the maxillary antrum, and this causes the disturbing feeling of having to do this piecemeal. These excisions are not routine, however, but are influenced by considerations such as location of the primary locus of the cancer, its size and the direction of spread, all of which are determined by opening the surgical specimen. If a portion of the infraorbital plate is removed, a comparable sling should be provided at this time from a piece of fascia lata. Removal of all the infraorbital plate will require more extensive reconstruction. One way is to fashion such a plate with a wafer of cancellous bone obtained from the iliac crest.

L   The raw surgical surfaces are covered with a thin split thickness skin graft which has been "pie crusted" extensively. When possible it is held in position at the periphery with a running stitch of chromic catgut. Even if not grafted, all the areas will slowly but eventually epithelialize. In the buccal area the cicatricial scarring will pull the cheek inward, and for this reason the surgeon should graft this area at least.

M   The subcutaneous tissue and the labial mucosa are approximated with interrupted stitches of 3-0 chromic catgut. It is important to approximate the vermilion border accurately because even a minimal discrepancy here will be obvious later. Fine nylon is used to close the skin. The operative defect is packed moderately firmly with fine-mesh petrolatum gauze. This keeps the skin graft in place, discourages the collection of serum underneath it and, as well, prevents fluids from being regurgitated through the nose.

N   No dressing is applied to the face wound but it is cleansed three times daily with a medicated ointment applied with cotton applicators.

    The patient is allowed free activity and may take oral fluids as desired. A small caliber plastic nasogastric feeding tube, placed in position in the operating room, is used to feed the patient until he can resume an adequate oral intake of food. The petrolatum gauze is removed on the third day and replaced twice daily with an obturator fashioned of Ivalon sponge. This material is easily trimmed, is soft when wet and can be easily and gently positioned. It is inert and inexpensive, and one sponge can be washed while the other is in position.

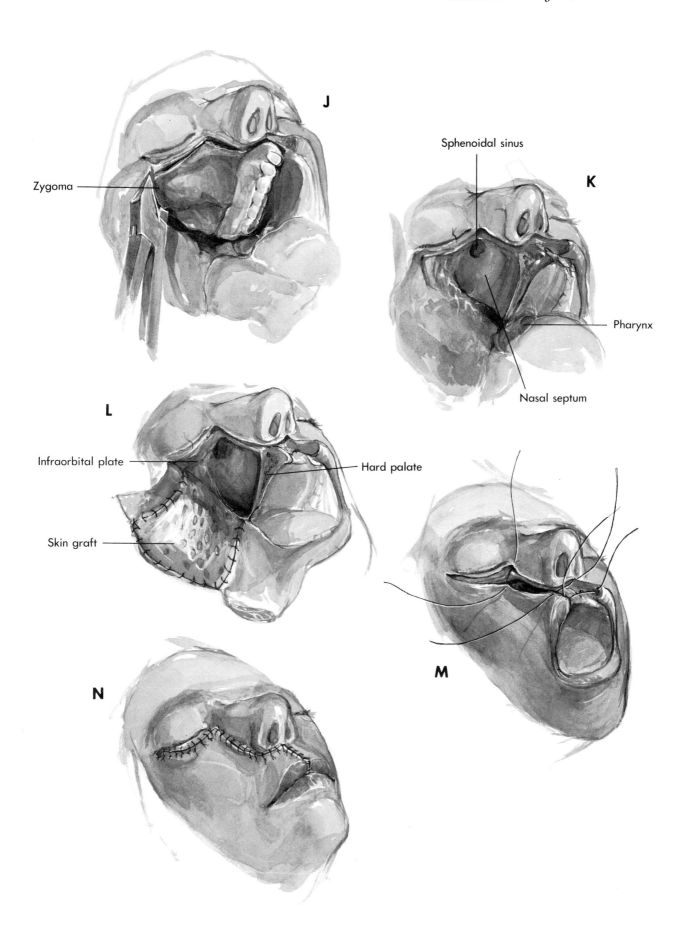

PAROTIDECTOMY

Advances in surgical procedures for excision of parotid tumors have not kept proper pace with those for other areas of the body, even though adequate anesthesia and other ancillary aids have become available and the operation hardly threatens life. Several reasons for this tardiness become apparent and understandable. There is natural reluctance to operate on, or even incise near, a nerve whose injury will produce an obvious and permanent testament to a technical error. This fosters in many a tendency to ignore these tumors — an attitude abetted by the lethargic growth rate of many of them. Often then when the patients do come to operation the tumors are "shelled out" along the plane of their pseudocapsule. Unfortunately, the benign mixed tumor, which is most often handled in this manner, has usually pierced the pseudocapsule so that numerous microscopic teats of tumor lie outside what is erroneously believed to be a confining capsule. The "shelling out" leaves behind a number of nidi which grow and reappear as multiple tumors within the operative field.

Surgery for this type of recurrence is associated, in turn, with a recurrence rate at least quadruple that of the initial operation. Furthermore, neglected or recurrent benign mixed tumors exhibit a disconcerting ability to become malignant. These circumstances influence some surgeons to shy away from these tumors but challenge others to attack the problem more aggressively. Finally, it has taken some time for the accumulation of sufficient information on the spectral clinical behavior of these various tumors to enable the surgeon to treat them with greater confidence and specificity and, consequently, better results.

Approximately 75 per cent of parotid tumors are benign. Of these about 60 per cent are mixed tumors, 5 per cent are Warthin's tumors, another 5 per cent being cysts, and another 5 per cent comprising a miscellany of lesions or inflammations. The remaining 25 per cent of parotid tumors are malignant and cover a wide range of lethality, about one-half being of minimal or moderate malignancy.

The clinician who treats patients with parotid tumors will recognize the difficulty often encountered in differentiating between the benign and the malignant, not to mention inflammatory processes and adjacent tumors that have nothing or little to do with the parotid gland. Since a full 10 per cent of parotidectomies, in retrospect, would not have been necessary had the correct diagnosis been known, it is essential that a concerted effort be made to keep surgical procedures to a minimum. The usual mass of or over the parotid gland is obvious; often, however, this may be sufficiently minimal or subtle in its diffuseness as to lull the unwary. Lymphomas, sarcoidosis, metastatic melanomas or epidermoid carcinomas, Sjögren's syndrome and Mikulicz's disease may first manifest themselves in the parotid gland area. Clearly, then, the physical examination should be general, with special emphasis on a thorough oropharyngeal examination to exclude a primary tumor in this area.

Although attempting to define the nature of a mass within or over the parotid salivary gland by palpation can be most difficult, there are some signs and symptoms that are helpful — but only helpful, not clearly diagnostic. Pain or redness usually indicates an acute inflammatory process; periodicity and local distress and swelling usually indicate chronic sialadenitis. Most hemangiomas and lymphangiomas are compressible; Warthin's tumors usually feel soft. Dryness of the eyes and arthritis in association with periodic bilateral parotid swelling should alert one to a possible diagnosis of Mikulicz's disease or Sjögren's syndrome. Drug ingestion may occasionally cause parotid swelling. A noninfectious parotid mass that causes facial nerve paralysis almost always indicates malignant disease. Firmness or a "rubber-like" feel to the tumor cannot, of itself, be of much help in differentiating between benign and malignant tumors. If one suspects a parotid salivary calculus, properly taken x-rays may demonstrate it. Sialography, properly performed and interpreted, is also valuable in diagnosing some parotid swellings. Finally, it must be remembered that the major cause of parotid swelling is mumps.

A surgeon can never be certain when he may have to sacrifice the facial nerve in order to properly treat a cancerous tumor of the parotid gland. The patient, therefore, should always be told of this possibility — the gravity of the presentation being influenced by the surgeon's confidence in what will probably be the microscopic diagnosis of the neoplasm. If there is a probability of facial nerve sacrifice, the patient will be encouraged by being informed of the availability (but without guarantee of success) of synchronous nerve grafting. Just as important, the patient should be gently advised of the possibility of transient or permanent paralysis as a result of injury to a branch of the facial nerve even if the tumor to be excised is benign. A surgeon who performs parotidectomy properly will appreciate the fact that this happens under the best of circumstances. Such undesirable iatrogenic sequelae can be kept to a minimum only by the surgeon who carefully examines the patient preoperatively, is thoroughly acquainted with the anatomy of this area and operates in accordance with sound surgical principles.

References

Anderson, R., and Byars, L. T.: Surgery of the Parotid Gland. St. Louis, The C. V. Mosby Co., 1965.
Beahrs, O. H., and Adson, M. D.: The surgical anatomy and technique of parotidectomy. Am. J. Surg. 95:885, 1958.
Davis, R. A., Anson, B. J., Budinger, J. M., and Kurth, L. E.: Surgical anatomy of the facial nerve and parotid gland based upon a study of 350 cervicofacial halves. Surg. Gynec. & Obst. 102:4 and 385, 1956.
Purcelli, F. M.: Exposure of the facial nerve in parotid surgery: A study of the use of the tympanomastoid suture as a landmark. Am. Surgeon 29:10 and 657, 1963.

Parotidectomy

A   This view of the skull, with the structures in the parotid area cut transversely, will demonstrate the anatomical relationships. The parotid gland is in an area of moderate anatomical complexity. Because of its intimate association with the facial nerve, however, it is necessary that in the performance of a parotidectomy the surgeon be conversant with this complexity and be able to perform precise and delicate surgery with confidence. The parotid gland lies in a fossa that is bordered by bony structures with variable completeness on all but the lateral and inferior sides. The anterior surface of the mastoid process lies posteriorly; posterosuperiorly, the external acoustic meatus; anterosuperiorly, the head of the mandible; and anteriorly, the ramus of the mandible. Deep to the parotid are the styloid process and the transverse process of the atlas.

The muscles that confine the parotid gland are, posteriorly, the upper portion of the sternocleidomastoid muscle, which also covers the lateral surface of the mastoid process. Medially are the posterior belly of the digastricus muscle, which originates from the medial aspect of the tip of the mastoid process, and those muscles arising from the styloid process, namely, the stylohyoid, styloglossus and stylopharyngeus. Only the more superficial stylohyoid muscle becomes pertinent in the usual exposure for a parotidectomy. Anteriorly, the masseter muscle that covers the ramus and angle of the mandible is itself overlapped posteriorly by the anterior portion of the parotid gland. The pterygoid muscles are related to the anterior aspect of the retromandibular portion of the gland.

The posterior auricular artery, a branch of the external carotid at the level of the digastricus muscle, courses posteriorly and superiorly to assume a position immediately in front of the mastoid process and thus lies in the direct line of dissection if this route is chosen for identifying the main trunk of the facial nerve. The external carotid artery assumes a more superficial position at the upper margin of the stylohyoid muscle and enters the parotid gland soon afterward.

The internal maxillary artery is seen running anteriorly deep to the ascending ramus of the mandible. The terminal portion of the parotid duct is shown at the point at which it has crossed the masseter muscle and at its anterior margin turns in sharply to pierce the buccinator muscle.

B   The jugular vein, like the internal carotid artery, does not even come into view in the performance of a parotidectomy, but some of the branches leading into it are important as landmarks. They are also sources of bleeding which can be dangerous, especially if one attempts to stop the bleeding with carelessly applied hemostats, "blind" stick-ties or electrocoagulation when working close to the facial nerve.

The posterior facial vein is formed near the root of the zygoma and passes downward behind the ramus of the mandible and through the parotid gland. In its course it receives about six branches before it bifurcates. An anterior ramus joins the anterior facial vein to form the usually short common facial vein, which empties into the internal jugular vein found running deep to the sternocleidomastoid muscle. The posterior ramus of the posterior facial vein joins with the smaller posterior auricular vein to form the external jugular vein, which is situated superficial to the sternocleidomastoid muscle.

The parotid gland, especially its larger superficial lobe, can have various shapes, the most common being that of an inverted triangle. Superiorly, it almost reaches the zygomatic arch; posteriorly, it reaches to and slightly overlaps the sternocleidomastoid muscle; anteriorly, it overlaps the masseter muscle, sometimes extending along the parotid duct. In about 15 per cent of patients accessory parotid tissue, discontinuous with the main mass, is found along the course of the parotid duct even up to the point at which it turns into the oral cavity.

The parotid gland has lateral, anterior and posterior surfaces, there being some disagreement on whether there is a fourth deep surface or whether the posterior and deep surfaces are one, creating a three-sided wedge with one surface facing the outside. Inferiorly and superiorly, the gland tapers to a border rather than a surface.

There have been described a superficial and a deep fascia with intervening septa

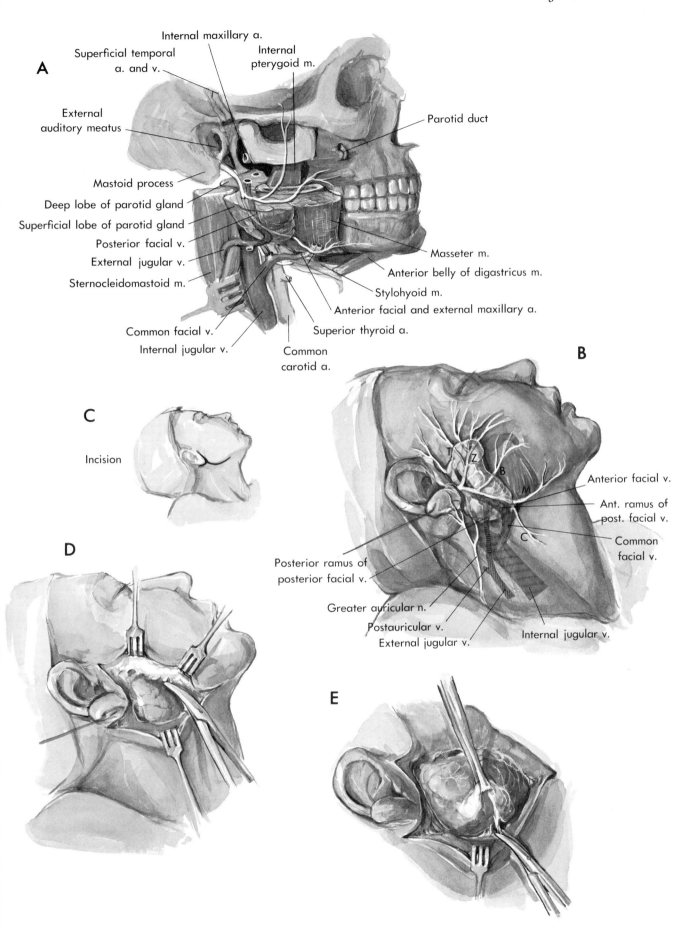

A

Internal maxillary a.

Superficial temporal a. and v.

Internal pterygoid m.

External auditory meatus

Parotid duct

Mastoid process

Deep lobe of parotid gland

Superficial lobe of parotid gland

Posterior facial v.

External jugular v.

Sternocleidomastoid m.

Masseter m.

Anterior belly of digastricus m.

Stylohyoid m.

Anterior facial and external maxillary a.

Common facial v.

Internal jugular v.

Superior thyroid a.

Common carotid a.

C

Incision

B

T Z B

M

Anterior facial v.

Ant. ramus of post. facial v.

C

Common facial v.

Posterior ramus of posterior facial v.

Greater auricular n.

Postauricular v.

External jugular v.

Internal jugular v.

D

E

which fuse peripherally to enclose the gland; the superficial fascia contains the platysma muscle, the deeper fascia enveloping the masseter muscle. This facial tissue and the connective tissue surrounding that portion of the facial nerve within the gland are of great value to the surgeon in developing the proper planes of dissection.

The facial nerve invariably emerges as a single trunk from the stylomastoid foramen, making its appearance to the surgeon 1 cm. deep to the anterior border of the mastoid process at a point 1 cm. from the tip of the process. It then divides into temporofacial and cervicofacial branches which divide further into (T) temporal, (Z) zygomatic, (B) buccal, (M) mandibular and (C) cervical branches. Further discussion on the facial nerve is to be found under Plate 3.

The greater auricular nerve emerges from the posterior portion of the sternocleidomastoid muscle at its midpoint and on its upward course swings around to lie on the superficial surface of the muscle and parallel and posterior to the external jugular vein. It trifurcates into mastoid, facial and auricular branches. This nerve is routinely divided during parotidectomy, the significance being the hypesthesia of the area postoperatively, especially of the earlobe. Patients can be annoyed by this, especially female patients who lose earrings or screw them on too tightly without knowing it.

C General anesthesia administered endotracheally is used routinely. Transfusion of blood is not necessary for patients having a superficial parotidectomy but may be needed if a total parotidectomy or an accessory radical neck dissection is performed. A small sandbag is placed under the shoulders of the patient and the head is rotated opposite the side being operated on.

A pledget of sterile cotton is placed in the external auditory canal and the area painted and draped to leave the side of the face and entire ear exposed. A Y-shaped incision is preferred because it offers wide exposure and can also be extended for the performance of a radical neck dissection if this becomes necessary. The incision is begun in front of the tragus, goes under and about 1 cm. from the base of the earlobe and then up behind the ear to a point about 2 cm. from the tip of the mastoid. From the lateralmost portion of the incision an arm is extended downward and forward, skirting the angle of the mandible and terminating several centimeters beyond this point.

D The anterior flap is made first so that small vessels emanating from the surface of the parotid gland are given time to stop bleeding spontaneously while the other flaps are being developed. Upward traction is applied to the skin edges with small rakes, and small Metzenbaum or even round-tipped manicure scissors are used for a spreading and cutting technique. The plane of the dissection proceeds just above the superficial parotid fascia. Small but distinct fibrous septa from the superficial surface of the parotid are encountered and divided while the flap is developed. The margins of the mobilization anteriorly extend to just short of the gland periphery. The earlobe is mobilized to the external auditory canal, folded upward and held in this position with a single stitch.

E The external jugular vein and the greater auricular nerve are divided. Bleeding points on the skin flaps are electrocoagulated and those on the gland are tied with 3-0 chromic catgut. The anterior border of the posterior belly of the digastric muscle is sought, keeping in mind the location of the various portions of the facial vein and of the cervical branch of the facial nerve.

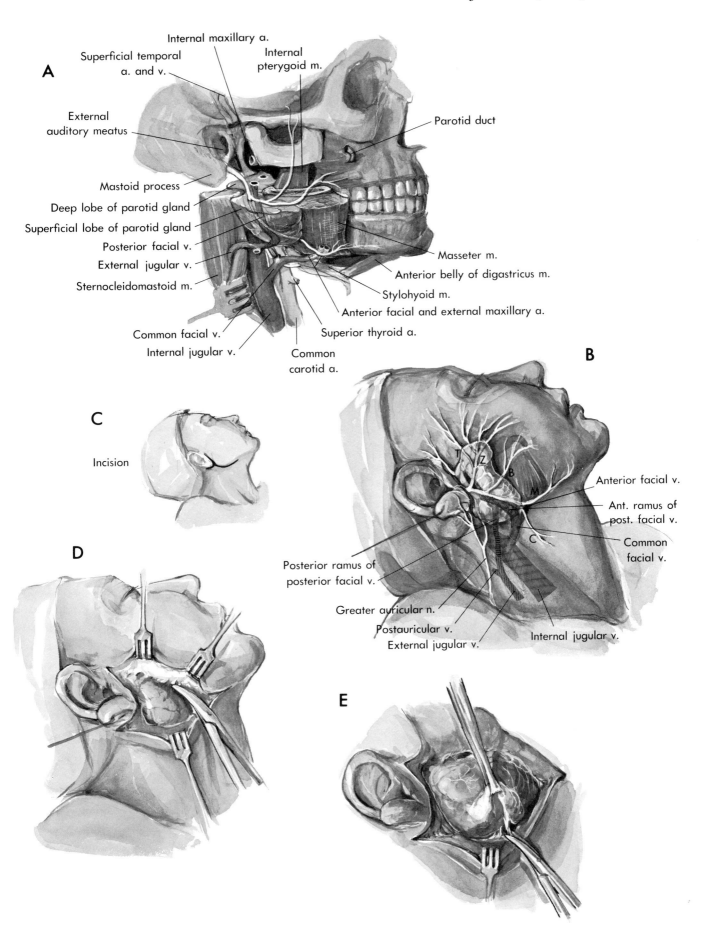

A

Superficial temporal a. and v.

Internal maxillary a.

Internal pterygoid m.

External auditory meatus

Parotid duct

Mastoid process

Deep lobe of parotid gland

Superficial lobe of parotid gland

Posterior facial v.

External jugular v.

Sternocleidomastoid m.

Masseter m.

Anterior belly of digastricus m.

Stylohyoid m.

Anterior facial and external maxillary a.

Superior thyroid a.

Common facial v.

Internal jugular v.

Common carotid a.

B

C

Incision

T Z B M C

Anterior facial v.

Ant. ramus of post. facial v.

Common facial v.

Posterior ramus of posterior facial v.

Greater auricular n.

Postauricular v.

External jugular v.

Internal jugular v.

D

E

F Two important objectives in performing a superficial parotid lobectomy are the adequate removal of the lobe and the confined tumor with proper safeguarding of the facial nerve. Uncertainty about a reliable and safe method of identifying the nerve has been the cause of inadequate surgery or reluctance to perform any.

The facial nerve can be identified either peripherally or centrally, certain factors favoring each approach. If given a choice, we prefer to identify the main nerve trunk and to proceed peripherally with the dissection. We believe that the main trunk is easier to locate than a peripheral branch, although, admittedly, injury to the main nerve trunk is a more serious accident. However, this is not so likely to happen as when attempting to locate a peripheral branch.

Although there are a number of valuable landmarks for locating the main trunk of the facial nerve, no single one can be constantly relied upon. The facial nerve can usually be found about 1 cm. deep to the anterior lateral border of the mastoid process from a point 1 cm. cephalad from the tip of the process. The nerve is the only structure in this area coursing in a posteroanterior direction and is 2 to 3 mm. in diameter. The styloid process may serve as an adequate guide to the location of the main trunk, but is absent or cannot be utilized in about half the patients and has the serious drawback of lying deep to the structure being sought. The nerve can also be found about 1 cm. medial to the inferolateral extreme of the tympanomastoid fissure. About 1 cm. anterior to the anterior margin of the mastoid process, the nerve gradually assumes a more superficial position—a point that must be remembered if the surgeon chooses to approach the main trunk here.

G₁ to G₄ Although the facial nerve is constant in emerging as a single trunk and in its primary divisions into temporofacial and cervicofacial trunks, there is considerable variation in the method and course of its subsequent ramifications. These line drawings demonstrate the more common variations. If one chooses to identify the main trunk of the nerve, specific knowledge of these variations is of limited practical value. They can hardly be too valuable to one choosing to isolate a peripheral branch, except to point up the considerable variation in their location and the tedious work involved in locating the nerves terminally, where they measure about 1 mm. in diameter. These drawings also show the variations in anastomoses between the branches. The mandibular branch anastomoses with other branches least commonly, so that injury to this branch is more certain to result in permanent paresis of the affected muscles.

H I The capsule at the inferoposterior margin of the parotid gland is grasped with Hayes Martin forceps or with Allis clamps and retracted anteriorly and superficially while it is separated from the sternocleidomastoid muscle and the origin of the posterior belly of the digastricus deep along the anterior margin of the mastoid process.

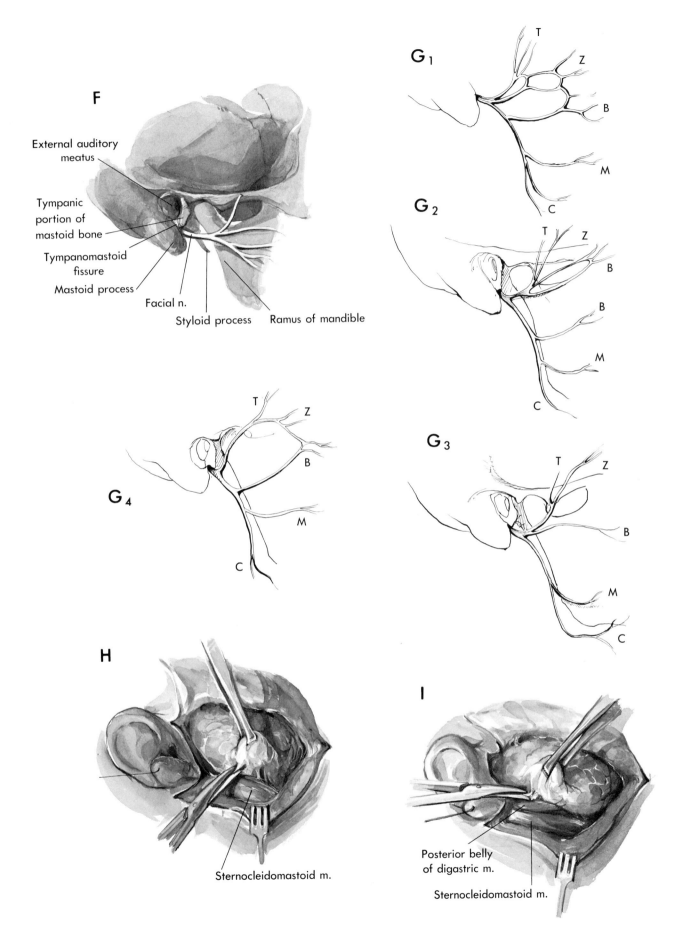

F

External auditory meatus

Tympanic portion of mastoid bone

Tympanomastoid fissure

Mastoid process

Facial n.

Styloid process

Ramus of mandible

G₁

T

Z

B

M

C

G₂

T

Z

B

B

M

C

G₃

T

Z

B

M

C

G₄

T

Z

B

M

C

H

Sternocleidomastoid m.

I

Posterior belly of digastric m.

Sternocleidomastoid m.

J
K
L
The dissection continues with the gland being retracted anteriorly and superficially and the nerve being uncovered from greater toward lesser trunks. In Figure K a spoon is shown being used since it can be an ideal retractor and is often held by the surgeon's free hand. A definite plane of dissection exists where the nerve traverses the gland. The surgeon should strive to remain in this plane for the sake of an easier dissection; he should also keep the nerve in constant view as he frees it. Venous bleeding is stopped by compression as one proceeds with the dissection. When handled in this fashion many such bleeding points stop spontaneously by the time the parotid lobe is removed. There should not be undue reliance on this method of hemostasis, however, as a bloody field is conducive to errors in interpretation as to what constitutes a nerve filament. If bleeders must be secured, it should be done with great care and with certainty that no nerves are traumatized.

M
The superficial lobe has been removed. Residual bleeding points are carefully clamped and tied with 4-0 chromic catgut. The letters indicate the various divisions of the exposed facial nerve.

N
Sometimes the tumor will be situated in the posterior portion of the gland, effectively thwarting the use of this route toward a safe exposure and dissection of the main trunk of the nerve. In such instances a retrograde dissection from a peripheral branch is necessary. For several reasons we prefer to use the cervical branch of the facial nerve for this purpose. It lies in proximity to and runs in the same direction as the posterior facial vein, the latter structure being relatively easy to find. Also, in the event the nerve is damaged in the course of initial dissection, the paralysis of the platysma muscle is of no consequence.

O
P
The posterior facial vein is identified and along with it the cervical branch of the facial nerve. The nerve is exposed retrogradely to a bifurcation, whereupon this branch is followed distally. In the process, the superficial lobe of the parotid and the contained tumor are reflected superiorly. The process of progressive retrograde dissection is continued until eventually the main trunk of the nerve is identified. The superior half of the dissection is now done, proceeding in a peripheral direction.

After hemostasis is assured, a small Penrose drain is exteriorized from the inferior aspect of the wound and the subcutaneous tissue is approximated with 4-0 chromic catgut. The skin is approximated with interrupted vertical mattress stitches of 4-0 nylon. A figure-of-eight pressure dressing is applied. The patient is observed immediately upon awakening for evidence that all branches of the nerve are functioning, since some hours later weakness or paresis of one or several branches may be present. If the surgeon has observed adequate function immediately postoperatively, the patient as well as the surgeon can be assured that the paresis is probably temporary. The drain is removed in two days, the stitches in five, and the patient discharged from the hospital. Salivary discharge from the drain site is practically always temporary.

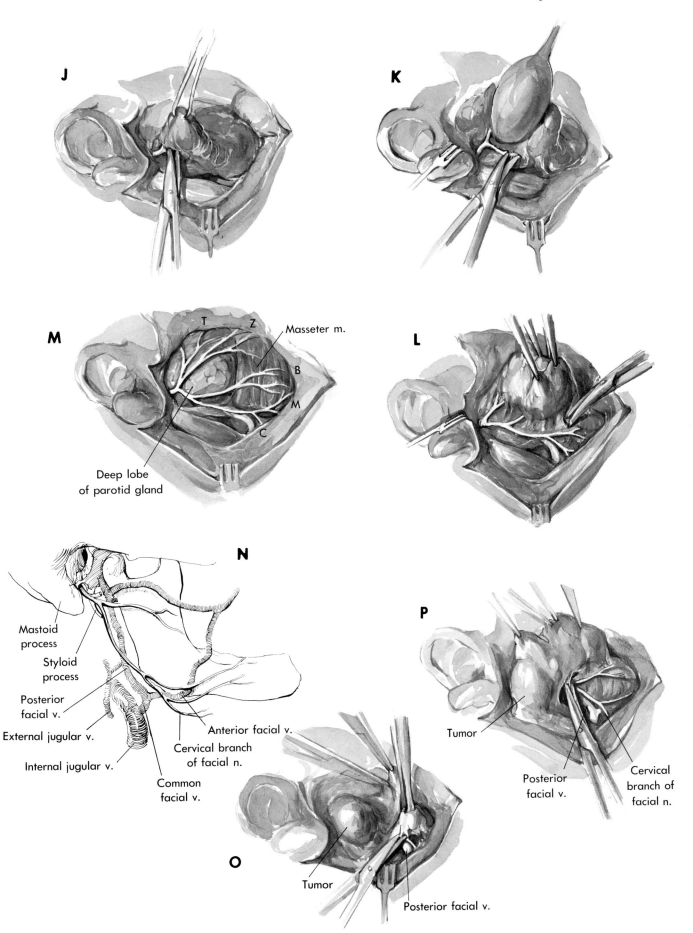

J

K

M

T Z Masseter m.

B

M

C

Deep lobe
of parotid gland

L

N

Mastoid
process

Styloid
process

Posterior
facial v.

External jugular v.

Internal jugular v.

Common
facial v.

Anterior facial v.

Cervical branch
of facial n.

P

Tumor

Posterior
facial v.

Cervical
branch
of facial
n.

Tumor

O

Posterior facial v.

RADICAL NECK DISSECTION

Radical neck dissection means different things to different people, as is true with many operations that do not involve the removal of a single organ but, instead, deal with the wide excision of certain areas of the body. The term is used here to designate the removal unilaterally of all of the lymph node bearing tissue in the cervical area superficial to the scalenus, levator scapulae and splenius capitis muscles and bound by the horizontal ramus of the mandible above, the anterior border of the trapezius in the back, the clavicle below and the midline anteriorly. The lymph nodes removed have been variously classified and include the following: the submaxillary nodes in the submaxillary triangle; the submental nodes located between the anterior bellies of the digastricus muscles; the superficial cervical group, which lies in proximity to the external jugular vein; the irregular and inconstant anterior cervical node found in front of the trachea and larynx; and, most important, the deep cervical nodes. The latter are the most numerous, the largest and form a chain along the carotid sheath from the base of the skull to the root of the neck; they also lie at the side of the trachea, larynx and esophagus. Lesser extensions or clusters are to be found along the spinal accessory nerve and the supraclavicular triangle in close relationship to the brachial plexus and subclavian vein. Additional tissues specifically resected in this operation are the sternocleidomastoid and omohyoid muscles, the internal jugular vein and the spinal accessory nerve.

Radical neck dissection is not to be equated with supra- or infra-omohyoid neck dissection, which indicates surgery cephalad or caudad to this muscle. A "modified" neck dissection usually designates something less than is stipulated above. Radical neck dissection can, of course, be performed in continuity with other procedures such as a glossectomy, mandibulectomy, parotidectomy, thyroidectomy or laryngectomy.

Proper requisites for a radical neck dissection include the following: (1) The primary cancer should be controlled, or controllable, either by surgery or irradiation unless, of course, one intends to excise simultaneously the primary cancer and to perform the radical neck dissection en bloc. Removal of the lymph node drainage of an uncontrolled primary tumor causes it to metastasize to aberrant sites, and there is minimal opportunity for a subsequent cure. (2) There are no distant metastases. (3) The cancer will be best treated by this operation rather than by a lesser one or by irradiation. (4) Fixation of lymph nodes to underlying structures constitutes involvement which is probably not resectable or has a minimal chance of cure by surgical means. (5) Prophylactic neck dissection not done simultaneously with excision of the primary lesion has limited application.

This operation is used most frequently in treatment of squamous cell cancer, usually metastatic from an intraoral source. Although radiotherapy plays a significant role in the treatment of primary squamous cell cancer, it has minimal curative application when the cancer has metastasized to the cervical lymph nodes. Additionally, intraoral squamous cell cancers metastasize primarily lymphogenously rather than hematogenously, so that an operation designed to excise the regional lymphatic channels and nodes is logical. Finally, in fewer than one-fourth of the patients with metastatic squamous cell cancer has the cancer progressed below the clavicles at the time of death. Although this does not mean that the malignancy will remain within the lymph nodes of the neck, the surgeon nonetheless has favorable opportunity to effect a cure with a radical neck dissection.

The term "therapeutic" neck dissection is used to signify that the cervical lymph nodes are palpable, and the term "prophylactic" is used for those operations done on necks in which they are not palpable. Obviously, prophylactic neck dissections will harvest a number of lymph nodes not clinically but later proved microscopically positive and thus will prove to have been therapeutic neck dissections. A prophylactic neck dissection would seem to be of value in treatment of cancers in which there is an appreciable incidence of microscopically positive nodes. It would also be of value if the excision of such microscopically involved nodes were attended by a higher cure rate than if one were to wait until such time as these nodes became palpable. Finally, a prophylactic neck dissection would be indicated if this procedure was a modest extension of an operation designed to excise a primary cancer even though there were not a substantial number of involved cervical nodes in the excised specimen.

Several types of cancers, which occur with some frequency and can kill with dismaying regularity, meet one or all of these criteria. Squamous cell cancer of the lateral floor of the mouth and/or the adjoining mandible or middle third of the tongue has a sufficiently high incidence of involving cervical lymph nodes, and the concomitant radical neck dissection can be done with only a modest addition to the duration and morbidity of the primary operation but with great benefit. Malignant melanoma of the skin of the neck is best treated by wide en bloc excision of the primary tumor and an underlying neck dissection even though this tumor also spreads hematogenously with great avidity. A thyroidectomy revealing a papillary or follicular cancer of the thyroid is often treated by extending the operation to include a radical neck dissection. This is done to remove nodes which, in a significant number of cases, although apparently uninvolved even when examined at the operating table, nonetheless contain cancer.

Patients requiring a radical neck dissection are often malnourished and dehydrated because of the discomfort caused by their oropharyngeal cancer or because of dysphagia resulting from radiotherapy to the primary lesions. Such deficits should be corrected with expediency but should not be a reason for significant delay of a curative operation.

The complications and safeguards of this operation have been well discussed elsewhere (Southwick and Slaughter, 1955) and are summarized here in brief fashion under their proper heading.

NERVES. As the neck is extended and the head is rotated away from the operative side, the *mandibular branch of the facial nerve* is pulled to a position below the lower border of the horizontal ramus of the mandible. It is deep to the platysma muscle and courses over the anterior facial vein and external maxillary artery; if severed, there is sagging at the angle of the mouth. The upper cord of the *brachial plexus* is liable to damage during dissection in this area. The *vagus nerve*, to be found within the carotid sheath, can easily be included with the jugular vein as the latter is ligated and divided. The nerve should be specifically identified before the vein is cut. The *phrenic nerve* is visible throughout its cervical course but remains under the deep cervical fascia and is safe from harm if this plane of dissection is maintained. The *spinal accessory nerve* is sacrificed at its insertion at the midpoint of the anterior border of the trapezius muscle and again as it exits from the skull next to the jugular vein. Its preservation requires a deliberate search for it and a careful dissection throughout its course. The *ansa hypoglossi nerve* is expendable. The *hypoglossal nerve* is looped transversely about 2 cm. cephalad and superficial to the bifurcation of the common carotid artery. The *lingual nerve* is liable to injury if, during the dissection of the middle of the submandibular triangle, it is pulled into the operative field by traction on the *chorda tympani nerve*. The *cervical sympathetic chain* is liable to damage during a retrotracheal and retroesophageal dissection for thyroid cancer.

VASCULAR STRUCTURES. The *common carotid artery* is easily identified and injury to it can be avoided. The *transverse scapular* and *transverse cervical* arteries are sometimes difficult to identify in the supraclavicular fat. Reckless clamping of a loose *thyrocervical trunk* or the high arching subclavian vessels may cause serious damage. The *jugular vein* is routinely divided; the proximal or chest side is doubly ligated because of the significant pressure that can be built up within it during coughing or straining. The relatively large *external jugular vein* has valves and also will not easily flow retrogradely. If partially cut, the incision remains open and it may suck in air to form emboli. The *thoracic duct* is probably cut more frequently than realized, with spontaneous clotting taking place; it should be sought for and preserved. Injury to it should be suspected if milky or clear fluid is seen in the lower medial operative field; if a tear is identified, the duct should be ligated.

MISCELLANEOUS. Transection of the lower portion of the *parotid gland* is part of routine node dissection. Saliva may drain from this area temporarily. A *pneumothorax* can occur if the apical pleura extends, or is pulled, supraclavicularly and cut.

References

Crile, G.: Excision of cancer of the head and neck. With special reference to the plan of dissection based on 132 operations. J.A.M.A. 47:22 and 1780, 1906.
Martin, H., Del Valle, B., Ehrlich, H., and Cahan, W. G.: Neck dissection. Cancer 4:441, 1951.
Southwick, H. W., and Slaughter, D. P.: Neck dissection: Complications and safeguards. S. Clin. North America 35:31, 1955.

Radical Neck Dissection

A   Most of the numerous anatomic landmarks are indicated.

1. Mandibular branch of facial nerve
2. Submaxillary salivary gland
3. Posterior belly of digastric muscle
4. Hypoglossal nerve
5. Parotid gland
6. Jugular vein
7. Sternocleidomastoid muscle (transected proximal end)
8. Spinal accessory nerve
9. Cervical sympathetic chain
10. Splenius capitis muscle
11. Levator scapulae muscle
12. Scalene muscle
13. Brachial plexus
14. Inferior belly of omohyoid muscle
15. Phrenic nerve
16. Thoracic duct
17. Jugular vein
18. Sternohyoid muscle
19. Vagus nerve
20. Superior belly of omohyoid muscle
21. Ansa hypoglossi
22. Common carotid artery
23. Internal carotid artery
24. Superior thyroid artery
25. External carotid artery
26. Mylohyoid muscle
27. Anterior belly of digastric muscle
28. Stylohyoid muscle

B   A double-Y incision is preferred. The extremes of the arms of the upper Y are the mastoid process posteriorly and the symphysis menti anteriorly. Those of the inferior Y are the junction of the trapezius and clavicle posteriorly and the midline anteriorly.

Although this incision is the easiest to make and provides the best exposure that can be maintained easily, variations from it may be necessary. One cause for variation may be the location of the tumor, such as an overlying malignant melanoma, which would be excised in continuity with the cervical contents. Another might dictate an attempt to encompass a biopsy incision. Although it would seem that the least important exception would be one based on esthetic considerations, this should not be dismissed lightly. Often, at minimal extra effort and no compromise of the operation, the postoperative appearance of the wound can be made more pleasing. Cross-hatching across the proposed incisions will make eventual wound approximation swifter and more accurate.

C   The skin flaps should include the platysma muscle, which is important in maintaining viability of the skin flaps. In the presence of an overlying malignant melanoma, the platysma muscle is excised along with the overlying skin. Sometimes the surgeon is confronted with a patient who has had a very limited operation with spillage of cancer cells into the operative field. In such an instance a definitive operation that will excise the cancer, yet not enter the "contaminated" area, will require an "enveloping" procedure. Here a secondary incision is made at the periphery of the primary one, and the dissection is maintained superficial to the platysma muscle. When the surgeon feels he is wide of the previous operative field he can then go deep to the platysma muscle and continue, remaining outside the previous operative field, thus "enveloping" all cancer-bearing tissue. Understandably, a greater incidence of flap necrosis is to be expected following this procedure.

D   The posterior flap is developed to the anterior border of the trapezius muscle. At its cephalic aspect, fibers of the sternocleidomastoid will be in intimate association with the dermis.

The medial flap is developed to the midline; this area is devoid of significant structures. The inferior flap is developed to the clavicle and the superior flap to the horizontal ramus of the mandible; they will require a stitch to keep them retracted. The medial and lateral flaps will lie out of the way. Throughout the operation electrocoagulation is relied on heavily for hemostasis of the smaller vessels and of practically all vessels on the specimen; the saving in time is substantial.

E   As the superior flap is developed, extra care to preserve the mandibular branch of the facial nerve will spare the patient an annoying postoperative deformity. With the assistant placing gentle traction on the flap and the surgeon applying countertraction on the neck tissue, a guarded, restrained dissection of the flap with the scalpel, in what amounts to a bloodless field, will reveal the nerve. Before the nerve and its course are identified, any small bleeders encountered in the vicinity should be clamped with exactness so as not to crush the nerve if it is adjacent.

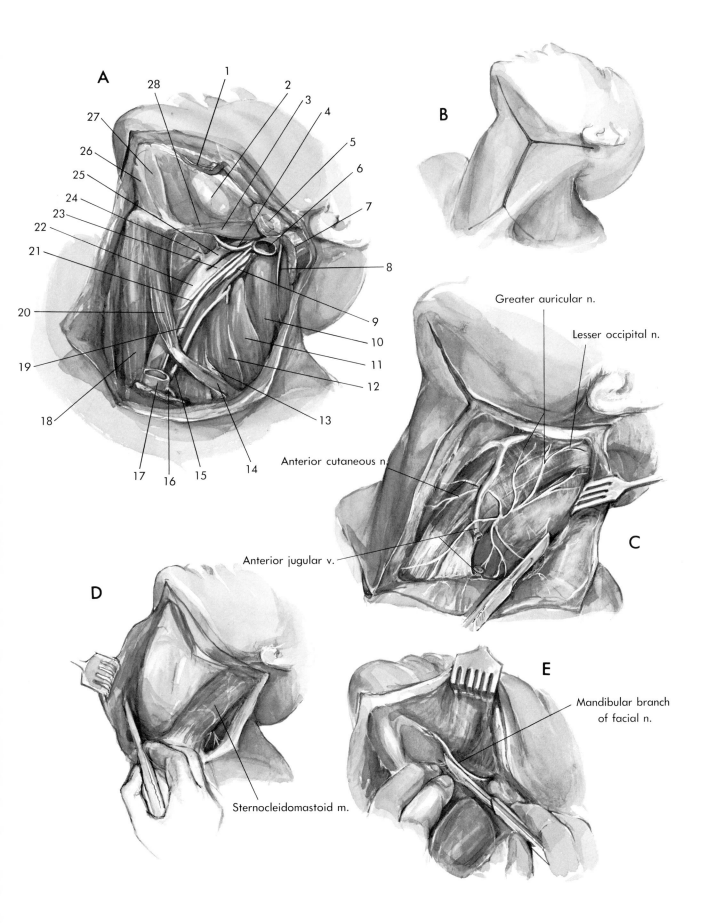

A

28 1 2 3 4 5 6 7 8 9 10 11 12 13 14 15 16 17 18 19 20 21 22 23 24 25 26 27

B

C

Greater auricular n.

Lesser occipital n.

Anterior cutaneous n.

Anterior jugular v.

D

Sternocleidomastoid m.

E

Mandibular branch of facial n.

F   When the mandibular branch of the facial nerve has been identified, the external maxillary artery and anterior facial vein are divided below it. The retracted cephalad end of the vein is then used to keep the nerve out of the operative field and harm's way. If the tumor has spread to the perivascular lymph nodes found at this location, the nerve, of course, will have to be sacrificed. This is usually encountered in clinical situations requiring excision of more than just the associated lymph nodes so that any deformity resulting from nerve loss is inconsequential.

G   The beginning of the formal dissection is often dictated by clinical considerations; electively we begin at the inferolateral aspect. As the dissection is carried forward toward the posterior edge of the sternocleidomastoid muscle, the inferior belly of the omohyoid muscle is encountered. In the window between this and the lateral edge of the sternocleidomastoid muscle, the phrenic nerve is visible.

H   The inferior belly of the omohyoid muscle is ligated and divided just above the clavicle. As this muscle and the fatty areolar tissue with the associated lymph nodes are retracted medially, a portion of the brachial plexus is exposed. If the brachial plexus is not readily visible or is situated more medially, it can be located by running the finger transversely over its presumed course and feeling the nerve trunks. This concern for locating the plexus is not an idle one as the nerve trunks can be tented by the retraction and brought into the path of the dissecting scissors. The apical pleura is deep and inferior to this point, but the possibility that it may extend superficially near the clavicle and may thus be inadvertently cut should be kept in mind. Because of impediment to venous flow some patients have a dusky face at the conclusion of surgery. The body below the neck is of normal color. However, in this eventuality one should not quickly dismiss the possibility of a pneumothorax.

I   The dissection continues along the anterior border of the trapezius muscle up to the mastoid process with constant retraction medially of the tissues to be removed. Venules in this area can be expected to ooze throughout the operation if they are not diligently clamped and electrocoagulated at this time. As the operation proceeds the mass of hemostats attached to the specimen will have to be shifted. To avoid dislodgment of important hemostats, all those not on the specimen should be secured now.

J   Attention is now turned to the sternocleidomastoid muscle, which inserts by a sternal and a clavicular head. It is separated from the underlying jugular vein by finger and the use of a Mixter clamp. It is divided about 1.0 cm. above its clavicular insertion. Bleeding is minimal, and hemostasis should be selective rather than ligation of the whole muscle mass.

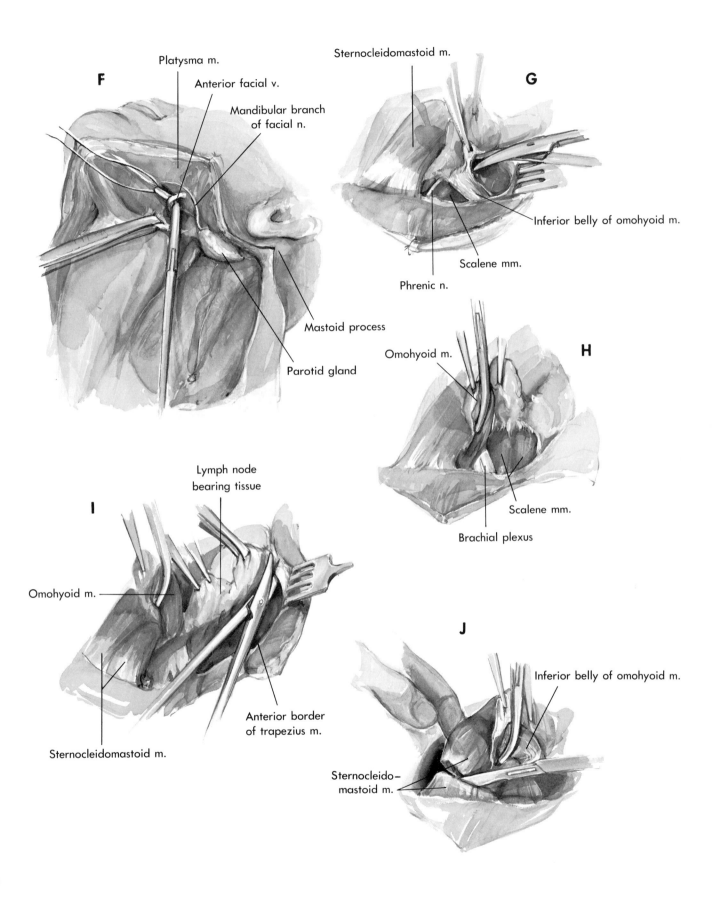

F

Platysma m.

Anterior facial v.

Mandibular branch of facial n.

Mastoid process

Parotid gland

G

Sternocleidomastoid m.

Inferior belly of omohyoid m.

Scalene mm.

Phrenic n.

H

Omohyoid m.

Scalene mm.

Brachial plexus

I

Lymph node bearing tissue

Omohyoid m.

Anterior border of trapezius m.

Sternocleidomastoid m.

J

Inferior belly of omohyoid m.

Sternocleido-mastoid m.

K   The previous step exposes the jugular vein, which is a cardinal point in beginning the inferior aspect of the dissection. This and the previous steps will also expose the subclavian vessels if they curve above the clavicle; awareness of this possibility will prevent their inadvertent injury. If this occurs, blind clamping and use of regular hemostats invite bigger tears. Arterial clamps should be used and the repair done with 5-0 arterial silk.

    From this point on the dissection will proceed alternately in a medial and cephalad direction. Countertraction on the hemostats attached to the specimen is essential to maintenance of exposure and the plane of dissection.

L
M   For safer encirclement of the jugular vein, the fatty areolar tissue superficial to it may be dissected upward for several centimeters. A curved forceps is used to get under the vein through the other side. A Hayes Martin thumb forceps is ideal for handling the vein and lifting it to be certain it is encircled rather than pierced. If a hole is made in this or any other major vein during the operation, there is risk of air embolism; accordingly, the hole should be plugged instantly by finger pressure.

N   The ligature is used to retract the jugular vein laterally. It is not at all rare to find that the vagus nerve has also been encircled and retracted; therefore, the nerve should be specifically identified before the jugular vein is divided.

O
P   The jugular vein is doubly ligated just above the clavicle. The more cephalad ligature is transfixed about 3 mm. cephalad to the first. A third ligature is applied even more cephalad and the vein divided between the latter two. In steps K to P the surgeon should remain aware of the location of the subclavian vein so that it is not damaged during the dissection and ligation of the jugular vein.

Q   The dissection continues along the carotid artery with awareness that the cervical sympathetic chain lies lateral and dorsal to it. The thoracic duct can usually be seen if it is sought. It is 2 to 4 mm. in diameter, a centimeter or two in length, curved or tortuous and translucent. Its presence may be recognized with the sudden appearance of lymphorrhea; apparently, most ducts so damaged heal with no untoward sequelae. Lymphatic fistula do occur, however, so that recognized tears should be secured and ligated with 3-0 silk.

R   In carrying on with the lateral aspect of the dissection, branches from the transverse cervical and scapular vessels are encountered and often have to be caught along with fatty areolar tissue rather than as individual vessels. The spinal accessory nerve may have been encountered before as shown in Figure I. It is located at the anterior border of the trapezius muscle and halfway between the clavicle and mastoid process. Often, contraction of the trapezius muscle may be the first sign that the nerve has been sectioned. If some type of neuroplasty is to be performed in an attempt to circumvent a shoulder drop, the dissection here is done with meticulous care.

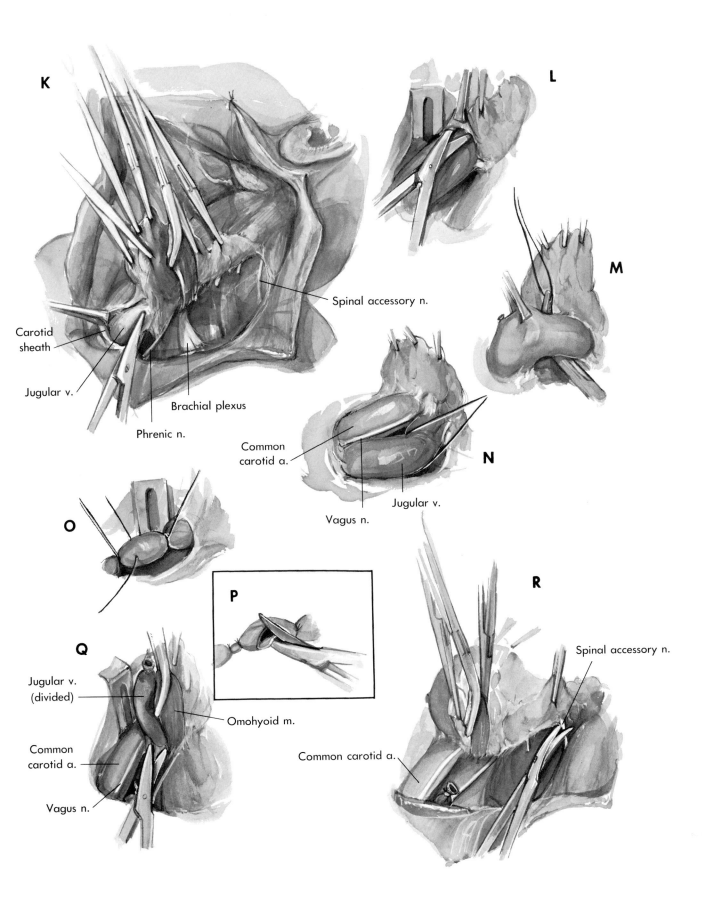

K

L

M

Spinal accessory n.

Carotid
sheath

Jugular v.

Brachial plexus

Phrenic n.

Common
carotid a.

N

Vagus n.

Jugular v.

O

Q

Jugular v.
(divided)

P

Omohyoid m.

Common
carotid a.

Vagus n.

R

Spinal accessory n.

Common carotid a.

S The dissection proceeds cephalad along the carotid artery while remaining within the carotid sheath. As the branches of the cervical plexus are sectioned, the mobility of the specimen improves perceptibly. The ansa hypoglossi nerve is not disturbed. As the omohyoid muscle is detached from the hyoid bone, the structures in the area of the carotid bifurcation are readily exposed. The other strap muscles are not disturbed. We do not practice routine anesthetization of the carotid bulb. The hypoglossal nerve is found approximately 2 cm. cephalad to the carotid bifurcation and looping in a direction transverse to the internal and external carotid arteries. Pharyngeal branches from the jugular vein are encountered ventral and caudal to the nerve. They are quite short and often sizable and if torn are difficult to secure without risk to the adjacent hypoglossal nerve. We tie them in continuity before dividing them. The superior laryngeal nerves are in this vicinity but are usually not encountered unless one must deviate from a "standard" radical neck dissection to seek nodes deep in this area. In this critical area cancer will all too often be attached to one of the several important structures; if this is the only deterrent to a curative operation, there should be no hesitancy in sacrificing any nerve or important structure.

T The dissection caudad to the posterior belly of the digastric muscle has progressed to the point at which the origin of the sternocleidomastoid muscle and the cephalic end of the jugular vein and spinal accessory nerve are to be divided next. The muscle is fibrous at this end and is essentially bloodless.

U
V The jugular vein is encircled by carefully passing a Mixter forceps around it just cephalad to the lower border of the posterior belly of the digastric muscle. Keep in mind that the vein runs deep to the muscle. In Figure V the muscle has been retracted to permit higher ligation of the vein. The digastric muscle itself can be sacrificed with impunity if necessary. A single tie of 2-0 silk is sufficient in this low pressure vein.

W The specimen is returned to its natural position and the dissection of the submaxillary triangle is begun. The dissection proceeds anteriorly on the level with the horizontal ramus of the mandible. This makes it necessary to go across the tail of the parotid gland in which are located several vessels, including the sizable posterior facial veins. Some of these vessels may have to be secured with a transfixion suture. If the surgeon does not go more cephalad than this, the facial nerve and its branches are safe from injury.

X When just past the parotid gland, the fatty areolar tissue comes easily as the dissection follows closely along the inferior aspect of the horizontal ramus of the mandible. Notice the reflected mandibular branch of the facial nerve.

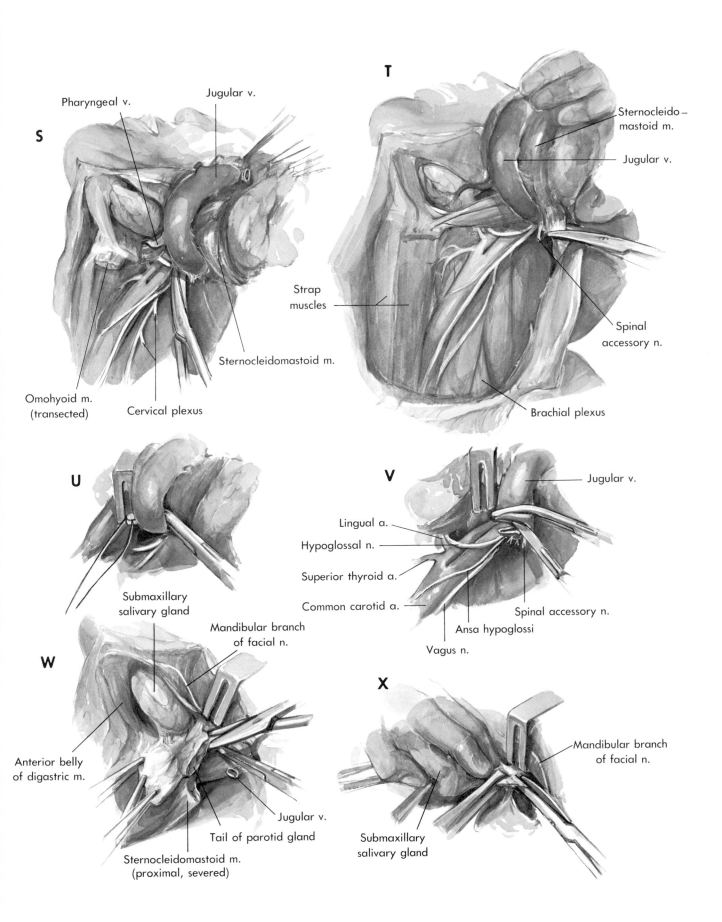

S
Pharyngeal v.
Jugular v.
Omohyoid m. (transected)
Cervical plexus
Sternocleidomastoid m.

T
Sternocleido-mastoid m.
Jugular v.
Strap muscles
Spinal accessory n.
Brachial plexus

U
Submaxillary salivary gland

V
Jugular v.
Lingual a.
Hypoglossal n.
Superior thyroid a.
Common carotid a.
Vagus n.
Ansa hypoglossi
Spinal accessory n.

W
Anterior belly of digastric m.
Mandibular branch of facial n.
Jugular v.
Tail of parotid gland
Sternocleidomastoid m. (proximal, severed)

X
Mandibular branch of facial n.
Submaxillary salivary gland

Y The submaxillary salivary gland can usually be dissected easily unless compromised by tumor in the vicinity. As the gland is retracted during the resection, care must be exercised so that the chorda tympani nerve which lies between the gland and lingual nerve does not pull the lingual nerve into the path of the dissecting scissors.

Z The anterior facial vein will have been divided early in the operation. The external maxillary artery will have been ligated as it passes deep to the posterior belly of the digastric and the stylohyoid muscles. Now these vessels with their associated lymph nodes are carried with the specimen. The duct of the submaxillary salivary gland is ligated with catgut and transected.

A₁ The dissection proceeds to the submental triangle. If any portion of the sublingual gland is herniated with the specimen, it should be transected and allowed to return to its natural position. The operation is completed by removing all fatty areolar tissue with accompanying lymph nodes to the opposite anterior belly of the digastric muscle.

B₁ The completed neck dissection is shown.
C₁   The wound is closed with narrow vertical mattress stitches which include the platysma muscle. Two catheters are exteriorized through inferiorly placed airtight counterincisions, anchored into position and placed on suction. Often there is minimal but sufficient oozing in the interval between completion of the dissection and closure of the wound that some blood clots collect under the flaps. These are flushed out by inserting the tip of a bulb syringe between two stitches and introducing 500 cc. of physiological saline solution under the skin flaps while maintaining suction. One thickness of a fine-mesh petrolatum gauze is placed over the incision; this helps to abort small air leaks. Otherwise, a minimal dressing is applied to the wound. The patient's head and thorax are kept elevated 30 degrees for most of the postoperative period. If the oral cavity has not been entered and if deglutition has not been compromised by nerve sacrifice in the neck, the patient is permitted to take oral nourishment as soon as desired.

Sacrifice of the jugular vein on only one side poses no problems postoperatively. If a contralateral radical neck dissection has been done previously, facial edema is more pronounced. Because cutaneous nerves are divided as part of the operation, there is remarkably little pain postoperatively. Stitches are removed on the seventh and ninth days unless this area has been irradiated, in which case they are left in longer. The patients are usually discharged from the hospital by the end of the second postoperative week.

A catastrophic complication which may occur if the operative area has received preoperative irradiation and develops wound infection is rupture of the carotid artery. This may be delayed, but usually occurs one week or more postoperatively. A patient who seems likely to develop this complication should be on "carotid precautions," i.e., absolutely constant surveillance by skilled and alert nursing staff. A sudden hemorrhage should be controlled digitally. Whole blood should be given to restore the blood pressure to normal for that patient and he should be taken to the operating room as soon as possible. When the blood pressure is normal, the wound should be reopened under general anesthesia. If a ruptured carotid artery is found, the artery should be ligated above and below the rupture and then divided. It will usually be necessary to ligate the common carotid artery proximally and the internal carotid artery distally. The incidence of paralysis is relatively low when the blood pressure has first been restored.

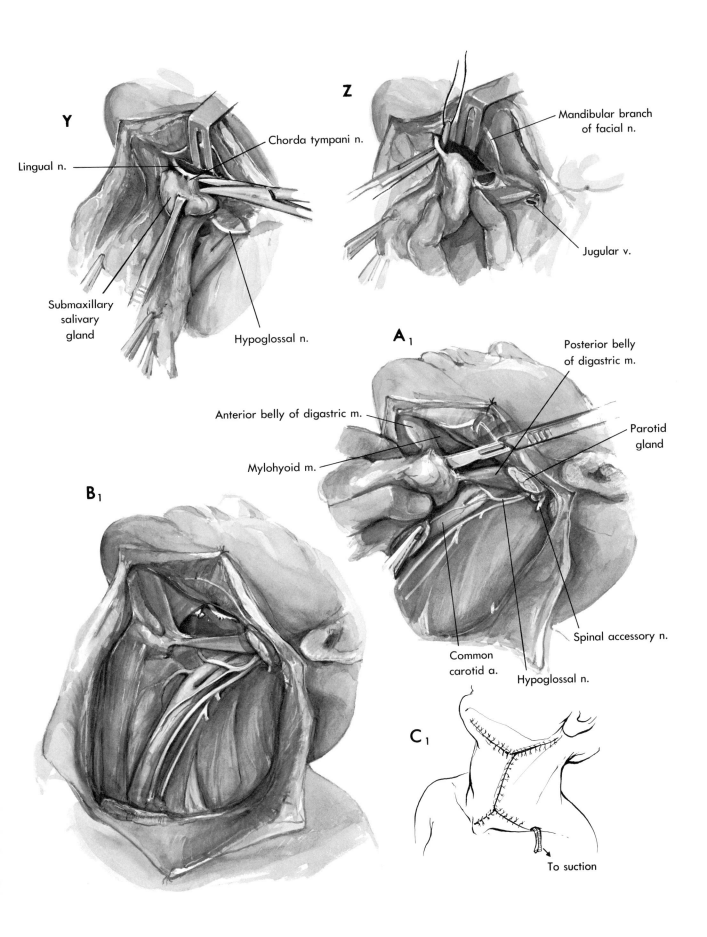

Y

Lingual n.

Chorda tympani n.

Submaxillary salivary gland

Hypoglossal n.

Z

Mandibular branch of facial n.

Jugular v.

A₁

Anterior belly of digastric m.

Mylohyoid m.

Posterior belly of digastric m.

Parotid gland

Common carotid a.

Hypoglossal n.

Spinal accessory n.

B₁

C₁

To suction

MONOBLOC NECK AND JAW RESECTION

When considering organs arising within or passing through the neck, one should recognize that they are unmatched elsewhere in the body for variations of embryonal origin, histological structure, physiological function or anatomical complexity. This makes it clear why surgical therapy of cancer of the head and neck requires not only a versatility of surgical skills but also a thorough grounding in surgical principles and basic sciences and a familiarity with the anatomy of the area.

Such terms as "monobloc neck and jaw resection" and "monobloc tongue resection" are replacing the popular and certainly more arresting one of "commando procedure." The latter term had its origin at the Memorial Hospital in New York around 1942 at the time of the Allied commando raids on Dieppe. The operation was being performed regularly at that time and the resident staff initiated the term for want of succinct terminology to describe the extensive surgery performed. The term "commando" is not, as some believe, a contraction of the words "combined" and "mandible."

The most common indication for the performance of the operation described herein is intraoral squamous cell cancer. It is performed for cancer of the anterior third of the tongue or the floor of the mouth only if cervical metastases are present. If the cancer is in the middle third of the tongue or the floor of the mouth it is technically necessary to obtain the more adequate exposure available with this operation. Also, it is reasonable to perform an in continuity neck dissection because of the appreciable yield of apparently normal nodes later proved microscopically involved with cancer. These reasons justify the modest enlargement of the operation in the absence of palpable cervical lymph nodes. With cancers of the posterior third of the tongue the primary lesion can be managed equally well by surgery or radiotherapy, the cervical metastases, if present, being removed by a standard radical neck dissection after the primary lesion has been controlled by radiotherapy. Squamous cell cancer of the mandible with cervical metastases or large gingival lesions without cervical lymph node involvement clinically are best treated with this operation. Finally, this operation is used for appropriate lesions that have recurred following radiotherapy.

This procedure is a natural development by extension of the classic radical neck dissection performed since the turn of the century. Although radical neck dissection itself was a new and radical procedure, the necessity for performing most of these combined operations under cumbersome local anesthesia and the high incidence of postoperative infection, hemorrhage and consequent mortality led many to recommend radium therapy, which was then becoming available. It became clear, however, that the lack of refinement of radiotherapy at that time and the fact that it could not be applied to neglected or advanced tumors or to those with osseous involvement left a void in the optimal treatment of these cancers. Furthermore, radiotherapy had, and continues to have, very limited application to squamous cell cancers that have metastasized to the cervical lymph nodes. In the latter part of the 1930's and early 1940's the availability of antimicrobial drugs, intravenous anesthesia, whole blood and the skin dermatome fostered the development by Dr. Hayes Martin and others of operations for therapy of head and neck cancer.

Because cancer of the head and neck remains relatively localized and is, therefore, amenable to cure by an operation for a considerable period after nodal deposits first appear, there have resulted a variety of radical operative procedures for its treatment. The radical neck portion of a monobloc neck and jaw procedure entails the removal of all the lymph node bearing tissue along with the sternocleidomastoid muscle, omohyoid muscle, jugular vein and submaxillary salivary gland. There are several reasons for a total, subtotal or marginal resection of the hemimandible. The foremost is cancerous invasion of the mandible. When the cancer involves the marrow cavity or neural canal, the entire hemimandible should be removed since cancer cells theoretically, and actually, may be found a considerable distance from the point of osseous invasion. Often resection of the mandible because of contiguous cancer permits better exposure of and access to the cancer. An equally important reason for resection of a portion of the mandible is to permit the shifting of soft tissues. This not only facilitates closure with less tension on the suture line but allows for greater mobility of the tongue, which otherwise would be sutured to the rigid mandible and be seriously hampered in its assistance with proper articulation. In short, although a horizontal ramus of the mandible is cosmetically more pleasing, its retention may seriously impair the patient's ability to eat and speak.

Nasotracheal anesthesia is desirable, preferably with a nonexplosive agent. Draping of the area is important and should be done in a manner that exposes the entire neck and mandible on the involved side. A medium-sized sandbag is placed under the shoulders. The skin is painted with a germicide such as Betadine, but it must be remembered that at the close of the operation the entire operative wound will be no cleaner than the oral cavity. The neck is extended and rotated away from the involved side. Electrocoagulation is used to control small bleeding vessels. This saves considerable operating time in a procedure of this magnitude and in our opinion does not retard wound healing or lead to any greater degree of serous exudation. Since the wound will be potentially contaminated, catgut is used for ligatures. Silk is used to ligate the jugular vein and other large vessels.

A clear airway is a necessity in all head and neck surgery. Preoperative consultation by the responsible anesthetist should be mandatory. The surgical team should be standing by during the induction of anesthesia. If the tracheal intubation is impossible or unduly difficult, a prompt tracheostomy is in order. In cases in which the anesthetist believes per oral intubation would be hazardous or impossible, the tracheostomy is done under local anesthesia before general anesthesia is induced.

References

Kremen, A. J.: Cancer of the tongue—A surgical technique for a primary combined en bloc resection of the tongue, floor of the mouth, and cervical lymphatics. Surgery 30:227, 1951.

Lore, J. M., Jr.: An Atlas of Head and Neck Surgery. Philadelphia, W. B. Saunders Co., 1962.

Martin, H.: Surgery of Head and Neck Tumors. New York, Hoeber Division, Harper & Bros., 1957.

Slaughter, D. P., Roeser, E. H., and Smejkal, W. F.: Excision of the mandible for neoplastic disease. Surgery 26:507, 1949.

Southwick, H. W., Slaughter, D. P., and Trevino, E. T.: Elective neck dissection for intra-oral cancers. A.M.A. Arch. Surg. 80:905, 1960.

Monobloc Neck and Jaw Resection

A The standard radical neck dissection will have been performed as described in the preceding chapter. Nasotracheal anesthesia is essential if the endotracheal tube is not to interfere with the oral aspect of the operation. Because of the abundant blood and mucus that will lie in the hypopharynx, the cuff on the endotracheal tube cannot be relied upon to prevent aspiration; packing the hypopharynx with gauze is a routine practice. The anterior limb of the upper horizontal neck incision is carried upward along the midline of the lower lip. The lip should be divided, since this step enhances the exposure of the intraoral area and facilitates the operation. If there is a compelling reason not to divide the lower lip, the anterior limb of the upper horizontal neck incision is extended if necessary to the lower point of the symphysis menti. When the buccogingival sulcus is divided as in Figure C, the entire cheek flap can be retracted cephalad. This less adequate exposure, however, is more suitable when a limited portion of the mandible is to be removed. If the mandible is to be left intact, the operation on the intraoral structures will be carried out after they have been herniated into the neck as in the pull-through operation. Digital support as depicted aids in making the incision and affords hemostasis.

B The buccal flap is dissected posteriorly and, except in case of buccal or encroaching gingival tumors, the incision is made in the buccogingival sulcus. The periosteum of the mandible is left attached to the buccal flap except for those portions of the mandible left in place. The postoperative appearance of the chin is more pleasing cosmetically if the mandible is resected somewhat lateral to the midline, so unless the mandible itself is involved, the mandible is not divided at the symphysis menti.

C The extent to which the buccal flap is mobilized depends on where the mandible will be sectioned. In this illustration all but the mental portion of the mandible is to be removed. Accordingly, the masseter muscle is sectioned at its insertion along the lateral inferoposterior aspect of the horizontal ramus of the mandible. If the cancer is situated more posteriorly and laterally, this muscle should be sectioned at a higher level.

D The facial nerve and parotid gland are included in the thick buccal flap, which is retracted upward, and thus are safe from harm. Scissors can be used to dissect the temporal muscle from its insertion in the coronoid process. Further dissection in this area will be easier after performance of steps E and F.

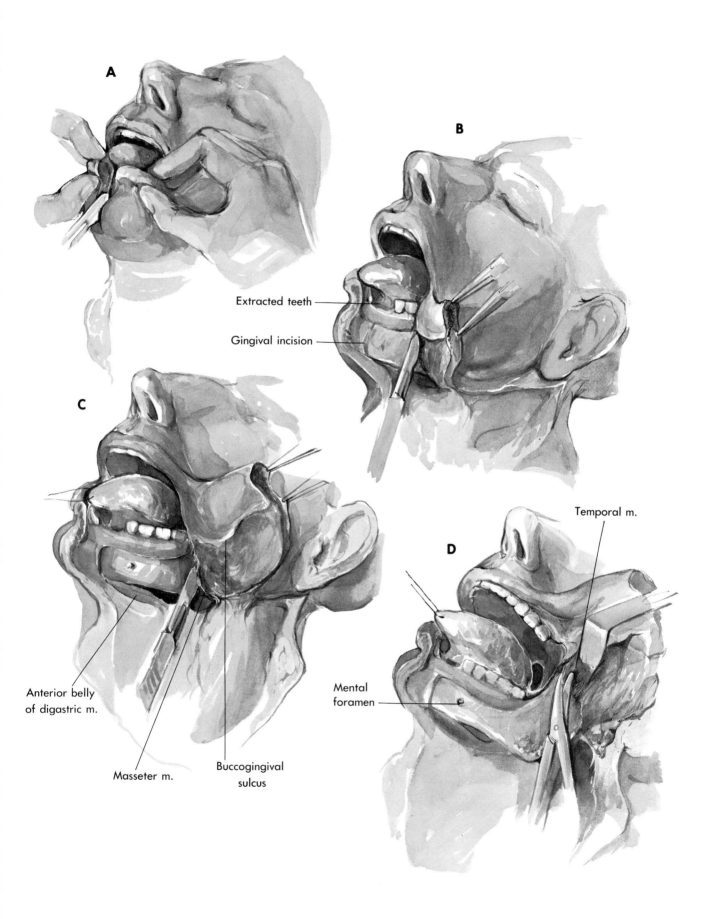

Extracted teeth

Gingival incision

Temporal m.

Mental foramen

Anterior belly
of digastric m.

Masseter m.

Buccogingival
sulcus

E A maneuver that may facilitate later closure is the extraction of the tooth anterior to the anticipated line of mandibular division. The gingiva will have been incised previously. Subperiosteal elevation of this gingiva anteriorly for a few millimeters and division of the mandible under this point will make loose tissue available for closure in this critical area; otherwise, an abruptly jutting tooth and a sharp mandibular edge may make satisfactory closure awkward (see Figures K and L). Before the surgeon divides the mandible with a Gigli saw, he should free the anterior belly of the digastric muscle. The external carotid artery has been tied in continuity to decrease hemorrhage. This is done distal to the origin of the superior thyroid artery.

F Traction is applied to the tongue by means of an atraumatic suture passed through the midline of its tip. An old towel clip, attached to the outer aspect of the severed mandible, is used to manipulate the mandible during the subsequent dissection. The extent of tongue resection depends on the extent and location of the cancer. In this instance the tumor is located at the point indicated by the asterisk (*) so the tip of the tongue has been left relatively free; the tongue incision has not come quite to the midline. If the cancer is ulcerated, its surface is electrocoagulated to diminish the number of viable cells which might become implanted in the operative wound. The sublingual gland is usually removed. (In this illustration the sublingual gland is intact.) When a limited or posterior tongue resection is performed, the line of excision may come close to the lingual nerve. It is often possible, without compromising the adequacy of resection around a cancer, to preserve the major branches of the lingual nerve. The lingual nerve passes between the hyoglossus muscle and the deep part of the submaxillary salivary gland. It then runs across the submaxillary duct and along the tongue, lying submucosally as it terminates at the tip of the tongue.

G The submaxillary salivary gland and associated lymph nodes are taken with the specimen as it is removed en bloc. The extent to which the mylohyoid muscle is excised depends on the location of the tumor; the medial wall of this muscle and the anterior belly of the digastricus muscle often are spared with more posterior tumors. Downward traction on the mandible facilitates division (usually with heavy scissors) of the insertion of the temporal muscle on the coronoid process and the ascending ramus of the mandible. The muscle is quite tendinous in this area and one can find himself dissecting along the fibers unless a sharp inward cut is made to separate them from the mandible.

H Continued downward lateral traction permits easier access medial to the mandible. This should not be done forcibly and the tongue incision should be complete to allow the mandible to come away freely. Cancers in the lateral floor of the mouth may fracture if the mandible is displaced too forcibly. Here the internal and external pterygoid muscles are divided; they are on stretch and are attached to the inner aspect of the angle of the mandible and to the mandibular condyle and joint capsule. Control of the internal maxillary artery is essential in this area; bleeding from its branches in the retracting pterygoid muscles as the muscles are cut sometimes obscures the identity of the specific structures being sectioned. Finally, the mandible is disarticulated.

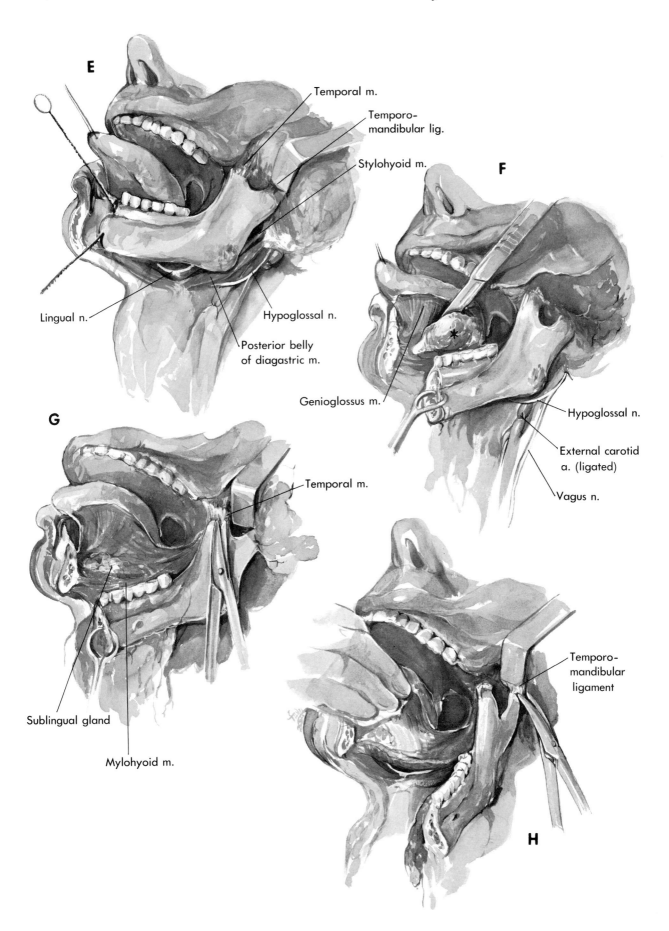

E

Temporal m.

Temporo-
mandibular lig.

Stylohyoid m.

F

Lingual n.

Hypoglossal n.

Posterior belly
of diagastric m.

Genioglossus m.

Hypoglossal n.

External carotid
a. (ligated)

Vagus n.

G

Temporal m.

Sublingual gland

Mylohyoid m.

Temporo-
mandibular
ligament

H

I   The primary lesion with a portion of the tongue, floor of mouth, mandible and the contents of a left radical neck dissection have been removed as a monobloc. The contours of the mucosal edges to be approximated vary with the location of the tumor and the extent of its resection. One has to examine the area for a while to determine the best way to bring the mucosal edges together so that there is minimal distortion of the soft palate, which is important to deglutition, and of the tip of the tongue, which is important in articulation.

J   Wound closure is begun posteriorly. Even if there is anticipated disparity in the length of the two edges to be apposed, priority is given to this posterior area to assure that it is closed with minimal tension. Avoidance of undue tissue displacement or distortion minimizes postoperative problems of deglutition. A two or even three layer closure is desirable. However, for the first several centimeters posteriorly it may be impossible to have more than a single layer of interrupted stitches of 3-0 chromic catgut.

K   The musculature of the tongue is sutured to the raw surface of the buccal flap in one or two layers with interrupted stitches of 3-0 chromic catgut. The free mucosal edge of the tongue is then sutured to the buccal mucosa at the previous buccogingival sulcus. The stitches are so placed and tied that the knots reside intraorally in the new buccogingival sulcus. Inevitably, the buccal, lingual and gingival incisions meet. This area, too, will resist closure in layers and is the reason for the attempts early in the operation (see Figure E) to provide some free gingival mucosa. In instances in which the anterior aspect of the tongue has been hemisected, the fashioning of a new free tip will allow for better articulation. If a new tip of the tongue is necessary, it is fashioned at this time and care is taken not to create one which is too long and may tend to protude through the lips. At about this point, or sooner, any disparity in length between the two mucosal edges will have to be compensated for during the placement of the stitches.

L   Subcutaneous stitches are necessary in the mental area. Sometimes removal of a 1 to 2 cm. wedge of the resultant excessive lower lip (as shown by the dotted line) will prevent lip drooping and subsequent drooling of saliva. This is not necessary when the anterior portion of the hemimandible remains. The wound is closed as in a standard radical neck dissection and suction drainage is instituted with a catheter under the flaps.

   A tracheostomy is routinely performed prior to removal of the endotracheal tube. The horizontal incision for the tracheostomy can be an extension of the mesial lower limb of the double-trifurcate cervical incision. A "tight" tracheostomy should be done to prevent or minimize leakage of air under the skin flaps. Alternately, if the initial radical neck incision is kept slightly away from the midline in its lower limit, the tracheostomy can be performed through a separate incision that has no communication with the radical neck dissection.

   Postoperatively the tracheostomy is given meticulous care since these patients may not be able to manipulate their saliva by virtue of the intraoral surgery or the sectioning of the nerve supply to the tongue. In addition, distortion of the tongue and palate may encourage mucus to run down into the larynx and trachea. High humidity and mucolytic agents are provided over the tracheostomy. The intraoral incision is kept relatively clean by having the nurse place a few milliliters of saline into the mouth and then having the patient lean toward the operated side to get this liquid in the new buccogingival gutter; it is then gently sucked out with a sterile catheter.

   The rapidity with which a patient may be able to take nourishment orally will depend on the factors mentioned previously. Solid food cannot be taken at this time and liquids usually cannot be directed properly by a tongue that has not regained its complete motor function. Mushy or ground foods are best because they are soft yet possess enough body not to flow too freely. A feeding tube in the stomach or esophagus is helpful. When the patient can swallow properly, the tracheostomy tube is occluded for 24 hours and then removed.

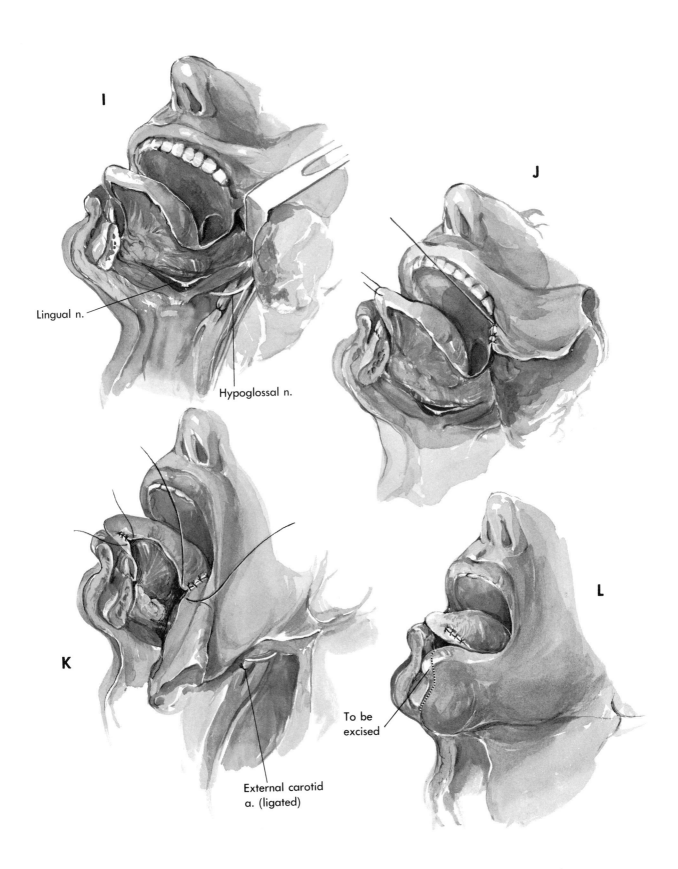

I

Lingual n.

Hypoglossal n.

J

K

External carotid
a. (ligated)

L

To be
excised

RADICAL THYROIDECTOMY

The polemic revolving around the proper therapy for cancer of the thyroid makes it clear that there is no proof that one treatment is clearly superior to another in all respects. The schism is greatest with respect to papillary cancer, which is the basis of the operative procedure illustrated in the following pages. After diagnostic biopsy, papillary cancer of the thyroid is treated by some with thyroid hormones only; at the other extreme, by routine total thyroidectomy, ipsilateral radical neck dissection and retrotracheal and retroesophageal dissection. One can understand, then, why even the choice of title for this section may cause some to scoff that the operation is not "radical" enough, but others may exclaim that for the cancer in question it is "radical" surgery, indeed.

There are a number of causes for this controversy, the principal cause being the tendency not to think in terms of the results of specific treatments for specific types of thyroid cancers. Instead, all too frequently an experience with thyroid cancer in general seems to influence decisions about specific patients, or specific experiences are applied generally. One example is the impressive but diverting influence of the pessimistic experience with anaplastic cancer of the thyroid, for which the cure rate is low regardless of the therapy used. On the other hand, papillary adenocarcinoma usually grows so slowly that practically any therapy (and in the absence of tracheal or esophageal obstruction, no therapy) will allow many patients to live for a considerable period. Certainly the usual statistics on three- or five-year survival rates (which frequently neglect to mention whether these patients are surviving with or without cancer present) following therapy for papillary cancer have limited value in proving the superiority of one treatment over another. Results of any therapy of papillary cancer of the thyroid should be assessed in terms of decades. There is also reluctance by many surgeons to perform "radical" or "mutilating" surgery on young patients when, in the limited experience of the surgeon concerned, there has not been driven home the fact that papillary cancer of the thyroid can actually kill the patient.

One argument for limited surgery is the fact that cancers of the thyroid that are 1 cm. or less in diameter, that do not have gross metastases at the time of surgery and that are treated by thyroid lobectomy have such a high rate of long-term survival that many surgeons find it difficult to justify the arbitrary recommendation of a radical neck dissection for any and all papillary cancers of the thyroid. It is true, of course, that a number of such patients will subsequently need surgery for the metastatic cancer that has by then become clinically apparent, and that such surgery would be more difficult and less neatly performed than if it had been done at the time of lobectomy. There is no overwhelming indication, though, that these patients will fare significantly less well than those having a "radical" operation initially.

Anyone feeling secure in the term "localized" papillary thyroid cancer or complacent about the ability of such cancers to metastasize must remember the high incidence of metastasis (approximately 68 per cent) to cervical lymph nodes which are clinically negative. Unless sizable, these nodes are soft and easily missed. On whole organ sectioning there is demonstrated a disconcertingly high frequency (up to approximately 80 per cent) of metastases (multifocal primary?) to the contralateral lobe. Notwithstanding this ominous information, it has not yet been demonstrated in a compelling way that the routine performance of a radical neck dissection is mandatory or even very beneficial in patients who have a small primary thyroid cancer and who have no gross involvement of the cervical lymph nodes at the time of thyroid lobectomy.

Radical neck dissection was initially conceived and used to treat oral epidermoid cancers that had metastasized to the cervical lymph nodes. One must remember, however, that metastatic deposits of epidermoid cancer are more widely distributed in the neck and occur at a more superficial plane than papillary cancer of the thyroid, which spreads to the retrotracheal and retroesophageal areas early and to the lateral cervical areas secondarily. Often the reason for failure to cure papillary cancer of the thyroid is nonresectable local invasion or the reluctance to resect vital structures immediately adjacent to the thyroid. Also, squamous cell cancer of the oral cavity spreads primarily lymphogenously so that the logic of a regional radical lymphadenectomy is obvious. Thyroid cancer spreads distantly by blood vessels with greater frequency, thus making radical local surgery futile with comparable frequency. In addition, squamous cell cancer remains in the cervical area with sufficient constancy, and if not excised kills the patient sufficiently soon, that an en bloc resection can effect a "cure" more dramatically and decisively than with papillary cancer of the thyroid. For these reasons some have felt that there is some misapplication of the original concept, if the classic radical neck dissection is used to treat papillary cancer of the thyroid gland. It certainly makes little scientific sense to see surgeons come within a millimeter of the tumor as it lies on the trachea or recurrent laryngeal nerve but then "radically" excise the sternocleidomastoid muscle at a point 10 cm. distant. Those against radical surgery correctly point to the local disfigurement, the morbidity to division of the 11th cranial nerve and the annoyance and possible sequelae of hypoparathyroidism. Many, of course, would pay this price for a cure, but the contention is that equally effective cures may be had more cheaply.

Certainly not the least reason for these changing attitudes is the rapidly increasing practice of administering thyroid extract to patients with thyroid cancer in expectation of supressing the secretion of thyroid stimulating hormone (TSH) by the pituitary and hopefully also supressing the hormone-dependent thyroid cancer itself. The rate of meaningful response is about 15 per cent, but the good results for long periods with this regimen cannot be ignored. Although it will not prove the panacea that many seem to feel, neither is it likely to become a vogue. Even those advocating radical local surgery are, in increasing numbers, administering TSH-supressive doses of thyroid to their patients postoperatively.

Clearly, many of the exponents of a particular therapy bring to their decision some element of emotional and social considerations along with a concept of an effective but not necessarily optimal therapeutic method. The procedure depicted in these pages is employed by us in the therapy of papillary cancer of the thyroid when no lymph nodes appear involved at the time of surgery. It entails a thyroid lobectomy, isthmectomy and subtotal contralateral lobectomy, and ipsilateral retrotracheal and retroesophageal dissection and cervical lymphadenectomy in continuity. If, however, the cervical lymph nodes are obviously grossly involved at the time of surgery we choose to sacrifice the sternocleidomastoid muscle and jugular vein. All these patients are placed on thyroid extract postoperatively.

References

Black, B. M., YaDeau, R. E., and Woolner, L. S.: Surgical treatment of thyroid carcinoma. Arch. Surg. 88:610, 1964.

Cole, W. H., Slaughter, D. P., and Majarakis, J. D.: Carcinoma of the thyroid gland. Surg. Gynec. & Obst. 89:349, 1949.

Frazell, E. L., and Foote, F. W.: Papillary cancer of the thyroid – A review of 25 years' experience. Cancer 11:5 and 895, 1958.

Hill, L. D., Kellogg, H., Jr., Crampton, J. H., Jones, H. W., and Baker, J. W.: Changing management of carcinoma of the thyroid. Am. J. Surg. 8:175, 1964.

Lindsay, S., and Chaikoff, I. L.: The effects of irradiation on the thyroid gland with particular reference to the induction of thyroid neoplasms: A review. Cancer Res. 24:1099, 1964.

Tollefsen, H. R., and DeCross, J. J.: Papillary carcinoma of the thyroid – The case for radical neck dissection. Am. J. Surg., 108:547, 1964.

Radical Thyroidectomy

A   During the course of this operation the exposure is admittedly more difficult to establish and maintain by virtue of the incision used and the fact that considerable dissection is carried out around the sternocleidomastoid muscle and jugular vein, which are retracted but are not resected. For this reason it is more necessary than ever that the surgeon possess an intimate knowledge of the anatomy of the neck if this operation is to be performed adequately and safely.

B   The standard collar incision can be extended toward the mastoid process in a hockey-stick fashion if it develops that the thyroid mass is cancerous. A shorter more cephalad but parallel incision may be necessary. A T extension from the primary incision toward the lateral aspect of the clavicle may be necessary for proper exposure. Of course, a standard double-Y incision may also be used. If there is to be an associated superior mediastinal dissection, a connecting midline sternal incision is added, but by then the considerations for the extensive involvement override esthetic consideration on the applicability of this restrained operation. The surgeon should excise with the specimen any biopsy incisions present, or adequately encompass the tract of a needle biopsy if this is how the diagnosis was made.

C   The incision may be started as the standard collar one and extended as the findings at operation dictate. If a single hockey-stick incision is used, it must be carried up to the mastoid process for adequate exposure. The submaxillary triangle is usually not entered in this operation. The standard collar incision is made somewhat more generous than usual on the side opposite the tumor; on the involved side it is made slightly short so that it can be swung smoothly into a hockey-stick configuration.

D   The superficial layer of the deep cervical fascia is incised along the anterior border of the sternocleidomastoid muscle in preparation for mobilization and division of the strap muscles. We recognize the professed wisdom of resecting the strap muscles over a cancerous thyroid lobe. This is really germane when one knows the diagnosis. Once the muscle is retracted or divided so that the underlying lobe can be examined and a proper diagnosis made, the value of resecting the overlying muscles is quickly minimized. If, in fact, it is beneficial or necessary to resect the strap muscles, then the depicted operation is itself inadequate. In any case, throughout this section the strap muscles will be shown divided and retracted.

E   The strap muscles are divided at the junction of their middle and lower thirds so as to disrupt their innervation minimally. The use of a crushing clamp at the point of division eliminates troublesome bleeding during closure, does not appear to affect recovery deleteriously and is an easy way to retract the muscles. Any veins seen running over the muscle should be secured with a suture ligature rather than depending for hemostasis entirely on the running stitch that will be used to reapproximate the muscles.

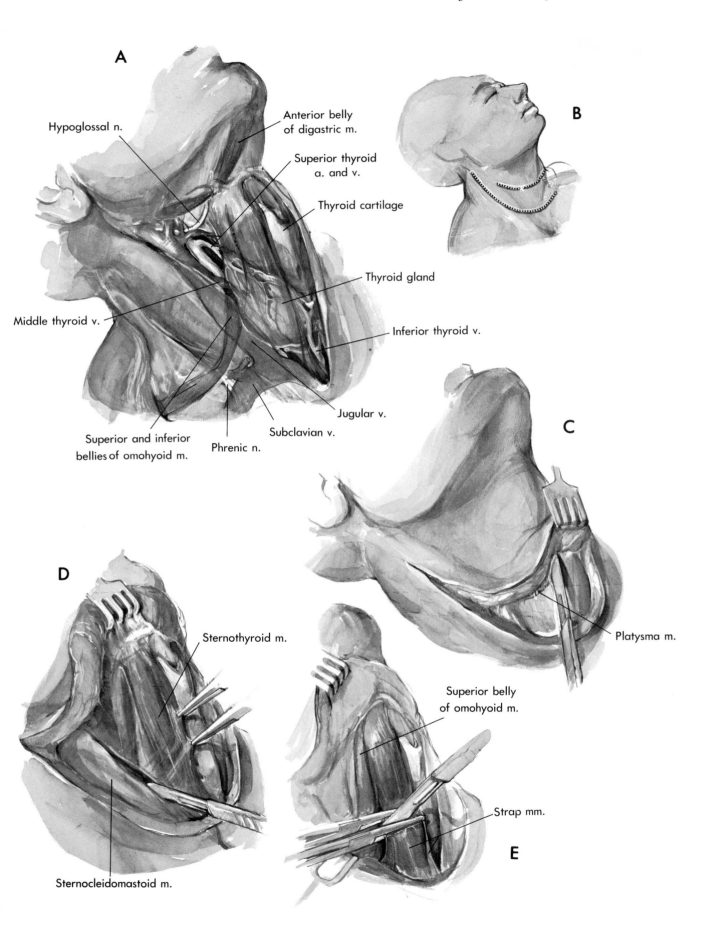

A

Hypoglossal n.

Anterior belly
of digastric m.

Superior thyroid
a. and v.

Thyroid cartilage

Thyroid gland

Inferior thyroid v.

Middle thyroid v.

Jugular v.

Subclavian v.

Superior and inferior
bellies of omohyoid m.

Phrenic n.

B

C

Platysma m.

D

Sternothyroid m.

Superior belly
of omohyoid m.

Strap mm.

E

Sternocleidomastoid m.

F   With division of the strap muscles on the side containing the tumor and retraction of those on the opposite side the thyroid can be adequately exposed and examined. Unfortunately, there is no consistently easy or dependable way to make a correct diagnosis at this point. The illustrated procedure indicates that the diagnosis is known so that, ideally, the operation can proceed as indicated in the following steps.

G   The dissection is begun on the lobe opposite the involved side. The strap muscles on this side are retracted so that the thyroid lobe can be mobilized. There certainly is no need to divide these strap muscles. Some of the vessels to this lobe may have to be ligated and divided for such mobility and also for better hemostasis. The location of the parathyroid glands is noted at this time.

H   The lobe is momentarily reflected medially so that the course of the recurrent laryngeal nerve can be noted. Since the surgery on this side will be intracapsular and well away from the nerve, it does not have to be identified as far along in its course as with a lobectomy. The thyroid lobe is divided so that the dorsal two-thirds and the associated parathyroid glands remain. The dissection within the posterior capsule not only minimizes injury to the recurrent laryngeal nerve but also to the parathyroid glands. A multiple clamping technique may be used as in patients with hyperthyroidism. However, these lobes are not so vascular or so big, and the previous ligation of the vessels reduces the amount of bleeding as the gland is cut.

I   As the anterior portion of the left thyroid lobe is reflected toward the right, sharp dissection is used to separate the isthmus from the trachea. We do not oversew the cut edge of the thyroid gland nor suture its capsule to the trachea so as to cover the cut surface. It is unwise on principle to apply any squeezing or crushing clamps to a thyroid lobe containing cancer. Not only may this initiate vascular embolization of cancer cells, but it may also be one of the ways a wound is seeded with such cells. A clamp or two are applied to the clinically uninvolved lobe for purposes of traction.

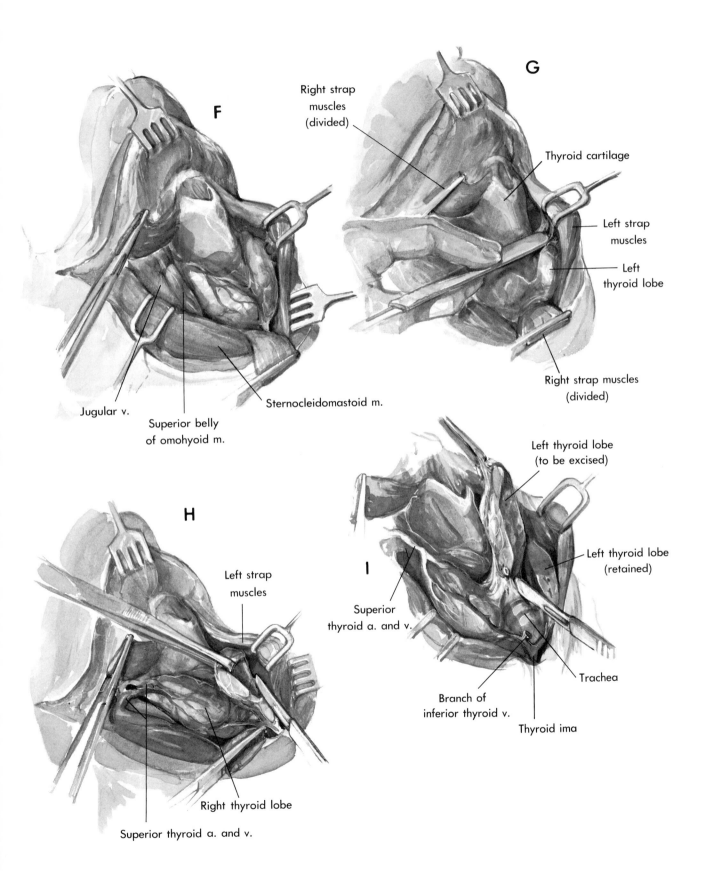

F

Right strap
muscles
(divided)

G

Thyroid cartilage

Left strap
muscles

Left
thyroid lobe

Right strap muscles
(divided)

Jugular v.

Superior belly
of omohyoid m.

Sternocleidomastoid m.

H

Left strap
muscles

I

Left thyroid lobe
(to be excised)

Left thyroid lobe
(retained)

Superior
thyroid a. and v.

Trachea

Branch of
inferior thyroid v.

Thyroid ima

Superior thyroid a. and v.

Right thyroid lobe

J This is the extent of surgery on the left neck. The head is rotated to the left and the right neck dissection is begun in the right inferolateral area, with the trapezius muscle being the lateral boundary of this dissection. The fatty areolar tissue, with the associated lymph nodes, is dissected medially. Branches of the transverse scapular and transverse cervical arteries are a danger in this area and should be clamped before being divided; otherwise, they will retract and it will take time to relocate and secure them.

K The dissection lateral to the sternocleidomastoid muscle extends from the supraclavicular area to the mastoid process. The tissue to be resected is rather scant toward the upper end. The spinal accessory nerve is preserved; metastatic tumor deposits are found in its vicinity sufficiently uncommonly and the morbidity of a drop-shoulder is sufficiently disabling and unsightly that it is reasonable to do this for the type of cancer and extent of involvement being treated. Preservation of the nerve is most difficult at its insertion, but it can be exposed easily here so that damage to it is avoidable.

L Up to this point the fatty areolar tissue with its associated lymph nodes will have been dissected on a plane almost as far as the anterior border of the sternocleidomastoid muscle as the dissection was carried on deep to this muscle. The inferior belly of the omohyoid muscle will have been divided early in the course of the dissection. This concludes the dissection lateral to the sternocleidomastoid muscle. Now with lateral retraction of the sternocleidomastoid muscle, the dissected tissue is shifted under and anterior to this muscle.

M With continued lateral retraction of the sternocleidomastoid muscle the dissection lateral to the great vessels of the neck is begun. Here the tissue is dissected off the scalene muscles with preservation of the phrenic nerve. Notice that the severed inferior belly of the omohyoid muscle has also been shifted anterior to the sternocleidomastoid muscle.

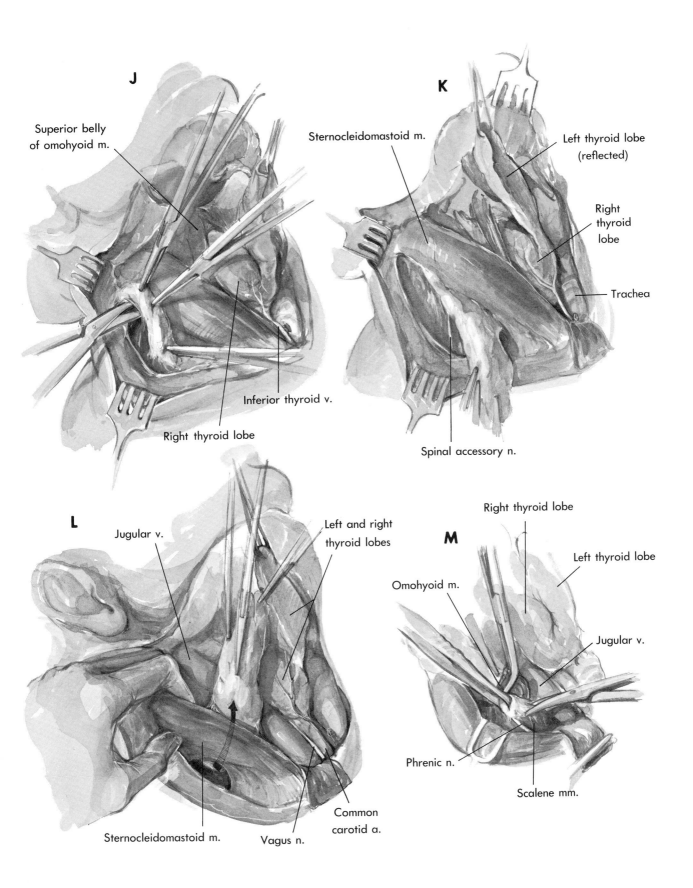

J

Superior belly of omohyoid m.

Inferior thyroid v.

Right thyroid lobe

K

Sternocleidomastoid m.

Left thyroid lobe (reflected)

Right thyroid lobe

Trachea

Spinal accessory n.

L

Jugular v.

Left and right thyroid lobes

Sternocleidomastoid m.

Vagus n.

Common carotid a.

M

Right thyroid lobe

Omohyoid m.

Left thyroid lobe

Jugular v.

Phrenic n.

Scalene mm.

N   The operation proceeds with the tissue being dissected about the carotid sheath in a medial and cephalad direction. Throughout the operation, emphasis shifts as the exposure is developed.

O   The inferior thyroid veins are divided and ligated with 3-0 silk. With the lower aspect of the carotid sheath cleansed of tissue, the recurrent laryngeal nerve is identified and preserved as the dissection proceeds in a cephalad direction. It is at this and the next steps that the retrotracheal and retroesophageal area is cleansed of fatty areolar tissue. Of course, the cervical sympathetic chain is preserved. Ordinarily, the latter is reasonably safe in its retroesophageal position. For better access to and dissection of this area, the trachea is displaced and rotated medially and the great vessels are retracted laterally. Traction on the tissue being excised may arc the sympathetic chain into the plane of dissection.

P   The inferior thyroid artery is ligated and divided just anterior to the common carotid artery. The middle thyroid vein will already have been divided and ligated. This frees the specimen and also exposes the point of entrance into the larynx of the recurrent laryngeal nerve. Small vessels may cause mild but troublesome bleeding at this crucial point so that the hemostats must be applied with exactness if injury to the nerve is to be avoided.

'Q   The specimen is returned to its normal position and the superior thyroid artery and vein divided and ligated with 3-0 silk. There are no other significant vessels that have to be divided. The hypoglossal nerve is identified as it crosses several centimeters cephalad to the carotid bifurcation at about the origin of the lingual artery.

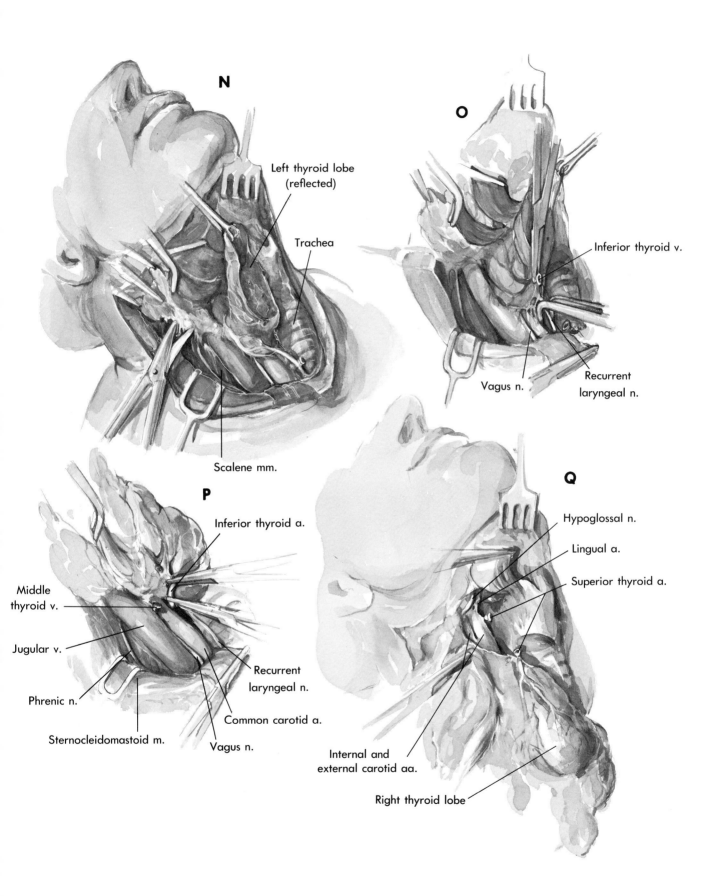

N

Left thyroid lobe
(reflected)

Trachea

Scalene mm.

O

Inferior thyroid v.

Vagus n.

Recurrent
laryngeal n.

P

Inferior thyroid a.

Middle
thyroid v.

Jugular v.

Phrenic n.

Sternocleidomastoid m.

Recurrent
laryngeal n.

Common carotid a.

Vagus n.

Q

Hypoglossal n.

Lingual a.

Superior thyroid a.

Internal and
external carotid aa.

Right thyroid lobe

R
S In order to be able to remove the specimen from around all sides of the great vessels, this cylinder of tissue with attached thyroid must at some point be split. Here it is being done on the anterior surface of the cylinder to the apex of the dissection, which is to the central tendon of the digastric muscle. In Figure R the scissors is shown at the apex of the slit commencing to cut the specimen on a line along the anterior half of its circumference. The result, shown in Figure S, is an unroofed jugular vein. The dissection about the carotid here is done in a manner to allow the specimen to lie superficial to it.

T The internal jugular vein is retracted laterally so that the specimen may be separated at its posterior circumference. Pharyngeal branches from the jugular vein are immediately adjacent, but traction may empty them of blood, making their detection difficult to the unwary. The medial half of the specimen, which contains the thyroid, is now swung under and lateral to the jugular vein.

U The jugular vein is now retracted medially at the apex of the dissection and the specimen amputated, with care being taken not to divide the spinal accessory nerve coursing near the vein. The incision is closed in two layers, the deeper one being the approximation of the platysma muscle. Since there is no great void to obliterate as with a radical neck dissection, insertion of catheters for postoperative suction is not really too useful in these cases. Instead, one or two small soft rubber drains are exteriorized through the lower aspect of the incision. The patients are watched for bleeding, unilateral paralysis of the vocal cord and hypoparathyroidism. The drains are removed on the second postoperative day, the stitches on the fifth and seventh days and the patient discharged soon afterward.

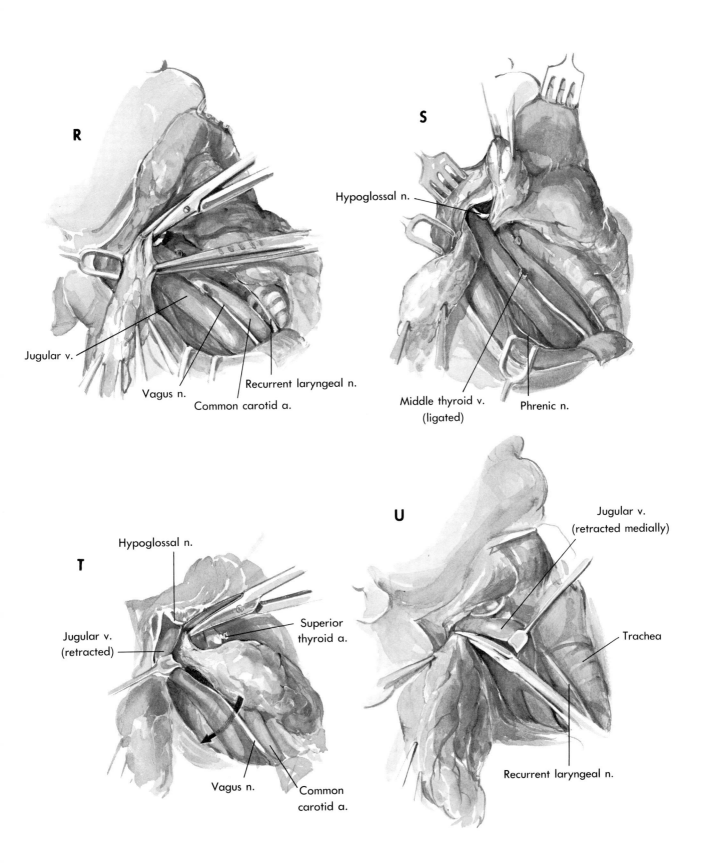

R

Jugular v.

Vagus n.

Common carotid a.

Recurrent laryngeal n.

S

Hypoglossal n.

Middle thyroid v.
(ligated)

Phrenic n.

T

Hypoglossal n.

Jugular v.
(retracted)

Superior
thyroid a.

Vagus n.

Common
carotid a.

U

Jugular v.
(retracted medially)

Trachea

Recurrent laryngeal n.

RADICAL LARYNGECTOMY

Impetus to the study of the larynx was given by the discovery of mirror laryngoscopy by a singing instructor, Manuel Garcia, in 1855. Prior to that time there had been only occasional references to laryngeal disease in the medical literature. A deluge of reports regarding laryngeal growths began to appear after the introduction of indirect laryngoscopy.

Alteration or loss of voice and the inexorable course of untreated laryngeal cancer have long been of major concern to both patient and physician. Restoration of vocal function, cure of cancer by radiotherapy or the permanent deprivation of voice by laryngectomy are dramatic episodes. It is natural, then, that in the past century considerable talent and effort should have been devoted to methods of treating cancer of the larynx.

The first laryngectomy was performed by Watson of Edinburgh in 1866 on a patient with destructive tertiary syphilis of the larynx. A successful laryngectomy for cancer was achieved subsequently by Billroth in 1873. From this date on there began a swing from "radical" to "conservative" thought regarding the proper therapy of laryngeal cancer which has continued to oscillate through the years up to this present writing. In the early years of this controversy, the high mortality rates that attended the procedure of laryngectomy were cited persistently by its detractors, and the successful results reported by its proponents could not be duplicated by other surgeons. The development of thyrotomy and vocal cord excision (termed laryngofissure) for the treatment of cancer confined to the vocal cord marked a distinct advance which, coincidentally, led to an appreciation of the behavioral differences of cordal and noncordal lesions. In 1878 Krishaber first proposed the classification of laryngeal cancer into intrinsic and extrinsic types. Although this distinction was significant and served well for many years, it was subject to different interpretations by various surgeons, with corresponding confusion in the reported operative results.

The high morbidity and mortality rates that accompanied the early laryngectomy, and the understandable reluctance of patients to be deprived of their voices, permitted radiotherapy to enjoy a therapeutic ascendancy. However, as reports of the untoward effects of radiotherapy began to appear, there gradually evolved a more thoughtful appraisal of its proper application.

A transformation developed in laryngeal surgery, as it has in all other major surgical endeavors. Some of these factors in improved surgery were: a better appreciation and understanding of cervical anatomy, improved anesthetic methods, the availability of ancillary laboratory procedures, the use of intravenous fluids, the wider and safer use of blood and the introduction of antibiotics. These factors made laryngectomy a relatively safe procedure, and the various modes of therapy could be evaluated more effectively. Radical neck dissection, an operation which originally was performed for palpable cervical metastases, was then successfully carried out as a primary procedure independently or in continuity with excision of the laryngeal cancer. The consequent spectacular rise in survival rates in patients with laryngeal cancer metastatic to cervical lymph nodes fully justified the adoption of more aggressive surgical measures. With improvement in the methods of rehabilitating patients with laryngectomies through the development of esophageal speech, the loss of one's larynx came to be regarded as something less than catastrophic.

The demonstration by Ogura of microscopic foci of cancer in nonpalpable cervical lymph nodes and the advocacy of elective neck dissection along with laryngectomy for lesions involving the rich lymph-bearing areas (epiglottis, arytenoids, aryepiglottic folds, ventricular bands and subglottic space) marked another significant advance. Expansion of the awareness of the lymphatic supply of the various portions of the larynx and application of this knowledge clinically has led to a revival of so-called conservation procedures. With these conservation operations, a relatively small but specific number of primary lesions and their associated lymphatic sites can be removed and voice and swallowing functions preserved. With correct selection of patients and skillful surgery, the cure rates become comparable to those obtained with sacrifice of the entire larynx.

Concurrent with these surgical advances in the treatment of laryngeal cancer, it has been demonstrated that radiotherapy, in expert hands, can offer cure rates for limited cordal cancer quite comparable to those of surgical excision.

Recent and current studies suggest that the use of preoperative radiotherapy for extensive primary lesions seems to have increased the operable salvage of patients with cer-

Page 52

tain cancers that, on first appraisal, had been regarded as incurable. It seems also that preoperative radiation may give slightly increased cure rates in the surgery of laryngeal cancer; however, this point is not yet definitely settled and needs further study and evaluation.

It now appears that surgery has reached a point of maximum effectiveness in dealing with laryngeal cancer and that methods of earlier detection or innovations in treatment will be needed to achieve even better results than the relatively good ones currently possible. Certainly, the high-risk patients with oral and laryngeal cancer, namely, the heavy smokers and those with a heavy intake of alcohol, need to be followed and watched most carefully if lesions are to be found early enough to be curable.

The most important aspect of laryngeal surgery is the maintenance of an adequate airway. If there is airway obstruction preoperatively, a tracheostomy, under local anesthesia, is mandatory before undertaking general anesthesia. The anesthetist must be certain that he is able to insert an endotracheal tube through the larynx before he anesthetizes a patient or else he must insist upon a tracheostomy for his endotracheal tube. If there is any doubt, the tracheostomy must be done first. It should be remembered that aseptic care should be provided postoperatively. Tracheostomy tubes and tracheal suction should be performed with good aseptic technique and appropriate cultures taken if there are any signs of respiratory tract infection. When a patient has a tracheostomy and is deprived of his usual cough mechanism and larynx, he is dependent on the persons caring for him for maintaining a clear airway. Additionally, one of the hazards in postoperative care is drying of the tracheal mucosa and obstruction with crusts. Maintenance of adequate humidification in the inspired air is mandatory. Not all tracheas and necks fit a standard tracheostomy tube; in consequence, an appropriately fitting tube must be used. To keep it clean of crusts sterile saline can be injected into the trachea in 5 cc. doses every one to four hours and a humid environment provided.

The other main problem in laryngeal and neck surgery relates to the need for viability of skin flaps and adequate, intact skin coverage. This is more difficult to obtain if extensive radiotherapy has been carried out before the surgery, since a radical neck dissection in continuity with laryngectomy leaves bare the carotid artery. Loss of skin coverage in this area is likely to result in carotid artery "blow-out." Untreated, this event has disastrous results; even prompt treatment by transfusion, maintenance of blood pressure and carotid ligation carries nearly a 35 per cent mortality rate, dependent upon the age of the patient.

References

Friedberg, S. A.: Recent trends in surgery of the larynx. S. Clin. North America 46:99, 1966.
Leroux, R. J.: Indications for radical surgery, partial surgery, radiotherapy and combined surgery and radiotherapy for cancer of the larynx and hypopharynx. Ann. Otol. Rhin. & Laryng. 65:137, 1956.
Ogura, J. H.: Surgical pathology of cancer of the larynx. Laryngoscope 65:867, 1955.
Schechter, D. C., and Morfit, H. M.: The evolution of surgical treatment of tumors of the larynx. Surgery 57:457, 1965.
Stevenson, R. S., and Guthrie, D.: A History of Otolaryngology. Edinburgh, E. & S. Livingstone, Ltd., 1949.

Radical Laryngectomy

Laryngectomy and radical neck dissection are procedures that have been performed separately for some time. However, the more advanced and demanding operation of combining these two procedures as an en bloc resection is being used with increasing frequency, with demonstration of the value in removing the cervical lymph nodes (even when they are not clinically palpable) on the same side as the laryngeal cancer. It is essential that there be a positive microscopic diagnosis of cancer before any such mutilating procedure is carried out. If preoperative radiotherapy has been administered, there is often a remarkable and unexpected regression of the cancer to the point that its continued presence at the time of operation is seriously in doubt. In such instances, only multiple and deep biopsies may suffice to reveal residual cancer. It would be up to the individual surgeon to decide whether to do this or to risk surgery on the rare patient who has been cured by preoperative radiotherapy.

A
B
There is a profusion of anatomical structures in this area and so many have to be disengaged or reapproximated that a thorough knowledge of the anatomical relationships is especially important. These two illustrations emphasize the anatomical structures and landmarks pertinent to the laryngectomy, the aspect of the radical neck dissection being complemented by the illustrations in that section. The larynx is over the 4th, 5th and 6th cervical vertebrae and is situated between the base of the tongue and the upper trachea. Its mucous membrane continues cephalad into the oropharynx, and caudad down into the trachea — a point of clinical concern with extracordal cancers that may spread submucosally to a point considerably beyond that of obvious mucosal involvement. The blood supply to the larynx is derived from the superior and inferior thyroid arteries and veins. The superior thyroid vein is removed in the course of excising the jugular vein during the radical neck dissection. The inferior thyroid vein must be secured separately at the root of the neck. The sequence of this operation permits ablation of the lymph node drainage and then of the vascular supply of the larynx before the larynx and tumor are manipulated.

The hyoid bone will be removed in its entirety. Notice the considerable number of muscles that have to be separated from its superior surface. The hypoglossal nerve starts its anterior swing at about the level at which the lingual artery branches from the external carotid artery and goes deep to the digastric and stylohyoid muscles. The infrahyoid or strap muscles will be excised on the involved side, but on the side opposite the laryngeal cancer all, save the thyrohyoid, are disengaged and left in place.

C
The patient is positioned as for a radical neck dissection, with the anesthesiologist making provision for removal of the orotracheal tube toward the end of the procedure and the insertion of a longer cuffed tube directly into the tracheostomy. Provisions are also made for transfusion of blood and electrolytic solutions. Endotracheally administered anesthesia is employed routinely. Some patients will have had a tracheostomy done preoperatively because of obstruction. We desist from the practice of some in performing a tracheostomy routinely in order to administer the anesthetic. Although this avoids trauma to the tumor and possible desquamation of its cells, there is no clear evidence that orotracheal intubation is detrimental to the patient, and for the present the cumbersome procedure of preliminary tracheostomy does not seem to be worthwhile. The skin flaps are fashioned as in a radical neck dissection. Sometimes it is desirable to have the inferomedial arm of the double-trifurcate incision fall short of the sternal notch so that the eventual tracheal stoma is made in an appropriately sized opening in the medial flap rather than in the primary neck incision.

The strap muscles effectively conceal the thyroid and most of the larynx. The greater auricular nerve is seen at the middle third of the posterior aspect of the sternocleidomastoid muscle as it swings to course cephalad on the superficial surface of the muscle.

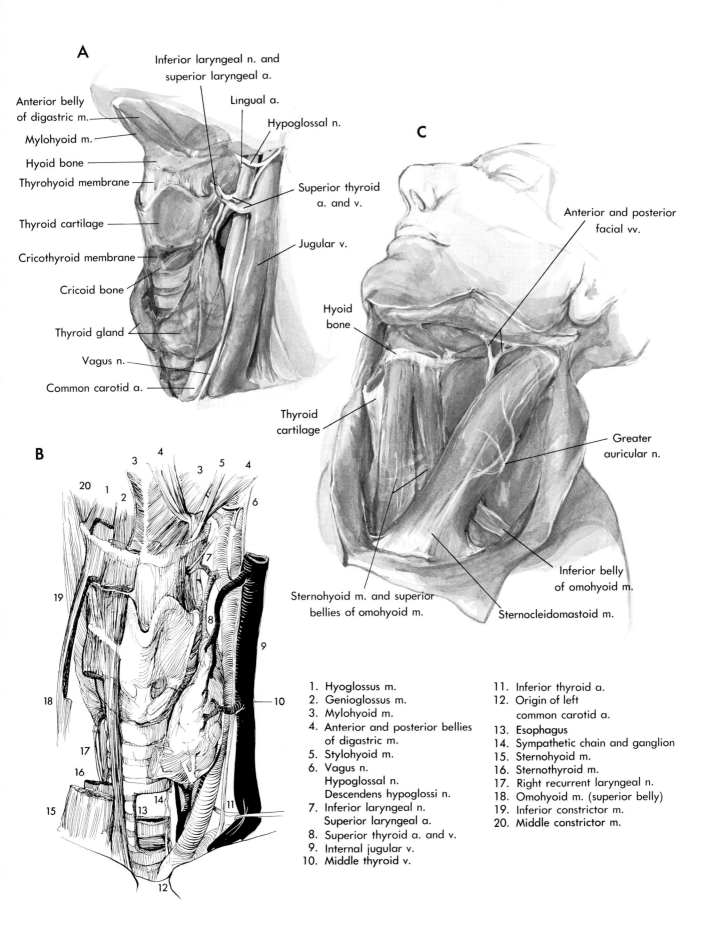

A

Inferior laryngeal n. and
superior laryngeal a.

Lingual a.

Hypoglossal n.

Anterior belly
of digastric m.

Mylohyoid m.

Hyoid bone

Thyrohyoid membrane

Superior thyroid
a. and v.

Thyroid cartilage

Jugular v.

Cricothyroid membrane

Cricoid bone

Thyroid gland

Vagus n.

Common carotid a.

C

Anterior and posterior
facial vv.

Hyoid
bone

Thyroid
cartilage

Greater
auricular n.

Inferior belly
of omohyoid m.

Sternohyoid m. and superior
bellies of omohyoid m.

Sternocleidomastoid m.

B

1. Hyoglossus m.
2. Genioglossus m.
3. Mylohyoid m.
4. Anterior and posterior bellies
   of digastric m.
5. Stylohyoid m.
6. Vagus n.
   Hypoglossal n.
   Descendens hypoglossi n.
7. Inferior laryngeal n.
   Superior laryngeal a.
8. Superior thyroid a. and v.
9. Internal jugular v.
10. Middle thyroid v.

11. Inferior thyroid a.
12. Origin of left
    common carotid a.
13. Esophagus
14. Sympathetic chain and ganglion
15. Sternohyoid m.
16. Sternothyroid m.
17. Right recurrent laryngeal n.
18. Omohyoid m. (superior belly)
19. Inferior constrictor m.
20. Middle constrictor m.

D The plan will be to proceed first with the radical neck dissection on the selected side, with the eventual pharyngeal entry on the uninvolved or lesser involved side. The procedure is begun by dissecting the fatty areolar tissue in the inferolateral area. The inferior belly of the omohyoid muscle is divided, and the dissection proceeds cephalad along the anterior border of the trapezius muscle. The spinal accessory nerve is found on the deep anterior surface of the junction of the middle and lower thirds of the trapezius muscle and is sacrificed. Since some of the fibers of the sternocleidomastoid muscle are intimately attached to the skin in the upper neck, it is reasonable to leave some behind rather than to try to remove all of them and so make the skin flap too thin in this area. Furthermore, this is rarely the area of cancerous deposits which must be skirted widely. As the dissection in the lower neck progresses medially, the transverse scapular and cervical arteries are encountered and divided. The brachial plexus will lie deep to this area.

The sternal and clavicular heads of the sternocleidomastoid muscle are divided about 1 cm. from their insertions. If a greater amount of muscle than this is left behind, it may become fibrotic and be confused postoperatively with residual or recurrent cancer. The sternohyoid and sternothyroid muscles are also divided at their lower ends. The carotid sheath is entered and the jugular vein encircled with the help of a Mixter gallbladder clamp. The vagus nerve can hug the internal jugular vein deceptively and be liable to injury, so it should be sought for and specifically identified before the vein is ligated and divided. Two ties of 2-0 silk secure the lower internal jugular vein and are applied about 2 mm. apart; a third tie is placed a centimeter more cephalad and the vein divided.

E The inferior thyroid vein is ligated and divided on the involved side since the thyroid
F lobe on this side is to be removed with the specimen. A small curved hemostat is insinuated under the isthmus toward the uninvolved side and straight hemostats are placed across the isthmus, whereupon it is divided between them. A transfixion stitch of catgut is used for hemostasis on the cut surface of the opposite isthmus, or vessels may be ligated individually and the anterior and posterior capsules of the thyroid approximated with continuous 3-0 chromic catgut. The inferior thyroid artery is divided next. The thyroid lobe is next dissected off the trachea to the first tracheal ring.

G The deep plane of the dissection remains just superficial to the deep cervical fascia. The specimen is dissected in a medial and cephalad direction, remaining superficial to the scalene muscles and sparing the phrenic nerve. The specimen has been freed to just beyond the carotid bifurcation, at which point the hypoglossal nerve is sought for and preserved. Next the sternocleidomastoid muscle is detached from its origin if this was not done completely earlier. The dissection continues in an anterior direction; the lower portion of the parotid gland is severed on a plane parallel to the horizontal ramus of the mandible. Division of the gland in this plane minimizes the risk of severing the mandibular branch of the facial nerve near its origin. Peripherally the nerve will have been freed to follow the upper neck flap. Several sizable branches of the facial vein are encountered and divided. As the specimen is carried over the carotid bifurcation, care is taken not to tear any of the veins from the pharynx since securing them can be troublesome and also poses a risk of injury to the hypoglossal nerve. The ansa hypoglossi nerve is severed at its origin and allowed to remain with the strap muscles which are sacrificed.

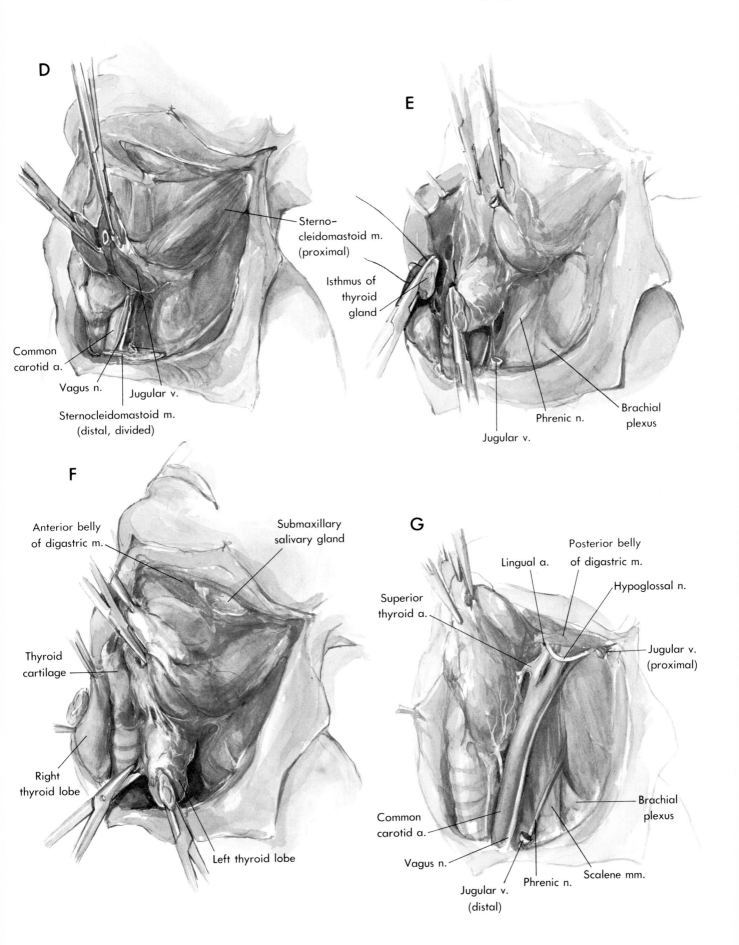

D

Sterno-
cleidomastoid m.
(proximal)

Isthmus of
thyroid
gland

Common
carotid a.

Vagus n.

Jugular v.

Sternocleidomastoid m.
(distal, divided)

E

Phrenic n.

Brachial
plexus

Jugular v.

F

Anterior belly
of digastric m.

Submaxillary
salivary gland

Thyroid
cartilage

Right
thyroid
lobe

Left thyroid lobe

G

Superior
thyroid a.

Lingual a.

Posterior belly
of digastric m.

Hypoglossal n.

Jugular v.
(proximal)

Common
carotid a.

Vagus n.

Jugular v.
(distal)

Phrenic n.

Brachial
plexus

Scalene mm.

H   The dissection of the submaxillary triangle is now carried out. The submaxillary salivary gland and associated lymph nodes are removed, and the salivary duct is ligated with catgut. In this and in Figure J can be seen the divided chorda tympani nerve. When the submaxillary salivary gland is retracted, the associated chorda tympani nerve may bow the attached lingual nerve into the operative field and it may be damaged. (Impaired sensation of taste of the anterior two-thirds of the tongue follows this unnecessary complication.) The middle thyroid vein is ligated and divided. The superior thyroid artery is divided at its origin and ligated with 2-0 silk. This releases the specimen considerably and substantially completes the radical neck dissection.

I   Although removal of the hyoid bone is not essential to an adequate cancer operation, its retention results in greater tension on the suture line during the subsequent pharyngeal closure. This leads to an increased incidence of postoperative pharyngocutaneous fistula — a serious and disabling complication. The muscles attached to the superior border of the hyoid bone are separated from it with the knife cutting directly on the bone. Although several scapel blades may be dulled in the process, it remains the best method for separating these muscles from the bone. This procedure is aided by downward traction on the specimen so that the suprahyoid muscles are made taut.

J   The greater horn of the hyoid bone should be removed in its entirety rather than cut across. A retained greater horn, by its discreteness and firmness, may be confused postoperatively with recurrent cancer. An effective way of bringing the horn to a more superficial position for skeletonization is to place a towel clip just deep to the bone and lift upward and medially. The dissection should continue close to the bone; dissection at a deeper plane will risk entry into the pharynx.

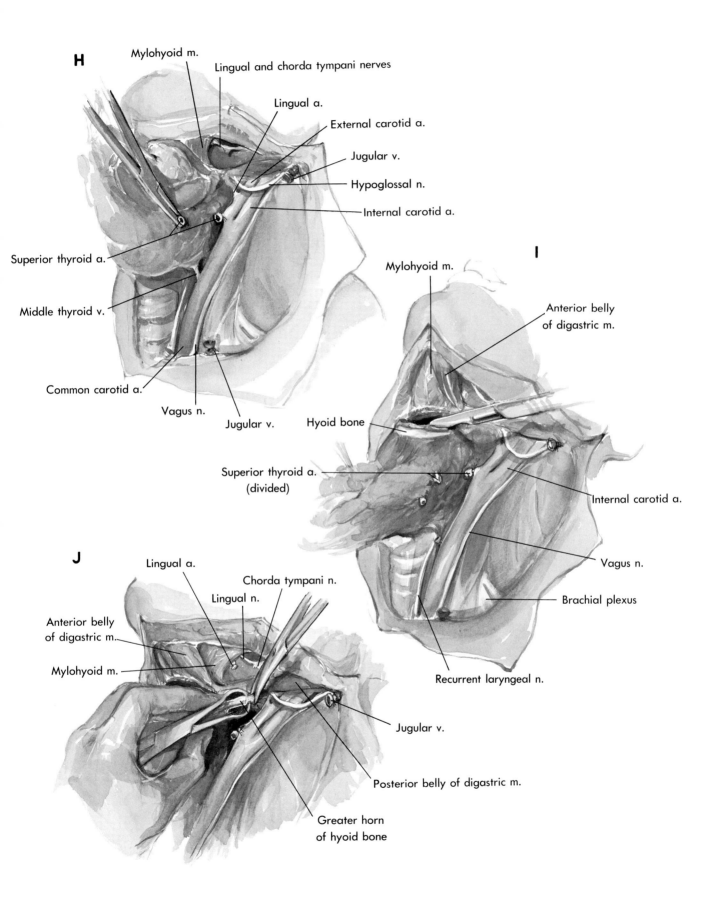

H

Mylohyoid m.

Lingual and chorda tympani nerves

Lingual a.

External carotid a.

Jugular v.

Hypoglossal n.

Internal carotid a.

Superior thyroid a.

Middle thyroid v.

Common carotid a.

Vagus n.

Jugular v.

I

Mylohyoid m.

Anterior belly of digastric m.

Superior thyroid a. (divided)

Hyoid bone

Internal carotid a.

Vagus n.

Brachial plexus

Recurrent laryngeal n.

J

Lingual a.

Chorda tympani n.

Lingual n.

Anterior belly of digastric m.

Mylohyoid m.

Jugular v.

Posterior belly of digastric m.

Greater horn of hyoid bone

K   The larynx is allowed to fall back into place. The superior laryngeal artery and internal laryngeal nerve are clamped, cut and ligated. Although the superior laryngeal artery most frequently branches off the superior thyroid artery, which has already been divided, it may have other origins or connections and will hemorrhage if neglected. It is quite necessary, of course, that it be specifically ligated on the opposite side also.

L
M   The specimen is swung to the left, exposing the side of the larynx less involved with cancer. The strap muscles are disengaged of their connection with the larynx with the intention of leaving them behind or, at the option of the surgeon, they can be left attached to the larynx to be excised with it. The omohyoid is then divided at its middle tendon. The paratracheal tissue to the cricoid cartilage is removed, and the thyroid lobe is disengaged from the trachea. A preferred method is to disconnect the strap muscles from the larynx and then, along with the underlying thyroid lobe plus the carotid sheath and sternocleidomastoid, retract them laterally. In Figure M the greater horn of the hyoid bone is being dissected free in the same fashion as on the opposite side.

N   The view of the laryngopharynx, when entered, is so different from that seen during laryngoscopy that even the experienced observer needs a moment for orientation. For this reason this view of the larynx, seen from a dorsal vantage point, is included here; we realize that only experience will generate confidence and speed in recognition of landmarks. The greater horn of the hyoid bone is immediately deep to the submucosa, justifying the need to skeletonize the greater horn (Figures J and M) during its mobilization if a "button-hole" in the mucosa is to be prevented. The line of mucosal incision for the laryngectomy is not shown since this would depend entirely on the location and extent of the cancer.

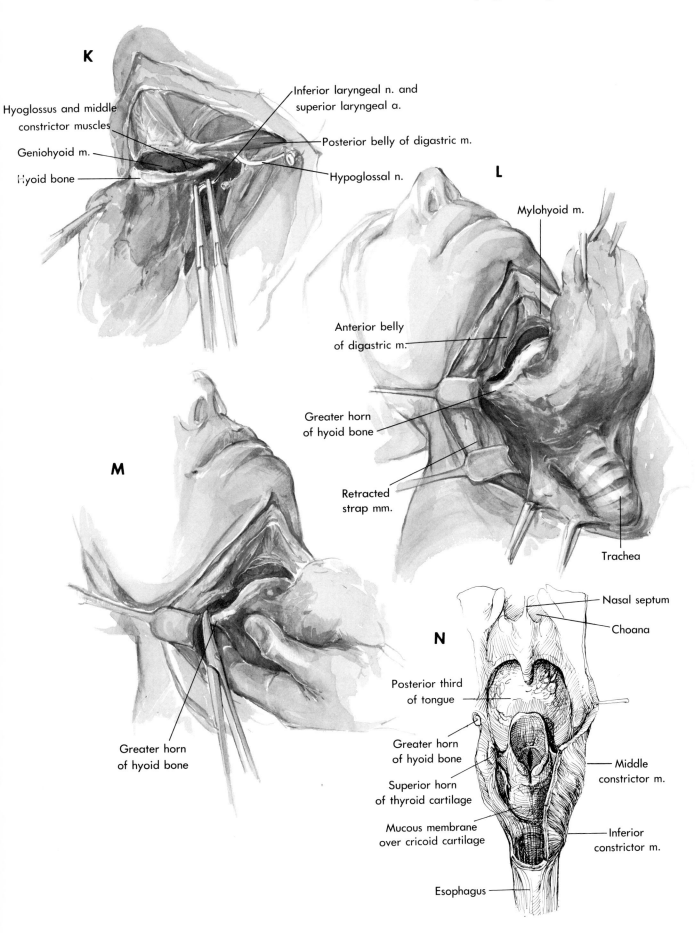

K

Hyoglossus and middle constrictor muscles

Geniohyoid m.

Hyoid bone

Inferior laryngeal n. and superior laryngeal a.

Posterior belly of digastric m.

Hypoglossal n.

L

Mylohyoid m.

Anterior belly of digastric m.

Greater horn of hyoid bone

Retracted strap mm.

Trachea

M

Greater horn of hyoid bone

N

Nasal septum

Choana

Posterior third of tongue

Greater horn of hyoid bone

Superior horn of thyroid cartilage

Mucous membrane over cricoid cartilage

Middle constrictor m.

Inferior constrictor m.

Esophagus

O   Preparations are now made for entry into the larynx. This is done on the side involved to a lesser degree, and so also on the side opposite the concomitant radical neck dissection. The tracheal cartilage is hooked with a tracheal hook and rotated rather severely in the opposite direction. An incision is made lightly over the inferior constrictor muscle just posterior to the thyroid cartilage. The pharyngeal mucosa will then pout through this incision. This is grasped with thumb forceps, herniated further and incised for entry into the pharynx.

P   Metzenbaum scissors are used to incise the constrictor muscles. The inferior aspect of the incision extends to the lowermost fibers of the inferior constrictor muscle. The incision is extended cephalad and turned medially just inside the greater horn of the hyoid bone, then continued along the upper border of the hyoid bone. Of course, the preoperative laryngoscopy may indicate a different course for the incision in accordance with the location of the tumor. Sufficient distortion of the specimen usually takes place as the operation proceeds so that it often is difficult to correlate the extralaryngeal incision with that on the mucosa which is dictated by the extent of cancerous involvement. For this reason it is often beneficial to incise the mucosa with the larynx maintained in a relatively natural position and to use this incision as the perimeter of the continuing dissection.

Q   The tracheal hook is applied to the left side of the larynx and the larynx rotated to the right. The division of the constrictor muscles proceeds downwardly and the mucosal incision is used as a guide. The stealthy submucosal spread of these cancers makes it necessary to provide an adequate margin of grossly normal tissue beyond the extent of the tumor. If there is any question about the adequacy of the excision, more tissue should be excised offhand. If excision of more tissue will create a serious problem in closure or reconstruction, microscopic examination of frozen sections from the periphery of the incision can help to substantiate the need for a wider excision.

R   The trachea must now be divided. This is done between tracheal rings and should not be so high as to cut into any subglottic extension of the tumor. An excessive length of trachea can, of course, be trimmed later. The endotracheal cuff balloon will be in this area, and care should be taken lest it be punctured and deprive the anesthesiologist of positive pressure before he and the surgeon are ready for the tube transfer. A long endotracheal tube is held in readiness. When the trachea is incised sufficiently, the anesthesiologist removes the current endotracheal tube, the new one is inserted through the tracheostomy and the balloon inflated. The proximal end is quickly passed under the drapes to the anesthesiologist so that the administration of the anesthetic is virtually uninterrupted. It is easy to insert the tube so far that it abuts the carina, with the possibility that this will prevent adequate ventilation. It will often be necessary to pack some gauze around the endotracheal tube to prevent seepage of blood into the trachea and to prevent the cuff balloon from popping out. If this occurs, the endotracheal tube can be stabilized with a stitch of 2-0 silk which is tied to it and then anchored to the anterior aspect of the uppermost tracheal ring. This portion of the trachea will be excised incidentally during tailoring for the tracheostomy (Figure Y).

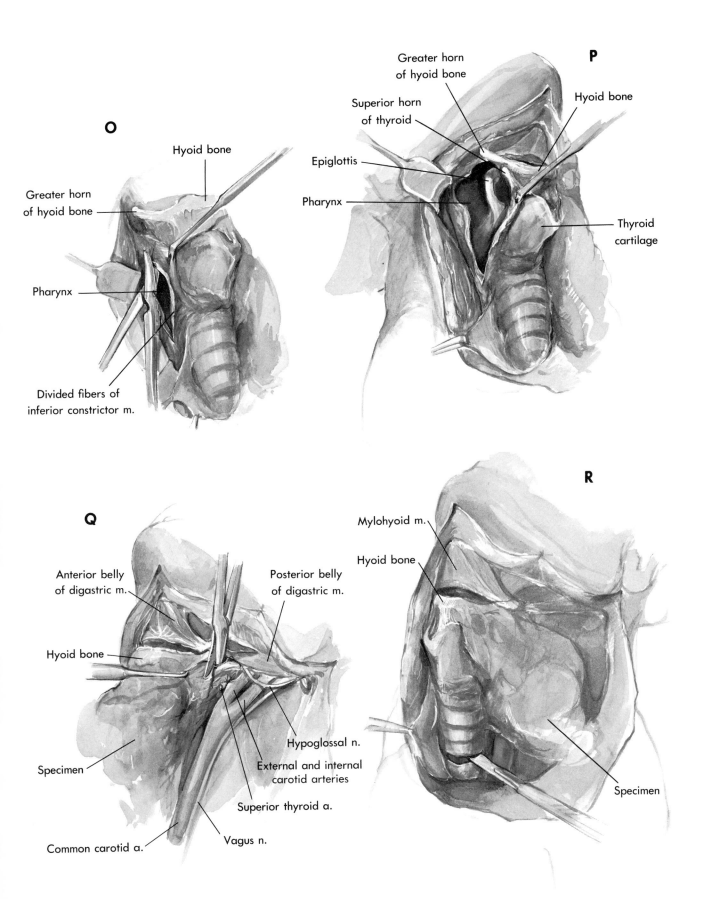

O

Hyoid bone

Greater horn
of hyoid bone

Pharynx

Divided fibers of
inferior constrictor m.

P

Greater horn
of hyoid bone

Superior horn
of thyroid

Hyoid bone

Epiglottis

Pharynx

Thyroid
cartilage

Q

Anterior belly
of digastric m.

Posterior belly
of digastric m.

Hyoid bone

Specimen

Hypoglossal n.

External and internal
carotid arteries

Superior thyroid a.

Common carotid a.

Vagus n.

R

Mylohyoid m.

Hyoid bone

Specimen

S
T

The trachea is incised to its membranous portion; it becomes critical, however, that the esophagus is not entered at this low point. (The longitudinal fibers of the esophagus will be recognized readily.) In addition, the dissection proceeds more easily once the proper plane has been reached. Some may prefer using a scissors in a spread-and-cut technique in this plane. The pharynx is entered near the postcricoid area but at a lower point if dictated by the proximity of cancer.

U
V

If all the fibers of the constrictor muscles have not been divided, this can now be done. The finger can be inserted into the pharynx to steady the tissue for guidance. Again, one can look inside and follow the mucosal incision. In Figure V the specimen has been removed. The resultant defect usually is T-shaped but obviously can be any bizarre shape. This is the time to examine the cut edges carefully and to have microscopic examination made of pieces removed from suspicious margins. A small caliber plastic feeding tube is introduced through the nose and directed distally down the esophagus under direct vision. It is easier to pass the tube at this time and certainly safer than trying to introduce it postoperatively when the patient cannot readily cooperate; gagging by the semiconscious patient may also place excess strain on the suture line. If passage of this tube is neglected now and it cannot be passed later, the patient is placed at a disadvantage from the standpoint of maintenance of nutrition; this tempts the surgeon to start oral feeding sooner than is desirable. It is essential that this tube not be allowed to come out until the surgeon wishes to remove it. A suture placed through the nose and tied to the tube aids retention.

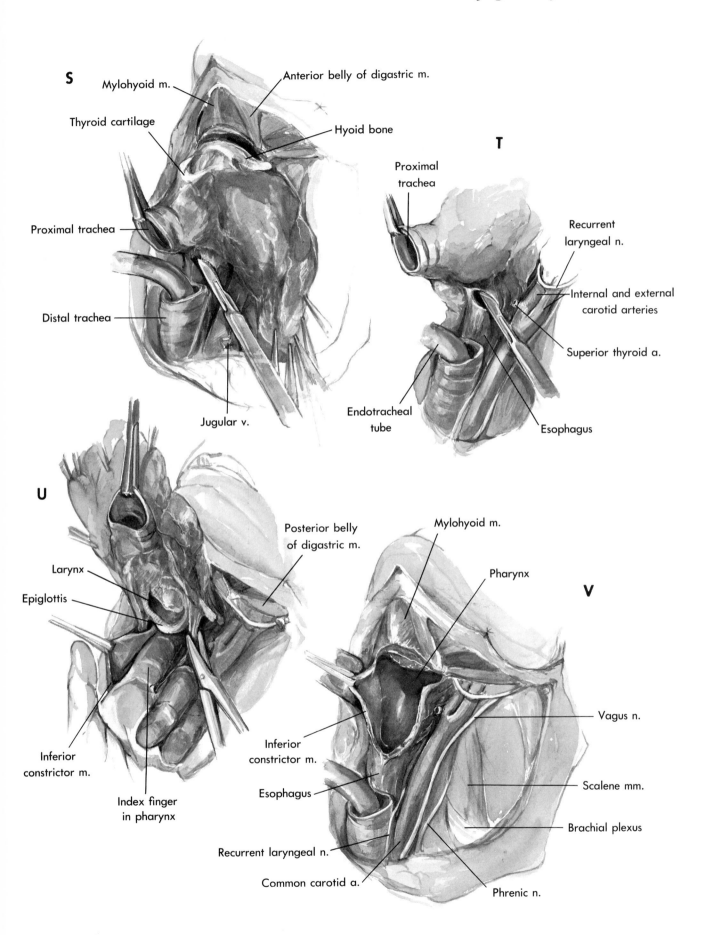

S

Mylohyoid m.

Anterior belly of digastric m.

Thyroid cartilage

Hyoid bone

Proximal trachea

T

Distal trachea

Proximal trachea

Recurrent laryngeal n.

Internal and external carotid arteries

Superior thyroid a.

Jugular v.

Endotracheal tube

Esophagus

U

Posterior belly of digastric m.

Mylohyoid m.

Larynx

Pharynx

Epiglottis

V

Vagus n.

Inferior constrictor m.

Inferior constrictor m.

Scalene mm.

Esophagus

Brachial plexus

Index finger in pharynx

Recurrent laryngeal n.

Common carotid a.

Phrenic n.

Radical Laryngectomy (continued)

W   The closure is done entirely with simple interrupted stitches of atraumatic 3-0 chromic catgut and is begun at the extremes of the trifurcate opening. Pharyngocutaneous fistula is one of the most serious postoperative complications and care in closure is important to its prevention. The mucosa must be coapted adequately but with care that the stitches are not tied too tightly with consequent necrosis of the intervening tissue. The end stitches should be retained after the first layer is placed, because the extremes of the closure can quickly retract, increasing the risk that the second layer will not be placed properly. The primary closure is in at least two layers. A critical point in the closure is in the meeting of the trifurcate lines. The strap muscles and other adjacent muscles or tissues are deliberately placed over the suture line so as to buttress this weak area.

X
Y   It is usually necessary to further mobilize the trachea from the esophagus so that the trachea can easily arch forward toward the skin surface. The trachea will also have to be beveled so that it meets the skin comfortably and at a right angle. The dashed line shows the proposed line of incision for tailoring the trachea.

Z
A_1
B_1   As is mentioned in the description of the development of the skin flaps, the infero-medial incision may be held short or directed to end over the medial third of the clavicle. The tracheostomy would thus end outside the suture line. In such an instance, a button of skin similar in diameter to that of the trachea is incised. The endotracheal tube is momentarily removed so that the trachea can be pulled through the skin opening as in Figure A_1. The trachea is sutured to the skin with interrupted stitches of 3-0 silk. Quadratically placed stitches (as in Figure B_1) are used to position the trachea properly and then additional stitches are placed as needed.

C_1   The trachea can, of course, be exited at the medial entrance of the lower incision. Suction drainage is a superior way to evacuate blood and serum and thus serves a most important function in maintaining contact between the skin flaps and the underlying tissue. One catheter is directed toward the mastoid process and another toward the submaxillary triangle. They are exteriorized through separate tight counterincisions and placed on suction while the patient is still on the operating table and the wound is being closed. The skin is closed in one layer with narrowly placed vertical mattress stitches of 3-0 silk. The slightly retracted platysma muscle is pulled forward so that it can be incorporated in this single layer closure. When the wound closure is completed, a bulb syringe is used to introduce several hundred milliliters of physiological saline solution into the wound. As this is aspirated it carries with it small blood clots that may have formed during the closure. A single thickness of fine-mesh petrolatum gauze is applied over the wound because this helps to seal small leaks.

A short tracheostomy tube is inserted. A tracheostomy tube permits better postoperative tracheal aspiration with less trauma to the stoma; also, a dressing can be applied with less risk of stomal occlusion. Tracheostomy tubes made of inert plastic material are gaining favor because they are as adequate as those made of silver and are less expensive. A light dressing is applied and the patient is transferred to a bed whose head is maintained at 30 degrees' elevation. The patient is fed by nasogastric tube until the fifth to seventh day, when oral liquids are permitted. If these are tolerated and there is no evidence of pharyngocutaneous fistula, more solid food is gradually permitted. In those patients who have not received neck irradiation, the stitches are removed on the ninth and eleventh days, and the patients usually leave the hospital by the fourteenth day.

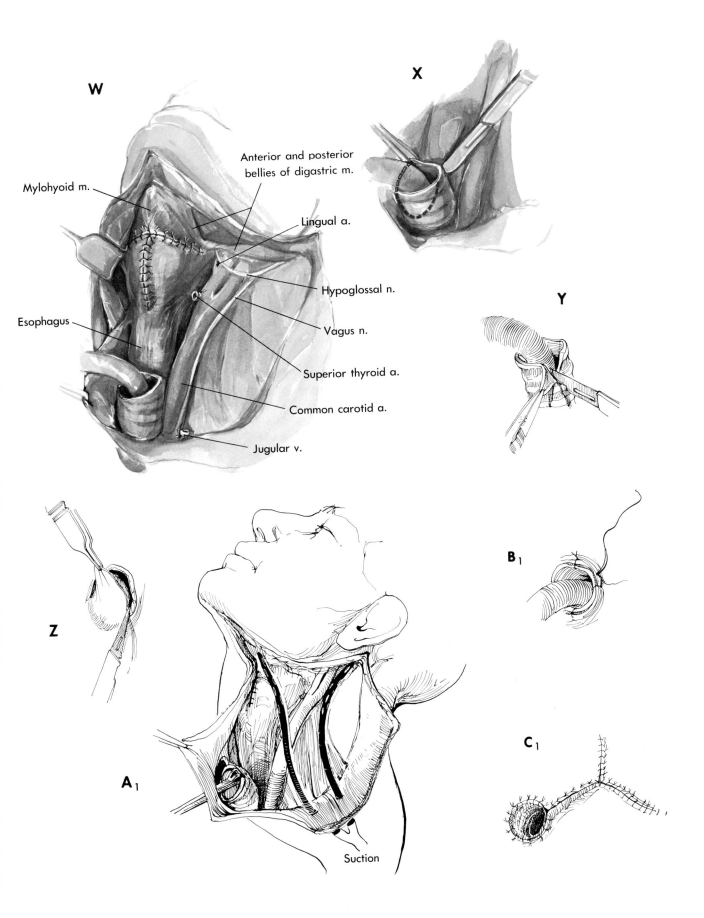

W

Mylohyoid m.

Anterior and posterior bellies of digastric m.

Lingual a.

Hypoglossal n.

Vagus n.

Esophagus

Superior thyroid a.

Common carotid a.

Jugular v.

X

Y

Z

A₁

Suction

B₁

C₁

CAROTID ENDARTERECTOMY

The contribution of carotid artery flow to cerebral function has been appreciated since early times, the word carotid being derived from the Greek work "karos," which means deep sleep.

A correlation between occlusion of the carotid artery and cerebral infarction was described in 1875 by Gowers and by others at the turn of the century. Obstruction of the internal carotid artery, however, was rarely diagnosed until 1937, when Egas Moniz and his associates demonstrated occlusion of the internal carotid artery by cerebral angiography. In 1954 Fisher recorded 28 cases of occlusive lesions of the carotid artery in a series of 432 consecutive autopsies on adults.

Interest in carotid surgery was stimulated by Eastcott, Pickering and Rob, who, in 1954, described reconstruction of the internal carotid artery in a patient with intermittent attacks of hemiplegia. Much investigative as well as clinical work has been done since that time because of the recognition of the importance of stenosis of the internal carotid artery in the production of cerebral symptoms.

The severity of the clinical picture often depends on the extent of extracranial as well as intracranial occlusive disease as well as on the anatomy of cerebral collateral circulation. Occasionally, a nonocclusive, ulcerated atheroma at the level of the carotid bifurcation, which appears relatively benign on arteriography, may be the source of an embolic lesion to the brain. Of equal importance is the realization that a completely occluded internal carotid artery may be present in a patient who is totally asymptomatic.

The diagnosis of stenosis of the internal carotid artery can be suspected in a patient who has transient attacks of light-headedness, blurring of vision, aphasia and weakness or numbness of extremities or in whom is found a firm carotid artery bifurcation, or a systolic thrill or bruit localized to the area of the bifurcation. A suspected diagnosis should be confirmed by carotid angiography in two planes employing serial filming. The carotid compression test, ophthalmodynamometric studies and electroencephalography may be of interest, but final judgment depends on visualization of the obstructive lesion.

The atheroma found at the bifurcation of the common carotid artery is segmental in the overwhelming majority of patients and is thus most suitable for endarterectomy. The operation of carotid endarterectomy has become fully established during the past decade and can result in total removal of atheromatous plaque with restoration of blood flow.

In the light of present knowledge of the complexities of cerebrovascular disease an attempt should be made to make carotid endarterectomy safe by careful attention to patient selection and operative technique. The hazard of operation is greatly increased in patients with acute stroke and in those with residual neurologic deficit. Controversy still exists as to the benefit of carotid surgery for those patients with acute stroke and for patients with carotid stenosis who are asymptomatic. Emergency surgery should be reserved for patients who manifest frequent and progressively longer lasting attacks of cerebral insufficiency and for those in whom carotid arteriograms demonstrate a hairline opening across the stenotic lesion.

Surgical exposure of the carotid bifurcation is best obtained through a longitudinal incision along the anterior border of the sternocleidomastoid muscle. Dissection of the carotid bifurcation should be accomplished by gentle manipulation to avoid complete obliteration of the lumen or the dislodgment of atheromatous debris. The integrity of brain tissue should be preserved at all cost during the performance of carotid endarterectomy. Artificial elevation of blood pressure and hypercarbia during the period the carotid artery is clamped have been advocated; however, the use of a temporary internal shunt has the advantage of maintaining carotid flow without dependence on other arterial channels or collateral flow. The shunt also facilitates repair of the internal carotid artery after completion of endarterectomy. The entire plaque should be removed, including the atheromatous projection over the normal intima distally. Once a thorough endarterectomy is accomplished, a primary repair without a patch graft is possible and preferred. Systemic use of heparin is necessary during carotid endarterectomy to prevent clot formation in the shunt or the distal arteries.

In summary, the cerebral infarct caused by thrombosis of the extracranial internal carotid artery is a distinct clinical entity. Removal of a predisposing atheroma prior to complete occlusion of the lumen, therefore, will decrease the incidence of disabling stroke. Emphasis should be placed on early diagnosis, proper case selection and meticulous surgical technique.

References

Eastcott, H. H. G., Pickering, G. W., and Rob, C. G.: Reconstruction of internal carotid artery in a patient with intermittent attacks of hemiplegia. Lancet 2:994, 1954.

Fisher, M.: Occlusion of the carotid artery: Further experiences. Arch. Neurol. & Psychiat. 72:187, 1954.

Gowers, W. R.: A case of simultaneous embolism of central retinal and middle cerebral arteries. Lancet 2:794, 1875.

Javid, H., and Julian, O. C.: Prevention of stroke by carotid and vertebral surgery. S. Clin. North America 51:1 and 113, 1967.

Carotid Endarterectomy

A   The performance of this operation requires a thorough knowledge not only of the anatomy of the carotid arteries but also of the surrounding structures, which abound in variety and importance. The operating surgeon should be well trained in blood vessel surgery. Both common carotid arteries arise in the thorax, the right one from the bifurcation of the innominate artery at the upper aspect of the sternoclavicular joint and the left from the highest point of the aortic arch. As they pass up into the neck, they are separated only by the trachea and are sufficiently similar that one description applies to both. As they proceed cephalad, they diverge, become more superficial and dorsal and assume a course roughly parallel to the anterior border of the sternocleidomastoid muscle. At the upper margin of the thyroid cartilage they bifurcate into the internal and external branches.

A sheath derived from the deep cervical fascia encloses the artery, the jugular vein, which lies lateral to it, and the vagus nerve, which lies between and dorsal to both. Septa in turn separate the nerve, artery and vein. In the lower neck the artery is deep to the strap muscles, but higher up only the anterior border of the sternocleidomastoid muscle lies over it. This illustration shows the carotid triangle within which most of the operation will be confined; it is bound by the sternocleidomastoid muscle posteriorally, the stylohyoid and posterior belly of the digastric muscle above and the anterior belly of the omohyoid muscle below. The descendens hypoglossi nerve is seen coursing over the common carotid artery; it should be spared if possible, but no serious sequelae follow its division.

The operation is usually performed under general anesthesia administered endotracheally. A small sandbag is placed under the shoulders and the head rotated away from the operative side. A longitudinal incision is made along the lower three-fourths of the medial border of the sternocleidomastoid muscle.

B   The anterior jugular vein may run across the line of exposure and require division. Branches of the greater auricular nerve should be spared, if encountered, at the upper aspect of the incision. The sternocleidomastoid muscle is retracted laterally. The dissection proceeds down to the outer adventitia of the common carotid artery and is continued in this plane. The superior thyroid artery, most frequently the first branch of the external carotid artery, is being mobilized. Usually it is not divided (as was done in this instance) unless this is necessary to effect a proper rotation of the carotid artery during the subsequent surgery. The lingual artery may need dissection and isolation but rarely division. The dissection is rarely carried low enough that the middle thyroid vein has to be divided. The undivided branches of the external carotid which are to be within the shunt are occluded by a doubly looped strand of 2-0 silk. The superficial dissection proceeds to just beyond the hypoglossal nerve, which crosses the external and internal carotid arteries 1 to 3 cm. cephalad to the bifurcation of the common carotid artery at about the level at which the lingual artery appears. As the lingual nerve is the motor nerve to the tongue, accidental injury to this nerve is a distressing complication. Since the vessels have to be visualized this high, a cardinal rule should be that the nerve be specifically identified rather than forgotten if not seen. If even higher exposure is needed, the nerve is mobilized off the carotid vessels and gently reflected cephalad; this may require intentional division of the restraining descendens hypoglossi nerve.

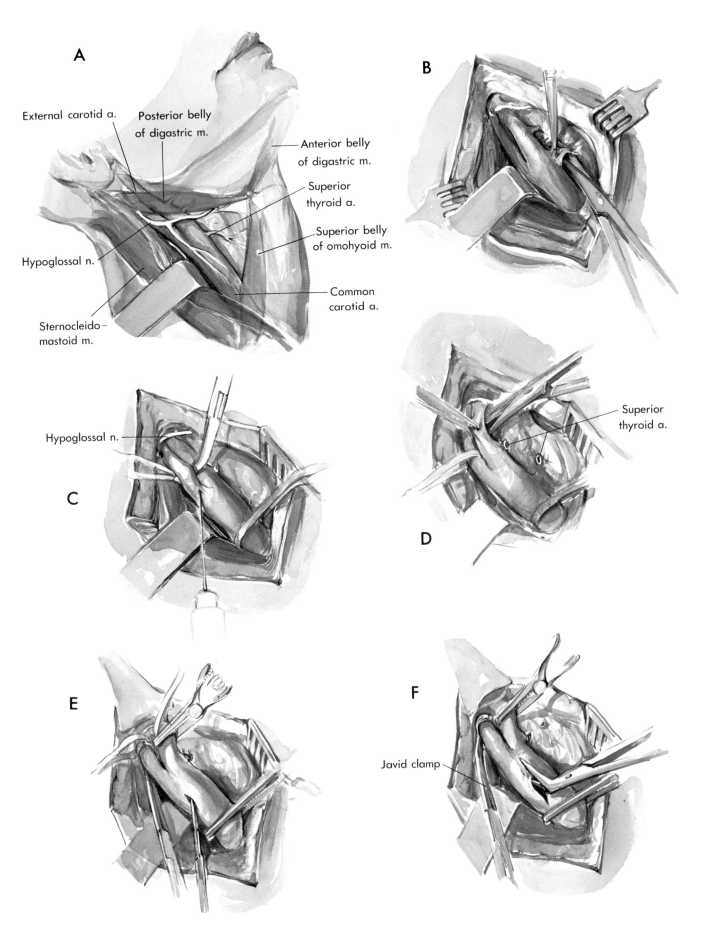

A

External carotid a.

Posterior belly
of digastric m.

Anterior belly
of digastric m.

Superior
thyroid a.

Superior belly
of omohyoid m.

Hypoglossal n.

Common
carotid a.

Sternocleido-
mastoid m.

B

Hypoglossal n.

C

Superior
thyroid a.

D

E

Javid clamp

F

C
D
A self-retaining retractor has been applied and, in addition, the sternocleidomastoid muscle has been retracted laterally. The common carotid artery is dissected free circumferentially and a ligature tape passed around it. The surgeon should visualize clearly the far side of the arterial dissection so that the subjacent vagus nerve is not injured. A ligature tape is being passed around the internal carotid artery. If, as is uncommonly the case, manipulation of the carotid bulb produces vasomotor changes, the adventitial tissue can be very lightly infiltrated with 1 per cent Xylocaine. In Figure D the proximal external carotid artery is being mobilized. When tapes have been passed around all three vessels, they are dissected to the extremes of the operative incision. The preoperative angiogram and finger palpation for a bruit will determine if the internal carotid artery has been exposed adequately since the surgeon should have under direct vision all the portion of the artery that is to have an endarterectomy. Sometimes an atheroma does not fade away soon enough as it extends upward from the bifurcation; this will necessitate exposure of the internal carotid artery to its fullest extent.

E
F
The patient is given heparin intravenously at 0.1 mg./kg. of body weight, but the total dose is not to exceed 50 mg. In accordance with the preference of the surgeon, the patient is made to breath a 5 per cent carbon dioxide during the period of occlusion for the vasodilatory effect of hypercarbia. The occlusion that follows is timed and an effort is made to keep it under three minutes. An arterial clamp is lightly applied to the common carotid artery and an arterial clamp or tourniquet is used to occlude the external carotid artery. A Javid clamp is placed in position in expectation of the shunt and a tourniquet placed just distal or proximal to this clamp. A longitudinal arteriotomy is made over the carotid bulb and extended in both directions with a 45 degree arteriotomy scissors.

The preferred shunt is made of tapered polyvinyl tubing. It is approximately 25 cm. in length, which allows for an adequate loop that will not be in the way of the surgeon. The end with the larger bore has an outside diameter of approximately 6 mm. and is inserted into the common carotid artery. The smaller end has an outside diameter of approximately 3 mm. and is inserted into the internal carotid artery. The ends of the shunt have a slight olive tip so that it becomes impossible for them to slip past and out of the snugly fitting Javid clamp. Smooth tips on the shunt preclude damage to the intima or dislodgment of an atheroma when the shunt is introduced.

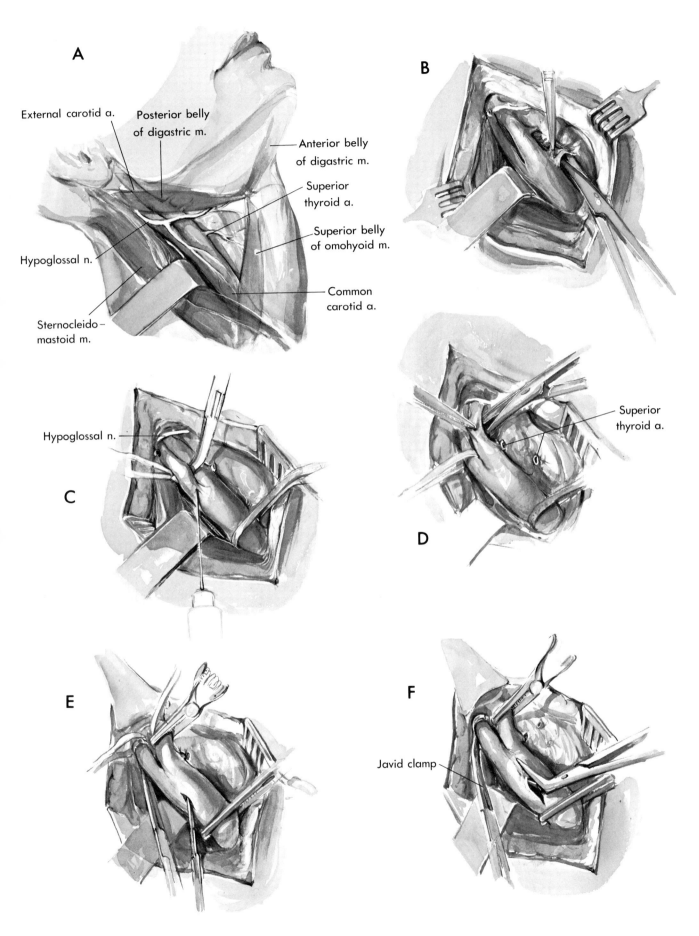

A

External carotid a.

Posterior belly
of digastric m.

Anterior belly
of digastric m.

Superior
thyroid a.

Superior belly
of omohyoid m.

Hypoglossal n.

Common
carotid a.

Sternocleido-
mastoid m.

B

C

Hypoglossal n.

D

Superior
thyroid a.

E

F

Javid clamp

G
H
I

The tourniquet is released, the Javid clamp is opened and the narrower end of the shunt is passed distally. The Javid clamp is closed, effectively preventing leakage around the shunt. The Javid clamp comes in two sizes (4 mm. and 8 mm. internal diameter), the larger for the common carotid artery and the smaller for the smaller internal carotid artery. These internal diameters of the encircling portion of the clamp hug the shunt tubing effectively in most instances; in the event the common carotid is significantly larger, the tourniquet illustrated in Figure I can be used. The tourniquet is released, and the tubing which has been allowed to fill retrogradely with blood is inserted as the tourniquet is relaxed, whereupon the tourniquet is retightened around the tube. The arrow in Figure I indicates the direction of blood flow in the looped shunt tubing, which has to be sufficiently long that it can be displaced to one side or another as necessary during the operation.

J
K
L

The arteriotomy usually has to be made along a diseased vessel. The endarterectomy is begun by teasing along the cut edge of the artery and finding the subintimal plane and then gently continuing to separate the atheroma in this plane. The atheroma has some substance and, if handled gently, can be peeled off quite intact. The atheroma extends a considerable distance, even to the aorta proximally, and has to be cut transversely at a convenient point, preferably where it may be relatively thin. The distal flow of blood eliminates the risk of an intramural dissection beginning at the point of transverse cutting. The atheroma is gently teased distally where it gradually thins out to blend with the thin, relatvely uninvolved intima. The specimen is separated by cutting transversely across the paper-thin intima. This distal transverse cut must be made cleanly and without leaving a free lip which can serve as the starting point of a subintimal dissection. Bits of atheroma or other debris are removed, lest they embolize or become nidi for clot formation. The opened cleaned vessel is flushed with heparinized saline from a syringe whose cannula is inserted to the level of tourniquet placement so that debris is rinsed out of these blind ends. The arteriotomy is now ready for closure.

M
N
O

A simple continuous stitch with 4-0 silk or 5-0 Tevdek is used to close the arteriotomy. Silk can be tied easily and securely, but does not glide so easily through tissue and may drag along some adventitial tissue. Tevdek has greater strength for equivalent suture size and traverses tissue smoothly, but requires greater skill and attention when tying knots. The stitching is begun at the distal internal carotid artery and the stitches are placed delicately so that the lumen of the vessel is allowed to remain at its greatest possible diameter. When the arteriotomy has been closed to the level of the common carotid artery, a second stitch is begun at the proximal end of the arteriotomy and is carried distally to a point at which the surgeon feels he has enough room to remove the shunt.

The proximal Javid clamp is loosened, the shunt removed and an arterial clamp reapplied lightly to the first tooth of the rachet. This is repeated distally except that the artery is reoccluded with a tourniquet. The external carotid artery remains occluded. The proximal stitch is progressed counterclockwise so that when the two sutures are tied they will lie flat. Just before the sutures are tied, the tourniquet on the internal carotid artery is released to allow backbleeding, so that the air bubbles and any overlooked debris in the internal carotid artery are flushed out. The sutures are now tied and the internal carotid is occluded at its origin with the fingers while first the external and then the common carotid vessels are released. Digital occlusion of the internal carotid artery is maintained for four or five pulse beats so that any residual air bubbles or atheromatous debris is harmlessly flushed into the external carotid artery. Compression of the internal carotid artery is now released. Gentle oozing from the suture line will subside with gentle nonoccluding pressure with moistened gauze; persistent points of bleeding can be sealed with single stitches.

A small soft rubber drain is placed along the arteriorrhaphy and exteriorized from the lower aspect of the incision. Protamine sulfate at half the dosage of heparin is administered, but if the arteriorrhaphy is prolonged or if the suture line seems unusually dry, protamine can be omitted. The subcutaneous tissue, including platysma muscle, is approximated with interrupted stitches of 3-0 chromic catgut and the skin with a continuous stitch of 4-0 nylon. The drain is removed the next day and the skin stitches on the fifth to seventh day.

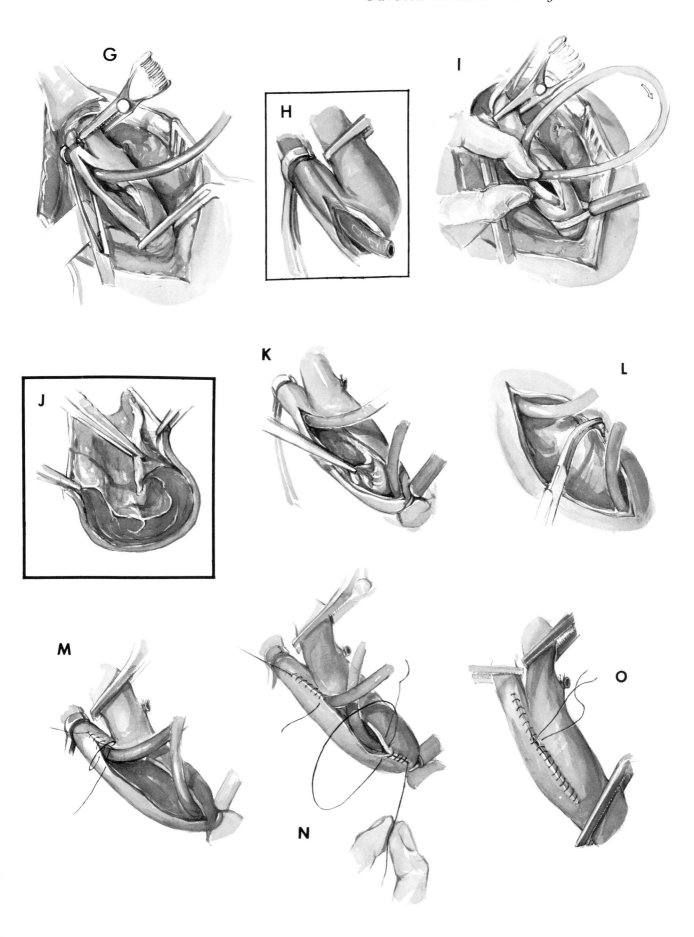

FOREQUARTER AMPUTATION

The intent of a forequarter amputation is to remove the entire upper limb, the shoulder girdle and its numberous muscular attachments plus the contents of the axillia and the low cervical area. Although it is a logically conceived operation that can be executed with a very low mortality, it remains a procedure that sounds forbidding to many surgeons and repugnant to all but desperately ill patients. Because it is so often done as an operation of desperation rather than one of election, the full potential of its benefits is sometimes clouded.

As would be expected from the predominance of mesenchymal tissue in the area, soft tissue sarcomas are the most common type treated by this operation. Skin cancers followed by osseous sarcomas are next in order of frequency of occurrence and, rarely, even huge benign tumors must be removed by this operation. Of all the tumors involving the arm, the soft tissue sarcomas are those most successfully treated by a forequarter amputation, especially those being treated initially rather than after multiple lesser operations. Although rhabdomyosarcomas are the most common type found, they unfortunately are attended by a low cure rate. They not only demand wide resection in keeping with the principle of going beyond the origin of the involved muscles, but they spread by vascular channels to recur, sometimes many years later. Synoviomas, unclassified sarcomas and angiosarcomas are less common varieties of soft tissue sarcomas with a low cure rate by any means of therapy. Neurilemomas and fibrosarcomas are two types occurring with reasonable frequency that can be successfully treated by surgery. The bone sarcomas constitute the smallest group, these being mostly osteogenic sarcomas and chondrosarcomas. Early hematogenous spread acounts for the very poor results from treatment of this group of tumors.

Metastases to axillary lymph nodes lower the cure rate in all the types considered. The belief by many that sarcomas do not metastasize to local lymph nodes is refuted by the reported incidence of up to 50 per cent metastasis with angiosarcomas and the 20 per cent incidence of metastasis to regional lymph nodes in the total group of soft tissue sarcomas.

Tumors of the skin of the arm, with the primary lesion in the arm or elsewhere, constitute the second most common indication for forequarter amputation. These tumors are largely malignant melanomas, with the primary tumor most commonly being in the arm; most of the remainder are adenocarcinomas, with the primary usually situated elsewhere. In most instances, the patients with these types of cancer of the arm present themselves for surgery with an extremity that is an extremely edematous, painful, fungating and otherwise useless appendage. The cancer is usually so extensive in distribution by metastases-in-transit or by direct extension that only such wide resection will excise all the grossly involved tissue. Less often, the cancer is so strategically situated about the vessels or nerves in the axilla that it can be excised only by a forequarter amputation.

There is such a wide histological variety of tumors arising in this area, each with its unique clinical behavior, that it would be unwise to expect this one operation to be equally effective against all. There are a number of factors—some common to all and others peculiar to specific tumors—that mitigate against a cure. Proximal recurrence in the stump is seen with tumors such as neurilemomas, synoviomas and fibrosarcomas that spread along neural or fascial sheaths. Although this type of recurrence is seen most commonly following conservative amputations, it can be seen after the highest resection. The tumor may recur locally simply because of a too limited resection (without amputation), and this recurrence will not be attributable to either proximal perineural or fascial spread. Borderline receptibility of a tumor defeats many attempts at cure. Although surgery on such patients is undesirable, often there is no reasonable alternative. The most disheartening group of patients are those who have been operated upon for early, apparently localized sarcomas and who later die of disseminated disease. Osteogenic sarcomas, angiosarcomas and rhabdomyosarcomas are the chief offenders in this category. Because of this characteristic of early hematogenous spread, we favor laminagrams of the lungs prior to operation so that metastases can be excluded with greater confidence.

The value of radiotherapy before surgery is being debated. Its most logical application would be immediately before disturbance of the tumor bed for biopsy. This would be a short noncurative dose but one which would presumably render any embolized cells much less viable or likely to "take" in their new environment. If there is an error in the preoperative diagnosis and the tumor is benign, the x-ray dose would not be harmful—at least in an adult. The risk would be greater in a patient with epiphyses that have not yet fused. Administration of a "curative" dose of x-ray (only after a confirmatory biopsy) before amputation has little merit for any lesion situated distal to the axilla because these tumors are not manipulated intraoperatively or else they can be effectively excluded by tourniquet on the proximal side of the tumor.

The question arises as to the superiority of forequarter amputation over disarticulation. In favor of a forequarter amputation is the recognition that the axillary lymph nodes can be removed in a most thorough fashion. Nerves, and of lesser importance, vessels, can be ligated at a higher level. It offers the best opportunity for resecting the most muscles in their entirety. A shoulder without the arm is essentially of esthetic value only, and its absence can be compensated for rather easily with a prosthesis. The disability from the two procedures is essentially similar, as are the postoperative morbidity and mortality.

The physical preparation of the patient is the same as for any other major operation. The disfigurement produced by this operation is inevitably psychically traumatic. The attitude of the surgeon is important in handling these patients; he must decide in his own mind, and beforehand, on the advisability of this operation so that it can be presented to the patient in a positive manner. The operation must not be forced on the patient, but neither should it be presented in so reticent a fashion that the patient has no support in making this very important decision.

References

Nadler, S. H., and Phelan, J. T.: A technique of interscapulothoracic amputation. Surg. Gynec. & Obst. *122*:359, 1966.
Pack, G. T.: Major exarticulations for malignant neoplasms of the extremities: Interscapulothoracic amputation, hip-joint disarticulation, and interilio-abdominal amputation; report of end results in 228 cases. J. Bone & Joint Surg. *38-A*:2 and 249, 1956.
Pack, G. T., McNeer, G., and Coley, B. L.: Interscapulothoracic amputation for malignant tumors of the upper extremity. Surg. Gynec. & Obst. 74:161, 1942.

Forequarter Amputation

A
B
General anesthesia by orotracheal intubation is used and the anesthesiologist must be prepared to cope with a deliberate entry into the thorax or even excision of a portion of it. A large bore plastic catheter should be inserted in a vein for rapid transfusion of blood if this becomes necessary. The patient is placed in the lateral position or a shade toward the supine if a difficult supraclavicular dissection is anticipated. Following preparation of the skin by a preferred method the patient is draped so as to leave the thorax exposed beyond the midline on both sides to the subcostal margin inferiorly and to include the lower two-thirds of the neck. The arm is also prepared and draped in a sterile fashion so that it can be moved during the course of the operation. Unless one is certain that the skin flaps will be adequate to cover the operative defect, the ipsilateral thigh should be prepared for donation of a skin graft.

The racquet-type incision depicted is one of several which can be used for a straight-forward forequarter amputation, but considerable digression from this may be necessary. This is especially true with patients who have had a previous radical mastectomy and in whom more of the skin of the anterior thorax must be removed. In such an instance, less skin is sacrificed posteriorly so that the resultant posterior larger flap may be used anteriorly. When cutaneous metastases are present near the operative field (usually from cancer of the breast or malignant melanoma), the breadth of skin excision must be very generous.

C
The anterior muscle groups that will have to be divided in this operation are shown. Included are the pectoralis major muscle, which arises from the sternum, the cartilage of all true ribs and the upper portion of the aponeurosis of the external oblique and converges to insert into the greater tuberosity of the humerus; and the pectoralis minor, which arises from the third to fifth ribs and passes upward to insert into the coracoid process. These muscles will be divided somewhere along their course, usually closer to their origin than to their insertion. The flat triangular trapezius muscle, which arises along a line from the external occipital protuberance to the spinous process of the last thoracic vertebra in the midline posteriorly, attaches itself to the lateral third of the clavicle, the acromion and the spine of the scapula. Anteriorly, this muscle is usually divided just cephalad to the clavicle. The sternocleidomastoid muscle usually has its lateral clavicular fibers divided; all of them may be divided if the clavicle is disarticulated. The need to remove more than the terminal fibers of this muscle suggests disease too extensive to resect. The subclavius muscle is of no consequence but should be left on any portion of retained clavicle. This and the remaining illustrations are those of a patient in the left lateral position as in Figures A and B. The dashed line that shows the position of the overlying racquet-type incision gives an idea of the amount of under-cutting necessary if one wishes to divide the underlying pectoralis major muscle at its origin. One need not make a fetish of such complete removal of the pectoralis major muscle in all cases since this is not necessary if the muscle is not involved with cancer.

D
The abundant anatomical cross-traffic is shown in this semidiagrammatic illustration. The common carotid artery is shown as it begins at the bifurcation of the innominate artery behind the sternoclavicular joint. On the left, of course, it arises from the highest portion of the arch of the aorta and is intrathoracic at its origin. The vertebral artery and the thyrocervical trunk are given off before the subclavian artery passes under the anterior scalene muscle. The thoracoacromial artery is the pertinent important vessel arising from the axillary artery. The axillary vein becomes the subclavian vein at the lateral border of the first rib and, as such, receives the anterior and external jugular veins. At the medial end of the clavicle it joins with the internal jugular vein to become the innominate vein. At this junction the subclavian vein also receives the right lymphatic duct, a structure of lesser magnitude than the thoracic duct on the left; nonetheless, both are important if the dissection proceeds this medially and if injury to them and consequent lymphorrhea are to be avoided. The composition and complexity of the brachial plexus change swiftly as it proceeds distally and there is not much to be gained by describing this anatomy since, in any case, it will be divided where necessary. The clavicle is the only bone usually worked on and will be sectioned at the junction of its middle and medial thirds, which is the point at which the clavicle crosses the vessels going to the arm. This demonstrates clearly that by disarticulation of the clavicle at the sternum one can dissect more medially if the occasion calls for it. This is particularly valuable for tumors that impinge on or invade the brachial plexus or for neural tumors that must be resected as far proximally as possible.

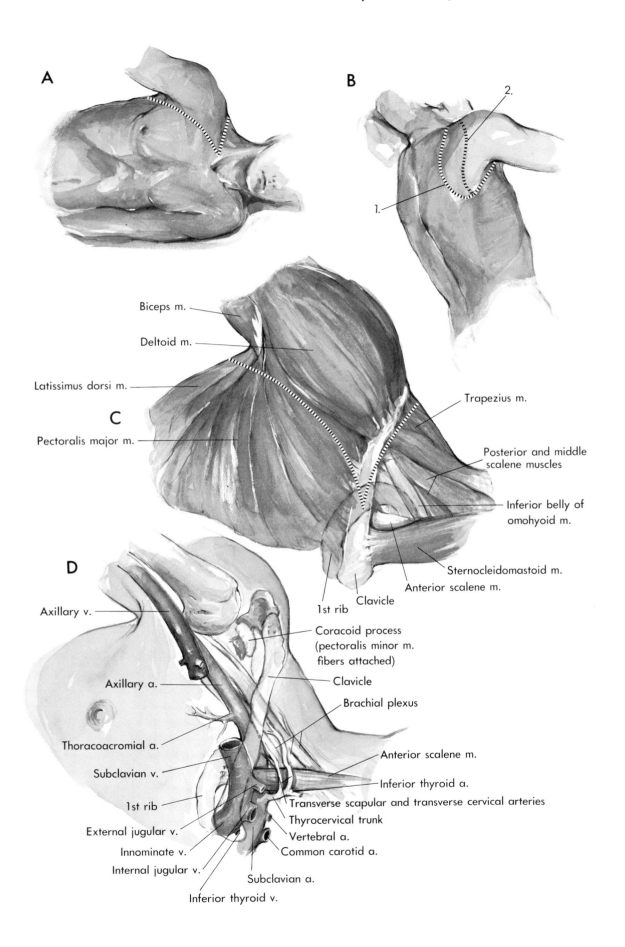

A

B

2.

1.

Biceps m.

Deltoid m.

Latissimus dorsi m.

C

Pectoralis major m.

Trapezius m.

Posterior and middle
scalene muscles

Inferior belly of
omohyoid m.

Sternocleidomastoid m.

Anterior scalene m.

1st rib

Clavicle

D

Axillary v.

Axillary a.

Thoracoacromial a.

Subclavian v.

1st rib

External jugular v.

Innominate v.

Internal jugular v.

Inferior thyroid v.

Subclavian a.

Common carotid a.

Vertebral a.

Thyrocervical trunk

Transverse scapular and transverse cervical arteries

Inferior thyroid a.

Anterior scalene m.

Brachial plexus

Clavicle

Coracoid process
(pectoralis minor m.
fibers attached)

E   The anterior portion of the incision is made first and the medial aspect of the clavicle exposed. The fibers of the pectoralis major muscle are separated from the caudal surface of the medial half of the clavicle. The incision need not remain close to the clavicle but can promptly be curved to run parallel to the sternum and at a variable distance lateral to it. The subclavius muscle is divided in line with the anticipated point of cutting the clavicle. Division of the tough costocoracoid membrane is also carried out at this time.

F   The superior aspect of the clavicle is freed next, and the lateral fibers of the clavicular head of the sternocleidomastoid muscle are divided. Deep to the clavicle at this point the anterior jugular vein is clamped, cut and ligated.

G
H   An avenue for the passage of the Gigli saw has to be made. The subclavian vein is closely subjacent, and care should be taken not to tear it because hemorrhage cannot be controlled easily or quickly. The safest way to separate the vein from the overlying clavicle is to go under the clavicle subperiosteally; when doing so, however, the periosteum should not be lifted more medially than the point of division of bone or there will be a risk of necrosis of the denuded bone. The Gigli saw is angled somewhat medially so that the cut edge of the retained clavicle is less sharp. In lesions involving the shoulder the entire clavicle is usually removed. In more peripheral lesions the technique of cutting the clavicle as depicted is satisfactory.

I   After the clavicle is divided the assistant can gently retract it caudally while the surgeon frees it from any underlying tissue. Branches of the transverse scapular or transverse cervical artery can be avulsed while doing this; the risk can be minimized by use of the finger to make certain tissue falls away as the clavicle is being retracted. The artery that lies more cephalad and deeper than the vein should be ligated first. The dissection to isolate the forequarter first encounters the branches of the thyrocervical trunk.

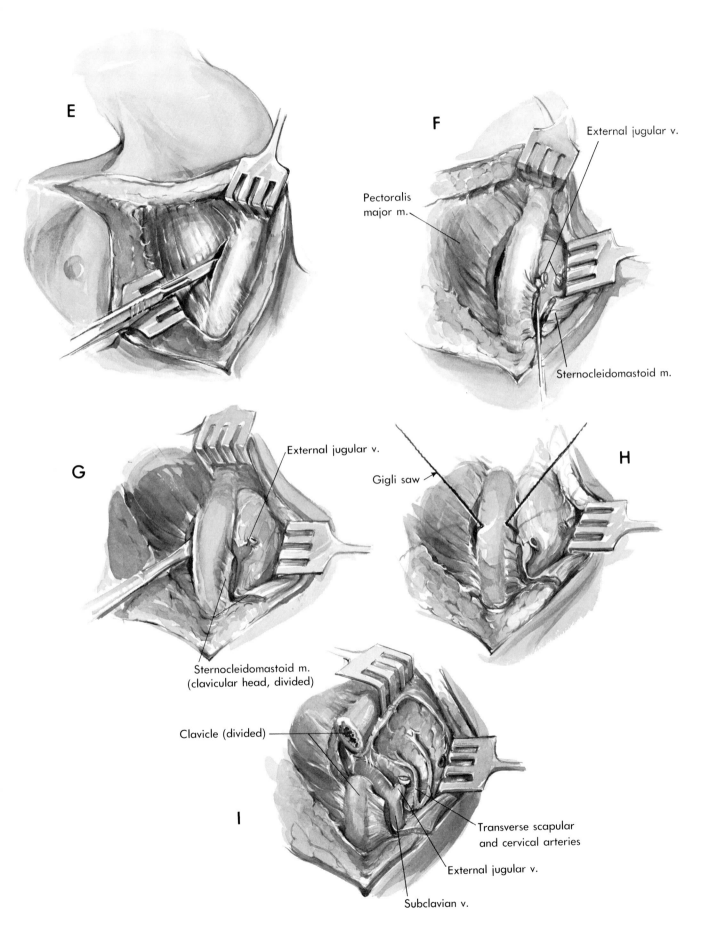

E

F

Pectoralis
major m.

External jugular v.

Sternocleidomastoid m.

G

External jugular v.

Gigli saw

H

Sternocleidomastoid m.
(clavicular head, divided)

Clavicle (divided)

I

Transverse scapular
and cervical arteries

External jugular v.

Subclavian v.

J   The artery must be ligated before the vein in order to avoid a congested arm and the consequent loss of the trapped blood. Early ligation of the vein is hardly as logical here as with cancer in other locations and certainly is not worth the attendant disadvantages. The artery is to be found cephalad to and deeper than the vein. One can expose the artery sufficiently to occlude it with a Potts arterial clamp and then proceed at leisure with the dissection of the overlying veins. The overlying areolar tissue is cleaned. The thyrocervical trunk is ligated proximal to its branching since a tie located at this point is less likely to slip off than one at the end of the severed vessel.

K   The subclavian artery is doubly ligated with 2-0 silk, the more distal ligature of the two being transfixed. An equally acceptable practice, especially if wound infection is probable or the area has been heavily irradiated, is to apply an arterial clamp, sever the artery and oversew it with 5-0 atraumatic arterial silk.

L   The sublcavian vein is doubly ligated with 2-0 silk. Both artery and vein, of course, can be ligated more medially if the clinical circumstances warrant. In order to obtain the necessary exposure for this it is necessary to disarticulate the clavicle and divide the anterior scalene muscle. Securing these vessels more medially is more difficult and more hazardous, especially with respect to the vein. In this position the phrenic nerve is immediately threatened and certainly should be spared. Even more medially the recurrent laryngeal nerve should be looked for and avoided.

M
N   The brachial plexus is simply sectioned without antecedent injections of the nerve trunks. Occasionally, a perineural vessel must be clamped and ligated. With neural tumors the plexus is sectioned as proximally as possible by lifting and retracting the anterior scalene muscle medially. The inferior belly of the omohyoid muscle is then divided.

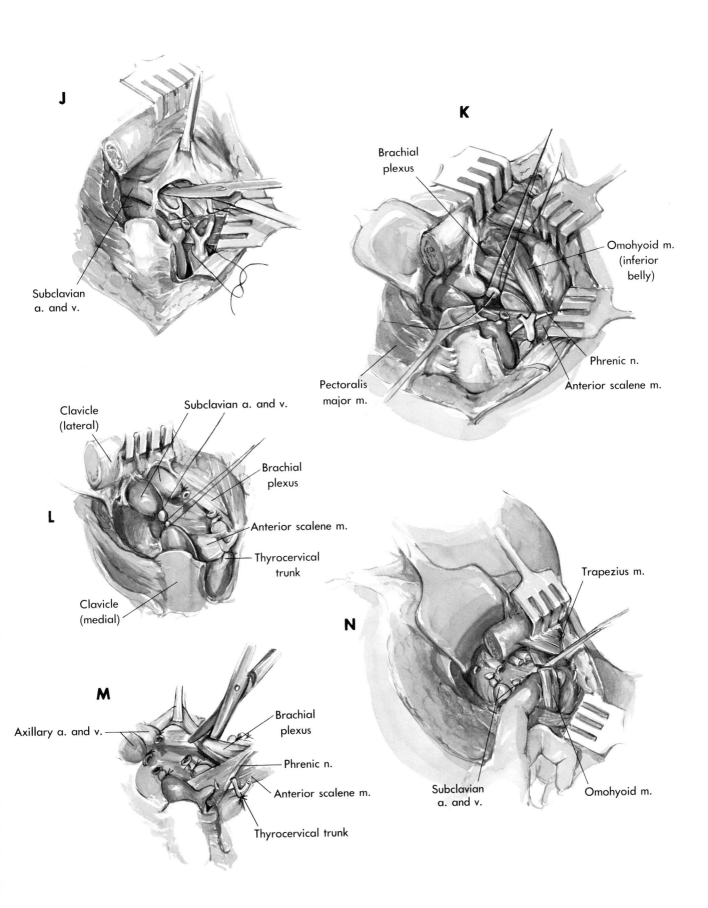

J

Subclavian
a. and v.

K

Brachial
plexus

Omohyoid m.
(inferior
belly)

Pectoralis
major m.

Phrenic n.

Anterior scalene m.

Clavicle
(lateral)

Subclavian a. and v.

Brachial
plexus

Anterior scalene m.

Thyrocervical
trunk

L

Clavicle
(medial)

Trapezius m.

N

Subclavian
a. and v.

Omohyoid m.

M

Axillary a. and v.

Brachial
plexus

Phrenic n.

Anterior scalene m.

Thyrocervical trunk

O   Division of the trapezius muscle is begun at its anterior aspect and close to the shoulder but must unhesitatingly be divided as close to its origin as possible if tumor in any way involves this muscle.

P
Q   The major and minor pectoral muscles are next divided. The muscle incision is slanted so that the cut muscle blends smoothly with the thoracic wall, effectively eliminating hollow areas wherein serum can accumulate. The pectoralis minor muscle will usually be excised in its entirety but the pectoral major muscle is not; it is sectioned in line with the overlying skin so that when an extensive amount of skin is sacrificed, the underlying muscle is also resected more radically.

     The arm is severely abducted by an assistant and, with the muscular and bony restraints gone, the entire shoulder is abducted. The long thoracic nerve is shown, but this will be sacrificed later along with the serratus anterior muscle which it innervates.

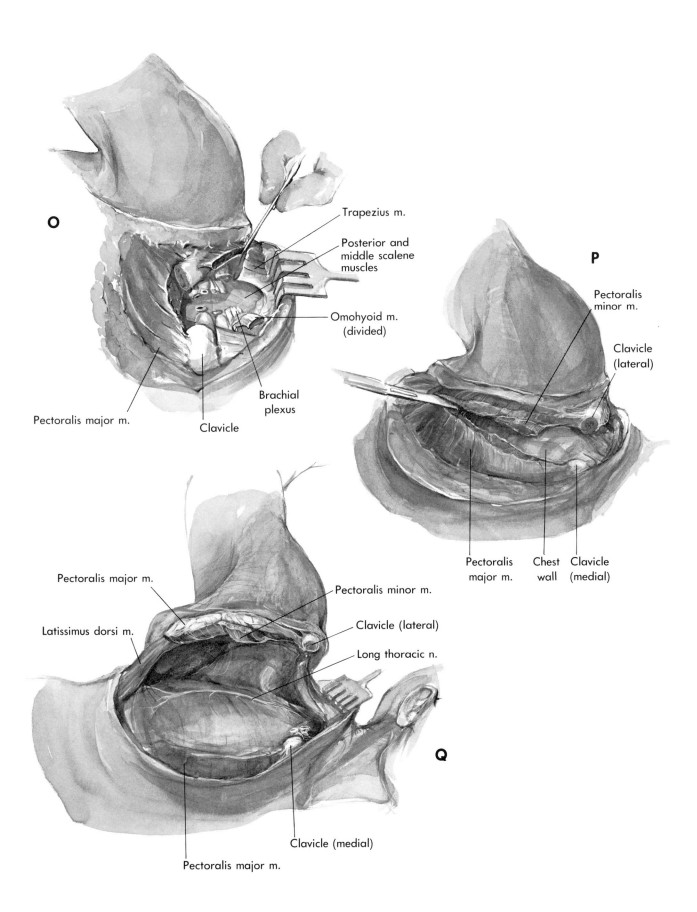

O

Trapezius m.

Posterior and middle scalene muscles

Omohyoid m. (divided)

Pectoralis major m.

Brachial plexus

Clavicle

P

Pectoralis minor m.

Clavicle (lateral)

Pectoralis major m.

Chest wall

Clavicle (medial)

Pectoralis major m.

Pectoralis minor m.

Latissimus dorsi m.

Clavicle (lateral)

Long thoracic n.

Q

Clavicle (medial)

Pectoralis major m.

R   The view and the field of operation now shift to the dorsal side of the patient. The path of the usual incision is shown. If more skin than this is to be sacrificed posteriorly, the surgeon can plan to compensate by leaving more skin anteriorly and, conversely, a larger anterior flap can be used if the posterior flap is short. A skin graft can be applied and easily maintained over this rigid convex surface, but one should assiduously avoid placing such a graft over the severed vessels or brachial plexus. Also, if a portion of thorax is removed, the defect is repaired with a sheet of fascia lata and every effort made to cover it with a full thickness flap of skin.

S
T   The dorsal musculature which is to be divided is shown in these two illustrations. The superficial layer includes the trapezius muscle, which has been described. The latissimus dorsi muscle already arises primarily through the lumbodorsal fascia, from the spinous processes of the vertebrae from the midthorax on down, from the posterior iliac crest and from fleshy digitations from the lower ribs. Its fibers curve around and overlap the inferior border of the scapula as they become a fasciculus inserting into the humerus. The levator scapulae, rhomboideus minor and rhomboideus major muscles arise at the midline of the back from the transverse processes of the upper cervical vertebrae and proceed in a generally downward direction to insert on the vertebral border of the scapula.

U   The assistant now pulls the arm and shoulder girdle forward so that the muscles attached to the scapula are put on tension. The latissimus dorsi muscle is incised across its thickest area. The trapezius muscle is divided along the vertebral border of the scapula so that it meets the incision made during the anterior dissection. The rhomboideus major and minor and the levator scapulae muscles now come into view and are divided in similar fashion.

V   Only the serratus anterior muscles now hold the shoulder girdle in place. The shoulder girdle is lifted and the serratus anterior muscles are divided at their origins.

W   Electrocautery and chromic catgut are used to effect complete hemostasis. The wound is closed with interrupted simple stitches of 3-0 silk. If the wound closure is tight, the skin flaps are held firmly against the chest wall; only a drain is exteriorized from the inferior aspect of the wound. If there is any looseness of the skin flaps we employ suction to the wound through two catheters exteriorized through snug counterincisions. A mild compression dressing is applied if deemed necessary.

     The patient is ambulated early and, as a rule, can begin oral nourishment the day after the operation. Normally, patients are discharged from the hospital by the second postoperative week.

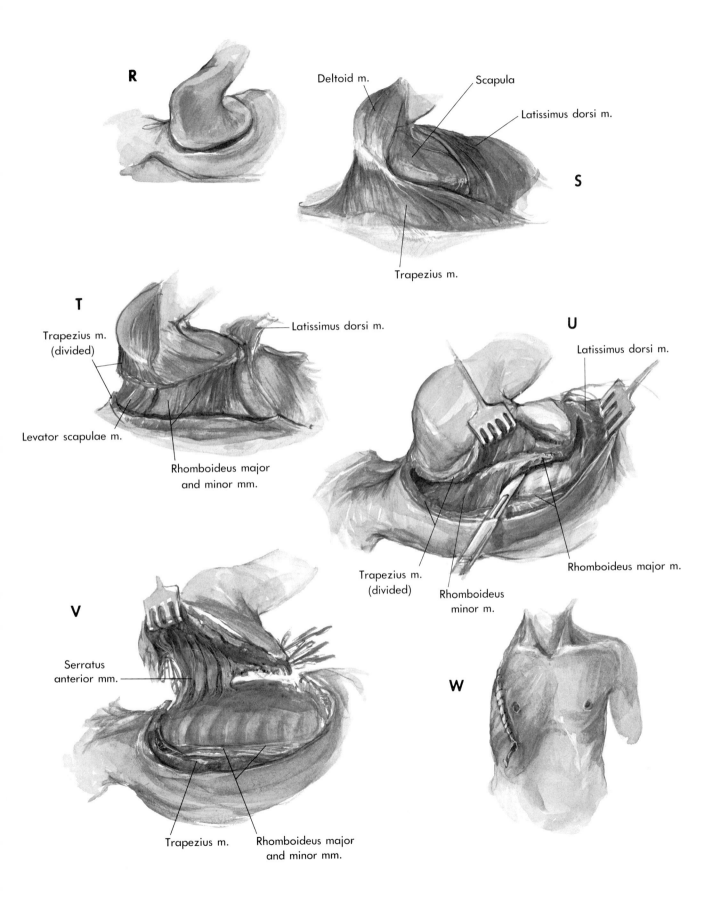

R

Deltoid m.

Scapula

Latissimus dorsi m.

S

Trapezius m.

T

Trapezius m.
(divided)

Latissimus dorsi m.

U

Latissimus dorsi m.

Levator scapulae m.

Rhomboideus major
and minor mm.

Trapezius m.
(divided)

Rhomboideus
minor m.

Rhomboideus major m.

V

Serratus
anterior mm.

W

Trapezius m.

Rhomboideus major
and minor mm.

RADICAL MASTECTOMY, EXTENDED

Carcinoma today attacks 15 per cent of the population of the United States, or nearly one person out of six. Carcinoma of the breast is the commonest and most lethal form among women. There is at present a dissatisfaction with the standard forms of surgical treatment of breast cancer since the patient reaching the surgeon has about a 60 per cent chance of surviving five years free of disease, and approximately a 40 per cent chance for a ten-year survival free of disease. Because it is thought that the disease rather than the treatment determines outcome, there has been interest in the use of radiotherapy alone, in simple mastectomy plus radiotherapy and in simple mastectomy alone.

As regards operative mortality rates, there should be no difference between simple mastectomy and radical mastectomy provided the surgery is done in an accredited hospital by a qualified surgeon assisted by a qualified anesthetist. Morbidity is greater among radical mastectomy patients primarily because of potential problems with mobilization of skin flaps and the possibility of edema of the arm. It would seem that the simple mastectomy for a curable carcinoma of the breast has little place since a patient with positive axillary or internal mammary lymph nodes can be cured of carcinoma by appropriate surgery. Radical mastectomy plus postoperative radiotherapy has not significantly raised the percentage of cures. Oophorectomy in the premenopausal female is helpful in delaying recurrence in those women whose breast carcinomas have spread to regional lymph nodes and beyond. Unfortunately, only about one third of breast carcinomas are markedly affected by the use of hormones. The use of male sex hormones in the premenopausal woman and the use of male or female sex hormones in the postmenopausal woman give varying results, as do the chemotherapeutic agents. In the hormone sensitive group, oophorectomy, adrenalectomy or hypophysectomy may have a marked benefit. Adrenalectomy and hypophysectomy are restricted to those patients who have a spread of carcinoma beyond the breast and its lymph node drainage.

At this moment carcinoma of the breast is most curable when treated by radical mastectomy or, when indicated, by extended radical mastectomy.

The operation of radical mastectomy was developed on the premise that radical local excision of a cancer en bloc with its lymph node drainage area would yield the greatest chance for a cure. The operation of radical mastectomy as it is commonly done was initiated and developed largely through the efforts of Halsted and Meyer. The standard operation presumes that the axillary lymph nodes drain the breast. The observation that the lymphatic drainage area of the breast was also into the internal mammary lymph node chains was put to clinical use by Urban. Urban in 1951 performed the first operation of extended radical mastectomy, which removes the subjacent internal mammary lymph node chain en bloc with a standard radical mastectomy. The Urban operation is particularly important and indicated for medial lesions, central lesions and when there are positive axillary lymph nodes. In these three situations the chance for internal mammary lymph node spread is high. By 1961 Urban had performed 610 extended radical mastectomies, with a 30-day postoperative mortality of two patients. Of these 610 patients 48 per cent had positive axillary lymph nodes, whereas 34 per cent had positive internal mammary lymph nodes. Eight per cent of all patients had only internal mammary lymph node metastases present. Sixteen per cent of all patients with negative axillary lymph nodes had positive internal mammary lymph nodes. These observations indicated that there was a place for extended radical mastectomy.

In Urban's series of 610 patients there were 390 patients available for a five-year follow-up study. In this group there were 54 per cent with positive lymph nodes, of which 48 per cent had positive axillary lymph nodes and 31 per cent positive internal mammary lymph nodes. Seventy-two per cent of these patients were living at the end of five years and 64 per cent were living and free of disease. Similar results were found in patients with only positive internal mammary lymph nodes or in patients with only positive axillary lymph nodes. The over-all five-year findings in 390 patients were 65 per cent living and 60 per cent living and free of disease.

There were 215 of Urban's 610 patients on whom a ten-year follow-up could be carried out. The follow-up was complicated by the fact that there was a 9 per cent incidence of new primary carcinomas developing in the opposite breast; additionally, 7 per cent died of diseases other than breast carcinoma. Of the 215 patients 56 per cent had lymph node metastases, 50 per cent of which occurred in the axilla and 32 per cent in the internal mammary nodes.

Fifty per cent of the 215 patients had survived and 47 per cent were free of disease at ten years. Patients with only internal mammary metastases did as well as patients with only axillary metastases. In both instances 48 per cent survived ten years and 46 per cent were free of disease.

A patient with a mass in the breast should be treated in the following way: The usual careful history and physical examination should be done and a chest x-ray obtained. Breast carcinoma metastases tend to involve the skin of the breast and the axillary or internal mammary lymph nodes; the carcinoma then spreads to lungs, bones or viscera. Chest x-rays should be taken to rule out pulmonary metastasis, and appropriate skeletal x-rays should be taken to evaluate any history of pain. A skeletal survey should be obtained if the lesion is marginally operable. A mammogram of the opposite breast may be valuable in locating additional occult lesions. If no contraindication exists, the patient should be taken to the operating room for a breast biopsy. This can be done by a needle aspiration if the lesion is of sufficient size and the staff pathologist is used to this type of biopsy; otherwise, an excisional biopsy and frozen section examination of the mass is indicated. If the frozen section is reported to be positive for breast carcinoma, a radical mastectomy should be done. However, if the lesion is medial or central, or if the axillary lymph nodes are positive, an extended radical mastectomy should be considered. Since the chest will be entered, higher morbidity can be expected. At present this operation should be carried out only by a well qualified surgeon in an accredited hospital. The chest defect will have to be stabilized. Urban has found that ox fascia has given satisfactory results, but fascia lata is better and can also be used, although this requires another incision.

If the extended radical mastectomy has been used, the usual postoperative precautions against chest complications should be observed. The intracostal catheter should be left in place until all air and serum are out of the thorax. Promotion of cough to avoid atelectasis is indicated. Additionally, the use of subcutaneous catheters should be applied with low suction to evacuate all subcutaneous serum or hematoma, so that the skin flaps will adhere. Elevation of the arm and elastic bandages from fingertips to axilla may relieve any lymphedema of the arm. Occasionally, a patient will be disabled by an extreme degree of lymphedema, which can be a most serious problem. A recently developed operation by Goldsmith seems to offer considerable help. In a small series of patients markedly incapacitated by lymphedema, transposition of the omentum has relieved the edema. Also rarely in this group of patients there will develop a lymphangiosarcoma of the extremity ten years or more postmastectomy.

References

Goldsmith, H. S., and de la Santos, R.: Omental transposition for the treatment of chronic lymphedema. Rev. Surg. 23:303, 1966.
Halsted, W. S.: The results of operation for the care of cancer of the breast performed at The Johns Hopkins Hospital from June 1889 to January 1894. Johns Hopkins Hosp. Rep. 4:297, 1894.
Meyer, W.: An improved method of the radical operation for carcinoma of the breast. Med. Rec. 46:746, 1894.
Statistical Report of End Results, 1949–1957. Memorial Hospital for Cancer and Allied Diseases and the James Ewing Hospital of the City of New York, 1965.
Urban, J. A.: Radical excision of the chest wall for mammary cancer. Cancer 4:1263, 1951.
Urban, J. A.: Extended radical mastectomy. Personal communication, 1967.

Radical Mastectomy, Extended

A   This semidiagrammatic rendition demonstrates the vascular anatomy pertinent to this procedure. The variations are sufficiently common, however, that the following should serve only as a guide. The internal mammary artery is given off at the caudad surface of the subclavian artery and in a slightly medialward direction. Once it passes the clavicle on its journey it proceeds directly caudally and about 1 cm. lateral to the lateral border of the sternum. It gives off perforating branches to the overlying muscles, breast and skin. At about the 6th intercostal space it divides into the laterally directed musculophrenic artery, and the main trunk continues caudally as the superior epigastric artery. A pair of veins accompany it down low but they unite into one vessel higher up which then remains medial to the artery before entering the subclavian vein.

   The supreme thoracic artery may or may not be present and may arise separately from the thoracoacromial artery. As mentioned later, it is encountered while advancing toward the 1st thoracic interspace. The thoracoacromial and lateral thoracic arteries are the two major vessels which are sacrificed. In addition, the dorsal thoracic from the subscapular must also be sacrificed.

B   There are three groups of lymph nodes draining the breast: the axillary, the internal mammary and the cervical. Cervical lymph node involvement with cancer indicates surgical incurability. The internal mammary lymph nodes are located subpleurally between the 1st and 6th costal cartilages, usually in the interspace. These nodes drain other areas in addition to the breast and also intercommunicate with those on the opposite side. The lymphatic duct, usually as a single trunk, accompanies the vessels; the left may empty directly into the thoracic vein and the right into the subclavian trunk, or they may enter into the respective junctions of the internal jugular and subclavian veins.

   The axillary lymph nodes, 15 to 30 in number, are the most important with respect to the operation. They can be subdivided into groups: group I is the lowest, group II is in the middle and group III is highest in the axilla. They have prognostic significance but the "classification" is of minimal value to the surgeon since all of them must be removed. The surgeon should tag the lymph nodes as being highest, midpoint and lowest in the axillary group so that the pathologist can identify and record their status with certainty.

C   Sooner or later even the most astute and experienced clinician will mistake a benign breast mass for a clinically certain cancer. For this reason we have never performed a radical mastectomy without microscopic confirmation of the presumed cancer. A needle biopsy of the mass and microscopic examination of the tissue the evening before surgery has some advantages if facilities and personnel are available for this practice. When open biopsy is to be done we prefer this to be excisional rather than incisional. With an excisional biopsy there is less pressure on the tumor, diminishing the risk of intravasation of cells, however small this risk may be. Incisional biopsy also carries the real risk of massaging the cancer to a greater degree with consequent embolization of the cancer cells. The rebuttal to this statement has been that a woman with breast cancer obviously massages this cancer within the breast during her daily movements, while dressing or even when sleeping in the prone position and that, therefore, cells have embolized long before the operation. This, of course, is true and probably accounts for many of the surgical failures to cure. It has been amply documented in the laboratory, however, that if cancer cells are "embolized" into an animal that is undergoing a "stress," such as surgical trauma or even an anesthetic, these embolic cells will "take" with greater frequency than in animals not "stressed" during the embolization. It appears, therefore, that although cancer cells may be embolized many times, those embolized during an operation are potentially the most lethal. There is no good reason not to apply this conclusion to humans and certainly little is lost by this attitude.

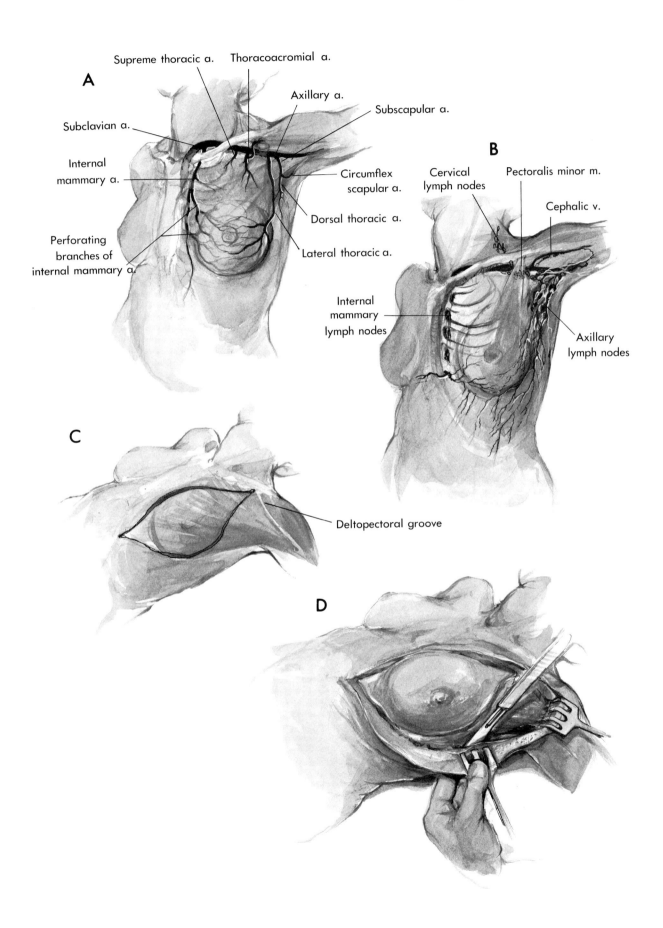

A

Supreme thoracic a.   Thoracoacromial a.

Subclavian a.

Internal
mammary a.

Perforating
branches of
internal mammary a.

Axillary a.

Subscapular a.

Circumflex
scapular a.

Dorsal thoracic a.

Lateral thoracic a.

B

Cervical
lymph nodes

Pectoralis minor m.

Cephalic v.

Internal
mammary
lymph nodes

Axillary
lymph nodes

C

Deltopectoral groove

D

We believe that an equally valid objection to incisional biopsy is the greater risk of contaminating the surgical wound with cancer cells. If one examines the bloody fluid that collects in the defect of an incisional biopsy, cancer cells often abound in it. Most surgeons will acknowledge that despite "baseball" stitches, rubber dams and other attempts to keep it confined, this cancer cell-laden fluid too often leaks out during the manipulations incident to a mastectomy to contaminate the wound. For this reason, when we feel compelled to perform an incisional biopsy, the biopsy wound is packed with a small sponge soaked in Zenker's solution. This quickly "fixes" and hopefully renders harmless all cells with which it comes in contact and, indeed, more effectively than does 95 per cent ethyl alcohol or 5 per cent formalin.

General anesthesia is preferably administered by endotracheal intubation. The thigh is prepared and draped in readiness for procuring a fascia lata graft. The arm on the operated side is abducted to a right angle and the other arm is kept at the patient's side. In order to avoid massaging the tumor, scrubbing of the breast is omitted and, instead, the operative field is painted with a solution of Betadine. The arm on the side to be operated is painted to the elbow and then pulled in the opposite direction so as to tilt the patient. The posterior thorax can then be painted to the midscapular line. A sterile drape and a second nonporous drape are placed on the table and the patient allowed to fall back in the supine position. After the painting is completed the area draped is bordered by the clavicle, the anterior border of the latissimus dorsi and the midsternal line and is somewhat below the subcostal border. The wound is now draped more narrowly for the biopsy, which is performed with instruments from a separate table. Following confirmation of the diagnosis, the confining drapes and the gloves of the operating team are changed and the operative area again painted with Betadine before proceeding with the radical mastectomy.

A variety of mastectomy incisions may be used, the vertical one being most compatible with maintenance of an adequate blood supply to the flaps. We prefer that the apex of the incision come to just above the clavicle rather than curve along the anterior axillary line. The incision is made at least 8 cm. peripheral to the cancer.

D   The lateral flap is developed first simply because it is easier to work here now rather than after the medial flap is made, from which blood and instruments get in the way.

The plane of dissection remains just superficial to the superficial fascia so that skin flaps are slightly more than full thickness skin. Although this is not shown, the assistants provide countertraction with the hemostats placed on the breast tissue. Use of the rake and left hand as shown permits good tactile evaluation by the surgeon as to how well the flap is being developed. We advise a short rapid stroke of the scalpel because the depth and direction of the cuts can be controlled better than with long sweeping strokes, which tend to cause terracing of the flaps. In the axilla the apocrine glands will be seen at the depth of the skin flap.

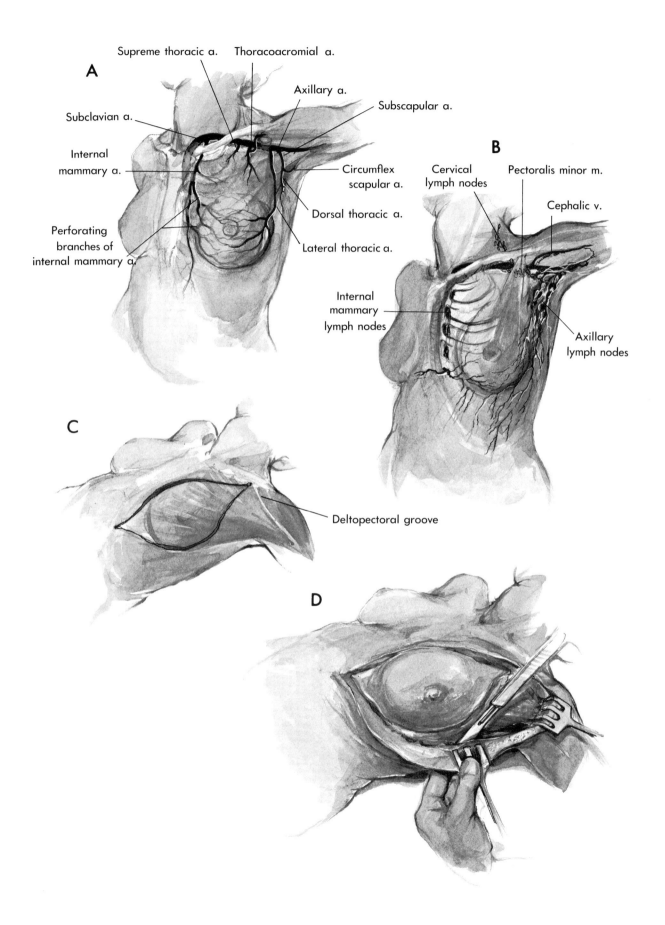

E The medial flap is developed next, with the assistant using one or two rakes for retraction. This must be in a ventral direction rather than toward the opposite side if "button-holing" of the skin is to be avoided. The thickness of the skin flaps is gradually increased in all parameters so that at about 8 cm. from the incision, or before reaching the periphery of the mobilization, they are full thickness, including most of the subcutaneous fat.

A laparotomy pad moistened with physiological saline solution is placed under each flap to prevent drying during the ensuing dissection.

F It is next necessary to disengage the insertion of the pectoralis major muscle, those fibers originating from the undersurface of the clavicle not being disturbed. The fascia over the pectoralis major muscle in the area of the clavicle is incised. Near the medial edge of the clavicle one can see the natural cleavage between the two parts of the muscle. If one keeps in mind the ontogenic development of an erect posture by the mammalian quadruped, it is easy to visualize how the pectoralis major muscle twists on its way toward a humeral insertion to accomodate the human posture. For the same reason, the clavicular position of the muscle overlaps the cephalic aspect of the sternal portion to an increasing degree as it passes toward the humerus.

If the cephalic vein has not been previously identified, attention is now focused on finding it. Once a start has been made with the spreading scissors, the pectoral fibers are separated by the blunt technique of an index finger hooked around them and proceeding toward the humerus. A medium Richardson retractor is ideal for exposing the termination of the muscle as it is cut by knife or scissors. The subclavian muscle is left intact.

G The latter maneuver exposes the clavipectoral fascia, which is incised along the lower border of the coracobrachial muscle. This exposes the tendon of the pectoralis minor muscle, which is divided from its insertion to the coracoid process of the scapula. The tissue is now dissected caudad en masse to the lower border of the axillary vein. Several small tributaries from the axillary artery will be encountered on the anterior aspect of the vein and should be secured. Although all soft tissue down to the underlying brachial plexus is removed with the specimen, the surgeon should be careful not to traumatize the plexus or the perineural vessels with too vigorous a dissection. The cephalic vein is, of course, preserved for its intrinsic value or in the event the axillary vein is damaged.

H We adhere to the sound principle of ligating the blood vessels early in the course of the operation and dissecting the tissue in a retrograde manner. The axillary dissection is begun at the lateral aspect of the vein and carried medially. All the tributaries coming off the inferior aspect of the axillary vein are divided. The subscapular vessels and nerve as well as the long thoracic and the thoracodorsal nerves are usually spared, but the thoracodorsal nerve should be taken without hesitation if there are grossly involved lymph nodes along its course.

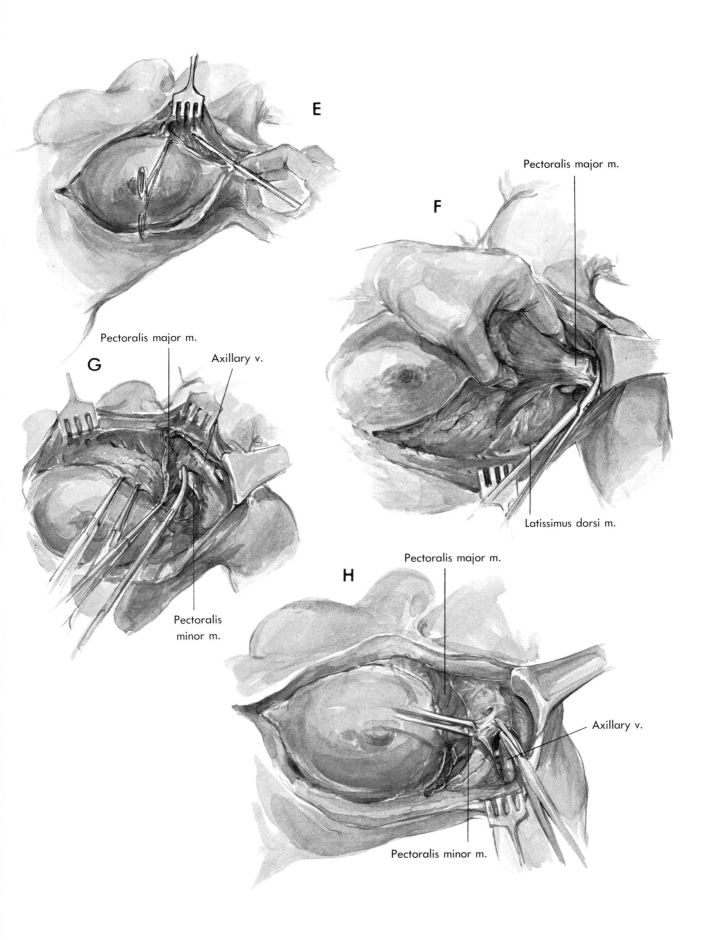

E

F

Pectoralis major m.

Latissimus dorsi m.

Pectoralis major m.

Axillary v.

G

Pectoralis
minor m.

Pectoralis major m.

H

Axillary v.

Pectoralis minor m.

I   The dissection of the apex of the axilla is carried out next while cleaning away all fatty areolar lymph node bearing tissue from the subscapular muscle. The subscapular vessels, the largest branches of the axillary, loop downward and give off the thoracodorsal branches before continuing more deeply as the circumflex scapular vessels. They should not be tented by excess traction on the thoracodorsal vessels lest they be accidentally cut.

J
K   The internal mammary chain is interrupted at the 1st and 6th interspaces, the upper one being done first. The origin of the uppermost fibers of the pectoralis major muscle must be divided to expose the area of the first interspace and the manubrial arch. The highest thoracic artery should be anticipated in this area; if lost, it will retract into the fibers of the subclavian muscle and prove difficult to secure. The fatty areolar tissue over this area is swept in a lateral and caudal direction so that the muscle fibers of the intercostal muscle of the 1st interspace are exposed. With fine strokes of the scalpel the muscle fibers are cut for a distance of 3 cm. lateral to the border of the sternum. A hemostat is used to separate the underlying fatty areolar tissue and to puncture the pleura directly lateral to the sternum. The index finger is inserted through this opening and the internal mammary vessels palpated laterally. If any involved lymph nodes are palpated cephalad to this opening, an internal mammary excision is of no value. In the absence of such involvement, the usual situation, the internal mammary artery and vein are ligated with 3-0 silk and, when divided, result in a 3 cm. intercostal opening.

L   This drawing shows the pectoral fascia and muscle fibers being cut to just medial to the lateral quarter of the sternum on the way down to the 6th interspace.

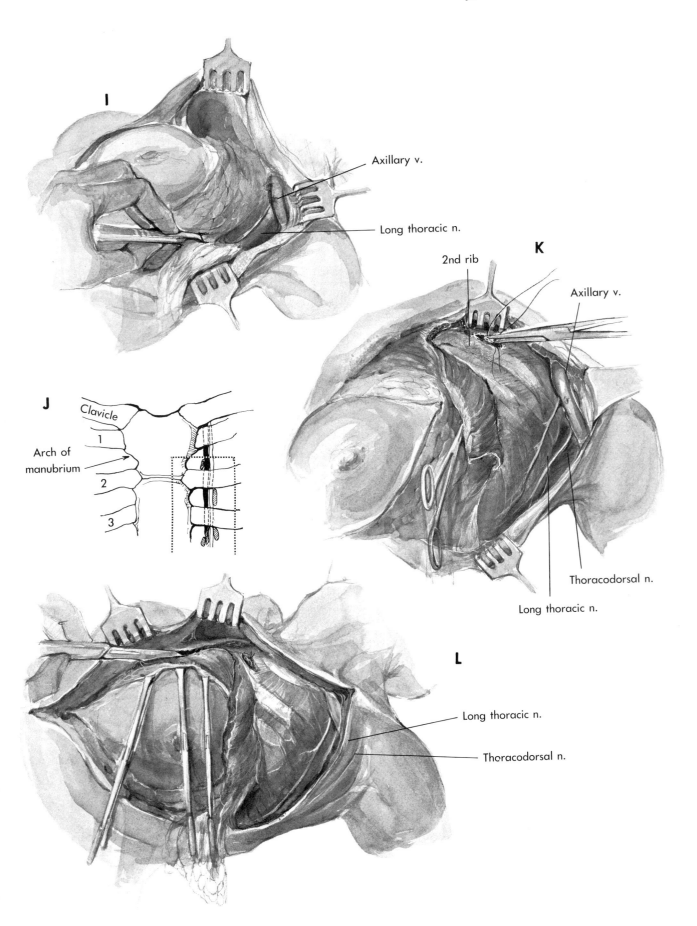

I

Axillary v.

Long thoracic n.

2nd rib

K

Axillary v.

Thoracodorsal n.

Long thoracic n.

J

Clavicle

Arch of
manubrium

1

2

3

L

Long thoracic n.

Thoracodorsal n.

M
N   At the lower aspect of the incision the fascia over the uppermost portion of the rectus abdominis muscle is removed. The 6th interspace is entered in the same manner as higher up and the internal mammary vessels are divided; there may be more than one internal mammary vessel at this level.

We prefer the oscillating saw to the Liebsche knife for cutting the sternum since it does not crush any bone during the cutting process. In Figure N there is indicated the portion of chest wall that is to be removed in continuity with the remainder of the specimen.

O   After the cross-cuts have been made at the level of the 2nd and 5th interspaces, a suitable instrument is used to pull the flap open partially; this is easy as the ribs here are cartilaginous. The individual ribs are divided from the inside with a scalpel so that the flap is now completely opened.

P   Bleeding from the sternal marrow is stopped with bone wax or electrocautery. The intercostal musculature is cut in line with the ribs, with the dissection proceeding laterally as the specimen now hangs off to the side. The axillary vessels and the internal mammary vessels and their perforating branches are ligated with 3-0 silk. For other smaller vessels electrocoagulation is effective and very time-saving.

The thoracic defect must be closed and stabilized. A variety of methods have been used to accomplish this. We have even simply replaced the skin flap over the defect with the result of risking some paradoxical respiration or a pneumothorax following necrosis of the overlying flap. Tantalum mesh has been used with good immediate results; however, this later fragments, with the possibility that slivers of metal will be extruded chronically through puncture sites, which remain infected during passage of the sliver. Ivalon, a polyvinyl formalin sponge, can be fashioned and applied easily but will not tolerate infection. Marlex mesh is the best synthetic prosthesis. Sliding rib grafts have been used by slitting laterally the upper half of the 2nd to the 6th ribs for a distance slightly greater than the width of the defect. A cross-cut frees this portion of the rib, which is slid medially and anchored at each end with wire. This technique is no better than a fascial graft alone in preventing paradoxical flapping of the overlying skin. By extending the mastectomy incision caudad a few extra centimeters and, in addition, retracting the skin flaps downwardly, an adequate piece of fascia from that over the rectus abdominis muscle can be obtained. There is no demonstrable loss in abdominal wall strength with the above procedure. One can also obtain a sheet of rectus fascia by cutting transversely and obtaining it from both recti. Some delicacy is required if one is not to excise all of the linea alba. In the last two methods one foregoes any advantage to excising the upper rectus sheath with the specimen.

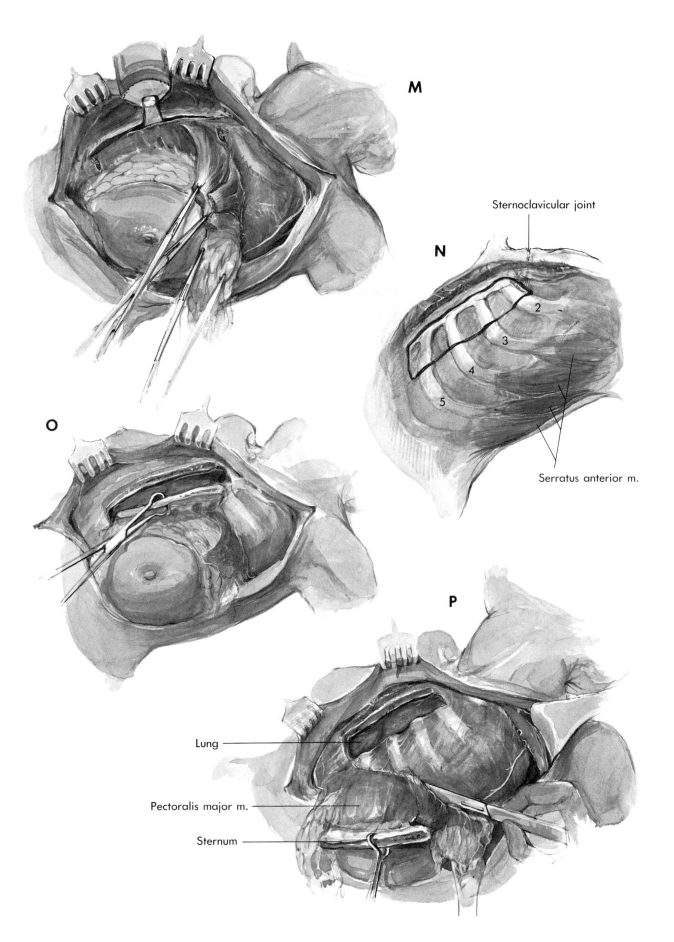

M

N

Sternoclavicular joint

2

3

4

5

Serratus anterior m.

O

P

Lung

Pectoralis major m.

Sternum

Q   In practice the two main sources of grafts are preserved bovine peritoneum and autogenous fascia. Bovine peritoneum has the advantages of ready availability and sufficient strength that it can be made leak-proof and well taut over the defect. To date there have been no reports of its not being accepted by the host. Procurement of autogenous fascia is illustrated here. When possible, a second operating team working distinctly separately can be used for this purpose so that there is no digression from the primary operation. The obvious disadvantages to the use of fascia lata are the need of a second operating team and the resultant scar over the thigh.

R   A longitudinal incision is made in the direct lateral aspect of the thigh. Once the fascia lata has been reached, the dissection laterally and just superficial to it proceeds with ease.

S
T   A piece of fasica lata is removed which is at least 2 cm. greater in both dimensions than the chest wall defect. Actually, only a modest skin incision is necessary because the undercut subcutaneous fat over the fascia lata permits shifting the opening in all directions as necessary to make the fascial cuts. The fascia will be thickest at its most posterior aspect. The fascial defect cannot and need not be closed. Hemostasis should be carried out carefully because this is a widely undercut wound which can accomodate a sizable accumulation of fluid. The subcutaneous tissue is approximated with 3-0 chromic catgut and the skin with interrupted vertical mattress stitches of 4-0 nylon. A drain is not used, but a pressure dressing is applied.

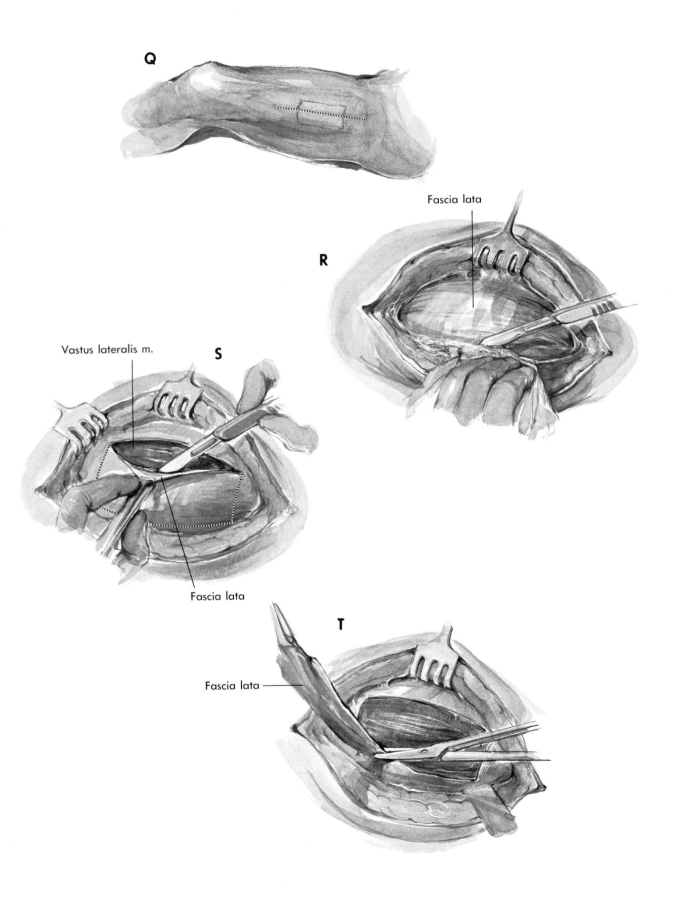

Q

Fascia lata

R

Vastus lateralis m.

S

Fascia lata

Fascia lata

T

U   Before beginning the repair of the thoracic defect, liquid blood and clots from the overlying surgery are removed from within the chest, care being taken not to rub or unduly traumatize the lung during the procedure. The intercostal vessels are examined at this time for assurance that all have been properly ligated; the thorax can accomodate a sizable amount of blood from a bleeding intercostal vessel without early overt signs of such an occurrence. Chest drainage is advisable. One chest tube is placed in the costophrenic angle at the midaxillary line and is connected to underwater chest drainage bottles.

V
W   The anesthesiologist is asked to expand the lung so that atelectatic areas can be aereated. They are allowed to collapse again slightly before the fascia lata is applied. The
X   purpose of the fascia lata is to provide a firm and leak-proof support. There are two perimeters to stitch. The central one anchors the fascia lata to the edge of the thoracic defect. If this anchoring is done on the pleural side, the marrow surface is covered and the fascia is on the same plane with the pleura. This, of course, results in a cavity, the thickness of the chest wall, between the fascia lata and the overlying skin, which fills with serum which wants to dissect under the rest of the sternal flap. We prefer to place the fascia lata flush with the outer surface of the thorax and to have the lung fill the space. Residual marrow bleeding has not been a problem, nor has the lung been damaged by coming in contact with the cut sternum. The interrupted inner stitches of 3-0 chromic catgut anchor the tightly drawn fascia to the cartilages and to the sternum. Peripherally, a continuous simple stitch of 3-0 chromic catgut is used to make the repair acceptably leak proof.

Y   Two subcutaneous catheters with multiple holes are exteriorized through tight counter-incisions lateral and caudad to the mastectomy incision. One is positioned under the axillary vessels pointing medially and the other is placed in the apex of the axilla. The edges are jockeyed into position with particular emphasis on an adequate amount of skin being available to collapse into and thus obliterate the infraclavicular space. We consider the early and sustained obliteration of this space to be an important requisite to prevent a collection of serous fluid and the accompanying undesirable sequelae. If possible, the suture line is made to fall away from the fascial graft. With the central or medially placed tumor for which this operation is used, often the resultant suture line is more medially situated than shown in this drawing. Narrowly placed simple stitches of 3-0 silk are used. Retention stitches are not used nor are the skin flaps secured to the chest wall with any stitches. Skin grafts are used as necessary with no serious concern if some or all of the skin graft lies over the fascial graft.

A chest x-ray is taken immediately after the operation to confirm complete re-expansion of the lung. Postoperatively, these patients experience slightly more discomfort than those with a classic radical mastectomy. The chest drainage tube can usually be removed in two to three days. Wound suction is maintained until there is assurance that the skin flaps will remain collapsed. Most patients are discharged before the end of the second week.

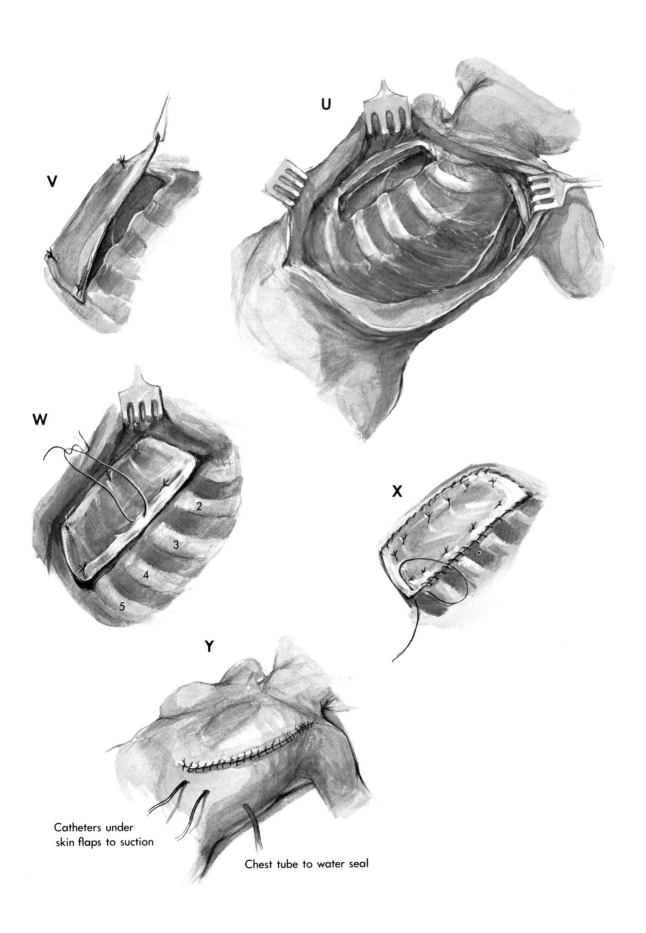

Catheters under
skin flaps to suction

Chest tube to water seal

MEDIASTINUM AND THYMECTOMY

The mediastinum, to the surgeon, is that area of the thorax below the neck, above the diaphragm and between the two pleural cavities. It is bounded anteriorly by the sternum and posteriorly by the spine. Since the anterior border of the spine is close to the anatomical middle of a normal patient, the mediastinum is located mostly anteriorly.

The mediastinum is enclosed with fascia that is continuous with the cervical fascia and continues down into the abdomen. This arrangement permits mediastinal air or infection ready access to both the neck and the abdomen.

The thoracic esophagus and trachea are most easily approached through the right thorax. The aorta, except for its ascending portion, is mostly in the left thorax. The heart and adjacent great vessels are largely anterior.

In operations on the mediastinum the surgeon must know all approaches and frequently use combined approaches. He may need a sternal-splitting incision (often combined with a "thyroid" incision), a trans-sternal incision into both hemithoraces, an anterior thoracotomy, a lateral thoracotomy or a posterior mediastinotomy.

Except for the posterior mediastinal area, a sternal-splitting incision is most universally acceptable for mediastinal lesions. This approach has the advantage of exposing the mediastinum without opening the pleural cavities, thus hopefully minimizing the respiratory complications. It is generally wise to drain the mediastinum with a catheter and water-seal drainage, just as is done in the usual thoracotomy.

The mediastinum is also unique in that it is constantly being wrung out both by respiration and by the beat of the heart. Since the mediastinal spaces to a considerable degree are continuous with those of the neck, a cervical mediastinotomy will drain the thoracic mediastinum if the proper spaces are entered and if the thoracic mediastinal infection is not walled off. Because the mediastinum is a closed space, a free perforation of the esophagus or trachea will usually promptly become a surgical emergency, with mediastinal tamponade.

A   This is an orientation drawing looking at the thorax and mediastinum from the anterior view and shows the sternal plate with its attached cartilage and xyphisternum. Immediately behind the sternal plate are the great veins. The left innominate vein joins the right innominate vein to descend as the superior vena cava and make up the right superior heart border. The inferior heart border is made up of the right atrium, with the inferior vena cava at the bottom angle. Just posterior to the great veins is the aortic arch. The innominate artery can be seen posterior and medial to the right innominate vein; it gives off the subclavian artery and the right common carotid artery. The left innominate vein is joined by a central vein from the thyroid region. The aortic arch swings to the left and gives off the left common carotid artery and the left subclavian artery posteriorly and then swings into the posterior mediastinum on the left anterolateral border of the spine. The pulmonary artery comes off in front of the aorta but, as it ascends in the mediastinum, goes behind the aorta. Its right branch, as mentioned, passes to the right lateral side, posterior to the ascending aortic arch and superior vena cava. The left pulmonary artery is the most cephalad portion of the left pulmonary hilum.

Also depicted are the pleural reflections. It can be seen that the mediastinal pleura on the right approaches the midline and overlies the cardiac silhouette anteriorly, whereas, on the left side, particularly in the inferior portion, the mediastinal pleura does not reach the midline. In the superior mediastinum, however, the mediastinal pleuras come very close together anteriorly. The tumors common to the anterior mediastinum are thyroid, possibly parathyroid, teratoid and thymic tumors. The thymus gland is an H-shaped structure, quite small in the adult, which lies straddling the vessels in the upper anterior mediastinum.

B   This depicts the approach to the anterior mediastinum via a sternal-splitting incision. Sometimes it is necessary to add to this a thyroid transverse incision, but it is not necessary if the surgery is confined to the thorax. The patient is supine on the operating table.

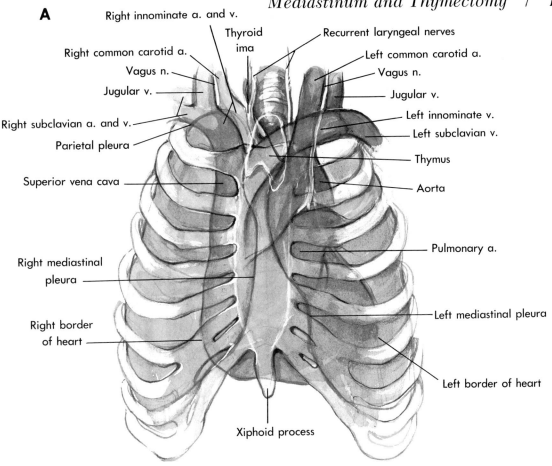

A

Right innominate a. and v.

Thyroid ima

Recurrent laryngeal nerves

Right common carotid a.

Left common carotid a.

Vagus n.

Vagus n.

Jugular v.

Jugular v.

Right subclavian a. and v.

Left innominate v.

Left subclavian v.

Parietal pleura

Thymus

Superior vena cava

Aorta

Pulmonary a.

Right mediastinal pleura

Left mediastinal pleura

Right border of heart

Left border of heart

Xiphoid process

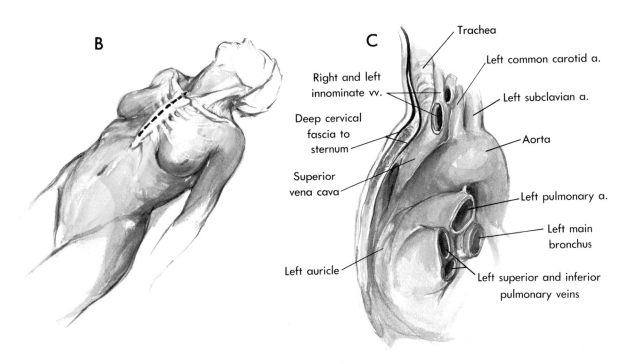

B

C

Trachea

Left common carotid a.

Right and left innominate vv.

Left subclavian a.

Deep cervical fascia to sternum

Aorta

Superior vena cava

Left pulmonary a.

Left main bronchus

Left auricle

Left superior and inferior pulmonary veins

C   This is a demonstration of the lateral anatomy in the region of the midportion of the sternum. It can be seen that the cervical fascia extends downward and invests the anterior and posterior part of the sternum. This fascia has to be incised to permit entry into the retrosternal space. Slightly lower there is a retrosternal space between the sternum and the great vessels. Here in the cervical region the trachea is subcutaneous but swings more posteriorly as it descends behind the aortic arch. It can also be seen that the veins are located anteriorly, the arteries more posteriorly and the pulmonary arteries posterior to the aortic arch.

D   In this figure an incision has been made through the skin and subcutaneous tissue in the midline down to the sternum. The pectoral muscles will not be encountered in the midline. The fascia over the sternum may be incised and retracted. At this point it is important to enter the retrosternal space. The scalpel depicts the incision in the prolonged sternal fascia attaching to the sternum. Caution must be exercised not to cut too deeply at this point since the central venous drainage of the thyroid may be immediately subjacent.

E   This is a lateral projection showing that a finger has entered the retrosternal space over the top of the sternum. It shows also how a Stryker oscillating saw is employed to saw through the midportion of the sternum.

F   This demonstrates an alternative instrument for cutting the central portion of the sternum, the Liebsche shears. Here the shears are protected posteriorly by the guard, and by advancing the instrument in a caudad fashion the sternum can be split.

G   The sternal sawing is begun in the suprasternal notch area and extended down toward the manubrium. It is helpful to utilize rake retractors to retract the cut sternum so that progress can be seen. The use of irrigating saline solution and suction helps to keep this field clear since there may be rather considerable bleeding from the raw surfaces of the sternum. If a nonexplosive anesthetic is used it may be very helpful to use electrocautery to help secure hemostasis from these raw bone areas. Otherwise, utilization of bone wax may help. The only significant danger in opening the sternum in this fashion is the possibility of injury to the great veins behind the sternum. The Stryker saw is so designed as to prevent this, and once the incision is started direct vision will permit the surgeon to see what he is cutting.

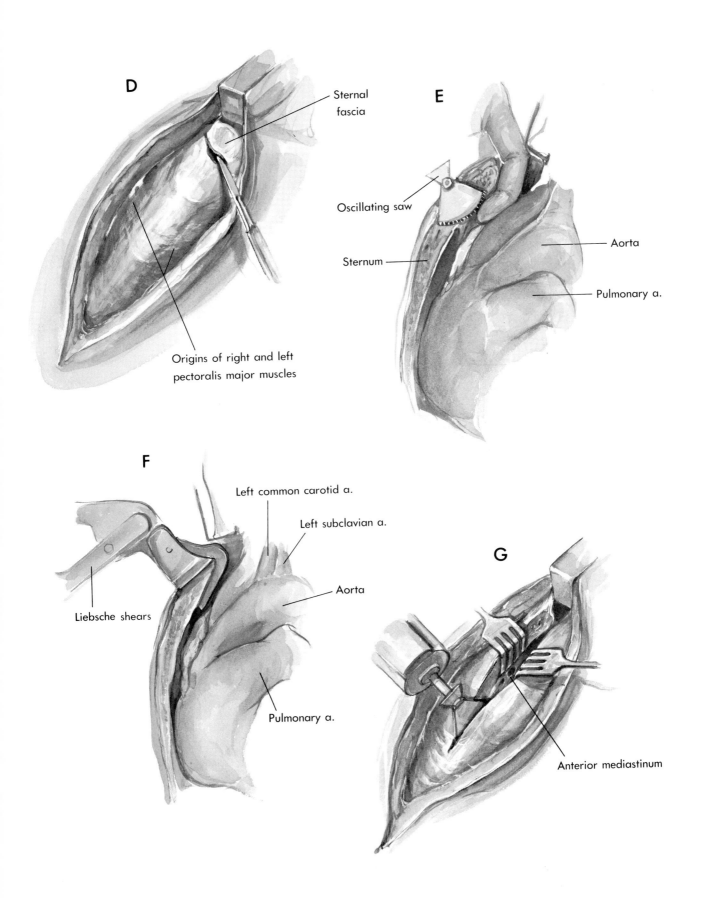

D

Sternal
fascia

Origins of right and left
pectoralis major muscles

E

Oscillating saw

Sternum

Aorta

Pulmonary a.

F

Left common carotid a.

Left subclavian a.

Aorta

Liebsche shears

Pulmonary a.

G

Anterior mediastinum

Mediastinum and Thymectomy (continued)

H   This semidiagrammatic rendition shows the blood supply of the thymus. The left portion of the sternum has been left in place as an aid to orientation. Most of the thymus has been removed to show the underlying vessels. The arterial supply to the thymus is primarily from the internal mammary artery. The venous drainage is multiple, with variation in the actual number and relative size of the veins. There is drainage into the internal mammary veins which, in turn, empty into the respective innominate veins. There is separate and direct drainage into the right and left innominate veins. There may also be drainage into the inferior thyroid vein, here shown as a single trunk. Opposite it is the unlabeled left superior intercostal vein.

I   The sternum has been split in its entirety and a self-retaining chest retractor has been inserted to spread the sternum. In this instance additional retraction is used in the soft tissue. The thumb forceps has picked up the right parietal pleura, and the right mediastinal pleura in its midanterior portion is being dissected from the mediastinal structures so that the thymus gland can be identified and removed.

J   The right pleura has been dissected laterally. With caution and care it is usually possible to do this without entering the pleural space. It is important to recognize any entry into the pleura so that appropriate counterdrainage with intercostal catheter and water seal can be instituted and the patient will not go to the recovery room with a unilateral or bilateral simple or tension pneumothorax. In this case, the right lower horn of the thymus gland has been identified. It has been retracted upward and lifted out as the lower horn of the thymus is dissected free. The vena cava and aortic arch can be seen immediately below. Although the blood supply of the thymus gland is as depicted, the location of vessels is inconstant. Vigilance is necessary to detect their presence; whatever vascular structures are encountered must be ligated as the dissection continues.

K   The thymus gland has been removed. It is important to remember that the superior lobes of the thymus gland extend up into the neck so that care must be taken when removing the gland. The retractor on the right is elevating the mediastinal pleura; the left innominate vein crossing the field is visible, as are the ascending aorta and the main pulmonary artery. The retractor on the left side is retracting the mediastinal pleura and left lung to the left. Ties are seen on the divided thymic veins draining into the thyroid ima and the left innominate vein.

   A small chest catheter is placed along the area of dissection, exteriorized through a tight stab incision and connected to water-seal bottles. The sternum is reapproximated with three to five stitches of Tevdek, the thickness of the suture being specifically fashioned for this task. The skin is closed with a continuous simple stitch of 3-0 silk.

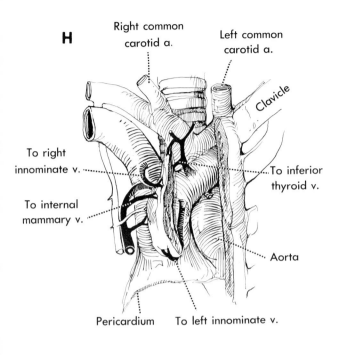

H

Right common carotid a.

Left common carotid a.

Clavicle

To right innominate v.

To inferior thyroid v.

To internal mammary v.

Aorta

Pericardium

To left innominate v.

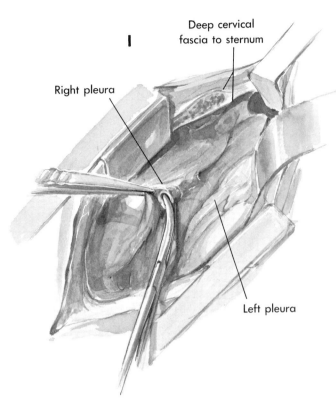

I

Deep cervical fascia to sternum

Right pleura

Left pleura

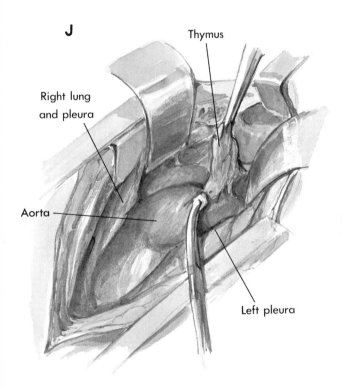

J

Thymus

Right lung and pleura

Aorta

Left pleura

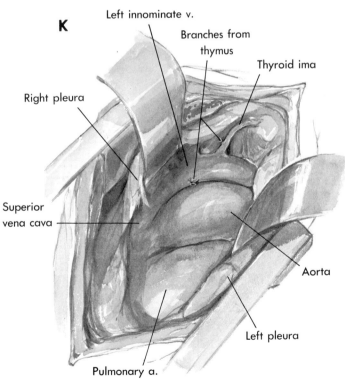

K

Left innominate v.

Branches from thymus

Thyroid ima

Right pleura

Superior vena cava

Aorta

Left pleura

Pulmonary a.

ORIENTATION TO THORAX

The right hemithorax depicted here is opened widely. The right thorax is the "venous chest," whereas the left thorax is the "arterial chest." The sympathetic chain runs along the anterolateral aspect of the spine. The anterior border of the vertebral bodies lies much closer to the anteroposterior middle of the chest than is usually realized. In the neck and upper thorax, the esophagus lies anterior to the spine. In the lower chest the esophagus is to the right of the spine and then courses to the left. However, in the open right thorax, the mediastinum will displace to the left in the left lateral decubitus position. Directly anterior to the esophagus is the trachea, which in the midchest branches into the right and left main bronchi. Directly anterior to the trachea is the superior vena cava. The azygos vein runs up the right anterolateral aspect of the spine, receiving intercostal vein tributaries, and passes anteriorly just cephalad to the lung hilum to join the superior vena cava. The inferior vena cava pierces the diaphragm anterior to the esophagus to enter the right atrium. The right inferior pulmonary vein is in the same frontal plane and directly caudad to the right main bronchus. The right main pulmonary artery passes posterior to the superior vena cava and joins the right lung hilum just anterior to the right main bronchus and just cephalad to it. The right superior pulmonary vein is caudad to the right main pulmonary artery and cephalad to the right inferior pulmonary vein. Both pulmonary veins lie in a frontal plane posterior to the superior and inferior vena cava. The heart fills most of the remaining anterior space. The thymus is in the anterior superior mediastinum.

The vagus and phrenic nerves are additional important structures. The right vagus nerve lies in the posterior portion of the carotid sheath and runs caudad in the neck posterior to the common carotid artery and internal jugular vein. It enters the thorax posterior to the carotid artery. It promptly branches into the right recurrent laryngeal nerve, which passes posteriorly to the right subclavian artery and ascends to the larynx in the right tracheoesophageal groove. The vagus continues caudad, crosses the trachea on its right side in a posterior direction and descends to the abdomen on the right side of the esophagus. The phrenic nerve is a branch of the fourth cervical nerve, which descends in the neck along the anterior border of the anterior scalene muscle, which it crosses in a "hand-in-pocket" fashion. It enters the thorax through the anterior part of the thoracic inlet. It descends along the right lateral side of the superior vena cava and passes caudad about 1 cm. anteriorly to the right lung hilum; at this point this nerve is very vulnerable to invasion by lung tumors. The phrenic nerve then runs caudad along the right anterolateral aspect of the pericardium. It innervates the diaphragm from the anteromedial aspect. The internal mammary vessels (the artery is from the subclavian artery) descend extrapleurally 1 cm. lateral to the lateral border of the sternum.

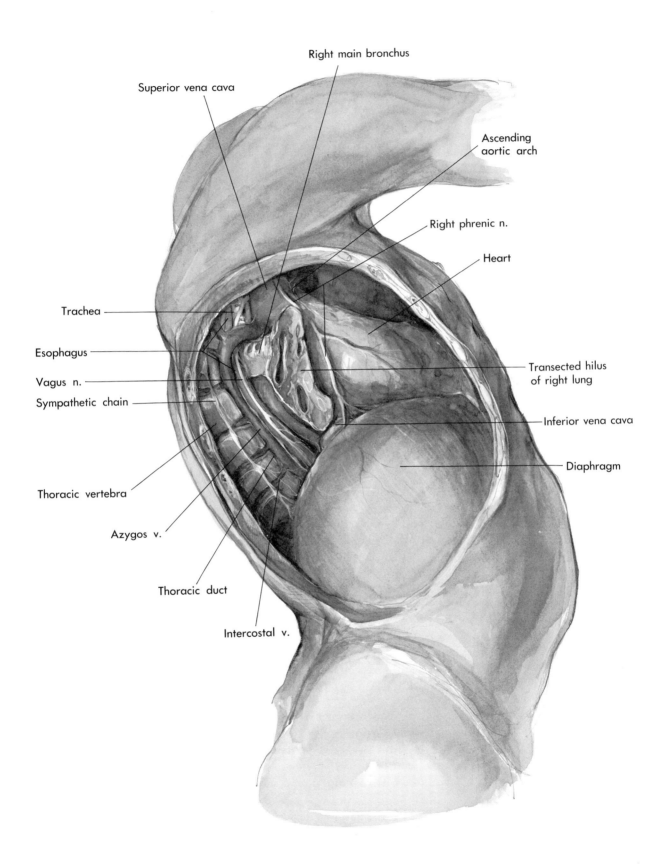

Right main bronchus

Superior vena cava

Ascending aortic arch

Right phrenic n.

Heart

Trachea

Esophagus

Vagus n.

Sympathetic chain

Transected hilus of right lung

Inferior vena cava

Diaphragm

Thoracic vertebra

Azygos v.

Thoracic duct

Intercostal v.

ORIENTATION TO LUNG

A
B
  These illustrations represent the right and left lungs and the Jackson-Huber classification of the bronchopulmonary segments. These are best seen in the opposite antero-oblique bronchogram of which this is a drawing representation. It will be noted that the right lung, being the larger, and representing 55 per cent of lung capacity, has ten bronchopulmonary segments, whereas the smaller left lung has eight bronchopulmonary segments. The right upper lobe contains the apical segment, the anterior segment, and the posterior segment; the right middle lobe contains the anterior and the lateral middle segments; and the right lower lobe contains the large superior segment and four basal segments located anteriorly, laterally, posteriorly and medially. On the left side the left upper lobe contains four bronchopulmonary segments. The left upper lobe bronchus bifurcates into the inferior and superior division. The inferior division, which is analogous to the right middle lobe, contains the superior and inferior lingular segments, whereas the superior division contains the anterior segment and the apico-posterior segment, which comes off as one branch and then subdivides into the apical and posterior subsegments. The left lower lobe bronchus gives off the large superior segment and has three basal segments: the anteromedial basal, the lateral basal and the posterior basal.

C
  This is a drawing of the lung hilum seen through a right thoracotomy. It can be seen that the esophagus is posteriorly to the left; the azygos vein crosses to join the superior vena cava just above the right lung hilum. It will be noted that the right main pulmonary artery is directly anterior and slightly cephalad to the right main bronchus. The superior pulmonary vein on the right side is directly caudad to the pulmonary artery and slightly anterior and cephalad to the inferior pulmonary vein. The right main bronchus on the right side runs down the longitudinal fissure; directly caudad to it is the right inferior pulmonary vein. The right atrium with its auricular appendage is anterior to the lung hilum, but the left atrium also is accessible through the right chest. The left atrium is directly posterior to the right atrium in the region where the right pulmonary veins insert into the left atrium posterior to the caval groove.

D
  This is the appearance of the great vessels seen from in front to depict the course of the right main pulmonary artery. It will be noted that the main pulmonary trunk is an anterior structure with the aorta rising behind it. However, as the ascending aorta rises in the thorax the pulmonary artery becomes more posterior and the right main pulmonary artery branch goes posterior to the aorta and the vena cava as it enters the right thorax. This means that exposure of the right pulmonary artery can be extrapericardial, or it can be intrapericardial but lateral to the vena cava, or it can be between the vena cava and the aorta. Occasionally, the approach might be between the aorta and the pulmonary truncus.

E
  This is the typical anatomy of the left hilum as seen through the left thorax. It will be noted that the left main pulmonary artery is directly cephalad to the left main bronchus. Directly caudad to the left main bronchus is the left inferior pulmonary vein. Just anterior to the left main bronchus and slightly overlapping either the pulmonary artery or the inferior pulmonary vein is the superior left pulmonary vein. These veins, likewise, enter the left atrium, which on this side shows the left auricular appendage.
  It can be seen that the vagus nerve enters the thorax anterior to the subclavian artery on the right and anterior to the aortic arch on the left and runs caudad posterior to the lung hila. The ligamentum arteriosum runs from the bifurcation of the main pulmonary artery to the concave side of the aortic arch just distal to the left subclavian artery. The left recurrent nerve can be found coming from the left vagus nerve looping caudad to the ligamentum arteriosum and coursing cephalad medially to the aortic arch. It runs cephalad in the tracheoesophageal groove to the larynx. On the right side the recurrent nerve runs caudad to the right subclavian artery in a posterior direction and then also runs cephalad to the larynx in the tracheoesophageal groove on the right.

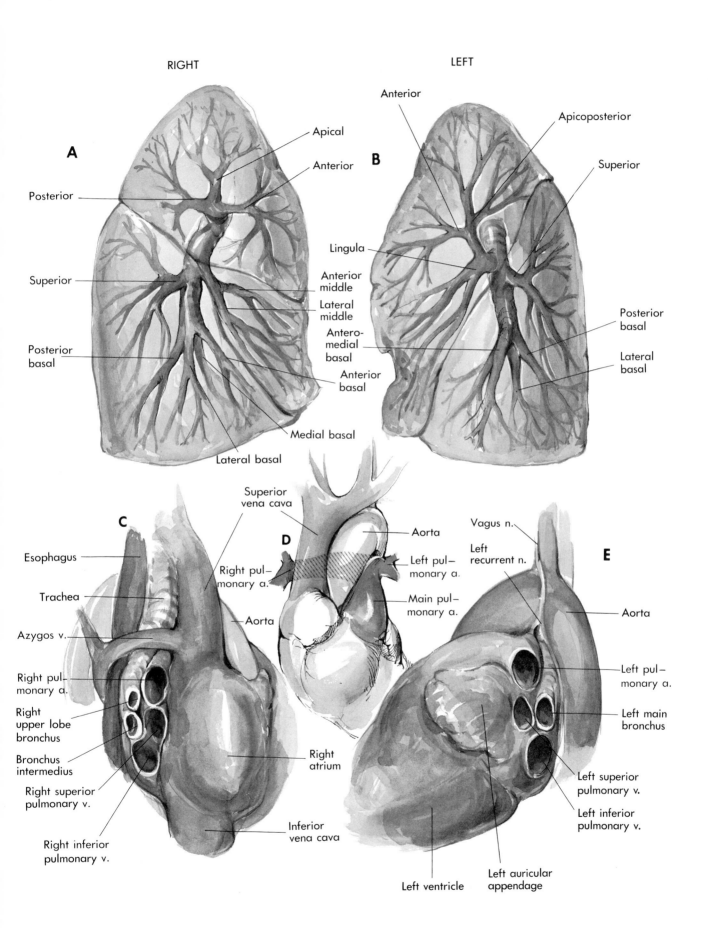

RIGHT

A

Posterior

Superior

Posterior
basal

Apical

Anterior

Anterior
middle

Lateral
middle

Antero-
medial
basal

Anterior
basal

Medial basal

Lateral basal

LEFT

B

Anterior

Apicoposterior

Superior

Lingula

Posterior
basal

Lateral
basal

C

Esophagus

Trachea

Azygos v.

Right pul-
monary a.

Right
upper lobe
bronchus

Bronchus
intermedius

Right superior
pulmonary v.

Right inferior
pulmonary v.

Superior
vena cava

D

Right pul-
monary a.

Aorta

Aorta

Left pul-
monary a.

Main pul-
monary a.

Right
atrium

Inferior
vena cava

Vagus n.

Left
recurrent n.

E

Aorta

Left pul-
monary a.

Left main
bronchus

Left superior
pulmonary v.

Left inferior
pulmonary v.

Left ventricle

Left auricular
appendage

RADICAL PNEUMONECTOMY

Pneumonectomy is now most commonly performed for primary malignant tumors of the lung, most frequently bronchogenic carcinoma. The operation is also performed when the lung has been destroyed and is a hazard to the patient, as in tuberculosis or bronchiectasis. These latter indications for resection have decreased as medical control of these diseases has improved. The successful resection of a lung requires a relatively normal contralateral lung if the patient is not to be a respiratory cripple. The operation of pneumonectomy will no doubt increase in popularity if and when homologous lung transplantation problems are solved.

There have been disagreements concerning the value of "simple" pneumonectomy versus "radical" pneumonectomy. The latter operation is a pneumonectomy plus an attempt to excise the mediastinal lymph nodes in continuity with the lung. The published reports of survivors so far have not indicated a statistically significant increased cure rate for carcinoma with use of the radical pneumonectomy, although we feel that in operations for cancer an effort should be made to remove the mediastinal lymph nodes.

The lung is a highly vascular structure and although pulmonary epidermoid carcinomas tend to spread by lymphatics to hilar and mediastinal lymph nodes, it is unfortunate that frequently the tumor has metastasized outside the thorax via blood vessels or lymphatics by the time surgery is performed. This high rate of extrathoracic metastasis is particularly likely to have occurred in the symptomatic lung tumors and poorly differentiated cell type tumors. The tendency for extrathorax metastasis to have occurred by the time of operation may be why radical pneumonectomy has produced no distinctly higher rate of "cure" than simple pneumonectomy.

There has also been controversy concerning the treatment of lung carcinoma by pneumonectomy or lobectomy. The published reports show approximately the same cure rate for lung cancer treated by either procedure. However, certain factors must be remembered when evaluating the choice of operation. Generally, a tumor is more localized when a lobectomy is possible than when a pneumonectomy is needed. Hence, patients treated by lobectomy may have less advanced disease. Ordinarily, patients with lung tumors treated by pneumonectomy run a surgical risk from 10 per cent to as high as 20 per cent, dependent upon the physiological status of the patient and the extent of resection, compared to a risk of less than 5 per cent from lobectomy in the same patient. It is apparent that a surgeon must expect an increase in his "cure" of resected carcinoma if he elects to do a pneumonectomy when a lobectomy could also be performed.

The less well differentiated carcinoma cell types, and especially the "oat cell" tumors, yield less success with surgical treatment. If the tumor is an adenocarcinoma, a careful search for a primary tumor elsewhere must be made. However, multiple primary tumors are relatively common, and a solitary lung tumor should be considered to be a new primary tumor rather than assumed to be a metastasis. Patients with primary tumors elsewhere are high risk patients to develop new lung tumors and should be carefully followed with this possibility in mind.

The improvement of surgical attack on lung carcinoma may be in two directions: one approach is to find the tumor earlier so that a simple lobectomy may be curative. Simple lobectomy in the "coin lesion" stage should be possible in over 90 per cent of the patients seen, with lymph nodes negative for tumor in about 75 per cent, and an expected "cure" in over 50 per cent. Patients alive and free of disease five years after resection are considered "cured," although those alive and free of disease three years after resection have a 90 per cent chance of also being five-year "cures." Few patients not surgically cured of lung carcinomas will live over 24 months. Most patients with inoperable lung tumors will not survive 12 months. Unfortunately, a high percentage of lung tumor patients coming to the hospital have advanced disease.

The other line of attack is to extend the surgical resection. Patients with proven metastases outside the chest cannot be cured by current surgical measures except for certain superior sulcus tumors, radical excision of which after preoperative irradiation has been shown by Paulson to be often curative. Preoperative irradiation of the thorax will not affect the extrathoracic spread of the disease, which has often already occurred in the symptomatic cancer. There are occasional instances when a "palliative resection" is indicated for cancer even though distant metastases are present, for example, a tumor with severe hemorrhage or a tumor with a lung abscess. A palliative pneumonectomy is rarely indicated.

Improvement in the surgical cure for lung carcinoma by extension of the operation or increase in the percentage of carcinomas resected needs further evaluation. In published figures approximately a third of symptomatic lung cancers are "inoperable" when first seen, a third are declared "inoperable" at the operating table and another third are resected. In the latter third, again about one third of those surviving operation will be "cured." Thus, 10 per cent or less (as low as 2 per cent) of symptomatic lung cancers are "cured" surgically.

Whether preoperative irradiation will improve the results with symptomatic lung tumors other than those of the superior sulcus is not definitely known. Radiation would not be expected to affect those patients whose tumors are already outside the thorax. Preoperative irradiation may improve the operability rate but it may also make it harder to assess the proper margin of resection at the time of operation. Some surgeons have felt that the postoperative morbidity rate is worsened by preoperative irradiation.

To date, adjuvant chemotherapy has not helped in lung carcinoma. This situation hopefully will change in the future as better cancericidal agents are developed. Recently, heart-lung by-pass equipment has been employed to extend the area of operability for tumors. This technique might be applicable to tracheal carinal resection, to resection of the left atrium or to replacement of the vena cava. Opportunity to use this equipment is limited and it has the disadvantage of requiring concomitant anticoagulation therapy.

An accurate diagnosis should be obtained before a pneumonectomy is considered. Bronchoscopy especially should be done. Only in the minority of bronchogenic carcinomas will a positive tissue diagnosis be obtained, but an accurate assessment of the state of the tracheo-bronchial tree, preferably by the operating surgeon, is of the utmost value. Even if positive tissue is unobtainable, the view of any pathological lesion and the collection of uncontaminated secretions for bacteriologic and cytologic study are valuable. A postbronchoscopy sputum and morning sputum are especially valuable for cytologic examination. Up to 80 per cent positive diagnosis can be expected by expert cytologists. A definitive diagnosis should be vigorously sought. If one does a thoracotomy for suspect tumors without a definitive diagnosis, unfortunately for the patient, a positive lymph node diagnosis can often be made by a mediastinal lymph node biopsy. Before doing a pneumonectomy, a biopsy by wedge excision or needle aspiration can be made. Only rarely and with extreme caution should a "blind" pneumonectomy be done.

The pneumonectomy patient should be studied preoperatively, with special attention given to respiratory bacteria present, since the postoperative empty thorax is more apt to be infected than if lung tissue is present to fill the space. Any infection should be as well controlled as possible. This is, of course, particularly important if the indications for pneumonectomy are tuberculosis or bronchiectasis. Attention should also be given to the respiratory reserve. Careful history, observation of respiration upon exercise and screening with function tests such as vital capacity, per cent vital capacity in one second, and maximum breathing capacity should be done. Special care should be taken to avoid removing the better lung in a patient with impaired respiratory reserve. At times bronchospirometry is indicated.

The cardiac status should be studied. Here again history and physical examination are most important. Roentgen examination of heart size should be done, and an electrocardiogram should always be obtained. Although patients with old myocardial infarctions will usually survive pneumonectomy, not often will they live to be "cures." Since at least 10 per cent of pneumonectomy patients will develop postoperative cardiac arrhythmia, a baseline ECG is mandatory. We have not felt that routine digitalis is indicated to prevent arrhythmia, as is advocated by other thoracic surgeons; however, careful observation of the postoperative cardiac rhythm is essential. Preoperative evidence of cor pulmonale or right heart strain should be sought. The presence of this condition should warn against pneumonectomy. At times cardiac catheterization, with measurement of the pulmonary artery pressure, or even performance of a "physiologic pneumonectomy," by studying pulmonary artery pressure change during balloon occlusion of the main pulmonary artery involved, will be helpful. The blood volume, fluid balance and hemoglobin should be in a normal range before pneumonectomy is undertaken.

Four pints of cross-matched blood should be on hand at the start of a pneumonectomy, with additional supplies readily available. Technical accidents during performance of pneumonectomy can cause excessive blood loss. It is particularly important that blood loss be measured, since patients having pneumonectomy tolerate overtransfusion very poorly. Blood should be given only if and when needed and in the amount lost. Monitoring central venous pressure during a pneumonectomy has been helpful to us.

The technical problems of pneumonectomy are complicated by the location of tumor close to the hilum. Usually in cases of tuberculosis the hilum is less involved. On the other hand, pneumonectomy for advanced unilateral bronchiectasis may be exceedingly difficult because of the firm, scarred lymphadenopathy that almost defies anatomical dissection. Extreme care must be taken in bronchiectasis since death in a patient with a benign lesion is particularly unfortunate. If the hilum is difficult to dissect, the intrapericardial approach should be used. This approach usually permits easier dissection, but it is very unforgiving of technical errors. One must avoid leaving a defect in the pericardium through which the heart might herniate fatally. It is equally dangerous to remove most of the pericardium while doing a pneumonectomy. In this instance the heart may twist on itself, obstructing the caval and pulmonary veins with fatal results. If necessary, a new pericardium should be fashioned and can probably best be done with autologous fascia lata.

Postoperatively one must be certain that the mediastinum is in the midline and that the pleural pressure in the empty thorax is a slightly negative mean pressure on quiet unassisted respiration. This state can be checked by an immediate postoperative chest film or by measurement of the pleural pressure with a pneumothorax machine with the patient supine and breathing spontaneously, or by means of an intercostal catheter with water-seal drainage. In the latter situation the chest tube should be clamped most of the time to avoid expulsion of the thoracic air, causing too negative pleural pressure. If for any reason thoracic bleeding or air leakage cannot be avoided, insertion of a chest tube is indicated. Acute gastric dilation should be avoided, especially in right pneumonectomy patients.

The most serious complications are hemorrhage (to be avoided by careful surgery), cardiac difficulty, empyema, and bronchopleural fistula.

In the operation to be depicted the tumor was at the lung root on the right side and required an intrapericardial resection and sacrifice of the right phrenic nerve along with the resected tumor.

It has been recommended that the venous drainage of the lung be obstructed before any significant manipulation of the lung. The motive for this approach is avoidance of hematogenous spread of tumor. There is some doubt whether careful surgical manipulation of the lung will disseminate tumor more than has already occurred with the coughing and straining of day-to-day living. In addition, the author has found that usually, when for technical reasons the venous drainage of lung tissue is obstructed first, one is troubled with engorged lung parenchyma that bleeds easily and interferes with the rest of the dissection. If for some reason the operation must be rapidly terminated before completion, one can stop without lung necrosis, even though the pulmonary artery has been transected, so long as the bronchial arteries are intact. A divided pulmonary artery produces an undesirable situation since the ultimate hypertrophy of the bronchial circulation will tend to add a peripheral arteriovenous fistula to the systemic circulation. The patient who needs a pneumonectomy, who is explored and who has a nonresectable condition often has a very stormy or fatal postoperative course. Thus, if a patient is explored for known disease, every attempt should be made to complete the operation. Insertion of radon seeds locally has at times given gratifying results.

The standard thoracic incision is that of the posterolateral approach. With this incision the patient is placed on his side with the underneath leg flexed to help keep the hips vertical. The hips are held vertical by adhesive strips fastened to the operating table. Appropriate pads or blankets are placed between the legs to prevent pressure points. The arms can be left free, folded in front of the face or extended on arm boards. Pressure points should be avoided, as should overextension with traction on the brachial plexus. The 6th rib is the landmark for a pneumonectomy; the 5th rib is the landmark for an upper lobectomy; and the 7th rib can be used for low thoracic problems or a combined approach to the upper abdomen.

The incision should be midway between the spinous processes and the vertebral border of the scapula and should be carried as cephalad as necessary. The incision continues about one inch below the angle of the scapula and then anteriorly toward the portion of the rib to be used. In a female patient the anterior portion of the incision is made in the lower breast fold. When the surgeon has severed the chest muscles, the ribs can readily be counted from above downward inside the chest wall musculature. We prefer an intercostal incision into the pleura in young people who have resilient ribs, but usually we resect a rib subperiosteally in older patients who have more rigid rib cages. A fractured rib will add to the discomfort of a thoracotomy and should be avoided if possible by use of incisions large enough for adequate exposure and then gradual opening of the rib-spreading retractor.

The anterior mediastinum is best approached with the patient supine, employing a sternal-splitting incision. In a condition in which the patient has excessive secretions, the prone position will occasionally be needed. In the prone position the hips must be elevated and fixed while the thorax is supported on the sternum and the face is in the neurosurgical cerebellar rest. The intratracheal tube must be carefully tied in. Gravity will drain the secretions. For most thoracic procedures it is advantageous to be able to dissect either anteriorly or posteriorly, as can be done in the lateral approach. The anterior and posterior approaches have certain technical limitations in the dissection.

Although the term bronchogenic carcinoma is firmly entrenched by usage in the medical literature, it should be remembered that certain primary lung carcinomas may not be bronchogenic in origin. For this reason the term "primary lung carcinoma" plus a description of the cell type is more accurate terminology.

References

Bloedorn, F. G., and Cowley, R. A.: Irradiation and surgery in the treatment of bronchogenic carcinoma. Surg. Gynec. & Obst. *111*:141, 1960.

Cahan, W., Watson, W., and Pool, J.: Radical pneumonectomy. J. Thoracic Surg. 22:449, 1951.

Graham, E. A., and Singer, J. J.: The successful removal of an entire lung for carcinoma of the bronchus. J.A.M.A. *101*:1371, 1933.

Moersch, H. J., and McDonald, J. R.: The significance of cell types in bronchogenic carcinoma. Dis. Chest 23:621, 1953.

Radical Pneumonectomy

A This illustration depicts the standard lateral approach and the position of the patient for a thoracotomy, with the patient lying on her side. The hips are kept directly vertical, usually with the aid of a sandbag and adhesive strapping to the table. The underneath leg is drawn upward to prevent the patient from rolling forward. Adequate padding is placed between the legs and the upper leg is left straight. Usually both hands are forward and in a comfortable position in front of the patient in a fashion not to interfere with the endotracheal tube and the anesthesia apparatus. The incision is periscapular.

B In the female the anterior part of the incision will be in the inframammary crease for cosmetic purposes. The posterior part of the incision is ordinarily midway between the spinous processes and the vertebral border of the scapula. The rib to be removed (or interspace to be entered) will dictate how high this incision is carried posteriorly. The standard approach for a pneumonectomy is either through the bed of the 6th rib or through the 5th or 6th interspace. In this case the 6th rib underlies the lower part of the scapula, and it is necessary to extend the incision posteriorly to at least the mid-portion of the scapula. This illustration demonstrates the anterior extent of this incision in the female, which in this case has been curved up in the inframammary fold so that the anterior part of the 5th or 6th rib can be approached. It is helpful to identify the rib or interspace to be used anteriorly before making the incision so that no unnecessary incision is made.

C This is essentially the same approach but in this case a male patient is shown; the anterior portion of the incision tends to follow the 6th rib anteriorly since the problem of the cosmetic appearance of the breast is not so significant.

D There are two sets of muscles anteriorly and two sets of muscles posteriorly which are encountered in this incision. Posteriorly the superficial muscle is the trapezius muscle. The muscles deep to the trapezius are the major and minor rhomboids. This drawing shows the incision of the trapezius muscle. Usually before doing this the auscultatory triangle with its fascia and lack of muscle has been entered and the cleavage plane found just outside the periosteum of the ribs. This can be cut with scalpel or scissors. There is some advantage to having a hand on either side so that hemostasis can be maintained with thumb and index finger if fair-sized vessels are encountered before they are clamped.

E This shows the two anterior muscles which are the latissimus dorsi superficially and the serratus anterior deep. These muscles are usually cut in single layers, but in less well developed persons they may readily be taken as one muscle layer.

F The muscle layers have been divided. Hemostasis is achieved either with the electrocautery or fine ligatures of black silk. The periosteum over the 6th rib has been incised with a scalpel and with the use of a periosteal elevator the periosteum is dissected cleanly from the rib. It is important to remember that the intercostal muscles insert as "hands in the pocket" and consequently freeing the cephalad edge of the rib is easiest if the periosteal elevator is moved anteriorly, whereas in freeing the caudad edge of the rib the dissection is easier if the periosteal elevator moves posteriorly. After the rib is freed in its entirety it can be resected or the incision can go through the bed of the periosteum without resecting the rib. As mentioned previously, rib removal or incision through the bed of the rib permits a better and more airtight closure of the thoracotomy incision. It also has the advantage that in older people the ribs spread slightly better than with an intercostal incision. However, in young adults or children, in whom the chest wall is more pliable, there are some advantages in the alternate use of the intercostal type incision.

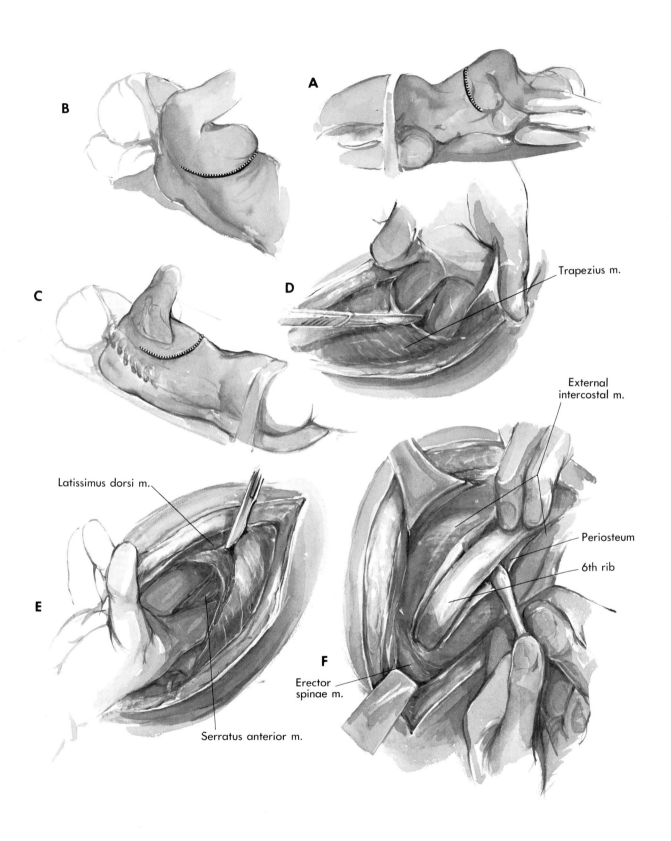

Trapezius m.

External
intercostal m.

Periosteum

6th rib

Latissimus dorsi m.

Serratus anterior m.

Erector
spinae m.

G A scapular retractor is holding the scapula cephalad. The posterior rib stump is visible. The pleura has been incised, usually with the scalpel, first making sure that there appears to be a free pleural space. The pleural opening is continued over the length of the rib, in this case following the longitudinal fissure, which can be seen. Normally, the longitudinal fissure lies directly under the 6th rib.

H In this drawing the retractor has been inserted in the pleural cavity and the rib spreading begun. The transverse fissure identifying the middle lobe as well as the upper and lower lobe can be seen. The rib stump is also prominent.

I In this drawing the posterior rib stump is being removed. This can be done before the chest has been entered but it is somewhat easier to do so after the chest has been opened and a brief exploratory palpation of the chest has been carried out to be certain that the operation will continue as scheduled. Here it is necessary to retract the spinal muscle of the thorax. This is done by dissecting the spinal muscle from the ribs and retracting it medially. After retraction the periosteal elevator is again used to free the periosteum from the rib back to the tip of the transverse process, which can be found close to and just caudad to the rib stump. Normally, the rib stump is cut flush with the tip of the transverse process to gain maximum exposure posteriorly. This has been done while the lung is being held away with a sponge-stick to protect the lung.

J The bared periosteum and pleura following the trimming of the rib stump is now being incised back to flush with the cut rib end. In similar fashion the anterior rib stump is freed and cut to the anterior limits of the incision. If the incision is carried close to the sternum one must be careful not to inadvertently injure the internal mammary vessels, which run 1 cm. lateral to the lateral border of the sternum. If for any reason one wished to continue the incision across the sternum, it would be necessary to ligate the internal mammary vessels. It would then be possible to cut the sternum, stopping just short of the internal mammary vessels on the opposite side. This maneuver gains considerable added exposure to the anterior aspect of the thorax.

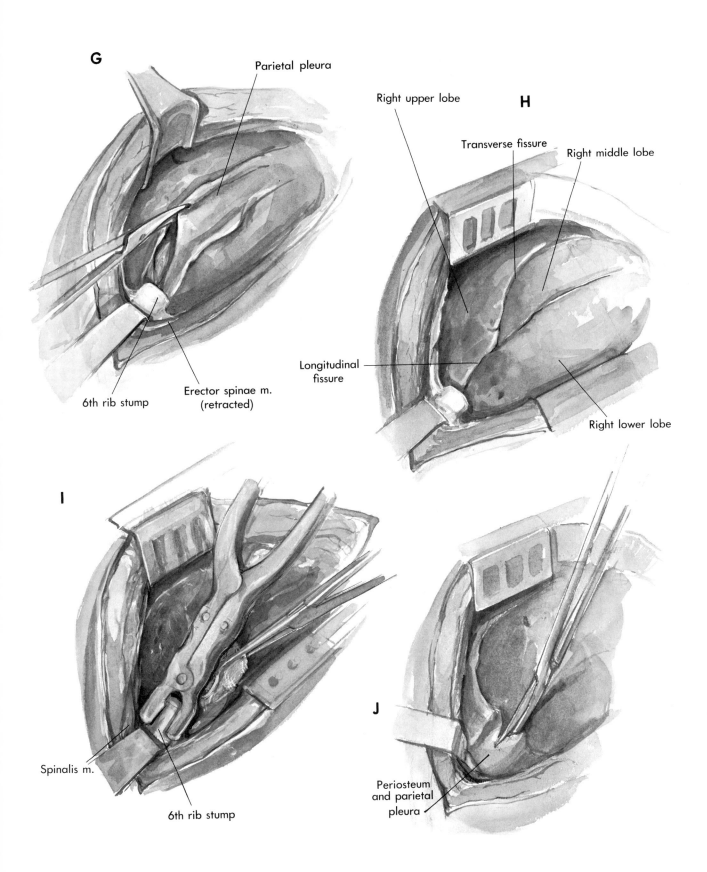

G

Parietal pleura

6th rib stump

Erector spinae m. (retracted)

H

Right upper lobe

Transverse fissure

Right middle lobe

Longitudinal fissure

Right lower lobe

I

Spinalis m.

6th rib stump

J

Periosteum and parietal pleura

K   The lung has been retracted anteriorly. It is important to remember that before beginning dissection in the thorax, all the anatomical structures should be carefully palpated. Since this is the right thorax, one should routinely examine the diaphragm and palpate the liver. The pericardium and heart should be examined, and thrills should be felt for in the various regions of the heart. The aorta, superior and inferior vena cava, phrenic nerve, vagus nerve and the region of the esophagus and azygos vein should be identified, and any tumor or suspected lymph nodes in the field should be gently and lightly palpated.

    In the case depicted, the exploration has been done, and the diagnosis of a lung tumor has been confirmed. Accordingly, the operative procedure has started by incision of the mediastinal pleura posterior to the lung hilum directly over the esophagus. It can be seen that this incision runs parallel to the anterior border of the spine which lies slightly posterior to it. The region of the azygos vein is being approached in the cephalad region of the lung hilum. It will be noted that the lower lobe has been retracted outward, showing that the inferior pulmonary ligament is divided. The medial portion of the lower lobe is attached to the mediastinum by reflections of pleura. This normally contains no significant structures, but there is usually a small blood vessel in the free edge of the inferior pulmonary ligament which must be ligated. One must be careful not to injure inadvertently the inferior pulmonary vein, which can be seen just faintly in the most caudad part of this hilum. The incision is stopped short of dividing the azygos vein, since the azygos vein is an important collateral venous system in case of superior vena cava obstruction. After the surgeon ascertains the situation here, it is wise to continue the incision around anteriorly to ascertain the condition of the anterior part of the hilum before partially committing oneself and dividing the azygos vein.

L   This drawing shows the lower lobe retracted posteriorly and cephalad. It is seen that the inferior pulmonary ligament is divided and also that the anterior mediastinal pleura over the hilum has been developed, revealing the anterior portion of the inferior pulmonary vein. The phrenic nerve which runs directly in front of the lung hilum and then diverges anteriorly on the pericardium can be seen prominently.

M   With this posterior and anterior exposure it has been felt so far that the lesion is operable. Accordingly, the azygos vein has been divided, usually with both a ligature and a reinforcing suture ligature. Now the status of the vena cava and the superior portion of the mediastinum must be ascertained before further commitment.

N   This drawing shows the usual relationships at the right lung hilum. The bronchus and inferior pulmonary vein lie in the same plane, with the vein directly caudad. The pulmonary artery is anterior to the bronchus and overlaps it in a cephalad direction. The superior pulmonary vein lies anterior to the bronchus and inferior vein; it lies directly between the pulmonary artery and the inferior vein.

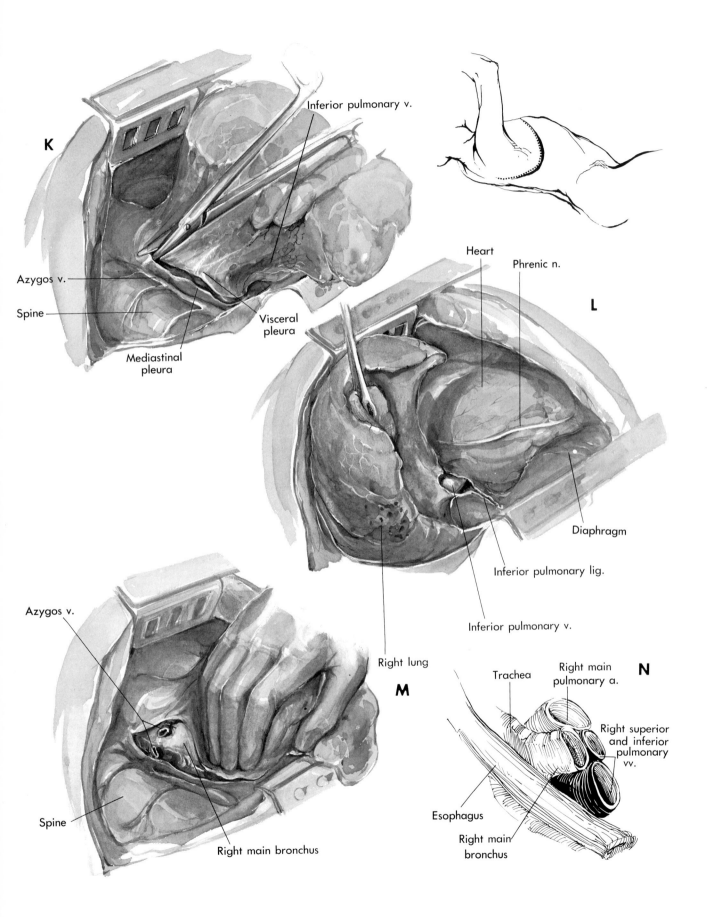

K

Inferior pulmonary v.

Azygos v.

Spine

Visceral pleura

Mediastinal pleura

Heart

Phrenic n.

L

Diaphragm

Inferior pulmonary lig.

Inferior pulmonary v.

Right lung

M

Azygos v.

Spine

Right main bronchus

N

Trachea

Right main pulmonary a.

Right superior and inferior pulmonary vv.

Esophagus

Right main bronchus

O   It will be seen here that the anterior mediastinum has been opened between the lung and the phrenic nerve. However, palpation has revealed that the tumor is located at this point and involves the pericardium where the vessels pierce it. Accordingly, it is felt that the situation inside the pericardium must be ascertained, for if this tumor is to be removed it will have to be done by an intrapericardial approach. In this case an incision is made anterior and parallel to the phrenic nerve. Considerable caution must be used in making the first entrance into the pericardium so that underlying structures such as the coronary vessels are not injured.

P   This shows that the pericardial incision has been made and extended and the pericardium retracted with sutures. It is important to remember that if a pneumonectomy is done, a total pericardectomy must not be done. A free heart without a pericardial cover can twist or obstruct in the absence of a lung to support it. Accordingly, as much pericardium as possible should be saved so that sufficient pericardial sling will be left; there can be no hole left in the pericardium large enough for the heart to prolapse. Visible inside the pericardium is the prominent right atrium.

Q   This diagram demonstrates the anatomy of the main blood vessels in the right lung hilum. The prominent superior vena cava can be seen coursing from left to right to enter the right atrium, which anteriorly has the auricular appendage. Caudad is the right ventricle, which lies in the right and anterior aspect of the heart. Directly anterior to the superior vena cava is the ascending aorta coursing upward from the heart, and beyond the aorta to the left can be seen the main pulmonary artery. The pulmonary artery branches and the right pulmonary artery comes into the right thorax posterior to the aorta and the superior vena cava. At this point the surgeon can dissect out the right pulmonary artery inside the pericardium just lateral to the vena cava or between the vena cava and the aorta. Care must be taken because the closer to the heart the more serious will be any laceration of these structures. It will be noted that the superior and inferior pulmonary veins which lie caudad to the right main pulmonary artery enter the left atrium, which in truth is the posterior atrium. The landmark for the entry of these veins into the left atrium is just behind the caval groove which separates the left atrium from the right atrium and is found posterior to the insertions of the superior and inferior venae cavae into the right atrium.

R   The pericardium has been opened widely. The dissecting sponge is used for most of the blunt dissection. If there is no tumor and the anatomy is otherwise relatively normal, blunt dissection will progress readily if the right cleavage planes are entered. In this case the superior vena cava has to be freed from the underlying pulmonary artery. The aorta is seen just beyond and anterior to the superior vena cava. It is seen that a small portion of the pulmonary artery is coming into view between the pericardium (which is grasped with forceps) and the superior vena cava. The lung has been retracted posteriorly with malleable retractors.

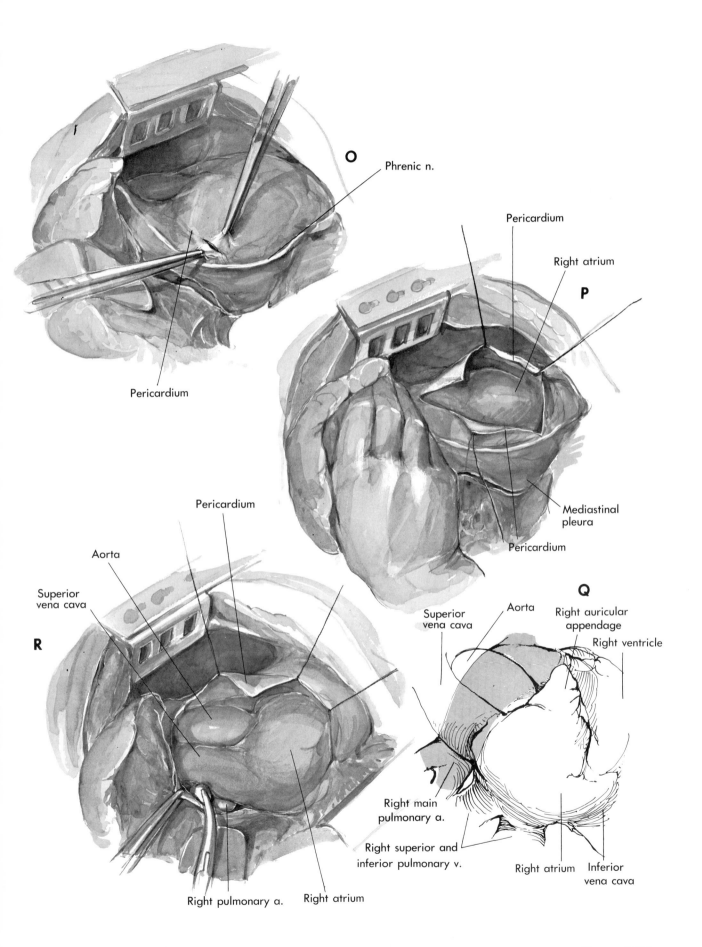

O

Phrenic n.

Pericardium

Pericardium

Right atrium

P

Mediastinal pleura

Pericardium

Pericardium

Aorta

Superior vena cava

R

Right pulmonary a.

Right atrium

Superior vena cava

Aorta

Right auricular appendage

Right ventricle

Q

Right main pulmonary a.

Right superior and inferior pulmonary v.

Right atrium

Inferior vena cava

S   The pulmonary artery has been dissected free lateral to the superior vena cava and a noncrushing Satinsky vascular clamp has been placed for proximal control of this vessel. After clamping of the pulmonary artery, the surgeon should carefully observe the condition of the patient. Should the systemic blood pressure drop significantly, this drop may be an ominous sign which precludes a pneumonectomy. However, if the patient's condition is relatively unchanged, the operation can proceed. The next step is to cut the pulmonary artery, allowing a good cuff of tissue distal to the Satinsky clamp. The cuff should consist of approximately 1 cm. of tissue to allow a safe and secure stump. It may, therefore, be quite difficult to achieve control of backbleeding from the lung after transection of this pulmonary artery. Since the bronchial arterial supply is still intact and the pulmonary venous blood supply is intact there may be significant bleeding. Sometimes it is necessary to dissect out and occlude the pulmonary veins to stop backbleeding, but usually it is possible to control it by pressure or a running suture.

T   The arterial suture is progressing. The suturing is being done with 4-0 atraumatic silk with an anchoring suture at the angle and an over-and-over suture going from left to right. After it has gone well around the angle to the right or caudad region it will return with a suture between each of the previous sutures and slightly superficial to it back to the cephalad angle where it will be tied. This is a relatively low pressure artery, and if the suture is well placed in a nondiseased artery there should be no significant bleeding. Slight bleeding can usually be controlled with gauze pressure while the tension on the suture line equalizes and some clotting occurs to halt the bleeding.

U
V   These depict an alternate method of securing the right pulmonary artery. In this case it was felt that there was inadequate artery to clamp and suture lateral to the superior vena cava. Accordingly, the vena cava is being retracted laterally and the pulmonary artery is freed up proximal to the vena cava. In Figure V the Satinsky clamp has been placed on the right main pulmonary artery between the superior vena cava, which is being retracted laterally with an umbilical tape, and the aorta, which is being retracted medially with a dissecting sponge. After placement of the clamp the vena cava would be retracted medially and the actual division and suture of the pulmonary artery carried out on the right lateral aspect of the superior vena cava.

W   The pulmonary artery has been secured and attention is now being focused on the inferior vein. It was felt that to remove this tumor the phrenic nerve would have to be sacrificed. Accordingly, the opening in the pericardium has been continued around caudad to the lung hilum and posteriorly to leave bare the left atrium and the pulmonary veins. This procedure should be done with caution since the pericardium is quite adherent to the major vessels where they pierce it. Normally, there is a free space between the posterior part of the left atrium and the pericardium, but the reflections onto the vessels call for careful blunt and sharp dissection. Here the incision in the pericardium has been carried cephalad posteriorly up to the main bronchus. This, combined with the anterior opening in the pericardium, should expose the left atrium and the pulmonary veins proximal to the tumor.

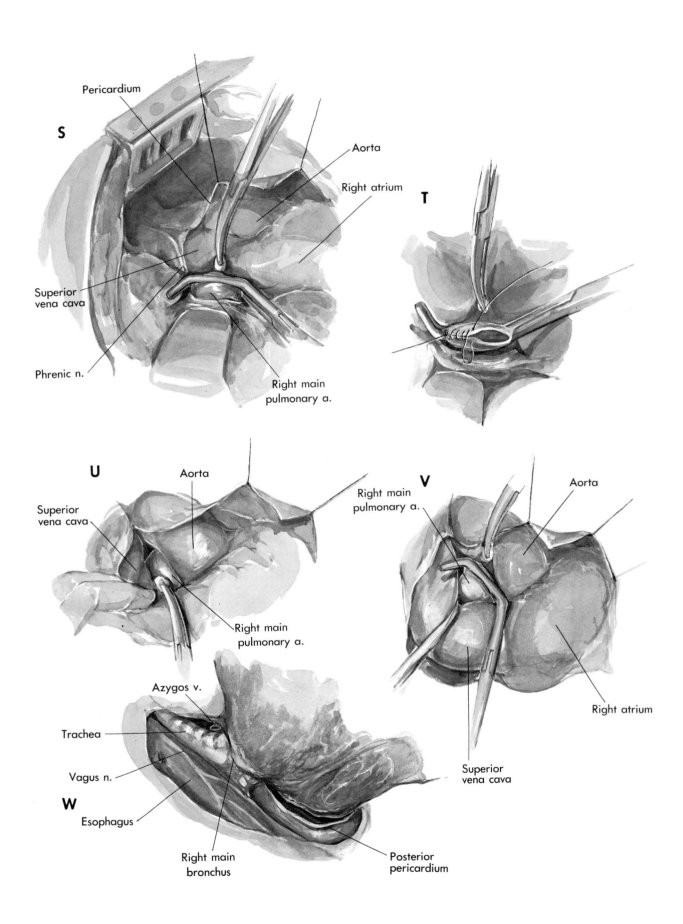

S

Pericardium

Aorta

Right atrium

T

Superior
vena cava

Phrenic n.

Right main
pulmonary a.

U Aorta

Superior
vena cava

Right main
pulmonary a.

Right main
pulmonary a.

V

Aorta

Right atrium

Superior
vena cava

Azygos v.

Trachea

Vagus n.

W

Esophagus

Right main
bronchus

Posterior
pericardium

X   The bronchus is being dissected free. The posterior wall of the left atrium can be seen through the opening in the posterior pericardium. The esophagus lies immediately posteriorly and is visible. The atrium is being dissected with a dissecting sponge between the superior pulmonary vein and the main bronchus. This must be done with considerable caution, particularly if the pneumonectomy is to be curative, and by going more proximal to the hilum it should be possible to get into normal tissue.

Y   This view shows that the lung has again been turned posteriorly after the left atrium and its junction with the superior and inferior pulmonary veins have been dissected free. A Satinsky clamp again has been placed on the left atrium at least 1 cm. proximal to the insertion of the two veins and in this case the left atrium is incised with a scalpel and both veins removed. Here again some backbleeding may ensue. If the bronchial artery input is still patent, this bleeding can be controlled by pressure or by appropriate suture ligature.

Z   This shows the start of the suture of the left atrium. Care should be taken that as much atrial stump as possible is available, preferably 1 cm. The suture material is 4-0 silk and the angle suture has been tied. An over-and-over continuous suture has begun from left to right and will be carried down around the caudad angle and then back over-and-over between and slightly superficial to each original stitch in the first row and tied to the original angle.

A_1 The atrium is secure and the Satinsky clamp is about to be removed. Here, too, the left atrium is a low pressure system and if care has been taken there should be no difficulty with bleeding from this area. Usually pressure will control any bleeding. Of course, should bleeding persist, additional interrupted mattress sutures should be placed to secure hemostasis.

B_1 The bronchus is being divided just distal to the bifurcation of the trachea. It is important in doing a pneumonectomy that there be no long, blind bronchial stump. Accordingly, the bronchus should be transected so that the row of sutures when placed will eliminate any pouch. In the case of the right main bronchus this is usually done 5 or 6 mm. distal to the bifurcation of the trachea and 5 or 6 mm. of bronchus taken in each bite of the suture. It is important that there be no prolonged lung leak. An alternate technique consists of placing noncrushing clamps such as the Allis on the cut bronchial stump. A third technique is to place angle sutures at either end of the bronchus and, by employing a cut-and-sew technique, to gradually divide and suture the bronchus to minimize air leaks. At any time during the operation the surgeon with his thumb and index finger can, if need be, compress the open bronchus so that the anesthetist can ventilate the other lung. If secretions have been a problem at the time the bronchus is opened, the surgeon has direct access and is able to clear the airway in the remaining lung with a suction catheter. This catheter should, of course, be considered dirty and be discarded after being used. Sutures of 2-0 silk are used with a fine or atraumatic needle.

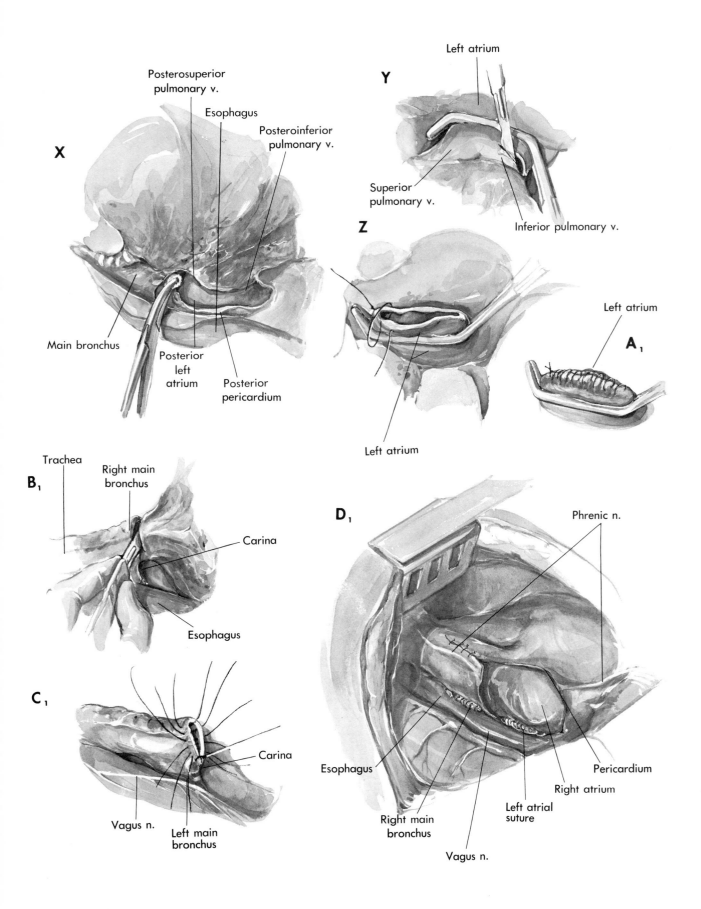

X
Posterosuperior pulmonary v.
Esophagus
Posteroinferior pulmonary v.
Main bronchus
Posterior left atrium
Posterior pericardium

Y
Left atrium
Superior pulmonary v.
Inferior pulmonary v.

Z
Left atrium

A₁
Left atrium

B₁
Trachea
Right main bronchus
Carina
Esophagus

C₁
Carina
Vagus n.
Left main bronchus

D₁
Phrenic n.
Esophagus
Right main bronchus
Vagus n.
Left atrial suture
Right atrium
Pericardium

C₁ This shows the medial angle suture tied and the rest of the sutures placed and ready for tying. This view is for illustrative purposes. Normally, the sutures are tied as placed.

D₁ This figure shows the defect in the pericardium, with the cephalad and caudad cut ends of the phrenic nerve. It will be noted that the defect in the pericardium has been approximated over the superior vena cava and that the defect is not large enough to permit herniation of the heart through it. This then needs no further support. The sutured left atrium is visible in the caudad part of the opening in the pericardium. The sutured pulmonary artery is not visible since it has retracted under the superior vena cava and the superior vena cava is being covered with the reapproximated pericardium. The bronchial stump can be seen cephalad to the left atrium, with the esophagus posterior to it coursing along the spine. At this point the bronchial stump should be tested under water for air leaks. If there are any air leaks, additional sutures are indicated. The thorax should be cleansed of blood· and serum. If one decides to use an intercostal catheter under water seal, which is not done routinely in a pneumonectomy, the catheter should be kept clamped and opened only when it is wished to measure or adjust the intrapleural pressures. The chest is closed in a usual fashion with interrupted silk sutures to the pleura and intercostal muscles if a rib removal technique has been used. Otherwise, pericostal catgut sutures are used for intercostal incisions, with a running catgut suture to close the intercostal muscles. The two muscle layers of the chest can be closed with interrupted sutures of silk or continuous sutures of catgut followed by the usual skin sutures.

If the pericardial defect is large enough to permit cardiac herniation, the defect should be repaired with autologous fascia or Marlex mesh. If much pericardium is removed, one must not close the pericardium tightly, since the heart might be compressed and tamponade produced.

If the tumor can be removed and a radical pneumonectomy is to be performed, the pleural incisions should extend from the apex of the thorax to the diaphragm. The right recurrent laryngeal nerve is identified. The lymph node bearing fatty tissue is divided just distal to this nerve and the area between the superior vena cava and trachea and then the area between the trachea and esophagus is dissected clear toward the hilum. The lymph tissue packet anterior to the esophagus is swept from the diaphragm up toward the lung hilum. The perihilar lymph tissue, including the subcarinal lymph nodes are all swept toward the specimen. Silver clips for hemostasis speed this dissection. Mapping the lymph node location for the pathologist aids in estimating the prognosis. It should be remembered that approximately one third of the patients with lung cancer at Memorial Hospital who survived for five years had positive lymph nodes in the specimen. Obviously, tumor in the lymph nodes does not necessarily indicate hopelessness. It is more difficult to dissect the mediastinal lymph nodes while doing a left thoracotomy, but one should attempt to dissect the fatty lymph node bearing tissue to the hilum of the specimen.

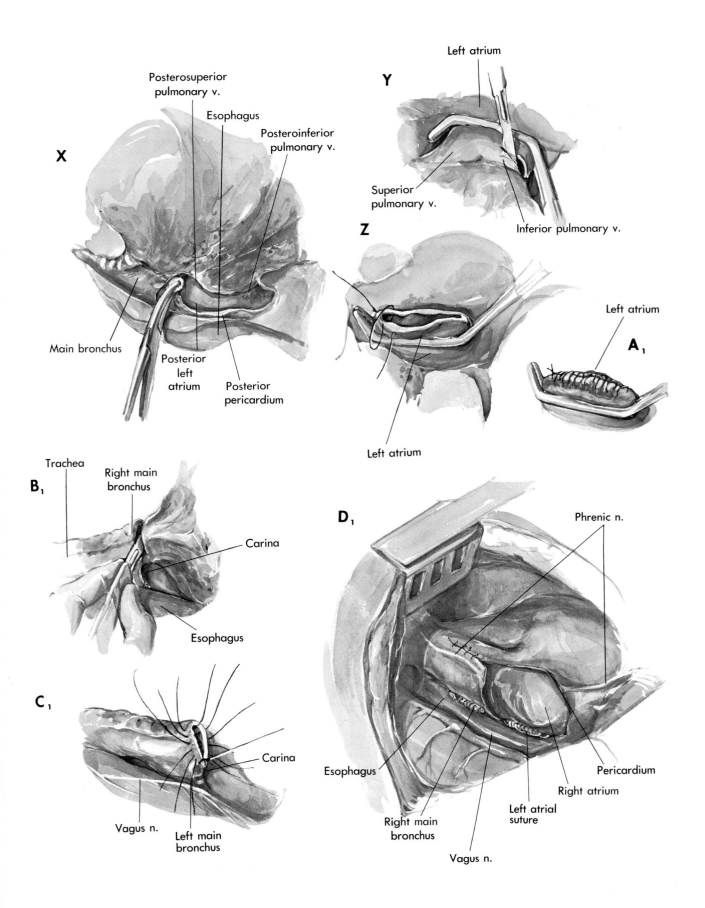

X

Posterosuperior pulmonary v.

Esophagus

Posteroinferior pulmonary v.

Main bronchus

Posterior left atrium

Posterior pericardium

Y

Left atrium

Superior pulmonary v.

Inferior pulmonary v.

Z

Left atrium

A₁

Left atrium

B₁

Trachea

Right main bronchus

Carina

Esophagus

C₁

Vagus n.

Carina

Left main bronchus

D₁

Phrenic n.

Esophagus

Right main bronchus

Vagus n.

Left atrial suture

Right atrium

Pericardium

PULMONARY LOBECTOMY—SLEEVE RESECTION

Pulmonary lobectomy is more commonly performed than pneumonectomy and should be a safer operation. A higher percentage of patients who undergo lobectomy have nonmalignant disease than is at present the case with pneumonectomy. In competent surgical hands the mortality rate will vary with the kinds of patients accepted for surgery, but in good risk patients the mortality rate should be under 1 per cent. The risk can be considerably higher in either poor risk patients or with less skillful, careful surgeons.

The potential indications for lobectomy are manifold but consist primarily of benign lesions or cancers. Tuberculosis, bronchiectasis, chronic lung abscess, granulomata (in which the lobectomy was for biopsy to rule out a neoplasm), deeply seated benign tumors and cystic disease make up the bulk of the benign lesions for which lobectomy may be indicated. The lobectomy is the treatment of choice for early bronchogenic carcinoma. It may also be indicated for a solitary metastatic lesion when the primary neoplasm has been controlled. Surprisingly, pulmonary resections in this latter situation give as good results as pulmonary resections for symptomatic primary bronchogenic carcinomas, namely, nearly 10 per cent "cures."

The lobectomy is also the treatment of choice for the suspect tumor lesion when the lymph nodes are negative and the lesion is too deeply situated to "wedge resect" for biopsy. The alternative here is either an incisional or a needle aspiration biopsy. Both carry risk of potential contamination and both may miss the tumor. Occasionally, one can do a segmentectomy for biopsy to conserve lung tissue. One should avoid segmentectomy in undiagnosed, uncontrolled granulomatous conditions since the postoperative morbidity may be considerably increased.

The chief benefit of lobectomy versus pneumonectomy is that it conserves the pulmonary reserve and leaves lung parenchyma to fill the hemithorax instead of leaving an empty hemithorax. The presence of lung tissue minimizes the risk of empyema and bronchopleural fistula. The lobectomy is thus the treatment of choice in the poor risk patient.

Because of the low operative mortality with lobectomy compared to pneumonectomy, there have been increased efforts by thoracic surgeons to accomplish with "radical" lobectomy what ordinarily in the past would have required pneumonectomy. In the case depicted here we show a radical right upper lobectomy with resection of a "sleeve" of the right main bronchus and a dissection of the visible mediastinal lymph nodes. This leaves the bronchus intermedius with the right middle lobe and right lower lobe intact.

A recent review of resected lung cancer cases at Memorial Hospital from 1947 through 1961 showed 453 resections. There were 302 pneumonectomies, 118 lobectomies and 33 wedge resections. The operative mortality for simple pneumonectomy was 19.8 per cent and for radical pneumonectomy, 15.6 per cent. With elimination of the operative deaths, the five-year survival rate for simple pneumonectomy was 30 per cent and for radical pneumonectomy, 35 per cent. The operative mortality for simple lobectomy was 11 per cent and for radical lobectomy, 13 per cent. With elimination of the operative deaths, the five-year suvival following 72 simple lobectomies was 17 per cent and following 46 radical lobectomies, 53 per cent. These data suggest that a radical lobectomy is the treatment of choice for lung cancer when feasible. The technique of mediastinal lymphadenectomy is the same as in radical pneumonectomy.

The depicted operation has the theoretical objection that retrograde lymph flow to the right middle lobe or right lower lobe may have left residual tumor. However, for lymph to flow retrogradely, it usually means that the regional lymphatics are already obstructed with metastatic tumor. If this be the case, the increased mortality from pneumonectomy will probably exceed the increased "cures" with pneumonectomy. However, this point is not yet definitely known. The situation on the left side is somewhat different in the case of a tumor in the left upper lobe. Here a left pneumonectomy is probably a better operation for carcinoma in a good risk patient than a left upper lobectomy. The left lung, representing only 45 per cent of the total respiratory function, also favors this procedure.

In poor risk patients "sleeve resections" of bronchi can be done in a variety of locations to preserve lung function. The role of preoperative irradiation with radical lobectomies is not yet definitely known; it seems to permit more lobectomies and to avoid pneumonectomies but probably has a higher complication rate.

One of the complications of bronchial anastomosis is subsequent stenosis. Follow-up by laminagraphy and bronchoscopy is important since dilatations can prevent complete stenosis. Large bronchi usually do not stenose if the anastomosis is technically well done. There is more difficulty with stenosis in small bronchi. Our experimental work indicates an advantage in not accurately reapproximating cartilaginous and membranous segments of bronchi. Misalignment turns the horseshoe-like cartilaginous rings, which then tend to hold the anastomosis open, since they are more resistant to contracture than the membranous portion of the bronchi.

References

Beattie, E. J., Jr.: The surgical treatment of lung tumors. Pneumonectomy or lobectomy? Surgery 42:1124, 1957.

Churchill, E., Soutter, L., and Scannell, J. G.: Surgical management of carcinoma of lung. J. Thoracic Surg. 20:349, 1950.

Jensik, R.: Preoperative irradiation and bronchopulmonary sleeve resection for lung cancer. S. Clin. North America 46:158, 1966.

Overholt, R.: Value of exploration in silent lung disease. Dis. Chest 20:111, 1951.

Paulson, D. L., Shaw, R. R., Kee, J. L., Mallams, J. T., and Collier, R. E.: Combined preoperative irradiation and resection for bronchogenic carcinoma. J. Thor. & Cardiovasc. Surg. 44:281, 1962.

Ramsey, H. E., Humphrey, C., Cahan, W. G., and Beattie, E. J., Jr.: The importance of radical lobectomy in lung cancer. (Submitted for publication.)

A   The incision has been made over the course of the 6th rib. In this illustration the periosteum of the right 6th rib is being incised to enter the right hemithorax.

B   This shows the location of the longitudinal and transverse fissures. The longitudinal fissure follows the course of the 6th rib, and the transverse fissure intersects the longitudinal fissure in the midaxillary line and travels horizontally in the 4th interspace.

C   The thorax is opened and the rib spreader is placed; the lung is retracted anteriorly with a malleable retractor. The mediastinal pleura has been opened anterior and parallel to the spine. Visible in the open mediastinal pleura is the esophagus with the bronchus anterior to it and the azygos vein crossing the esophagus in the cephalad portion of the mediastinal exposure. The superior vena cava can be seen anteriorly joining the azygos vein. The mediastinal pleura should be opened from the thoracic apex to the diaphragm to permit the removal of all the visible lymph nodes, as in the radical pneumonectomy.

D   The azygos vein has been dissected out and the technique of acquiring hemostasis without clamping vessels is demonstrated. The Mixter gallbladder clamp is a very convenient instrument for passing under vessels or around vessels and grasping the intended ligature. After the vessel has been ligated both proximally and distally it is usually wise to reinforce each with a suture ligature placed distally and then to divide the vessel, having achieved hemostasis. The azygos is a direct major branch of the superior vena cava and should be treated with due caution.

E   The lung has been moved posteriorly so that the anterior aspect of the lung hilum can be dissected. In this instance the ligated stump of the azygos vein can be seen in the cephalad portion of the incision. The mediastinal pleura in front of the hilum but posterior to the phrenic nerve has been incised. This depicts the development of the proper cleavage plane over the pulmonary artery, which is established by picking up the loose adventitial tissue and incising it. Again the surgeon finds that the Mixter gallbladder clamp is convenient for passing along the vessel or across the vessel under the areolar tissue in the proper cleavage plane. The spread tissue is then incised with scissors.

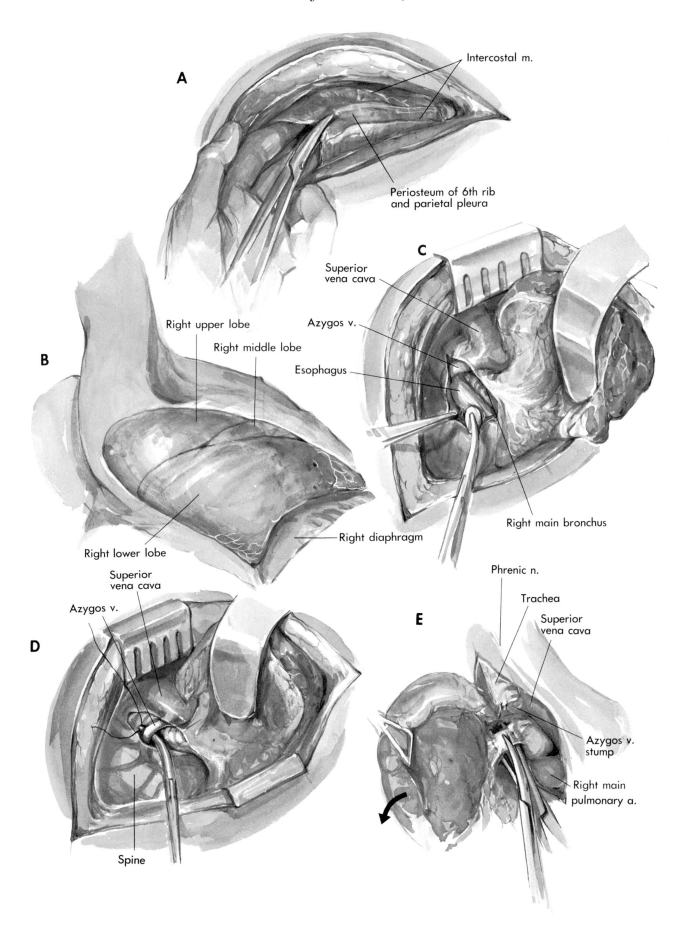

A

Intercostal m.

Periosteum of 6th rib and parietal pleura

B

Right upper lobe

Right middle lobe

Right lower lobe

Right diaphragm

C

Superior vena cava

Azygos v.

Esophagus

Right main bronchus

D

Superior vena cava

Azygos v.

Spine

E

Phrenic n.

Trachea

Superior vena cava

Azygos v. stump

Right main pulmonary a.

F   The establishment of the proper cleavage planes over the vessels is continued since it was found (Figure E) that there was still a layer of tissue on the pulmonary artery. The superior pulmonary vein is immediately caudad to this pulmonary artery and the trachea and right main bronchus are cephalad and posterior. We are starting to look for the arterial branches to the right upper lobe.

G   This shows further development of the pulmonary artery. The branches to the right upper lobe are being sought further. In such a situation it is better to do the early dissection distal, rather than proximal. If there is injury or damage to a vessel, it is better to have peripheral damage rather than proximal damage which might be difficult to control. Should damage occur to a major pulmonary vessel, hemostasis should be obtained digitally while careful proximal dissection is carried out; injudicious, blind and hasty placing of hemostats must be avoided.

H   Now the main pulmonary artery has been dissected free since it will have to be temporarily occluded while the sleeve resection of the bronchus is carried out. A Mixter gallbladder clamp is placed deep to the main pulmonary artery and an umbilical tape is being passed around it.

I   The umbilical tape is in place on the proximal portion of the right main pulmonary artery and dissection is now being carried distally, identifying the branches of the right upper lobe. In this illustration the apical and anterior branches are coming into view. There is considerable anomaly in the blood supply to lung segments, and each case must be considered individually and dissected cautiously.

J   A Mixter clamp has been placed deep to the apical anterior segmental arterial branch and 2-0 silk is being passed around the vessel.

K   It is seen that the apical anterior segmental artery has been doubly ligated close to the main pulmonary artery and proximal to the bifurcation of this branch artery. A distal ligature on the apical segment is in place while the clamp in this instance is passing a ligature around the anterior segmental arterial branch. Here a suture ligature is not necessary since a ligature should not slip over a bifurcating vessel. However, were it necessary to ligate and divide a pulmonary artery with no branches to utilize, it is safer to reinforce the ligature with a suture ligature.

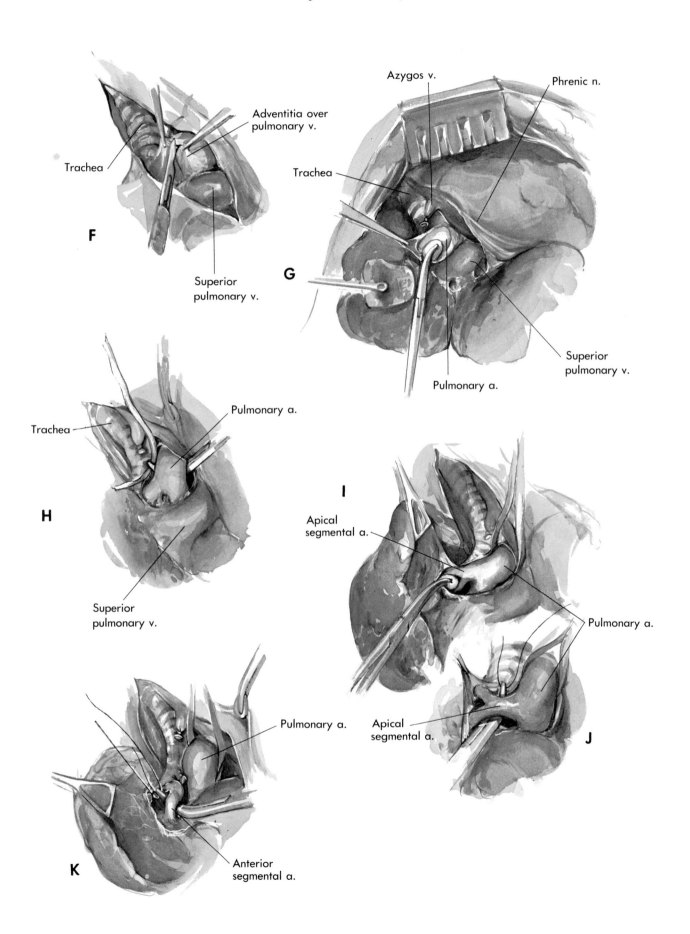

F

Trachea

Adventitia over
pulmonary v.

Superior
pulmonary v.

G

Azygos v.

Phrenic n.

Trachea

Superior
pulmonary v.

Pulmonary a.

H

Trachea

Pulmonary a.

Superior
pulmonary v.

I

Apical
segmental a.

Pulmonary a.

Apical
segmental a.

J

K

Pulmonary a.

Anterior
segmental a.

L   The artery has been divided and the stump can be seen. The venous drainage of the upper lobe into the superior pulmonary vein can be seen. This superior pulmonary vein also drains part of the middle lobe, and at this point the veins are not being divided.

M   The lung has now been moved anteriorly and we are approaching the hilum posteriorly. The dissecting sponge is clearing the bifurcation of the trachea. The trachea can be seen extending cephalad to the left. The right main bronchus is seen extending to the right. The right upper lobe bronchus with the tumor involvement nearly flush with the main bronchus can be seen.

N   The left main bronchus has been dissected free with a combination of sharp and blunt and finger dissection. The Mixter gallbladder clamp is around the left main bronchus and is drawing an umbilical tape around it.

O   This shows the umbilical tape in place around the left main bronchus. The dissecting sponge is developing the fissure between the right upper lobe and the right middle lobe, thus clarifying the bronchus intermedius. The plan will be to anastomose the bronchus intermedius to the trachea. At this point clear identification of the bronchus intermedius is indicated. The structure that is visible just under the dissecting sponge is the posterior aspect of venous drainage of the upper part of the middle lobe. All visible lymph nodes on the bronchus intermedius should be dissected to the right upper lobe and removed with the specimen.

P   In this illustration the specimen and lung have been turned posteriorly again and we are dissecting the anterior part of the lung hilum. The stump of the arterial apical anterior branch can be seen. The venous branches of the superior vein are being dissected out so that the venous drainage from the right middle lobe into the superior pulmonary vein can be seen.

Q   A ligature has been placed flush with the upper lobe venous drainage into the superior pulmonary vein and a second ligature is being passed.

R   The venous drainage from the right upper lobe has been ligated doubly and the three branches of the vein cut peripherally to the ligatures. The arterial branch to the posterior segment comes into view. This has been ligated close to the main pulmonary artery and the second ligature has been placed around this posterior arterial segment in preparation for ligation.

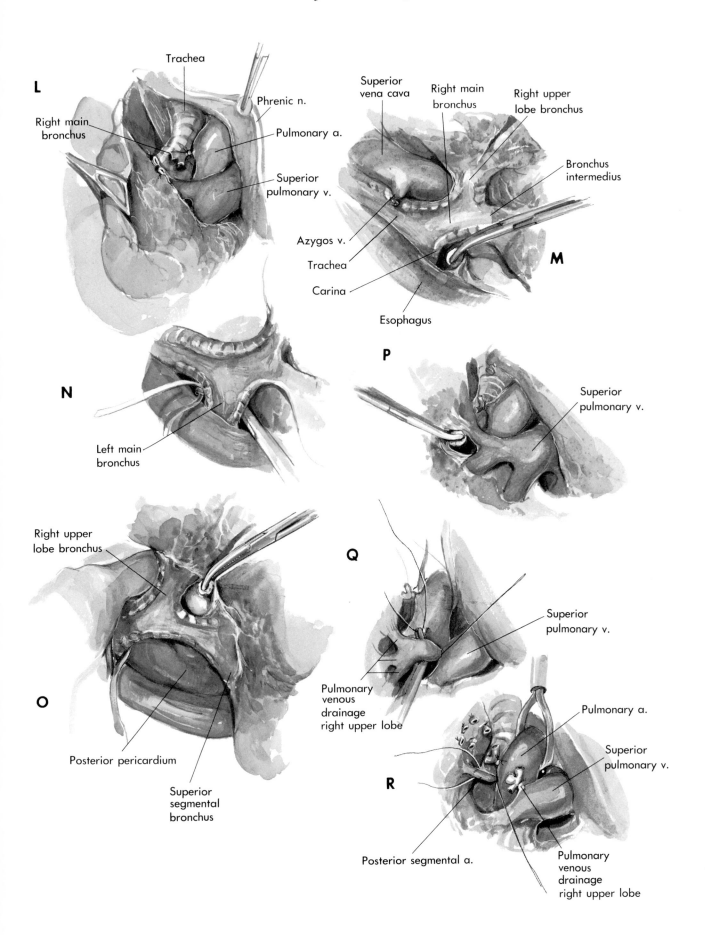

L

Trachea

Phrenic n.

Right main bronchus

Pulmonary a.

Superior pulmonary v.

Superior vena cava

Right main bronchus

Right upper lobe bronchus

Bronchus intermedius

Azygos v.

Trachea

Carina

Esophagus

M

N

Left main bronchus

P

Superior pulmonary v.

Q

Pulmonary venous drainage right upper lobe

Superior pulmonary v.

Right upper lobe bronchus

O

Posterior pericardium

Superior segmental bronchus

R

Pulmonary a.

Superior pulmonary v.

Posterior segmental a.

Pulmonary venous drainage right upper lobe

S The ligated stumps of both artery and vein to and from the right upper lobe can be seen. Additionally, the umbilical tape which has had a segment of rubber catheter passed over it has been advanced down to occlude the main pulmonary artery on the right.

T The intratracheal tube which is somewhat longer than normal has had its balloon deflated and, with digital guidance, has been advanced into the left main bronchus. The umbilical tape around the left main bronchus is about to be tied down to maintain airtight closure so that the left lung can be ventilated. The anesthetist must hold or firmly anchor the endotracheal tube in this new, advanced position.

U The umbilical tape has been tied around the left main bronchus to secure the position of the endotracheal tube. The bronchus intermedius is now being divided with a scalpel.

V The right main bronchus has been cut across approximately 5 mm. distal to the bifurcation of the trachea, and now the specimen is about to be removed. The thumb forceps is holding the sleeve of the resected main bronchus. The posterior aspect of the main pulmonary artery with its ligated branches can be seen. The scissors are cutting loose the residual adherence between the upper and middle lobes.

W The beginning of the bronchial anastomosis is underway. The first suture is placed utilizing 2-0 silk so that the cartilaginous ring on the medial aspect is united.

X This shows that the anterior row of sutures in the cartilaginous portions has been completed. The sutures have been ligated and tied as we have placed them. The lateral angle suture is placed and is ready to be tied.

Y The cartilaginous anastomosis is completed except for the membranous portion. Here a suction catheter is being placed to clean out any blood or serum.

Z The completed anastomosis is shown. In this case the umbilical tape ligature around the left main bronchus has been removed. The endotracheal tube has been withdrawn back into the trachea. The tracheal balloon has been reinflated, and ventilation of the right middle and lower lobe has begun. (At this point it is wise to check the integrity of the bronchial anastomosis under saline for air leaks so that they can be repaired.) Finally, the temporary occluding ligature around the main pulmonary artery has been removed. We are now ready for closure of the chest. It is important, since an upper lobectomy has been done, to divide the inferior pulmonary ligament to permit the right middle and lower lobes to rise cephalad in the chest. Ordinarily, two intercostal catheters are placed, preferably in the anterior axillary line. The anterior tube should run posteriorly to drain the costophrenic angle. The more posterior tube should run to the apex to vent the air from the apex. These are sutured to the skin and kept under water seal until removed. The chest is closed in the usual fashion.

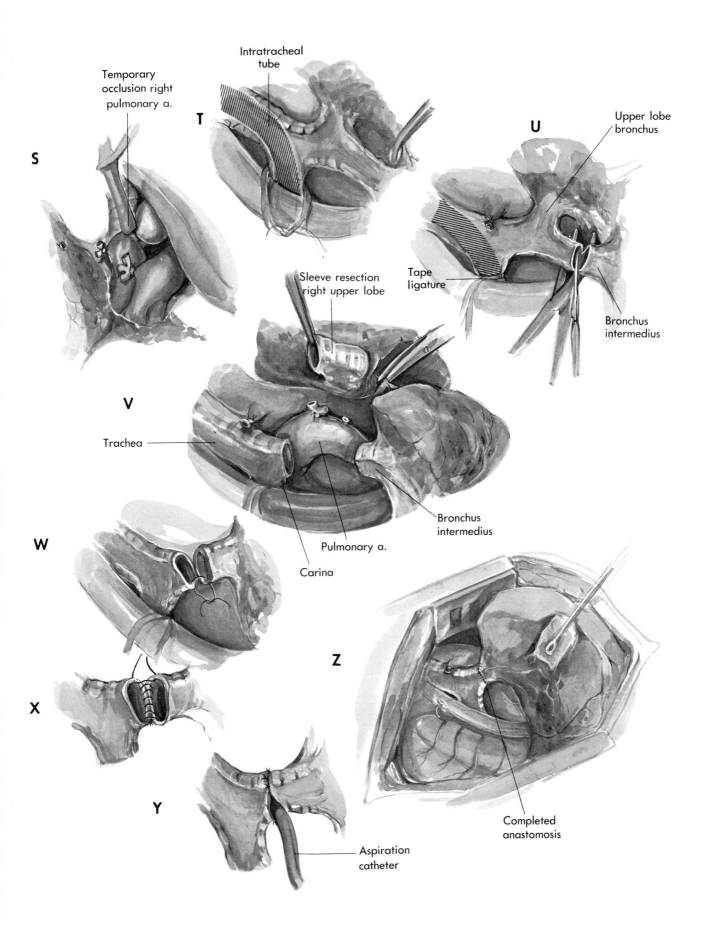

Temporary
occlusion right
pulmonary a.

Intratracheal
tube

S

T

U

Upper lobe
bronchus

Sleeve resection
right upper lobe

Tape
ligature

Bronchus
intermedius

V

Trachea

Bronchus
intermedius

Pulmonary a.

Carina

W

Z

X

Y

Completed
anastomosis

Aspiration
catheter

PULMONARY SEGMENTECTOMY

The lung, like the liver, is a unique organ with a dual blood supply. The chief vascular supply is formed by the pulmonary arteries and veins which compose a low pressure system with venous blood. These low pressure vessels tend to be fragile, and hemostasis should be obtained before they are divided. The usual surgical technique of clamp, cut and ligate is unwise; vessels should either be appropriately ligated in continuity and cut, or they should be clamped with a noncrushing vascular clamp, cut and sutured with fine, atraumatic continuous sutures. A torn major pulmonary vessel will produce a major and perhaps fatal hemorrhage. In cases of accidental hemorrhage, grasping the vessel with the fingers, replacing the blood loss and gaining adequate proximal exposure should be lifesaving.

The parenchyma of the lung is nourished by the bronchial arteries, which are systemic arteries with high pressure containing oxygenated blood. These vessels accompany the major bronchi. The bronchial vessels may be large and surgically troublesome if the pulmonary artery is obstructed. The bronchial veins are small and not very significant except in case of pulmonary vein obstruction. The bronchial veins drain into the azygos venous system. The pulmonary vascular and bronchial vascular systems communicate at arteriolar level. This collateral communication will preserve the lung viability if either system is ligated or obstructed.

Segmentectomy has been developed by modern thoracic surgeons from increased knowledge of the anatomy of the lung. All surgeons operating on the lung should be familiar with the Jackson-Huber classification of the bronchopulmonary segments, which depicts ten segments in the right lung and eight segments in the left lung. This is the normal situation, but many patients differ in small or large part from the norm. It is essential that careful, complete, preoperative bronchograms be obtained when segmentectomy is contemplated. The bronchogram is an essential map for the surgeon during the operation.

Just as each segmental bronchus may vary, so do the arteries accompanying the bronchi. Generally, the artery lies anterior and cephalad to its respective bronchus, but there may be more than one artery to a segment or the artery may come as a branch from a neighboring segment. A surgeon should beware of dividing an artery that is larger than expected. The surgeon should dissect out clearly the adjacent proximal and distal arterial branches so that no accident occurs which could turn a segmentectomy into a lobectomy or physiologic pneumonectomy. Segments drain peripherally to the segmental veins. The veins run in the intersegmental planes and coalesce anteriorly to form the left or right superior or inferior pulmonary veins. The inferior pulmonary veins are normally the most caudad structure in the lung hilum, immediately caudad to the main bronchus. The superior veins lie anterior to the bronchus, usually between the main pulmonary artery and the inferior pulmonary vein. There may be a common pulmonary vein rather than a superior and inferior vein. In the latter situation ligation of a main pulmonary vein could interrupt almost all the venous drainage of a lung with disastrous effects to that lung. The pattern of the segmental veins has great variety. The usual surgical technique is to identify the proper bronchus, divide it and all the arteries directly supplying this segment, to avoid division of a major arterial branch to an adjacent segment, and then to perform the "traction dissection." Only those veins draining the segment should be removed. This "traction dissection" may be difficult or impossible if the disease crosses the segmental plane. Proper surgical judgment and the proper planning of the surgical attack is mandatory.

The case depicted here is a left apicoposterior segmentectomy for tuberculosis. Any segment can be removed in this fashion. The usual diseases treated by segmentectomy are tuberculosis and bronchiectasis; some of the indications are left lower lobectomy plus lingulectomy for bronchiectasis, basal segmentectomy for bronchiectasis, apical and posterior segmentectomy for tuberculosis, upper lobectomy plus superior segmentectomy for tuberculosis, and other combinations. At times a segmentectomy biopsy may be indicated for an indeterminate lesion when this procedure can remove the lesion without breaking into the disease and causing gross contamination.

When the disease process is bilateral, lung conservation is particularly important. Diminished pulmonary function may likewise dictate conservation of lung tissue. There is more postoperative morbidity from a segmentectomy than from a lobectomy because of the frequency of persistent air leak. Adequate pleural drainage (two or more chest tubes), prompt re-expansion of the lung, avoidance of atelectasis and good preoperative preparation are all especially important. If it is apparent that the remaining lung tissue will not fill the hemithorax, a preliminary thoracoplasty or subsequent thoracoplasty may be indicated. Air leaks are particularly troublesome in emphysematous patients. In persistent air leaks bacteriologic culture of the chest drainage, the use of appropriate antibiotics based upon respiratory bacterial cultures and good preparation of the patient for surgery may spell the difference between life and death.

The use of an intercostal drainage catheter is optional in a pneumonectomy. In other thoracic operations we feel that two chest catheters are mandatory. One catheter should go to the apex via the anterior thorax to insure the evacuation of air. The other catheter should go from the anterior thorax to the base posteriorly to insure the drainage of blood or serum. The catheters should be connected by appropriate large bore tubing to water-seal drainage bottles. The catheters and tubing should be positioned so that they are not readily lain on, they should not be kinked, and they should descend with some slackness to the water-seal bottles without rising and falling loops. The use of suction is optional, but in case of a rapid air leak, suction is usually necessary.

The main concern postoperatively is the avoidance of atelectasis, which is best prevented by the relief of pain with appropriate narcotics and enforcing an effective cough. Sterile nasotracheal aspiration is indicated when the patient will not cough. Bronchoscopy should usually be performed if atelectasis occurs. Adequate hydration, adequate humidification of the inspired air and the use of expectorants aid in keeping the respiratory mucus thin and easy to expectorate. For patients with impaired respiratory reserve, mechanically assisted respiration via a tracheostomy tube may be lifesaving. In the care of a tracheostomy, meticulous asepsis along with bacteriologic monitoring of the airway bacteria should be employed. The measurement of the tidal volume and the gas tensions of arterial blood are necessary.

References

Blades, B.: Conservation of lung tissue by partial lobectomy. Ann. Surg. *118*:353, 1943.
Boyden, E. A.: The intrahilar and related segmental anatomy of the lung. Surgery *18*:828, 1946.
Jackson, C. L., and Huber, J. F.: Correlated applied anatomy of the bronchial tree and lungs with a system of nomenclature. Dis. Chest, *9*:319, 1943.
Kent, E., and Blades, B.: Anatomic approach to pulmonary resection. Ann. Surg. *116*:782, 1942.
Overholt, R. H., Woods, F. M., and Ramsay, B. N.: Segmental pulmonary resection. J. Thoracic Surg. *19*:207, 1950.

Pulmonary Segmentectomy

A   This depicts a patient lying on his right side for a left thoracotomy. The appropriate periscapular incision is indicated by the dotted line since it is planned to do a segmentectomy of the upper lobe. In this case the 5th rib will be removed to gain higher access to the thorax.

B   Here the anatomy is depicted. The aortic arch can be seen sweeping around in the lower right-hand side of the picture, with the subclavian artery extending cephalad to the right. The vagus nerve can be seen crossing the aortic arch and the recurrent nerve branch going anteriorly. The vagus nerve continues down along the anterior aspect of the descending aorta and joins the esophagus. The pulmonary artery on the left side runs in the longitudinal fissure. Accordingly, one separates the upper and lower lobes and by incising the pleura in this region can dissect out the pulmonary artery. In this picture this is being done. The main pulmonary artery is seen, as are the arterial branches to the left upper lobe. The left main bronchus, which is immediately caudad to the pulmonary artery, can be seen; dotted lines indicate the inferior and superior segmental bronchi, which in this case go on to give off from the superior division the anterior segment and the apicoposterior segment. An apicoposterior segmentectomy is planned in this case. The usual and important landmark to identify accurately is the bronchi, because one should divide only those arterial branches definitely accompanying the bronchi. Usually, arteries lie anterior and cephalad to the respective bronchi, but since there is considerable variation, careful dissection and exposure are indicated before ligation of the vessels. In this case it can be seen that there are four arterial branches. Commonly, the apical branch comes off first, followed by the posterior branch, the anterior branch and the lingular branch or branches. However, this arrangement can be different and it is not unusual to find that the posterior branch comes off the apical branch or that it comes off at the same level.

C   The dissection has begun. The mediastinal pleura anterior to the lung hilum is being opened. The lung is being retracted caudad. (Later, the upper lobe is retracted anteriorly and the lower lobe is retracted posteriorly so that the incision can be continued in the fissure.) The vagus nerve is seen posteriorly, the phrenic nerve anteriorly and the main pulmonary artery in the depths of the dissection.

D   In this drawing the technique of developing the plane in the fissure with the Mixter gallbladder clamp prior to incision is demonstrated.

E   The phrenic nerve is seen coursing from right above to left below. The main pulmonary artery here is seen to the right. The superior pulmonary vein is to the left. In this case the entire lung is being reflected posteriorly.

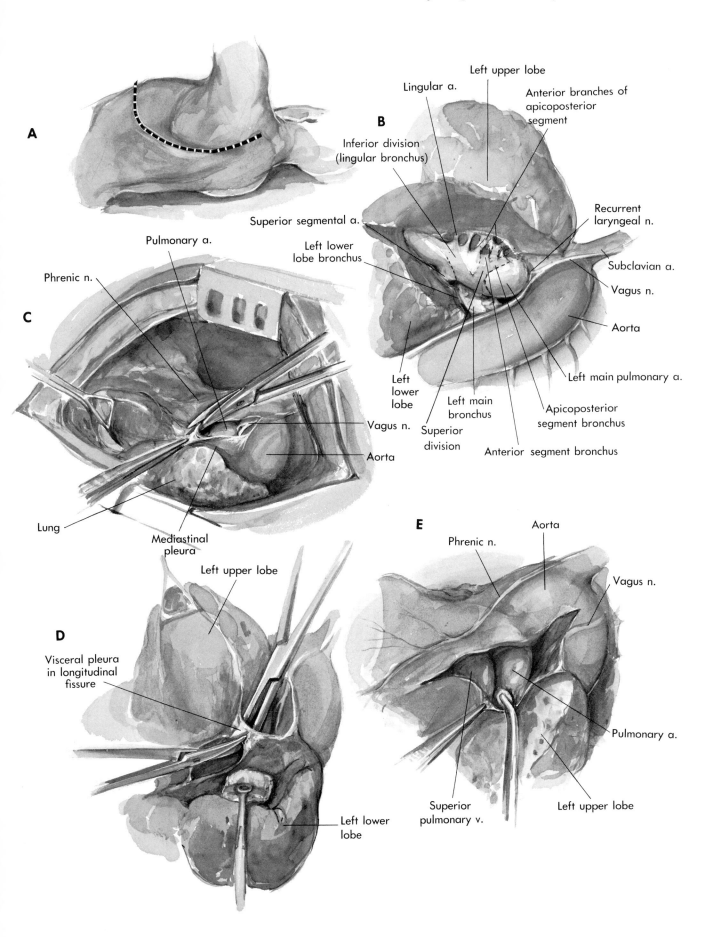

A

Pulmonary a.

Phrenic n.

C

Lung

Mediastinal pleura

Left upper lobe

D

Visceral pleura in longitudinal fissure

Left lower lobe

Lingular a.

Left upper lobe

Inferior division (lingular bronchus)

Anterior branches of apicoposterior segment

B

Superior segmental a.

Left lower lobe bronchus

Recurrent laryngeal n.

Subclavian a.

Vagus n.

Aorta

Left main pulmonary a.

Left lower lobe

Left main bronchus

Superior division

Apicoposterior segment bronchus

Anterior segment bronchus

Vagus n.

Aorta

E

Phrenic n.

Aorta

Vagus n.

Pulmonary a.

Superior pulmonary v.

Left upper lobe

F   The upper lobe is being retracted upward to the left while the lower lobe is being retracted downward to the right and the main pulmonary artery is exposed. The branches are being dissected free.

G   The division of the branches has been begun. Careful inspection has demonstrated that the farthest vessel to the observer's left is the lingular artery, whereas the highest and first vessel to the viewer's right is the anterior artery. The vessel which has been ligated and is in the course of having a distal ligature placed is the posterior branch.

H   There can be seen the distal stumps of three vessels which have been ligated. The intact vessel on the left is the lingular artery; the intact vessel on the right is the anterior artery. As has already been pointed out, there is considerable variation in the origin of these vessels and in every case their origin and distribution should be determined before division.

I   The lung has again been retracted caudad so that the superior pulmonary vein is in view. The incision has been carried down through the pleura over it and with a combination of sharp and blunt dissection the most cephalad branch, which clearly came from the apicoposterior region, is being ligated. As an alternative method one could divide the arterial supply and bronchial supply and merely ligate those veins left holding the segment in place after the usual traction segmentectomy. However, since there is obviously one major branch involved here, it is considered better to ligate this individually before proceeding.

J   The stump of the doubly ligated (or ligated plus suture ligature) apicoposterior venous branch is shown. The two venous branches coming from the anterior segment and lingula have been left intact.

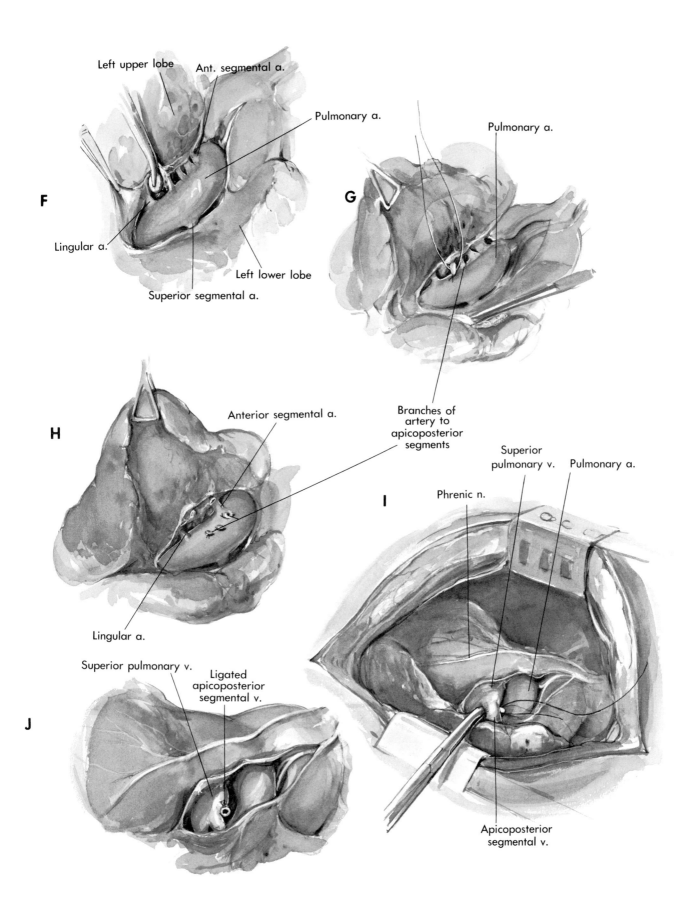

F

Left upper lobe   Ant. segmental a.

Pulmonary a.

Lingular a.

Left lower lobe

Superior segmental a.

G

Pulmonary a.

Branches of
artery to
apicoposterior
segments

H

Anterior segmental a.

Lingular a.

I

Phrenic n.

Superior
pulmonary v.   Pulmonary a.

Apicoposterior
segmental v.

J

Superior pulmonary v.

Ligated
apicoposterior
segmental v.

K   The bronchus to the upper lobe is being identified and the apicoposterior branch of the superior division found.

L   The branches of the bronchus have been found. They have been clamped with the Satinsky clamp. At this point the anatomy can be checked by having the anesthetist inflate the lung to be certain that the remaining segments inflate while the bronchus to be divided is clamped. This has proved to be the case, and now the scalpel will cut the apicoposterior segmental bronchus just proximal to its bifurcation.

M   The cut apicoposterior segmental bronchus can be seen. To the left can be seen the lingular inferior division bronchus. To the right and above is the anterior bronchus going to the forepart of the left upper lobe.

N   The stump of the sutured apicoposterior bronchus can be seen directly anterior to the three arterial stumps on the main pulmonary artery. It is sutured with interrupted 3-0 silk sutures not tied too tightly. The clamps are on the distal apicoposterior bronchus in the upper clamp. The lower clamp is on the distal venous segment. The traction segmentectomy has just begun. It is wise to keep the lung inflated as the traction segmentectomy begins so that one can judge the areas that are to remain behind. Careful palpation will tell which areas are to be removed, and caution must be taken that the diseased area is not broken into during the segmentectomy. With firm pull primarily on the bronchus the segment is being withdrawn. One can be certain of being in the correct cleavage planes if the intersegmental veins come into view.

O   The clamp in the lower portion of the illustration is on one branch of the intersegmental vein and it will have to be ligated.

P   The apicoposterior segment has been removed. The Duval noncrushing clamps are lifting the anterior segment for demonstration purposes. To the left in the drawing is the undisturbed lingula. Seen as branches of the pulmonary artery are the lingular artery and the anterior segmental artery, with the sutured stump of the apicoposterior segmental bronchus just visible. The chest is closed in routine fashion; care is taken to stop as many of the air leaks as possible by ligature. The morbidity from air leak is somewhat higher in segmentectomy than in lobectomy, and adequate chest drainage catheters must be used in addition to the usual chest closure.

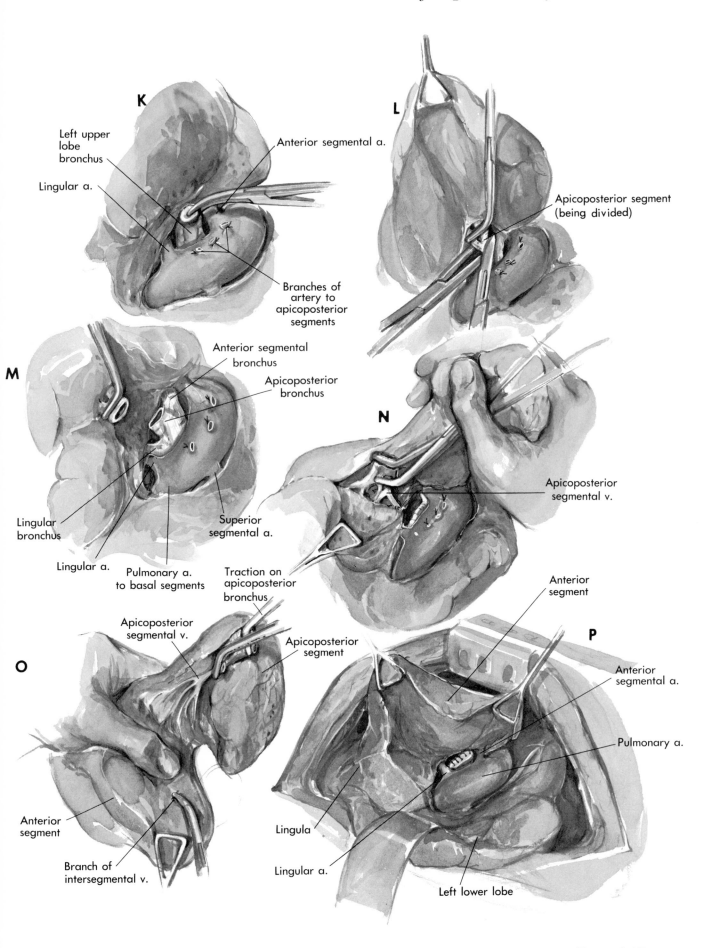

K

Left upper
lobe
bronchus

Anterior segmental a.

Lingular a.

Branches of
artery to
apicoposterior
segments

L

Apicoposterior segment
(being divided)

M

Anterior segmental
bronchus

Apicoposterior
bronchus

Lingular
bronchus

Lingular a.

Pulmonary a.
to basal segments

Superior
segmental a.

N

Apicoposterior
segmental v.

Traction on
apicoposterior
bronchus

Apicoposterior
segmental v.

Apicoposterior
segment

O

Anterior
segment

Branch of
intersegmental v.

Anterior
segment

Anterior
segmental a.

P

Pulmonary a.

Lingula

Lingular a.

Left lower lobe

ESOPHAGECTOMY

Operations on the esophagus can result in considerable morbidity and mortality. Since the esophagus is primarily a conduit to carry liquids and solids from the oral cavity to the stomach, its dysfunction results from obstruction or from esophagitis caused by reflux of acidic gastric contents into the esophageal lumen. The surgical procedures performed on the esophagus are therefore done to relieve or prevent obstruction or to relieve or prevent esophagitis.

For surgical purposes it is well to consider the esophagus as composed of four quarters. The upper quarter is the cervical esophagus above the sternal notch. The second quarter is the esophagus behind the sternal notch and above the aortic arch. The third quarter of the esophagus is in the right thorax from the aortic arch distal to the deviation of the esophagus to the left side. The lowest quarter of the esophagus is in the left lower thorax and transverses the esophageal hiatus of the diaphragm into the abdominal cavity where it joins the stomach at the cardia.

Of the acquired forms of esophageal obstruction, obstruction by malignant tumor is the most difficult for palliation and for care of the patient. Most carcinomas of the esophagus are epidermoid in type, although in approximately 5 per cent of patients an adenocarcinoma may be found. Adenocarcinoma is usually found in the lower quarter, but may be found elsewhere in the esophagus and is often associated with ectopic gastric mucosa.

As an organ, the esophagus is readily distensible in the lateral direction. It has no true serosa and its outer layer is longitudinal muscle fibers. Its blood supply is segmental from mediastinal arteries and from the pharyngeal and stomach vessels. In general, the blood supply is sufficiently adequate that the entire esophagus can be mobilized without necrosis provided the blood supply from the stomach and the pharynx is not disturbed.

Carcinomas of the esophagus tend to be rather advanced by the time the patient develops symptoms of obstruction. All symptoms of dysphagia or reflux esophagitis require immediate diagnosis if carcinoma is to be found in its early form. The tumor tends to spread to regional lymph nodes but can also extend considerable distances up or down the esophagus through the lymphatics of the esophageal wall. The tumor tends to drain upward to the supraclavicular nodes and downward to the cardiac nodes around the left gastric artery supplying the stomach.

The surgical cure rate for carcinoma of the esophagus is distressingly low, and much of the surgery is palliative. It is essential that a surgical operation with a low cure rate have a relatively low morbidity and mortality rate. Most of the morbidity and mortality from surgery on the esophagus is related to leakage from the anastomosis line. If surgery is to be done, the safest procedure must be used.

The diagnosis of lesions of the esophagus begins with a careful history and physical examination for symptoms of esophageal obstruction or gastric regurgitation into the esophagus. Search for distant metastases must be made. Esophageal fluoroscopy and roentgenograms with appropriate contrast media as well as esophagoscopy should be carried out in all patients with significant symptoms or objective findings of esophageal disease. If the mucosa of the esophagus is involved, a biopsy should be made through the esophagoscope. Great care must be taken not to perforate the esophagus since this accident is usually a surgical emergency requiring drainage or surgical closure. If the esophageal mucosa is intact, caution in biopsy is advisable. Esophageal cells properly collected and examined by an expert cytologist should be diagnostic in 95 per cent of cases of esophageal carcinoma.

A gastrostomy under local anesthesia for feeding purposes usually is performed first; major surgery on the esophagus is delayed until the surgeon is convinced that the patient has reached his optimum condition for surgery. Abdominal exploration is prognostically valuable.

Surgical excision of the upper quarter of the esophagus has not given a satisfactory rate of cure or palliation of the esophageal obstruction. The operation that has been used most has been a local excision of the esophagus with construction of a skin-tube graft to connect the pharynx to the distal esophagus just above the sternal notch. The local excision usually performed has not been an adequate procedure since it has been desirable to save the larynx. The skin tube has not been a satisfactory conduit and is plagued with strictures and obstruction. The cervical esophagus is a relatively superficial structure and heavy doses of radiation from supervoltage sources have been almost as successful as surgery in terms of palliation and five-year survival rate. Combined radiotherapy and operation should be considered. Perhaps radiotherapy combined with the surgical approach and bowel grafts will have application in the future.

Carcinomas of the second and third quarters of the esophagus are not so amenable to palliation by radiation because of their deeper location. Surgical excision of the thoracic area of the esophagus has not been accompanied by a satisfactory "cure rate." There is interest at present in combining preoperative radiation and surgical excision. The excisional surgery is performed some four to six weeks after conclusion of a full radiation course or immediately after a short radiation course. The safest operation is a two-stage procedure with nearly total esophagectomy through the right thorax and reconstruction of the esophagus by interposition of the colon extrapleurally between the cervical esophagus and the stomach. An irradiated esophagus should not be anastomosed inside the thorax. The two-stage procedure avoids any anastomotic leak into the thorax, which is usually a fatal complication.

Carcinomas of the lower quarter of the esophagus, as mentioned previously, may be adenocarcinoma. The tumor may also be adenocarcinoma of the stomach with extension upward into the lower esophagus. Carcinomas of the lowest quarter of the esophagus seem best treated by operation through the left thorax, with resection of the lower esophagus and upper stomach and reconstruction of the alimentary tract by anastomosing the stomach to the residual esophagus near the aortic arch.

A gastrostomy will often be necessary for feeding purposes prior to surgery or during radiation therapy. Our usual procedure is to perform a gastrostomy under local or, if possible, general anesthesia and to treat the lesion with 6000 to 7000 rads of cobalt radiation. This has increased resectability. More recently we have decreased the radiotherapy dose to 4500 rads administered over a period of four weeks.

Approximately four to six weeks after completion of the radiation course, which in itself takes four to six weeks, a right thoracotomy is done. If the tumor cannot be removed, the procedure is terminated. In a later stage a colon by-pass procedure can be performed if the condition and probable duration of survival of the patient warrant it. The entire thoracic esophagus is removed if the tumor is operable. The patient is allowed to recover from the esophagectomy operation. He should have evidence of weight gain, be in satisfactory nutritional status with no obvious signs of nonresectability or incurability. Usually this interval period is a month or two. During this interval a salivary drainage fistula is created in the neck and the patient is fed through the gastrostomy. A preoperative barium enema examination to demonstrate a normal colon is mandatory. The bowel is prepared with an insoluble sulfa drug plus cleansing enemas for four or five days prior to the anticipated operation. When an optimum point for repair is reached, the patient is operated upon again and the colon interposed substernally. Occasionally, the good risk patient may have the colon interposed two weeks after the completion of radiotherapy and before the esophagectomy. This shortens the period of disability, but a cervical leak into the mediastinum, which is not scarred closed, may be hazardous.

References

Scanlon, E. F., Morton, D. R., Walker, J. M., and Watson, W. L.: The case against segmental resection for oesophageal carcinoma. Surg. Gynec. & Obst. *101*:290, 1955.
Torek, F.: The first successful case of resection of the thoracic portion of the esophagus for carcinoma. Surg. Gynec. & Obst. *16*:614, 1913.

Esophagectomy

Most patients with cancer of the esophagus are unable to swallow a normal intake of food and are malnourished. Uncommonly these patients may even be unable to swallow their saliva and will need a cervical esophagostomy. Such "spit fistulas" are undesirable and should be done with considerable reluctance. It is possible that x-ray therapy before the thoracotomy may cause enough shrinkage of the tumor to relieve a complete obstruction; the edema which precedes shrinkage may cause a complete but temporary blockage. The cervical esophagostomy is shown in this plate. Even if there is to be no antecedent cervical esophagostomy, many patients require a gastrostomy. It is much easier to nourish these patients swiftly and to a more normal nutritional state by this device. If the gastrostomy can be performed under general anesthesia, the surgeon has the opportunity to assess the liver, and the abdominal cavity in general, for metastatic deposits. Finding such deposits would preclude a curative esophagectomy, and the surgeon can concentrate on the merits of a palliative colon interposition. In addition to distant metastases, other criteria of relative noncurability or nonresectability include recurrent laryngeal nerve involvement, mediastinitis or paraesophageal abscess from presumed perforation of the cancer and tracheal invasion as evidenced by hemopytysis or by tracheoesophageal fistula.

If an esophagectomy is performed, the accompanying vagotomy will result in annoying gastric atony and retarded emptying while the patient waits for the colon interposition and the accompanying pyloroplasty. Therefore, if the patient's condition can tolerate it, the pyloroplasty can be performed at this time. This will provide a better functioning gastrostomy between the time of exploratory celiotomy and colon interposition and shorten the duration of the operation at the time of this last procedure. This is how this series of illustrations is presented even though it can frequently be performed in two stages.

A   The cervical incision is made along the anterior border of the sternocleidomastoid muscle about two-thirds of the way to the mastoid process. The greater auricular nerve will be encountered at the upper end of the incision and should be spared. The superficial cervical fascia is incised so that the sternocleidomastoid muscle can be retracted laterally.

B   The carotid sheath is exposed but not dissected. The middle thyroid vein is ligated in continuity and then divided. The inferior belly of the omohyoid muscle may have to be divided to obtain this exposure. Preferably it should be retracted upward. The inferior thyroid artery contributes sufficiently to the nourishment of the cervical esophagus and, for the sake of better viability of this portion of the esophagus during the later anastomosis, should be preserved if at all possible.

C   The thyroid gland can now be rotated medially, exposing the recurrent laryngeal nerve, which is preserved. Sometimes it is necessary to divide some of the strap muscles before the thyroid can be rotated.

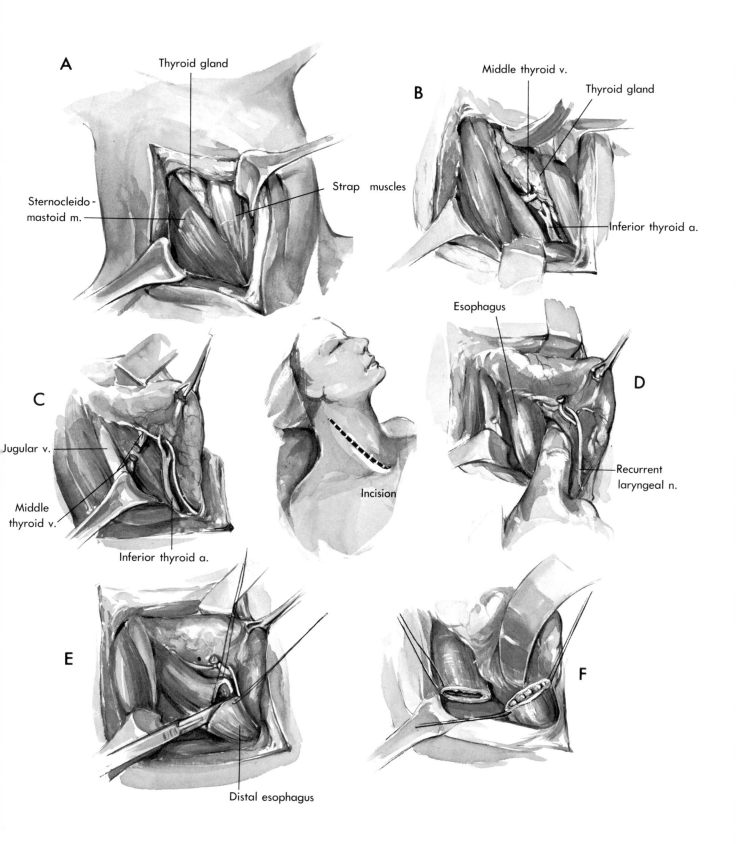

A

Thyroid gland

Sternocleido-mastoid m.

Strap muscles

B

Middle thyroid v.

Thyroid gland

Inferior thyroid a.

C

Jugular v.

Middle thyroid v.

Inferior thyroid a.

Incision

Esophagus

D

Recurrent laryngeal n.

E

Distal esophagus

F

D   The finger is placed on the cervical prevertebral fascia and the esophagus dissected away from it. The overlying trachea is gently separated from the cervical esophagus. The vessels to this portion of the esophagus come from the inferior thyroid artery and usually do not require ligation.

E
F   Because the esophagus lacks a serosa it is more fragile than the intestine and should be handled gently. This is especially true if an immediate esophagocolic anastomosis is to be performed and the esophagus is to be in prime condition. Here, atraumatic sutures are used to manipulate the esophagus as it is divided. The distal end is closed with interrupted stitches of 3-0 silk and left in place. The proximal portion is stitched to the skin circumferentially with interrupted 3-0 silk.

With the patient whose nutritional general condition is satisfactory, the sequence of operations can begin with the esophagectomy; that is the assumption under which these plates will be presented.

The patient is placed on the left side 45 degrees from true lateral so that incisions can be made in the right neck and chest and the abdomen. The left arm is extended forward while the right arm is draped in a sterile manner, swung over the head and supported on the anesthesia screen, but left available for later movement when the neck must be fully exposed. Self-adhesive clear plastic drapes are best for covering the immediate operative sites; the remainder of the area should be draped in the usual fashion.

This operation lends itself to two operating teams, with one on the left side of the patient working in the abdomen. The abdomen must be opened first to explore for metastases that would make it unnecessary to open the thorax. A long midline incision is made, starting well up the xiphisternum. The usual thorough exploration is conducted, with particular attention focused on the lesser curvature of the stomach and the celiac axis. The finding of involved lymph nodes only here does not mitigate against an attempt at curative surgery. The thorax is also opened at this time. For the sake of illustrative continuity the thoracic portion of the operation is shown in the next two plates even though both the thorax and abdomen are theaters for simultaneous action.

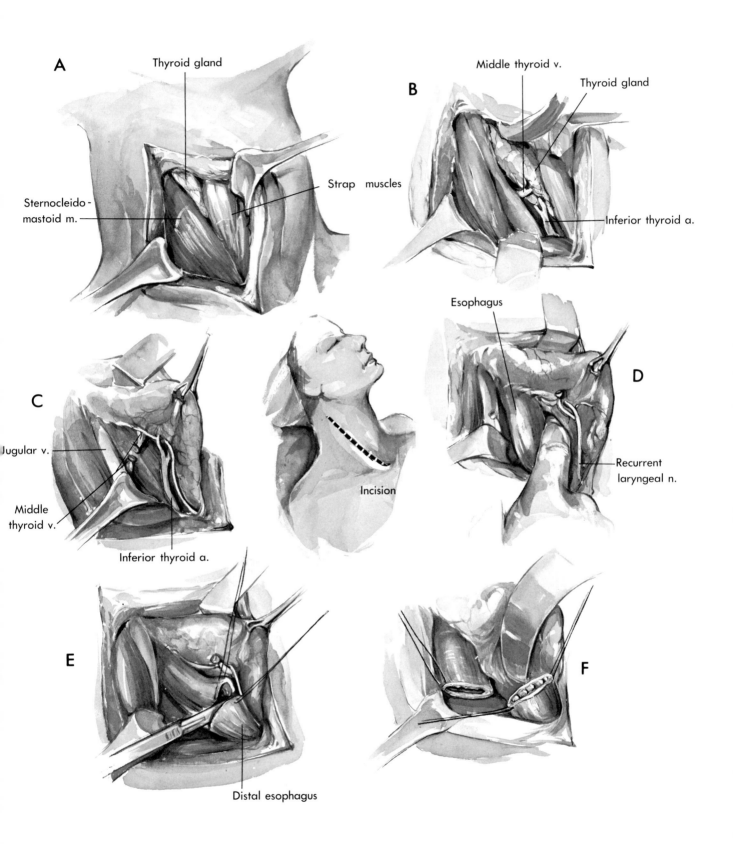

A

Thyroid gland

Sternocleido-
mastoid m.

Strap muscles

B

Middle thyroid v.

Thyroid gland

Inferior thyroid a.

C

Jugular v.

Middle
thyroid v.

Inferior thyroid a.

Incision

Esophagus

D

Recurrent
laryngeal n.

E

Distal esophagus

F

G   The right thorax is entered through the 5th or 6th rib, which is excised subperiosteally. The collapsed lung is covered with a moist gauze pad and reflected anteriorly; the mediastinal pleura is incised. Ligation and division of the azygos vein results in ample exposure of all but the extreme upper and lower ends of the thoracic esophagus.

H   A pledget of gauze at the tip of an eight-inch curved hemostat is an excellent instrument to use in starting the dissection of the esophagus off the spine posteriorly and the aorta medially. A linen tape is placed around the esophagus to help to lift it forward and to maintain this plane of dissection, which goes smoothly in the absence of para-esophageal inflammation.

I   The lymph nodes in the area of the tracheal bifurcation should be included in the excised specimen, which has now been mobilized for almost its full length. If the thoracic duct is cut (often opalescent to milky fluid will signal this accident), it should be ligated or oversewn, as the case may necessitate, with atraumatic 4-0 silk. Inadvertent entry into the opposite chest through a tear in the mediastinal pleura should be recognized and the anesthetist warned. A mental note should be made to insert a chest tube on this side connected to an under-water seal drainage apparatus at the conclusion of the operation.

J   When the abdominal and thoracic approaches are combined, the hand in the abdomen can assist in making the opening in the esophageal hiatus. If there has already been a preliminary abdominal entry for a gastrostomy and possibly pyloroplasty, the esophagogastric area is mobilized entirely from within the chest. Traction on the esophageal hiatus will deliver some of the cardia of the stomach into view.

K   The division of the terminal esophagus is done between Kocher clamps after the surgical field is protected adequately with large gauze pads against possible contamination from any gastric spillage. Several Babcock forceps may be needed to anchor the stomach and prevent its retraction into the abdomen.

    Following division of the terminal esophagus a tie is placed proximal to the proximal clamp and the latter removed. A horizontal basting stitch is applied under the distal clamps and will effectively prevent leakage after clamp removal. Prior to removal of the clamp excess tissue is trimmed away.

L
M   A simple through-and-through running stitch is placed across the free edges of the divided distal esophagus. A row of interrupted simple stitches of 3-0 silk is applied to
N   the seromuscular layer of the esophagogastric junction. Notice the trifurcate stitch in Figure M which is used to invert the ends. The stomach is replaced in the abdominal cavity and the diaphragmatic defect closed with interrupted simple stitches of 2-0 silk.

O   Attention is now directed to the cervical area. The reader is referred to Plate 1 for details of dissecting the cervical esophagus. When there is a dual approach through chest and neck, the esophagus and the thoracic inlet can be dissected more easily and more surely in the same plane. With gentle pulling from above and coaxing from below the entire thoracic esophagus is "snaked" out of the chest.

    The reader is again asked to appreciate the somewhat overlapping or juxtaposition of the illustrations and descriptive text, which is dictated by the sequences which are possible for performing this procedure, or which the surgeon may choose to follow. If only the thoracic esophagectomy is to be performed, the esophagus is divided at this time at a point about 2 cm. below the clavicle and the cervical esophagostomy made as low as possible.

    If the colon interposition is to be done at this time, the esophagus which is now out of the chest is left as is for easier manipulation during the esophagocolostomy. The chest is closed in the preferred manner.

    The next series of plates will show the abdominal aspects of the operation. The celiotomy incision is made before the thoracic to permit examination for metastases that would make a thoracotomy fruitless. The reader will remember that a previous celiotomy, with incidental exploration, may have been done for the purpose of providing a feeding gastrostomy, or only abdominal and cervical incisions may be made for a palliative esophagocolostomy.

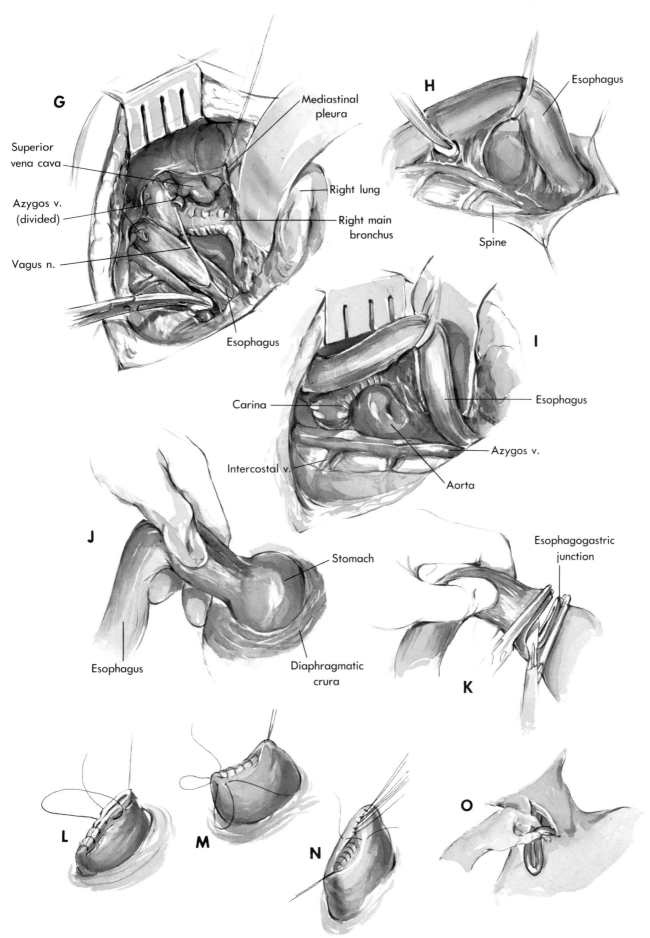

G

Mediastinal pleura

Superior vena cava

Azygos v. (divided)

Vagus n.

Right lung

Right main bronchus

Esophagus

H

Esophagus

Spine

I

Carina

Intercostal v.

Esophagus

Azygos v.

Aorta

J

Stomach

Esophagus

Diaphragmatic crura

Esophagogastric junction

K

L   M   N   O

Esophagectomy (continued)

P These illustrations show the abdominal incision and the portion of the right colon to
Q be mobilized. Pertinent comments on the use of the left colon or small bowel as esophageal substitutes are in the discussion of Plate 4.

R Prior to mobilization of the colon the surgeon must examine the large bowel to ascertain which side he wishes to use. Factors that will influence this decision are the length of available colon, the caliber of the colon lumen relative to that of the esophagus, poor or aberrant vascularity of the segment in mind, inflammation (example: diverticulitis or even diverticulosis), especially on the left side, previous operative procedures and, finally, the habitus of the patient. In this instance the right colon was chosen; here it is being displaced medially while its relatively avascular peritoneal reflection is being incised. The colon conduit between esophagus and stomach functions by gravity. Thus isoperistaltic and antiperistaltic segments function equally well. However, it is essential that there be adequate colon without redundancy. It is essential that careful measurements be made before cutting the bowel.

S The mobilization is continued across the hepatic flexure of the colon and then to the gastrocolic omentum. The dissection is conducted inside the gastroepiploic vessels as this is a more avascular area. The omentum up to the left transverse colon (if not all of it) is removed so that there will be an unencumbered length of transverse colon for the subsequent cologastrostomy.

An opening in the avascular area of the gastrohepatic omentum can be made now for later passage of the colon segment through it.

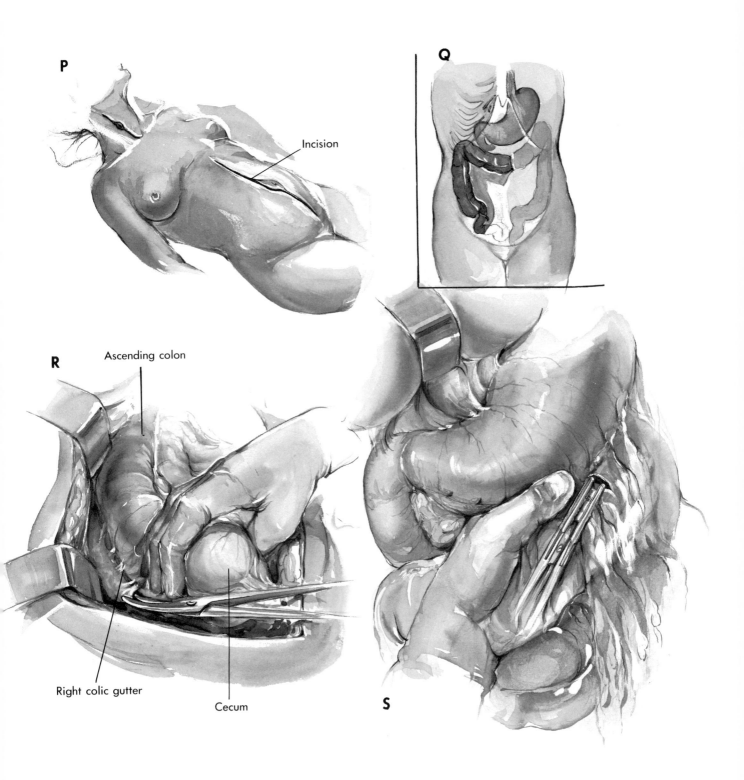

P

Incision

Q

R

Ascending colon

Right colic gutter

Cecum

S

T   After the right colon has been fully mobilized it is held up so that there is light behind its mesentery causing it to be transilluminated. The vasculature can be inspected and the vessels one contemplates ligating are dissected free. They are occluded by a bull-dog clamp while other chores are attended to. This maneuver predicts the ability of the bowel to survive with the midcolic artery as its sole source of blood supply and should be a routine prelude to further surgery in this area.

U   The surgeon must be thoroughly acquainted with the usual vascular pattern of the large bowel. There is shown here the most common pattern for the right colon and the right side of the transverse colon. The middle colic artery is given off at almost the origin of the superior mesentric artery. The transverse colon has been raised so that the middle colic artery, whose natural course is caudad, appears here to be traveling cephalad. The right colic artery courses laterally toward the midascending colon and the ileocolic artery to the cecal area. The marginal artery is shown intact but sometimes this may not be so.

V_1
V_2
V_3 Depicted here are some variations in the vasculature of the right colon. In Figure V_1 the middle colic and right colic arteries arise from a common trunk so that to gain colon length, the right colic would have to be divided at its bifurcation with the middle colic artery. In Figure V_2 there is no right colic artery, the middle colic and ileocolic arteries supplying the right colon through a larger marginal artery. In Figure V_3 the right colic and ileocolic arteries arise from a common trunk with early arborization and a meager marginal artery.

W   One of the advantages of using the left colon is its more predictably longer length, although it may not appear so in this instance of a rounded splenic flexure. Also, the marginal artery of Drummond is more predictable in its presence and adequacy; the vascular pattern is also more constant. In addition, the left colon is more nearly the diameter of the esophagus to which it will be anastomosed. If used, the left colon and its mesentery would be incised along the dashed lines numbered 1 and 2, with the distal end (2) destined to lie in the neck.

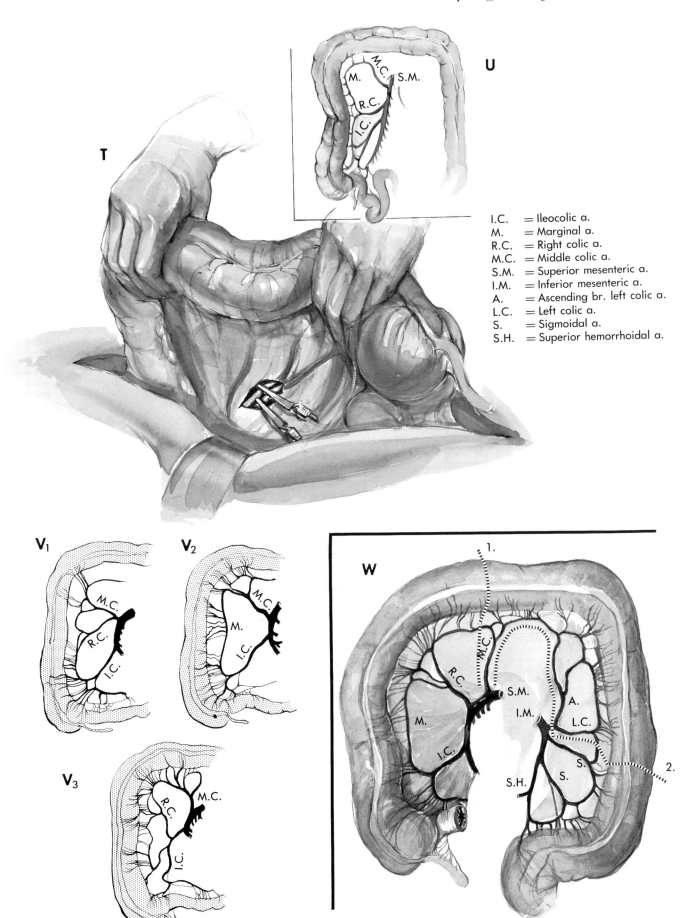

I.C. = Ileocolic a.
M. = Marginal a.
R.C. = Right colic a.
M.C. = Middle colic a.
S.M. = Superior mesenteric a.
I.M. = Inferior mesenteric a.
A. = Ascending br. left colic a.
L.C. = Left colic a.
S. = Sigmoidal a.
S.H. = Superior hemorrhoidal a.

X When the decision is made to use the right colon, the ileum is divided about 5 cm. from the ileocecal valve. A Kocher clamp is placed on the proximal side; the distal side is tied with a linen tape and the ends left long for possible later use in pulling the colon up into the neck. Usually, however, the traction is applied to the appendix. In children in whom this operation is sometimes applicable, large ileocecal lymph nodes may have to be excised to enable the colon to pass through the substernal tunnel.

The greatest care should be exercised that the marginal vessels are not damaged. The amount of mesentery left attached, however, should not be so much that the colonic segment becomes too thick. In this instance the right colic artery was found to be expendable when a clamp on it and the ileocolic artery were well tolerated. Nevertheless, it is left intact initially so that if a sufficient length of colon is available it need not be disturbed. If this does not allow for mobilization of a sufficient length of colon, it can be divided (dashed line) with the knowledge that this is a safe move.

The transverse colon is divided between Kocher clamps placed well distal to the middle colic artery. Injury or impedance to the flow of the middle colic artery is obviously a serious complication. There is a dangerous lack of emphasis on the equal importance of maintenance of an adequate venous outflow; the veins are more easily compressed or occluded by torsion. Infarction of the right colon by venous thrombosis is no less a catastrophe than infarction by arterial occlusion.

The ileocolic anastomosis may be performed in various ways. If properly performed, none is really unacceptable or unphysiologic. The end-to-end anastomosis seems to be most logical for allowing easy propulsion from ileum into colon; it also involves the making of only one anastomosis. However, it requires compensation for the usual disparity between the two bowels. An end-to-side anastomosis is a meaningless mimicking of the natural state. The above types of anastomoses plus the side-to-end carry the risk of having to work at the mesenteric border of either or both bowels. Placement of the stitches at an adequate depth for proper inversion of the seromuscular layer at this point may result in ischemia sufficient to lead to necrosis and leakage. Technical temerity may cause the same problem from inadequate closure.

When safety from leakage and stenosis at the anastomosis are given a high priority, a side-to-side connection would seem to be best for the average surgeon. One need not be concerned with injury to the mesenteric vessels while performing the anastomosis, disparity in bowel lumina is no problem, the anastomotic opening can be made as large as desired with no concern about stenosis and probably less chance of obstruction by torsion. As is obvious, we use an end-to-end anastomosis, feeling we can overcome its disadvantages and make use of its time-saving virtues.

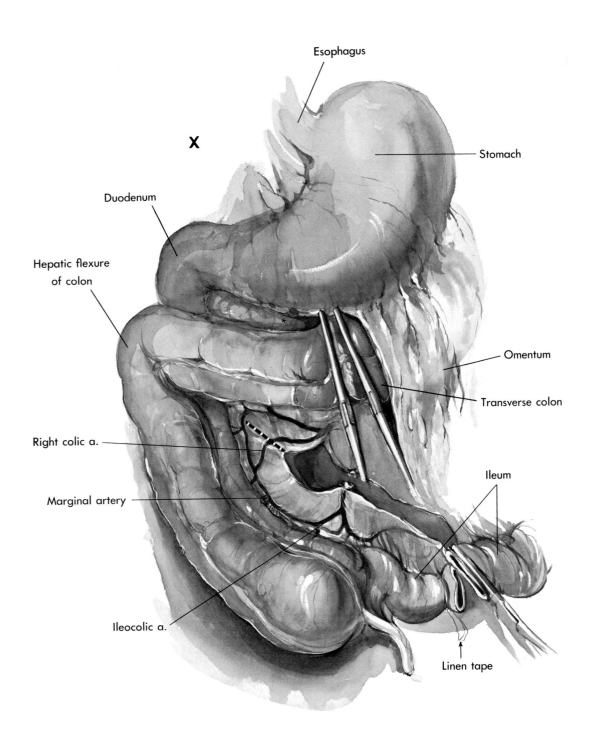

Esophagus

X

Stomach

Duodenum

Hepatic flexure
of colon

Omentum

Transverse colon

Right colic a.

Ileum

Marginal artery

Ileocolic a.

Linen tape

Y The posterior row of interrupted (or continuous) stitches is placed first. The ileum, which is almost always narrower than the colon, should be centered on the latter. The correction of the discrepancy in their lumina by stitch placement should start at this point so that there is a uniform puckering throughout the circumference of the colon rather than in any one big arch of the circumference, an occurrence which may prove awkward to handle.

Z
A₁
B₁
C₁
Excess tissue is trimmed and the anastomosis continued into an open method with adequate isolation of the site with large moistened abdominal pads. Atraumatic 4-0 chromic catgut is used for the mucosal anastomosis. We have no hesitancy in using a continuous simple stitch, which is begun posteriorly in the center with two separate strands. A Connell stitch is used at each corner and so placed that as the two sutures approach each other on the anterior row one is progressing clockwise and the other in a counterclockwise manner; as they meet they can be tied simply and without any bulging of mucosa. If the surgeon remains alert that the assistant does not pull on the stitch every time it is handed to him, "purse stringing" of the anastomosis is no problem. The anterior closure through the seromuscular layer is performed with simple interrupted stitches of 2-0 silk.

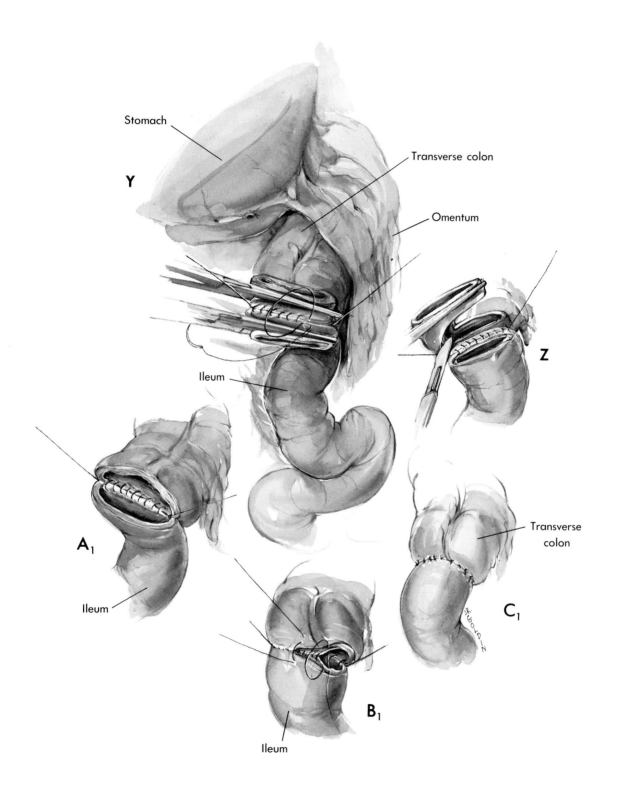

Stomach

Y

Transverse colon

Omentum

Z

Ileum

A₁

Ileum

B₁

Ileum

Transverse
colon

C₁

D₁
E₁
F₁

A previous cervical esophagostomy has been made. This will have to be "taken down" as illustrated. Some scar tissue will obliterate some of the landmarks which now are not too important so long as one continues the dissection close to the esophagus. At the thoracic outlet such scar tissue will make pleural entry less likely. The sternal insertion of the deep cervical fascia must be incised and this opening enlarged. The fingers are unmatched for this function. If necessary, the lateral fibers of the strap muscles can be divided to provide this room. Bone should not be removed unless there is no other recourse, because an indolent osteomyelitis can develop in this area.

G₁

The abdominal opening of the retrosternal tunnel is now begun; the skin incision should have been well over the xyphisternum. The peritoneum is grasped with hemostats, made taut and transversely oriented, with cutting and spreading movements made with the scissors in tissue which is rather loose and avascular. This is done for about the length of the scissors' blades.

H₁
I₁

The retrosternal tunnel is now developed entirely by the fingers and then the hand. From above one should strive for a four-finger opening if possible; below, a large tunnel is possible and, in fact, necessary. A correspondingly narrower tunnel is necessary in children, and the fingers of one hand can span the distance. The sagittal view in Figure H₁ shows how the fingers work toward each other in establishing the substernal tunnel. The hand progressing upward from below has to have all fingers and thumb held together tightly if it is to fit into this confined space. Gentleness should be used to prevent entry into either pleural cavity. The left pleural reflection is farther laterally than the right; hence, the dissection should be to the left of the midline as pictured.

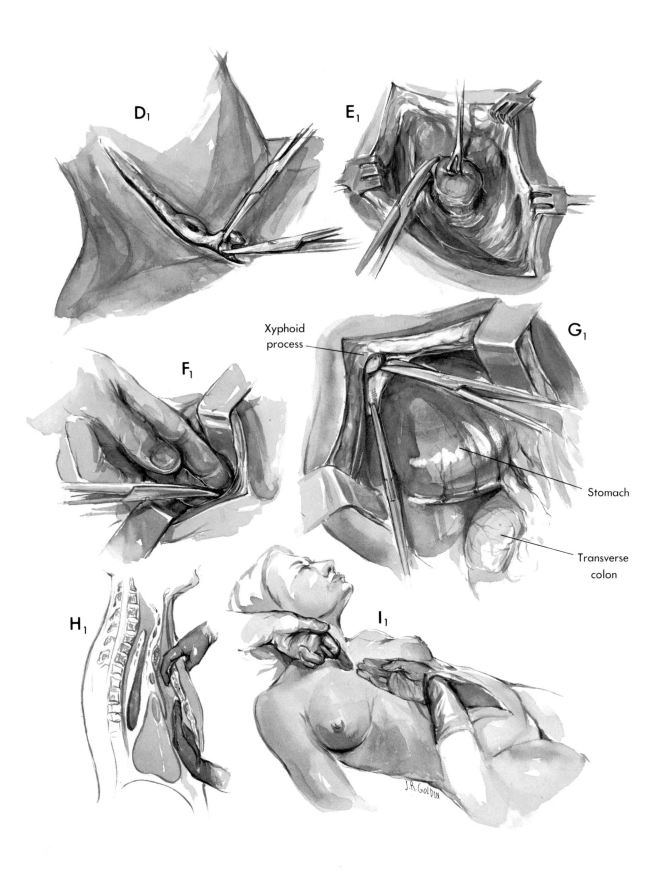

D₁

E₁

Xyphoid
process

F₁

G₁

Stomach

Transverse
colon

H₁

I₁

J.R. GOLDIN

J_1 The mobilized right colon is swung right laterally and upward so that the cecum is now cephalad. With the appendix as the leading point, the colon is passed dorsal to the stomach before it is introduced into the lower retrosternal aperture. Crossing anterior to the stomach is fraught with the danger of causing strangulation or compression of the blood supply to the colon by any gastric postoperative dilatation.

    With gentle and careful bimanual manipulation, the colon is shepherded through the retrosternal tunnel. The vessels of the colon segment are inspected carefully at this time for excessive tension, torsion or compression or for signs of venous engorgement. In fact, once this stage of the operation has been reached most failures of viability are caused by impedance to venous outflow rather than by inadequate arterial inflow.

K_1
L_1
M_1 The cecum has come to the furthest cephalad point in the neck. The thought of using the ileum for the anastomosis should be abandoned because the ileum is less vascular at this point, the anastomosis is more difficult to make and it is necessary to pull the colon up more tightly for the better vascularity of the most terminal portion of the ileum to reach the esophageal opening. The ileum, therefore, is removed and the defect closed in two layers; the inner with a continuous stitch of 3-0 chromic catgut and the outer with interrupted simple stitches of 3-0 silk.

N_1
O_1 The base of the appendix will be the site of esophagocolic anastomosis. Accordingly, an appendectomy is performed, with the cecal defect made equal in circumference to that of the esophagus. Interrupted simple stitches of 4-0 silk will be used throughout for this anastomosis so as to reduce to a minimum any reaction to suture material. In Figure O_1 the posterior row of stitches through the seromuscularis has been placed with the knots facing to the outside. If there has been a previous cervical esophagostomy, the rosette of mucosa which has been convenient for handling and positioning the esophagus is now trimmed off.

P_1
Q_1 Figure P_1 illustrates that it is simple to place the posterior mucosal row of stitches so that the knots reside within the lumen. Those in the anterior row are similarly placed, but the last few are not tied until all are in position lest there will be no room in which to manuever the last several stitches.

    The second anterior row of simple interrupted stitches is being placed (Figure Q_1) in a fashion which has the cecum overlying the esophagus. If there has been a previous cervical esophagostomy, the resultant paraesophageal scar tissue will make available somewhat more substantial tissue for the esophageal bite by the needle. Otherwise, the lack of a serosa on the esophagus makes it necessary that the stitches through the musculature of the esophagus be placed with great care.

R_1 At the completion of the anastomosis, the cecum may need some adjustment since the amount within the neck may be excessive. The colon may need to be retracted somewhat back into the abdomen; great care should be exercised during adjustment so that there is no tension on the anastomosis. The latter maneuver reduces even more the tension on the middle colic vessels. A small drain is exteriorized through a dependent counterincision and the wound closed for all but its central portion with interrupted vertical mattress stitches of 3-0 silk. This allows the surgeon to observe the viability of the esophagus and colon and the integrity of the anastomosis. In 24 or 48 hours, if all appears to be well, these stitches are tied. Venous thrombosis or engorgement results in a dusky to obviously necrotic colon; arterial insufficiency can result in a pale pink colon with a deceptive appearance of viability.

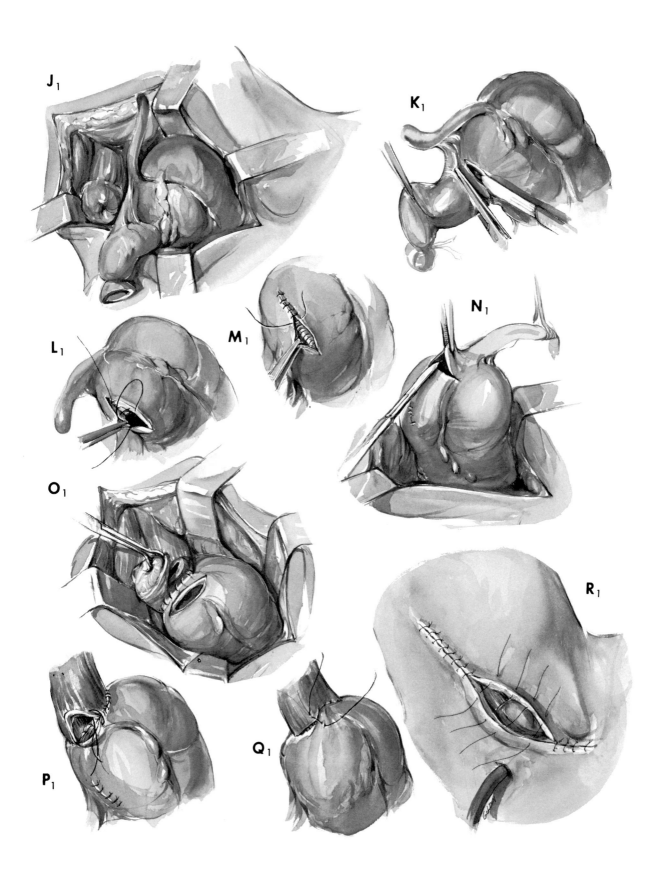

S₁ This semidiagrammatic rendition shows how the right colon is swung laterally and upward as it is placed in position. This causes the vessels to be on the right side. In fact, if the ileal mesentery appears in the neck at other than a direct lateral position the surgeon must assume that torsion exists somewhere.

T₁ The colon will have been brought behind the stomach and through the gastrohepatic ligament. A site is chosen on the anterior and cephalad aspect of the antrum for the cologastrostomy. There should be no excess colon between the tunnel and this site; otherwise, the excess colon will hang in a J-shape fashion. Inasmuch as this interposed colon works solely by gravity, any path other than a straight line from esophagus to stomach will pose later problems in food transit. The posterior row of 3-0 black silk stitches is preceded here by two anchoring stitches. Careful technique during the performance of the earlier gastrostomy will have reduced the number of adhesions which now have to be lysed.

U₁
V₁
W₁
X₁ The anastomosis is performed as indicated. A continuous simple stitch is used throughout the anastomosis, except the anterior one through the seromuscular layer, in which interrupted 3-0 silk is used. Atraumatic 3-0 chromic catgut is used for the mucosal layer. A gastrostomy is made if one is not already in place. A Y-shaped tube is inserted with one arm directed cephalad into almost the entire length of the colon. Positioning of the tube is easier if it is done before the anterior aspect of the cologastric anastomosis is completed. This serves the sole purpose of aspirating swallowed air, which may distend the colon in this relatively rigid place and impede its venous flow, thereby leading to necrosis.

The abdomen is now ready for closure. A medium-sized soft drain is placed adjacent to the retrosternal colon and exteriorized through a counterincision. One drain is placed in the right colic gutter and another to sweep over both the anastomoses. They are exteriorized through counterincisions in the right hypochondrium. The abdominal wound is closed with through-and-through heavy gauge nylon; a concurrent continuous stitch of 1-0 chromic catgut is used to approximate more accurately the linea alba.

An x-ray of the chest is taken in the operating room or promptly in the recovery room to make certain that no pneumothorax is present on either side. The esophagocolic anastomosis in the neck not infrequently will leak. This is not of serious consequence if the area is well drained. However, the incidence of strictured anastomoses will increase with the incidence of leaks. If the anastomotic lumen is lost, dilatations will become difficult or impossible. A valuable aid is to have a braided silk thread passed at the time of operation through the colon and out the mouth, and through the stomach out the gastrostomy. Both ends are then tied together. This thread is a valuable guide for later dilatations if needed. If the thread is not needed, it is easily removed about three weeks postoperatively.

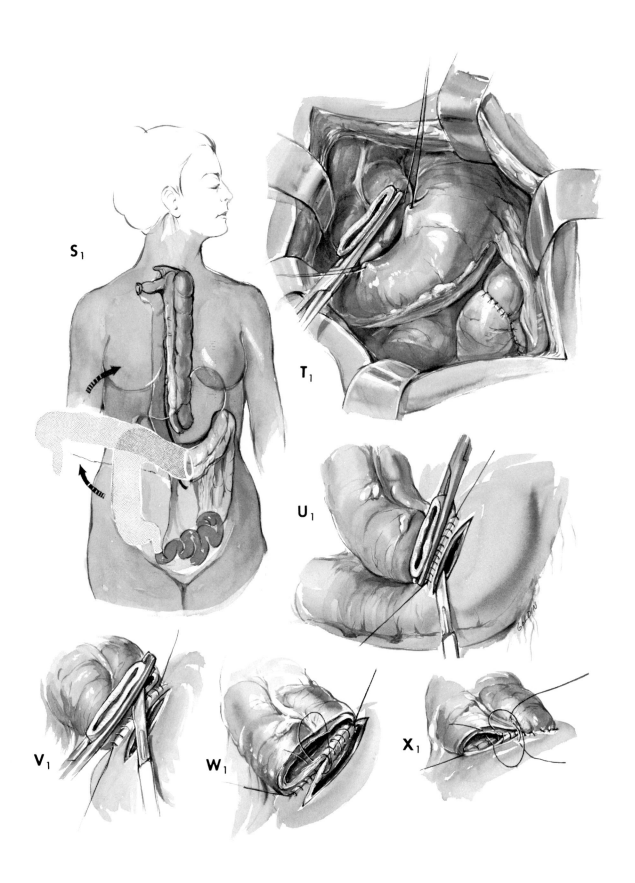

S₁

T₁

U₁

V₁

W₁

X₁

Esophagectomy (continued)

This diagram shows the various intestinal realignments and anastomoses. It is uncommon to have a colon fall through the retrosternal area so straight and true.

When peristalsis is adequate, the patient is fed through the gastrostomy, but not so early or in such amounts that the patient will regurgitate into the retrosternal colon. Nothing is given orally for 10 to 12 days until healing is complete. Ordinarily by three weeks all tubes have been removed, and patients are taking a soft diet by mouth and can return home.

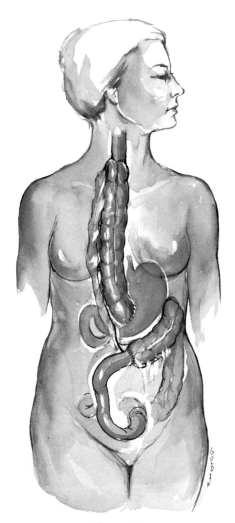

Plate 10

ESOPHAGEAL HIATAL HERNIORRHAPHY

An esophageal hiatus hernia is the commonest of all diaphragmatic hernias. It is usually found as an acquired hernia in adults.

The commonest hernia in the newborn infant is the hernia through the dome of the diaphragm known as the foramen of Bochdalek. This hernia is usually not associated with a hernial sac and, since the abdominal viscera may rise into the thorax and then become distended with air, it is a hernia that may prove rapidly fatal if it is not recognized and treated surgically. The least common diaphragmatic hernia of infancy is the hernia in the sternocostal region, either left or right side, through the foramen of Morgagni. These are relatively rare hernias and invariably there is a hernial sac of peritoneum.

It is now being recognized that esophageal hiatus hernias also occur in infancy and may, indeed, be symptomatic. An infant who constantly regurgitates after feeding and who fails to thrive and gain weight in the first few months of life may have an esophageal hiatus hernia. For this reason, in infants with these symptoms the pediatrician should always consider a congenital esophageal hiatus hernia in his differential diagnosis.

In the adult large hernias through the diaphragm, if not of the esophageal or the costosternal type, are usually traumatic. The traumatic hernias are not associated with a peritoneal hernia sac and, if not recognized, may have grave consequences. The costosternal hernia may not be recognized until adult life. Many patients come to operation because of the physician's inability to diagnose accurately a mass in the anterior mediastinum.

The esophageal hiatus hernias appear with increasing frequency as age increases and they can be demonstrated in the majority of aged patients. This is a sliding hernia, as the cardia and stomach slide posteriorly and retroperitoneally up into the chest in such fashion that the anterior part of the hernia is invested with a hernial sac. Most of these hernias produce insufficient discomfort to warrant surgical correction. Symptoms are usually related to regurgitation of gastric contents into the esophagus, which is interpreted by the patient as substernal distress after meals or on lying down.

Since the same dermatomes innervate the esophageal hiatus area, the biliary system and the coronary vessels of the heart, it may be difficult at times to distinguish among the distress of an esophageal hiatus hernia, biliary dysfunction and coronary artery disease. Usually the patient with minimal symptoms from a hiatus hernia will respond well to medical management, which consists of antacids, a bland diet, elevation of the head of the bed while sleeping and avoidance of eating or drinking directly prior to bedtime. However, a minority of those with hernias will have complaints not relieved by medical management. These complaints usually fall into two categories: esophagitis or bleeding. There may be sufficient regurgitation of gastric juice, particularly when its acid level is high, to produce severe inflammation and possible ulceration of the esophageal mucosa. The esophagitis may be quite painful and disabling. If this condition is neglected, it may result in considerable scarring in the esophagus with the resultant so-called acquired short esophagus, since the scarred esophagus not only decreases in diameter but shortens in length. The shortening of the esophagus has the undesirable feature of making it impossible to replace the cardia below the diaphragm.

The other problem from uncontrolled esophageal hiatus hernia is related to bleeding, either from the esophagus or from the stomach. Ulceration in the stomach is prone to occur in that portion above the diaphragm and is probably related to increased acid production and stasis in this segment. When patients are encountered who have had chronic bleeding from the gastrointestinal tract and the source of the bleeding is obscure, one cause which should be considered and carefully sought is the possibility of an esophageal hiatus hernia.

Incarceration and perforation of esophageal hiatus hernias are quite rare. However, incarceration, strangulation or perforation of traumatic diaphragmatic hernias is less rare and is especially difficult to diagnose since the symptomatology appears to be abdominal and yet the physical examination of the abdomen tends to be negative.

In evaluating a patient with an esophageal hiatus hernia, the usual history, physical examination and routine laboratory work should be done. Of particular importance is a careful upper gastrointestinal x-ray series to ascertain the condition of the esophagus, the position of the cardia and the status of the stomach and duodenum. Other lesions, such as duodenal ulcer and pyloric stenosis, should be particularly sought for. The stool should be examined for occult blood. If there is evidence of blood loss in the gastrointestinal tract, a proctosigmoidoscopy and barium enema are indicated. Evaluation of the heart, including an electrocardiogram, and a cholecystogram to evaluate the gallbladder are in order. The gastric acidity should be measured in the fasting state and after stimulation by histamine; the gastric juice should also be examined for evidence of blood. If there is evidence of significant symptoms of esophageal disease, an esophagoscopy should be carried out before any surgical repair of the hernia. Even if surgery is not contemplated, it is important to assess the condition of the esophagus by esophagoscopy. At esophagoscopy, one has to be cautious about biopsy of ulcerations in the esophagus for fear of perforation. However, esophageal washings for cytologic examination should be helpful. (Tumors seem to occur more frequently in the diseased esophagus than in a normal esophagus.) Esophagoscopy should include a search for the condition of gastroesophagus; there is some question whether gastric mucosa in the esophagus is a congenital lesion or whether there may be repair of esophageal ulcerations by gastric mucosa coming up from the stomach.

It is our feeling that patients with esophageal hiatus hernia who do not respond well to medical management, or who have persistent bleeding and persistent esophagitis, should be offered surgical repair unless they are considered poor surgical risks.

There has been some controversy as to whether esophageal hiatus hernias should be repaired transthoracically or transabdominally. It is our feeling that if there is significant associated abdominal pathology, the operation should be performed transabdominally. However, if thorough and careful evaluation fails to reveal abdominal pathology, it is simpler and associated with less morbidity in proper hands to repair the hernia transthoracically. This is particularly true of the esophageal hiatus hernias that need repair in infancy. The liver in infancy is relatively large, and considerable dissection of the left lobe of the liver is needed for adequate exposure of the hiatus hernia transabdominally in the infant. Infants tolerate thoracic surgery well, and the exposure of a hiatus hernia through the thorax in the infant is very simple. Usually all that has to be done in the repair of the esophageal hiatus hernias of infancy is to tighten the esophageal hiatus by approximating the crus of the diaphragm with moderately heavy suture material in such fashion that the hiatus will admit a fingertip; extensive dissections and repair are not necessary.

If the decision is to repair the hiatus hernia transthoracically, the classic method has been to use the technique of Allison. This consists in freeing the esophagus and herniated stomach and of opening the sac as far around the esophageal gastric junction as possible and using this tissue where it joins the esophagus just above the cardia to suture to the diaphragmatic hiatus. The esophageal hiatus is tightened by sutures approximating the crus posterior to the cardia with heavy suture material. The esophageal hiatus as reconstructed should permit a tight fingertip to pass in addition to the esophagus. A counterincision in the dome of the diaphragm may also be used for traction and to anchor the stomach to the undersurface of the diaphragm around the cardia in such fashion as to help to hold the cardia below the diaphragm. A more recent modification, by Belsey, has been helpful in preventing regurgitation. This consists of suturing the left wall of the esophagus to the right side of the fundus in such fashion that the angle of entry of the esophagus into the stomach is made more acute. In consequence, when the stomach distends, the distention has a tendency to occlude the cardia rather than to make it patulous.

If there is a diseased pylorus and significant delay in gastric emptying, it is necessary to combine the hiatus hernia repair with a drainage procedure for the stomach. The drainage procedure can be either a pyloroplasty or a gastroenterostomy. However, in the latter procedure, if the gastric acidity was high, a vagotomy would also be indicated. We have not felt that in the standard esophageal hiatus hernia repaired surgically there was need for combining a vagotomy and a gastroenterostomy with the herniorrhaphy. However, a vagotomy and drainage have given good results when the standard esophageal hiatus herniorrhaphy could not be carried out because of a "short" esophagus. The neglected esophageal hiatus hernia, in addition to producing a short esophagus and a nonreducible hiatus hernia, may also cause a stricture in the esophagus. It has been our policy to perform vagotomies and gastric drainage procedures in these patients and then wait to see if the apparent stricture improved. Some of the strictures are associated with acute ulceration, and if the ulceration responds to the vagotomy and drainage procedures, there will be less "stricture." However, if after the vagotomy and drainage it becomes apparent that there is a true stricture, attempts at esophageal dilatation should then be made.

Page 174

The resection of the cardia should be avoided as long as possible since the cardia is a better sphincter than we can devise. In an occasional case, when there is an intractable stricture not responding to the aforementioned therapy, it may be necessary to interpose bowel, usually colon, between the esophagus and the stomach so that the patient may eat normally again.

After the esophageal hernia repair, it is important postoperatively to keep the stomach decompressed for a time until peristalsis is regained. The return of peristalsis may be prolonged if a vagotomy has been done. In such cases, a decompressing gastrostomy is valuable. Once peristalsis has begun, we normally start the patient on a liquid diet and keep him on a soft diet for the next two or three weeks. Not infrequently the patient may have some difficulty swallowing solid food in the early postoperative period, particularly if the repair has been snug. This ordinarily will correct itself over a period of time and is usually a favorable sign. Before discharge home, a repeat esophagogram should be obtained to ascertain the status of the hiatus hernia. Approximately 85 per cent of hernia repairs should be permanent. Usually if the hernia is going to recur, it will do so in the first six to 12 months. The repair of a recurrent hiatus hernia is less satisfactory than the first attempt. If the first repair has been carried out by a competent surgeon, the standard hernia repair is not likely to be successful the second time. If the patient is sufficiently symptomatic, one may have to rely on vagotomy and gastric drainage procedures as a secondary choice. The placement of a silver clip at the level of the cardia and two clips on the diaphragmatic hiatus may be helpful in following the patient postoperatively in cases in which recurrence of the lesion is expected to occur.

References

Allison, P. R.: Reflux esophagitis, sliding hiatus hernia, and the anatomy of repair. Surg. Gynec. & Obst. 92:419, 1951.
Belsey, R.: Functional disease of the esophagus. J. Thorac. & Cardiovasc. Surg. 52:164, 1966.
Clagett, O. T.: Present concepts regarding the surgical treatment of esophageal hiatus lesions. Ann. Roy. Coll. Surg. Eng. 38:195, 1966.

A   General endotracheal anesthesia is utilized and the patient is placed 45 degrees from the true right lateral decubitus position. A pillow is placed between the legs, the left leg being flexed at the hip and knee. The patient is stabilized with 3-in. adhesive tape which is placed across the hip and knees and anchored to the operating table. Both arms are in front of the patient with the elbows bent. A nasogastric tube is passed, normally while the patient is awake and able to assist with its passage by swallowing a small amount of water. If a painful esophagitis precludes this, the tube is passed after the patient has been anesthetized. This tube decompresses the stomach pre- and post-operatively and makes handling of the esophagus somewhat easier. A lateral thoracotomy incision is made over the approximate level of the 8th rib. The incision extends upward to about the level of the auscultatory triangle. The latissimus dorsi muscle is then transected. There are two methods by which the pleural space may be entered. The incision can be carried through the 7th intercostal space utilizing an intercostal incision, or the 8th rib may be removed in a subperiosteal fashion. The rib spreader should be opened slowly and periodically throughout the early stages of the dissection to prevent any unnecessary breaking of ribs.

B   When the pleural cavity has been entered, the left lower lobe is gently retracted upward; at its lowermost attachment one can readily see the inferior pulmonary ligament. This ligament is partially cut sharply with the scissors and then dissected up to the level of the inferior pulmonary vein. The latter portion of the dissection can be readily carried out using a stick sponge or a sponge dissector, locally referred to as a "peanut" and consisting of a pledget of gauze at the tip of an 8-in. curved hemostat. There may be small arterial bleeders present in the inferior pulmonary ligament and these should be ligated as indicated with 3-0 silk.

    A moist laparotomy pad is placed over the left lower lobe and lingula and they are retracted cephalad with malleable retractors. This maneuver readily brings into view the diaphragm, hernial sac, aorta and phrenic nerve.

C   The mediastinal pleura over the lowermost portion of the esophagus is cut in a T-shape with a scissors. This incision is extended along the lower part of the esophagus, and just above the diaphragm is carried slightly anteriorly as well as posteriorly. Sharp dissection is continued to free the lateral portion of the lower esophagus for a distance of about 8 to 10 cm. Small arterial branches will be noted coming off the aorta supplying the lower portion of the esophagus; these must be carefully identified, ligated in continuity with 3-0 silk and transected, but only for whatever exposure seems necessary.

D   By use of blunt finger dissection the remainder of the lower esophagus can be dissected free from the surrounding mediastinal tissues and right pleura. This should be done carefully so that the vagi are left in their normal anatomic positions and the right pleural space is not entered. A Penrose drain is then placed around the esophagus to facilitate further dissection of the sac and the posterior aspects of the crura.

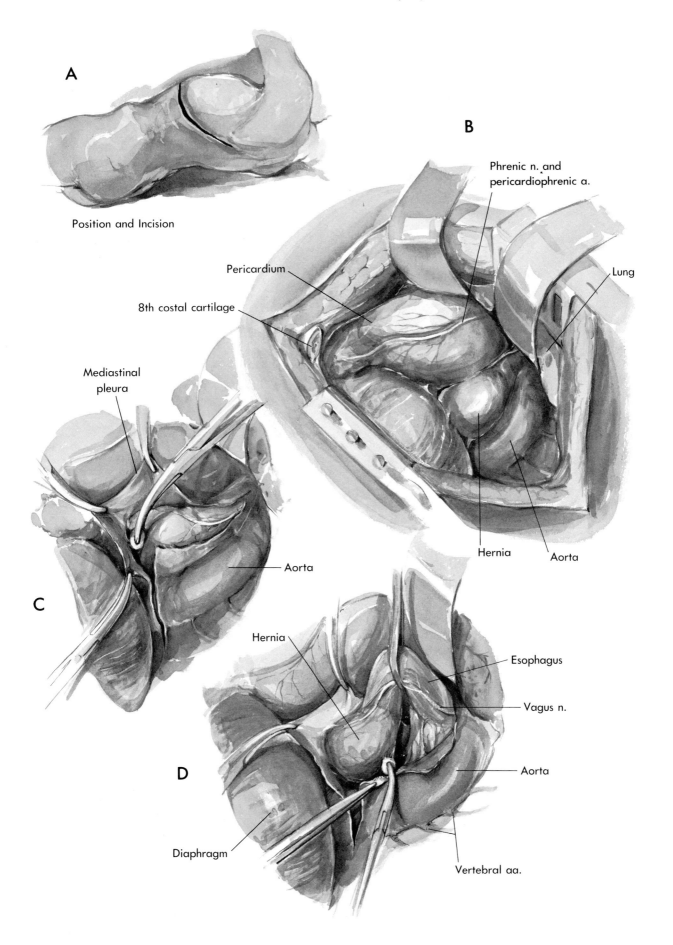

A

Position and Incision

B

Phrenic n. and pericardiophrenic a.

Pericardium

8th costal cartilage

Lung

Mediastinal pleura

Hernia

Aorta

C

Aorta

D

Hernia

Esophagus

Vagus n.

Aorta

Diaphragm

Vertebral aa.

E
F
G

The medial and lateral components of the right crus are now dissected; this is begun with scissors and the tissue over the crura pushed away bluntly with a pledget of gauze at the tip of an 8-in. forceps. One must be careful that the lateral component of the crus is not attenuated or destroyed by the dissection because this tissue sometimes is not substantial and, if greatly distorted, would make repair of the crus most difficult. The medial component of the crus usually has to be freed from the parietal pericardium until a firm fascial component is well delineated. This is readily felt with the thumb and index finger.

A counterincision is now made in the diaphragm. This incision must be made in a location in which the least number of fibers of the phrenic nerve will be severed. The phrenic nerve descends along the lateral wall of the pericardium, pierces the diaphragm and then on its undersurface sends radiating arcs posteriorly. The counterincision, therefore, must be made medial or lateral to these sweeping arcs. The dashed line in Figure E indicates the location of the counterincision used by the authors. Care must be taken that the underlying spleen is not injured. Two silk sutures are placed in the pleural surface of the diaphragm and used to tent up the diaphragm which is then incised with a knife. The remainder of the counterincision is then easily completed with scissors for a length of about 4 in. The diaphragm has an excellent arterial supply and often these vessels are transected in making the counterincision; bleeders should be transfixed with suture ligatures of 2-0 black silk.

H

The index finger is next passed through the counterincision and up into the hernial sac. The hernial sac and the attachment of the attenuated phrenoesophageal ligament to the esophagus are readily ascertained, especially with the finger stretching the hernia and surrounding tissue from within.

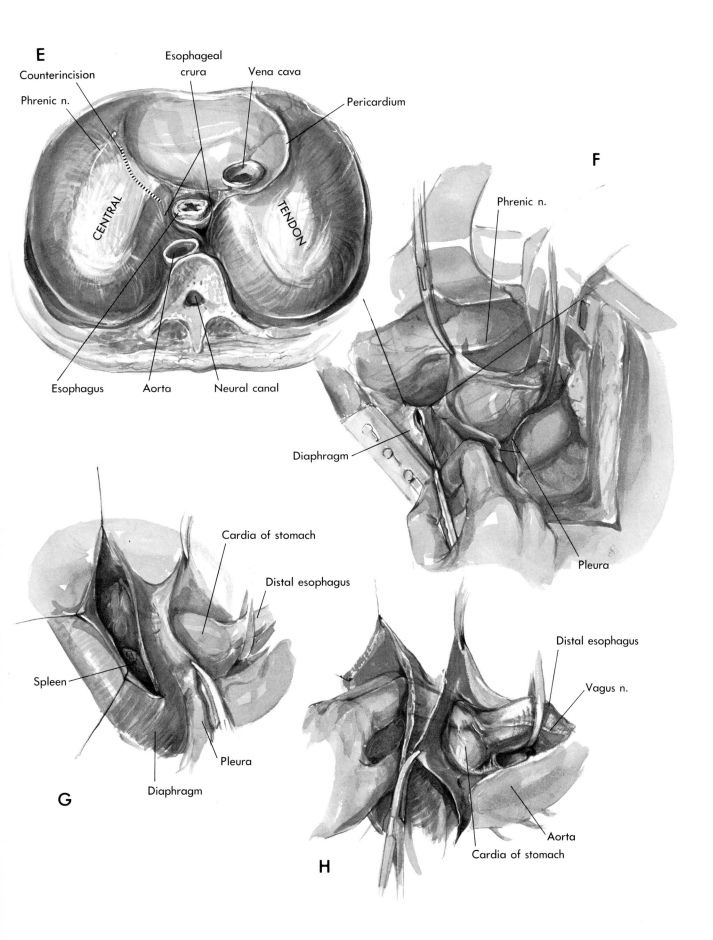

E

Counterincision

Esophageal crura

Vena cava

Phrenic n.

Pericardium

CENTRAL

TENDON

Esophagus

Aorta

Neural canal

F

Phrenic n.

Diaphragm

Pleura

Cardia of stomach

Distal esophagus

Spleen

Pleura

Diaphragm

G

Distal esophagus

Vagus n.

Aorta

Cardia of stomach

H

I   The sac is opened and transected so that a cuff of phrenoesophageal ligament remains attached to the esophagus. The hernial sac is cut laterally, anteriorly and medially; there is no sac posteriorly. This trimming is carried down to the crura. At times we have not trimmed the sac but have used it to sew to the new hiatus.

J   The posterior aspect of the esophagogastric junction is then dissected free. Care must be taken that all arterial bleeders are ligated, as posterior bleeding can become troublesome. Opening the sac will also facilitate further dissection of the medial component of the right crus, and if previous dissection has not been adequate, this can now be accomplished.

K   The posterior crural stitches of zero silk are now placed. Silk of this thickness is used since this heavy material has much less tendency to cut through the muscle fibers of the crus. Usually it is necessary to place only two or three horizontal mattress stitches posterior to the esophagus. If the crural fibers are brought together obliquely, this places too much stress on one of the components of the crus and there is considerable tendency for the suture to pull out. The sutures must also be placed in substantial tissue so that they will hold. Actually, the crural fibers should not be cleaned too thoroughly from their esophageal edge so that during placement of the crural stitches the needle can include peritoneum and pleura in its bites; this helps to buttress the crural fibers against the shearing effect of the stitches. Occasionally, the lateral component of the right crus may have to be sutured to the left crus. The crural stitches are allowed to hang free and are not tied until later in the procedures, or all but the one closest to the esophagus are tied.

L   A series of stitches will now be placed so that when they are tied the phrenoesophageal ligament will come to lie and be anchored to the undersurface of the esophageal crura. These consist of mattress stitches of 2-0 black silk. They are first placed through the phrenoesophageal ligament near the esophagus, keeping in mind that a good bite of tissue must be taken in placement of each stitch to insure its holding. The needle is passed through the esophageal hiatus, the tip of the needle engaging the undersurface of the diaphragm approximately 0.5 to 1.0 cm. from the crural edge. The other end of the suture strand is threaded on a needle and brought through the diaphragm 3 to 4 mm. from its partner as a mattress stitch. These stitches are placed laterally, anteriorly and medially and will number approximately eight to ten in number. As there is no posterior attachment of the phrenoesophageal ligament and hernial sac, stitches obviously cannot be placed in this small area. After placement of the stitches through the phrenoesophageal ligament and the diaphragm, the Penrose drain is passed through the esophageal hiatus and down into the peritoneal cavity and passed out into the chest again through the counterincision in the diaphragm. Tension is placed on the Penrose drain; the esophagogastric junction which has been encircled by the rubber drain is readily pulled through the esophageal crura so that it now lies beneath the diaphragm. The stitches through the phrenoesophageal ligament and diaphragm are now tied securely. Tension on the Penrose drain is then relaxed and the esophagogastric junction will be seen to lie firmly and securely in place below the diaphragm.

    The crural sutures are tied now if this has not already been done. These should not be tied tightly as they will cause muscle necrosis and in time will cut through the crural fibers, which could lead to recurrence of the hernia. After the posterior crural sutures have been tied, the esophageal hiatus should admit the tip of the index finger posteriorly to the level of the distal interphalangeal joint.

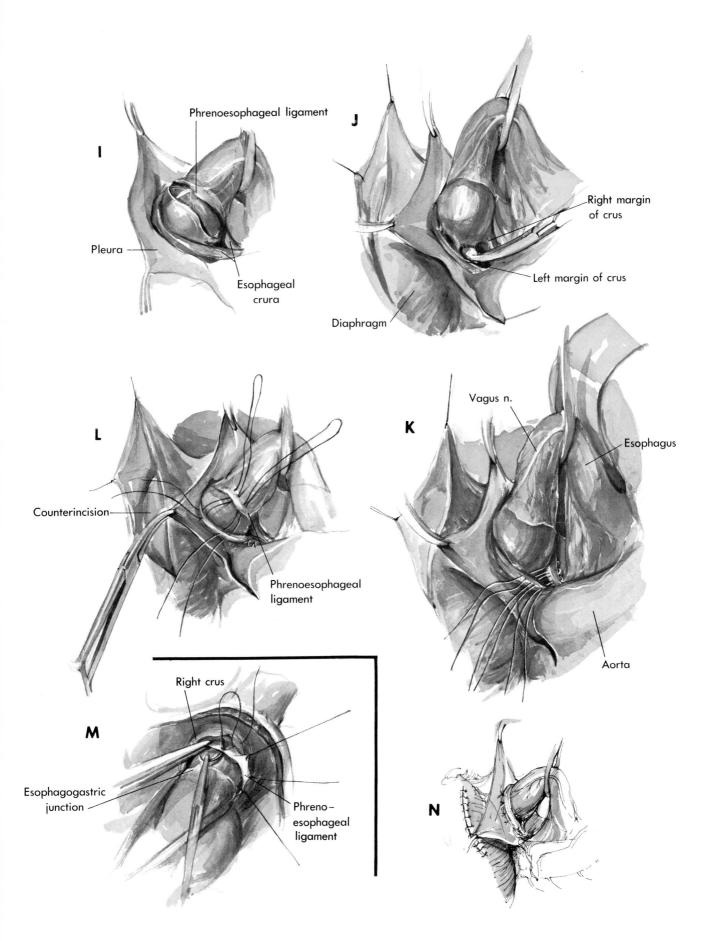

I

Phrenoesophageal ligament

Pleura

Esophageal crura

J

Right margin of crus

Left margin of crus

Diaphragm

L

Counterincision

Phrenoesophageal ligament

K

Vagus n.

Esophagus

Aorta

M

Right crus

Esophagogastric junction

Phreno-esophageal ligament

N

M   On a few occasions it is possible to gain considerable exposure and vision through the counterincision in the diaphragm. In such instances the phrenoesophageal ligament can be stitched to the undersurface of the esophageal crura under direct vision with simple interrupted stitches of 2-0 silk. If regurgitation has been a serious problem, two or three sutures uniting the left lateral terminal esophagus to the medial aspect of the gastric fundus will change the angle of entry and help to correct the problem.

N   The counterincision in the diaphragm is then closed with interrupted figure-of-eight stitches of 2-0 black silk. One must be careful to include both the peritoneal and pleural surfaces of the diaphragm in the stitch. Iatrogenic diaphragmatic hernia can occur through the counterincision so it must be closed carefully. A second row of stitches is used for this closure to insure against disruption of this suture line. The area of dissection is carefully inspected to make certain all bleeding points have been ligated. The excess pleura shown here is trimmed at this time. A single No. 28 chest catheter is introduced intercostally just above the diaphragm and placed so that it lies adjacent to the area of lower esophageal dissection. The chest is closed in an appropriate manner.

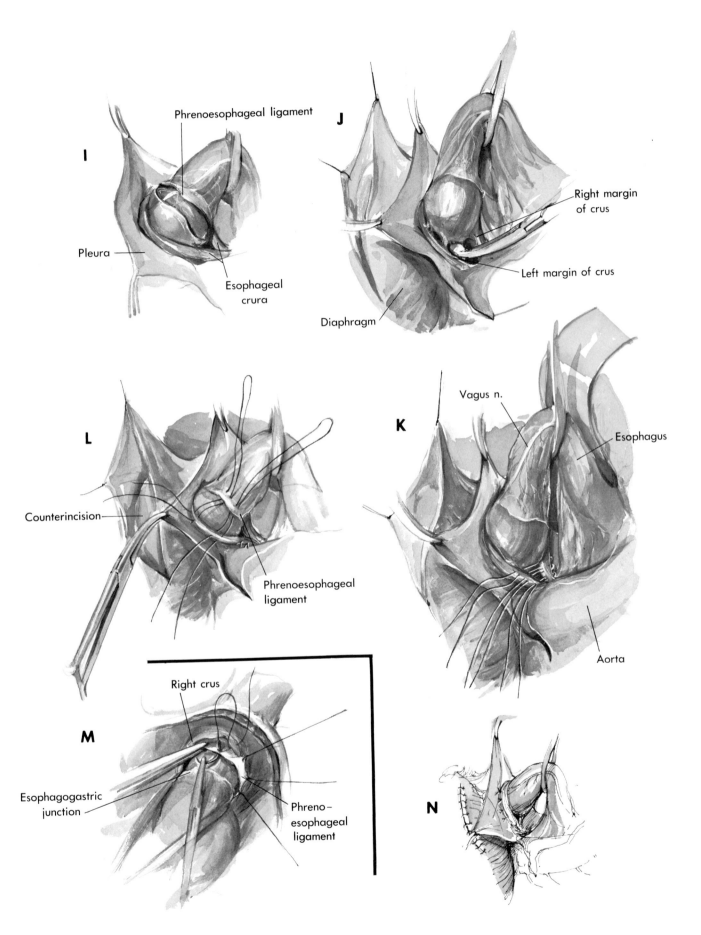

I

Phrenoesophageal ligament

Pleura

Esophageal crura

J

Right margin of crus

Left margin of crus

Diaphragm

L

Counterincision

Phrenoesophageal ligament

K

Vagus n.

Esophagus

Aorta

M

Right crus

Esophagogastric junction

Phreno-esophageal ligament

N

Hiatal Herniorrhaphy, Transabdominal

Regardless of the route used to repair an esophageal hiatus hernia, it is vital that the surgeon be thoroughly familiar with the anatomy of this area both below and above the diaphragm. Although one route may be preferred and used more commonly, it is necessary to be versatile so as to be able to apply the technique necessary to fit the circumstances of the case.

The abdominal approach is more difficult and less effective in obese patients in whom developing and maintaining the proper exposure can be a trial. Lysis of adhesions from previous upper abdominal surgery may consume an inordinate amount of time and will certainly result in a greater loss of blood. Most patients who have a recurrence from a previous transabdominal repair should have the recurrence treated by the thoracic route. Proceeding through the abdomen again to dissect free the previous abdominal repair constitutes a difficult if not a hazardous operation and may not leave the surgeon with properly identifiable tissue. In elderly patients with emphysema or other causes of compromised pulmonary reserve, the abdominal approach may result in fewer postoperative respiratory difficulties.

The abdominal approach naturally allows the surgeon to explore the peritoneal cavity for unsuspected or unrelated problems or to evaluate and correct known and related disease, which occurs in as many as 40 per cent of patients. The most commonly associated problems are duodenal ulcer, cholecystitis and cholelithiasis, all of which can be taken care of during this time electively or as a necessary part of the operation. The colonic diverticulitis which also occurs with considerable regularity in these patients is rarely corrected at this time.

A   This illustration is a coronal cut through the hernia to demonstrate its component parts and relationships. The pouch of peritoneum that comprises an esophageal hiatus hernia is in front and to the right of the stomach. Notice that the anterior wall of the cardia of the stomach comprises the posterior wall of the hernial sac. The esophagogastric junction is, of course, located a variable distance from the esophageal hiatus, just as the latter may be widened minimally or to the point of severe attenuation of the crural fibers.

The transversalis fascia of the abdominal cavity and the mediastinal fascia from the thorax fuse at the esophageal hiatus to become the phrenoesophageal ligament which is attached to the esophagus. Use of this ligament is an integral part of most types of repair. Although it is an anatomic entity and the use of it in the repair is conceptually sound, it often is severely attenuated or difficult to identify from the mediastinal pleura. The latter can usually be easily separated from it, as is shown in the plates on transthoracic repair. Prolonged and severe esophagitis may fuse the phrenoesophageal ligament and mediastinal pleura so that they cannot be separated.

B   A long left paramedian rectus muscle reflecting incision is used and carried to the side of the xiphoid process which can be excised with impunity if it is large and in the way. A midline incision is as adequate, and both will allow for ample exposure for the performance of any associated operation.

The first step in gaining exposure of the esophagogastric junction is mobilization of the left lobe of the liver. The left lobe is retracted toward the patient's right, and the thin avascular triangular ligament of this lobe is incised to just short of the inferior vena cava. The medial portion of the left lobe is then folded dorsally on itself and laparotomy pads placed over it; it is held in this position with a Deaver retractor. If the left lobe is too thick for such folding or extends too far to the left, it can be retracted cephalad with a large Harrington retractor; this is broader than a Deaver, not flexible, its edges are less sharp and the handle is better suited for prolonged and comfortable retraction. It is well suited for exposing this area for other procedures such as vagotomy. Notice the inferior phrenic vein which courses more ventral to the left triangular ligament and can easily be avoided.

C
D   With gentle traction on the stomach a sufficient portion of the hernial sac will present itself so that it can be grasped with Babcock forceps and delivered in its entirety into the peritoneal cavity. The esophagogastric junction will perforce have been delivered below the esophageal hiatus. The peritoneum over the esophagogastric junction is then cut transversely with scissors.

Page 184

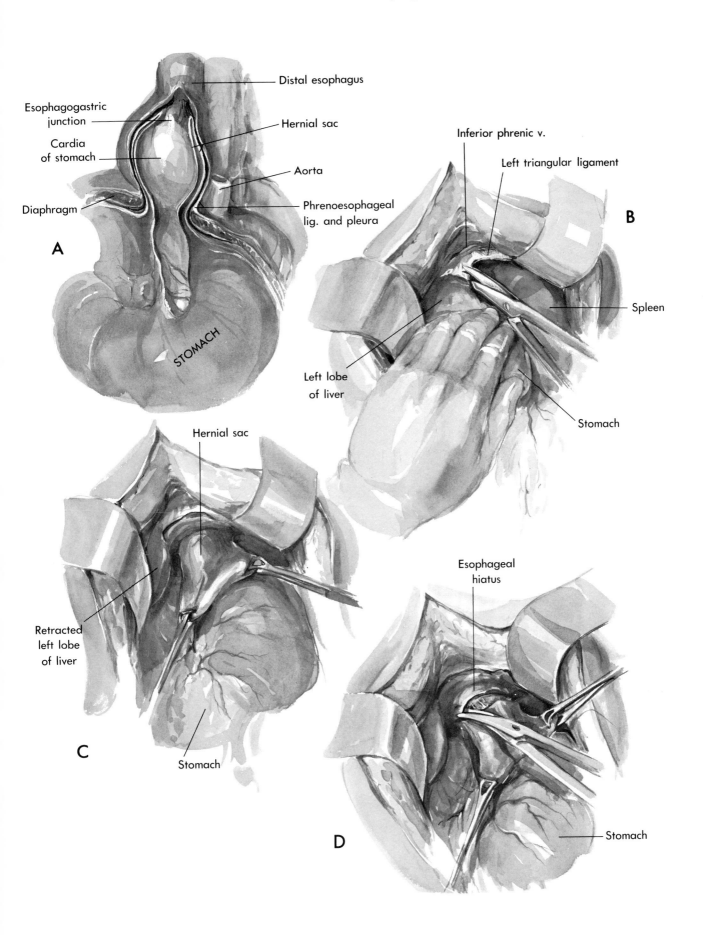

A

Distal esophagus

Esophagogastric junction

Hernial sac

Cardia of stomach

Aorta

Diaphragm

Phrenoesophageal lig. and pleura

STOMACH

B

Inferior phrenic v.

Left triangular ligament

Spleen

Left lobe of liver

Stomach

C

Hernial sac

Retracted left lobe of liver

Stomach

D

Esophageal hiatus

Stomach

Hiatal Herniorrhaphy, Transabdominal (continued)

E   The left index finger is used to encircle the esophagus; through this opening a small rubber drain is passed and used for traction. All of any remaining peritoneum is divided and the traction is sustained; the esophagogastric junction can be made to migrate 3 to 5 cm. below the esophageal hiatus in the diaphragm.

F   Esophagitis, high gastric acid secretion and current or quiescent duodenal ulcer are some of the reasons for choosing to perform a vagotomy and an emptying procedure at this time. The vagi are easily located and isolated. Several silver clips are placed distally and proximally and an intervening segment excised.

G   The crura must next be identified and prepared for approximation. The esophagogastric junction is severely displaced to the left, bringing into view the right margin of the hiatus. Sutures will readily cut through muscle only, especially the thinner right marginal fibers; it is therefore advisable not to clear the crura too thoroughly so that the muscle fibers can be buttressed by the peritoneum which is included in the bite of the needle.

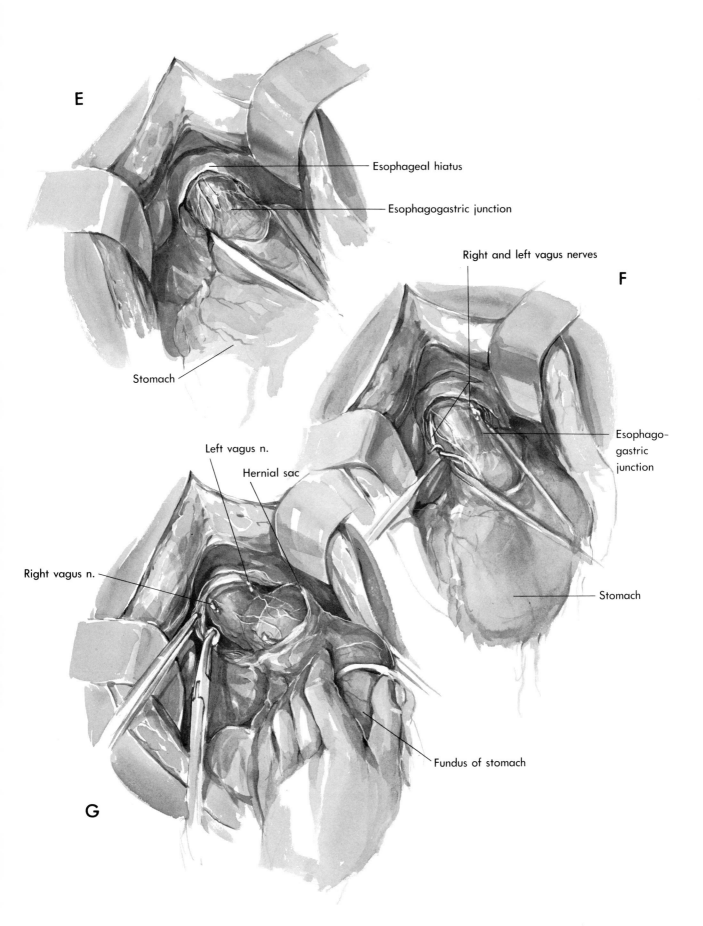

E

Esophageal hiatus

Esophagogastric junction

Stomach

Right and left vagus nerves

F

Esophago-gastric junction

Stomach

Left vagus n.

Hernial sac

Right vagus n.

Fundus of stomach

G

H   This illustration shows the operative area denuded of peritoneum and fatty tissue and with the stomach and liver omitted. The esophageal hiatus is in the shape of an inverted tear-drop. The rounded margin is located anteriorly, with the acutely angled margin located posteriorly; this is the "weak" area wherein the crural fibers must be approximated. The esophageal hiatus is almost always comprised of fibers from the right crus, those of the left margin usually being thicker than those of the right. Notice how the muscle fibers of the right crus are arranged as a sling as they form the esophageal hiatus.

I

J   Three or four stitches of zero silk are usually sufficient for repair of the hiatus which, after correction, should allow the index finger to pass easily next to the esophagus. The heavy silk is definitely preferred over fine silk, which will cut through the muscle fibers more easily. The surgeon should be cognizant of the nearby inferior vena cava during placement of these stitches. For exceptionally lax crural fibers it may be necessary to place one or two stitches anteriorly to take up the slack. However, the purchase on this tissue is poor when attempting to effect a repair in this fashion so that we attempt to carry out the repair entirely posteriorly. A recent modification has been to suture with several stitches the lesser curvature of the stomach distal to the cardia to the fascia over the crura and the descending aorta. The lesser curvature of the stomach has touch fascial tissue which, if anchored below the esophageal hiatus, is further insurance against recurrence of the hernia.

K   If the phrenoesophageal ligament can be identified as such, its available free edge is anchored to the crural fibers.

L   Several additional maneuvers may add to the benefits of the repair. One is to reconstruct the acute esophagogastric angle by placing several stitches of 3-0 silk between the cardia of the stomach and the adjacent esophagus. In addition, the cardia is attached to the undersurface of the diaphragm with similar suture material. The area is not reperitonealized. If there is associated intra-abdominal disease to be corrected it is done next. A pyloroplasty or gastrojejunostomy, whichever the surgeon chooses, is done in the usual manner. Because of the possible prolonged gastric atony secondary to the vagotomy, a gastrostomy is performed and the tube is exteriorized through a counter-incision in the left hypochondrium. The abdominal incision is closed in the usual manner.

   Postoperatively oral intake is witheld until peristalsis returns and until there is no evidence of gastric retention. The patient may experience difficulty in swallowing food for a while, but this should not be too disconcerting and most likely is due to edema about the crura, or swelling about an esophagitis not yet completely subsided. If the repair was done properly this should subside within a few weeks. Before being discharged, the patient should have an examination of the esophagus and stomach with barium to evaluate the repair and to serve as a basis for comparison should some symptoms persist or recur.

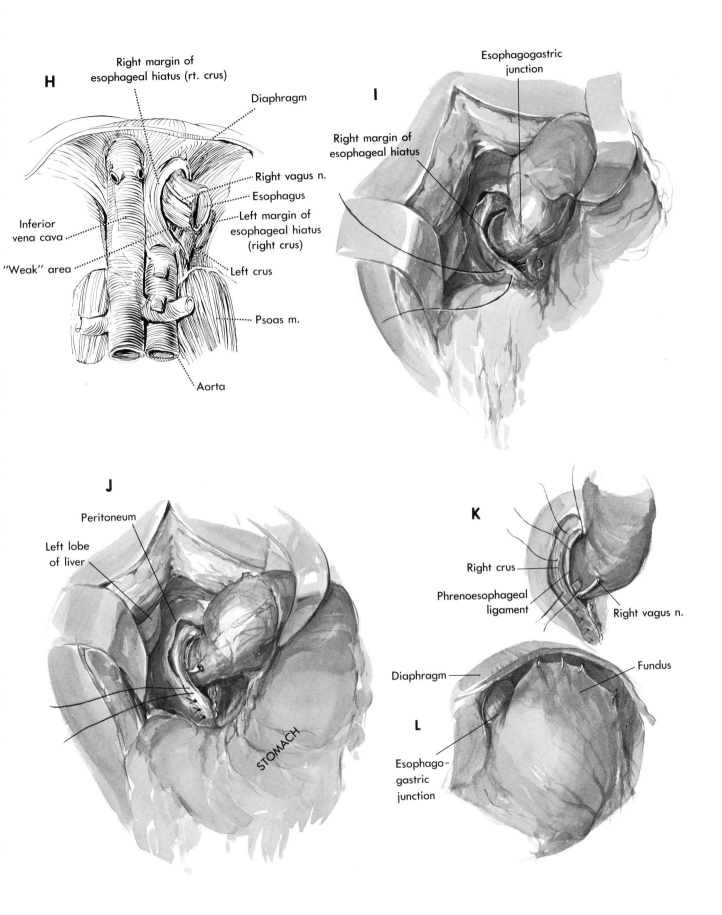

H

Right margin of esophageal hiatus (rt. crus)

Diaphragm

Right vagus n.

Esophagus

Left margin of esophageal hiatus (right crus)

Left crus

Inferior vena cava

"Weak" area

Psoas m.

Aorta

I

Esophagogastric junction

Right margin of esophageal hiatus

J

Peritoneum

Left lobe of liver

STOMACH

K

Right crus

Phrenoesophageal ligament

Right vagus n.

L

Diaphragm

Fundus

Esophago-gastric junction

TOTAL GASTRECTOMY

Stomach cancer has been decreasing steadily in incidence in the United States, probably as a result of dietary changes in this country. This is in contrast to the situation in Japan, where 50 per cent of the males and 33 per cent of the females who develop cancer suffer from gastric cancer. Adults in the United States have less gastric carcinoma, but they have an increased incidence of colonic carcinoma, probably the penalty of the richer diet of a more affluent society. Modern civilization is accompanied by a high incidence of peptic ulcer and its attendant problems, but the surgical treatment of peptic ulcer seldom requires a total or near total gastrectomy. The patient bleeding to death from multiple gastric "stress" ulcers usually would not be helped by a total gastrectomy. Operable gastric carcinoma, however, calls for radical surgery.

There is a long list of distinguished European and American surgeons who have made significant contributions to the refinement of gastric surgery for carcinoma. They are too many to list, but the references for this section note the most prominent contributions. Brunschwig was among the first to recommend not only a radical resection of the stomach to the esophagus and duodenum but also to resect radically at the lesser and greater curvatures.

The stomach is a hollow viscus which initiates the process of digestion. Food arrives from the mouth mixed with saliva which contains ptyalin, a starch splitting enzyme. Between the esophagus, which is primarily a conduit, and the stomach, is a sphincter, the cardia. A low pressure of 10 cm. of water on the esophageal side will open the cardia, but 30 to 40 cm. of water pressure are needed on the gastric side to permit reflux. In benign lesions this sphincter should be preserved. The stomach produces hydrochloric acid from its parietal cells and proteolytic enzymes from its chief cells. Hydrochloric acid is an excellent germicide and, normally, the gastric contents leaving the stomach are sterile. In the absence of gastric hydrochloric acid (as is frequently seen in carcinoma), bacteria can proliferate and may seriously contaminate the operative field during gastric surgery.

At the distal end of the stomach is the pylorus. This, too, is a valve; it opens to permit the acidified gastric contents to enter the alkaline duodenum. This valve tends to prevent reflux. The duodenum is subject to acid digestion, as is the jejunum. The colon is resistant to acid digestion and is thus useful for upper gastrointestinal reconstruction. The secretion of hydrochloric acid by the stomach is under central nervous system control via the vagus nerves. Hydrochloric acid is also stimulated mechanically by the presence of food in the antrum of the stomach. This explains why antrectomy is valuable in ulcer control and why leaving the antrum in an antral exclusion operation is highly undesirable. Hydrochloric acid in the duodenum stimulates the release of the hormone secretin by the duodenum. Secretin, in turn, stimulates pancreatic secretion.

Cancer of the stomach is an insidious disease usually diagnosed late. It is commoner in patients with hypochlorhydria. Any patient with hypochlorhydria should have an upper gastrointestinal series of x-rays every six months. Any patient with persistent dyspepsia should be suspect. After the usual history, physical examination and collection of laboratory data, an upper gastrointestinal series should be done. A gastric ulcer that does not heal completely after a few weeks of medical treatment should be considered possible carcinoma. Gastric cytology and gastroscopy may confirm the diagnosis prior to operation. If the diagnosis is not known, an exploratory laparotomy is indicated. Frequently biopsy of a lymph node will be positive for carcinoma. If there is no extragastric spread and the lesion is doubtful, an excisional biopsy of the lesion can be taken. If the diagnosis is positive for gastric carcinoma and the lesion is removable in a good risk patient, radical surgery is indicated.

It should be remembered that gastric cancer can cross the cardia and can also cross the pylorus. Along the greater curvature the omentum and spleen should be removed. Any adherent viscera such as colon, small intestine and pancreas can also be removed en bloc. On the lesser curvature the celiac axis should be dissected clear. The left gastric and splenic arteries can be removed, but the hepatic artery should be spared. The mesentery of the stomach and the left lobe of the liver can be removed.

Usually the duodenal stump can be closed. If its closure is insecure, a catheter should be left as a drain in the duodenum. The exposure of the esophagus may require a thoracic extension of the incision. The jejunum as a Roux-en-Y is the usual form of anastomosis to the esophagus. A pouch created by a loop of jejunum of some length with an enteroenterostomy may help to prevent the dumping syndrome.

The best results after a total gastrectomy come from prevention of oral intake for two weeks, decompression of the new stomach and maintenance of nutrition by a distal feeding jejunostomy.

Since patients with gastric carcinoma tend to be in poor nutritional status, careful fluid balance with measurement of serum electrolytes preoperatively and every two days postoperatively is in order. In the patient without gastric hydrochloric acid, consideration of bowel preparation is in order; especially careful surgical technique to avoid contamination is valuable.

References

Brunschwig, A.: Radical surgery for gastric cancer. J. Nat. Cancer Inst. 5:365, 1945.

Brunschwig, A.: Radical resections of advanced intra-abdominal cancer. Summary of results in 100 patients. Am. Surgeon *122*:923, 1945.

Billroth, T.: Ueber einen neuen Fall von gelungener Resektion des carcinomatösen Pylorus. Wien. med. Wchnschr. *31*:1427, 1881. (Billroth I.)

Billroth, T.: Zur Casuistik und Statistik der Magenresektionen und Gastroenterostomieen. Arch. klin. Chir. *32*:616, 1885. (Billroth II.)

Graham, R. R.: A technique for total gastrectomy. Surgery 8:257, 1940.

Lahey, F. H.: Complete removal of the stomach for malignancy, with a report of five surgically successful cases. Surg. Gynec. & Obst. 67:213, 1938.

Meyer, H. W.: Intrathoracic esophagojejunostomy for total gastrectomy with lower esophagectomy for carcinoma. Surgery 12:115, 1942.

Mikulicz-Radecki, J. von.: Zur operativen Behandlung der Pylorusstenose. Chirurgenkongress, 1887. (Pyloroplasty.)

Paine, J. R., and Wangensteen, O. H.: The necessity for constant suction to inlying nasal tubes for effectual decompression or drainage of upper gastro-intestinal tract; with comments upon drainage of other body cavities. Surg. Gynec. & Obst. 57:601, 1933.

Pean, J. E.: De l'ablation des tumeurs de l'estomoc par la gastrectomie. Gaz. d. hôp. 52:473, 1879.

Petz, A. de.: Aseptic technique of stomach resections. Ann. Surg. 86:385, 1927.

Polya, E. A.: Zur Stumpfversorgung nach Magenresektion. Zentralbl. Chir. 38:892, 1911.

Schlatter, C.: Ueber Ernaehrung und Verdauung nach vollstaendiger Entfernung des Magens-Oesophagoenterostomie beim Menschen. Beit. klin. Chir. *19*:757. (Total gastrectomy.)

Total Gastrectomy

A
B

The blood supply to the stomach is abundant. Lymph nodes also abound in this area and can be found in intimate proximity to adjoining organs or to the vessels supplying them. Performing a total gastrectomy is a major operation, but to do so for cancer of the stomach means the aggressive but careful and methodical removal of these nodal deposits — an obligation requiring technical skill and thorough knowledge of the anatomy of this area if the operation is to be done properly.

In these two illustrations the liver, greater and lesser omenta and peritoneum have been removed for greater anatomic clarity. The blood supply to the stomach is derived from the right gastric artery, which branches off the hepatic artery and courses along the lesser curvature of the stomach to meet the left gastric artery given off at the celiac axis.

The right gastroepiploic artery, a branch of the gastroduodenal artery, courses along the greater curvature of the stomach to meet with the left gastroepiploic artery, which is a branch of the splenic artery. In addition, the stomach receives the short gastric branches from the splenic artery.

The venous drainage of the stomach is into the portal venous system. The coronary vein, to be found along the lesser curvature of the stomach, and the pyloric vein empty separately into the portal vein. The right gastroepiploic vein empties into the superior mesenteric either directly or via the middle colic vein. The left gastroepiploic and short gastric veins drain into the splenic vein. The gastroepiploic vessels nourish the greater omentum. The intimate relationship of the splenic and omental vessels to those of the stomach dictates the need to routinely excise the omentum and usually the spleen in the performance of a gastrectomy for cancer.

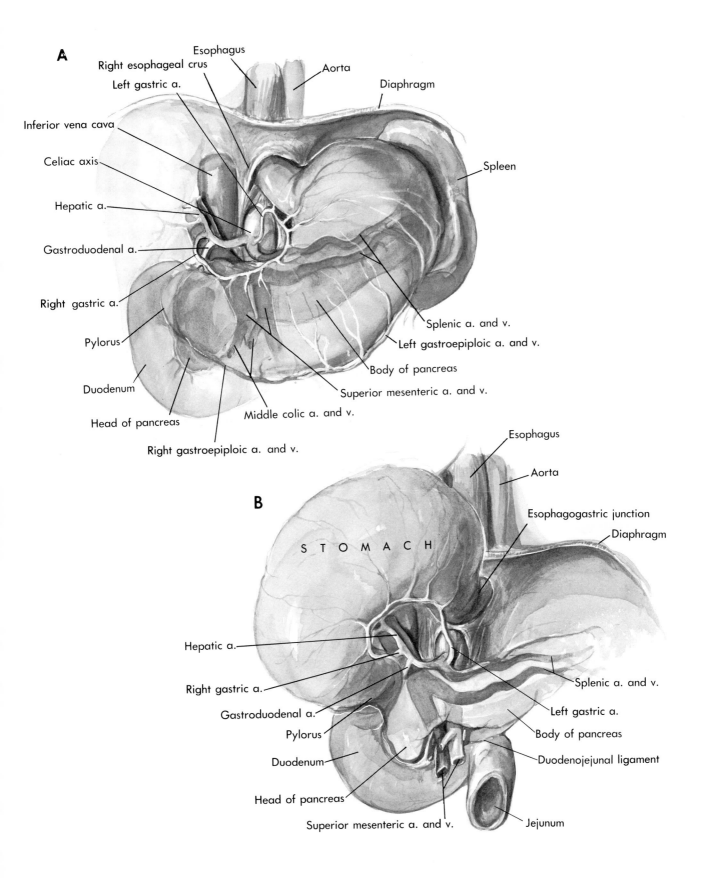

A

Esophagus
Right esophageal crus
Left gastric a.
Aorta
Diaphragm
Inferior vena cava
Celiac axis
Spleen
Hepatic a.
Gastroduodenal a.
Right gastric a.
Splenic a. and v.
Pylorus
Left gastroepiploic a. and v.
Duodenum
Body of pancreas
Head of pancreas
Superior mesenteric a. and v.
Middle colic a. and v.
Right gastroepiploic a. and v.

B

Esophagus
Aorta
Esophagogastric junction
Diaphragm
STOMACH
Hepatic a.
Right gastric a.
Splenic a. and v.
Gastroduodenal a.
Left gastric a.
Pylorus
Body of pancreas
Duodenum
Duodenojejunal ligament
Head of pancreas
Superior mesenteric a. and v.
Jejunum

Total Gastrectomy (continued)

C
C₁
General anesthesia is administered by endotracheal intubation and the patient placed in the supine position. If the surgeon is certain of a thoracoabdominal approach, the patient is tilted slightly to the right. The left arm is protected with padding and folded over the face and incorporated with the anesthesia screen. The right arm remains at the side and into it is placed a venous catheter of large caliber. The entire anterior abdomen and thorax are prepared, delineated with towels and covered with an adhesive transparant plastic drape. Figure C₁ depicts the several incisions that may be used. The transverse incision (a) is the least desirable. It takes longer to open and close, the exposure is usually not so ample as with other incisions, and it is awkward to extend into the thorax. The oblique incision (b) extends into the thorax easily and naturally but, as with the transverse, takes longer to establish and to close.

In any case, only the abdomen should be opened first, and we prefer a left paramedian or midline incision (c, d). The latter is swift and simple to make and virtually bloodless. It is expected that this midline incision will be closed with through-and-through nylon stitches, the linea alba being approximated with a continuous stitch of 1-0 or zero chromic catgut. Although such a closure is cruder than the others, and is followed by a higher incidence of ventral herniation, its advantages overcome these drawbacks. It seems reasonable not to spend the inordinate amount of time necessary to make and close the transverse and oblique incisions but to put this time to better use toward the intent of this already long operation. That oblique or transverse incisions close more firmly and do not lend themselves to evisceration can be countered by the knowledge that evisceration almost cannot occur in midline incisions closed as described, even in these debilitated patients. A realistic acceptance of the present cure rate following gastrectomy for cancer will indicate that not many patients are likely to complain of a ventral hernia if it should happen to occur.

D
On opening the peritoneal cavity, note is made of any excess free fluid. A methodical exploration of the peritoneal cavity is carried out, with the search being more diligent in areas prone to metastases. Distant metastases to the liver and drop metastases to the pelvis indicate incurability, whereas involvement of the transverse colon or the pancreas, especially the body or tail, lend themselves to a curative en bloc removal with the stomach. The gastrohepatic ligament and the retroduodenal area are common sites of lymph node involvement, as would be expected because of the presence in this area of vessels to or from the stomach. The stomach is evaluated last. Metastases do not, of course, preclude resection of the involved portion of the stomach for present or anticipated signs and symptoms of obstruction, but they eliminate the need to remove regional nodes or adjacent organs. Involvement of the lower half of the stomach can usually be handled adequately entirely through the abdomen. Higher lesions require the wide exposure and deliberate dissection which can be carried out best through a thoracoabdominal incision.

If the decision is for a wider exposure, the incision is angled toward the left over the 9th interspace. For an even wider exposure and elimination as well of the postoperative pain of any rib fracture, the incision is carried over the 9th rib with the intention of removing it subperiosteally. The costal cartilage is cut across in the indicated V-shape or is fashioned in this manner during the closure. This stabilizes the reunited ends and eliminates the annoying clicking often experienced when the cartilaginous cut is smooth and in a single plane.

E
E₁
Sometimes just division of the costal arch without entry into the pleural cavity will produce the necessary added exposure. The placement of the diaphragmatic incision is dictated by distribution of the phrenic nerve. Within the thorax the phrenic nerve descends laterally between the pericardium and mediastinal pleura, penetrates the diaphragm and sends branches posteriorly as sweeping arcs. An incision of the diaphragm must avoid these branches so that the incision usually used approaches the esophagus in a wide sweep in order to avoid them (dotted line, Figure E₁). An alternate method is to stay inside the main trunk of the nerve as is shown in Figure E₁. If this method is to be used the nerve and the accompanying pericardiophrenic artery must be separated for a considerable distance proximally so that as the diaphragmatic incision is made the nerve will follow laterally rather than be stretched and rendered ineffective. A separate thoracotomy can also be made. This has the advantage of leaving the costal arch intact, but the exposure is not quite so wide.

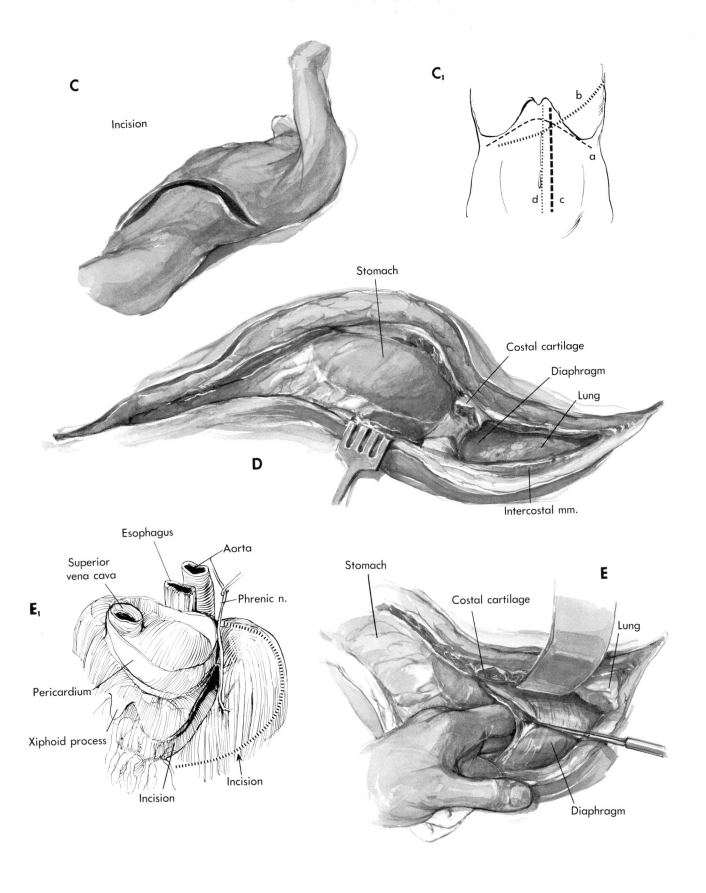

C

Incision

C₁

b

a

d   c

Stomach

Costal cartilage

Diaphragm

Lung

D

Intercostal mm.

Esophagus

Aorta

Superior
vena cava

Phrenic n.

E₁

Pericardium

Xiphoid process

Incision

Incision

Stomach

Costal cartilage

E

Lung

Diaphragm

F
G
As the diaphragm is incised, bleeding points are clamped with hemostats and secured with figure-of-eight transfixion stitches using 3-0 silk. The chest wall spreader is positioned and opened as the diaphragm is cut to permit this. The incision is carried through the esophageal crus and a medium soft Penrose drain placed around the esophagogastric junction.

H
The vagi are isolated several centimeters proximal to the esophagogastric junction and divided; the proximal trunks are ligated with 3-0 silk.

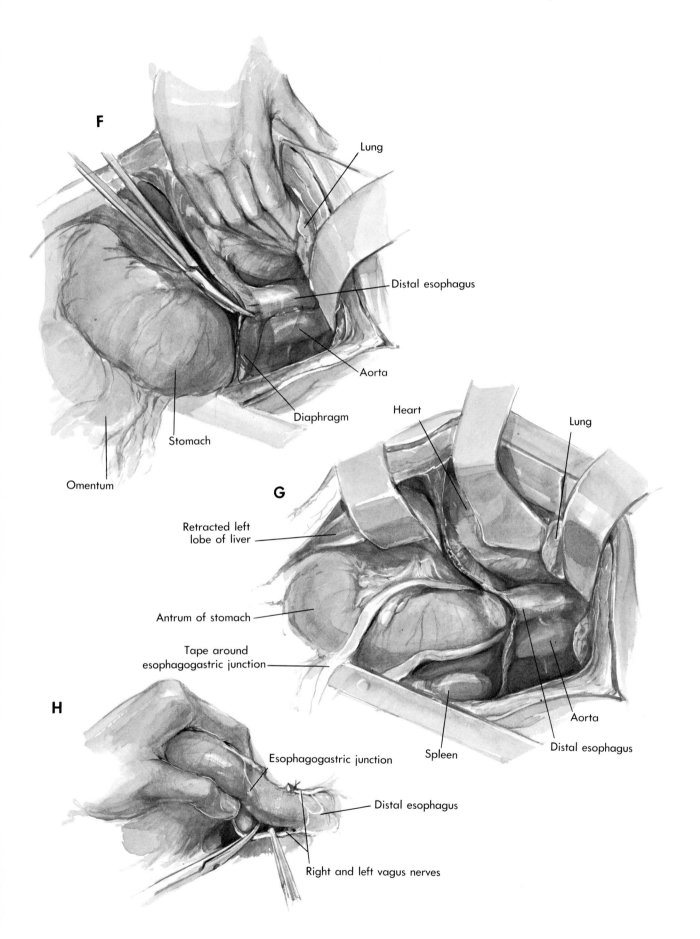

F

Lung

Distal esophagus

Aorta

Diaphragm

Stomach

Omentum

Heart

Lung

G

Retracted left
lobe of liver

Antrum of stomach

Tape around
esophagogastric junction

Aorta

Distal esophagus

Spleen

H

Esophagogastric junction

Distal esophagus

Right and left vagus nerves

I   The soft Penrose drain is used to lift the terminal esophagus while its dorsal surface is dissected of fatty areolar tissue and any associated lymph nodes. The esophagus, in contrast to the remainder of the intestinal tract down to the rectum, lacks a serosa and so does not hold stitches well. For this reason, anastomoses between the esophagus and another portion of the intestine are plagued with a greater incidence of suture line disruption and leakage. With this reality in mind, a total gastrectomy should be done for sufficient reason and not as a fetish. Often, if the stomach in this area is not involved, or if the esophagogastric area can be dissected cleanly with assurance, it may seem reasonable to leave a very small cuff of stomach behind. The improved integrity of a subsequent anastomosis to this cuff containing serosa may, in carefully selected and evaluated cases, greatly overcome the apparent drawback of the less radical resection.

J
K
L   A splenectomy is indicated and performed for all but limited antral lesions. The spleen is mobilized from any of its lateral attachments and along with the tail of the pancreas is rotated medially. The splenic artery and then the vein are isolated just off the tail of the pancreas so as to allow resection of the splenic artery and a maximal amount of splenic hilum; they are then clamped, cut and ligated with 2-0 silk. In Figure K the vessels are shown clamped, cut and ready for ligation. An alternate technique would ligate the vessels, achieve hemostasis, and divide the vessels without using clamps. Figure L shows division of the splenocolic ligament. The spleen now remains attached to the stomach by the short gastric vessels.

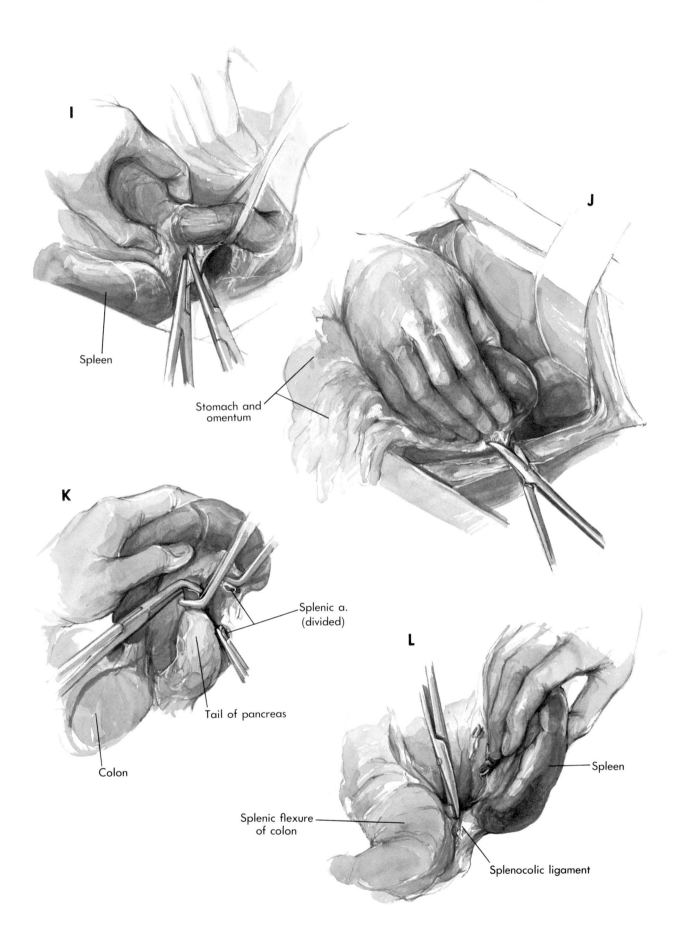

I

Spleen

Stomach and
omentum

J

K

Splenic a.
(divided)

Tail of pancreas

Colon

L

Spleen

Splenic flexure
of colon

Splenocolic ligament

M   In the introductory plates it was pointed out that the blood supply to the greater omentum is derived from the right and left gastroepiploic vessels. It is necessary, therefore, that the greater omentum be removed in its entirety when performing a total gastrectomy. If one stays close to the colon during this dissection it can be done swiftly and with minimal loss of blood. One should identify the colon blood supply and, of course, avoid it.

N   When the whole of the greater omentum has been freed it is swung cephalad and with a Mixter forceps the right gastroepiploic artery is isolated at its origin from the gastroduodenal artery, clamped and divided and ligated with 2-0 silk.

O   The duodenum is freed from any underlying pancreatic tissue, two small Payr clamps are placed across the selected site and the duodenum is divided with a scalpel. By use of the clamp on the stomach side as a handle, the stomach is reflected upward and medially. The fatty areolar lymph node bearing tissue located in this retroduodenal area is freed so that it can be removed with the stomach.

P   The duodenum is closed at this time. A horizontal mattress stitch of 3-0 chromic cat-
P₁ gut is applied under the clamp. Any excess tissue superficial to the Payr clamp is excised and the clamp removed. In Figure P₁ the corner of the duodenum is being inverted; this is repeated at the other end. The duodenal closure is completed with interrupted stitches of 3-0 silk through the seromuscularis.

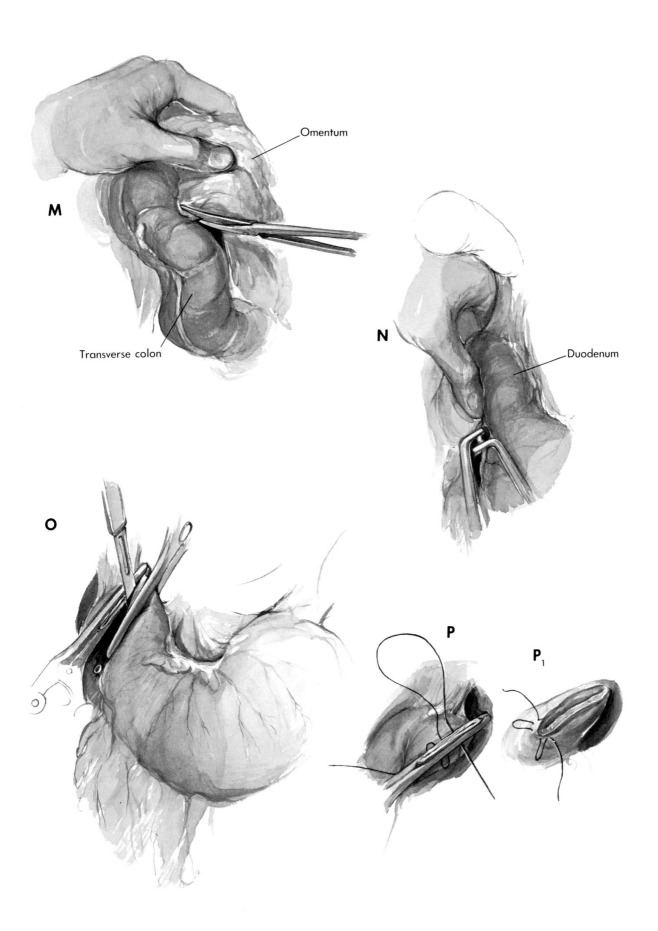

M

Omentum

Transverse colon

N

Duodenum

O

P

P₁

Q
R The right gastric artery is divided at its origin from the hepatic artery. One method is to identify and isolate it with the stomach and duodenum in their natural position as depicted in Figure Q. Simple ligation of this vessel has, on several occasions, led to secondary hemorrhage, presumably from digestion of the vessel distal to the ligature by pancreatic enzymes in this area, incidental to the retropancreatic and retroduodenal dissection. As a precaution, this vessel is occluded with a Potts clamp and oversewn with 5-0 arterial silk (Figure R).

S It has been demonstrated in "second-look" operations performed on patients having a curative gastrectomy for cancer that the gastrohepatic omentum is a common site of residual cancer. This and the retropancreatic area are often either ignored or not dissected thoroughly in the usual gastrectomy for cancer. Unfortunately, they are the most difficult areas to dissect. This combination of abundant nodal deposits, early nodal involvement and relative difficulty of dissection combine to defeat a curative gastrectomy if the surgeon is not methodical and thorough in dissecting this area. The hepatic artery has been cleaned of surrounding tissue and the dissection proceeds cephalad, remaining close to the liver and sweeping the tissue medially, at which point the left gastric artery is divided. Next the celiac axis is dissected clear of lymph node tissue as thoroughly as possible.

T This illustration depicts a method of isolating and dividing the right gastric artery from behind the stomach while it is reflected cephalad and toward the patient's right. This may be necessary when one wishes to gain access to the artery without cutting through a thick gastrohepatic omentum or any one portion of it containing involved lymph nodes.

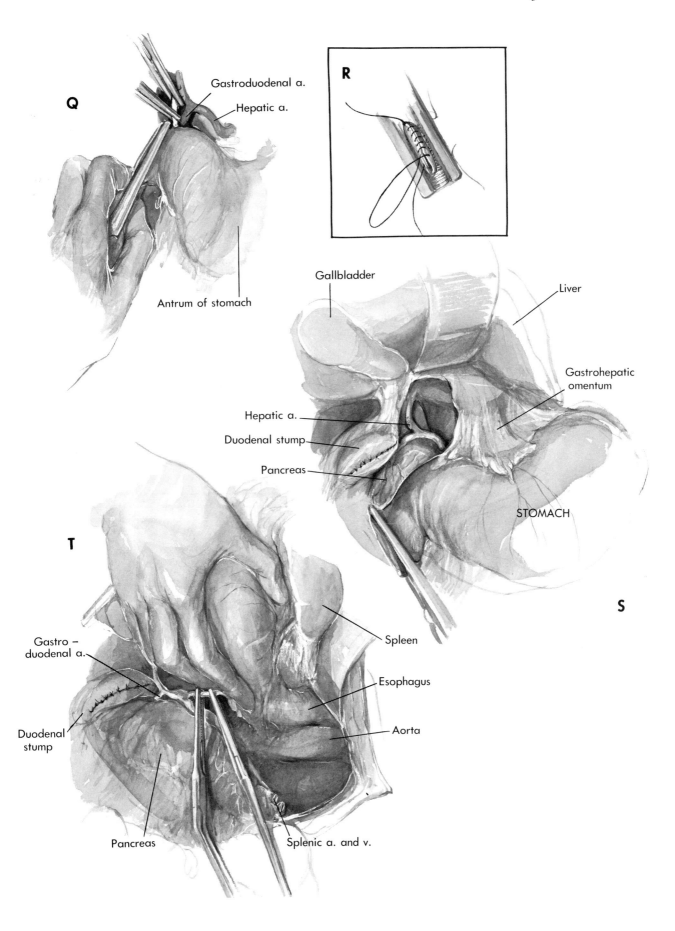

Q

Gastroduodenal a.

Hepatic a.

Antrum of stomach

R

Gallbladder

Liver

Gastrohepatic omentum

Hepatic a.

Duodenal stump

Pancreas

STOMACH

S

T

Gastro – duodenal a.

Duodenal stump

Pancreas

Spleen

Esophagus

Aorta

Splenic a. and v.

U   The artist's vantage point has shifted so that it now is on the patient's right side. With dissection of the gastrohepatic omentum and celiac axis, the stomach remains attached only by the esophagus. The stomach is used as a tractor and to stabilize the esophagus for the anastomosis. A window is made in an avascular area of the transverse colon, and a loop of jejunum (as close as possible to the ligament of Treitz but without tension) is brought through this window. The anastomosis between the muscularis of the esophagus and the seromuscular layer of the jejunum is made with atraumatic 3-0 silk. The two anchoring stitches are placed first.

V   The anastomosis is made in three layers if at all possible. The first and outer one is
W   made with interrupted simple stitches. Figure V shows the needle transversing the
X   longitudinal esophageal muscle fibers in an oblique manner. We believe this is probably less conducive to stitches cutting through the esophageal musculature than longitudinal stitches and less devitalizing than transverse stitches. With a No. 15 scalpel blade, the seromuscular tissue of the jejunum is incised about 3 mm. away from the first suture line until the submucosa and mucosa pout into the incision. The muscularis of the esophagus is incised in a similar manner. This layer is approximated with interrupted stitches of 3-0 silk.

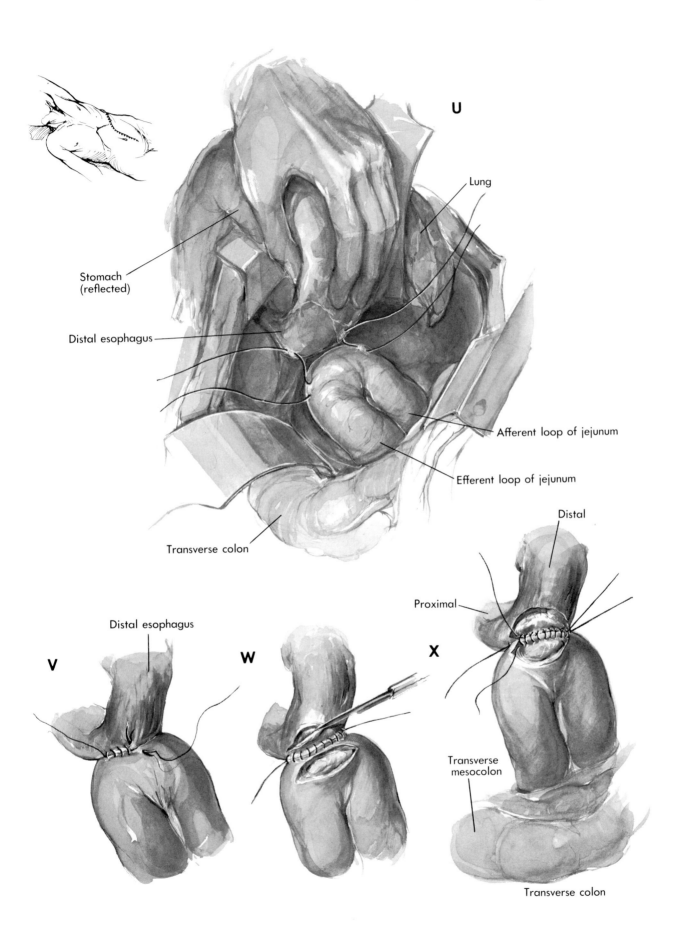

U

Lung

Stomach
(reflected)

Distal esophagus

Afferent loop of jejunum

Efferent loop of jejunum

Transverse colon

Distal

Proximal

V

Distal esophagus

W

X

Transverse
mesocolon

Transverse colon

Total Gastrectomy *(continued)*

Y to C₁

The posterior mucosal anastomosis is made with a continuous stitch of 4-0 chromic catgut. In Figure Z the specimen is amputated, and the anterior anastomosis completed as in Figure A_1. The second and third anterior layers are made with interrupted simple stitches of 4-0 silk as depicted in Figures B_1 and C_1

D to G₁

A variety of esophagojejunal anastomoses can be used, just as a variety of reservoirs can be constructed. Here the lumina of the jejunal limbs immediately adjacent to the esophagus are to be joined. In Figure D_1 the limbs are approximated for a length of 10 cm. with a continuous or interrupted seromuscular stitch using 3-0 silk. The intestine is opened as in E_1 and the mucosa approximated with a continuous stitch of 3-0 chromic catgut as in Figure F_1. After the anterior mucosal layer has been closed, the seromuscularis is approximated with interrupted stitches of 3-0 silk.

The jejunum on either side of the esophagojejunal anastomosis is anchored to the diaphragm so that the weight of the jejunum is not transmitted directly to the anastomosis. A feeding jejunostomy is made. The jejunum distal to the esophagojejunostomy should be decompressed. A nasal decompressive tube can be used or a transabdominal jejunal tube can be passed proximally.

A chest drainage tube is exteriorized on the left and attached to under-water seal drainage. The chest is closed in the usual manner. A Chaffin tube is placed next to the esophagojejunal anastomosis and exteriorized through a counterincision. Large Penrose drains from the duodenal stump and from the left subphrenic space are similarly exteriorized. If the abdominal incision has been in the midline, the closure is performed with through-and-through stitches of heavy gauge nylon with synchronous approximation of the linea alba with 1-0 chromic catgut.

The chest tube is removed by the third postoperative day when drainage has ceased. Jejunal feeding is begun with the return of peristalsis. Our results have been best when nothing is taken by mouth for 12 days. If the esophagogram is normal at this time, liquids are begun. A soft diet is started a few days later and continued for a few weeks. Careful balance of fluids and electrolytes is indicated. Hyponatremia as a result of salt restriction during the first 48 hours should be avoided. Extensive operations such as this are prone to sequester fluid in injured tissue and to present problems in management. Barring complications, most patients leave the hospital by the middle of the third postoperative week.

Page 206

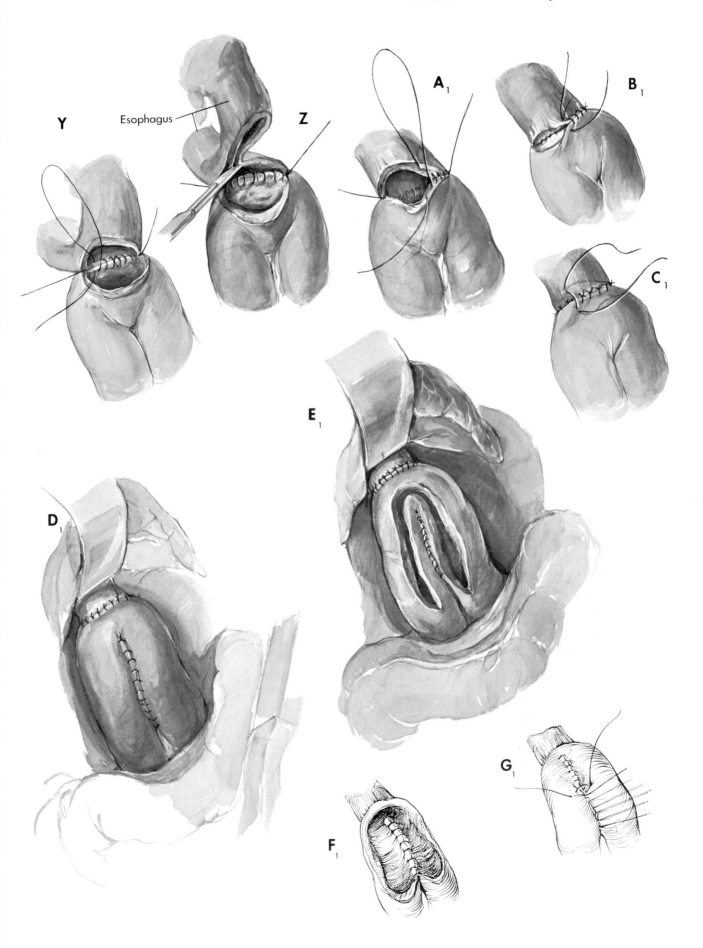

Esophagus

HEPATECTOMY

Resection of the major portions of the liver has been hazardous because of the extreme vascularity of the liver and the softness of its parenchyma. However, with surgical skill and knowledge of the liver structure, and with an anatomical approach to the hilum, a surgeon can remove large portions of the liver. The normal liver has enormous powers of regeneration. If up to 80 per cent of the liver is resected, the remaining liver over a period of weeks to months will hypertrophy to nearly its preoperative size.

Like the lung the liver has a dual blood supply. Its systemic blood supply is via the hepatic artery which, in turn, is a branch of the celiac axis. The hepatic artery lies in the left anterior portion of the gastrohepatic ligament. Normally, the hepatic artery branches into a right and left hepatic artery. A surgeon should dissect out clearly the pattern of the hepatic artery and its branches before proceeding. Interrupting the hepatic artery close to the liver parenchyma is usually fatal; however, ligation of the hepatic artery at its source may permit liver survival via collateral arteries.

The second blood supply to the liver is through the portal vein. The portal vein provides venous blood, enriched by absorbed nutriment during the processes of digestion. Each liver lobule thus receives arterial and venous blood at its periphery. The hepatic veins form from its center and drain into the inferior vena cava. There are communications in the liver between the systemic arteries and the portal veins. In cirrhosis the hepatic venous block not only obstructs the portal vein and causes portal hypertension, but the block to systemic outflow may cause the arterial blood to drain retrograde into the portal vein, with aggravation of the portal hypertension. In the normal human ligation of the portal vein is compatible with survival, but this procedure is fatal in the dog. The portal vein and its branches lie in the posterior portion of the gastrohepatic ligament.

A hepatic arteriogram and a cholangiogram permit the mapping of liver anatomy. In theory, a hepatic segmentectomy is as feasible as a lung segmentectomy. In actual fact, however, a segmentectomy of the liver presents additional problems; one is that cleavage planes between the liver segments are not discrete and are not so readily dissectible as in the lung. Additionally, a serious problem in liver segmentectomy is the hazardous configuration of the hepatic veins.

Hepatic veins tend to be short and are often large, usually numerous and without any standard anatomic pattern. Since the inferior vena cava runs in a groove on the posterior surface of the liver, the hepatic veins tend to be obscured and to lie in the liver parenchyma. One helpful anatomic feature is that the hepatic veins draining the left lobe tend to enter the inferior vena cava to the left of the midline, whereas the hepatic veins draining the right lobe tend to enter the inferior vena cava to the right of the midline.

Unfortunately, the liver is intolerant of arrested circulation; 30 minutes or less of arrest in a normothermic liver may result in irreversible shock. Moderate hypothermia prolongs the safe period of ischemia, but we have found this to be variable in different patients and we would not exceed 30 minutes. If possible, total arrest of liver circulation should be avoided.

The greatest hazard in liver resection is causing uncontrollable hemorrhage from the vena cava in attempting to secure the hepatic veins. Since two thirds of cardiac venous return comes from the inferior vena cava, the inferior vena cava cannot be cross-clamped more than momentarily. If extreme danger in handling a hepatic vein is apparent, a venovenous bypass without systemic anticoagulation can be tried along with a safe period of interrupted circulation to the liver. In the usual operable case these measures should not be necessary.

The indications for hepatectomy are usually metastatic disease from an abdominal tumor and, occasionally, a primary liver tumor. A left lobectomy performed cautiously by an experienced surgeon carries a surgical risk of approximately 10 per cent. The reported mortality for a right lobe hepatectomy has been approximately 33 per cent. More extensive liver resections will have higher risks. The operation should be done only when the diagnosis is known and under the most favorable circumstances by a skilled surgical team.

References

Brunschwig, A.: Hepatic lobectomy. Am. J. Surg. 97:148, 1959.
Pack, G. T., and Baker, H. W.: Total right hepatic lobectomy. Report of a case. Am. Surgeon 138:253, 1953.
Wayson, E. C., and Forster, J. H.: Surgical anatomy of the liver. Surg. Clin. North America 44:1263, 1964.

A   The liver, the largest organ in the body, occupies most of the right hypochondrium, some of the epigastrium and even the left hypochondrium. Five ligaments connect it with the undersurface of the diaphragm and the anterior abdominal wall: they are the two lateral triangular ligaments, the coronary ligament, which runs the entire width of the liver, and the falciform and round ligaments. At least four of them are involved with a left or right lobectomy. There is considerable variation in the shape of the liver but the right lobe is always the larger and fills all the underside of the right diaphragm. Before the performance of a right or left hepatectomy it is necessary to interrupt the appropriate branch of the hepatic artery, portal vein and bile duct. It is essential, therefore, that one be acquainted with the normal anatomy as well as with the numerous variations which can be encountered at the porta hepatis.

B$_1$
B$_2$ Although most surgeons perform a considerable amount of extrahepatic biliary surgery, the anatomic knowledge necessary for this is inadequate if one is to operate on the liver itself. Contrary to external appearances, the liver is not divided into left and right lobes by the falciform ligament but by a fissure which runs from the gallbladder fossa to the inferior vena cava and which is not discernible externally. The left lobe is itself divided into medial and lateral segments by the falciform ligament and each segment is further subdivided into inferior and superior areas. The medial segment of the left lobe has been known as the quadrate lobe. The right lobe is divided into anterior and posterior segments, each in turn divided into superior and inferior areas. These divisions of the liver are established by the division of the portal vein within the liver. Each of these areas has its particular arterial, portal and biliary duct system, which is quite constant and in contrast to the situation when they are in an extrahepatic position. There is essentially no cross-circulation of blood or bile between the areas mentioned except that the quadrate lobe has blood vessels and bile ducts from both sides.

C$_1$
C$_2$ This arrangement is not followed with any fidelity by the hepatic venous system. These vessels are larger than any of the conduits that enter the liver through the porta hepatis, are generally at the intersegmental planes and run at right angles to them. Also, there are three channels draining hepatic venous blood in contrast to the bifurcate hepatic artery, portal vein and bile duct system. The hepatic vein on the right enters the vena cava on the right, and the middle and left ones enter more caudally and on the left. The latter two may join immediately before entering the vena cava. Much smaller branches from the quadrate lobe enter the vena cava directly. In addition, there is considerable variation in the numerous smaller vessels entering the vena cava.

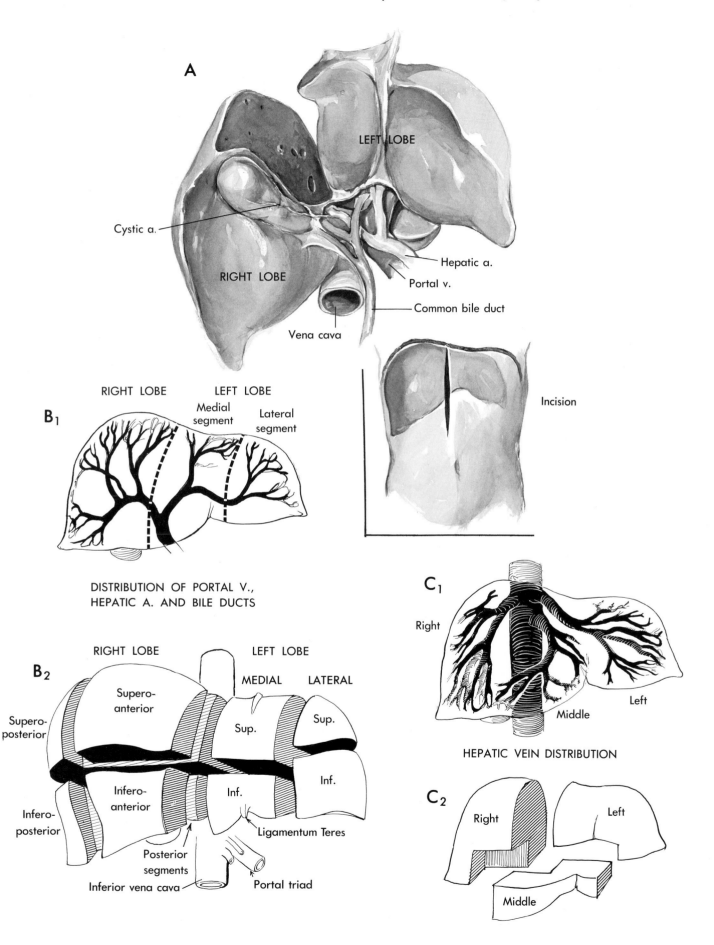

A

Cystic a.

Hepatic a.

Portal v.

Common bile duct

LEFT LOBE

RIGHT LOBE

Vena cava

Incision

B₁

RIGHT LOBE   LEFT LOBE

Medial segment   Lateral segment

DISTRIBUTION OF PORTAL V.,
HEPATIC A. AND BILE DUCTS

C₁

Right

Middle

Left

HEPATIC VEIN DISTRIBUTION

B₂

RIGHT LOBE   LEFT LOBE

MEDIAL   LATERAL

Supero-posterior

Supero-anterior

Sup.

Sup.

Inf.

Infero-anterior

Inf.

Inf.

Infero-posterior

Ligamentum Teres

Posterior segments

Inferior vena cava

Portal triad

C₂

Right

Left

Middle

Figures C$_1$ and C$_2$ show the areas drained by the three hepatic veins. The right hepatic vein drains all of the right lobe except the inferior area of the anterior segment. The left hepatic vein drains all of the left lobe except the inferior area of the middle segment. The middle hepatic vein drains the remainder.

The considerable disparity in the distribution of the afferent and efferent systems makes it necessary for the surgeon to accomodate to both during the performance of hepatic surgery. All areas deprived of arterial supply must, of course, be removed. Although arterial deprivation to a portion of the liver is a constant risk, it is easier to make the error of leaving behind an area devoid of venous drainage or of injuring a hepatic vein with serious jeopardy to that portion being drained by this vein, even though the arterial supply to the segment is intact. For example, during a right hepatic lobectomy, dissection too far to the left of the vena cava may result in damage to the left lobe unless the plane of dissection remains in line with the falciform ligament.

In essence, one can see that there is a severe limitation to the number of planes one can follow in resecting portions of the liver. It can be between the right and left lobes, through the falciform ligament or any part lateral to it or, very uncommonly, excision of the right and middle lobes can be done, but with great risk of injury to the left hepatic vein. Otherwise, excisions are wedge or scallop in shape, are usually limited to the free anterior border of the liver and most commonly are done for metastatic cancer.

General anesthesia is used, and the anesthesiologist must keep in mind that a good portion of the liver will be removed during the procedure and also that the operation will produce some degree of postoperative dysfunction of the liver that remains. Accordingly, anesthetics metabolized mainly by the liver should be avoided. For a left hepatic lobectomy the patient is placed in a supine position. Large bore plastic catheters are positioned preferably in the two arms even though one arm has a blood pressure cuff on it. If a hepatic vein is torn or cut with resultant brisk hemorrhage, transfusions of blood under pressure into the inferior vena cava would be less effective than if delivered to the superior vena cava through an arm vein. A long right paramedian incision is used. Factors such as body build and tumor size and location may make it necessary to extend the incision across the chest in a hockey-stick fashion.

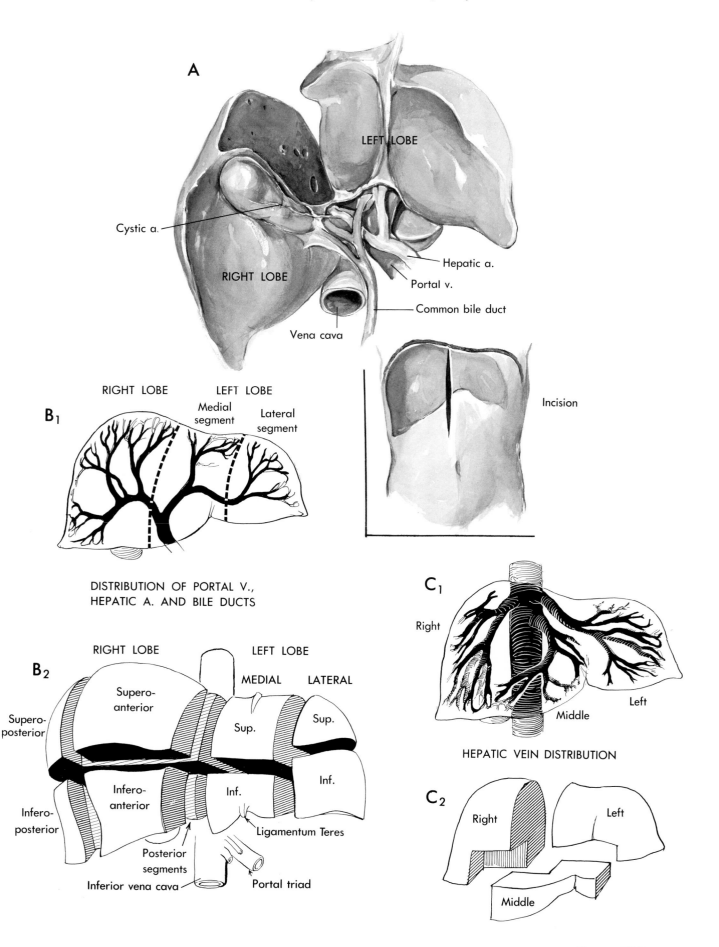

A

LEFT LOBE

Cystic a.

Hepatic a.

Portal v.

Common bile duct

RIGHT LOBE

Vena cava

Incision

B₁

RIGHT LOBE   LEFT LOBE

Medial   Lateral
segment   segment

DISTRIBUTION OF PORTAL V.,
HEPATIC A. AND BILE DUCTS

C₁

Right

Middle   Left

HEPATIC VEIN DISTRIBUTION

B₂

RIGHT LOBE   LEFT LOBE

MEDIAL   LATERAL

Supero-
posterior

Supero-
anterior

Sup.   Sup.

Inf.   Inf.

Infero-
posterior

Infero-
anterior

Inf.

Ligamentum Teres

Posterior
segments

Inferior vena cava   Portal triad

C₂

Right   Left

Middle

D   Even if the diagnosis was established during a previous recent celiotomy, a thorough exploration of the peritoneal cavity should be made again for any extrahepatic metastases even though their absence most likely was influential in prompting this second operation. If any are found at this time their presence eliminates the chance of cure but does not exclude the possibility of palliation. The round and falciform ligaments are divided at the time of entry. The left triangular ligament is divided to just short of the vena cava. This is avascular tissue unless collateral veins are present. If so, these must be occluded by electrocautery or ligature or a considerable amount of blood will be lost by the end of the operation.

E   The gastrohepatic omentum is divided so that the left lobe of the liver is now mobile.

F
G   The left hepatic artery is identified next. The dissection must be carried to the liver substance to be certain that a vessel has not been interrupted proximal to a point of division. The critical consideration here is to make certain of the presence of the right and left hepatic arteries and to carry on with the dissection distal to the bifurcation.

     There is abundant anatomic variation in the porta hepatis—a situation making the dissection of vessels and ducts here hardly routine. Three such variations are diagrammed here and are coded as follows: LG = Left gastric a., Sp = Splenic a., SM = Superior mesenteric a., GD = Gastroduodenal a., RG = Right gastric a. Surgeons are well aware of the dangers these variations of the hepatic artery pose to safe biliary surgery. The danger is greatly diminished if, above all, the identification of vessels at the point of entry into the liver is accurate. There are practically always three vessels to the liver, the variations being in their point of origin or in the presence of accessory vessels. This results in errors of ligating too few rather than too many vessels. This statement is applicable in the performance of a lobectomy and providing the division of the vessels takes place at a point just before their entry into the liver substance.

H   The left hepatic bile duct is isolated and divided next. As mentioned previously, there is practically no cross-circulation of the bile ducts between the various areas so attention must be paid to prevention of occlusion of the bile drainage of any portion of the tissue that is left behind. The dashed line indicates the anticipated line of incision.

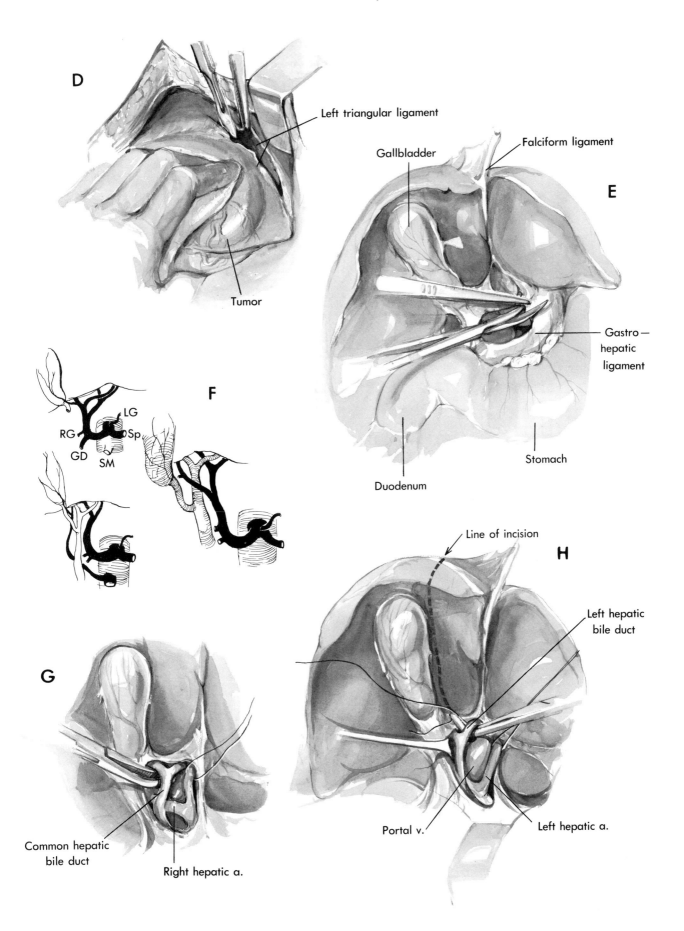

D

Left triangular ligament

Tumor

Gallbladder

Falciform ligament

E

Gastro—
hepatic
ligament

Duodenum

Stomach

F

LG

RG

GD   SM   Sp

Line of incision

H

Left hepatic
bile duct

G

Portal v.

Left hepatic a.

Common hepatic
bile duct

Right hepatic a.

I   The left hepatic duct is divided quite close to its union with the right duct and doubly ligated with 3-0 silk. This will permit lateral retraction of the right duct and medial retraction of the still intact left hepatic artery to expose the left branch of the portal vein.

J
K   The left hepatic artery is doubly ligated in continuity with 2-0 silk and divided. A Mixter hemostat is used to dissect the left portal vein, which is then ligated with similar material and divided. It is not necessary during any portion of the operation to dissect the cystic artery. Once it is identified, it and the common and right hepatic arteries are displaced with a vein retractor to expose the underlying portal vein.

L   It is now possible to bring most of the left lobe of the liver outside the peritoneal cavity, especially if there is some yielding of the falciform ligament. If there is undue rigidity, however, this maneuver might twist and occlude the vena cava sufficiently to reduce cardiac inflow. The left triangular ligament is now divided to the inferior vena cava under direct vision.

M   By this time, some color changes in the liver surface will have taken place as a result of vessel division and these will serve as a further guide as to where the liver should be divided. Usually it is on a line from the left border of the gallbladder to the vena cava. Although the scapel is used to incise Glisson's capsule, the deeper portion of the liver can be separated with the noncutting side of the blade or the scapel handle itself.

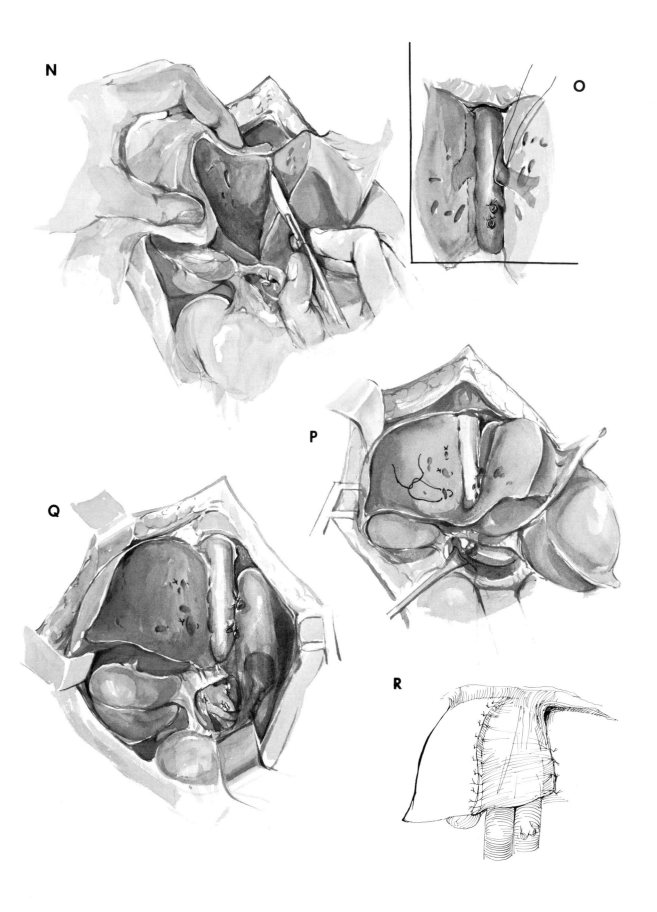

Hepatic Lobectomy, Right

A   The performance of a right hepatic lobectomy requires the adequate exposure that can be obtained only with a thoracoabdominal incision. The abdominal portion is always done first even if there has been a recent celiotomy indicating the need for this operation. The abdominal exploration is again as thorough as during the initial evaluation because, in the intervening period, however short, new or previously undetected lesions may have become manifest.

B   When, after the abdominal exploration, the surgeon still feels that the operation is indicated or feasible, the incision is extended into the thorax over the course of the 9th rib. The thoracic incision need not be extensive; specifically, the diaphragm does not have to be incised for too great a length. This will expose all but the nonperitonealized portion of the liver to direct view. Evidence of portal hypertension in the absence of cirrhosis should alert the surgeon to the probability of involvement beyond the right lobe in the depth of the liver.

C
D   The reader is referred to the previous section on left hepatic lobectomy for a discussion of the intrahepatic distribution of bile ducts, arteries and portal and hepatic veins. Of more critical importance is the recognition of the vagaries of the vasculature at the porta hepatis.

The porta hepatis is freed of fatty areolar tissue, exposing the hepatic artery, portal vein and bile ducts as close to the liver as possible so that their distribution can be determined with absolute certainty. The cystic duct and artery are ligated with 2-0 silk and divided. Next, the more superficially located right hepatic duct is tied first, followed by ligation of the right hepatic artery and then the right branch of the portal vein. All are tied in continuity in this sequence with 2-0 silk. Shortly following division of the artery and vein, a line of demarcation will develop, indicating the plane at which the transection of the liver should take place.

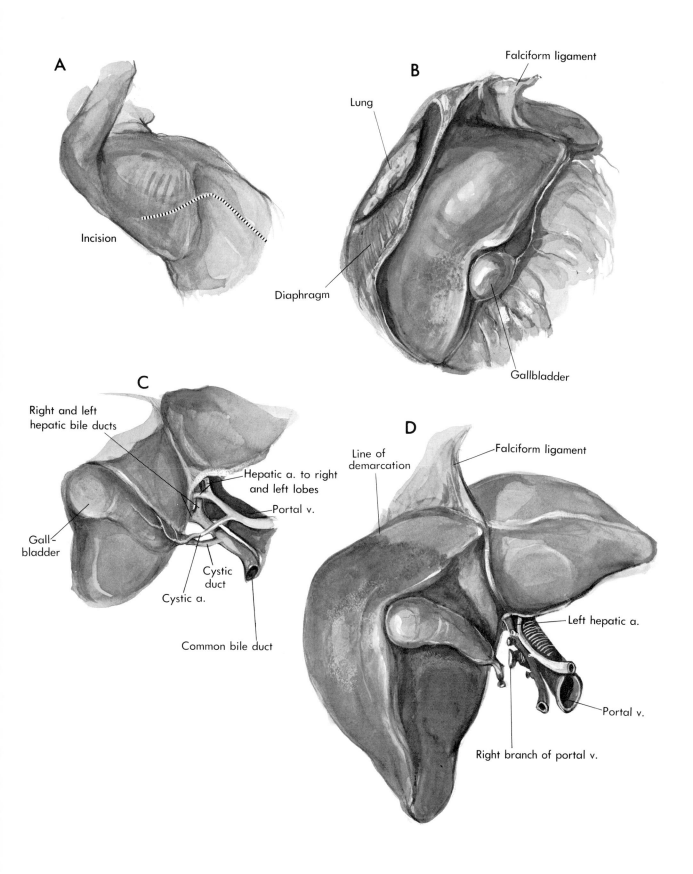

A

Incision

B

Falciform ligament

Lung

Diaphragm

Gallbladder

C

Right and left
hepatic bile ducts

Hepatic a. to right
and left lobes

Portal v.

Gall-
bladder

Cystic
duct

Cystic a.

Common bile duct

D

Line of
demarcation

Falciform ligament

Left hepatic a.

Portal v.

Right branch of portal v.

E   In this illustration the liver is omitted. As is indicated by the shaded area, a variable but considerable portion of the dorsal aspect of the liver is not peritonealized. In this case practically all the adrenal gland was covered by the liver. Three hepatic veins are shown here but those of the lateral and medial segments of the left lobe may unite a centimeter or two before they enter the vena cava as one. Although the hepatic veins usually enter just 1 or 2 cm. from the upper border of the liver, the exposure and their safe occlusion can be obtained only by the longer route to be described.

F   A moistened laparatomy pad is placed over the right lobe and the assistant retracts and rotates it medially. This exposes the right triangular ligament which is incised so that the surgical approach is from behind the right lobe. It is usually relatively avascular but can also be traversed by collateral vessels, which must be individually secured.

G   The previous step frees the liver so that it can be separated easily from the underlying structures to the lateral border of the inferior vena cava. One should not avulse the adrenal gland, which will remain in place if the plane of dissection is developed superficial to it. The adrenal arteries and inferior phrenic vein should not be torn. Six or eight short paired veins which are 2 to 4 mm. in diameter enter the vena cava directly from the liver and must be carefully isolated and ligated with 2-0 silk in continuity and divided if rotation of the liver is to continue. Notice the right hepatic vein which is being exposed just below the upper border of the liver.

H
I   The dissection now concentrates on isolating the right hepatic vein. A note of caution is in order; the surgeon must remain aware that, with continued medialward rotation of the right lobe and consequent traction on the right hepatic vein, the vena cava at about this point may become twisted and occluded. The right hepatic vein is carefully isolated, clamped doubly with angled Potts vascular clamps and divided. The vessel is oversewn with arterial 4-0 silk. We prefer this method of securing this vein because it requires less mobilization of it than is necessary when one must free enough of it to ligate it.

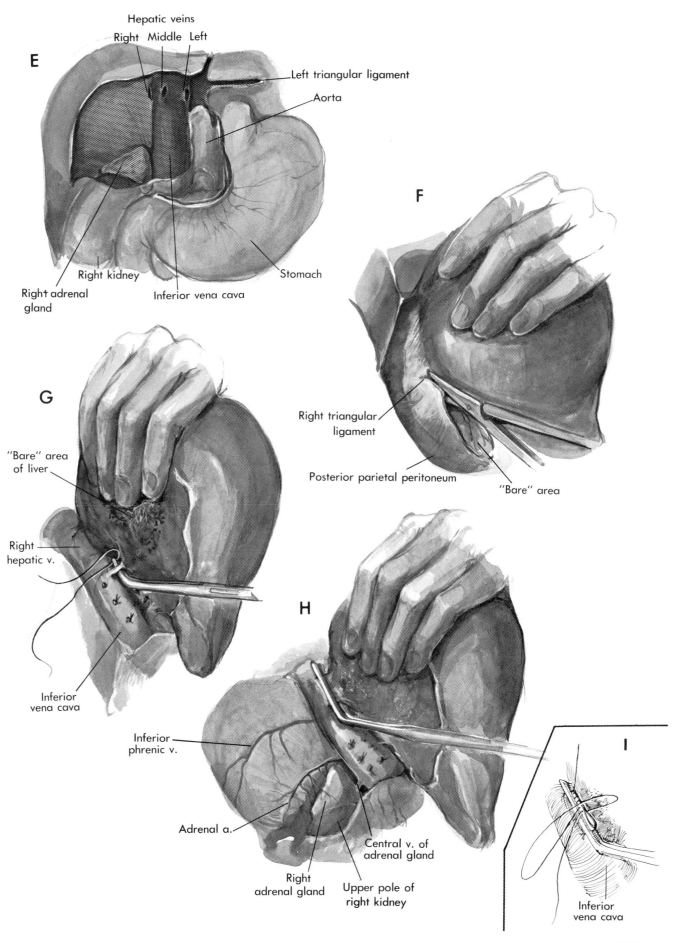

E

Hepatic veins
Right Middle Left
Left triangular ligament
Aorta
Right kidney
Stomach
Right adrenal gland
Inferior vena cava

F

Right triangular ligament
Posterior parietal peritoneum
"Bare" area

G

"Bare" area of liver
Right hepatic v.
Inferior vena cava

H

Inferior phrenic v.
Adrenal a.
Right adrenal gland
Upper pole of right kidney
Central v. of adrenal gland

I

Inferior vena cava

J   The right lobe of the liver is returned to its normal position and Glisson's capsule is incised with a scalpel. The remainder of the division along the line of demarcation is done in a blunt manner, the scalpel handle being ideal for this purpose. In this fashion resistance is felt when any sizable vessels are encountered. These are dissected free for a short distance to each side of the line of cleavage, tied in continuity with 3-0 silk and divided. Those vessels not suited for such handling, or torn in the process of blunt dissection, are secured with figure-of-eight suture ligatures of atraumatic 3-0 silk.

K   On occasion the bulk of the tumor in the right lobe will not permit sufficient rotation of the right lobe for accurate dissection of the right hepatic vein; or, the inferior vena cava is promptly occluded as the large, or too rigid, right lobe is reflected for the necessary dissection. In such situations the right hepatic vein can be approached from the front at the depth of the cleavage between the right and left lobes. As the cleft between the lobes is being developed, the vein is watched for as it enters the vena cava laterally. It is dissected free for just a short length, occluded with an angled Potts clamp and divided. It is oversewn with 4-0 arterial silk.

L   The right lobe of the liver can now be removed. The raw cut area of the liver is inspected for open vessels and whether they are leaking bile or blood, they are secured. As illustrated at the conclusion of the previous section, this raw area may be covered by Glisson's capsule salvaged from the surface of the right lobe at the beginning of the operation. A chest tube is exteriorized through an intercostal space in the right costophrenic sulcus and attached to under-water seal drainage. The diaphragm is closed in two layers with interrupted 2-0 silk. The costal arch is notched at the point of division and approximated with Tevdek suture material. The chest incision is closed in a preferred manner dependent upon whether an intercostal incision was made or a segment of rib excised. A Chaffin tube and two large Penrose drains are positioned in the operative field and exteriorized through a counterincision in the right upper quadrant. The abdomen is closed securely in the preferred manner.

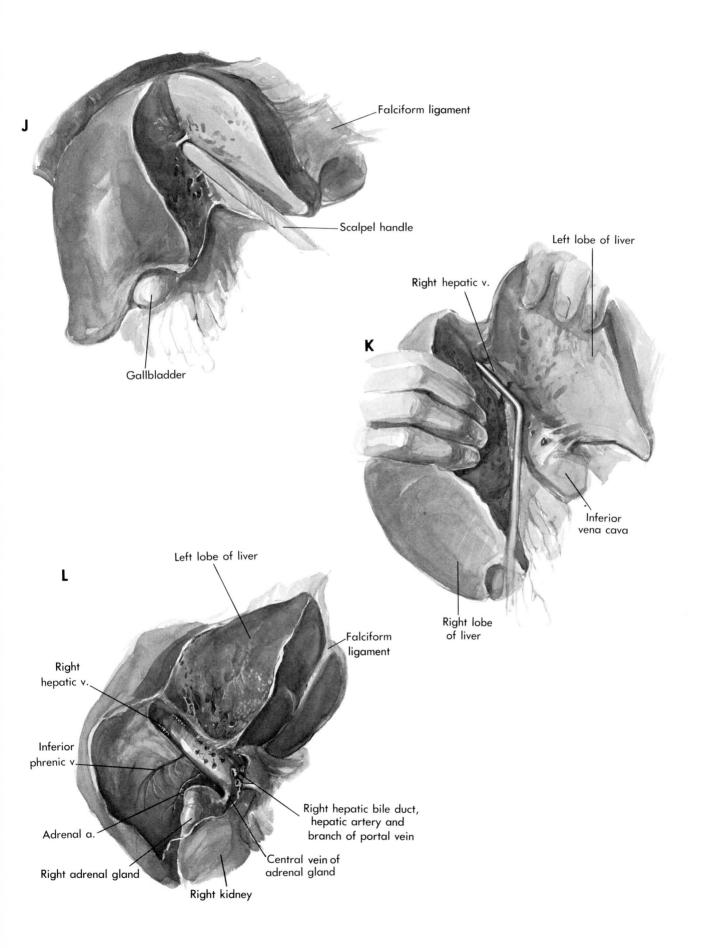

J

Falciform ligament

Scalpel handle

GallblADder

Left lobe of liver

Right hepatic v.

K

Inferior
vena cava

Right lobe
of liver

Left lobe of liver

L

Falciform
ligament

Right
hepatic v.

Inferior
phrenic v.

Right hepatic bile duct,
hepatic artery and
branch of portal vein

Adrenal a.

Right adrenal gland

Central vein of
adrenal gland

Right kidney

RECONSTRUCTION OF BILE DUCT STRICTURE

Operative errors are of many types. Most are not serious and cause no distress if unnoticed or ignored. Some are serious and can be fatal if not corrected immediately or ultimately. Some errors are calamitous and can only be prevented; they defy repair.

A stricture of the common bile duct, when a consequence of a surgical error, is unique in that it may have any or all of the above characteristics. When a stricture of the bile duct produces signs and symptoms they can often be managed by medical means only. When such treatment is ineffective, however, the time of correction of a stricture requires fine clinical judgment in deciding if a particular patient needs an operation and when that patient is in the optimum condition for it. A stricture of the common duct is reparable, but the operation can be one of the most difficult from the standpoint of technical skill, sheer stamina and surgical judgment. Even then the results can be disappointing.

Stricture of the common bile duct can be caused by inflammation such as from a long impacted stone and by chronic inflammation from bile leakage around a T-tube or from pancreatitis. Anomalies in the area of the porta hepatis may lead to operative accidents. Most strictures, however, are the result of trauma to the duct in the performance of an ordinary cholecystectomy and occur because of failure to adhere to certain principles necessary for safe gallbladder surgery. These minimal requisites include: an adequate abdominal incision and visualization of the field of operation, proper retraction, exact hemostasis and, above all, definite identification of a structure before it is divided. Implicit is the need to know thoroughly the vagaries of the anatomy in this area.

The more common causes of trauma to the duct are: excessive traction on the cystic duct with consequent tenting and clamping of the common duct at this juncture; "blind" clamping in the presence of hemorrhage about the cystic artery with consequent damage to the bile duct, hepatic artery or portal vein in the immediate vicinity, thus compounding the difficulty; the placement of suture ligatures which in their sweep include more than the intended vessel; the division of structures without their proper identification when confronted with anomalous anatomy. It is quite evident that prevention is the best treatment for stricture of the common bile duct.

The use of broad spectrum antibiotics has made it possible to avoid surgery altogether in some patients afflicted minimally or to gain valuable time while preparing a patient for a necessary operation. A considerable portion of this operation involves the lysis of numerous adhesions with consequent oozing of blood from numerous sites. The intraoperative blood loss can be considerable. It is of the utmost importance, therefore, that any hypoprothrombinemia be corrected, usually by the administration of vitamin K. Anemia is corrected by transfusions of whole blood.

As with other operations of equal magnitude, the critical part of it, such as anastomosis, is carried out after a tedious dissection. For this reason it is prudent to schedule this as the only operation of the day. During its performance one has to resist the restlessness which breeds recklessness after a few hours of seeming fruitless dissection and search. Similarly, the surgeon must be able to recognize the futility of an approach so that an alternate one can be followed and executed properly. An example is knowing when to abandon the search for a distal duct or the dissection of a distal segment which in the end would not be suitable for a primary anastomosis and to proceed with a Roux-en-Y jejunal anastomosis.

References

Child, C. G., and Lindenauer, S. M.: Repair of bile duct strictures. Michigan Med. 65:454, 1966.
Cole, W. H., Ireneus, C., Jr., and Reynolds, J. T.: Stricture of common bile duct: Studies in 122 cases. Ann. Surg. *142*: 537, 1955.
Lahey, F. H.: Stricture of common and hepatic ducts. Ann. Surg. *105*:765, 1937.
Madden, J. L., and McCann, W. J.: Reconstruction of the common bile duct by end-to-end anastomosis without the use of an internal splint or stent support. Surg. Gynec. & Obst. *112*:305, 1961.

A The incision used is either paramedian or subcostal in location and is influenced by the one already present. All else being equal, a long right paramedian rectus muscle reflecting incision offers the greatest flexibility and widest exposure and is to be preferred.

B This cross-cut illustration of the portal triad demonstrates the usual relationships of duct, artery and vein, with the vein lying most dorsally and the artery medial to the duct. However, the scarring of the previous operation(s) and the possibility that anomalous courses of these conduits or their tributaries may have been the reason for initial operative difficulty should amply warn the surgeon to expect considerable digressions from what is usual.

C
D With whatever incision is used, it is desirable to extend it beyond its previous extremes so that, if possible, the peritoneal cavity can be entered in a virginal area. The hepatic flexure of the transverse colon may be stuck fast immediately under the peritoneum; thus, there is risk of entry into the colon if one elects to enter the abdomen directly over the site of the presumed stricture. It is unusual for the hepatic flexure of the colon not to be adherent to the undersurface and leading edge of the liver. When freeing a colon so attached, the surgeon should stay just on Glisson's capsule and risk entering the liver rather than enter the colon and risk contamination of the entire broad operative field during the ensuing several hours. The edge of the liver may not be readily apparent, especially with a subcostal incision that reveals a broad brand of adhesions anchoring this edge to the subcostal margin. Usually a free edge is found medially over the left lobe or, less desirably, at the lateral aspect of the right lobe. If a finger can be insinuated above this band of scar so that it lies on uninvolved liver, the finger acts as an excellent bimanual guide during division of this scar. The scar in the subhepatic area can be so dense that only a scalpel will cut it. It is preferred, however, that scissors be used because the spread and cut technique will reveal areas of less tissue resistance, and hence possible natural planes, more than will the sharp cut of the knife.

It is a fortunate circumstance if a T-tube is within a portion of the common duct or within a subhepatic fistula. Such a tube is left in place as the easiest and surest guide to the duct.

When sufficient scar tissue has been lysed to allow reasonable orientation, the exposure can be widened. The proximal stump of the ligamentum teres is found and grasped with a curved six-inch forceps to pull the liver downward and upward. Sometimes perihepatic adhesions will prevent this. If they are few and ventral in location, they can be lysed to advantage; if numerous and over the dome, it is wiser to leave them alone. A moist laparotomy pad is placed on the undersurface of the liver and an appropriately sized Deaver retractor with a pistol grip is placed in position. These ideal retractors should be available in a variety of widths and lengths if they are to be used to retract exactly and effectively.

It will be necessary to mobilize the duodenum by the Kocher maneuver so as to expose the fullest length of common duct. The duodenum may be adherent to the undersurface of the liver so that it completely covers the portal triad. It will have to be freed with care so that peels of seromuscularis are not left behind.

The hepatic artery can be located by palpating for it; the portal vein can be assumed to lie deep to this and the common duct situated lateral to both. A No. 23 needle is inserted slowly in the area presumed to contain the duct and suction is applied with insertion and withdrawal. Sometimes only small amounts of bile may be aspirated; this is often hidden by blood within the needle. The fluid should be expelled on gauze, against which bile is seen more readily. If it reveals the location of the duct, the needle is left in place for the subsequent dissection.

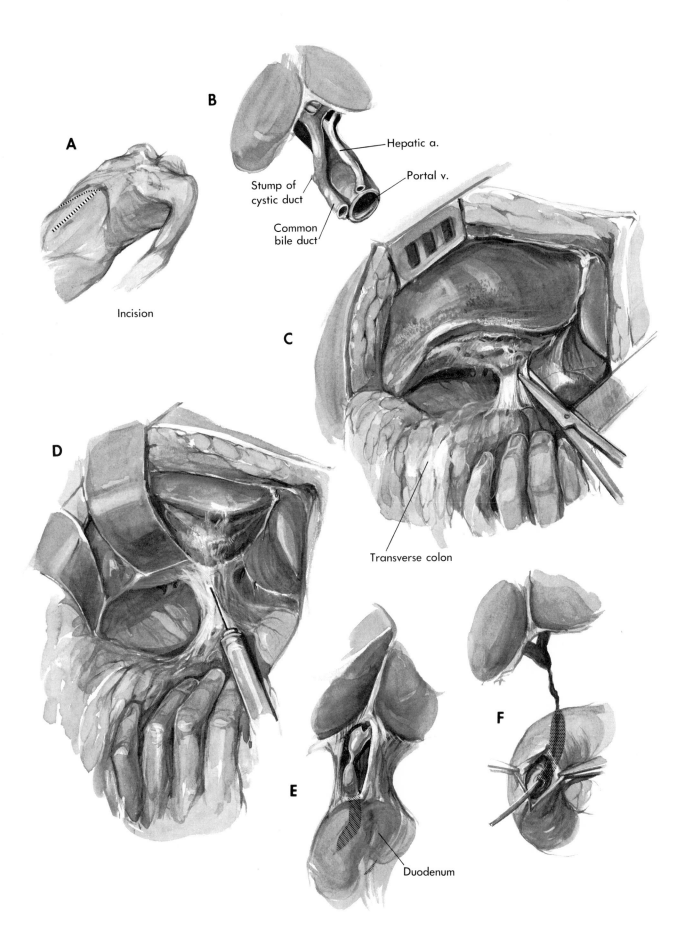

A

Incision

B

Stump of
cystic duct

Hepatic a.

Portal v.

Common
bile duct

C

Transverse colon

D

E

Duodenum

F

E   By palpation and inspection the hepatic artery is identified or freed sufficiently so that it is not jeopardized during the subsequent dissection. Here a relatively narrow stricture is shown. The shaded area indicates the length of common duct which is exposed by the Kocher maneuver.

F   The duct, of course, may be obliterated for a greater distance than is shown here and be difficult to identify. This distal segment may be approached retrogradely through the duodenum. This serves two important functions: It helps to identify the distal duct for a swifter and safer dissection. It also may indicate that so much of the distal duct is destroyed, and thus unavailable for a primary end-to-end anastomosis, that no more time need be wasted in dissecting it free. The surgeon can then proceed forthwith to prepare for a choledochojejunostomy.

     The ampulla is distinctly more firm than the surrounding tissue and can sometimes be located by palpation. The stricture precludes the free flow of bile as an aid in locating the duct opening. Gentle massage of the area may produce a few drops of clear pancreatic juice from the duct orifice. A fine probe is inserted into the ampulla first and is then followed with a minimal sphincterotomy so that a large groove director or Bake's dilator can be advanced retrogradely. The duodenotomy is closed in two layers, the mucosa with a continuous stitch of 3-0 chromic catgut and the seromuscularis with interrupted stitches of 3-0 silk.

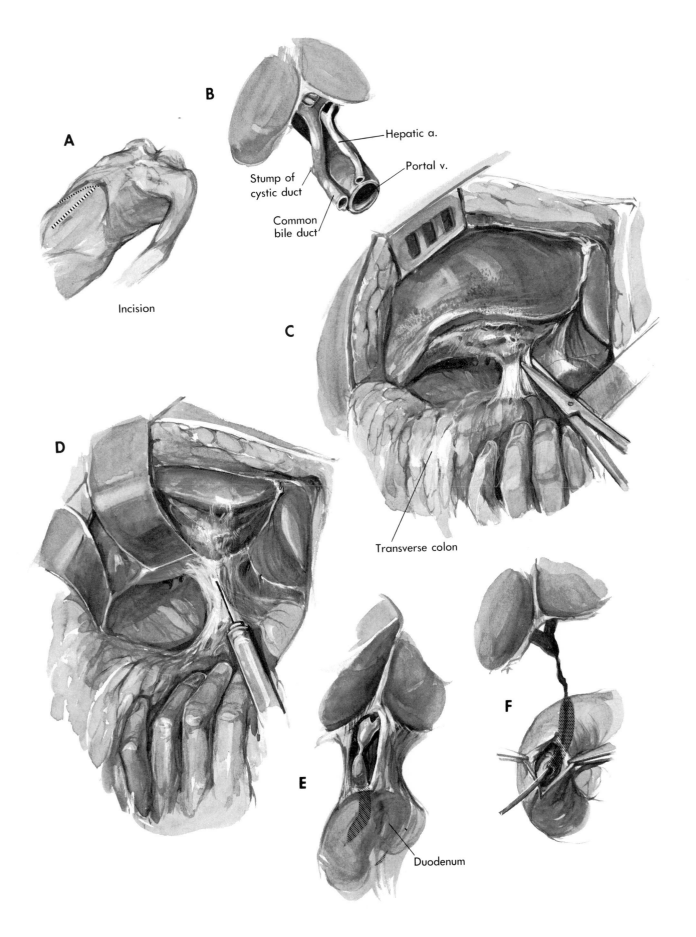

A

Incision

B

Hepatic a.

Portal v.

Stump of
cystic duct

Common
bile duct

C

Transverse colon

D

E

Duodenum

F

G_1
to
G_4

An end-to-end anastomosis is the preferred type of reconstruction and is chosen if good proximal and distal ducts can be obtained and if they can be anastomosed without tension on the suture line. Unfortunately, most cases are not this favorable. Interrupted stitches are used throughout. In this magnified drawing the two anchoring stitches of 4-0 silk are in place with three to six additional stitches (depending on the size of the ducts) used to effect the approximation of the serosa (G_1). Sometimes tying the anchoring stitches obscures the view for placement of the subsequent ones. It is then advisable to delay tying them until all are in position. The mucosal layer is closed with interrupted stitches of 4-0 chromic catgut. Prior to the anterior closure, a T-tube is introduced into the duct from a point distal to the anastomosis. If the anastomosis is sufficiently close to the hepatic ducts, the proximal limb of the T-tube is split so that a limb goes up each duct. The anterior anastomosis is completed and the hole for introduction of the T-tube closed with 4-0 chromic catgut.

Figure G_4 shows the wedge of rubber we remove from directly opposite the long limb of all T-tubes — even from those used in ordinary common duct surgery. When the T-tube is removed later, this notch will allow the tube to come out more smoothly and probably with less trauma to the duct.

H_1
to
H_3

If there is insufficient duct distally for an end-to-end ductal anastomosis, then a Roux-en-Y choledochojejunostomy is performed. If the diameter of the proximal duct is adequate so that there is minimal puckering of the jejunum with an end-to-end choledochojejunostomy, this anastomosis is used. Again a two-layer closure is used and a T-tube positioned as shown. The jejunum can be brought into position through the mesocolon or in front of the transverse colon according to the preference of the surgeon and the dictates of local factors. The jejunojejunostomy is done in two layers.

I_1
to
I_3

If the short proximal duct is not dilated, the disparity between ductal and jejunal lumens may be difficult to reconcile. An end-to-side choledochojejunostomy is then performed, as the jejunal opening can be made in the desired dimensions. The proximal jejunum is closed in two layers. The opening in the side of the jejunum to receive the duct should be an adequate distance from the closed end where impingement by the inverted tissue might otherwise interfere with duct drainage. Figure I_3 demonstrates how the jejunum proximal and distal to the anastomosis can be anchored so that the weight of the jejunum is not on the suture line.

J_1
to
J_3

This trio of drawings shows the method of Lahey for making a common channel of two separate ducts when the stricture has destroyed all the common hepatic bile duct. Two layers of interrupted stitches of 4-0 silk are used to approximate the serosa. The cut is then made between these two layers as is shown in Figure J_1. The mucosa is sutured from the inside with 4-0 chromic catgut when the common channel has been created as in J_2. The resultant "common" duct can be anastomosed to the jejunum in the manner already described.

Throughout the operation blood loss, which may be considerable, is measured and replaced accordingly. A urinary catheter is in position and urinary output is maintained by infusion of clear liquids as necessary.

The T-tube is exteriorized through a counterincision separate from that used for the Penrose drains. One drain is placed in proximity but not in contact with the anastomosis. Another is placed in the retroduodenal area if it has been dissected and if there is any concern about pancreatic leakage. Accidental removal of a T-tube is a serious matter so that it should be secured in a manner known by the surgeon to be most foolproof. Postoperative abdominal distention can displace T-tubes and should be prevented and adequate slack of the T-tube left intra-abdominally.

The length of time the T-tube is to be left in position is a highly debatable point. It is difficult to justify an arbitrary period. In those strictures which are limited and in which the anastomosis is done optimally, and which are not followed by postoperative complications, the tube can be removed in two to three weeks. If the repair is done under circumstances in which a stenosis of the anastomosis is probable, and the physical presence of the tube will minimize this, then it should be left in place for up to one year.

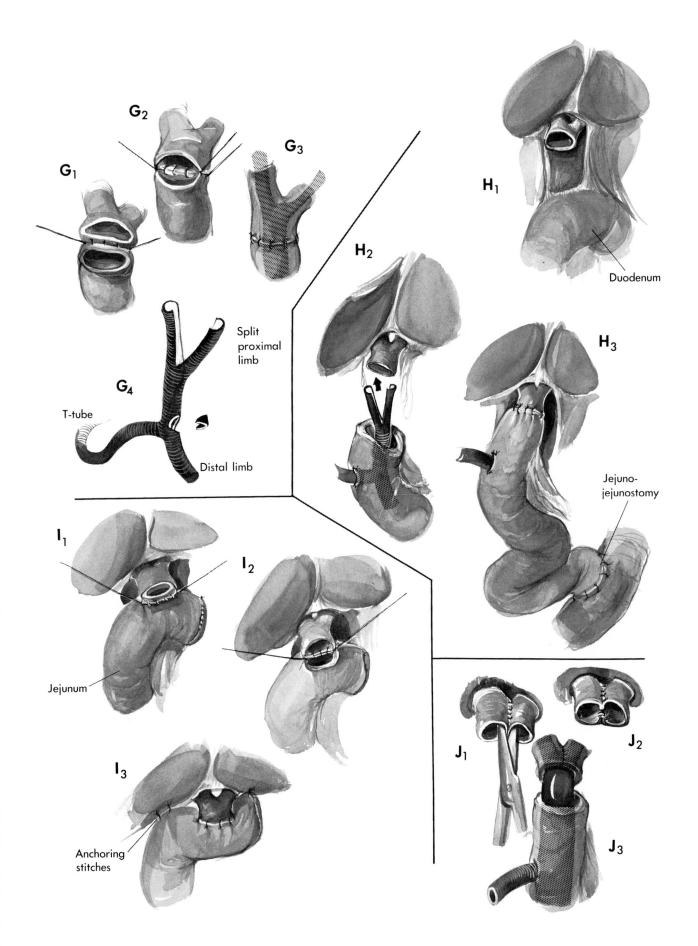

G₁

G₂

G₃

G₄

T-tube

Split proximal limb

Distal limb

H₁

Duodenum

H₂

H₃

Jejuno-jejunostomy

I₁

I₂

Jejunum

I₃

Anchoring stitches

J₁

J₂

J₃

PORTAL HYPERTENSION

Portal hypertension is a syndrome caused by an increase in portal pressure, leading to esophagogastric varices, splenomegaly and often hepatomegaly and ascites. An increase in pressure occurs in the portal system proximal to any obstruction within it. Based on the site of obstruction, portal hypertension has been classified as suprahepatic, intrahepatic and subhepatic.

Suprahepatic portal hypertension may result from cardiac failure, pulmonary fibrosis and hepatic vein occlusion. Portal hypertension associated with cardiopulmonary pathology is a relatively unimportant surgical consideration, for the disease either is amenable to medical therapy promptly or, if not, death usually occurs before esophageal varices present serious problems. Suprahepatic portal hypertension due to thrombosis or compression of the hepatic veins, known as the Budd-Chiari syndrome, is characterized by the prompt appearance of massive ascites and extensive esophagogastric varices. The prognosis of these patients is very poor and, because of the involvement of the portal vein and many of its radicles, surgery is seldom considered.

Intrahepatic portal hypertension accounts for approximately 80 per cent of all cases of portal hypertension requiring surgical treatment, and cirrhosis is by far the most common cause in this group.

Subhepatic portal hypertension is usually due to thrombosis of the portal, splenic or superior mesenteric veins and is seen more commonly in children and young adults.

The surgical treatment of portal hypertension has been directed primarily toward the control of bleeding from esophageal varices. Intractable ascites and severe hypersplenism associated with cirrhosis are less common indications for portal decompression. Once it has been established that a patient has bled from esophageal varices, he is evaluated and elective shunt surgery considered. From the clinical point of view, a patient in reasonably good nutritional status, without ascites or jaundice, would be considered a suitable candidate. Regarding certain basic biochemical parameters of liver function, an ideal candidate for shunt surgery should have a serum albumin higher than 3 gm., a bilirubin of less than 2 mg./100 ml., a bromsulfalein retention less than 25 per cent, and a prothrombin time greater than 50 per cent of normal. If these clinical and laboratory criteria are adhered to, the mortality of shunt surgery is low. Nonetheless, in well over a third of the patients included in the large series reported in the literature, these optimal conditions have not existed. However, it was believed that the risk of further hemorrhage was greater than the mortality of the contemplated procedure in each individual case, and therefore operation was carried out.

In the past, ascites had been considered a serious contraindication to operation, but in recent years it has been recognized that shunt surgery, particularly if it affords decompression of both the hepatic and the splanchnic beds, will result in a reversal of a previously intractable ascites. Once a patient has been selected as suitable for shunt surgery, a period of preoperative preparation varying from a few days to several weeks should be utilized to achieve maximum improvement in liver functions and the general physical condition of the patient.

The common objective of all shunt procedures is to reduce portal venous pressure by diversion of blood from the obstructed splanchnic bed into the systemic venous system. A portacaval shunt is the most frequently employed, during which procedure the portal vein is anastomosed to the inferior vena cava. In intrahepatic portal hypertension, the procedure of choice is a portacaval shunt, and in patients with portal vein thrombosis a splenorenal shunt is the preferred operation. Recently, repeated success has been demonstrated with the division of the inferior vena cava below the renal veins and anastomosis of the proximal divided end of the inferior vena cava to the side of the superior mesenteric vein. It should be emphasized that not infrequently in patients with subhepatic portal hypertension the opportunity for portal decompression by a venous shunt does not exist and, therefore, other modalities of treatment, such as esophagogastric surgery, have been carried out.

End-to-side portacaval shunt has gained increasing popularity in the past two decades. The side-to-side variety, however, appears to be superior in the management of the ascites associated with cirrhosis and portal hypertension. This is based on the need for decompression of both the splanchnic and the intrahepatic vascular beds in the presence of intractable ascites. The rationale for this combined hepatic and splanchnic decompression relates to the severe outflow obstruction in the liver as the important factor in the pathogenesis of cirrhotic ascites. The double barrel portacaval shunt, in which the portal vein is divided and the two divided ends are anastomosed to the side of the inferior vena cava, has been recommended to achieve the largest possible side-to-side anastomosis between these two venous systems. The end-to-side portacaval shunt is also unfavorable in patients in whom the portal vein functions as an outflow tract for the liver.

Determination of the portal, splanchnic and hepatic pressures at the time of surgery will be helpful in determining whether an end-to-side or side-to-side portacaval shunt should be employed. The portal pressure refers to the measurement of the unobstructed portal bed, splanchnic pressure to the pressure on the intestinal side of the temporarily occluded portal vein, and hepatic pressure to readings taken on the hepatic side of the temporarily occluded portal vein. In the majority of patients, the portal pressure will be significantly elevated in portal hypertension, and upon clamping the portal vein the splanchnic pressure will show a rise as opposed to the hepatic pressure, which usually shows several centimeters of decline during the temporary occlusion of the portal vein. In a much smaller group of patients, clamping the portal vein at the time of surgery results in no change or even a significant elevation of the hepatic pressure. In this small group of patients the portal vein must be functioning as an outflow tract, in which case an end-to-side portacaval anastomosis will then be contraindicated.

When the extrahepatic portal obstruction is limited to the portal vein, a centrally placed splenorenal shunt close to the vena cava through a left thoracoabdominal incision has a good chance of remaining patent. When the splenic vein is obstructed or is unavailable because of a previous splenectomy, the side-to-end superior mesenteric to vena cava shunt has been of considerable value.

In children with portal hypertension due to postnecrotic or posthepatitic cirrhosis, or hepatic involvement from fibrocystic disease of the pancreas, improvement in nutrition, regression of esophageal varices and disappearance of ascites and hypersplenism have frequently followed successful shunt procedures. Children with portal hypertension due to congenital biliary atresia have the least favorable outlook. Shunting procedures are generally not advised in these patients as the disease rarely permits survival beyond two years of age.

References

Blakemore, A. H., and Lord, J. W.: The technique of using vitallium tubes in establishing portacaval shunts for portal hypertension. Ann. Surg. *122*:476, 1945.

Linton, R. R., Ellis, D. S., and Geary, J. E.: Critical comparative analysis of early and late results of splenorenal and direct portacaval shunts performed in 169 patients with portal cirrhosis. Ann. Surg. *154*:446, 1961.

McDermott, W. V., Jr.: Treatment of cirrhotic ascites by combined hepatic and portal decompression. New England J. Med. *259*:897, 1958.

Voorhees, A. B., and Blakemore, A. H.: Clinical experience with superior mesenteric vein–inferior vena cava shunt in the treatment of portal hypertension. Surgery *51*:35, 1962.

Portacaval Shunt

A A portacaval shunt must frequently be done on patients already quite ill from the systemic effects of their chronic disease or from a recent episode of hemorrhage. Most of them, therefore, can overcome only minimal errors in surgical judgment or technique. Postoperative complications exact a high toll, and these patients do not easily tolerate a second portal decompressing operation should the first one fail. Since shunts performed on a prophylactic basis have not proved a sound investment or gained favor, the surgeon does not have the opportunity to operate on these patients when they are presumably less seriously afflicted. These reasons for discouraging surgery are supplemented by the difficulty encountered at the time of operation in obtaining and maintaining the exposure of the surgical field. There is also the need to pay constant attention to details and to accept the task of the sometimes slow, tedious stopping of venous bleeding from vessels whose size and number are not encountered or are of no concern in most other operations.

B An adequate length of the portal vein is essential for a successful anastomosis and repair of torn tributaries can compromise these prerequisites. Although the extra-hepatic portal vein probably is not plagued with as many variations as the hepatic artery, equal vigilance is needed to detect them. Certainly, unsuspected tributaries can be torn more easily. The portal hypertension present hinders the cessation of bleeding usually seen with nonligated smaller veins.

The splenic and superior mesenteric veins meet dorsal to the pancreas to form the portal vein which continues as such for 6 to 7 cm. before dividing into left and right branches, each immediately entering the liver. It remains singular in only 10 per cent of patients. The diameter of the portal vein is normally about 1 cm. but it may be greater in a patient with portal hypertension. Approximately two-thirds of the time it is entered by the coronary and pyloric veins which form a loop that hugs the lesser curvature of the stomach and receives branches or is a continuation of the left gastric vein, the esophageal plexus and the short gastric veins. To a lesser extent these two veins enter at the junction of the inferior mesenteric and splenic veins or into the splenic vein itself. Whatever tributaries the portal vein has enter on its medial side.

C The portal vein lies medial and dorsal to the common bile duct and hepatic artery. These structures run along the right border of the gastrohepatic ligament. The arrow points to the foramen of Winslow. Considerable fibro-adipose tissue and some lymph nodes may be found on the intestinal side of the portal vein. This illustration shows how dissection of the portal vein may be carried out by retracting the common bile duct and hepatic artery medially and anteriorly for adequate exposure without performing any dissection on the hepatic artery or common bile duct.

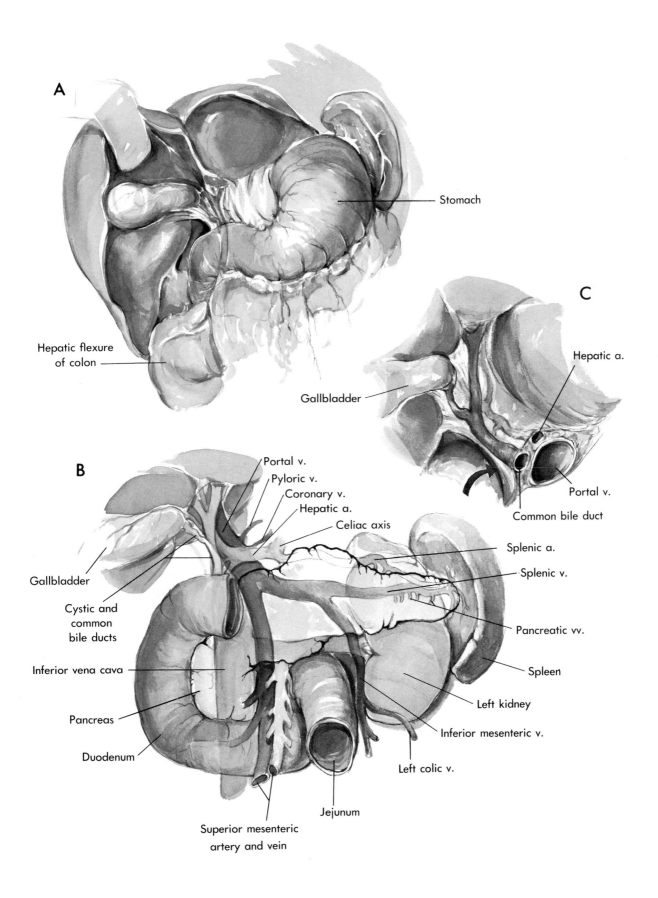

A

Stomach

Hepatic flexure
of colon

C

Gallbladder

Hepatic a.

Portal v.

Common bile duct

B

Portal v.
Pyloric v.
Coronary v.
Hepatic a.
Celiac axis

Gallbladder

Cystic and
common
bile ducts

Inferior vena cava

Pancreas

Duodenum

Splenic a.

Splenic v.

Pancreatic vv.

Spleen

Left kidney

Inferior mesenteric v.

Left colic v.

Superior mesenteric
artery and vein

Jejunum

D   The patient is placed in the supine position, and general anesthesia with endotracheal intubation is used. Unless the surgeon has information from a recent celiotomy or the patient has had a previous splenectomy, splenoportography is done at this time. This enables the surgeon to obtain the fullest information on the portal venous system and thus maintain flexibility in his approach. The skin in the area over the left 9th interspace at the anterior axillary line is prepared in the preferred way. A No. 22 spinal needle is inserted at this point and as it enters the peritoneum is directed cephalad or caudad so that it transverses the longitudinal axis of the spleen. The stylet is removed, the needle is flushed lightly with saline, about 25 ml. of 45 per cent Hypaque is injected rapidly and, just at the conclusion of the injection, the first film is taken. It is essential that respirations cease while the x-rays are being taken. It is advisable to take several subsequent films at close intervals after this initial injection. While the x-rays are being developed and interpreted, the torso is prepared widely for the anticipated operation. An adhesive plastic drape is ideal for this area where drapes soon become wet with ascitic fluid.

A thoracoabdominal incision unquestionably provides the best exposure, but the increased postoperative morbidity as a result of division of the diaphragm and the entry into the thorax has influenced many surgeons to perform the operation entirely abdominally.

E   An elliptical transverse incision is used, extending from the midaxillary line on the right to at least the left midclavicular line. The distance from the subcostal margin is dictated by the position of the lower border of the liver. Free fluid is almost invariably found in the peritoneal cavity even in those patients not being operated on for relief of ascites. The usual thorough exploration of the peritoneal cavity is carried out and the surgeon remains alert for the possibility of a multicentric hepatic malignancy which can be missed in an already nodular liver. Since ulcers are frequently seen in these patients, the duodenum deserves special attention. If stones are found within the gallbladder, a cholecystectomy should be performed at the conclusion of the operation. If a liver biopsy is contemplated it should be obtained now rather than later in the operation because the handling of the liver may produce factitious microscopic changes. A small caliber cork bore is used to obtain a through-and-through core of tissue somewhat away from the liver edge and the hole is plugged with a similarly shaped core of Gelfoam. If one is satisfied that the edge of the liver is representative, an ellipse of tissue can be excised and the cut edge oversewn with atraumatic 3-0 chromic catgut, foregoing mattress stitching of the liver.

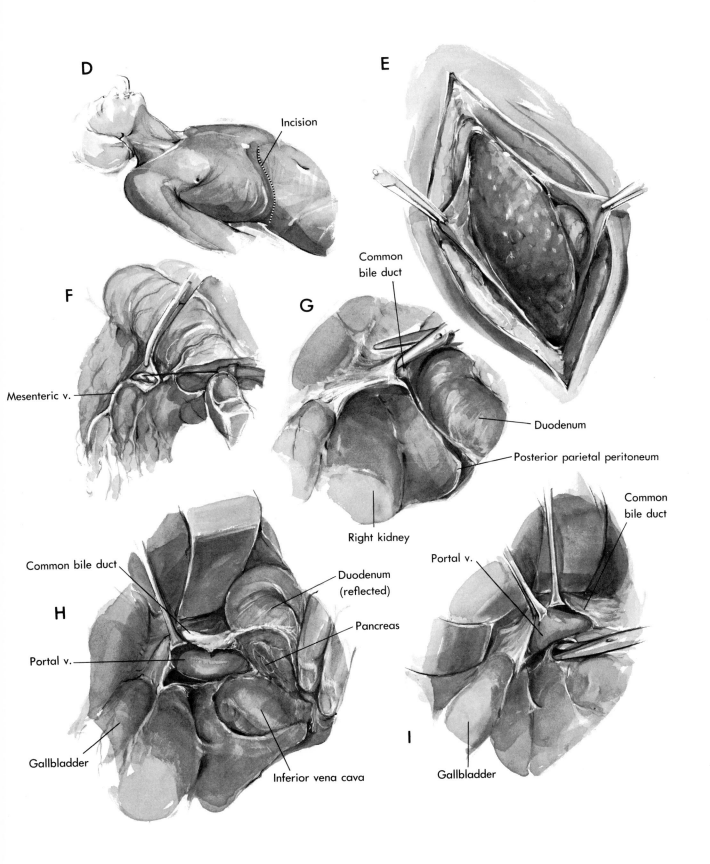

D

Incision

E

Common
bile duct

F

Mesenteric v.

G

Duodenum

Posterior parietal peritoneum

Right kidney

Common
bile duct

Common bile duct

Duodenum
(reflected)

Portal v.

Pancreas

Portal v.

H

Gallbladder

Inferior vena cava

I

Gallbladder

F   The portal venous pressure is taken at this time through a portal tributary, usually a jejunal vein. A disposable spinal tap manometer is adequate. The needle is inserted into an exposed vein and patency of the saline-filled manometer is determined by fluctuations consonant with respirations. Readings are obtained in at least two vessels. Portal venograms may also be obtained at this time if deemed necessary, keeping in mind that the splenoportogram may not necessarily have visualized an otherwise patent vein. In the event the portal vein is proved to be occluded and the surgeon chooses to do a splenorenal shunt the incision can be extended to the left and into the thorax for proper exposure through a thoracoabdominal incision.

G   The visceral surface of the liver is covered with two thicknesses of moist laparotomy pads and retracted cephalad with a wide Deaver retractor. Often a distended gallbladder hampers development of the exposure, but with pressure from the retractors it gradually empties. The hepatic flexure of the colon and the small bowel are retracted caudad. The portal vein can be further assessed as well as located bidigitally with the index finger within and the thumb over the foramen of Winslow. The turgid vessel can be compressed but bounces back quickly. The duodenum is mobilized only if it is really necessary. Whereas the posterior parietal peritoneum lateral to the duodenum is usually avascular and can be cut without concern for prolonged bleeding, the collateral veins and venules create just such a problem. It is, therefore, necessary to employ a clamp-cut-and-tie technique if the Kocher maneuver is employed. The peritoneum over the portal triad is shown being cut so that mobilization of the portal vein can begin.

H   The common bile duct has been freed from the portal vein and along with the hepatic
I   artery is being retracted anteriorly and medially with long vein retractors, the ideal instrument for this. In the retroduodenal area there may be excessive fatty areolar lymphatic tissue which has to be excised for proper exposure and mobilization. This should be ligated prior to division to minimize lymphorrhea. The portal vein is mobilized circumferentially and the surgeon remains ever vigilant for tributaries which will not only bleed briskly if cut but will require suturing and excessive handling of that portion of the vein which must be maintained in optimal condition. The coronary and pyloric veins enter on its medial side.

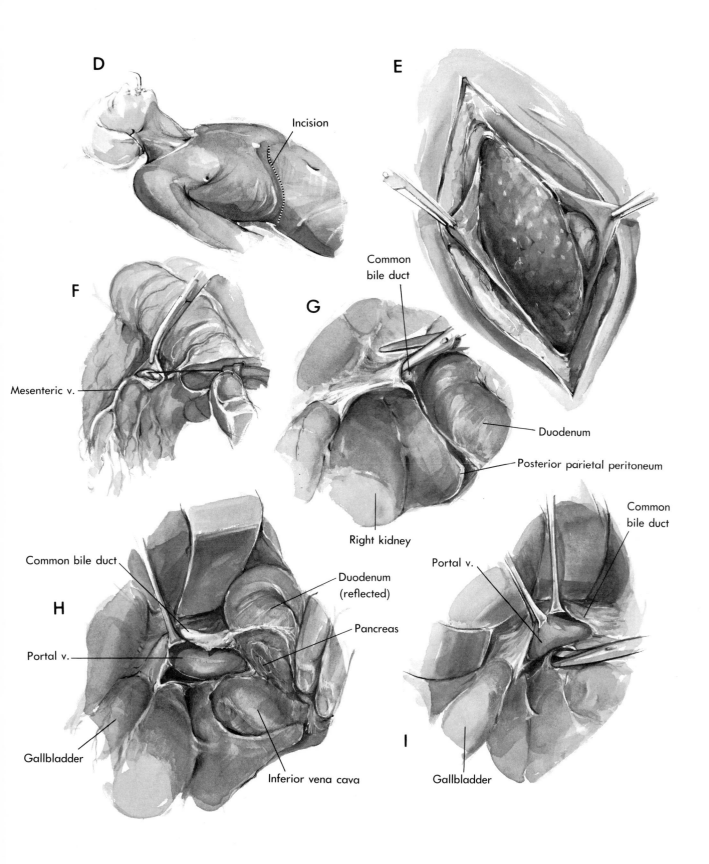

D

Incision

E

F

Mesenteric v.

G

Common
bile duct

Duodenum

Posterior parietal peritoneum

Right kidney

Common bile duct

H

Portal v.

Gallbladder

Duodenum
(reflected)

Pancreas

Inferior vena cava

Common
bile duct

Portal v.

I

Gallbladder

J
K
A small soft rubber drain is passed around the portal vein and is used for gentle retraction to expose the various surfaces of the vein. Gauze pledgets at the tip of an eight-inch hemostat are ideal for this circumferential dissection. The parietal peritoneum over the vena cava is incised and dissected free with scissors and the vena cava exposed from the level of the renal vein and upward to the liver. It is not advisable to expose the posterior and medial surfaces of the vena cava; to do so may incite unnecessary bleeding.

L
A straight or angled Potts arterial clamp is applied to the intestinal side of the portal vein. There is frequently difficulty in obtaining an adequate length of portal vein so that the anastomosis can be performed without tension and with the proper sweep and the angle of union with the vena cava. For this reason the portal vein must be tied as close to the liver as possible. This is done with 2-0 silk, which is sufficient for this relatively low-pressure system.

M_1
M_2
Sometimes an enlarged caudate lobe will cover the vena cava in such a fashion that it is necessary to bend the portal vein excessively so that it meets the vena cava at a more caudal site. This causes it to kink—a situation certain of failure and obviously unacceptable. Before removing a portion of the caudate lobe it is necessary to free it from the underlying vena cava. The previously mentioned pledgets of gauze at the tip of a curved hemostat can be used to tease apart the liver and vena cava. While doing this the surgeon should look for and secure the one or two pairs of short veins entering this portion of the liver from the vena cava. Mattress stitches are needed to stop the usually steady ooze of blood from the cut liver surface.

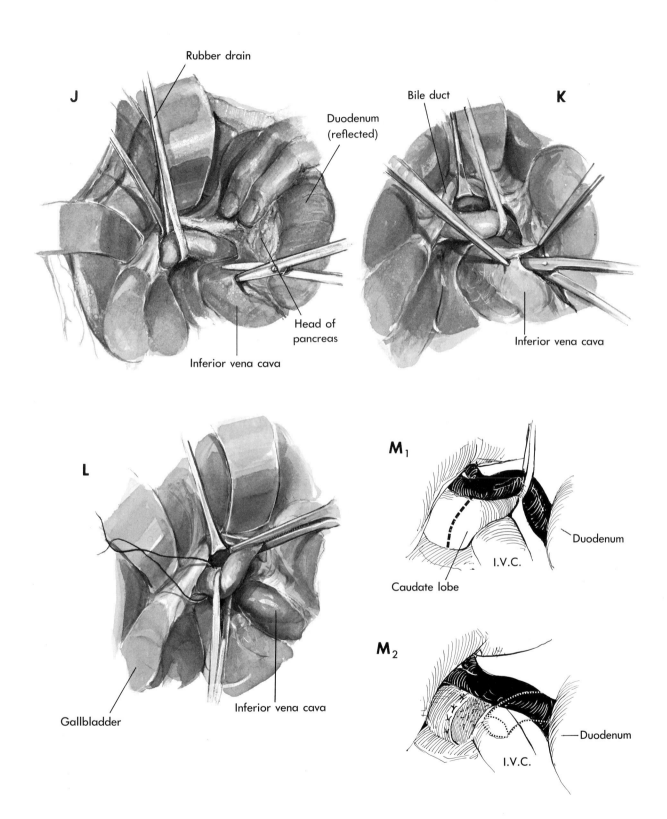

J

Rubber drain

Duodenum (reflected)

Head of pancreas

Inferior vena cava

K

Bile duct

Inferior vena cava

L

Gallbladder

Inferior vena cava

M₁

Duodenum

I.V.C.

Caudate lobe

M₂

Duodenum

I.V.C.

N
O

The Potts clamp is applied first as close as possible on the intestinal side of the portal vein and the tie on the liver side is secured. The portal vein is divided cleanly, leaving a 3 mm. cuff on the liver side.

P
to
V

A Satinsky clamp is used to isolate that portion of the inferior vena cava which can best meet with the portal vein. Although an oval piece of vena cava can be cut out straight away, the more deliberate method shown is more accurate. Figures P and Q show the opening of the vena cava, which in Figure R is being fashioned into an oval that will accurately accomodate the portal vein. The oval is on the long axis of the vena cava. A simple slit in the vena cava has long since been found to be undesirable and is more likely to become occluded. The open vessels are flushed with heparinized saline. There are a number of proper and adequate vascular anastomotic techniques, and the reader is urged to use the one with which he is most facile. The stitches are begun on the far or medial sides of the vessels. The two separate, or one double-needle strand of atraumatic 4-0 silk is used and so placed that all knots are on the outside. A simple stitch is used. An assistant is charged with holding the Potts clamps so that there is no tension on the suture line. At one of the corners (U) an everting Connell stitch is used so that as the separate strands approach (V) from each end they rotate in opposite directions; when they are tied there is no distortion as is seen when tying strands that have terminated on the same side of a vessel. The guidelines (T) can be applied before or immediately after beginning the anastomosis (S); however, they are not utilized in the anastomosis. In performing venous anastomoses it is particularly important that sutures be accurately placed and proper tension maintained so that a minimum of suture material is "free" or available inside the lumen, since this might increase the chances of causing blood clots.

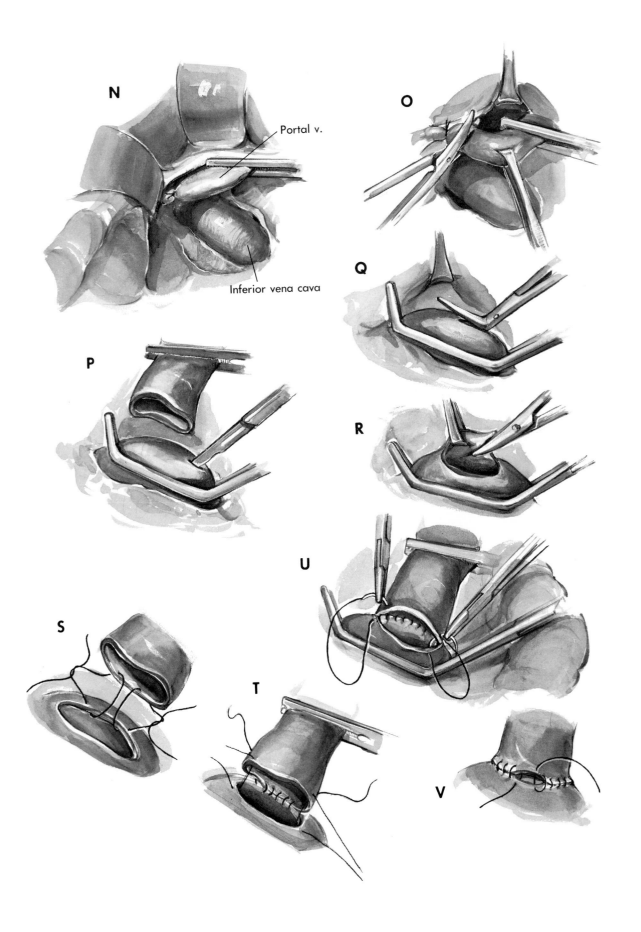

N

Portal v.

Inferior vena cava

O

Q

P

R

U

S

T

V

W With completion of the anastomosis the caval clamp is removed first; this is followed quickly by removal of the one on the portal vein. Any oozing from the suture line can be stopped by very gentle pressure for several minutes with a piece of moistened gauze. Any persistent bleeding point can be sealed with individual stitches, but the vessels should not be clamped while this is being done. The wound is not drained routinely. The peritoneum is closed with a continuous stitch of zero chromic catgut and the remainder of the wound in layers with interrupted stitches of 2-0 silk.

X_1
X_2 A double-barreled portacaval shunt is technically more difficult because the liver and intestinal side of the portal vein must be brought to the vena cava for the anastomosis. It is necessary that the maximal length of vein be mobilized and that neither limb be created at the expense of its partner. The portal vein on the intestinal side is anastomosed first so that its success can be more assured. As with the other types of anastomoses, one must be certain that the course and seating of the vein are proper and will not result in twisting or kinking when the clamps are removed.

Y_1
to
Y_5 A side-to-side anastomosis again makes it mandatory that the maximum length of vein be mobilized if excessive tension on the suture line is to be avoided. The anastomosis is done as before, with special care that the stitches are placed well at the cephalad and caudal aspects of the anastomosis where the tension is greatest.

Z We have never been faced with the need to connect the portal and caval systems with a graft but do feel that without question this should be an autogenous graft, probably fashioned from the saphenous vein.

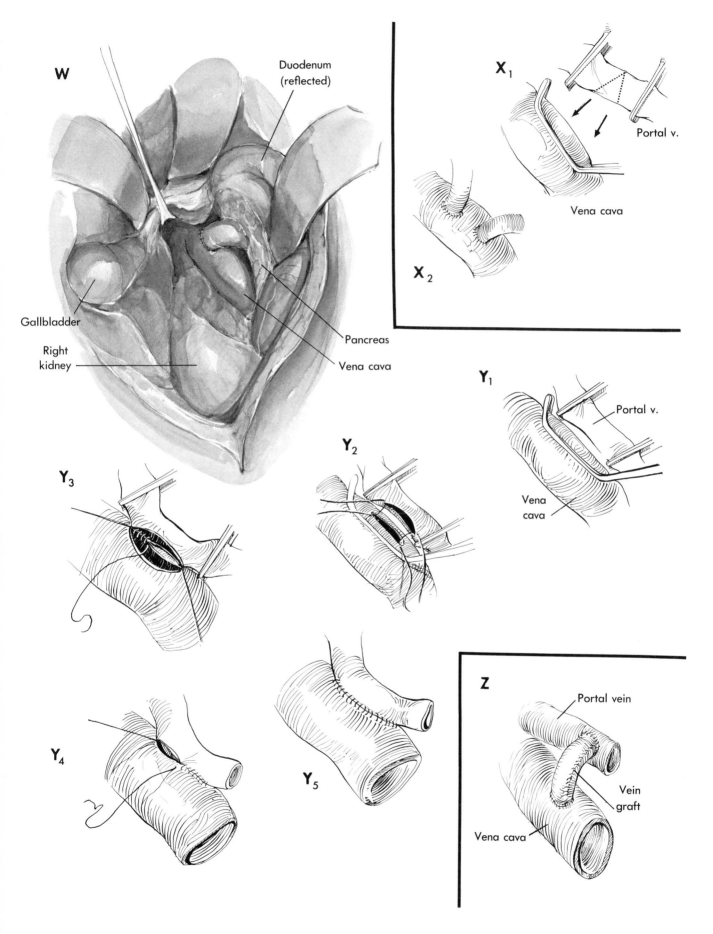

W

Duodenum
(reflected)

Gallbladder

Right
kidney

Pancreas

Vena cava

X₁

Portal v.

Vena cava

X₂

Y₁

Portal v.

Vena
cava

Y₂

Y₃

Y₄

Y₅

Z

Portal vein

Vein
graft

Vena cava

Splenorenal Shunt

A   Although a surgeon may prefer a certain type of portal decompression operation, any of several may have to be used by election or necessity. Obviously, shunt surgery should not be attempted unless the surgeon has the ability to perform any one of them and also has a thorough knowledge of the vascular anatomy of the upper abdomen. A normal size spleen is shown here, but there may be a variable degree of splenomegaly. The splenic vein issues from the splenic hilus as several tributaries and courses toward the right on a position caudad to the splenic artery, remaining behind the pancreas throughout its course. There empty into it the left gastroepiploic vein, the short gastric veins, some pancreatic veins and the inferior mesenteric vein before it joins with the superior mesenteric vein to form the portal vein. Deep to it lie the left kidney and adrenal gland and the aorta.

B   The patient is positioned on his right side and at a 45 degree angle from the true supine. Large sandbags are used at the shoulder and hip for support. Three-inch tape is placed across the hips and anchored to the operating table so that the patient can be maintained in this position. The left arm is padded, folded over the head and attached to the anesthesia screen with proper support. A large bore venous catheter should be in position. Since a distended stomach would interfere with the operation it is kept deflated with an inlying nasogastric tube in spite of the theoretic and real risk in doing so in the presence of the esophageal varices. An abdominothoracic incision is utilized, the abdominal being made first to assess operability and to exclude nonremediable causes of portal hypertension such as cancer. The abdominal incision is extended obliquely from the midline of the abdomen through the 8th or 9th interspace. The diaphragm is incised toward the esophageal hiatus, with care being taken not to damage the phrenic nerve and remembering that sizable collateral veins may be encountered.

C   The usual exploration of the peritoneal cavity is carried out. The status of the spleno-
D   portal system must be known so that if there is any doubt on this point a splenoporto-gram may be done at this more convenient time under direct vision. Portal pressures are obtained through a mesenteric vein. Division of the gastrocolic omentum is begun at the midtransverse colon and on the relatively avascular gastric side of the arcades of the gastroepiploic vessels.

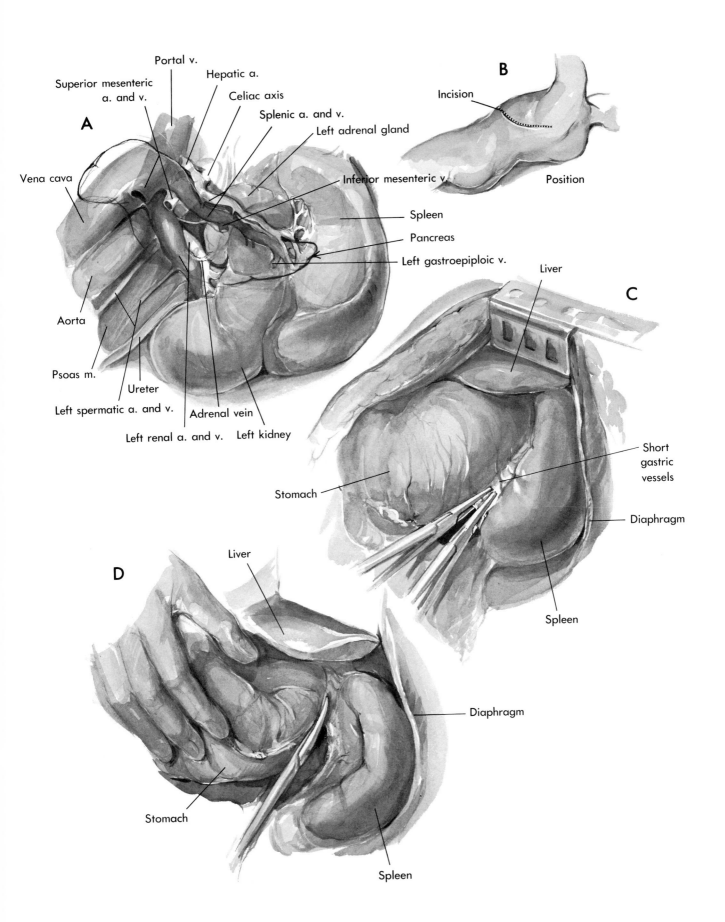

A

Portal v.
Superior mesenteric a. and v.
Hepatic a.
Celiac axis
Splenic a. and v.
Left adrenal gland
Vena cava
Inferior mesenteric v.
Spleen
Pancreas
Left gastroepiploic v.
Aorta
Psoas m.
Ureter
Left spermatic a. and v.
Adrenal vein
Left renal a. and v.
Left kidney

B

Incision
Position

C

Liver
Short gastric vessels
Diaphragm
Stomach
Spleen

D

Liver
Diaphragm
Stomach
Spleen

E
F
The short gastric vessels are divided in their entirety so that the greater curvature of the stomach is entirely free. In Figure E the usually large uppermost short gastric vessels are being clamped. The splenocolic ligament is clamped and divided. Normally avascular areas may be extensively traversed by collateral venules which, because of the hypertension, will bleed copiously when transected. For this reason, no blunt dissection is carried out in these operations and far more clamping and ligating of tissue is practiced. Electrocoagulation is used for oozing points.

G
The stomach is reflected medially and the splenic flexure of the colon displaced downward. The peritoneum over the hilar vessels is incised and dissection of the vessels begun. The artery is isolated first and tied with 2-0 silk or looped with a linen tie and left open so that it can keep the splenic vein and its tributaries turgid for easier dissection. The splenic vein is isolated next. This is done slightly away from the hilus and over the single vein rather than becoming involved with a time-consuming dissection of its tributaries, coming off the spleen.

H
The spleen is reflected medially and any lateral attachments divided. Although this is normally an avascular area, extensive collateral vessels make it necessary to clamp this tissue before its division and ligation. The problem is aggravated if there are any perisplenic adhesions or if the spleen is quite large. If such involvement is present and the blood loss threatens to become excessive, the splenic artery is ligated.

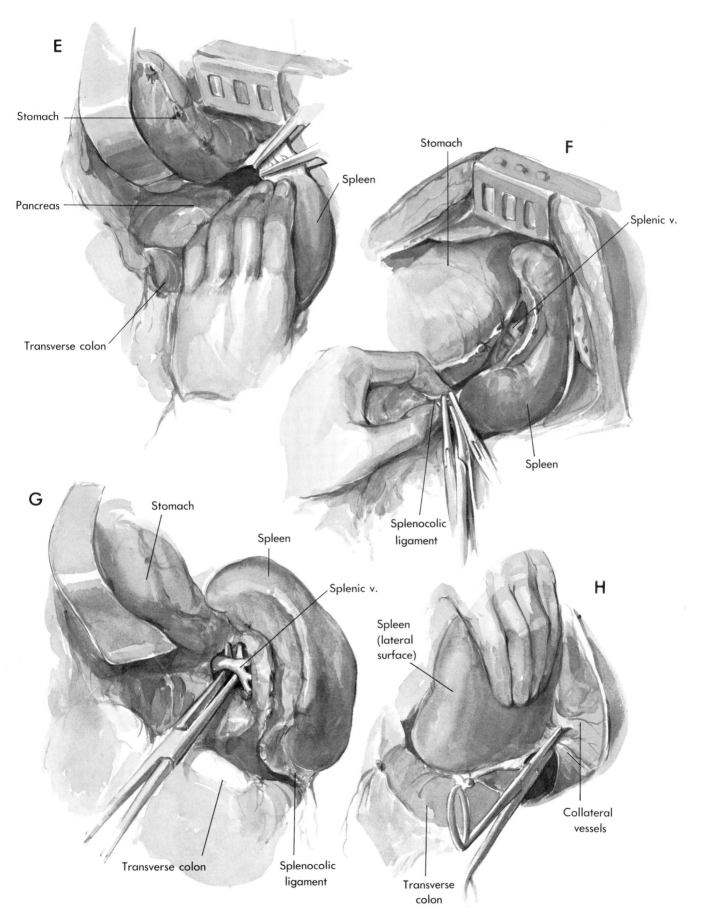

E

Stomach

Pancreas

Transverse colon

Spleen

F

Stomach

Splenic v.

Spleen

Splenocolic ligament

G

Stomach

Spleen

Splenic v.

Transverse colon

Splenocolic ligament

H

Spleen (lateral surface)

Collateral vessels

Transverse colon

I   The spleen is reflected even more to the right and the posterior parietal peritoneum at the tail of the pancreas incised so that this portion of the pancreas can also be reflected. A spring Potts clamp is now placed on the splenic vein close to the hilum and the spleen is amputated. Five milliliters of saline containing 10 mg. of heparin are injected into the vein immediately proximal to the clamp and the vein reclamped just proximal to the needle punctures, all this being done on a portion of the vein that is not to be used.

J
K
L   The splenectomy results in the wide exposure which is necessary for the proper mobilization of the splenic vein. The vein is delicately teased away from the pancreas, and the pancreatic veins isolated with an Adson hemostat. These short pancreatic veins are clamped, divided and ligated with 5-0 silk. If they are particularly short they are tied in continuity before being divided. Tearing of these tributaries can, cumulatively, become serious by virtue of the blood loss, consumption of time securing these bleeders and the possible compromise of the lumen of the splenic vein when repairing the tears. The splenic vein is mobilized medially to the point where it is joined by the inferior mesenteric vein.

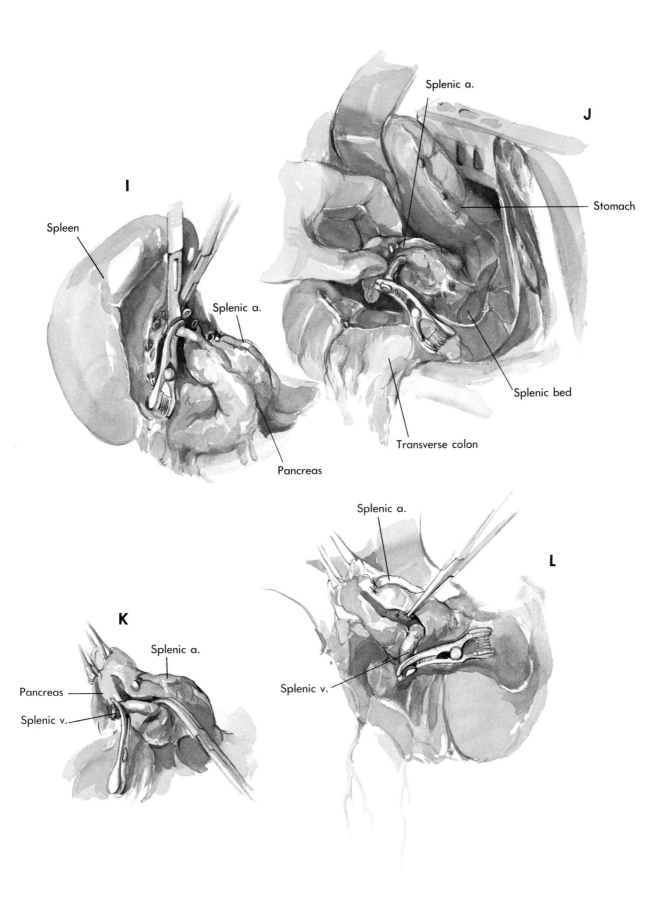

I

Spleen

Splenic a.

Pancreas

J

Splenic a.

Stomach

Splenic bed

Transverse colon

K

Splenic a.

Pancreas

Splenic v.

L

Splenic a.

Splenic v.

M
N The renal vein is prepared in its middle third for the anastomosis. The tail of the pancreas is temporarily displaced cephalad and the posterior parietal peritoneum over the renal vein is incised to the vena cava. The entire kidney need not be mobilized. The spermatic and adrenal veins are susceptible to injury and are spared if possible but can be ligated with impunity if they appear to interfere with the contemplated anastomotic site.

O A Satinsky clamp is applied over a portion of the renal vein and the splenic vein brought into position. At this time the downward curve of the splenic vein is observed since the surgeon must feel confident that there will be no kinking or twisting which encourages thrombosis. If there is any doubt about this, the vein is mobilized further so that it can make a smooth downward sweep. The tail of the pancreas is held out of the way by grasping the peripancreatic fatty areolar tissue with Babcock forceps.

P
Q
R An oval window suitable to receive the splenic vein is cut away from the renal vein with a sharp curved scissors in a method similar to that used in the portacaval anastomosis. The vessels are joined by anchoring stitches at the ends of the oval and the posterior anastomosis is placed first. Atraumatic 5-0 silk is used and the bites of the needle are about 1.5 mm. apart and about 1.0 mm. from the cut edge. Smooth-tipped vein hooks are used to manipulate the vessel edges during placement of the anterior row of stitches. Often it may not be possible to partially occlude the renal vein during the anastomosis. If total occlusion is necessary this must be preceded by occlusion of the artery. The short period of renal ischemia during performance of the anastomosis is not harmful if 30 minutes or so.

S The clamp on the renal vein is removed first and followed promptly by removal of that on the splenic artery. Oozing from the suture line will stop if pressure is applied for a moment with a moist sponge. The pancreas is examined carefully for any trauma. If the tip of the tail has been transected, the defect is sutured with atraumatic 3-0 silk. Portal pressure is again determined to assess the immediate effect on it by the shunt.

A chest catheter is exteriorized at the costophrenic angle in the midaxillary line and connected to an under-water seal. The diaphragmatic incision is repaired in two layers with interrupted stitches of 2-0 silk. The costal cartilages are notched before being approximated. A soft rubber drain is placed in the splenic bed and is made to pass by the tail of the pancreas on its way to the outside through a counterincision. The remainder of the wound is closed in the preferred fashion.

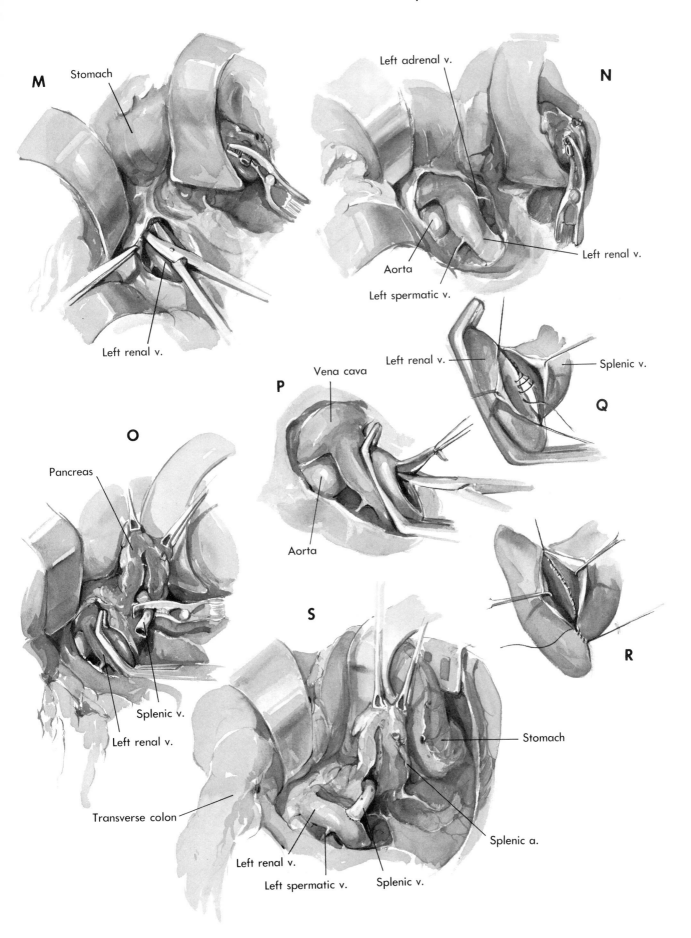

M

Stomach

Left renal v.

N

Left adrenal v.

Aorta

Left spermatic v.

Left renal v.

O

Pancreas

Splenic v.

Left renal v.

P

Vena cava

Aorta

Q

Left renal v.

Splenic v.

R

S

Transverse colon

Left renal v.

Left spermatic v.

Splenic v.

Stomach

Splenic a.

PANCREAS

The pancreas is both an endocrine and exocrine organ. The surgical diseases it is subject to are frequently not readily diagnosed.

The endocrine function of the pancreas is to produce insulin to help control glucose metabolism by the body. Failure of its endocrine function results in diabetes mellitus, which is not a disease amenable to surgical therapy since the pancreas cannot yet be transplanted. The overproduction of insulin by the pancreas, as occurs with a pancreatic adenoma, is a condition amenable to surgery. It is important to recognize that other lesions such as thoracic neoplasms can also produce insulin-like compounds that can cause hypoglycemia. The pancreatic lesion that produces an oversecretion of insulin with resultant hypoglycemia is a beta-cell adenoma. Adenomas may be multiple and they may be small, which makes complete discovery and total excision difficult. If the adenomas are multiple or cannot be found and the diagnosis seems certain, the treatment of choice is a subtotal pancreatectomy, which leaves some of the head of the pancreas intact.

The pancreatic tumors of the Zollinger-Ellison syndrome are non-beta-cell tumors. They are frequently malignant (47 per cent) and produce the hormone gastrin, which causes the stomach to secrete hydrochloric acid at a maximal rate. These pancreatic tumors can be suspected whenever it is found that the stomach is already producing a maximum volume of gastric juice with maximum acidity not increased by exogenous histamine stimulation.

The exocrine function of the pancreas is to produce digestive enzymes. The most important digestive enzymes are amylase, lipase, trypsin and chymotrypsin. The 24-hour volume of pancreatic juice is 500 to 1500 cc.; this is alkaline in reaction because of its high bicarbonate concentration. The alkalinity is valuable in neutralizing the acid gastric contents and in promoting an optimum environment for enzyme activity.

Carcinoma of the pancreas is a serious problem. If the tumor is in the tail, it is usually undiagnosed until the tumor has spread widely and is not amenable to surgical cure. Carcinoma of the head of the pancreas is diagnosed sooner since it tends to obstruct the bile ducts and to produce jaundice, but surgical removal of cancer of the pancreatic head has not had a high percentage of cures. Carcinoma of the duodenum at the ampulla of Vater is a lesion much more susceptible to cure. This lesion requires resection of the head of the pancreas.

Of the benign exocrine lesions of the pancreas, the most important is pancreatitis. It is thought that pancreatitis occurs when there is obstruction to the pancreatic exocrine function (pancreatic duct obstruction) caused by activation of its digestive enzymes by bile reflux.

The typical pancreatitis patient has either biliary tract disease or else overdrinks ethyl alcohol. Alcohol stimulates gastric acidity via the duodenal production of the hormone secretin. Vomiting and retching raise ductal pressure. Pancreatic reflux may occur with a mixture of bile and pancreatic juice in those persons whose bile ducts and pancreatic ducts join proximal to the ampulla of Vater, or when a gallstone obstructs the ampulla. In spite of these hypotheses the exact mechanism whereby biliary disease or alcoholism produces pancreatitis in man is not definitely known. Methyl alcohol ingestion can cause pancreatitis.

In the presence of acute pancreatitis an elevated serum and urinary level of pancreatic enzymes (amylase) can be found. Usually, acute pancreatitis is not a surgical disease; fasting, intestinal decompression and rest will frequently bring about subsidence of the symptoms. Biliary pathology should be electively corrected. Occasionally, pancreatitis is fulminant and fatal. Peritoneal dialysis and massive fluid, plasma and blood replacement may be helpful.

The necrosis and inflammation associated with pancreatitis may cause blockage of the pancreatic duct and cyst formation in the pancreas. Internal drainage of the cyst into the stomach or into defunctionalized small intestine will be indicated if the cyst persists. If sphincterotomy of the sphincter of Oddi will prevent biliary reflux into the pancreas, it should be done.

If recurrent attacks of pancreatitis occur, the diseased gland may produce severe pain. Anatomically, there is typically a series of ductal obstructions and dilatations. The diagnosis of chronic pancreatitis may be difficult to make unless calcification is seen in the pancreas or pancreatic exocrine deficiencies are demonstrated. Duodenal aspiration may show a lack of bicarbonate in the pancreatic juice. Severe pancreatic deficiency will be evidenced by malabsorption of fats. This can be detected by feeding test doses of radioactive tagged fats and quantitating the per cent absorbed. Other diseases may also produce steatorrhea. An important surgical disease is "abdominal angina," in which food produces crampy pain and fatty diarrhea. This can be caused by arterial obstruction, usually to two of the three major arterial supplies to the gastrointestinal tract, i.e., the celiac axis, the superior mesenteric or the inferior mesenteric artery. It is important at all exploratory laparotomies that surgeons routinely and carefully evaluate the abdominal arterial pulses.

Operations on the pancreas are difficult and somewhat hazardous. The tail of the pancreas is relatively simple to resect, but even here there may be serious complications from leakage of digestive juices. The pancreatic stump must be drained well, or the gland should be inserted into the lumen of bowel.

Resection of the head of the pancreas is complicated by the fact that the alimentary tract must be reconstructed with provision for drainage of bile and pancreatic juice into the bowel. The presence of the superior mesenteric vessels, which lie in intimate contact with the pancreas, complicates and restricts the performance of a total pancreatectomy.

References

General

Doubilet, H.: The physiological basis for the surgical management of acute and chronic pancreatitis. Surg. Clin. North America 38:505, 1958.

Porter, M. R.: Changes in pancreatic physiology incident to pancreatic disease or surgery. Surg. Clin. North America 38:487, 1958.

Warren, K. W.: Complications of pancreatic surgery. Surg. Clin. North America 37:683, 1957.

Pancreatitis

Child, C. G., III, and Kahn, D. R.: Current status of therapy of pancreatitis. J.A.M.A. 179:363, 1962.

Doubilet, H., and Mulholland, J. H.: Surgical treatment of chronic pancreatitis. J.A.M.A. 175:177, 1961.

DuVal, M. K., Jr.: Pancreaticojejunostomy for chronic pancreatitis. Surgery 41:1019, 1957.

DuVal, M. K., Jr., and Enquist, I. A.: The surgical treatment of chronic pancreatitis by pancreaticojejunostomy: An 8-year reappraisal. Surgery 50:965, 1961.

Gillesby, W. J., and Puestow, C. B.: Surgery for chronic recurrent pancreatitis. Surg. Clin. North America 41:83, 1961.

Puestow, C. B., and Gillesby, W. J.: Retrograde surgical drainage of pancreas for chronic relapsing pancreatitis. A.M.A. Arch. Surg. 76:898, 1958.

Pancreatectomy

Child, C. G., III, and Fry, W. J.: Current status of pancreatectomies. Surg. Clin. North America 42:1353, 1962.

Whipple, A. O.: Observations on radical surgery for lesions of the pancreas. Surg. Gynec. & Obst. 82:623, 1946.

Whipple, A. O., et al.: Treatment of carcinoma of the ampulla of Vater. Ann. Surg. 102:763, 1935.

Adenoma

Whipple, A. O., and Frantz, V.: Adenoma of islet cells with hyperinsulinism. Ann. Surg. 101:1299, 1935.

Zollinger-Ellison Syndrome

Ellison, E., and Carey, L.: Diagnosis and management of the Zollinger-Ellison syndrome. Am. J. Surg. 105:383, 1963.

Zollinger, R., and Ellison, E.: Primary peptic ulceration of the jejunum associated with islet cell tumors of the pancreas. Ann. Surg. 142:709, 1955.

Pancreaticoduodenectomy

A Several types of incisions may be used. Although a right paramedian muscle reflecting incision probably allows slightly more latitude, a midline incision is easier to make and is essentially bloodless. In an operation of this magnitude, such an incision should be closed with through and through stitches. More accurate apposition of the linea alba with a continuous suture of 1-0 chromic catgut may reduce the incidence of postoperative ventral herniation. The acknowledged increased incidence of early and late postoperative ventral herniation with such an incision is of minimal importance in such a group of patients when compared to the advantages it offers. The transverse incision allows for easier access to organs in the upper abdomen and probably has the least risk of postoperative dehiscence. It does take longer to make and to close, and maintaining exposure does not seem so easy.

B The general topographic relationships are shown here. The length of the retroduodenal common duct allows for subsequent sectioning at an adequate distance from an ampullary or duodenal tumor. Notice that the hepatic flexure of the colon may overlie some of the second and third portions of the duodenum. The transverse colon and its associated transverse mesocolon have been removed to show some of the underlying anatomy. The transected root of the mesentery of the small bowel makes more obvious the manner in which the duodenum passes under the superior mesenteric artery and vein and over the aorta. The spleen is not shown.

C The most difficult aspect of the operation is the control of bleeding, especially from tributaries from the superior mesenteric artery and vein. The hepatic artery is seen giving off the gastroduodenal artery, which, in turn, gives off the superior pancreaticoduodenal artery, which then meets the inferior pancreaticoduodenal artery from the superior mesenteric artery. The right and left gastric arteries are also shown. It is important to keep in mind the numerous anatomic variations that may be present. A misjudgment in the location of such a vessel would most likely be important as a cause of bleeding rather than of necrosis.

D Aspiration of a distended gallbladder with a large bore needle is carried out at the onset of the operation. This step will facilitate the exposure; if there is any question about the disease present, the needle will serve for a cholecystocholedochogram. Aspiration of bile and the reinstillation of contrast material 25 cc. in excess of the volume of bile will enable the surgeon to visualize the bile ducts and may help to exclude the presence of a stone as the cause of the jaundice.

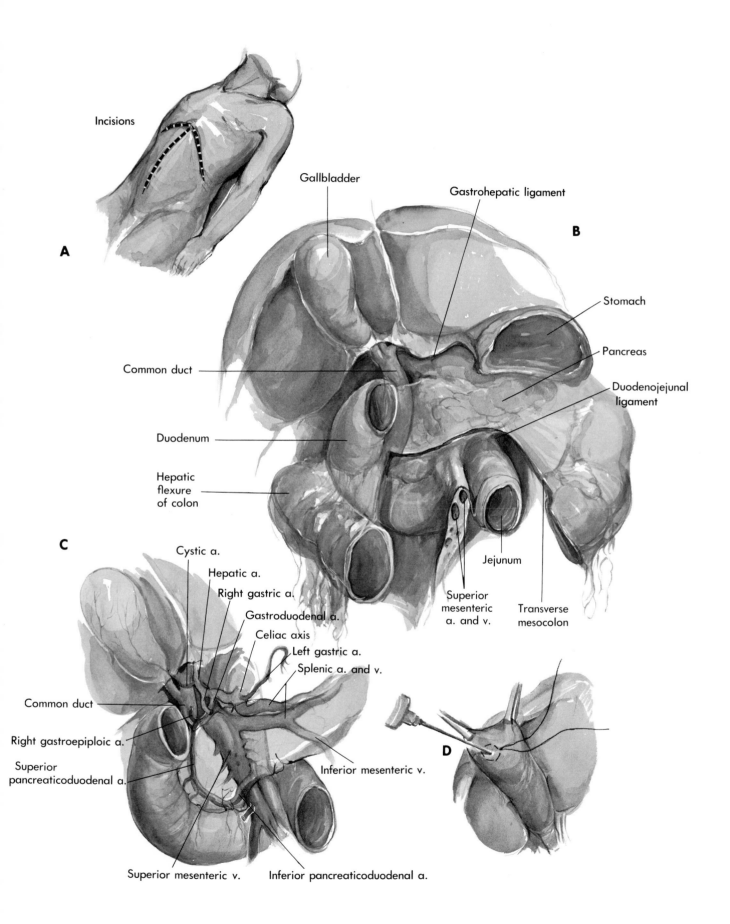

Incisions

A

Gallbladder

Gastrohepatic ligament

B

Stomach

Pancreas

Common duct

Duodenojejunal
ligament

Duodenum

Hepatic
flexure
of colon

Jejunum

Superior
mesenteric
a. and v.

Transverse
mesocolon

C

Cystic a.

Hepatic a.

Right gastric a.

Gastroduodenal a.

Celiac axis

Left gastric a.

Splenic a. and v.

Common duct

Right gastroepiploic a.

Superior
pancreaticoduodenal a.

Inferior mesenteric v.

D

Superior mesenteric v.

Inferior pancreaticoduodenal a.

E The root of the transverse mesocolon is divided as it crosses over the right kidney, the second portion of the duodenum and up to the left of the superior mesenteric vessels. The dissection along the designated lower border of the body of the pancreas is relatively void of vessels. At this point, involvement of the superior mesenteric vessels with tumor is assessed. This also permits a preliminary inspection of the posteroinferior aspect of the pancreas as well as of the vena cava and aorta. If any of these vessels is involved with tumor as manifested by no significant cleavage between their anterior surfaces and the posterior aspect of the pancreas, the tumor can be considered as nonresectable and the major procedure abandoned gracefully.

F The duodenum is mobilized by incising the lateral parietal peritoneum from the superior mesenteric vessels inferiorly, past the right free margin of the hepatoduodenal ligament to the origin of the gastroduodenal artery. Most of the remainder of the duodenal mobilization is performed by using blunt dissection.

G The superior mesenteric vessels as well as the vena cava can be further examined for tumor involvement by palpating them posterior and cephalad to the pancreas. Again, if there is no cleavage between the portal vein and the dorsal surface of the pancreas, the tumor can be considered as nonresectable. Although a portion of the portal vein so involved can be resected with the tumor and a portacaval anastomosis performed, this is a rare exception.

H Confirming the presence of a resectable cancer of the head of the pancreas can be a vexing problem. This is less so with lesions involving the ampulla of Vater, the terminal common duct (duct of Wirsung) or the peri-Vaterian duodenal mucosa. A duodenotomy is necessary to obtain tissue for a microscopic diagnosis of all but the lesions of the terminal common duct. The operative field should be walled off with gauze pads during this aspect of the operation to minimize the possibility of seeding raw areas with cancer cells. Once the biopsy specimen is obtained, the duodenum is closed, the instruments discarded and the gloves changed before proceeding. Some surgeons recommend pancreatectomy for tumor on gross findings alone. We have preferred to seek a tissue diagnosis. At times, however, a decision will have to be made by clinical judgment.

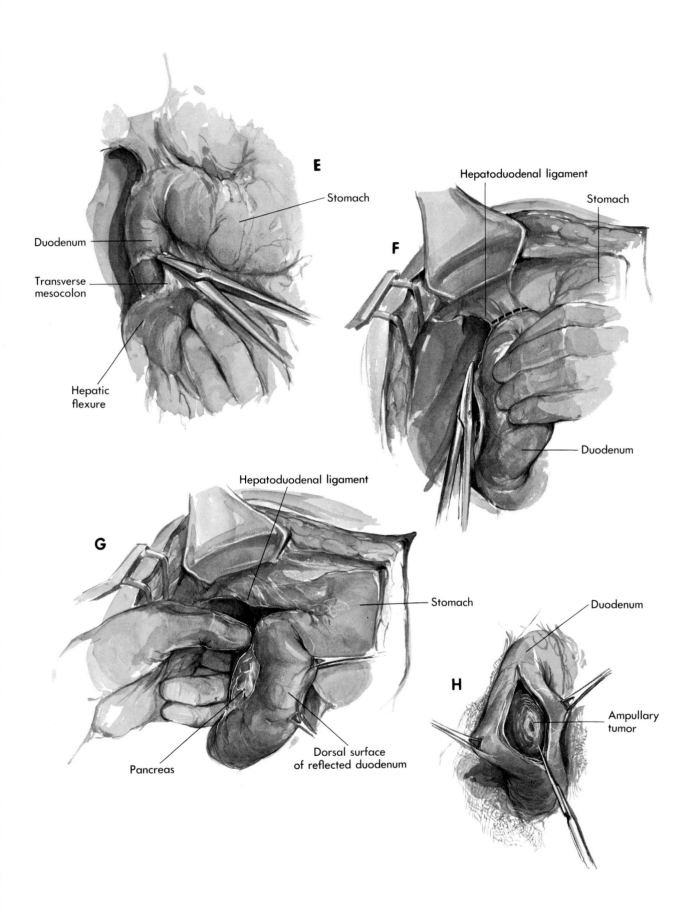

E

Stomach

Duodenum

Transverse
mesocolon

Hepatic
flexure

F

Hepatoduodenal ligament

Stomach

Duodenum

G

Hepatoduodenal ligament

Stomach

Pancreas

Dorsal surface
of reflected duodenum

H

Duodenum

Ampullary
tumor

I   The dilated common duct is circumferentially dissected at this stage. Usually the point of division is above the entrance of the cystic duct for cancer of the distal common duct; for cancer of other sites considered in this section, the necessity for division above this point would probably mean extensive involvement and would indicate an incurable if not a nonresectable tumor.

J   The common duct is encircled with a soft rubber drain for retraction and preliminary dissection from the portal vein. Because of a mild inflammatory reaction around a chronically distended common duct, care is necessary here to prevent injury to the portal vein and consequent troublesome hemorrhage.

K   We chose to section the common duct at this time because, of the several major structures that have to be sectioned, the severed common duct can still be used for the performance of a choledochojejunostomy if it is decided shortly thereafter that the tumor is nonresectable or that the operation must be terminated for other reasons.

L   Sectioning of the common duct at this stage (K) allows for rotation of the head of the pancreas and attached structures for easier and more accurate ligation of branches from the superior mesenteric vessels. Only the more lateral branches can be adequately exposed for dissection, ligation and division at this time. The remainder will be so handled later (Plate 6). These branches are short, will tear easily from their relatively fixed position in the pancreas and certainly lead to troublesome bleeding if torn. Ligation in continuity is, in our opinion, the safest and, in the long run, the swiftest way to proceed through this difficult aspect of the operation.

For ductal or ampullary tumors, the divided distal common duct may profitably be closed with a continuous simple stitch to prevent tumor spillage.

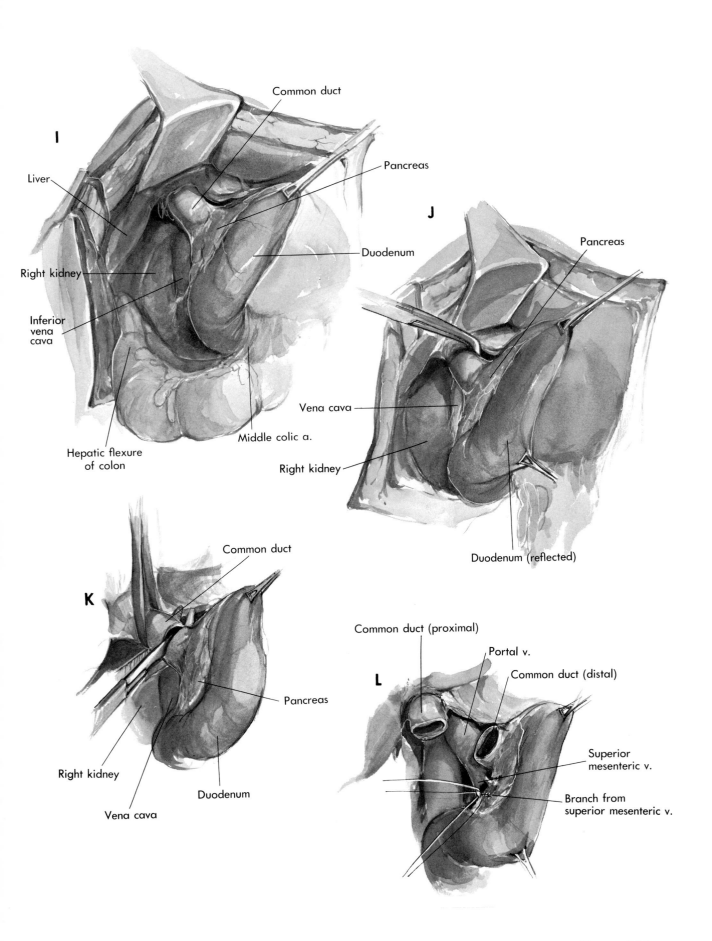

I

Liver

Right kidney

Inferior
vena
cava

Hepatic flexure
of colon

Common duct

Pancreas

Duodenum

Middle colic a.

J

Pancreas

Vena cava

Right kidney

Duodenum (reflected)

K

Common duct

Pancreas

Right kidney

Vena cava

Duodenum

L

Common duct (proximal)

Portal v.

Common duct (distal)

Superior
mesenteric v.

Branch from
superior mesenteric v.

M   The gastrocolic ligament is next divided just outside the gastroepiploic arch through at least the second short gastric branches. Traction on the stomach downward and to the right facilitates this exposure.

N   After the stomach is freed along its greater curvature it is elevated, exposing the pancreas fully. Minor adhesions between the pancreas and the stomach are often present and are readily divided. The mobilization need not be so thorough in the area shared by the antrum and the head of the pancreas if there is a risk of cutting into the cancer. This exposure will now make possible definitive surgery on the pancreas itself and readies the stomach for the transection which is also a part of the procedure.

O
P   The next step involves passing a small soft rubber drain under the body of the pancreas. This is done most safely just to the left of the superior mesenteric artery, which also coincides with the subsequent optimum site of division of the pancreas. Keeping to the left of the superior mesenteric artery and vein is of the utmost importance, as tearing of a branch from these vessels means copious bleeding with minimal exposure at this point for their identification and ligation. At this stage, the inferior pancreaticoduodenal artery from the superior mesenteric artery should be identified, ligated in continuity and divided.

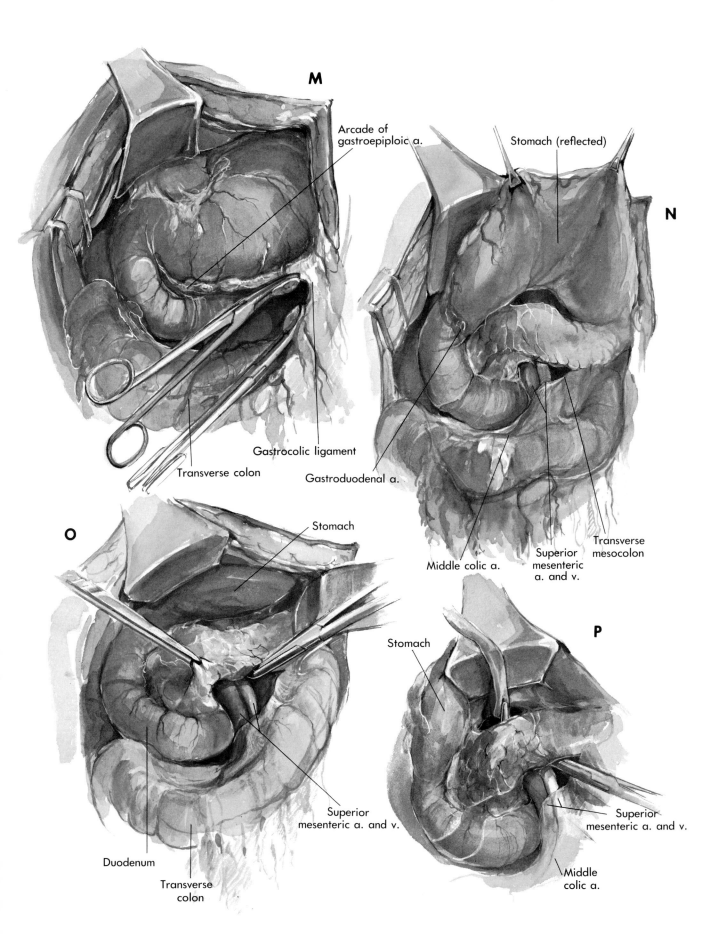

M

Arcade of
gastroepiploic a.

Stomach (reflected)

N

Gastrocolic ligament

Transverse colon

Gastroduodenal a.

Middle colic a.

Superior
mesenteric
a. and v.

Transverse
mesocolon

O

Stomach

Superior
mesenteric a. and v.

Stomach

P

Superior
mesenteric a. and v.

Duodenum

Transverse
colon

Middle
colic a.

Q   Cephalad to the body of the pancreas and along the lesser curvature of the stomach can be seen the celiac axis, and the splenic, hepatic and gastroduodenal arteries. Dissecting in this area, with the stomach reflected upward or in its natural position, depends on the preference of the surgeon. In more obese patients (who have a fatty lesser omentum) it is easier to reach these vessels by the manner shown.

R   We show the stomach in its natural position. The gastroduodenal artery is now divided and the distal end is simply ligated, the proximal end being oversewn with 6-0 arterial silk. The reason for this is that pancreatic leakage, which might otherwise have been nonfatal in this area, has resulted in digestion of this sizable artery proximal to the simple ligature with fatal hemorrhage. Notice the use of a noncrushing arterial clamp on the proximal side of the vessel that is to be oversewn.

S   The left gastric artery is isolated just above the angula incisura. Since the left gastric artery is closely adjacent to the stomach, it is necessary to incise the peritoneum of the gastrohepatic omentum in order to identify the artery more easily.

T   An approximately 50 per cent gastric resection is performed. The Payr clamp is just distal to the double row of von Petz staples and holds the portion of the stomach which eventually is to be removed. The von Petz staples are particularly applicable here as they confine the stomach secretions for the considerable time the remainder of the operation is in progress.

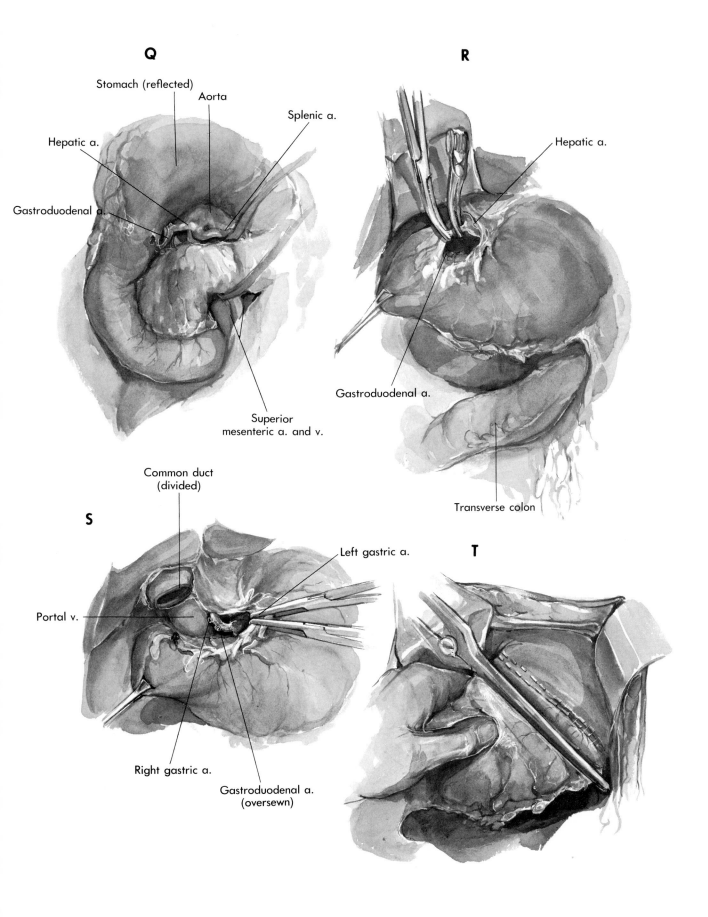

Q

Stomach (reflected)

Aorta

Splenic a.

Hepatic a.

Gastroduodenal a.

Superior
mesenteric a. and v.

R

Hepatic a.

Gastroduodenal a.

Transverse colon

S

Common duct
(divided)

Left gastric a.

Portal v.

Right gastric a.

Gastroduodenal a.
(oversewn)

T

U   Following division of the stomach, the antrum is reflected laterally. The walls of the lesser curvature of the stomach are inverted now or later with simple interrupted stitches of 2-0 black silk to a residual opening of about 4 cm. for the future stoma. The staples, in the portion not inverted, are left in place until just before the gastrojejunostomy is performed.

V   The pancreas is now divided. Digital pressure is effective for temporary hemostasis while these vessels are secured with transfixion stitches of 3-0 black silk. The pancreatic duct will be dilated and the juice within it may be under increased pressure.

W   With lateral reflection of the head of the pancreas, ligation and division of tributaries from the superior mesenteric vein can be completed. Sometimes it is easier to divide the pancreas more to the left of the superior mesenteric vessels and to complete ligation and division of branches from these vessels by reflecting the head of the pancreas toward the right.

X   Continued reflection of the head and neck of the divided pancreas to the right and gentle traction of the superior mesenteric vessels to the left will allow for safer and swifter dissection of an often stubbornly situated uncinate process. A vein retractor fulfills its function admirably here in keeping the superior mesenteric vessels out of the way.

Y   The fourth portion of the duodenum and the first portion of the jejunum are mobilized by first dividing the duodenojejunal ligament (Treitz). Here it is shown being done from the left of the superior mesenteric vessels. However, the maneuver of gentle traction of the jejunum toward the right from the right side and under the superior mesenteric artery and vein will permit a similar dissection.

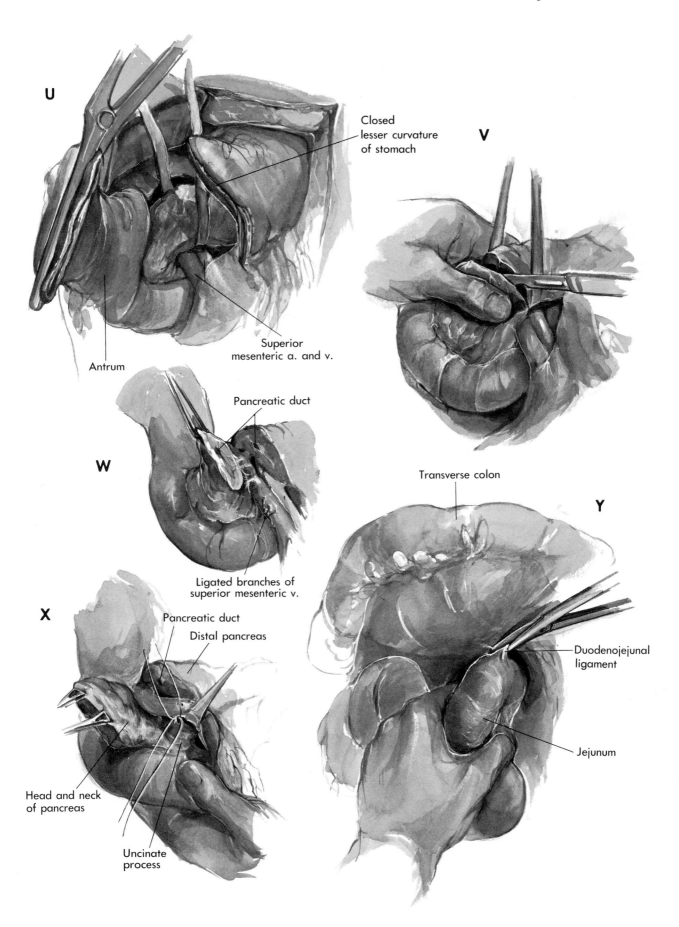

U

Closed
lesser curvature
of stomach

V

Antrum

Superior
mesenteric a. and v.

Pancreatic duct

W

Ligated branches of
superior mesenteric v.

Transverse colon

Y

X

Pancreatic duct

Distal pancreas

Duodenojejunal
ligament

Jejunum

Head and neck
of pancreas

Uncinate
process

Z   The mobilized proximal jejunum is brought toward the right under the superior mesenteric artery and vein and divided immediately distal to the duodenojejunal ligament. The portion of the jejunum marked with an asterisk (*) will subsequently be used for the pancreaticojejunostomy.

A₁   Transection of the jejunum now allows withdrawal of the proximal jejunum and fourth portion of the duodenum toward the right. The distal jejunum has been returned to its normal position to be used in the subsequent reconstruction.

B₁   The completed destructive aspect of the operation is shown to illustrate the absence of distal stomach, head and neck of pancreas, all the duodenum, some proximal jejunum, distal common duct and the accompanying lymph nodes. The gallbladder is not shown and could be removed anytime it is convenient.

C₁   The reconstructive phase of the operation begins by passing the proximal jejunum through the mesenteric window. The asterisk (*) marks the same spot as in Figure Z. We prefer, when possible, an end-to-end pancreaticojejunostomy; this anastomosis is performed first. The transected end of the pancreas is inspected at this time and further mobilized as necessary so that there is an approximately 2 cm. free margin of pancreas.

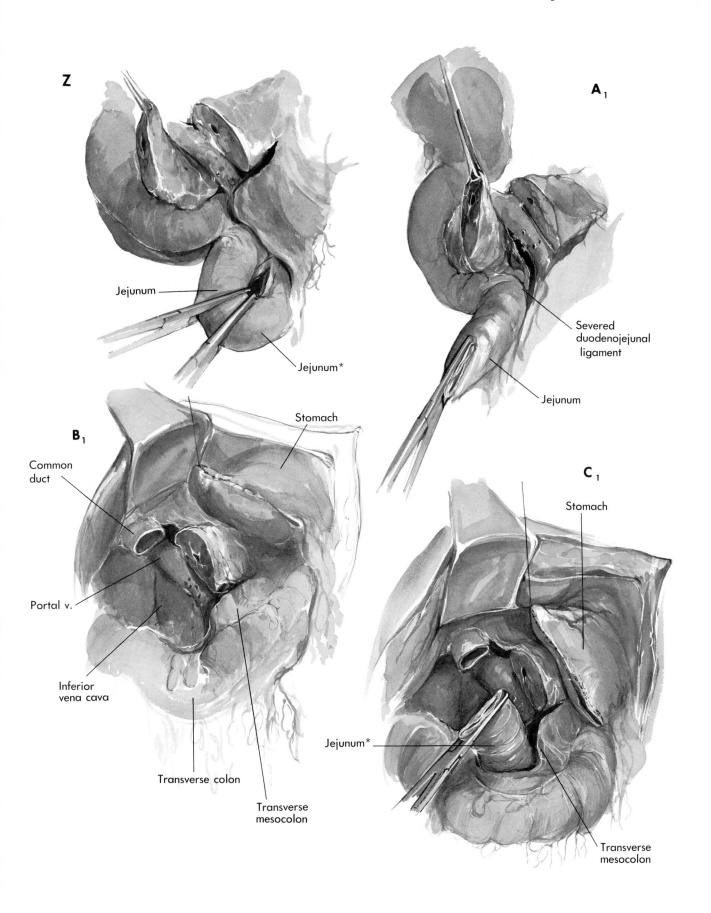

Z

Jejunum

Jejunum*

A₁

Severed
duodenojejunal
ligament

Jejunum

B₁

Common
duct

Portal v.

Inferior
vena cava

Stomach

Transverse colon

Transverse
mesocolon

C₁

Stomach

Jejunum*

Transverse
mesocolon

D$_1$ The posterior surfaces of the jejunum and pancreas are approximated about 1 cm. from
E$_1$ their respective edges with interrupted stitches of 3-0 black silk.

F$_1$ The jejunal mucosa and the capsule of the divided pancreas are approximated with a
G$_1$ continuous stitch of atraumatic 3-0 chromic catgut as shown here. Some choose to
use interrupted stitches of atraumatic 3-0 black silk.

H$_1$ The second anterior pancreaticojejunal row of stitches continues with interrupted
I$_1$ atraumatic 3-0 black silk. They also are placed 1 cm. back of the respective free edges
and engage the seromuscular edge of the jejunum and the capsule of the pancreas.
This causes "telescoping" of the free edges so that they lie within the jejunum, leading
to a decreased incidence of anastomotic leakage.

J$_1$ The end-to-side choledochojejunostomy is performed next. A posterior row of inter-
K$_1$ rupted simple stitches made with 4-0 black silk is followed by a second layer using continuous 4-0 chromic catgut to appose the mucosa. The continuous suture technique
is superior to interrupted sutures for protection against leakage. However, great care
should be exercised that, during placement, the sutures do not "purse-string" the anastomosis. If the duct is not dilated, an interrupted technique had best be used. Figure
K$_1$ shows both anterior layers of stitches being placed. Accurate suture placement and
care not to invaginate an excessive amount of tissue make the preferred two-layer
closure possible.

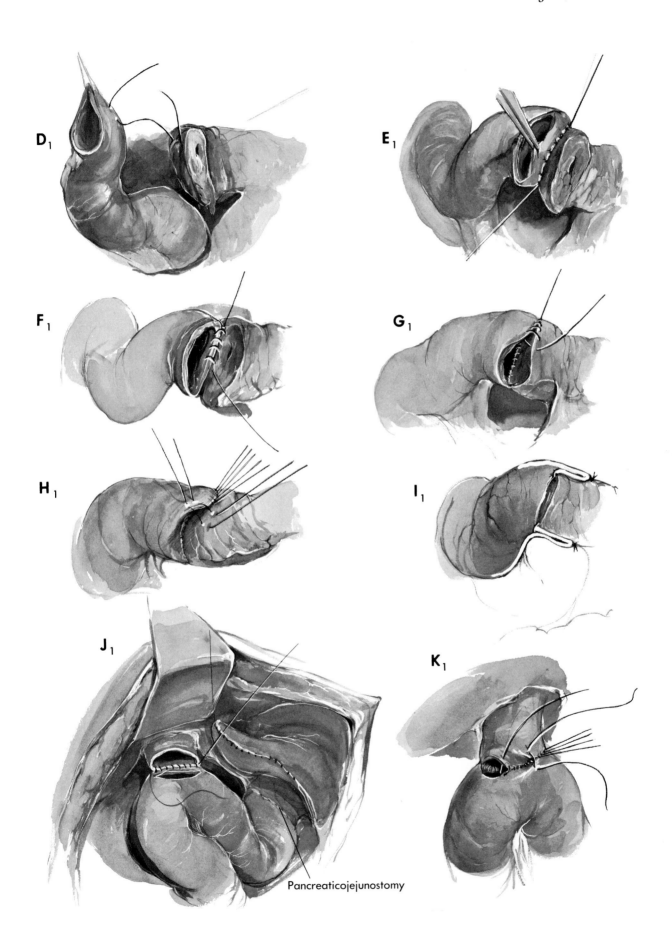

D₁

E₁

F₁

G₁

H₁

I₁

J₁

Pancreaticojejunostomy

K₁

L_1 The Polya-Hoffmeister gastrojejunostomy is performed in two layers following trimming of the stapled free edge of the stomach. The suturing of the seromuscular layer is performed with continuous or interrupted stitch using 3-0 black silk; the mucosa is approximated with a continuous stitch of atraumatic 3-0 chromic catgut. The mesocolic defect is repaired with interrupted stitches of 3-0 chromic catgut to obviate internal herniation. There should be sufficient length of jejunum distal to the choledochojejunal anastomosis to prevent the retrograde travel of food up and into the biliary radicals. Ordinarily a loop of about 25 cm. will suffice.

M_1 The completed operation is shown. If a gastrostomy can be performed with ease, it will certainly increase the postoperative comfort of the patient. It is our feeling that a gastrostomy also decreases postoperative nasopharyngeal and pulmonary complications. Soft rubber drains and one Chaffin tube from the pancreaticojejunostomy, placed so as to include in their sweep the two other anastomoses, are exteriorized through a counterincision in the right upper quadrant. The incision is closed in the manner prescribed in Plate 1.

N_1
O_1
P_1 There are a number of alternate ways to perform the reconstructive aspects of the operation which may be dictated by the circumstances of the operation. Three are depicted here. In Figure N_1 the cut pancreas is simply oversewn, with no provision for exocrine discharge. An end-to-end choledochojejunostomy is performed if the common duct is dilated and the jejunum rather small. Or, the jejunum can be closed and an end-to-side choledochojejunostomy performed. An in continuity gastrojejunostomy is performed.

     Figure O_1 shows the pancreas anastomosed to the side of the jejunum and, in contrast to the procedure described in this section, it follows rather than precedes the biliary anastomosis. The procedure depicted in Figure P_1 is least desirable because of the greater incidence of gastrojejunal anastomotic ulceration and of ascending cholangitis.

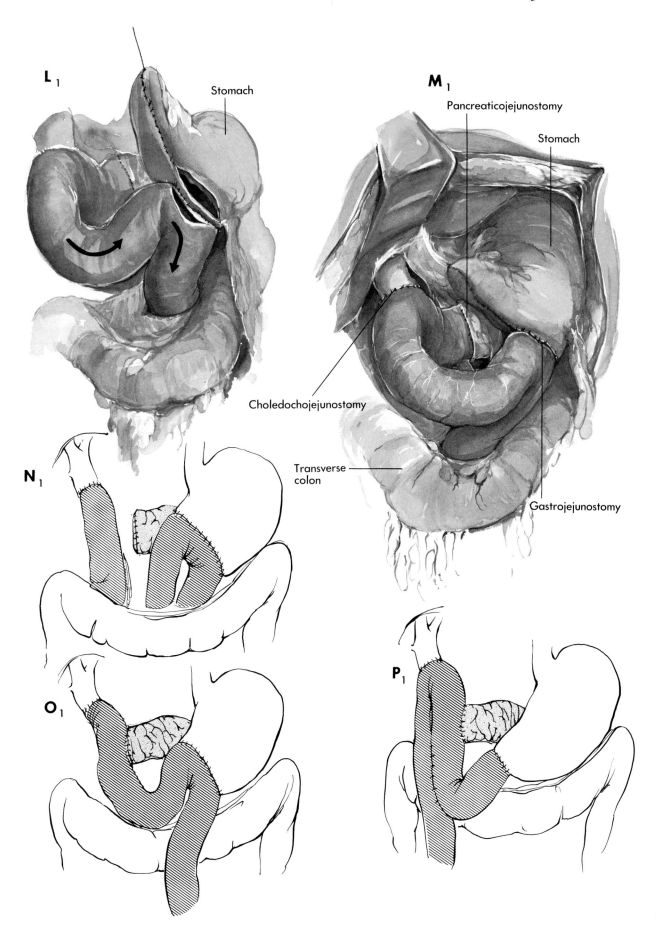

L₁

Stomach

M₁

Pancreaticojejunostomy

Stomach

Choledochojejunostomy

Transverse colon

Gastrojejunostomy

N₁

O₁

P₁

Pancreaticojejunostomy

A   A variety of operations have been devised to relieve pancreatic duct obstruction. The one emphasized in this section is that popularized by Puestow and Gillesby. This illustration shows the anatomic relationships of the pancreas that are of importance in the performance of this operation. The spleen hugs the tail of the pancreas closely, making splenectomy a routine necessity for the several types of pancreaticojejunostomy performed most commonly. In the procedure described the splenic vessels will accompany the pancreas into the jejunum so that a splenectomy is obligatory. Even if the anastomosis were to be end-to-end between pancreas and jejunum, the dissection necessary to spare the spleen and then proceed with the subsequent anastomosis is too tedious and hazardous.

The superior mesenteric vein is vulnerable to injury when the pancreas is mobilized. The splenic artery runs along the upper border of the pancreas, giving off branches to the pancreas, with the splenic vein just below the artery. The superior mesenteric artery and vein mark the point to which the pancreas should be mobilized even though the enveloping jejunum will extend farther to the right. It is apparent at the outset that it may be necessary to cover with the jejunum more of the pancreas anteriorly than has been mobilized posteriorly.

B   Many patients with chronic pancreatitis will have had previous operations that will influence the abdominal incision to be used. The preferred incision is the left paramedian with reflection of the rectus abdominis muscle. Portal hypertension, especially in association with adhesions from any previous surgery, can make this incision time consuming. As usual upon opening the peritoneal cavity, an exploration is first carried out and particular attention is given to the liver and the extrahepatic biliary system.

C   Next the stomach is freed along the greater curvature by separating it from the omentum. This is done by dividing along the relatively avascular area distal to the gastroepiploic vessels and extending from the angula incisura of the stomach on the right to the left to include the short gastric vessels. Adhesions between the posterior aspect of the stomach and the anterior surface of the pancreas are more numerous than usual but can be lysed by blunt and sharp technique.

D   The vascular supply to the spleen is interrupted with the spleen in situ or after it has been delivered into the wound, depending on the severity of the perisplenic adhesions. The lesser tributaries are ligated in continuity and divided. The main vessels can be individually isolated and divided or clamped and divided as shown, with tailoring at a later time when the tip of the pancreas is amputated.

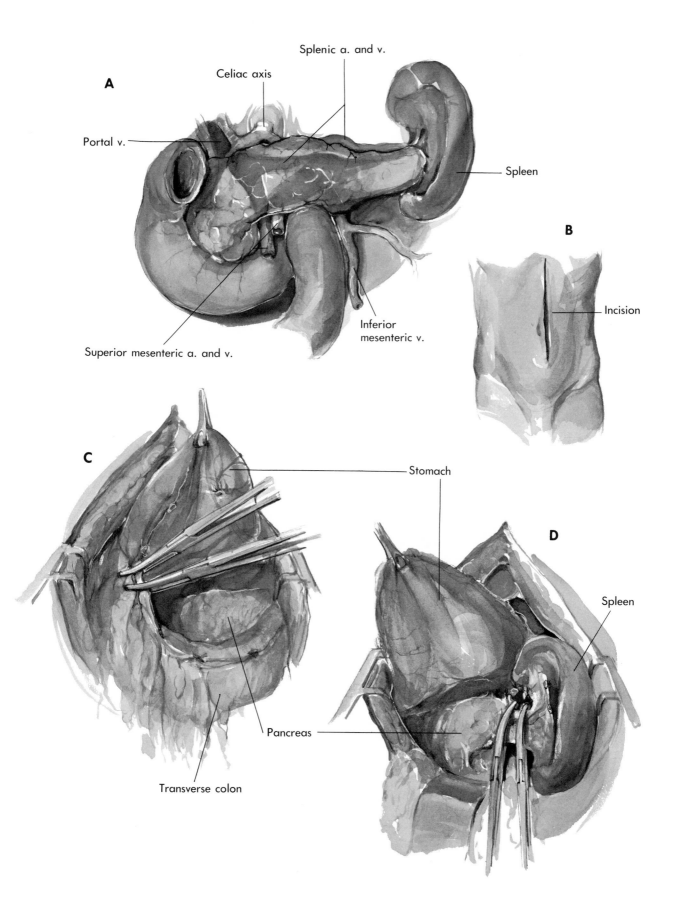

A

Celiac axis

Splenic a. and v.

Portal v.

Spleen

Superior mesenteric a. and v.

Inferior mesenteric v.

B

Incision

C

Stomach

D

Spleen

Pancreas

Transverse colon

E   With the spleen removed, the transverse colon displaced downward and the stomach upward, the portion of the pancreas to be mobilized is in full view. Its mobilization is begun along the relatively avascular inferior border and toward its tail.

F   This dissection is relatively bloodless. Rarely, with portal hypertension, varices (veins of Sappey) which may be present in this retroperitoneal location are a distinct hazard, commanding careful dissection and ligation.

G
H   The dissection continues dorsally as far to the right as the superior mesenteric vessels. It is quite unnecessary and certainly hazardous and time consuming to attempt to gain more mobility of the pancreas by dissecting it free of the superior mesenteric artery or vein. At this point, the splenic artery and vein can be ligated and divided just proximal to where the pancreatic tail will be amputated.

I
J   The pancreas is amputated 1 to 2 cm. from its tip. Pressure by fingers of the left hand are the best means of obtaining temporary hemostasis. With periodic release of this pressure, individual bleeding points are detected and secured with suture ligatures of atraumatic 3-0 chromic catgut. The pancreatic duct is usually dilated and can be seen easily or its presence indicated by a spurt of pancreatic juice under pressure. Although a dilated duct is almost always found if one is persistent, further transverse incisions in the tail may be necessary to locate the duct. Puestow advocates making three to four longitudinal incisions across the long axis of the pancreas to one half its depth and as far right as the superior mesenteric vessels in the rare instance in which a duct cannot be found.

K   When the pancreatic duct is found, a blunt-tip probe is used to determine its direction and degree of patency. There is no point in persisting with the probing if an early constriction is met, as the extent of disease will be defined in the subsequent steps.

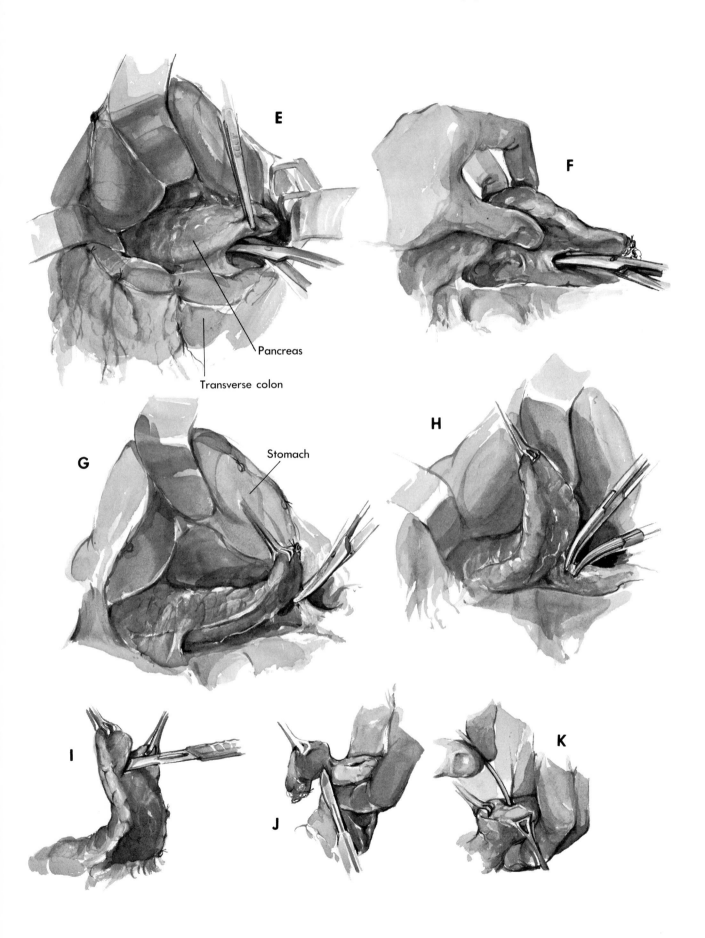

E

F

Pancreas

Transverse colon

G

Stomach

H

I

J

K

L   With a grooved probe in place the duct can be opened as illustrated. Otherwise a blunt-tipped bandage scissors may be used to find one's way and to cut open an irregularly scarred duct. Since the stenotic portions of the duct may be quite narrow, the surgeon must be forceful and gentle while advancing the scissors. Digital compression remains the most effective way to maintain hemostasis as individual bleeding points along the duct are secured with suture ligatures of atraumatic 3-0 chromic catgut. One continues with incision, compression, suture ligation, followed by further incision until the duct is opened to a point at which it appears normal and which usually means going to the right of the superior mesenteric vessels and reaching the ducts of Wirsung and Santorini. If there is diffuse bleeding along the cut edge of the pancreas, bleeding can be effectively controlled with a continuous suture of atraumatic catgut. However, since this suture technique may occlude the small tributaries of the main duct, it should be used only when absolutely necessary.

M   The duct is now fully opened, showing the "chain-o'lakes" effect produced by the erratic constrictions with intervening dilatations so characteristic of this disease. Minimal to extensive calcification may be found, but calcification is not in the ductal system but rather in the parenchyma. It is futile and too traumatic to attempt to remove calcification. Reportedly, some calcification will disappear later. Preparation of the pancreas is now complete.

N   The transverse colon is reflected upward, and the proximal jejunum identified and prepared for division.

O   The site of division is approximately 20 cm. from the duodenojejunal ligament. The clamp to be placed on the distal jejunal limb is brought through a window in the avascular portion of the transverse mesocolon as it is to be brought back through this window.

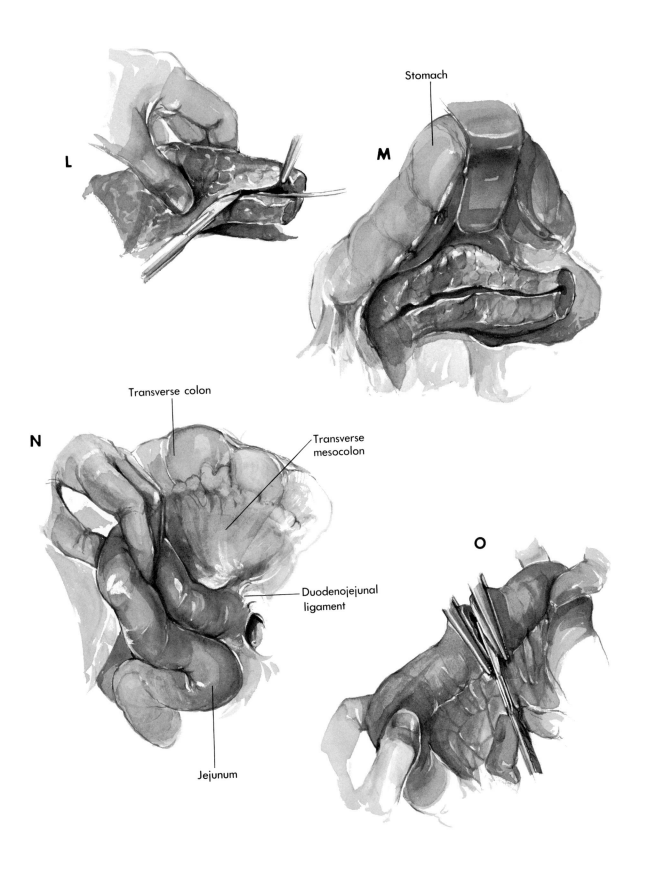

L

M

Stomach

N

Transverse colon

Transverse
mesocolon

Duodenojejunal
ligament

O

Jejunum

P
Q
Some guidance and traction of the transected tail of the pancreas into the jejunum will be necessary for the remainder of the procedure. Here, a suture of 3-0 chromic catgut is placed in the pancreas as shown. The needle is held as shown (P), with the point on the convex side of the curved needle holder. It can thus be advanced easily inside the jejunum. This distance is predetermined and should exceed by at least several centimeters the length of unroofed pancreatic duct; otherwise, this traction stitch will thwart the surgeon in pulling the jejunum far enough to the right. When this distance has been reached, the needle holder is turned (Q) so that the point of the needle can be brought through the bowel wall. Both ends of the traction suture may be brought through in the manner shown, or the ends may be brought through separately as shown in Figures R and S. In the latter case the ends can be tied and will thus serve as an anchoring suture. The mesocolic window should not constrict the vasculature of the jejunum going through it.

R
The suture attached to the pancreas is held while the accordion-like jejunum which is beginning to envelop the pancreas is gently pulled toward the right.

S
The free end of the jejunum is anchored to the pancreas at a point to the right of the unroofed duct with interrupted sutures of atraumatic 3-0 black silk. They are placed about 1 cm. apart. The superior mesenteric vessels may sometimes prevent the surgeon from bringing the jejunum far enough to the right so that the unroofed duct at the head of the pancreas may be covered. In such a case, the jejunum can be fish-mouthed at the point it comes in contact with the vessels. A several-centimeter slit will usually be sufficient to allow the additional jejunum necessary to cover all the exposed duct.

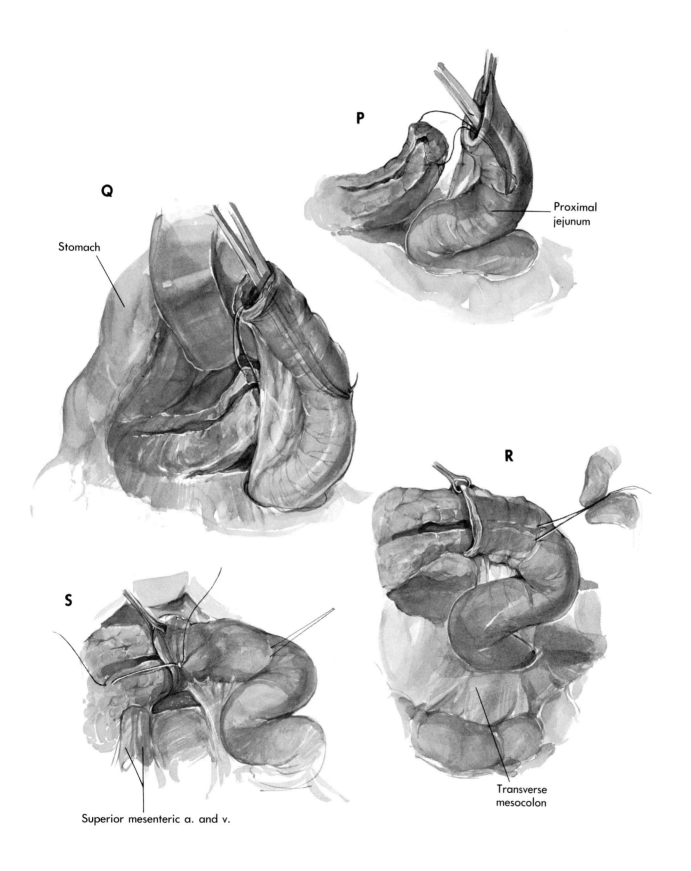

P

Proximal
jejunum

Q

Stomach

R

S

Superior mesenteric a. and v.

Transverse
mesocolon

T   When the placement of sutures on the ventral surface has been completed, the jejunum and pancreas are reflected toward the right and the jejunum sutured to the dorsal surface of the pancreas in a similar fashion.

U   The pancreas and jejunum have been returned to their previous position and the pancreaticojejunostomy has been completed.

V   A Roux-en-Y jejunojejunostomy is performed in as proximal a position as possible. Whenever possible we do a gastrostomy. A soft rubber drain is placed at the site of the pancreaticojejunostomy and exteriorized through a counterincision. The abdominal incision is closed in a usual fashion.

    A variety of procedures have been advocated and used for relieving the pancreatic ductal obstruction of chronic pancreatitis. None, in our opinion, has as wide an applicability as the one described.

W   The main differences between the procedure illustrated here and the one just described are: The spleen is not removed, nor the tail of the pancreas. There is a side-to-side anastomosis between the pancreatic duct and the jejunum (here begun), and the duct is not unroofed completely. A modification of this is to split the jejunum and suture its edges to the superior and inferior margins of the pancreas. Otherwise, the direction of jejunal peristalsis and the Roux-en-Y jejunojejunostomy are as in the Puestow procedure. In this and in the next two procedures, the jejunum is brought into position through the mesocolon.

    The disadvantages are the increased risk of leakage along such an extensive suture line. Also, the duct is not opened so extensively, though this is not an impossible accomplishment.

X   This operation was the early one used to drain the pancreatic duct in a retrograde direction. This fails to relieve the obstructions created by the "chain o'lakes" effect and will thus not relieve the patient and will lead to early recurrence. Even if one is confident that the duct is patent all the way to the head of the pancreas, subsequent duct constriction from scarring will lead to recurrence. Cicatricial stenosis of the duct where it is transected will, all too frequently, defeat the intent of the operation.

Y   This operation utilizes an isolated loop of jejunum which is anastomosed side-to-side to the pancreatic duct. It drains pancreatic secretions into a more physiologic location, the duodenum, via a jejunoduodenostomy. The jejunal continuity distally is maintained by an end-to-end jejunojejunostomy. This operation cannot be applied easily to drainage of the entirely opened pancreatic duct. Drainage of the pancreatic secretions into the duodenum is not a critical advantage.

Z   This illustration demonstrates the use of the gastric antrum as the draining receptacle for pancreatic secretions. It is necessary to amputate the pancreas generously and to unroof the duct of the remainder of the pancreas before making a snugly fitting opening on the dorsal aspect of the antrum and positioning the pancreas within the stomach. A vagotomy is necessary.

    The reader can see that the enduring success of the Puestow operation is attributable in great measure to the fact that the pancreatic duct is unroofed extensively, tending to preclude the subsequent development of stenosis and obstruction, and that this extensively unroofed duct is covered and drained in a manner which has proved to be safe and effective. The necessary splenectomy and the drainage of pancreatic secretions into the jejunum by a Roux-en-Y anastomosis have not been detrimental to this success.

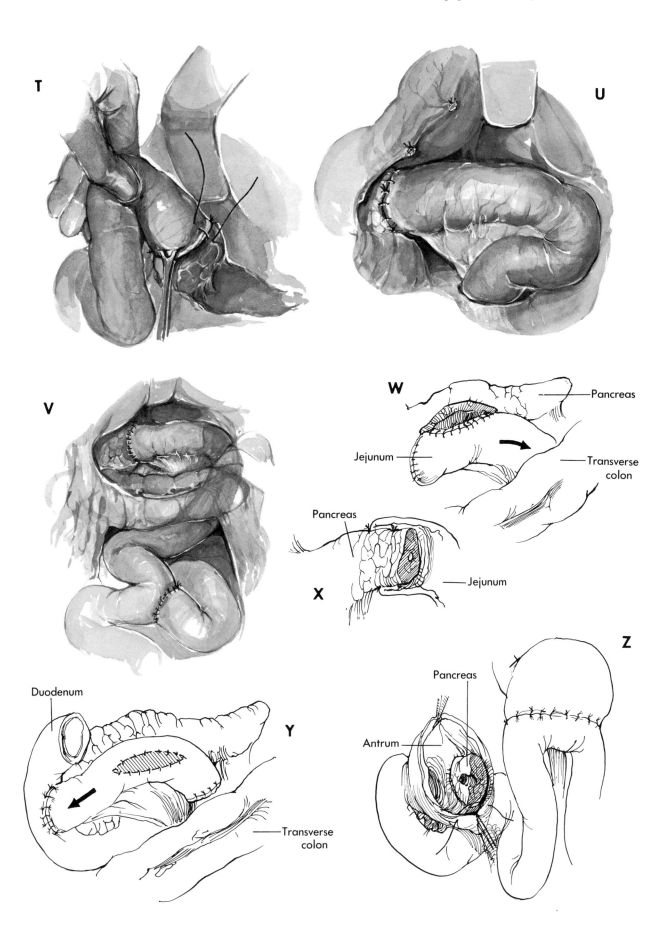

T

U

V

W

Pancreas

Jejunum

Transverse
colon

Pancreas

Jejunum

X

Duodenum

Y

Transverse
colon

Pancreas

Antrum

Z

ADRENALECTOMY

The adrenal gland is functionally two endocrine glands. The medulla secretes epinephrine and norepinephrine, which are sympathomimetic drugs. Their action produces constriction of blood vessels, an increase in pulse rate and elevation of blood pressure. These changes produce complex alterations in the pattern of blood flow. Pheochromocytomas are functional tumors of the adrenal medulla. Patients with pheochromocytoma typically present with episodic hypertension, usually of severe degree; hypertension that responds to a Regitine test suggests such a functional tumor. Laminagrams of a pyelogram or roentgen views of a retroperitoneal carbon dioxide insufflation may demonstrate an enlarged adrenal gland and confirm the suspected diagnosis. It is important to realize that functional adrenal medullary tissue may be ectopically placed along the urogenital ridge and must be sought for in patients exhibiting signs of a pheochromocytoma who have normal adrenal glands. The approach to a pheochromocytoma is usually best made transperitoneally with a ventral laparotomy.

The adrenal cortex produces a variety of hormones which may be divided into those with androgen, estrogen, mineralocorticoid and glucocorticoid effects. The androgenic hormones can produce virilism in females or precocious puberty in males. The estrogenic hormones may feminize men. Excessive mineral corticoids produce hyperaldosteronism characterized by hypertension with low serum potassium levels. Excessive glucocorticoids produce the clinical picture of Cushing's syndrome with moon facies, trunk obesity, striae, hypertension and weakness.

The glucocorticoid hormones are controlled by the pituitary gland by means of the adenocortotropic hormone (ACTH). There are certain extrapituitary sources of ACTH, such as carcinoma of the lung or pancreas. Dysfunction of the adrenal cortex may be secondary to excess ACTH causing adrenal hyperplasia or may be primary due to an adenoma or carcinoma of the adrenal cortex. The glucocorticoid hormones can be estimated by the daily urinary excretion of 17-hydroxycorticosteroids, which normally range from 3 to 12 mg. The excessive production of ACTH by the pituitary can be suppressed by the administration of the synthetic steroid, Dexamethasone, which helps to define the cause of the Cushing's syndrome. Dexamethasone suppresses pituitary stimulated excessive adrenal cortex function but does not affect the primary adrenal cortex cancer.

References

Conn, J. W.: Primary aldosteronism, a new clinical syndrome. J. Lab. & Clin. Med. 45:3, 1955.
Emlet, J. R., Grimson, K. S., Bell, D. M., and Orgain, E. S.: The use of piperoxan and Regitine as routine tests in patients with hypertension. J.A.M.A. 146:1383, 1951.
Scott, H. W., Foster, J. H., Liddle, G., and Davidson, E. T.: Cushing's syndrome due to adreno-cortical tumor. Ann. Surg. 162:505, 1965.

A   The adrenal glands are well ensconced in the body, sometimes to the discomfiture of the surgeon who tries to reach them. They lie on lumbar slips of the diaphragm to which they are attached more firmly than to the kidneys at about the level of the 11th thoracic vertebra. The relationships of the right adrenal gland are to the vena cava medially, to the kidney inferiorly and to the liver and sometimes the vena cava and the non-peritonealized portion of the liver anteriorly. The left adrenal gland is more medial and cephalad in location than the right and lies closer to the aorta. Anteriorly it is covered by the posterior surface of the stomach, the posterior surface of the pancreas and the splenic vessels. The adrenal glands have a rich blood supply from three arteries which are branches from the aorta, the renal artery and the inferior phrenic artery.

Although easy surgical routes to the adrenals are available, they often may not be feasible by virtue of the indication for the operation. If aberrant adrenal tumors are to be looked for, the abdominal route is the only one to be used. Generally, however, the abdominal route is the most traumatic to the patient and trying to the surgeon.

B   The patient is prepared preoperatively for the endocrine loss incident to the operation. The following program is followed rather routinely: Twelve hours preoperatively 100 mg. of cortisone is given intramuscularly. On the morning of surgery 100 mg. of cortisone is given again intramuscularly. Just before beginning the operation an infusion of 1000 cc. of 5 per cent dextrose in water is begun in which are placed 100 mg. of hydrocortisone. This infusion is usually given over six hours but the rate is adjusted as necessary. A separate arm vein is used for infusion of other necessary fluids.

A long left paramedian rectus muscle retracting incision is used. In this instance it extends to the pubis because an oophorectomy was also performed. Incidentally, the abdominal approach is not necessarily the best one if both ovaries are also to be removed. With some patients a separate incision in the flank for the adrenalectomy and one lower abdominal incision for the ovaries, with the patient repositioned each time, has been a wise choice with respect to duration of operation, blood loss and post-operative morbidity.

C
D   The peritoneal cavity is opened and an exploration is conducted for metastases. If ectopic adrenal tissue is being sought, the region of the renal hilum and vessels is carefully palpated. The para-aortic tissue down to the aortic bifurcation is examined with care.

The left adrenal gland is being done first. We prefer reflecting the spleen, the tail of the pancreas and the greater curvature of the stomach medially. This reflection is done by the assistant who stands on the patient's right side. The surgeon may choose to stand on the patient's right side for a better view of the left suprarenal area; in such instances, the left hand is occupied with retracting the overlying structures. The spleen may be torn and have to be removed, but this should delay the major operation for only a short while.

An alternate approach to the left adrenal is to mobilize the greater curvature of the stomach and to displace it cephalad and the pancreas and splenic vessels caudad for direct access to the adrenal. This is cumbersome and not usually productive of adequate exposure.

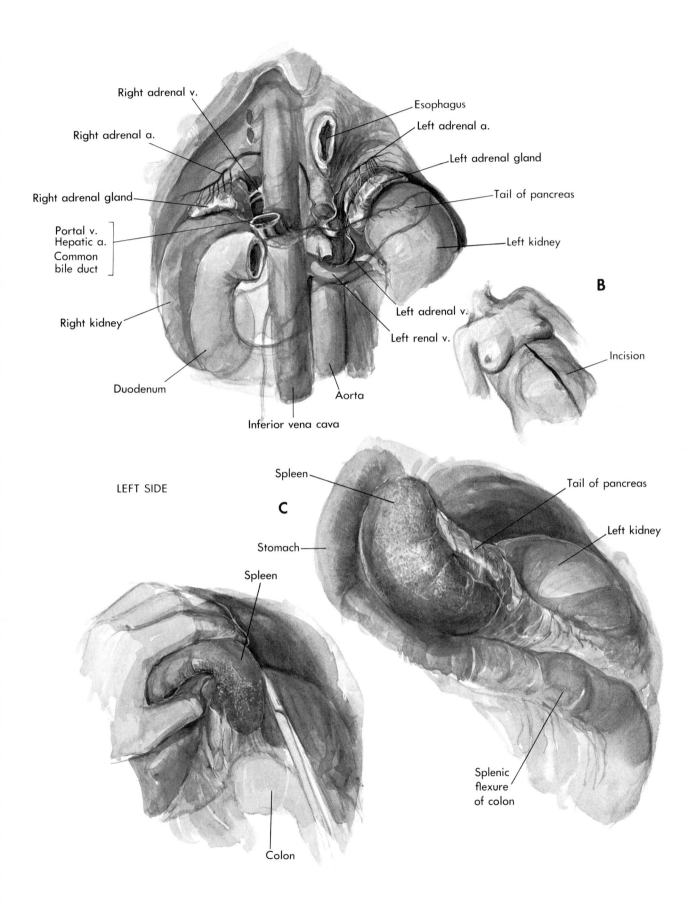

Right adrenal v.

Right adrenal a.

Right adrenal gland

Portal v.
Hepatic a.
Common
bile duct

Right kidney

Duodenum

Inferior vena cava

Esophagus

Left adrenal a.

Left adrenal gland

Tail of pancreas

Left kidney

B

Left adrenal v.

Left renal v.

Aorta

Incision

LEFT SIDE

C

Spleen

Stomach

Spleen

Colon

Tail of pancreas

Left kidney

Splenic
flexure
of colon

E   This line drawing shows the relationships of the left adrenal gland under the posterior parietal peritoneum as well as one of the several adrenal arteries, neither being very sizable. If these vessels are severed close to the gland they can be expected to stop bleeding spontaneously. The central vein most commonly courses caudally to empty into the left renal vein. Familiarity with the venous drainage enables a surgeon to isolate and ligate the vein early when removing a pheochromocytoma, thus minimizing wild fluctuations in the blood pressure during even minimal manipulation of the tumor.

F   The exposure of the suprarenal area is excellent with this approach. The adrenal gland can usually be palpated through the posterior parietal peritoneum. If not, the peritoneum is incised transversely just above the kidney, the leading edge of the adrenal being delivered easily in this fashion. Blunt and sharp dissection is used to free the adrenal, with silver clips being applied to the arterioles. The central vein is usually singular, but considerable hemorrhage can occur from lesser accessory veins. The central vein is tied in continuity with 2-0 silk and the gland removed. One adrenal still remains, and the surgeon should be aware that it may be significantly damaged by metastatic cancer from the breast and that, in effect, the patient has just had near-total physiologic adrenal ablation.

H
I   Exposure and removal of the right adrenal gland is more difficult than on the left side. The undersurface of the liver is covered with a moistened laparotomy pad and a Deaver retractor used to expose the furthest medial recess next to the vena cava. The portal triad is retracted medially. A moistened laparotomy pad is placed on the kidney and it is displaced caudally with the hand, which frequently helps to bring the adrenal with it somewhat, or at least to widen the avenue to it. The posterior parietal peritoneum over the adrenal is incised and the gland dissected as on the opposite side.

J   Again, the arterial supply to the gland is abundant but the arterioles are not large. We prefer to occlude them with silver clips. The central vein, usually singular, is rarely longer than 1 cm. and drains directly into the vena cava. As with the right side, it should be tied in continuity with 2-0 silk before being divided.

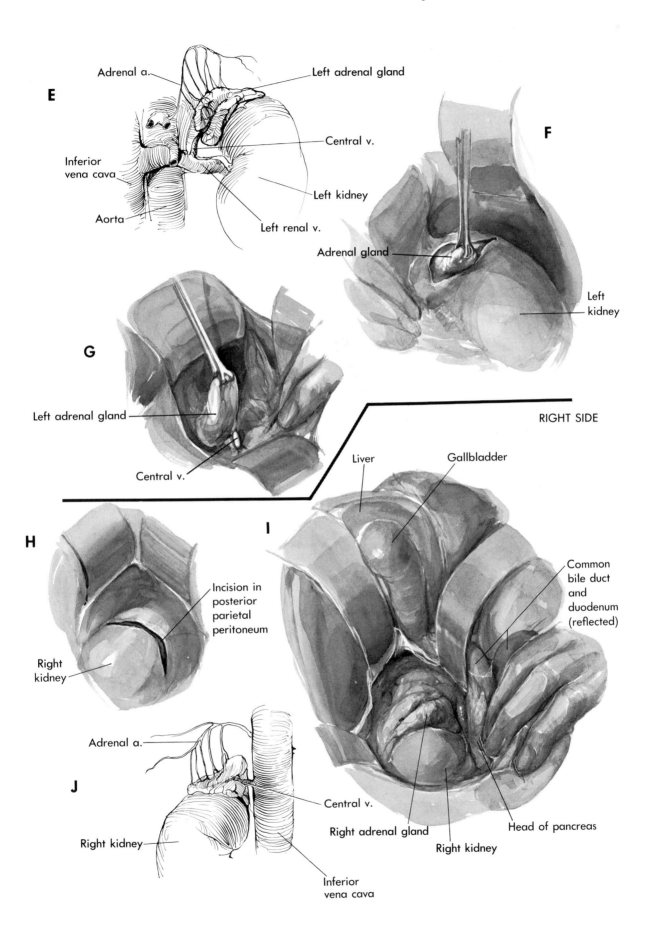

E

Adrenal a.

Left adrenal gland

Central v.

Inferior
vena cava

Left kidney

Aorta

Left renal v.

F

Adrenal gland

Left
kidney

G

Left adrenal gland

Central v.

RIGHT SIDE

Liver

Gallbladder

H

Incision in
posterior
parietal
peritoneum

Right
kidney

I

Common
bile duct
and
duodenum
(reflected)

Adrenal a.

J

Central v.

Right kidney

Right adrenal gland

Head of pancreas

Right kidney

Inferior
vena cava

Adrenalectomy — Flank

A   Save for a thoracoabdominal approach, the one through the flank offers the widest exposure for performance of a routine adrenalectomy. This is especially true on the right side and, on balance, is the one to be preferred. If a choice can be had, it is also the approach that is probably the least traumatic to the patient. In this posterior oblique view of the back, a window has been cut out of the latissimus dorsi muscle, the major muscle that has to be divided in the performance of this operation. The window permits viewing the underlying muscles. Some fibers of the internal oblique muscle will have to be divided anteriorly. The serratus posteroinferior muscles and the intercostal muscles will have to be disengaged while making the incision.

B   This semitransparent rendition shows some of the relationships of the right adrenal gland. The vena cava is on its anterior border; inferiorly it lies on the kidney. On its anterior surface the gland is covered by the duodenum, the undersurface of the liver and, sometimes, the inferior vena cava. The gland is positioned between the 11th and 12th ribs posteriorly, although this relationship varies considerably. The dashed line traces the costophrenic sulcus, although this too can be varied. This illustration demonstrates how the pleural reflections will have to be displaced cephalad if intrapleural injury is to be avoided. Some fibers of the diaphragm must also be transected but they are inconsequential.

C   Proper positioning of the patient is an important ancillary consideration if the optimum exposure is to be obtained at the proper time. The patient is placed in the direct lateral position. If the patient is somewhat obese, a slight ventral tilt will encourage the abdominal visceral bulk to fall away: if the patient is not obese, a slight dorsal tilt will permit somewhat better visualization of the wound depth. The break in the table is at the level of the 12th rib. Having it lower or higher than this is useless or detrimental in that the kidney rest, when raised, may elevate the chest or pelvis and cause a narrowing of the space between the last rib and the iliac crest. The under leg is folded, the upper kept straight, and a pillow is placed between them. Three-inch tape is placed across the hips and attached to the table to anchor the patient. A similar piece of tape is placed across the shoulder and used to determine the tilt of the upper torso.

The incision is carried along the course of the 12th rib, starting 3 to 5 cm. from the midline in the back and extending to the anterior axillary line. The right adrenalectomy is potentially more dangerous and is usually done first.

D
E   Bleeding points in the skin and subcutaneous fat are clamped and electrocoagulated. The fingers are insinuated under the latissimus dorsi muscle and it is divided to the sacrospinalis muscle in line with the skin incision. This exposes the last rib (Figure E).

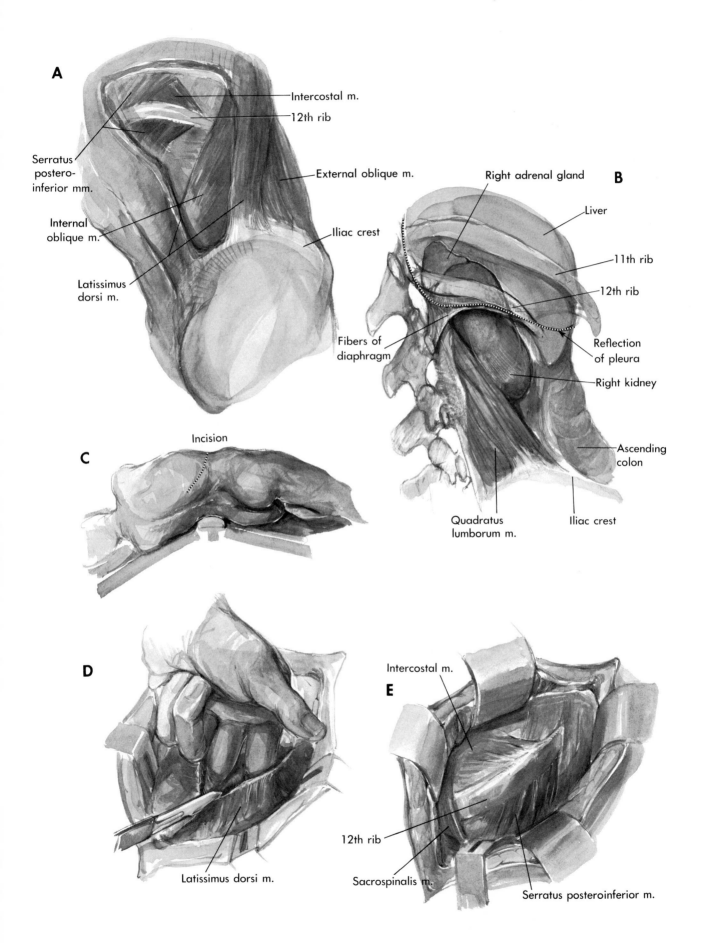

A

Serratus postero-inferior mm.

Intercostal m.

12th rib

External oblique m.

Iliac crest

Internal oblique m.

Latissimus dorsi m.

B

Right adrenal gland

Liver

11th rib

12th rib

Reflection of pleura

Fibers of diaphragm

Right kidney

Ascending colon

Quadratus lumborum m.

Iliac crest

C

Incision

D

Latissimus dorsi m.

E

Intercostal m.

12th rib

Sacrospinalis m.

Serratus posteroinferior m.

F   The table is broken at this time. The 12th rib is excised subperiosteally to its articulation. It is not necessary to incise routinely any of the sacrospinalis musculature, but occasionally incising some of the lateralmost fibers is helpful.

G   As the bed of the 12th rib is incised, the surgeon should remain alert for the location of the costophrenic sulcus. The two surfaces of the pleura are often difficult to see at this point and the only signal that the pleural cavity has been entered may be the hissing sound of air being sucked in. The anesthesiologist can be asked to inflate the patient's lungs to a maximum so that the extremes of the costophrenic sulcus can be detected as the lungs reach this point. This sulcus may course more caudally as one goes posteriorly; once the sulcus is identified it cannot be assumed that it will follow a course parallel to the rib. In the presence of pleural fluid, the surgeon may deliberately choose to make a small opening into the pleural cavity to evacuate this fluid.

H   The kidney rest is now elevated. Gerota's fascia is incised, the perirenal fat is spread with the fingers and the adrenal gland, which is a slightly more orange-yellow color than the surrounding fat, is sought. In patients with abundant perirenal fat this may not be a simple matter. The adrenal gland is considerably more firm than the surrounding fat. Although this is not so discernible at this stage of the dissection, it can be an important means whereby one can identify the gland in otherwise formless fat. On the left side, the tail of a thin pancreas may confuse the issue.

I   Once an edge of the gland is freed it is grasped gently with Babcock forceps. No other type of forceps will serve for grasping without tearing the gland, an event associated with modest but most annoying bleeding. If the gland is not being removed because of cancerous involvement, the dissection can best be carried out close to its capsule. This is a gentle, teasing, spreading dissection of the tissue with the scissors, forceps and even the tip of the suction tube. Most of this dissection is relatively bloodless; arterioles are best secured with silver clips.

J   On the right side the central vein can be expected to be about 1 cm. in length and to course directly medially into the vena cava. On the left side it will course directly caudally toward the left renal vein. The vein is tied in continuity with 2-0 silk and transected.

K   Hemostasis must be assured as there is minimal firmness of surrounding tissue to restrain bleeding. If the pleura has been opened, a small catheter is inserted into the pleural cavity and the pleura is closed now to the catheter with continuous simple stitches of atraumatic 3-0 chromic catgut. The table is made flat. Gerota's fascia is closed with continuous catgut. The intercostal muscles and latissimus dorsi muscles are sewn with interrupted stitches of 2-0 chromic catgut. The skin is closed with interrupted vertical mattress stitches of 3-0 silk. The anesthesiologist is asked to inflate the lungs fully while, simultaneously, the intrapleural catheter is removed. An intercostal catheter attached to water-seal drainage can be placed through a thoracic counter-incision if drainage is expected.

     If there is entry into the pleural cavity an x-ray of the chest is taken in the recovery room to check for proper expansion of the lungs. Postoperatively the surgeon must be alert to the real possibility that symptoms of shock may be due to adrenal insufficiency rather than to blood loss. Drains are removed in 48 hours. Most patients can be weaned to a maintenance dose of cortisone by the time they are sent home on the tenth postoperative day.

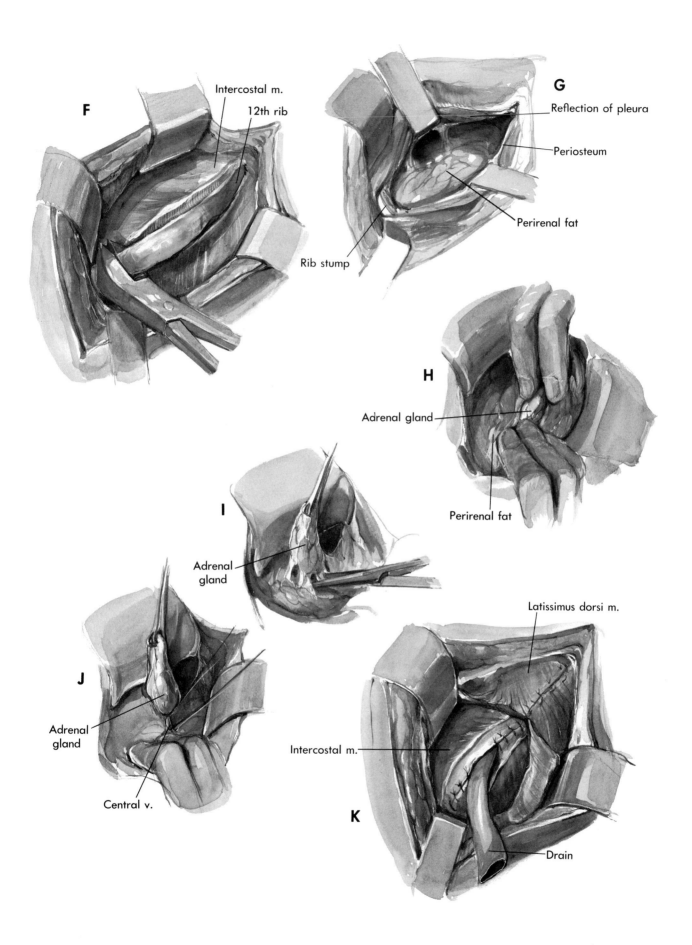

F

Intercostal m.

12th rib

G

Reflection of pleura

Periosteum

Perirenal fat

Rib stump

H

Adrenal gland

Perirenal fat

I

Adrenal gland

J

Adrenal gland

Central v.

Latissimus dorsi m.

Intercostal m.

K

Drain

Adrenalectomy — Dorsal

A   This semidiagrammatic phantom drawing demonstrates the structures surrounding the adrenal gland that have to be displaced or traversed in removing the adrenal through the dorsal approach. The posterior reflection of the pleura is usually at the level of the 12th rib. If, therefore, the approach is through the bed of the 12th rib, the pleura often can be reflected upward without intrapleural entry. Notice also that diaphragmatic fibers reach this low, but few have to be cut if entry is made over the 12th rib. The adrenal gland is more closely subjacent to the 11th rib and if this approach is used the pleura is entered intentionally and more fibers of the diaphragm must be cut.

B
C   If the choice is to go in through the bed of the 11th rib, the skin incision is made over this rib (1). If, however, only the 12th rib will be excised, the incision is curvilinear and located paravertebrally from the 10th rib to the iliac crest (2). It is important to position the patient so that ventilation is unimpeded and adequate and so that the normal lumbar lordosis is reversed and maximum exposure is available.

D   The skin and subcutaneous tissue have been incised and bleeding points have already been clamped and electrocoagulated. The latissimus dorsi muscle is cut practically transverse to the direction of its fibers. Bleeding vessels are clamped and ligated with 3-0 chromic catgut. The periosteum over the 11th rib is being incised in preparation for excising this rib subperiosteally.

E   The rib has been excised for its entire length and the pleural cavity entered. The lung is displaced cephalad and the diaphragm is incised along a level with the 11th interspace where its fibers are sparse. Deep to this, Gerota's fascia is incised to reveal the perirenal fat.

F   The adrenal gland (here the right one) is located and mobilized, with the anticipation that the short central vein will course centrally toward the vena cava. The arterioles to the gland are clamped with silver clips. Less desirably, they can be cut and ignored with assurance that most will stop bleeding spontaneously. The vein is tied in continuity with 2-0 silk before it is divided. On the left side the vein will be found to course caudally to enter the left renal vein and is handled in a similar manner.

G   With hemostasis assured, the wounds are closed in layers. The diaphragmatic incision is reapproximated with interrupted horizontal mattress stitches of 2-0 silk. The periosteal bed is closed with a continuous stitch of 2-0 chromic catgut. Prior to completion of this closure, a medium-sized catheter is exteriorized from the pleural cavity. The latissimus dorsi muscle is closed with interrupted 2-0 chromic catgut and the skin with interrupted vertical mattress stitches of 3-0 silk. The anesthesiologist is then asked to expand the lungs maximally, at which time the catheter is removed.

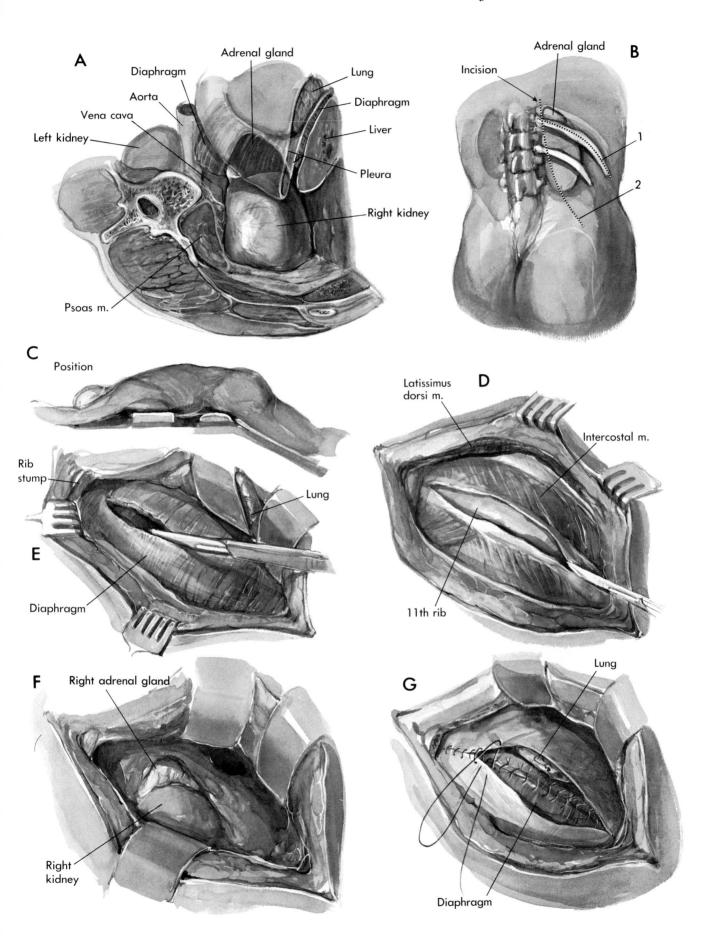

A

Adrenal gland

Diaphragm

Aorta

Vena cava

Left kidney

Lung

Diaphragm

Liver

Pleura

Right kidney

Psoas m.

B

Incision

Adrenal gland

1

2

C

Position

Rib stump

Lung

E

Diaphragm

D

Latissimus dorsi m.

Intercostal m.

11th rib

F

Right adrenal gland

Right kidney

G

Lung

Diaphragm

RADICAL NEPHRECTOMY

Renal neoplasms account for 1.3 per cent of all malignant neoplasms. They are slightly commoner in males than females. Of the cancers of the genitourinary tract, kidney cancers comprise about 10 per cent. A radical nephrectomy is indicated for an operable carcinoma of the kidney. If the tumor is papillary and arises in the collecting system of the kidney, a total ureterectomy is also indicated. The Wilms' tumor is the commonest kidney tumor of infancy and childhood. A radical nephrectomy with chemotherapy and with optional radiation therapy is the present treatment of choice. The commonest presenting complaint of renal carcinoma in adults is hematuria, either gross or microscopic. A mass is reported to be present in 40 to 80 per cent of the adult patients with this lesion. In the infant or child with a Wilms' tumor, a mass is usually the presenting complaint. If local or distant metastases occur, pain is frequent.

The patient suspected of having renal carcinoma should have the usual history taken and be given a thorough physical examination. The routine laboratory work should include a urinary Papanicolaou smear and culture. An intravenous pyelogram should be done. The tumor, if present, is usually seen on the intravenous pyelogram. If the diagnosis is in doubt, a renal arteriogram is the most helpful diagnostic technique. The arteriogram is approximately 95 per cent accurate and thus usually establishes the diagnosis. Urine cytology is of little value in diagnosing renal cell cancer but is a great help in diagnosing bladder cancer or renal pelvis cancer. Cystoscopy and retrograde ureteral catheterization are chiefly indicated to delineate the function of the opposite kidney if its function is in doubt. Serum calcium and phosphate should be evaluated since some kidney cancers present a hyperparathyroid-like picture.

The chief differential diagnosis in a suspect renal carcinoma is that of a renal cyst. If the diagnosis is in doubt, an exploratory operation is indicated. If the lesion seems to be a cyst, a needle aspiration should be done. If clear fluid is obtained, the cyst should be opened and the diagnosis confirmed. If the fluid aspirated is bloody and the lesion is consistent with a tumor, an excision of the kidney is indicated. A partial nephrectomy should be considered if the total kidney function is seriously impaired.

Gustave Simon of Heidelberg is given credit for having performed the first planned and successful nephrectomy. The operation was performed in a woman with a ureterovaginal fistula. In the century that has elapsed since this early effort, improvements in preoperative and postoperative care, in anesthesia and in operative technique have combined to produce a progressive drop in operative mortality from nephrectomy, so that the risk now is about 1 per cent. In the past 20 years there has been an exploration of extended operations for the control of kidney cancer. The extensive procedure which has been widely utilized in the treatment of renal adenocarcinoma has been designated "radical nephrectomy." This operation entails the intact removal of Gerota's fascia with the enclosed perirenal fat and kidney, including the adrenal gland in the case of an upper pole neoplasm, and the systematic dissection of the regional lymph nodes along the great vessels from the level of the diaphragm to the aortic bifurcation.

The rationale of this extended operation for renal adenocarcinoma is dependent upon recognition of three important local features of the tumor: (1) There is a tendency toward direct perirenal extension. Such perirenal extension is probably a function of the grade of the tumor and certainly a function of its size, being more common in the larger renal adenocarcinomas. (2) There is a tendency toward direct venous invasion. Tumor thrombosis of the major renal veins is identifiable in approximately 50 per cent of all patients. (3) There is a tendency toward lymphatic spread. Regional lymph node involvement is identifiable in about 20 per cent of patients with renal adenocarcinoma.

Adequate exposure is the prime consideration in radical nephrectomy. The choice of incision in obtaining such adequate exposure will depend upon the body build of the patient, the size and location of the tumor, and such special considerations in the individual patient as previous diseases or operations.

In 1948 Mortenson described the use of a thoracoabdominal incision for the removal of a large renal tumor. Chute and Soutter were the first in this country to report the use of this exposure for the removal of renal tumors. The incision combines transthoracic and transabdominal exposures. With the patient in the lateral or the anterolateral position the incision is made from the lateral margin of the rectus muscle at about the level of the umbilicus posteriorly, superiorly and laterally over the 10th or 11th ribs to the rib angle. The pleural cavity is entered through the bed of the subperiosteally resected rib. The diaphragm and abdominal muscles are incised in line with the incision opening the peritoneal cavity.

In a disease with as varied a natural history as renal adenocarcinoma, it is not yet possible to assess the influence of radical nephrectomy in contrast to simple nephrectomy in the treatment of renal cancer. It is safe to say that the extended operation has not increased morbidity or mortality and that some tumors which could not have been removed by other techniques have been excised with extended procedures. Robson has published experiences with a small series of patients treated by radical nephrectomy suggesting improved survival. The final evaluation of the procedure must await further experiences.

Whitmore reported on 215 patients with kidney cancers treated in the 30 years from 1927 through 1957 at Memorial Center. One hundred thirty-six patients presented without metastasis and 79 cases had metastases. Whitmore categorized the tumors in four stages: (A) encapsulated tumor; (B) tumor within the kidney; (C) the tumor invading the renal capsule and adjacent structures; and (D) the tumor had produced distant metastases. In stage A, five of seven (71 per cent) were living and well at five years; in stage B, 22 of 34 (69 per cent) were living and well at five years; in stage C, there were 36 patients of whom 11 (31 per cent) were living and well at five years; in stage D, two of 10 patients (20 per cent) were living and well at five years. Whitmore concluded that radical nephrectomy was probably better than simple nephrectomy but that the absolute proof was not yet available.

It is also important to remember that cancer of the kidney may be bilateral in 5 to 10 per cent of Wilms' tumors and less than 5 per cent of renal cell cancers. Thus, a bilateral nephrectomy in stages, with the use of either a kidney transplant or chronic renal dialysis, is occasionally a consideration. It does seem that radical nephrectomy is to be preferred to simple nephrectomy. Wide exposure is needed. The hilum should be handled by an individual ligation technique and not by mass ligation. One can occlude the inferior vena cava above the renal veins if the renal arteries are also clamped. This maneuver permits inferior vena cava reconstruction. The normal kidney remaining can be protected from ischemia for 30 to 60 minutes by local or total body hypothermia.

References

Chute, R., and Soutter, L.: Thoraco-abdominal nephrectomy for large kidney tumors. J. Urol. *61*:688, 1949.
Mortenson, H.: Transthoracic nephrectomy. J. Urol. *60*:855, 1948.
Simon, G.: Exstirpation einer Niere am Menschen. Deutsche. Klin. *22*:137, 1870.
Whitmore, W. F.: Renal Neoplasms. Monographs on Surgery. Baltimore, The Williams & Wilkins Co., 1952.
Whitmore, W. F., and Krause, C.: Survival following nephrectomy for renal cell cancer. *In* King, J. S. (ed.): Renal Neoplasia. Boston, Little, Brown and Co., 1967.

Radical Nephrectomy

A   There is a considerable amount of anatomic complexity in both renal areas. The kidneys lie paravertebrally in the dorsal aspect of the abdomen behind the parietal peritoneum and are surrounded by adipose and areolar tissue. For the sake of greater clarity this tissue, which also bears the lymph nodes in the hilar area, has been omitted in this view of the left side. In marked contrast to a nephrectomy for noncancerous involvement, a radical nephrectomy entails excision of the perinephric tissue and thus mandatory exposure of most of the numerous topographic relationships of this organ. Those which are valuable to the surgeon are illustrated here.

Structures on which the kidneys lie posteriorly include the diaphragm, the quadratus lumborum and the psoas major muscles. On the right side this includes the 12th rib, whereas on the left it is both the 11th and 12th ribs. Anteriorly, the right kidney is covered mostly by the liver and to a lesser extent by the duodenum and the hepatic flexure of the colon. The left is covered by the spleen, pancreas, stomach and, to a variable degree, by the splenic flexure of the colon. Both are capped by the adrenal glands. The medial borders of the kidneys barely override the lateral borders of the psoas muscles.

The celiac axis, superior mesenteric artery and renal arteries exit from the aorta in close sequence. In at least 10 per cent of instances more than one renal artery is given off on each side. One of the several sources of an adrenal artery is shown. The left renal vein crosses ventral to the aorta on its way to the vena cava and the right renal artery posterior to the inferior vena cava on its way to the kidney. The internal spermatic artery and vein communicate with the renal vessels on the left but on the right with the aorta and vena cava.

B   General endotracheal anesthesia is used, preferably a gas that is nonexplosive so that electrocoagulation can be used. The patient is tilted with the side to be operated elevated about 25 degrees and supported with several small sandbags. The leg on the side to be operated is flexed over the opposite leg and a pillow placed between them. The arm is positioned away from the side of the patient and, after it is padded sufficiently, is supported on the anesthesia screen. The incision is made over the course of the 10th rib. The line of proposed incision is cross-hatched as an aid to later closure; surprising displacement of the wound edges can occur with flank incisions.

C
D   Most blood vessels encountered to this point are small and can be electrocoagulated. The incision is carried several centimeters posterior to the latissimus dorsi muscle and parallel to the fibers of the serratus anterior muscle so that very few of them have to be divided. The 10th rib is excised subperiosteally. The anterior border of the latissimus dorsi muscle is retracted strongly so that as much as possible of the rib can be removed.

E   The incision is continued through the bed of the rib with resultant entry into the chest at the costophrenic sulcus. Here the lung has collapsed sufficiently that the diaphragm is visible immediately. The incision is extended anteriorly along the fibers of the external oblique muscle. Some fibers of the internal oblique muscle must be cut, but those of the transversus can mostly be spread apart.

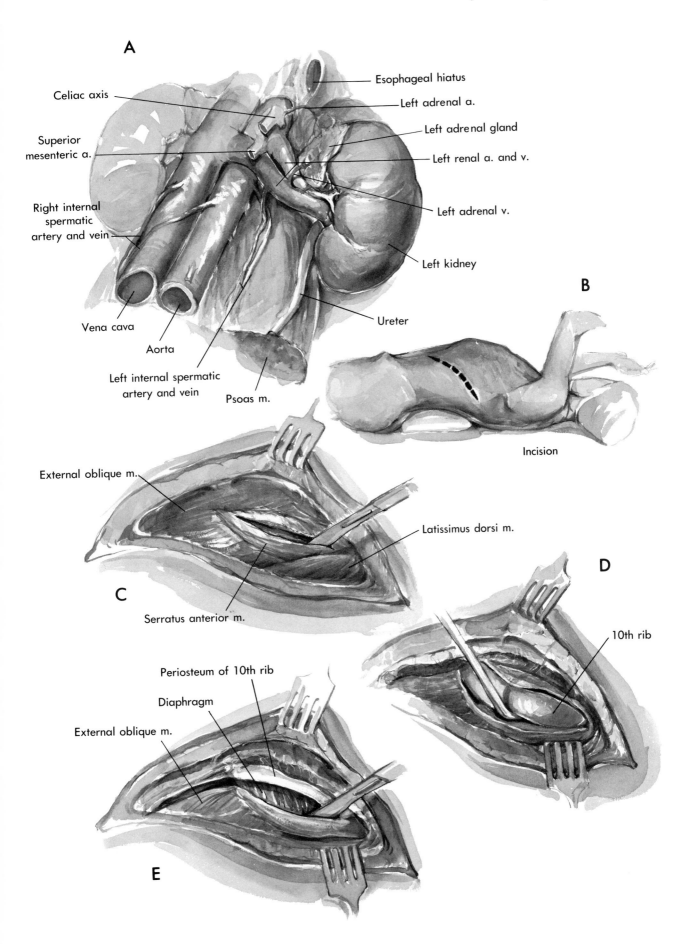

A

Celiac axis

Superior
mesenteric a.

Right internal
spermatic
artery and vein

Vena cava

Aorta

Left internal spermatic
artery and vein

Psoas m.

Esophageal hiatus

Left adrenal a.

Left adrenal gland

Left renal a. and v.

Left adrenal v.

Left kidney

Ureter

B

Incision

C

External oblique m.

Serratus anterior m.

Latissimus dorsi m.

D

10th rib

E

Periosteum of 10th rib

Diaphragm

External oblique m.

F   The fibers of the diaphragm are divided, as it turns out transverse to their long axis. The phrenic nerve should be sought and spared. More fibers of the phrenic nerve will be spared if the diaphragmatic incision is curved, with the convexity laterally.

G   When the incision is extended to its fullest through all layers and the wound spread, the spleen will dominate the operative field. It is fortunate if there are no perinephric diaphragmatic adhesions; they are annoying in their capacity to bleed if ripped. It is much less likely that a renal tumor is curable if it has grown anteriorly and has penetrated the posterior parietal peritoneum and become intimate with the overlying structures. However, peritoneal adhesions may simulate peritoneal invasion. In any case, if the renal pedicle is free there should be no hesitancy in removing en bloc all or portions of the adjacent structures such as the spleen, the splenic flexure of the colon or the tail of the pancreas.

H   For the remainder of the operation retractors such as the Ferguson or Mayo type with shallow blades should be used on the medial side of the incision. Deaver or malleable retractors pose an excessive risk of lacerating the spleen and making a splenectomy mandatory. The assistant's hand is excellent for providing safe and well controlled retraction. The splenocolic ligament is divided; a vessel within it requires ligation of the ligament. Downward traction on the splenic flexure of the colon or upward traction on the spleen while working on the splenocolic ligament should be gentle or an attached portion of the splenic capsule will be torn.

I
J   The gastrocolic ligament is divided next, the line of dissection being in the relatively avascular area inside the gastroepiploic artery and vein. Following this maneuver, the short gastric vessels are divided and ligated so that the colon and stomach can be displaced downward and medially, respectively (Figure J). The body and tail of the pancreas are also exposed.

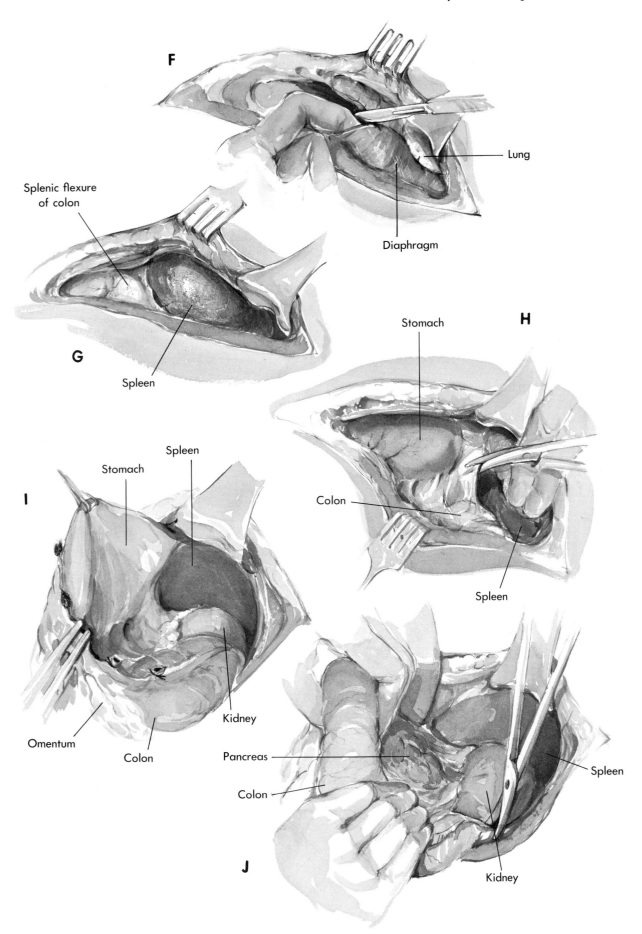

F

Lung

Diaphragm

Splenic flexure
of colon

G

Spleen

Stomach

H

Colon

Spleen

Spleen

Stomach

I

Kidney

Omentum

Colon

Pancreas

Colon

Spleen

Kidney

J

K   Most of the malignant tumors of the kidney are adenocarcinomas, a group notorious for their propensity to venous embolization. The venous invasion by these tumors is mostly microscopic but can be seen grossly in many removed specimens. The ability of these cells to break off during manipulation of the kidney has been demonstrated by recovery of a great number of such cells in the upper inferior vena cava. Notice that to this point the kidney itself has not been handled in order to bring it into the operative field but, instead, the overlying structures have been displaced. The ability to maneuver around the kidney is one of the dividends of this generous incision and particular approach.

L   The immediate next intent is to secure the blood supply of the tumor-laden kidney. The posterior parietal peritoneum is incised over the aorta and any fatty areolar lymph node bearing tissue is dissected laterally to the edge of the aorta.

M   The renal vein must be ligated as early as possible, but the artery must be ligated
N   before the vein if congestion of the kidney (and loss of the trapped blood) is to be avoided. In these two illustrations, the fatty areolar tissue in the area has been deleted for illustrative purposes. A Mixter forceps is used to encircle these vessels and, with ligatures at the root of both artery and vein, they are ligated essentially simultaneously with 2-0 silk. A transfixion ligature is applied to the artery. Note again that 10 per cent of kidneys have multiple renal arteries. The internal spermatic vein is tied in continuity. The adrenal gland will be excised as part of a proper cancer operation, but also because its venous drainage must be sacrificed. During the dissection the adrenal arteries can be occluded with silver clips, but most will stop bleeding spontaneously when cut.

O   The dissection continues with displacement of the tissue laterally over the psoas. One must remain alert for accessory vessels, especially on the right side, for if divided unknowingly they can be particularly vexing for the surgeon who may have to find the loose ends under the vena cava.

P   There is depicted here a continuation of the lateral and inferior dissection of the ureter, the internal spermatic vein and the associated fatty areolar tissue. The ilioinguinal and genitofemoral nerves coursing along on the underlying psoas muscle remain behind unharmed.

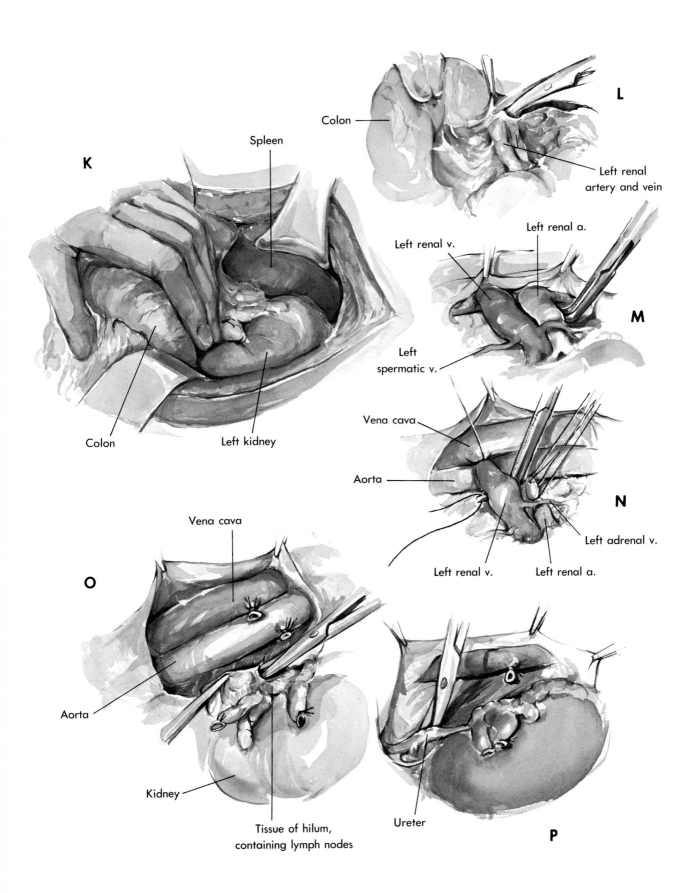

K

Spleen

Colon

Colon

Left kidney

L

Left renal
artery and vein

M

Left renal v.

Left renal a.

Left
spermatic v.

N

Vena cava

Aorta

Left renal v.

Left renal a.

Left adrenal v.

O

Vena cava

Aorta

Kidney

Tissue of hilum,
containing lymph nodes

P

Ureter

Q Up to this point the dissection of the cancerous kidney has been from a medial to lateral direction and in keeping with the principle of early sequestration of its blood supply and of removal of the lymphatic channels toward their point of origin. Now the kidney is mobilized at its upper pole by incising the peritoneum and perirenal fascia. The adrenal gland lies within the encountered perirenal fat and is excised, and it is at this point that some of the arterioles to the adrenal gland are found. At the completion of this portion of the dissection the base of the operative field will be the posterior insertions of the diaphragm.

R Any remaining lateral attachments are severed and the kidney lifted so as to resume the caudal dissection begun in Figure P. In the previous two and in the following illustrations the kidney needs to be handled for the sake of convenience. The kidney is now so mobile that this should entail no risk.

S The distal point at which the ureter is divided depends largely on the cell type of the cancer being excised. Since in this instance it is an adenocarcinoma, the ureter is divided proximal to the ureterovesical junction, and the distal portion is ligated with 3-0 chromic catgut. Squamous cell or papillary cancers have the predilection of metastasizing or growing down the ureteral lymphatics and appearing as recurrences in the ureteral stump. For such cancers, therefore, the practice is to excise the ureter in its entirety along with a button of urinary bladder. In expectation of this the incision is initially made longer so that the ureterovesicular junction can be reached easily.

T A soft rubber drain is placed in the renal fossa and exteriorized through a posteriorly placed counterincision. The operative site is checked for residual bleeding and the organs replaced in their normal position. A right angle chest tube is exteriorized at the posterior axillary line at the 11th interspace and attached to an under-water seal drainage. It is anchored to the skin securely. The lung is examined for areas of atelectasis and these areas are aerated. The diaphragmatic incision is reapproximated with interrupted horizontal mattress stitches of 2-0 silk.

U
V The peritoneum is closed with a continuous stitch of 1-0 chromic catgut up to the diaphragmatic repair. The intercostal muscles are approximated in a similar manner. The fascia is sewn with interrupted simple stitches of 2-0 silk. The skin is closed in a preferred manner and a large dressing applied so the ample drainage will not soak through.

An x-ray of the chest should be taken in the recovery room to confirm that the lung on the operated side is expanded. Entry into the thorax and surgery under the diaphragm combine to produce a high incidence of left lower lung complications if the clinician is not aggressive in measures to prevent this. Patients are taught preoperatively to breathe deeply and are urged to do so early and regularly postoperatively. Early ambulation is more difficult to enforce than with a thoracic or abdominal incision, but the rewards in decreased postoperative complications are appreciable when such a regimen is followed.

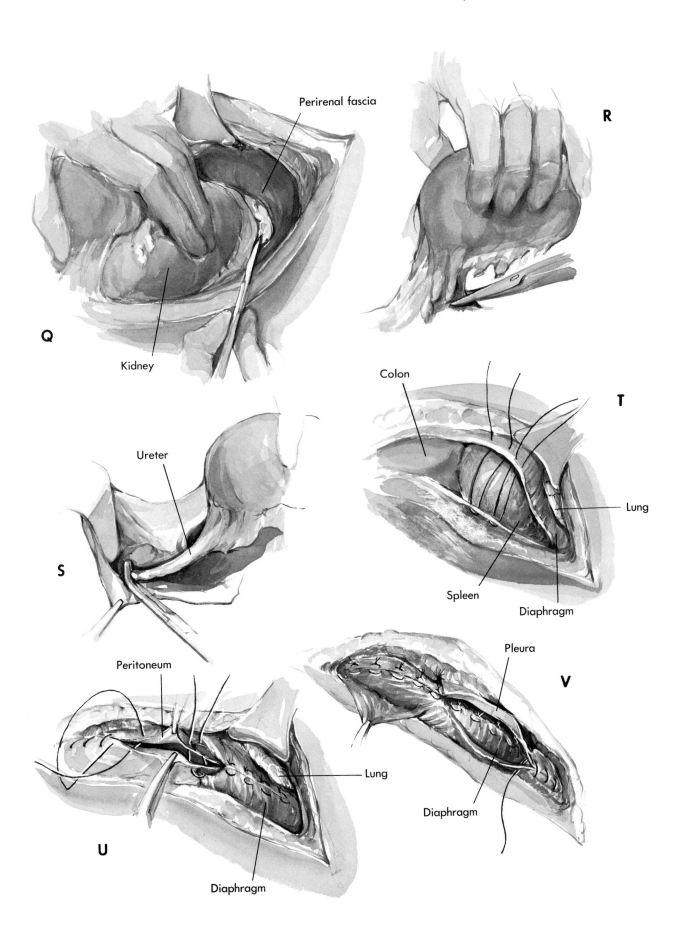

TOTAL COLECTOMY

It is noteworthy that total excision of the colon is most frequently performed for inflammatory disease or the presence of precancerous lesions rather than for cancerous involvement.

The commonest indication for total colectomy is ulcerative colitis and its complications of toxic megacolon, hemorrhage and perforation, resulting in permanent disruption of intestinal continuity by ileostomy. On occasion, massive life-threatening hemorrhage from pancolonic diverticular disease is best treated by colectomy when the bleeding source(s) cannot be identified by multiple colotomies or "compartmentalization" of the colon with intestinal clamps. Familial polyposis offers an absolute indication for total colectomy. Here, however, intestinal continuity is commonly re-established by ileoproctostomy or cecoproctostomy. Other relative indications for total colectomy are: (1) the presence of several polyps in all three segments of the colon, (2) a manifest proclivity for polyp formation following transabdominal polypectomy, (3) colonic cancer coexisting with polyps in other segments of the colon, and (4) when cancer in a long redundant sigmoidal loop has become adherent to the cecum or ascending colon.

The performance of a total colectomy is in itself usually not technically difficult, but the desperate illness and severe debilitation of the patients upon whom such urgent or emergent surgery is performed demand a high degree of clinical judgment and technical skill. The widespread use of corticosteroids in the therapy of ulcerative colitis undoubtedly has enabled many patients to postpone an inevitable operation and others to be maintained in remission or a state of health reasonably close to remission. Concurrently, however, there is now that group whose corticosteroid dosage is increased almost beyond reason to keep pace with a deteriorating disease state, or they are sustained on heavy doses for an inordinate length of time. By the time both internist and patient acknowledge the need of a colectomy, the patient may be desperately ill indeed.

For elective cases, preoperative antimicrobial agents are used and combined with cleansing of the lower bowel by dietary and mechanical agents as circumstances of the disease warrant.

Exposure is gained through a generous left paramedian incision extending from the pubic ramus to almost the left costal margin. The colon is mobilized by dividing the parietal attachments. In performing a colectomy for ulcerative colitis the gastrocolic omentum is transected, thus permitting the omentum to be removed intact with the colon, thereby reducing the risk of small bowel obstruction from an ensnaring omentum. The mesocolon and its contained vessels are divided at a convenient distance from the colon only when the resection is for inflammatory or benign lesions. In contrast, colectomy for cancer requires an en bloc resection of the lymph nodes and vessels beginning at the root of the mesentery. Reperitonealization of the colic gutters is not required and, in fact, is inadvisable. The most distal segment of the ileum free of disease by frozen section microscopy at surgery is employed to fashion an ileostomy after Brooke's technique, which provides rapid maturation of the stoma.

Reconstruction of the intestinal tract following total colectomy for familial polyposis is accomplished between the terminal ileum and rectum, the disparity of bowel diameters being reduced by slitting of the antimesenteric border of the ileum. The rectum also may contain polyps, but it is not removed. These are within easy reach of the proctoscope and, after an initial fulguration of those present (usually not all at one time), additional polyps can easily be fulgurated as they may appear. As the patient advances in age, they reappear less commonly. Indeed, total regression has been observed in the rectal segment. An important advantage of an ileoproctostomy is the sparing of the patient, often an adolescent, the handicap of an ileostomy. For multiple polyps in all segments of the colon, but when the cecum is spared, cecoproctostomy can be done. It is technically easier to perform, allows adequate inspection by proctoscopy and is usually accompanied by more normal bowel habits.

In highly selected patients with ulcerative colitis in whom a diseased rectum is spared, the reconstruction of the intestinal tract by ileoproctostomy might be attempted. However, the generally disappointing results following this procedure have prompted the majority of American surgeons to perform a one- or two-stage panproctocolectomy.

References

Brooke, B. N.: The management of an ileostomy—including its complications. Lancet 2:102, 1952.
Ferguson, L. K., and Nusbaum, M.: The technique of total colectomy and ileostomy. Surgery 57:915, 1965.
Van Prohaska, J., and Siderius, N. J.: The surgical rehabilitation of patients with chronic ulcerative colitis. Am. J. Surg. *103*:42, 1962.

Total Colectomy

A Total colectomy is usually a straightforward procedure and, although always a major operation, can easily be one of desperation in patients critically ill with fulminating ulcerative colitis. The success of the operation will then depend on many factors, not the least being the ability of the surgeon to bring into play basic surgical principles and refined operative skill.

The colon receives its blood supply from the superior and inferior mesenteric arteries in the following manner: The superior mesenteric artery arises from the aorta 1 to 2 cm. below the celiac axis, passes under the body of the pancreas, but over its uncinate process as well as over the transverse portion of the duodenum, and gently curves on its course to the right iliac fossa. It is accompanied by the superior mesenteric vein along its right border. From its convex or left side it gives off eight to 12 branches which supply the small bowel. The ileocolic artery is the last branch of the concave or lateral side of the superior mesenteric artery. It divides into descending and ascending branches, the latter anastomosing with the terminal branches of the superior mesenteric and the descending anastomosing with the right colic artery. The right colic artery is given off at about the midpoint of the ascending colon. It too divides into descending and ascending branches, the latter anastomosing with the middle colic artery. The middle colic artery is given off just as the superior mesenteric appears from under the pancreas and divides into a right branch which anastomoses with the right colic artery and a left which anastomoses with the ascending branch of the left colic artery. These anastomoses constitute the marginal artery which lies about 3 cm. from the mesenteric edge of the bowel.

The remainder of the colon is supplied by the inferior mesenteric artery which is smaller than the superior and which arises from the aorta at the level of the 3rd lumbar vertebra or approximately 4 cm. from the aortic bifurcation. The left colic artery is the first branch of the inferior mesenteric artery. It divides into an ascending branch which anastomoses with the left branch of the middle colic and a descending branch which anastomoses with the highest of the two or three sigmoidal arteries. The inferior mesenteric artery finally becomes the superior hemorrhoidal artery. The inferior mesenteric vein is shown taking its cephalad course to empty into the splenic vein.

B
C A left paramedian incision is used to leave the right side entirely free of scars which may hamper the proper construction of an ileostomy and because, once the right colon is mobilized, it can be delivered into the wound easily. In Figure B the right colon is being displaced medially by hand as the lateral peritoneal reflection is incised. In some patients with a friable toxic megacolon heavy with fluid and air, even the hand cannot be used with confidence. In such instances a double purse-string suture of 2-0 silk may have to be applied and through it the colon aspirated of liquid and air so that it can be manipulated. When this is done, the area about the aspiration site is heavily protected with laparotomy pads. The mobilization of the right colon exposes the psoas muscle, the right kidney and ureter, the spermatic or ovarian vessels and the second and third portions of the duodenum. In Figure C the phrenocolic and hepatocolic ligaments are clamped before being divided because the vessels within them can bleed persistently if not ligated.

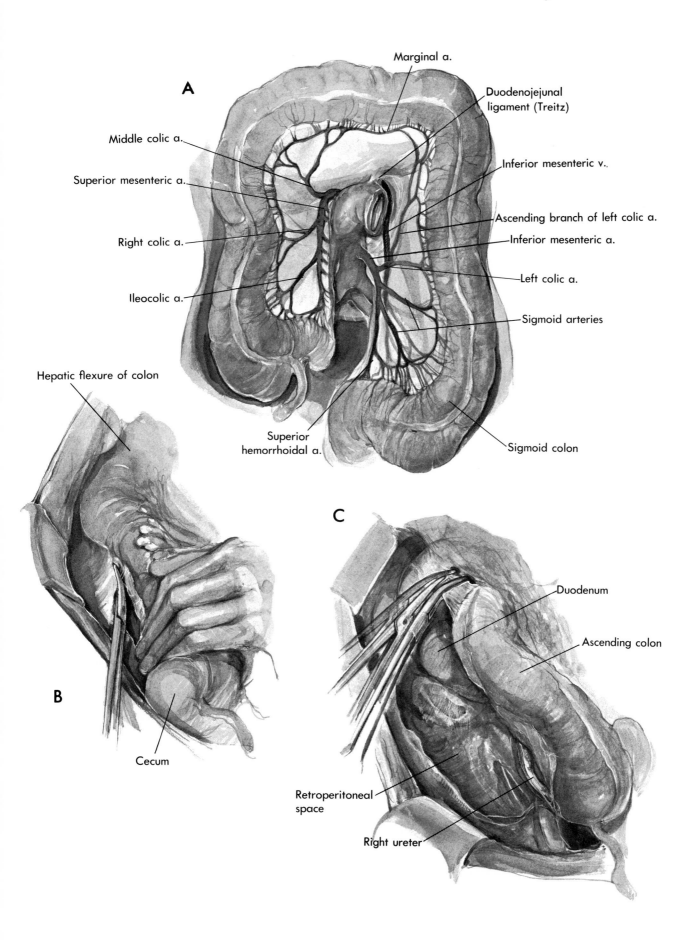

A

Marginal a.

Duodenojejunal ligament (Treitz)

Middle colic a.

Superior mesenteric a.

Right colic a.

Ileocolic a.

Inferior mesenteric v.

Ascending branch of left colic a.

Inferior mesenteric a.

Left colic a.

Sigmoid arteries

Hepatic flexure of colon

Superior hemorrhoidal a.

Sigmoid colon

B

Cecum

C

Duodenum

Ascending colon

Retroperitoneal space

Right ureter

D The entire right colon has been mobilized. If the operation is being performed for chronic inflammatory disease, the pericolic inflammation will not permit easy separation of the colon so that the right ureter and retroperitoneal portion of the duodenum become liable to injury.

E The extensive denuding of this area invites a retained omentum to become adherent, and this may lead to troublesome postoperative complications. It is, therefore, removed along with the colon. The gastrocolic omentum is being divided on the more avascular stomach side of the gastroepiploic vessels.

F The colon is returned to its normal position so that its vasculature can be divided.
G Remaining proximal to the vascular arcades requires that only three sets of vessels, the ileocolic, the right colic and the middle colic, be divided. They are ligated with 2-0 silk.

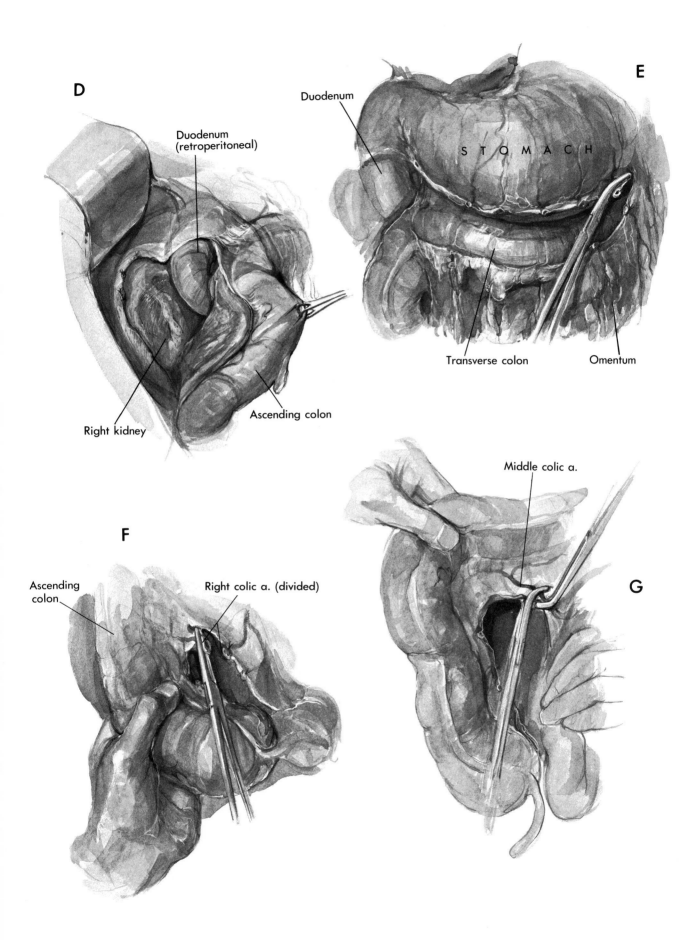

D

Duodenum
(retroperitoneal)

E

Duodenum

S T O M A C H

Transverse colon

Omentum

Right kidney

Ascending colon

F

Middle colic a.

Ascending
colon

Right colic a. (divided)

G

H
I

The operation shifts to the descending colon, which is retracted medially as the peritoneal reflection is incised up to the splenic flexure. Normally this is an avascular area wherein incision of the peritoneum and mobilization of the colon can proceed with dispatch and with little concern for persistent bleeding. In the presence of ulcerative colitis, however, numerous small collateral vessels may be present. Usually packing the area with moistened laparatomy pads will be sufficient for hemostasis, with ligation being necessary for the larger vessels or those vessels which persist in bleeding. The hand is placed near the splenic flexure as shown, and the index finger insinuated under the splenocolic ligament. This is clamped, cut, and ligated with 2-0 chromic catgut. If the splenic flexure is unusually high, one is tempted to pull too hard on the colon in order to bring the splenocolic ligament into better view; this increases the risk of tearing the splenic capsule in this area.

J

Here the splenocolic ligament is shown being divided.

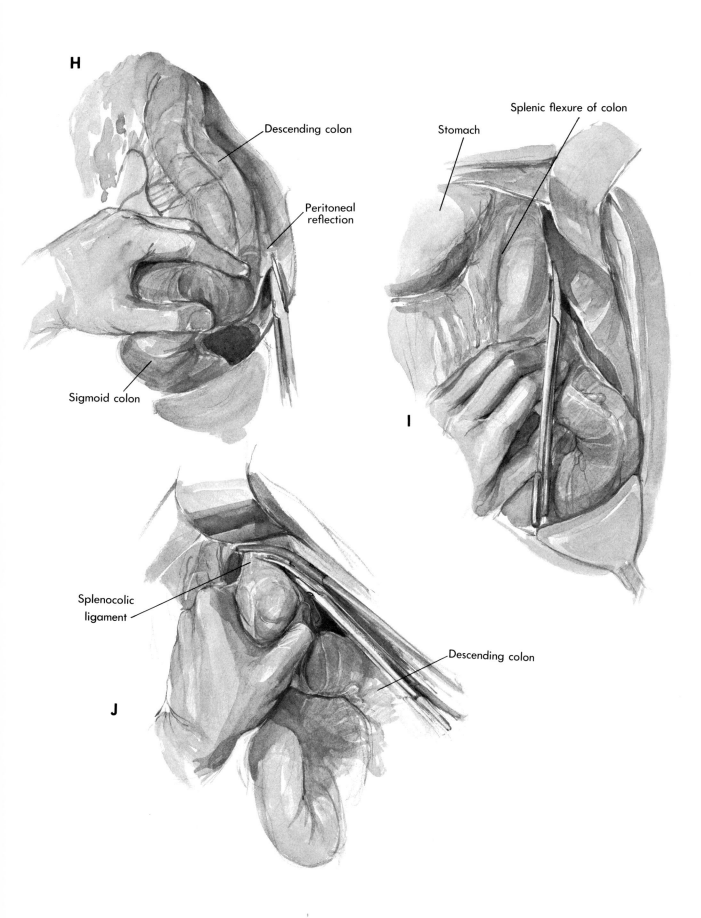

H

Descending colon

Peritoneal
reflection

Sigmoid colon

Splenic flexure of colon

Stomach

I

Splenocolic
ligament

Descending colon

J

K   The sigmoid colon is detached from its lateral fixation and displaced medially as its mesentery is separated from the underlying psoas muscle, spermatic or ovarian vessels and ureter.

L   The left colon has been repositioned so as to lie naturally and its vasculature ligated.
M   In Figure L the artery and vein are being isolated where they are single trunks, allowing a more expeditious operation. Notice the window cut into the mesentery to allow the separate ligation of the inferior mesenteric vein. Sometimes in obese individuals or those with a thick mesentery it is desirable to divide the vessels at a position closer to the bowel (Figure M).

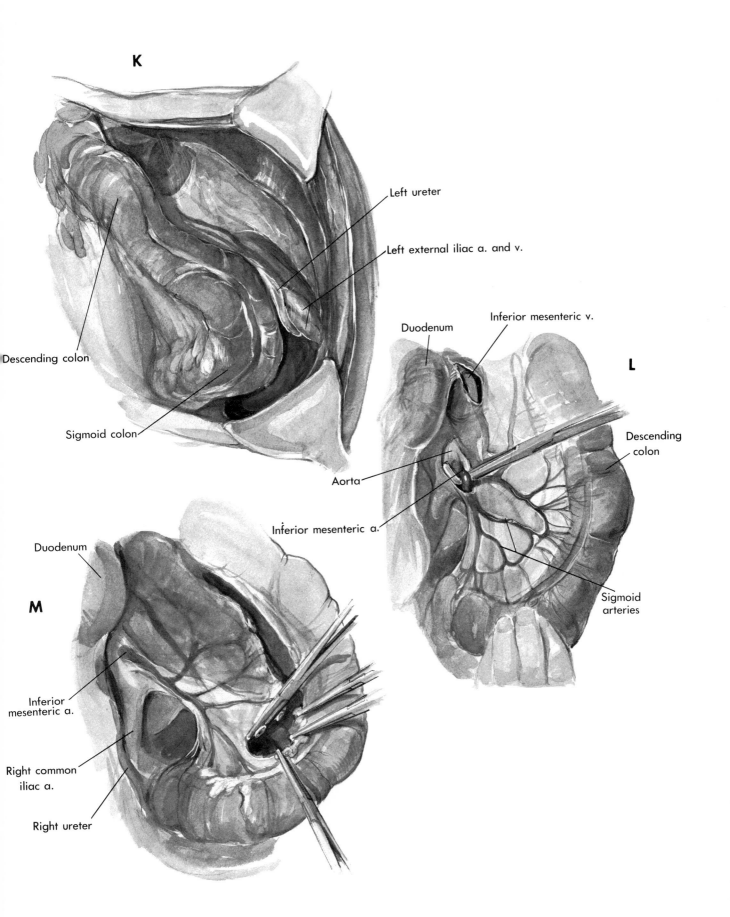

K

Left ureter

Left external iliac a. and v.

Duodenum

Inferior mesenteric v.

L

Descending colon

Descending colon

Aorta

Sigmoid colon

Inferior mesenteric a.

Sigmoid arteries

Duodenum

M

Inferior mesenteric a.

Right common iliac a.

Right ureter

N   The view shifts as indicated by the figure in the left upper corner. The mesosigmoid is clamped and divided down to the peritoneal reflection. If the surgeon is certain that the rectum is to be removed at this time or later, it is desirable to carry the present dissection to below the peritoneal reflection. This is obviously necessary with a synchronous resection of the rectum or with a metachronous resection in which it is advisable to dissassociate the rectum from the peritoneum, allowing a later perineal removal of the rectum without entry into the peritoneal cavity. If one intends to attempt a later ileorectal anastomosis, the colon is divided at the peritoneal reflection and oversewn in two layers, the outer being with interrupted 2-0 silk. In this illustration the middle hemorrhoidal vessels are being clamped, divided and ligated.

O   The upper rectum is being divided between Kocher clamps. If the rectum is to be
P   removed at this time it is tied with a linen tape distal to the Kocher clamp, amputated and the stump covered with a rubber dam which is held in place with a tie of heavy silk. The rectal stump is replaced in the true pelvis as in Figure P. If the rectum is to be removed at a later date, it is not tied at all but oversewn in two layers, the outer with interrupted stitches of 2-0 silk, and it is replaced in the true pelvis.

Q   The pelvic peritoneum is closed with continuous 3-0 chromic catgut. Of course, the peritoneum would not have been incised in this manner nor require such a closure if the rectum were retained for later anastomoses with the ileum.

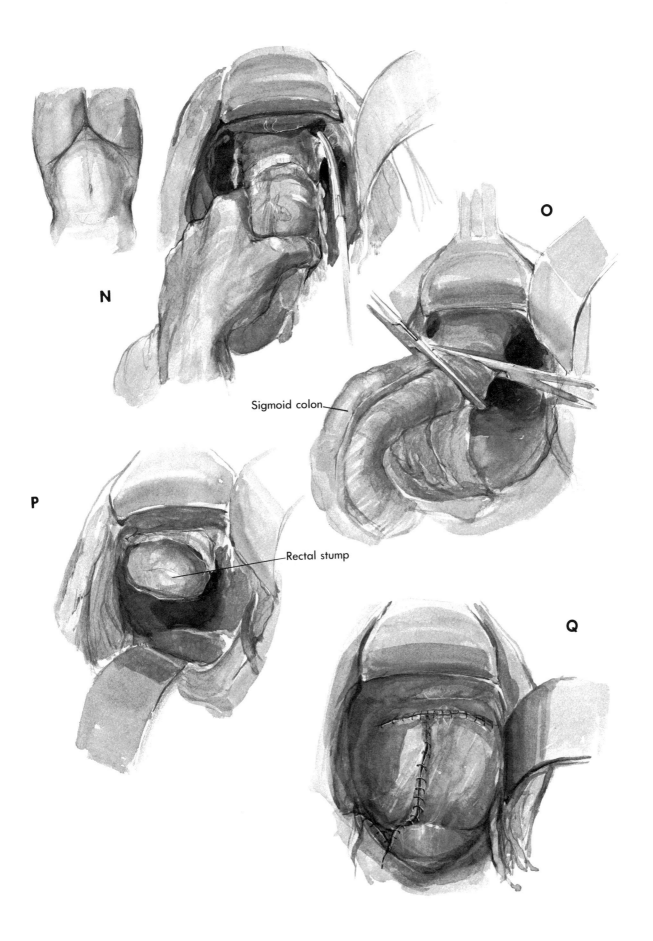

N

O

Sigmoid colon

P

Rectal stump

Q

R
S

Division of the ileum is left until last since it will coincide with the subsequent construction of the ileostomy. If, at the commencement of the dissection, there is uncertainty about the level of ileal involvement it is proper to divide the ileum then so that microscopic examination of this tissue can be carried out while the remainder of the operation proceeds.

The site of the ileal stoma should be chosen with care preoperatively. The ileostomy is best placed midpoint between the umbilicus and anterior iliac spine. It should be on a smooth surface without scars or natural skin creases. The patient should be examined for the latter while lying down as well as when standing and leaning over. A circular piece of skin, fascia and peritoneum equal in diameter to that of the ileum is cut out at the selected spot on the abdomen.

The skin, anterior rectus sheath and peritoneum are grasped and held in proper line while this cut is being made so that the cut through the various layers will remain in line later. Dissociation between tissue planes results in a shearing effect with obstruction of the terminal ileum. The tip of the Payr clamp is inserted through the abdominal opening to grasp the ileum before it is divided, or is inserted to grasp it after it has been divided so as to pull it to the outside. Before this is done, hemostasis in this hole must be absolute if infection in this area and later in the ileum is to be avoided. An intestinal clamp has been placed proximally to guard against massive spillage during this manipulation.

T

The hiatus lateral to the ileum is a source of internal herniation or volvulus. It is closed by attaching the mesentery of the ileum to the abdominal wall as shown. This is done with interrupted stitches and so placed that they do not disturb the ileum in its course.

U
to
X

Simple exteriorization of the ileum is attended by inflammation with proximal progression and subsequent dysfunction of the terminal ileum. This is obviated by eversion of the ileum so that no serosa remains exposed. The exteriorized ileum is trimmed to a length of 4 cm. The phantom drawing in Figure V shows the Babcock forceps grasping the mucosa at a point halfway down so that it can be everted as in Figure W. Stitches are placed so that they anchor the ileum and keep the mucosa everted, with no suture remaining buried. The needle traverses the free edge of the mucosa, then the seromuscularis of the underlying ileum at the skin level and then the skin itself.

The left and right colic gutters are drained, with care being taken to keep the counterincision on the right, well to the side so that it does not interfere with, or infect, the ileostomy. The abdomen is closed in a usual manner, but because these patients may be cachectic or being treated with corticosteroids, retention sutures are used. The ileostomy bag is immediately placed in position.

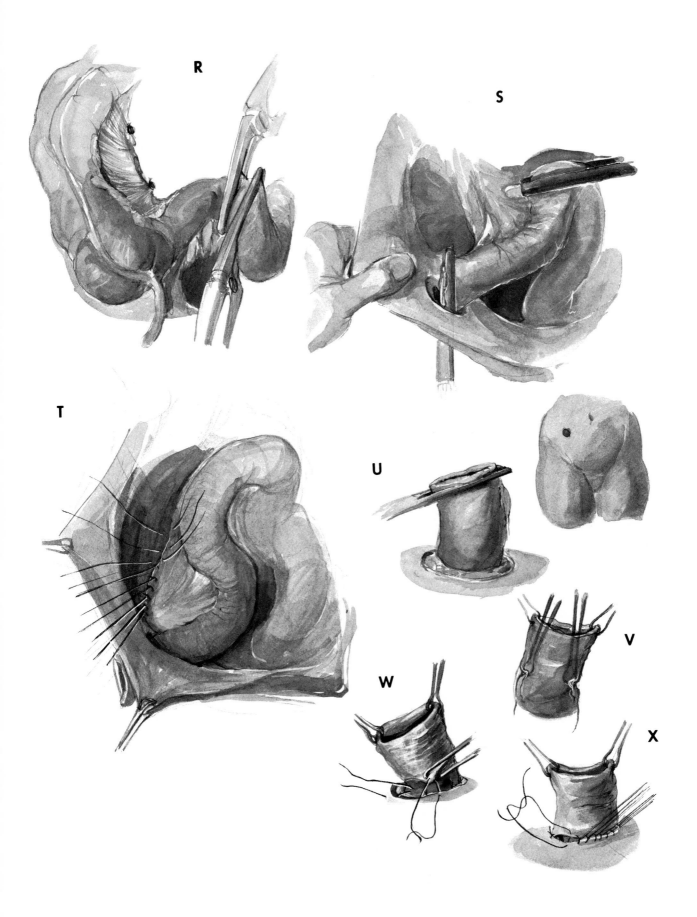

ABDOMINOPERINEAL RESECTION

Curative surgery for adenocarcinoma of the rectum by abdominoperineal resection is based upon the knowledge of tumor behavior and is commonly employed for lesions at or below the peritoneal reflection. The biological characteristics of this lesion are well established and are predictable. In contrast to the prolonged natural course of papillary thyroid cancer, for example, the average natural life expectancy of patients harboring untreated rectal cancer is relatively short, lasting approximately 27 months from the time of presumed clinical onset. It is insignificantly altered by primary radiation alone or in combination with colostomy. Surgery remains the most effective treatment of rectal cancer. With the growing relative rarity of gastric carcinoma in the United States, the colon carcinomas in both men and women have become the most important gastrointestinal tumors.

The tumor is relatively slow growing (about two thirds are Broder's grades I or II) and extends usually no more than 3 cm. longitudinally within the bowel wall. Nevertheless, at surgery, two thirds of the patients already have lymph node involvement in one or both components of the dual lymphatic system, and in almost three quarters of patients the tumor has penetrated all layers of the bowel wall. One out of ten patients has distant organ spread. These observations combined with a working knowledge of pelvic anatomy comprise the essential elements for an intelligent surgical attack against rectal cancer in an otherwise healthy patient.

The patient's bowel is mechanically cleansed and prepared with an antimicrobial agent. The operation as illustrated is subject to occasional modification dictated by the surgical disease and the structural characteristics of the patient, or both. Synchronous combined resections are becoming more commonplace and are proportionate to the increasing number of skilled residents assigned to our service. Division of the inferior mesenteric artery at its aortic take-off, with distal resection of the mesentery and rectum, as opposed to transecting the artery beyond the left colic is not routinely done in patients with a low lying Dukes' C lesion. We believe, under these circumstances, that it adds more risk and offers no greater chance of cure. This is particularly true in the obese patient. It is our contention that the critical factor governing cure rates in this situation is the extent of lateral pelvic spread rather than superior hemorrhoidal–inferior mesenteric node involvement. The bony confines of a narrow pelvis not infrequently preclude the operative excision of lateral cancer spread, but actually operative manipulation contributes to a greater risk of local recurrence. Unfortunately, residual tumor recurrence under these circumstances takes place in up to 50 per cent of patients. This observation is dependent upon and varies directly with the degree of tumor anaplasticity and its proximity to the anus. No effort is made to close the perineum tightly in these patients. The wound is packed widely opened. However, we try to approximate the perineum in selected patients with an apparent early lesion which is located a reasonable distance above the dentate line. A Penrose or sump drain should be employed in these patients to prevent the accumulation of fluids. In continuity resection of the posterior vaginal vault or the seminal vesicles and a portion of the prostate is done in the case of penetrating lesions. A previously inserted urethral catheter serves as a landmark.

Whenever possible, the pelvic peritoneum is reconstructed without tension. This may be accomplished by providing additional pelvic parietal peritoneum in continuity through finger dissection from the pelvic walls. Wide excision of a large rectal tumor at the reflection, which, in the female, would include the uterus and ovaries en bloc, might leave inadequate pelvic peritoneum for closure. In this instance, a rubber tampon inserted from below would be adequate to support the abdominal viscera. The packing can be gradually withdrawn beginning on the seventh postoperative day.

The high incidence (3 to 18 per cent) of ovarian metastases in colorectal cancer has led us to perform concomitantly bilateral oophorectomy with or without hysterectomy in all women who have gross abnormalities of one or both ovaries; when the uterus or ovary is adherent to the tumor; when the tumor has invaded the bowel serosa or peritoneal implants are present; and, finally, when a palliative resection is performed in the presence of metastases or there is other evidence of widespread disease.

Provisional ligature of the hypogastric arteries is usually not done except possibly in the presence of a large tumor irradiated previous to surgery.

The terminal colostomy is sutured to a horizontally placed elliptical skin stoma. This tends to coapt the mucosal edges when not in use, thus reducing the amount of exposed moist mucosa. Adjunctive chemotherapy is not being used. However, encouraged by the favorable 10-year survival rates of patients with Dukes' C rectal cancer who received preoperative radiation and abdominoperineal resection as reported by Deddish and his associates at the Memorial Hospital in New York and others, we have been using this adjunct. Two thousand rads are given during the immediate preoperative period. No significant technical problems have been encountered that could be attributed solely to the use of radiation.

Employing the principles and techniques herein described, we have achieved a five-year survival rate of 50.9 per cent for all patients admitted with a diagnosis of rectal cancer and on whom an abdominoperineal resection was performed.

References

Daland, E. M., Welch, C. E., and Nathanson, L.: One hundred untreated cancers of the rectum. New England J. Med. 214:451, 1936.

dePeyster, F. A., and Gilchrist, R. K.: Pathology and manifestations of cancer of the colon and rectum. In Turell, R. (ed.): Diseases of the Colon and Anorectum. Philadelphia, W. B. Saunders Co., 1959, Chapter 19.

Fletcher, W. S., Allen, C. V., and Dunphy, J. E.: Preoperative irradiation for carcinoma of the colon and rectum. Am. J. Surg. 109:76, 1965.

Morson, B. C., Vaughan, E. G., and Bussey, H. J. R.: Pelvic recurrence after excision of rectum for carcinoma. Brit. M. J. 5348:13, 1963.

Quan, S. H., Deddish, M. R., and Stearns, M. W., Jr.: The effect of preoperative roentgen therapy upon 10 and 5 year results of the surgical treatment of cancer of the rectum. Surg. Gynec. & Obst. 111:507, 1960.

Shimkin, M. B., and Cutler, S. J.: End results in cancer of the rectum. Dis. Colon & Rectum 7:502, 1964.

Abdominoperineal Resection

A   The pertinent anatomic structures to be encountered in the abdominal portion of the operation are shown. The pubic symphysis (*) is at the top of the illustration. The right ureter is rarely in jeopardy, but the left can easily be damaged during mobilization of the sigmoid colon. Sometimes, however, it is necessary to catheterize the ureters for easier identification. An intravenous urogram will show the location and number of ureters. In addition, a cystoscopy is advisable for rectal lesions that are located anteriorly. The inferior mesenteric artery is shown as it typically arises approximately 4 cm. from the aortic bifurcation. The left colic artery is given off approximately 5 cm. from the origin of the inferior mesenteric artery. The left colic artery then divides into an ascending and descending branch. Preservation of this bifurcation when ligating the descending branch at its origin from the left colic artery helps to assure blood supply to the distal sigmoid via the marginal artery. There is considerable variation in the vascular anatomy of this area which must be taken into account to assure a viable colostomy. When the mesentery is fat the major vessels can be better palpated than seen.

B   A left paramedian rectus muscle reflecting incision is preferred, with the patient in moderate Trendelenburg position. The symphysis pubis is at the (*). After the peritoneal cavity is entered the surgeon should look for any excess amounts of free fluid. The exploration should be methodical and thorough, with particular attention being paid to both lobes of the liver, the mesentery of the left colon, any evidence of tumor having invaded through the bowel wall into the pelvic peritoneum, and the presence of any other primary cancers. The presence of several metastatic nodules in the liver need not preclude the advisability of an abdominoperineal resection. This is especially true if the primary lesion is moderately large and the metastases are small. The terminal illness will be attended by tenesmus, rectal bleeding, perineal pain and may require a colostomy for obstruction before the patient succumbs to cancer within the liver.

C   For illustrative purposes the edges of the incision are not covered with double thickness laparotomy pads as is customary with all celiotomies.

    The small intestine preferably is confined to the upper peritoneal cavity with moistened laparotomy pads. In some instances the small intestine may be eviscerated and covered with moist pads, but it must also be watched for torsion or excess tension. We prefer ligation of the vascular supply as soon as resectability has been determined and before dissection and its attendant manipulation is begun. Although it is probably more realistic to request this maneuver with intestinal cancers above the peritoneal reflection, nevertheless, we attempt to practice it routinely. Through a short incision in the peritoneum of the mesentery, the inferior mesenteric artery is isolated, ligated and divided just distal to the origin of the left colic artery. The inferior mesenteric vein just lateral, but not parallel to it, is also ligated and divided at this time with 2-0 silk. The usual position of the ureter is shown by the asterisk.

D   The sigmoid is mobilized by reflecting it medially and incising the mesentery at the lateral peritoneal reflection.

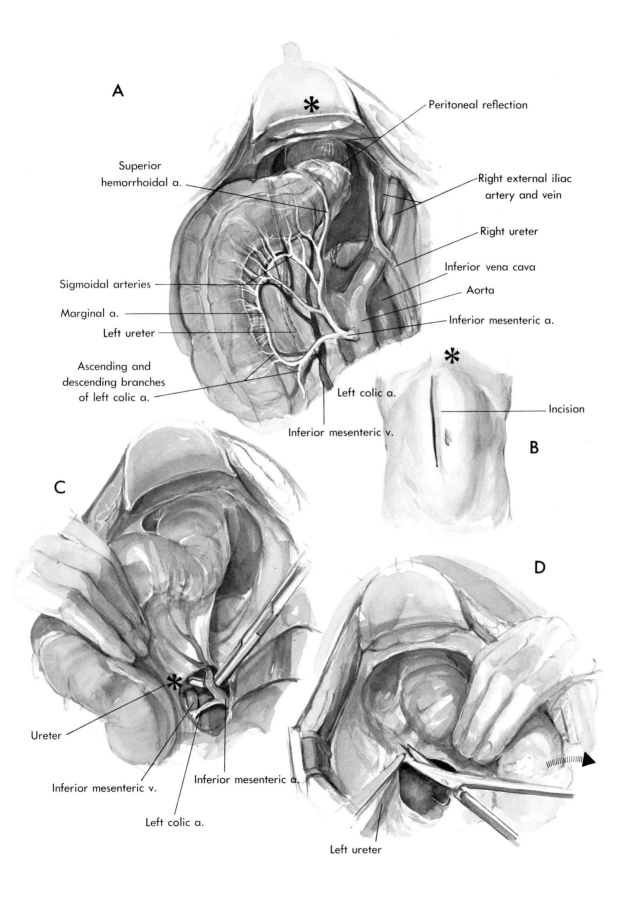

A

Peritoneal reflection

Superior
hemorrhoidal a.

Right external iliac
artery and vein

Right ureter

Inferior vena cava

Sigmoidal arteries

Aorta

Marginal a.

Inferior mesenteric a.

Left ureter

Ascending and
descending branches
of left colic a.

Left colic a.

Inferior mesenteric v.

Incision

B

C

D

Ureter

Inferior mesenteric v.

Inferior mesenteric a.

Left colic a.

Left ureter

E   Incision of the peritoneum over the mesosigmoid is continued downward to and across the rectovesical or rectouterine sulcus. Traction on the sigmoid makes the mesosigmoid taut and easier to cut accurately. The left ureter and iliac vessels are thus exposed and should not be injured. This dissection allows the surgeon to free the mesocolon to the midline.

F   The sigmoid is reflected to the left and again traction put upon it so that it can be cut more easily. Here traction is by hand, but it is often more convenient to do so with a linen tape passed through the mesosigmoid at a point selected for the future division and construction of the colostomy. The peritoneum over the mesosigmoid is incised so as to meet its counterpart from the left. Again the ureter just lateral to the peritoneal incision as well as the iliac vessels must be looked for and guarded from injury.

G   With the peritoneum incised the mesosigmoid is divided between curved hemostats. In obese individuals there may be considerable tissue to clamp and this should be done gently to avoid tearing vessels within it. The ligatures are of 2-0 silk.

H   The mesosigmoid is divided by sharp technique, with clamping and ligating of all tissue to just below the sacral promontory but avoiding the midsacral vessels. The dissection in the hollow of the sacrum can then be carried out by careful but firm blunt dissection. When in the right plane, the ease and feel of the dissection is unmistakable and the surgeon will save time and avoid trouble if he is careful in establishing this plane. One must not dissect dorsal to the presacral fascia or tear the sacral veins in this area as the hemorrhage can be considerable. If this does occur, the surgeon should be wary of the grave temptation of prolonged suction of blood while seeking to find or secure the bleeding point. Packing of the sacral hollow is a reliable way to stop bleeding temporarily while the patient is transfused. The field is then exposed piecemeal and bleeding vessels ligated or stitched as they are encountered.

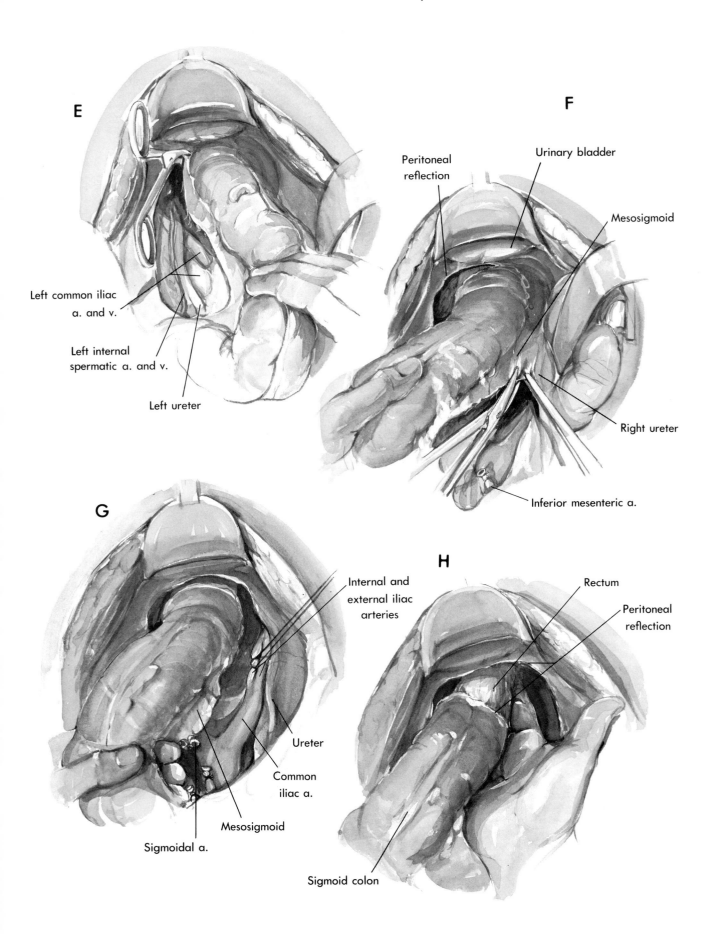

E

Left common iliac
a. and v.

Left internal
spermatic a. and v.

Left ureter

F

Peritoneal
reflection

Urinary bladder

Mesosigmoid

Right ureter

Inferior mesenteric a.

G

Internal and
external iliac
arteries

Ureter

Common
iliac a.

Mesosigmoid

Sigmoidal a.

H

Rectum

Peritoneal
reflection

Sigmoid colon

I   This sagittal view shows the hand in the hollow of the sacrum bluntly dissecting the rectum to, or just below, the coccyx. Dissection to this level during the abdominal stage of the operation will greatly facilitate the perineal dissection. Injudicious or excessive handling of the tumor (which is not shown) should be avoided in the relatively narrow confines of the pelvis. Admittedly some massaging of the tumor in such circumstances is virtually impossible to avoid. Anteriorly the dissection should stay on the rectal side of Denonvilliers' fascia except when the location of the tumor precludes this plane of dissection.

J   The anterior dissection is begun by sharp technique for a few centimeters until the correct plane of dissection has been established, but then must shift to the use of blunt technique. Separation of the urinary bladder from the rectum should be carried down at least past the seminal vesicles and preferably past the posterior surface of the prostate. In the female the dissection in the rectovaginal septum is carried down to the midpoint of the vagina.

K   With traction on the sigmoid (and rectum) the lateral rectal stalks containing the
L   middle hemorrhoidal vessels are exposed, clamped, cut and ligated as laterally as possible with 2-0 silk. The abdominal mobilization has been completed. The hollow of the sacrum is packed with several large surgical pads to minimize bleeding and to induce clotting within small vessels while the sigmoid is being divided and the ends covered.

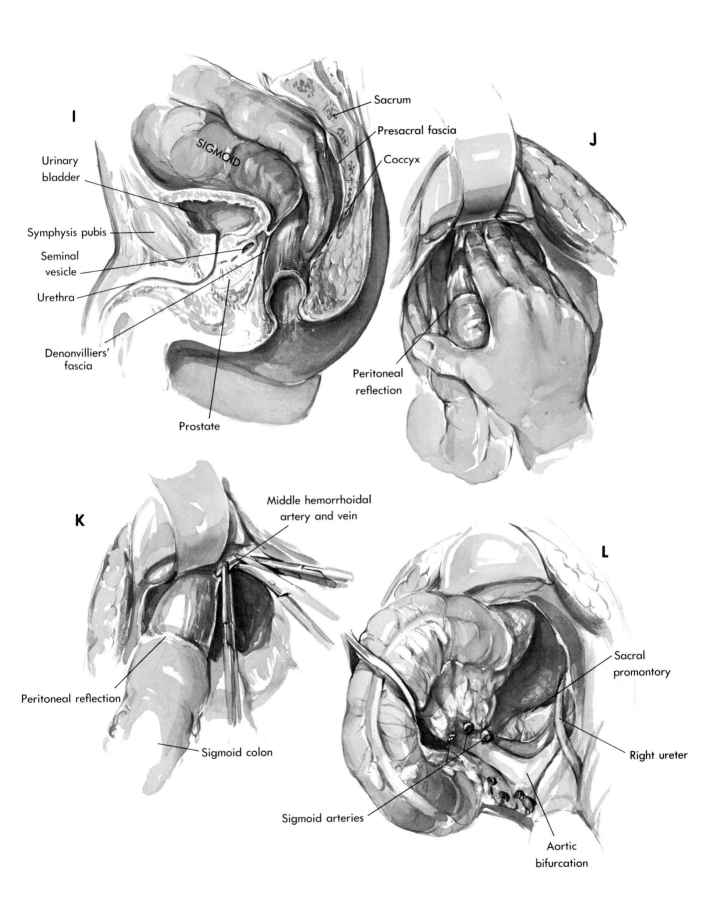

I

Urinary
bladder

Symphysis pubis

Seminal
vesicle

Urethra

Denonvilliers'
fascia

Prostate

SIGMOID

Sacrum

Presacral fascia

Coccyx

J

Peritoneal
reflection

K

Middle hemorrhoidal
artery and vein

L

Peritoneal reflection

Sigmoid colon

Sigmoid arteries

Sacral
promontory

Right ureter

Aortic
bifurcation

M   The portion of the bowel to be divided is carefully isolated from the remainder of the operative field with large laparotomy pads. Several practices can be followed in dividing the sigmoid. We prefer placing ties of heavy linen tape several centimeters apart and dividing the bowel between the ties with a scalpel. Both ends are then covered with small rubber dams which are secured with heavy black silk. This allows less subsequent contamination than simply oversewing the divided sigmoid.

N   The rubber dam used to cover the divided bowel is shown. The sigmoid and rectum are placed in the pelvis. Any excess of sigmoid that would prevent its being placed in the pelvis should be excised. A circular piece of skin of appropriate size is excised for the colostomy. Generally, this is positioned best at a point midway between the umbilicus and the left anterior iliac spine; however, body build and contours, scars and length of colon excised are influencing factors. The subcutaneous fat is spread and a similar piece of fascia is removed. The muscles are simply spread and the peritoneum incised and stretched. A clamp is passed into the peritoneal cavity through the colostomy opening and is used to pull the sigmoid out of the peritoneal cavity. The sigmoid should make a gentle sweep as it comes to the outside; therefore, if the proximal sigmoid is excessively long, it should be exteriorized and trimmed as necessary rather than permitted to remain intraperitoneally. These considerations now will make postoperative irrigation and function of the colostomy easier. The defect lateral to the sigmoid is closed by approximating the visceral and parietal peritoneum with a continuous stitch of 3-0 chromic catgut. The colostomy is surrounded by iodoform gauze and then by pads thickly impregnated with zinc oxide ointment. The serosa of the sigmoid colostomy may be anchored to this gauze as insurance against retraction, but if there is a question about excessive pull on the sigmoid, a Payr clamp is used to hold the sigmoid in place. The rubber dam is removed 24 to 48 hours later. Leaving it clamped for a longer period than this provides no greater safety because by now the bowel serosa is sufficiently adherent to surrounding tissue to effectively seal the peritoneal cavity from any feces that may spill next to the colostomy and through the zinc oxide impregnated gauze. In fact, it is advisable to open the bowel as soon as peristalsis appears because an unrelieved active colon will distend and foreshorten, and with the abdominal wall pushing forward there is a tendency for the sigmoid to pull inward.

O   The most accessible peritoneum for a reperitonealization of the pelvis is over the bladder anteriorly. Lateral mobilization will also help to release available peritoneum. In females in whom no alternative is feasible the uterus may be tipped backward to help to close this defect.

P   The pelvic peritoneum is approximated with a continuous stitch of 2-0 chromic catgut. No drains are used. The abdomen is closed with continuous and interrupted 1-0 chromic catgut for the peritoneum; the anterior rectus sheath is repaired with interrupted simple stitches of 2-0 silk and the skin with interrupted vertical mattress stitches of 3-0 silk. Retention sutures are optional.

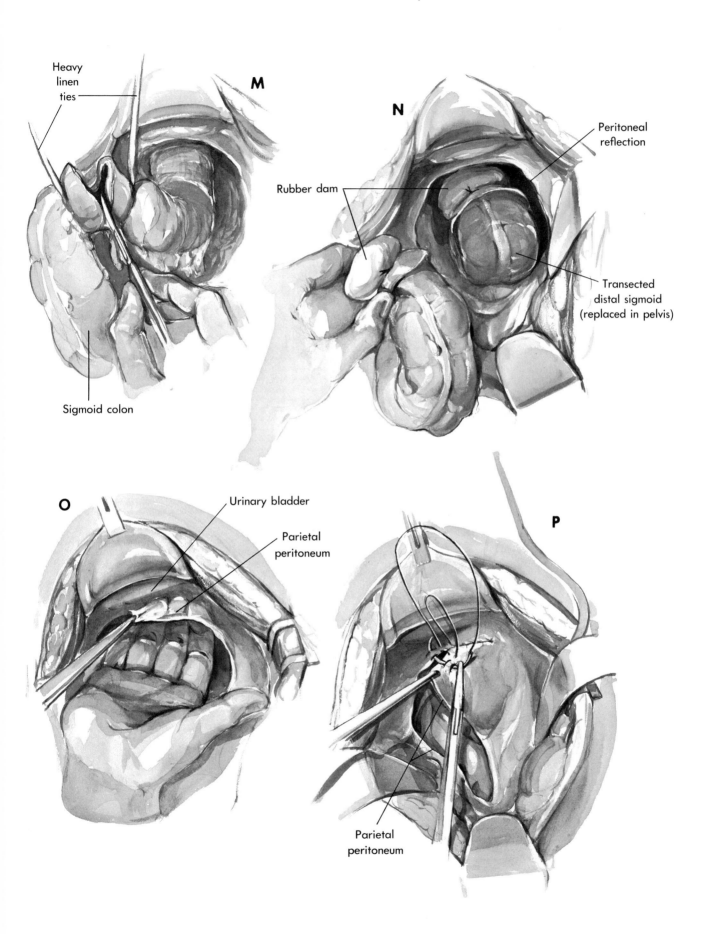

Heavy
linen
ties

M

Sigmoid colon

N

Rubber dam

Peritoneal
reflection

Transected
distal sigmoid
(replaced in pelvis)

O

Urinary bladder

Parietal
peritoneum

P

Parietal
peritoneum

Q
R
Although several positions may be used for the perineal dissection the lithotomy position is the least disturbing to the patient from the cardiorespiratory standpoint and even then it is advisable to have the patient gradually brought back from the Trendelenburg position. The patient's buttocks should extend several inches over the edge of the table. Some of the pertinent anatomy is shown (Q). After the patient is positioned, a purse-string suture (Figure R) is used to seal the anus, after which the area is cleansed and draped. A urinary catheter will have been in position.

S
The elliptical perineal incision extends from the ischeal tuberosities (*) laterally to the coccyx posteriorly and to the perineal region anteriorly. The coccyx need be excised only infrequently and when more exposure is clearly necessary.

T
U
The inferior hemorrhoidal arteries and branches from the internal pudendal vessels are clamped, cut and ligated, allowing access to the ischeorectal space, from which all the fat is removed. This exposes the inferior surface of the levator ani muscles.

V
The presacral fascia is incised, permitting entry into the pelvic cavity. With the patient in the lithotomy position the blood accumulated in the hollow of the pelvis will pour out, sometimes leading the unwary to think that brisk active bleeding is present.

W
The finger is hooked over the levator ani muscles, which are clamped and divided as laterally as possible.

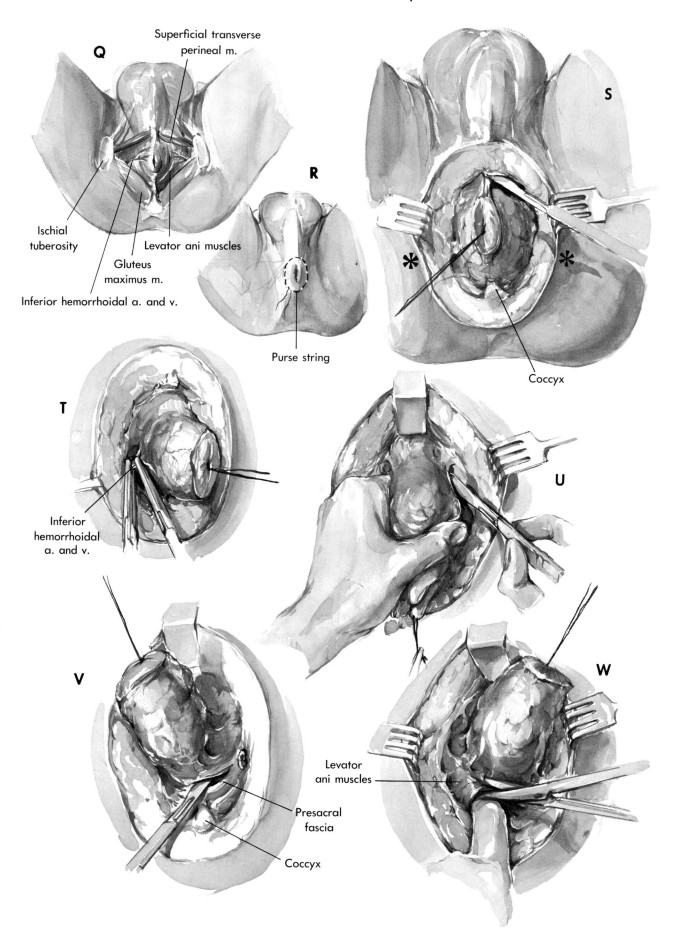

Q

Superficial transverse
perineal m.

Ischial
tuberosity

Gluteus
maximus m.

Levator ani muscles

Inferior hemorrhoidal a. and v.

R

Purse string

S

*

*

Coccyx

T

Inferior
hemorrhoidal
a. and v.

U

V

Presacral
fascia

Coccyx

W

Levator
ani muscles

X   The levator ani muscles are divided as far anteriorly as the superficial transverse perineal muscles where the latter are divided, resulting in the anterior levators holding the specimen in place. The dissection can be completed with sharp technique in the following manner while retracting the rectum dorsally.

Y
Z   With the hand in the hollow of the sacrum, the distal sigmoid colon is delivered (Figure Z) so that essentially all the specimen is exteriorized. The laparotomy pads are removed and counted.

A₁   With a finger behind this portion of the levator ani muscles a more accurate dissection can be carried out and with less risk of urethral trauma in the male. In the female vaginal tissue may be taken if indicated by virtue of proximity of the tumor.

B₁   Significant bleeding points are secured. A large rubber dam backed by long rolls of fluffed gauze is used to fill the pelvic space and to apply mild pressure for hemostasis, while at the same time supporting the new pelvic floor. The wound may be partly closed anteriorly and posteriorly if it is reasonably dry and there is sufficient tissue to effect such a closure.

With a finger behind this portion of the levator ani muscles a more accurate dissection Postoperatively the bladder should be kept decompressed, with catheter drainage for several days until it is clear that the bladder function is normal. The residual urine will have to be measured once or twice after the catheter is removed. The perineal pack is removed in two to three days if the perineal wound has been left open, and then sitz baths are begun while the wound granulates in. Sexual function in the male is usually disrupted, and the operation requires an informed consent from younger males.

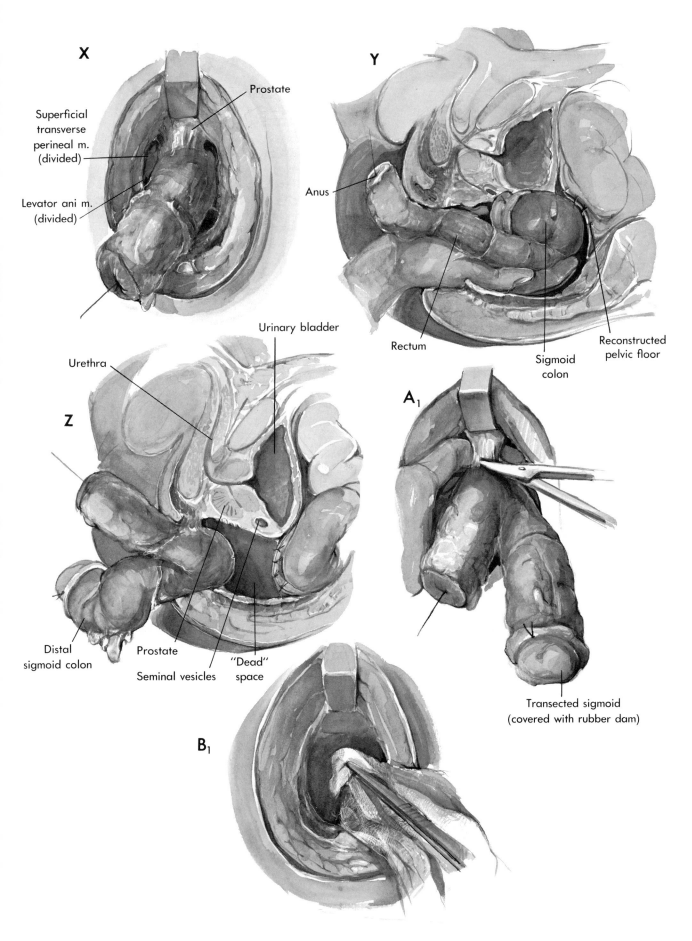

X

Superficial
transverse
perineal m.
(divided)

Levator ani m.
(divided)

Prostate

Y

Anus

Rectum

Sigmoid
colon

Reconstructed
pelvic floor

Urethra

Urinary bladder

Z

Distal
sigmoid colon

Prostate

Seminal vesicles

"Dead"
space

A₁

Transected sigmoid
(covered with rubber dam)

B₁

RADICAL ABDOMINAL HYSTERECTOMY WITH PELVIC LYMPHADENECTOMY

Radical surgery for the treatment of carcinoma of the cervix dates back to 1898 when Wertheim first performed the extensive abdominal operation that bears his name. In 1901 Schauta performed the first radical hysterectomy for cervical cancer by the vaginal route. Prior to these two pioneering efforts, simple hysterectomy by either the abdominal or vaginal route was the only surgical answer to this disease and the five-year survival rate was about 10 per cent. With the introduction of the above-mentioned more radical procedures, the survival rate increased fourfold. This fourfold improvement in the therapy of carcinoma of the cervix has never been equaled.

In later years Wertheim ceased to dissect routinely the pelvic lymph nodes. He did it only after palpation and inspection, removing only those lymph nodes that appeared to him to be palpably involved. The reason for this divergence from the original concept was that when lymphadenectomy was performed, the morbidity rate increased considerably and the mortality rate was about 20 per cent. The morbidity rate and the mortality rate (2.3 per cent) of the Schauta procedure were considerably less; however, the great drawback of the radical vaginal procedure was the fact that the surgeon could not resect the pelvic lymph nodes, whereas in the abdominal operation assessment and excision of nodes was possible. For many years the Wertheim operation remained the treatment of choice if a cure was sought aggressively. However, in the absence of modern anesthetic methods, knowledge of fluid balance, antibiotics, the ready use of blood transfusions and other ancillary aids so important to radical surgery, the morbidity and mortality of this operation were forbidding to most clinicians. Quite naturally, with the advent of radiotherapy, the treatment of cancer of the cervix by radical operations lost favor.

In 1939 Meigs, discontent with some of the sequelae of radiotherapy, reinstituted the surgical approach in the therapy of squamous cancer of the cervix and, in 1944, described his technique which he designated as a "Radical Abdominal Hysterectomy with Bilateral Pelvic Node Dissection." Largely because of a series of articles subsequently published by Meigs and his followers describing their successes, radical surgery for the treatment of cancer of the cervix again gained popularity. The five-year survival rate, free of cancer for Stage I involvement, increased to 80 per cent, and the operative mortality decreased to a level comparable with that of any other major operation.

Cervical carcinoma spreads by direct extension into the paracervical and paravaginal tissues with concurrent involvement of the intervening lymphatic channels. It tends, however, to remain confined to the pelvis; metastases to lung, bone and liver do occur, but with far less frequency than one might expect. For this reason it is accepted by most surgeons that a radical hysterectomy and pelvic node dissection achieves the maximum cure rate when the cervical cancer is sufficiently confined as to place it in Stages I or IIA of the International Classification.

The preoperative investigation and evaluation of the patient's general physical condition is most important. Any abnormalities found during this preoperative period should be properly corrected: anemia or low total blood volume is suitably treated by transfusion; electrolyte imbalance is restored; and any associated infection is treated as necessary. A careful and precise pelvic examination, including rectovaginal-abdominal palpation is mandatory; one must appreciate the fact that this is of primary importance in determining the extent and operability of the lesion prior to surgical exploration. The gastrointestinal and urinary tracts should be adequately examined preoperatively because carcinoma of the cervix is in close anatomic relationship.

A cystoscopy is performed, with thorough and methodical evaluation of the posterior aspect of the bladder to evaluate any anterior progression of the cancer. Areas of edema in the bladder may indicate underlying tumor as well as inflammation. Therefore, a biopsy should be taken of any abnormality or possible tumor-bearing area so as to be as certain as possible of the presence or absence of cancer in this area. An intravenous urogram is also mandatory because the ureters may be involved by parametrial spread of the cancer, a condition which can exist with few or no clinical signs or symptoms. If ureteral obstruction exists, this will indicate that, at the least, an anterior exenteration will be necessary to excise all the cancer. This urogram will also be used as a standard for postoperative follow-up studies of the urinary tract.

Page 336

A proctoscopy is performed on all patients. Invasion of the rectum, as evidenced by firmness or fixity of the rectum opposite the cervix, should alert the surgeon to the probable inapplicability of this operation and the possibility that a posterior pelvic exenteration might be more in order. These patients are given insoluble sulfonamides orally and are placed on a low-residue diet and then on liquids for two days preoperatively; this minimizes the undesirable consequences of rectal entry during the posterior dissection. It also results in an effectively decompressed small and large bowel which, as a consequence, is manipulated less and also is displaced out of the pelvis more easily. The investigation and preparation of these patients do not otherwise differ significantly from those for patients undergoing other types of major surgery.

During the operation good exposure, meticulous handling of tissues, careful dissection and a thorough knowledge of the anatomy are essential for success. The danger of injury to the urinary tract and the lower intestinal tract is always present. The greatest number of complications associated with this operation are those of the urinary tract. Constant awareness and care is necessary if one is to avoid mechanical injury to the lower third of the ureters and to the bladder. Restrained aggressiveness is necessary when dissecting the lower ureters so that they do not suffer ischemia and necrosis because of interference with their blood supply.

Radiotherapy has again come into vogue for treatment of Stage I and Stage IIA cervical cancers and in expert hands gives cures similar to surgery. The problem is that staging of cervical cancer with surgery is relatively accurate, whereas staging by the radiotherapist is much less accurate, being based in main on a pelvic examination. More extensive, controlled clinical trials will be needed to resolve this controversy. The answer may prove that the treatment is optional—either surgery or radiotherapy in expert hands. Combined therapy may be needed in more advanced cases.

References

Brunschwig, A.: Complete excision of pelvic viscera for advanced carcinoma; A one-stage abdominoperineal operation with end colostomy and bilateral ureteral implantation into colon above the colostomy. Cancer *1*:177, 1948.

Fletcher, G. H.: Female pelvis, uterine cervix. *In* Fletcher, G. H.: Textbook of Radiotherapy. Philadelphia, Lea & Febiger, 1966, Chapter 10.

Friedell, G. H., and Parsons, L.: The spread of cancer of the uterine cervix as seen in giant histological sections. Cancer *14*:42, 1961.

Liu, W., and Meigs, J. V.: Radical hysterectomy and pelvic lymphadenectomy. Am. J. Obst. & Gynec. 69:1, 1955.

McCall, L.: Surgical management of invasive carcinoma of the uterine cervix: The vaginal approach. Ann. Acad. Sc. 97:3 and 835, 1962.

Meigs, J. V.: Carcinoma of the cervix—the Wertheim operation. Surg. Gynec. & Obst. 78:195, 1944.

Williams, T. J.: Preoperative and postoperative care in radical pelvic surgery. Clin. Obst. & Gynec. 8:3, 1965.

A   The patient is shaved from nipples to midthighs, including the perineum. The vagina is cleansed with Betadine or the germicide of choice followed by the optional placement against the cervix of two sponges soaked in absolute alcohol. A straight catheter is inserted into the bladder, any urine is drained, 10 cc. of indigo carmine is introduced into the bladder and the catheter is removed. If there is an intraoperative bladder laceration, the leaking dye will help indicate this mishap.

The surgeon stands on the left side of the patient. A low midline or paramedian incision is the only reasonable one for this operation. It should extend clear to the symphysis pubis and for several inches above the umbilicus because it is just as easy to close a generous incision. Such an incision has the advantage of making the exposure and dissection easier, better and safer. Furthermore, it is impossible to perform this operation properly without adequate and maintained exposure. It can be extended for work in any other part of the abdomen as dictated by the circumstances. A preoperative low residue diet results in a more decompressed bowel that can be retracted with greater ease and, consequently, less postoperative ileus. Sometimes a cecum with low peritonealization or a redundant sigmoid may interfere with adequate exposure. These should be mobilized by dividing their respective peritoneal attachments so that they can be displaced cephalad and maintained there with moistened laparotomy pads. The patient is placed in the Trendelenburg position.

B
C   The exploration of the peritoneal cavity should be thorough, with particular attention given to the pelvic peritoneum for evidence of metastasis, induration or an excess of free fluid. The iliac lymph nodes are palpated for enlargement or fixation. The cervix and paracervical tissue and the adjoining area of the bladder are palpated with care to determine the presence and extent of lateral spread and the degree to which it may be fixed to these structures. The ureters are examined for evidence of any dilatation, which should quickly arouse suspicion of blockage by tumor.

A tenaculum is applied to the fundus of the uterus so that it can be manipulated. This is acceptable in a patient with cervical cancer but would risk exudation of cancer cells in a case of adenocarcinoma of the fundus. An alternate way is to grasp each round ligament and fallopian tube close to the uterus with curved six-inch hemostats. The hemostats are tied together and used as tractors. Squamous cancer of the cervix rarely metastasizes to the round ligaments, so they are ligated and divided several centimeters from their origin from the uterus. The uterus is retracted cephalad, the peritoneum over the vesicouterine sulcus incised and this plane developed down to the body of the uterus. It is a relatively avascular plane and lends itself well to blunt dissection. The ovarian artery and vein and the infundibulopelvic ligament are clamped, cut and ligated with 3-0 chromic catgut. The ends of this ligature are left long, a hemostat attached, and the hemostat placed over the side of the abdomen to act as a gentle retractor.

It is well to re-emphasize that adequate excision of the local paracervical tissue is every bit as important as a proper lymphadenectomy. Indeed, an aggressive approach in excising local tissue involved with cancer will salvage more patients than similar aggressiveness for patients with lymph node involvement. A hysterectomy performed discontinuously from the lymphadenectomy has gained some following because it offers improved exposure and greater ease for the lymphadenectomy. It is questionable whether it is a safer approach to this problem; the most serious indictment is that it cuts across all lymphatic channels.

D   The parietal peritoneum is incised laterally to meet with the anterior incision. The above steps are carried out bilaterally, resulting in considerable mobilization of the uterus.

E   The ureter is mobilized with constant care not to "strip" it excessively, as excessive surgical trauma to the paraureteral vessels is not only in itself an important cause of ureteral necrosis but will complement other conditions conducive to the formation of fistulas. A fine nontoothed forceps is used and the ureter itself is never grasped. The para-ureteral tissue is handled instead with proper precautions since this tissue is fragile and will avulse easily.

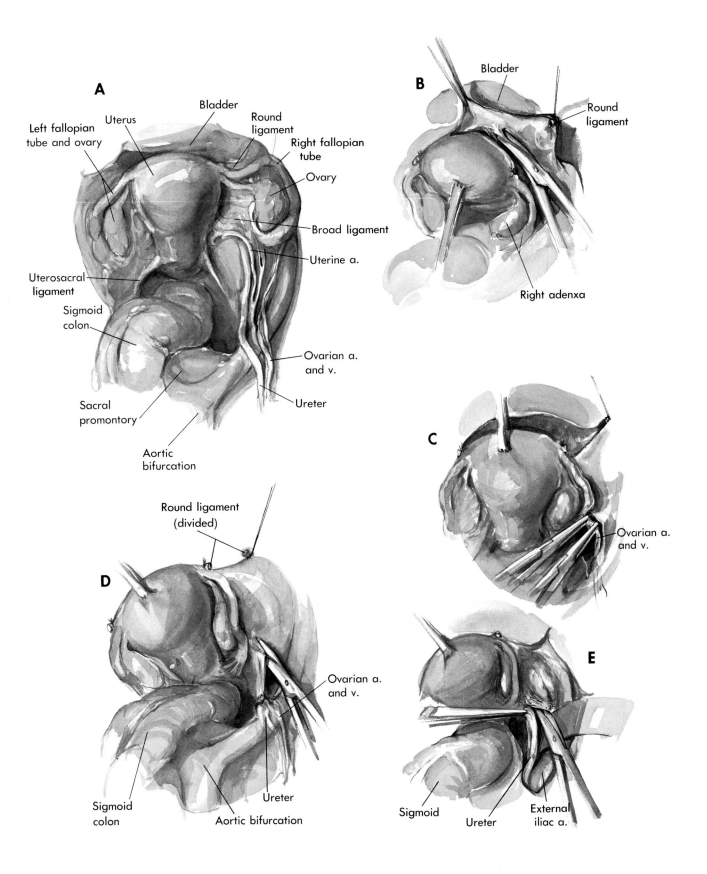

A

Left fallopian tube and ovary

Uterus

Bladder

Round ligament

Right fallopian tube

Ovary

Broad ligament

Uterine a.

Uterosacral ligament

Sigmoid colon

Ovarian a. and v.

Ureter

Sacral promontory

Aortic bifurcation

B

Bladder

Round ligament

Right adenxa

C

Ovarian a. and v.

D

Round ligament (divided)

Ovarian a. and v.

Ureter

Sigmoid colon

Aortic bifurcation

E

Sigmoid

Ureter

External iliac a.

Radical Hysterectomy (continued)

F   The ureter is freed to just past the uterine artery. The dissection below this point will be done later in the procedure. The web of tissue below this contains the uterine artery, superior vesical artery and the obliterated hypogastric artery, all of which arise from the internal iliac artery. Only the uterine artery is clamped, cut and ligated, along with the associated web of connective tissue, leaving intact the superior vesical arteries to the bladder.

G   One needs the peritoneum for subsequent peritonealization, but there certainly should be no hesitancy in removing it if it is involved or it jeopardizes the lymphadenectomy. A small soft rubber drain is passed under the ureter so that it can be manipulated with the least trauma. While the ureter is displaced medially, the peritoneum is cut transversely to the lateral border of the iliac artery and then easily freed from the underlying tissue. If there has been previous irradiation with thickening and adherence of the peritoneum to the underlying tissue, one can contemplate a difficult dissection which is hazardous because of the risk of damaging the underlying vessels. A stitch is placed through each free corner of the mobilized peritoneum and hemostats attached to them and allowed to hang over the side, thus effectively maintaining the exposure over the iliac vessels.

H
I   The pelvic lymphadenectomy is begun lateral to the iliac artery and toward the medial edge of the psoas muscle. The uterus and ureter are displaced toward the opposite side during the dissection, which is begun at the upper lateral border of the common iliac artery. A plane of dissection is established within the outer adventitia. The fatty areolar lymph node bearing tissue is then easily excised by a technique that combines spreading and cutting and a sweeping movement with the partially opened scissors. Experience is necessary to make this an easy and relatively swift technique. The endopelvic fascia, which forms part of the vascular sheath, is incised so as to free the vessels. One or two small vessels may restrain the external iliac vessels to a lateral position. These should be divided so that the external iliac vessels may be displaced medially for the sake of a better dissection as well as for accessibility to the veins in the event they are injured.

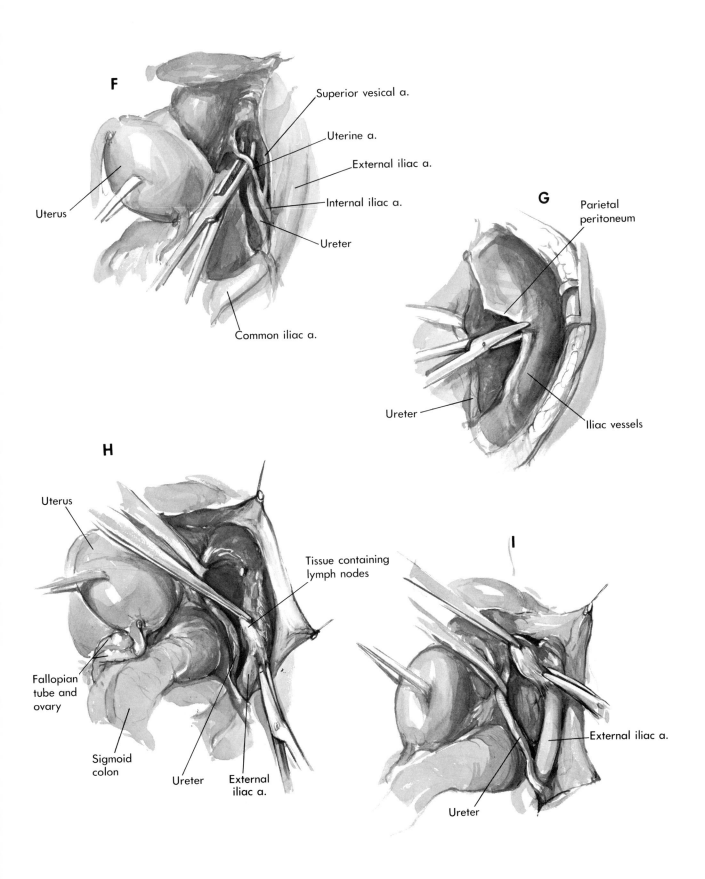

F

Superior vesical a.

Uterine a.

External iliac a.

Internal iliac a.

Ureter

Uterus

Common iliac a.

G

Parietal peritoneum

Ureter

Iliac vessels

H

Uterus

Tissue containing lymph nodes

Fallopian tube and ovary

Sigmoid colon

Ureter

External iliac a.

I

External iliac a.

Ureter

J The dissection of the areolar tissue surrounding the external iliac vessels is carried distally to their termination and then dorsally to the levator muscles. A vein retractor is used to displace these vessels laterally during this dissection. The obturator fascia must next be cleaned of its fatty areolar tissue. The deep portion of the endopelvic fascia which forms the remainder of the vascular sheath is incised to provide access to the obturator internus muscle. As the dissection proceeds over the obturator muscle the greatest risk is the tearing of the obturator veins which are inconstant in their anatomic location. This certainly is one area in which it is profitable to spend extra time to perform the dissection with deliberate care. We prefer to tie the obturator veins in continuity before division since they are fragile and clamps tear them easily. If they are torn from the iliac vessels or from the obturator fossa, there may be considerable bleeding by virtue of their size and the difficulty encountered in either ligating them or suturing the tear. Tears in the iliac vein can best be handled by prompt pressure over the tear, followed by pressure proximal and distal to this point. With the tear effectively isolated it can then be repaired with 5-0 arterial silk. If at all possible, an everting stitch should be used for repair of the veins so that the intima has a smooth surface rather than one which will encourage the formation of a clot at the suture line with possible later thrombosis and embolization. An obturator vein torn off at the obturator fossa will retract and not be amenable to clamping. Immediate hemostasis can be obtained, however, by pressure on the obturator fossa with a sponge stick. The aperture and the deeper veins are sewn with a suture ligature of atraumatic 3-0 chromic catgut, which is usually sufficient to stop venous bleeding. Blind clamping can damage the obturator nerve as can a recklessly placed stitch.

The obturator nerve, which is 2 to 3 mm. in diameter, makes its appearance into the pelvis medial to the psoas muscle at the pelvic brim. It then passes behind the iliac vessels to lie lateral to the hypogastric artery and vein, from where it proceeds downward and can be found at the midpoint of the obturator fossa. The iliac vessels are retracted laterally and upward; the nodal dissection is begun laterally and, with gentle traction on this tissue, proceeds medially and off the lateral wall of the pelvis.

Unilateral trauma to the obturator nerve is tolerable, but if the nerves are damaged bilaterally the resultant internal rotation of the thighs makes walking very difficult. If the obturator fossa is involved with cancerous lymph nodes and fixed to adjacent tissue, there is no chance for cure by surgery. In such an instance a silver clip is applied to aid the radiotherapist. Involvement by tumor of the external iliac vessels also precludes cure by surgery according to present surgical reports. It is not reasonable to resect the vein and to replace it with a vein graft even though this may be technically feasible. The vein can be sacrificed if this be the only limit to complete excision of the cancer. Lymphedema of the leg is an inevitable consequence if cancer involvement around the iliac vessels is left untreated. Again a silver clip is applied so that the radiotherapist can be certain of treating this site accurately.

K The attention of the surgeon is now directed back to the bifurcation of the common iliac vessel where nodes are to be found between the vessels. The tissue is grasped with fine tissue forceps and gently dissected in a medial direction. There can be seen the obturator nerve which courses caudally and then laterally to enter the obturator foramen. The ureter is still displaced medially while the dissection continues medially over the internal iliac vessels.

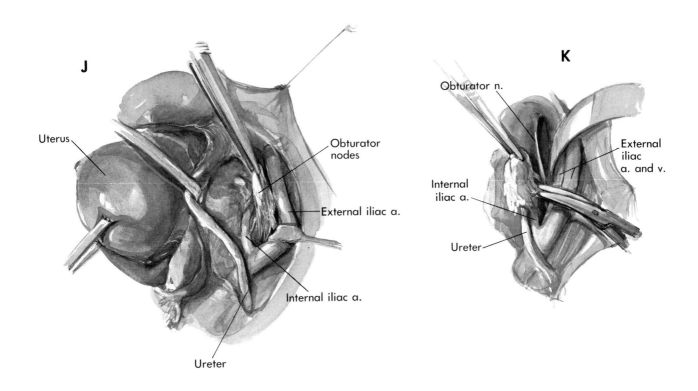

J

Uterus

Obturator
nodes

External iliac a.

Internal iliac a.

Ureter

K

Obturator n.

External
iliac
a. and v.

Internal
iliac a.

Ureter

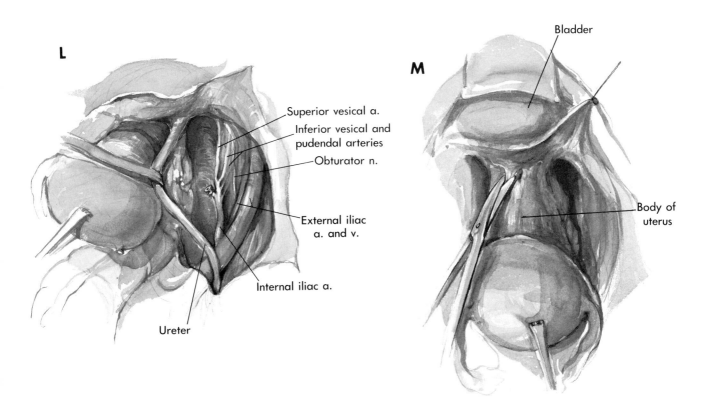

L

Superior vesical a.

Inferior vesical and
pudendal arteries

Obturator n.

External iliac
a. and v.

Internal iliac a.

Ureter

M

Bladder

Body of
uterus

L All lymph node bearing tissue has now been dissected off the iliac vessels and their tributaries. For artistic purposes the fatty areolar lymph node bearing tissue has been minimized so that one can observe more clearly the pertinent anatomy in this area. There can be seen the external and internal iliac artery and vein, the uterine artery having already been ligated and divided.

Notice that only the uterine artery, coming off the internal iliac, has been sacrificed, and that the superior and inferior vesical arteries are left intact to nourish more adequately the urinary bladder. Additionally, the inferior pudendal arteries have not been disturbed. Again, for artistic purposes, the ureter is shown to be denuded reasonably thoroughly, but the surgeon must use caution and the judgment of previous experience to determine to what degree this is advisable in any particular patient in view of the seriousness of ureteral necrosis and subsequent formation of a ureter fistula as a result of aggressive ureteral dissection. A similar lymph node dissection is repeated on the opposite side.

M With the lymph node dissection having been completed bilaterally, the tenaculum is attached to the fundus of the uterus and retracted in a cephalad direction. This brings the vesicouterine sulcus into a more superficial position in preparation for mobilization of the anterior portion of the body of the uterus and the cervix. Sometimes it is advantageous to proceed with the separation of the uterus and bladder after the posterior dissection (Plate 4, Figures Q and R), which permits the uterus to be pulled farther out of the pelvis, thus facilitating an easier dissection of the distal ureters. The peritoneum over the vesicouterine junction has already been incised. The dissection is begun with scissors, although in the absence of fibrosis the tissue can be spread as easily with the finger. If one remains near the midline, the dissection is relatively bloodless. The separation is continued to at least 2 cm. below the cervix; however, if there is evidence of anterior vaginal involvement, the separation continues to at least 2 cm. beyond the cancer.

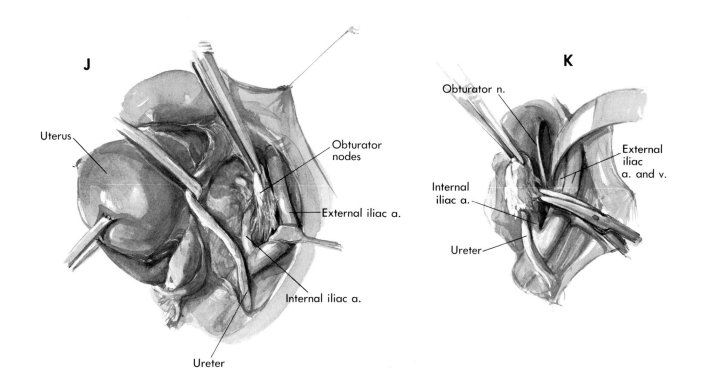

J

Uterus

Obturator
nodes

External iliac a.

Internal iliac a.

Ureter

K

Obturator n.

External
iliac
a. and v.

Internal
iliac a.

Ureter

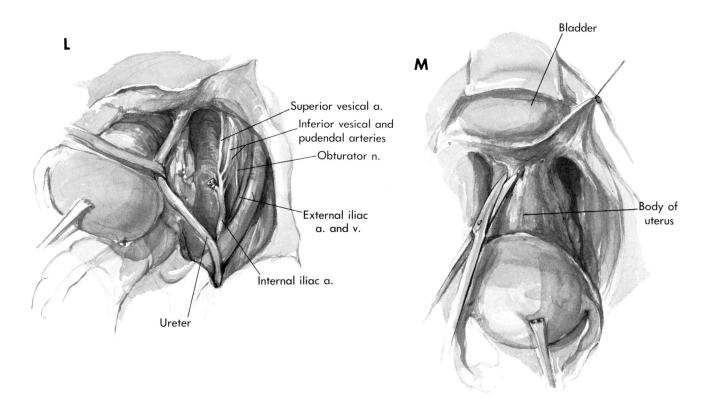

L

Superior vesical a.

Inferior vesical and
pudendal arteries

Obturator n.

External iliac
a. and v.

Internal iliac a.

Ureter

M

Bladder

Body of
uterus

N
O
P
The ureters will have been freed from the pelvic brim to the point at which they are crossed by the uterine artery. This is probably the most awkward area to dissect adequately and neatly, yet reluctance to do just that may jeopardize the adequacy of cancer removal or add to the postoperative morbidity. The medial stump of the uterine artery, or tissue adjacent to it, is grasped with forceps and retracted cephalad and medially. This places the cardinal ligament and associated tissue crossing over the ureters on tension, facilitating its deliberate and careful dissection. An Adson hemostat is used to tunnel gently under this tissue, which is the superficial layer of the vesicouterine ligament (P). The ureter is unroofed by clamping and cutting only a small portion of tissue at any one time. If the amount of tissue grasped and ligated each time is excessive it may distort and possibly obstruct the adjacent ureter. This procedure is continued until the entire ureter is uncovered to the bladder. If the ureteral branch from the uterine artery is encountered at this time it has to be ligated. Ureteral fistulae occur most commonly in this area and, although many factors contribute to this unfortunate complication, careful attention to detail and gentle handling of tissue is an important factor in decreased occurrence.

Q
R
Considerable caudal and upward traction is now applied, exposing the cul-de-sac of Douglas. The peritoneum in the sulcus is incised and either a pledget of gauze on the tip of an eight-inch hemostat or the finger around which gauze has been wrapped can be used to gently separate this tissue. If the right plane of dissection is not found, the surgeon will recognize it by the considerable bleeding and the difficulty in proceeding with the separation of tissue. Care in finding this right plane, therefore, will be rewarded by an easy and swift dissection, which is carried to approximately 2 cm. beyond the cervix. If the surgeon encounters difficulty with this plane of separation but feels that it is necessary to continue, he must exercise extreme caution not to enter the rectum. In Figure R there are indicated the uterosacral ligaments; these are grasped with Mixter forceps, divided and ligated with 2-0 chromic catgut. This completes the major portion of the dissection and leaves the uterus attached only to the vagina.

S
The uterus is returned to its natural position with the tenaculum pulling in a cephalad direction. Transection of the vagina is begun. One must be careful not to leave the patient with an excessively short vagina; it is also improper to compromise at this time on the wideness of the resection. Certainly, later recurrence of squamous cancer at the vaginal cuff is a difficult situation to handle, and any method of therapy has a low incidence of cure. The surgeon must keep this in mind while going widely beyond this tumor yet without excessive sacrifice of vaginal length. If the vagina must be sacrificed, it is possible to reconstruct the vagina in a young woman by means of a segment of colon as a gut, with repair of the colon by a colocolotomy. The paracervical tissue is seen attached to the lateral body of the uterus and has the characteristic appearance which has often been described as the "whiskers" of Franz Joseph.

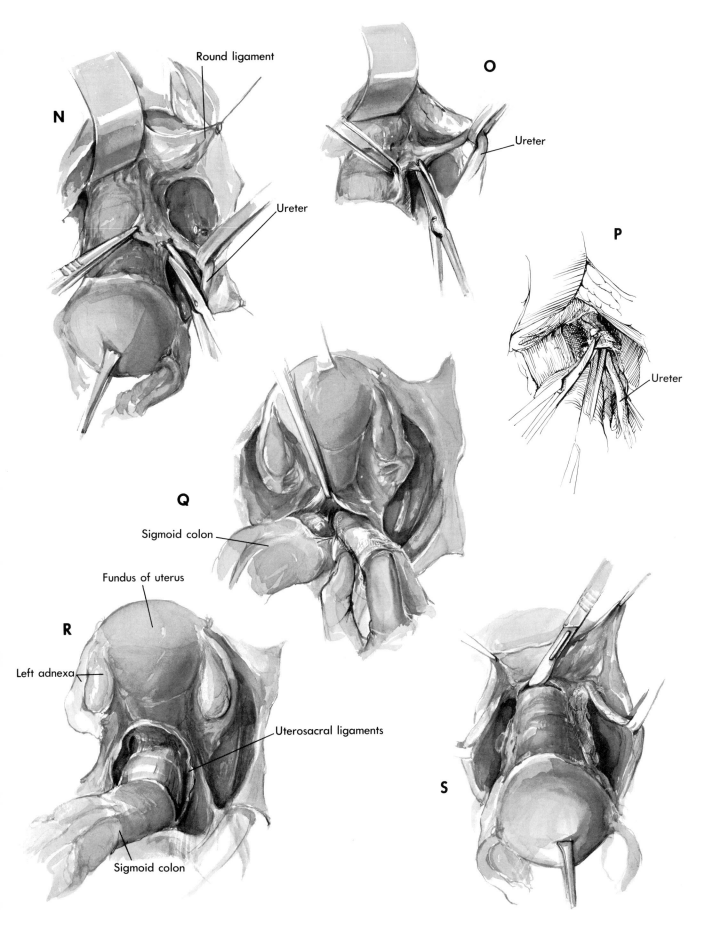

Round ligament

N

O

Ureter

Ureter

P

Ureter

Q

Sigmoid colon

Fundus of uterus

R

Left adnexa

Uterosacral ligaments

Sigmoid colon

S

T
U
V

As the vagina is incised its free edges are grasped with Kocher hemostats which act to keep the rim of the vagina open since it otherwise may retract. In addition, they act as hemostats while the operation is being carried further. In Figure U the index finger and thumb encircle the neck of the uterus and pull it somewhat upward, allowing the surgeon to have a direct view of the cervix to make certain that the vagina is being divided an adequate distance from the cancer. After the uterus is removed, the vaginal cuffs on both the specimen and that remaining are carefully examined for proximity of the cancer. If there is any question on this point, additional tissue is excised from the vaginal cuff and sent for microscopic examination of frozen sections. In Figure V a hemostatic simple or locking stitch is used, inasmuch as individual ligation of bleeding vessels in the area is virtually impossible and certainly time consuming. Such a hemostatic stitch may cause slight additional necrosis of tissue, but this will be sloughed out postoperatively through the vagina. This type of healing will not lead to any significant scarring and shortening of the healed vagina. The reader will remember that a pledget of gauze soaked in absolute alcohol had been placed in the vagina at the beginning of the operation. This is left in place and not retrieved through the abdomen because it might contaminate the pelvic area.

W

It has been our practice in the past to leave the vagina open, as this defect will heal without difficulty while allowing a ready postoperative egress of serohemorrhagic fluid. Two medium soft rubber drains are brought lateral to the rectum and over the ureters as they are positioned under the iliac vessels. They are adjusted so that along their course they will effectively drain the uterovesicular area in the event of fistula formation. The current practice is to close the vagina without drainage if the operative field is exceptionally dry. Otherwise, the vagina is closed around a catheter which is placed on suction for 24 hours.

X

A simple stitch of atraumatic 3-0 chromic catgut is used to reperitonealize the pelvis. This is usually accomplished without difficulty, especially if during the development of the exposure of the iliac vessels the peritoneum was not excised widely but was unfolded with the help of laterally directed cuts. The viscera are carefully repositioned and the peritoneum closed with a continuous stitch of 2-0 chromic catgut. The anterior rectus sheath is closed with interrupted 2-0 silk and the skin with vertical mattress stitches of 3-0 silk. While this is being done the patient is slowly returned to the horizontal position. A Foley catheter is left in place.

Postoperatively these patients are handled essentially the same as any other patient who has undergone a major procedure. A nasogastric tube is not used routinely, the decision to do so being influenced by the difficulty of the dissection, the handling of the viscera and the postoperative clinical course of the patient. Certainly, it is more desirable to keep the patient decompressed prophylactically than to have distention occur postoperatively with the attendant pulmonary complications and the increased incidence of dehiscence or later ventral herniation. The greatest attention should be directed toward the urinary bladder to see that it is empty at all times. We prefer to leave the Foley catheter in place for at least 12 days, at which time we perform a continuous drip intravenous pyelogram to make certain that the ureters and bladder are intact; the catheter can then be taken out, but the patient should be watched for signs of urinary retention.

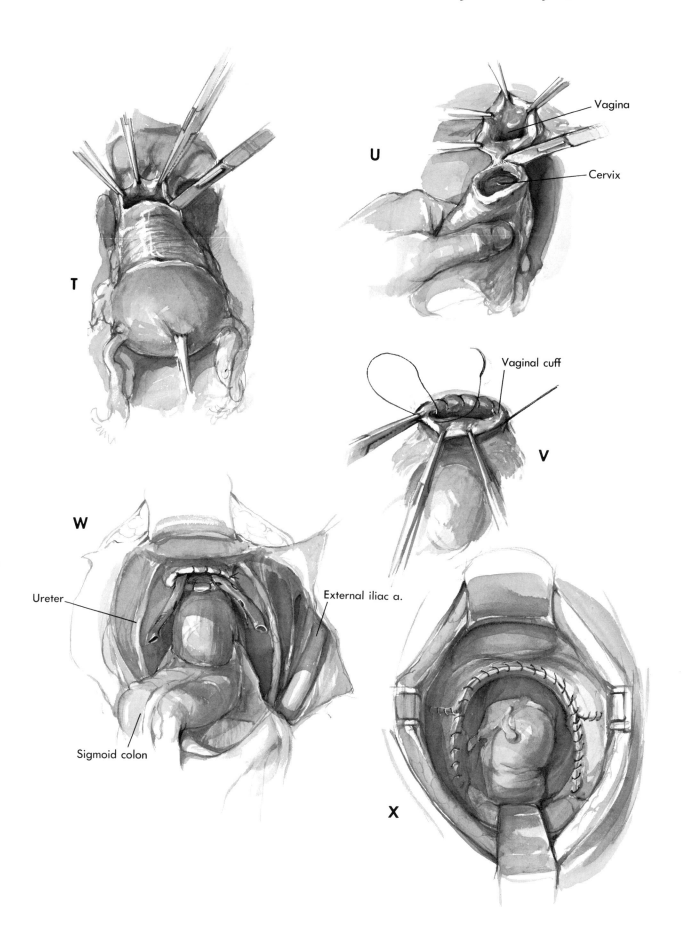

T

U

Vagina

Cervix

Vaginal cuff

V

W

Ureter

External iliac a.

Sigmoid colon

X

URINARY DIVERSION

Urinary diversion is made necessary by a variety of conditions, benign or malignant, congenital or acquired, and arising within or from outside the urinary bladder. Prior to the more effective control or management of prostatic or bladder cancer, ureterosigmoidostomy was used to divert the urine because it was, next to a suprapubic cystostomy, nephrostomy or ureterocutaneous anastomosis, the least major operation available for internal diversion. Furthermore, it could be done so that it would lie extraperitoneally – a decisive advantage prior to the availability of antibiotics. The problems of hyperchloremic acidosis could usually be controlled, but those of ascending infection stimulated the refinement of ureteroenteric anastomoses that would resist regurgitation of intestinal contents. At present these problems with ureterosigmoidostomy can be controlled more effectively, but the applicability of the operation has lessened.

With the advent of more major pelvic surgery, specifically pelvic exenteration, the use of ureterosigmoidostomy resulted in a "wet" colostomy which was quite unsatisfactory. As a consequence, there were developed urine conduits that were dissociated from the fecal stream yet did not have the disadvantages of cutaneous ureterostomies, which are plagued with ascending infection and stenosis at the ureterocutaneous stoma.

The ileal (Bricker) conduit is more widely used and has become the preferred method of diversion. It is only a conduit and is incontinent, thus requiring that a bag be worn to collect the constant flow of urine. Stasis and infection are prevented by the modest length (15 to 20 cm.) and volume of the ileal segment and by the peristalsis, which is directed toward the outside.

The ileocecal (Gilchrist) bladder is meant to be a reservoir without leakage. Its capacity can be predetermined to a degree by the site at which the ascending colon is divided and the resulting size of the "bladder." The ileocecal valve, the peristalsis of the ileum toward the cecum from the ileal stoma, and the placement of the ileum so that it courses in a cephalad direction allow patients enough capacity without leakage that they need catheterize the reservoir only every six hours. The deliberate retention of urine, however, requires greater vigilance against electrolyte imbalance and causes more concern about ascending infection. For some time postoperatively the patient must contend with the considerable amount of mucus secreted by the colonic mucosa.

With the resurgence of the use of earlier cystectomy for cancers of the urinary bladder, one can expect urinary conduits or reservoirs to be used with increasing frequency. Preoperative evaluation of the patient who is a candidate for some type of urinary diversion is similar to that of any patient considered for a major surgical procedure. However, specific attention and careful inspection must be made of an intravenous urogram or, if this is inadequate, of a retrograde pyelogram. These visual studies of the urinary tract prior to operation will determine the presence or absence of any anomalies, such as duplications of the ureter and the diameter and the point of occlusion of the ureters, all of which would be important to know at the time of the surgical procedure.

The complications of the ileal conduit are mainly those of the associated procedures such as cystectomy or pelvic exenteration. Those relating to the conduit itself are primarily small bowel obstruction which, in almost all instances, is best handled by long tube, gastrointestinal intubation. In the few instances in which a urinary fistula occurs, reoperation will be necessary. Late complications of the ileal conduit are mainly reflected in the stoma and are best handled as they develop. The two most common complications are stricture of the stoma, which requires surgical revision but is usually a minor procedure and can be done under local anesthesia, and skin reactions around the stoma with a reactive hyperkeratosis. This latter is usually caused by a poorly fitting urine bag, which allows urine to come into constant contact with the skin; it is best treated by removal of the collecting bag for a week to ten days, and then a refitting of the bag. Electrolyte imbalance occurs only if the original conduit is of such great length that sufficient reabsorption can occur or if the conduit has turned into a reservoir as a result of unrecognized stricture of the stoma. At present even though the primary condition for which the urine was diverted has been controlled, there still is a small percentage per year of survivors who will develop serious kidney damage. This problem needs further study.

References

Bricker, E. M.: Symposium on clinical surgery; bladder substitution after pelvic evisceration. Surg. Clin. North America 30:1511, 1950.
Gilchrist, R. K., and Merricks, J. W.: Construction of a substitute bladder and urethra. Surg. Clin. North America 36:1131, 1956.

A   Some of the topographic relationships that may aid in the construction of an ileal conduit are shown. The portion of the ileum intended as the conduit is inside the heavy dashed lines. The conduit will lie dorsal or under the reanastomosed ileum so that its distal end will have to make its way anteriorly in order to come to the outside. One can see how an ileum and cecum that are somewhat low will lie heavily on the end of the conduit, causing it to kink or even to obstruct. The problem can be overcome by mobilizing the cecum and displacing it medially, with the conduit coursing to the right of the cecum before coming to the outside.

     Maintenance of viability of the ureters is essential to the success of this operation, and since they need not be mobilized or dissected extensively this should not be a problem. The reader will remember the multiple origin of the blood supply to the ureter from the renal, spermatic, hypogastric and inferior vesical arteries. The ureters course along the medial borders of the psoas muscles and the bifurcation of the common iliac vessels before entering the pelvis. At the pelvic aperture, the left ureter lies behind the sigmoid and its mesentery.

B   A left paramedian or midline incision is used. It is important to give adequate thought to the site of the ileostomy so that it will be surrounded by flat skin. The esthetic success of the operation necessitates that the appliance for urine collection be fitted and glued properly postoperatively and with minimal leakage. This means that the stoma should not be too close to the umbilicus or anterior iliac spine and that deep natural skin creases must be avoided.

C   The posterior parietal peritoneum over the iliac bifurcation is incised to expose the
D   ureters. The dissection must not be so thorough that it removes the adventitial tissue and the associated blood vessels from the ureter or so that the adventitial tissue is traumatized with thrombosis of these vessels. If there is to be pelvic surgery, the internal iliac vessels are ligated at this point to reduce the degree of subsequent bleeding. As it would be technically awkward and clinically hazardous to deal with an acute appendicitis in such patients, an appendectomy is performed routinely and in a preferred manner.

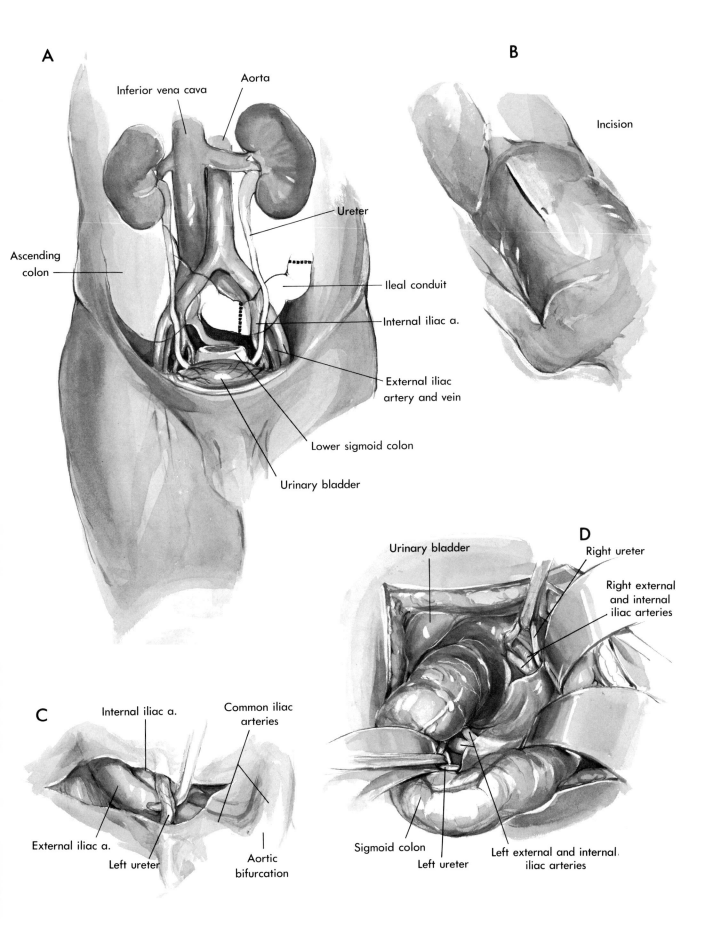

A

Inferior vena cava

Aorta

Ureter

Ascending
colon

Ileal conduit

Internal iliac a.

External iliac
artery and vein

Lower sigmoid colon

Urinary bladder

B

Incision

C

Internal iliac a.

Common iliac
arteries

External iliac a.

Left ureter

Aortic
bifurcation

D

Urinary bladder

Right ureter

Right external
and internal
iliac arteries

Sigmoid colon

Left ureter

Left external and internal
iliac arteries

E A section of terminal ileum is chosen at a distance of about 20 cm. from the ileocecal valve. Sometimes this portion of the small intestine will show chronic changes consequent to radiotherapy to the pelvis. Ileum so affected often lacks pliability and there is greater resultant stress on the uretero-ileal anastomosis and a greater tendency of the bowel to kink. In such an instance, a more proximal segment is chosen even if one has to go up to the jejunum. There is no indication that one portion of bowel chosen is significantly different physiologically from another portion. It is important, however, that from whatever level the segment is chosen it truly serve as a conduit and not as a reservoir.

F The necessary length of ileum is about 12 to 20 cm. This is influenced by the anatomy of the patient, the length and thickness of the mesentery and the thickness of the abdominal wall the conduit must transverse. It is rarely necessary to have a length in excess of 20 cm.; any conduit longer than this begins to defeat the intended purpose of having urine flow out forthwith and it remains instead a commodious receptacle.

G The mesentery need not be divided too far proximally. Furthermore, this practice is a wise precaution against jeopardizing the blood supply to this segment.

H
H₁ The operative field is walled off with large gauze pads and the small intestine divided between closely spaced Kocher clamps. Figure H₁ shows how the mesentery is cut in a stepwise fashion in patients with a thick abdominal wall. This tailoring of the mesentery makes available a few more centimeters of distal ileum with an adequate blood supply so that the ileal stoma can be made to reach the skin surface without undue tension.

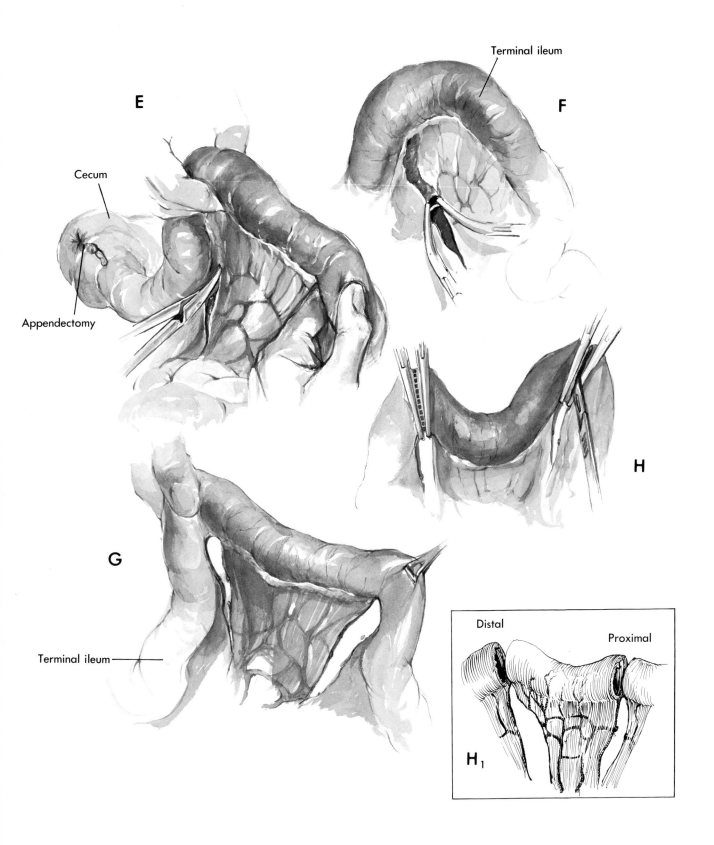

E

Cecum

Appendectomy

F

Terminal ileum

H

G

Terminal ileum

Distal

Proximal

H₁

I
J
It is essential that the conduit be positioned dorsal to the divided ileum. In Figure I the proximal end of the conduit is being closed with a continuous stitch of 3-0 chromic catgut. In such a proximal dead-end and low pressure segment we have no hesitancy about leaving in place that portion of the bowel crushed by the Kocher clamp. The stitches are placed just proximal to this crushed portion. In Figure J a row of interrupted simple stitches of atraumatic 3-0 silk is being applied through the seromuscular layer.

K
Reconstruction of the ileal stream is now begun. Both Kocher clamps are rotated outwardly so that the apposing serosa is in better view, and interrupted simple stitches of 3-0 silk are placed about 7 mm. apart and 3 mm. from the clamps.

L
M
Following placement of the posterior row of stitches through the seromuscularis, the intestine is transected immediately adjacent to the clamps. A clean cut results if the scapel slides along the metal of the clamp. The seromuscularis stitches at each end are retained for stabilization. The bowel is opened about 5 mm. from the seromuscular suture line and the mucosa approximated with a continuous simple stitch of 4-0 chromic catgut. When utilizing a time-saving continuous stitch, the surgeon must guard against his assistant's pulling the free end of the suture between stitches and inadvertently "purse-stringing" the anastomosis; otherwise, interrupted stitches are used for the seromuscular and mucosal layers.

N
The anterior row of interrupted seromuscular stitches of 3-0 silk is now applied. Experience and judgment will enable one to do this without invagination of excessive tissue and a resultant obstructive "diaphragm."

O
The mesenteric defect is closed with a continuous stitch of atraumatic 3-0 chromic catgut, and again there should be minimal tension on the free end of the suture during its placement. The mesentery should be caught just inside its cut edge; sometimes careless placing of the needle too wide from this edge results in occlusion of a marginal vessel which is necessary for viability of the ileum at the anastomosis. Equally frustrating is the careless piercing of one of these vessels with a resultant hematoma and all the tribulations attendant to correcting this easily avoidable and time-consuming error.

P
The reanastomosed ileum has been elevated with the conduit dorsal to it. The mesenteric opening at the site of reanastomosis should be sufficiently large that there is no chance that the blood vessels to the conduit will be constricted. Too ample an opening may pose a real threat to herniation of bowel through it. Sometimes it is better not to suture the entire length of the divided mesentery to itself but to leave a generous opening proximally and then to apply interrupted stitches from the periphery of this opening to the mesentery of the conduit. This helps also to prevent tension of the conduit on its mesentery. This suturing is best left until the operation has been completed and the conduit exteriorized because the reanastomosed ileum and conduit with their respective mesenteries will then be in their natural position. The needle bites should be applied with great care if injury to the mesenteric vessels is to be avoided.

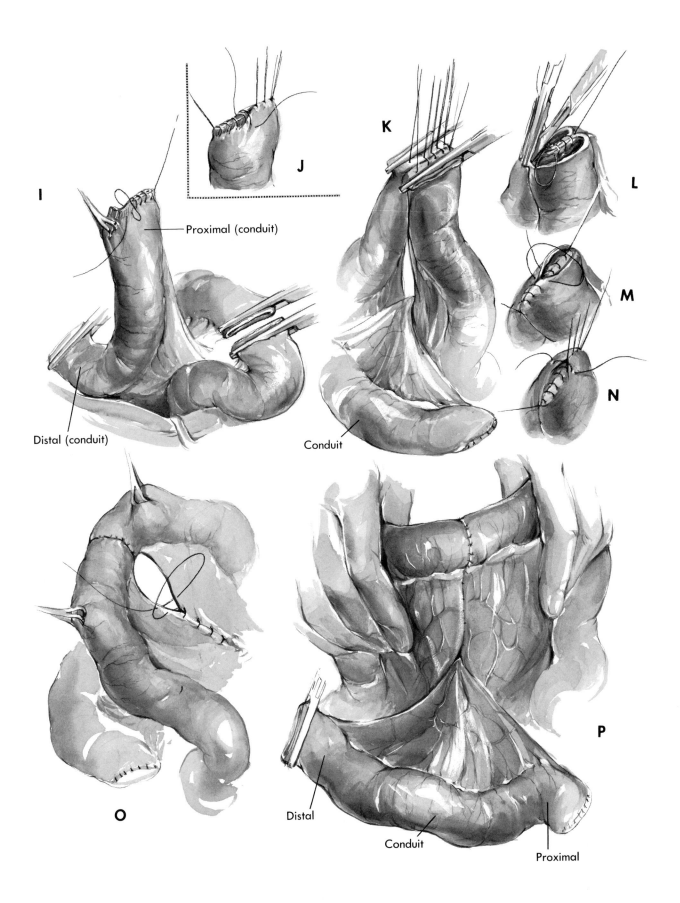

I

J

K

L

M

N

Proximal (conduit)

Distal (conduit)

Conduit

O

P

Distal

Conduit

Proximal

Q   At the beginning of the operation the ureters are identified as they cross the bifurcation of the iliac vessels. They are transected 3 to 4 cm. distal to this point and the distal ureter tied with chromic catgut. The proximal ureter is then free for a distance of 4 or 5 cm. The ureter is divided and a single stitch is passed through its rim for traction and manipulation. The conduit is allowed to fall in its natural position and the remaining bowel retracted because the subsequent steps demand ample exposure for their exact, adequate and easy execution.

R   There usually is a sufficient excess of ureter that one can plan on trimming off a few millimeters prior to the anastomosis. For this reason there is no hesitancy is applying fine instruments to the terminal ureter (here an Allis clamp is on the adventitia) so that it can be manipulated accurately. The left ureter is anastomosed first and close to the proximal end of the conduit. A first transverse row of interrupted stitches of 4-0 silk is applied between the serosa of the bowel and the adventitia of the ureter. They are placed about 1.5 cm. from the cut end of the ureter and usually three or four stitches will suffice.

S   A longitudinal slit about 1 cm. long is made proximally and on the ventral side of the ureter. This spatulation results in a bigger diameter of the terminal ureter and less likelihood that a modest postoperative uretero-ileal stenosis will be harmful clinically. This spatulation is not necessary, however, if the ureter is already hydronephrotic.

T   The ileal opening is made next and this should correspond in size to the diameter of the spatulated ureter. It makes no difference in the resultant shape of the opening whether the cut into the ileum is made transverse or parallel to the long axis of the ileum. Here an eight-inch curved hemostat is used to supply internal support. Any bleeding encountered can be stopped by momentary pressure or by the stitches of the anastomosis; clamping and ligating simply add to the amount of dead and foreign tissue in this area.

U   The inner anastomosis is performed with interrupted 4-0 chromic catgut. The first stitch is placed between the apex of the spatulating cut in the ureter and the dorsalmost point of the ileal opening. This and the remaining stitches go through the entire thickness of the ureter and bowel and 2 mm. from each edge. The ileal mucosa may protrude excessively if the suction that is applied to keep the field dry is too strong. In such circumstances the surgeon must not place the needle through the bowel wall in one movement and thus include in the stitch too much of the prolapsed mucosa. Instead, the needle can be put through the seromuscular layer and then the mucosa pushed back in toward the lumen so that its edge is in line to be caught by the needle. The needle will go from inside to outside of the ureter and from outside to inside of the ileum so that the knots will eventually be inside the ileal lumen. Any excess of traumatized portion of ureter is trimmed off at this time. The ureter is now sufficiently stable that handling it with instruments is quite unnecessary. A fine forceps may be used for counterpressure as the needle is passed without the need to actually grasp the tissue with instruments.

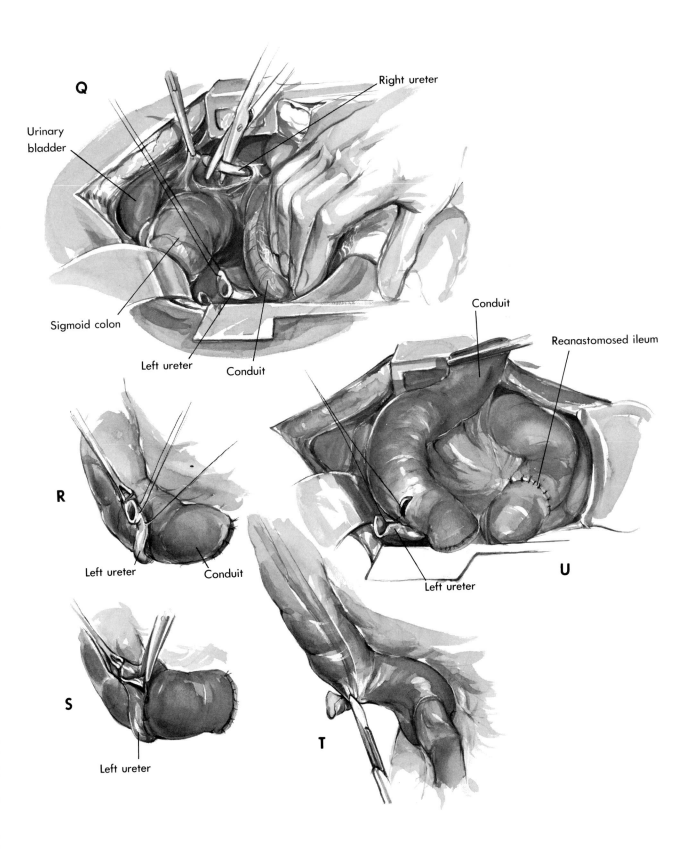

Q

Urinary bladder

Right ureter

Sigmoid colon

Left ureter

Conduit

R

Left ureter

Conduit

S

Left ureter

T

Conduit

Reanastomosed ileum

Left ureter

U

V
W

We prefer to splint the uretero-ileal anastomosis with ureteral catheters because it is a simple maneuver that is not harmful and may be beneficial. The benefit is in knowing postoperatively, in the event of anuria, that the cause is not twisting or kinking of the ureters or obstruction of the anastomosis by swelling. The catheter, which has been threaded up the ureter, is pulled through the partially completed uretero-ileal anastomosis and then to the outside. As can be seen in Figure W the main concern would be with the possible deleterious effect to healing from the catheter lying on the anastomosis.

X

The ureteral catheter is anchored to the opening of the conduit to prevent its inadvertent dislodgment.

Y

The uretero-ileal anastomosis is being completed and, as can be seen, the ties will reside inside the lumen. The next to the last stitch can be placed but not tied so that visibility is not impaired for placement of the last one. As the last stitch is tied and cut, the free ends will protrude outwardly, but with a fine forceps can be directed toward the lumen where they belong.

Z

The anastomosis is completed by placing the anterior row of stitches between the adventitia of the ureter and the seromuscular layer of the ileum. A similar anastomosis is carried out on the right side with an attempt to insert this ureter as far to the left as possible. If the rectum and some sigmoid have been removed and a colostomy performed, the hiatus between the mesosigmoid and the posterior parietal peritoneum is closed with interrupted simple stitches of 4-0 chromic catgut.

A_1
B_1

The site for exteriorization of the conduit will have been chosen at the beginning of the operation. A button of skin and subcutaneous fat is excised in adequate diameter to allow unrestricted passage of the ileum. Similar pieces of fascia and peritoneum have to be excised, but before this is done, they should be pulled medially so that all the openings are in proper alignment. Otherwise, there may be a shearing effect along the various layers of the abdominal wall, leading to obstruction of the conduit. An Allis forceps is used to pull the ileum gently through the abdominal wall while the conduit is observed for kinking, twisting or excess tension. When the natural position between the conduit and intestine has been determined, the mesentery of the conduit is carefully anchored to that of the overlying ileum. Figure P in Plate 3 shows this relationship well. It is not advisable to attempt to eliminate the hiatus lateral to the exiting conduit as one does with an ileostomy.

The ileum is stitched to the skin with interrupted stitches of 3-0 chromic catgut; these traverse through full thickness of skin and ileum. They are placed about 1 cm. apart and tied gently so as not to strangulate ileal tissue.

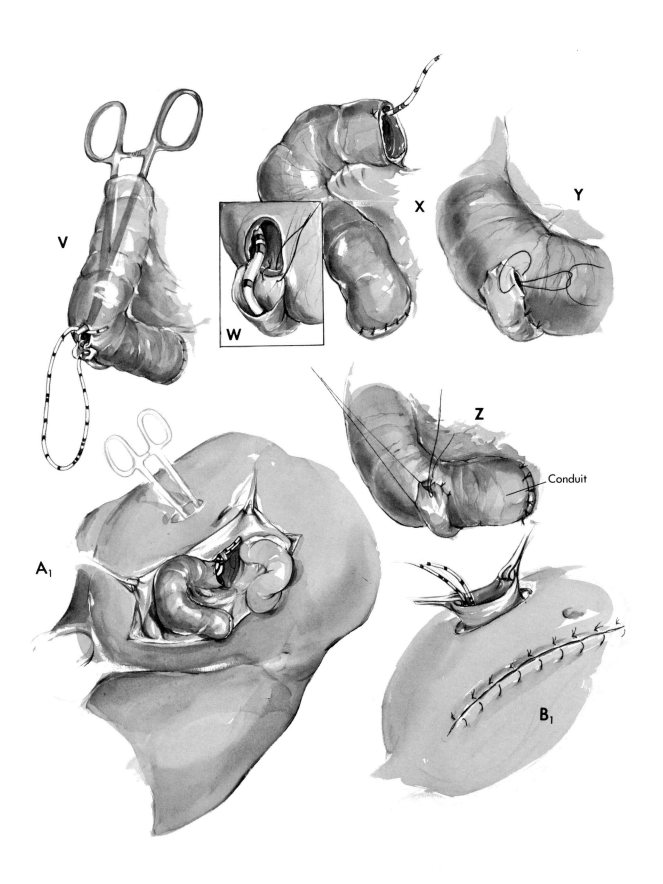

V

W

X

Y

Z

Conduit

A₁

B₁

Ileocecal Bladder

A The vascular anatomy of the right colon assumes major importance in this procedure. The most common vascular pattern is shown here, and the surgeon would do well to become familiar with the possible variations. It is not necessary, however, to perform an aortogram to learn its pattern beforehand. It is essential, of course, that a relatively recent intravenous urogram be available. On occasion it may be necessary to deal with a double ureter on one side. It is also wise to perform a barium enema to exclude colonic disease and to ascertain the size and proper location of the right colon. Evidence at this time or at the time of surgery that the terminal ileum has been damaged by radio-therapy should alert a surgeon to be prepared to construct an alternate type of urinary conduit or reservoir. A right colon containing feces is a decided handicap, and special precautions should be taken to avoid this possibility.

A left paramedian muscle reflecting incision is preferred. During this exploration the surgeon can assess the resectability of the cancer, and if curative surgery cannot be performed, the ileocecal bladder can be constructed as a palliative measure. One may choose to construct only the ileocecal bladder at this time and to perform the destructive operation several weeks later.

B
C When present, the appendix is removed in the usual manner. The right colon is mobilized by incising the right lateral peritoneal reflection. The mobilized colon is held up so that, with transillumination, the surgeon can more clearly visualize the vessels going to the terminal ileum and cecum.

D Intestinal clamps are applied on either side of the points of planned division. On the ascending colon this is about 22 to 25 cm. distal to the ileocecal valve or the point at which the resultant colonic volume would be approximately 600 ml. The vascular pattern of the right colon further influences this point of division. The ileum is divided approximately 15 cm. from the ileocecal valve. This is sufficiently long to prevent loss of urine yet short enough for the catheter to reach the urine reservoir with ease.

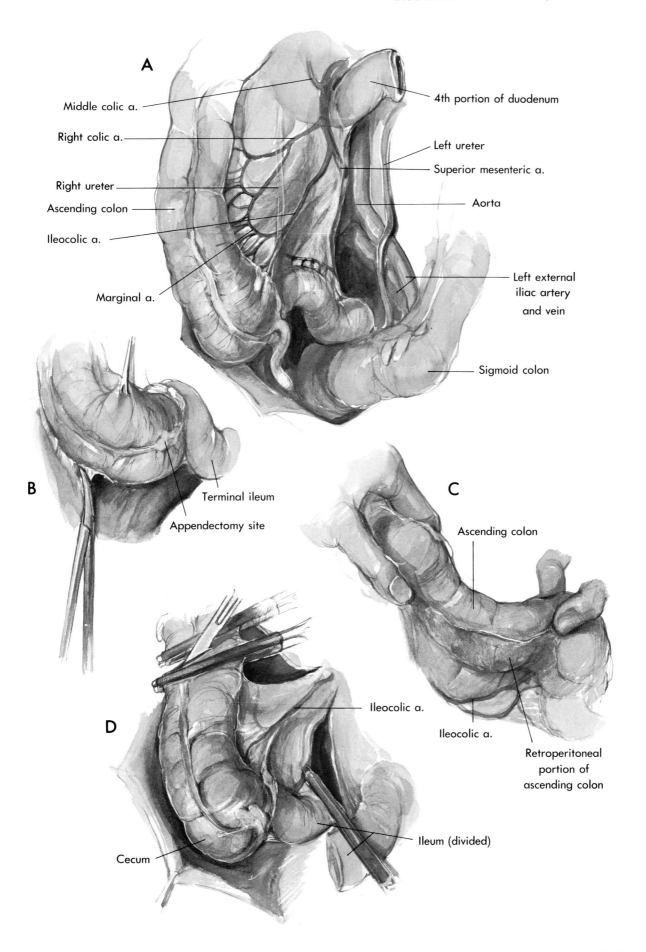

A

Middle colic a.

Right colic a.

Right ureter

Ascending colon

Ileocolic a.

Marginal a.

4th portion of duodenum

Left ureter

Superior mesenteric a.

Aorta

Left external
iliac artery
and vein

Sigmoid colon

B

Terminal ileum

Appendectomy site

C

Ascending colon

Ileocolic a.

Ileocolic a.

Retroperitoneal
portion of
ascending colon

D

Cecum

Ileum (divided)

E
F
The ends of the divided colon are closed in two layers, the mucosal with a continuous simple stitch of 3-0 atraumatic chromic catgut and the seromuscular with a similar stitch of 3-0 atraumatic catgut. Silk should not be used on the ileocecal bladder—even on the seromuscular layer. It has been disconcerting, on examination of the interior of the ileocecal bladder at a later time with a cystoscope, to see the silk being extruded into the bladder lumen or, on several occasions, serving as the nidus for a bladder stone.

A variety of ileo-intestinal anastomoses are available. The side-to-side anastomosis shown here has the least risk of loss of viability of intestine at the site of anastomosis. Stitches can be placed without concern that they might compromise a nutrient vessel in the mesentery. Also, the anastomotic size can always be made of adequate dimensions. The need to close two open ends of intestine before proceeding with the anastomosis takes a little extra time. The "blind loop" syndrome is no problem in these cases.

G
The reservoir is now ready for positioning. If a colostomy is present or is anticipated on the left side (the usual circumstance), the ileostomy must be positioned on the right side. In the absence of a colostomy the ileocecum need be turned only 90 degrees counterclockwise on its mesentery on a sagittal plane in order to have the ileum exit at the left lower quadrant and for the reservoir to lie horizontally. This maneuver does not cause kinking of the ileocolic vessels.

H
If the left lower quadrant cannot be used for the ileostomy, the ileocecal bladder must be turned in two planes in order to have the ileum exit in the right lower quadrant. To permit this, the cecum is rotated 90 degrees clockwise and then it is rotated 180 degrees on its long axis toward the pelvis so that its ventral surface becomes dorsal.

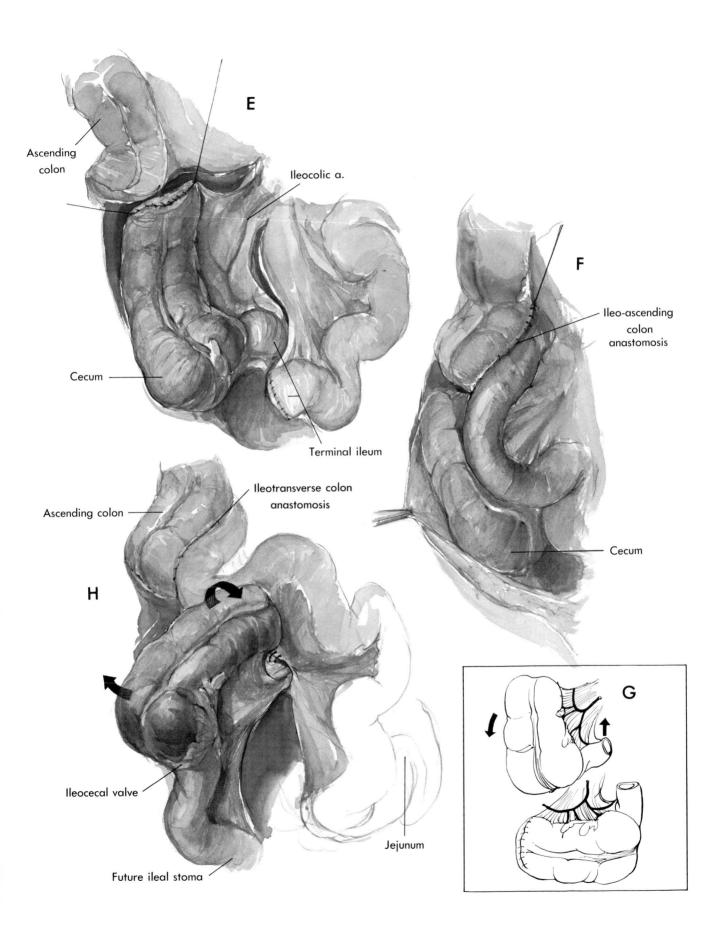

Ascending
colon

E

Ileocolic a.

Cecum

Terminal ileum

F

Ileo-ascending
colon
anastomosis

Cecum

Ascending colon

Ileotransverse colon
anastomosis

H

Ileocecal valve

Jejunum

G

Future ileal stoma

I
J

These illustrations show the completion of the rotation of the ileocecal bladder so that the ileum can exit in the right lower quadrant. Interestingly, the ileocolic vessels tolerate this twisting extremely well, in no instance making it necessary to abandon the maneuver or leading to later avascular necrosis of the bladder which is supplied by this twisted pedicle. The mesenteries of the reanastomosed ascending colon and terminal ileum are approximated with a continuous stitch of 3-0 chromic catgut to obviate internal herniation. The mesentery of the ileum is sutured to the peritoneum of the lateral abdominal wall to forestall a similar postoperative occurrence.

K
L

The ileocecal bladder is lifted so that the ureters may be prepared for anastomosis. The posterior parietal peritoneum over both ureters is incised longitudinally and the ureters ligated with 2-0 chromic catgut as distally as possible. The bladder is now allowed to fall into its new position so that the site of the ureterocolic anastomosis can be determined. The colon is grasped with Babcock forceps on either side of the proposed right ureterocolic anastomosis and an incision made transverse to its long axis. The seromuscular incision is 1.5 to 2.0 cm. in length and the mucosal opening is sufficient in size to just admit the ureter.

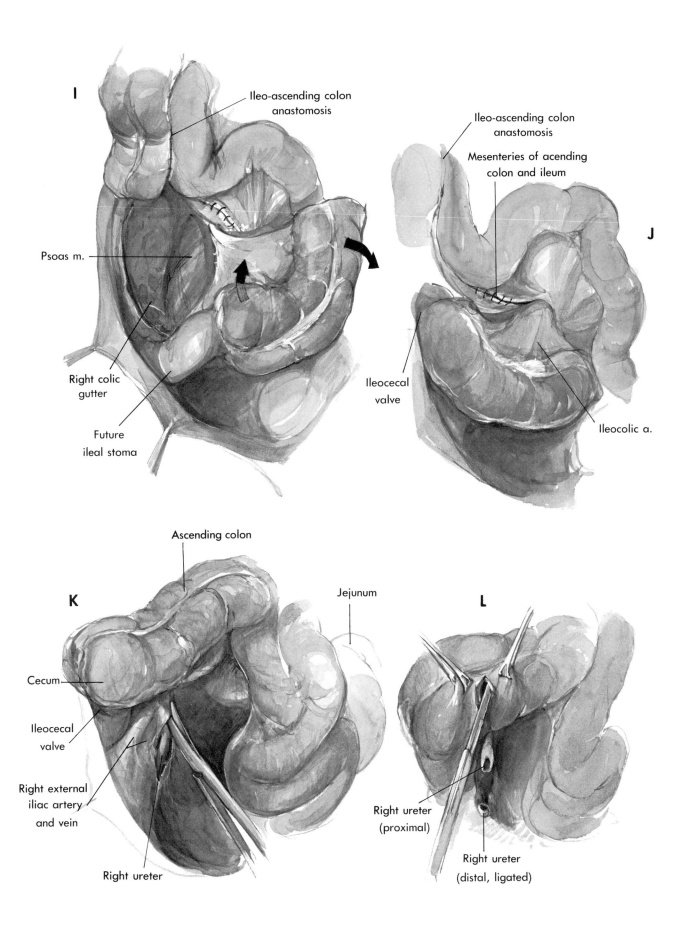

I

Ileo-ascending colon
anastomosis

Psoas m.

Right colic
gutter

Future
ileal stoma

Ileo-ascending colon
anastomosis

Mesenteries of acending
colon and ileum

J

Ileocecal
valve

Ileocolic a.

Ascending colon

Jejunum

K

L

Cecum

Ileocecal
valve

Right external
iliac artery
and vein

Right ureter

Right ureter
(proximal)

Right ureter
(distal, ligated)

M
N
The ureter is spatulated by making a 6 to 8 mm. slit on its ventral surface. Two stitches of atraumatic 3-0 chromic catgut are each passed first into the colon as indicated and then out through the newly made opening. Each strand is passed through a respective corner of the spatulated ureter, whereupon it is returned to the colon lumen through the opening and out again right next to each point of original entry. These sutures will be used to guide the ureter to the colon and to anchor it there.

O
This phantom drawing shows the spatulated shape assumed by the ureter as it is anchored in place. The ureter itself is not otherwise anchored with stitches to the surrounding tissue. If the mucosal opening is excessive it is repaired with interrupted stitches of 4-0 chromic catgut. The seromuscular incision is reapproximated over the ureter with interrupted simple stitches of 4-0 chromic catgut so that a tunneling effect is created. This is quite effective in about 95 per cent of patients in preventing regurgitation of urine from a distended cecum.

The reader will recognize this as an alternate method of performing a ureterocolostomy. The length of the ureter must be just enough to make an easy sweep around the upturned cecum. If the length of ureter is excessive, it may kink as the cecum is returned to its final position.

P
The new bladder is returned to its final position and supported in place with stitches of catgut between it and the posterior parietal peritoneum. It is desirable to have the reservoir lying below the sacral promontory so that the ileum takes a cephalad course to exit at the right lower quadrant. This insures against spillage from the reservoir should the ileocecal valve not be completely competent.

The reader is referred to the previous section for information on delivering the left ureter and handling the free edge of the mesentery of the colon in the event of a colostomy. Medium-sized soft rubber drains are placed in the vicinity of each ureterocolic anastomosis and exteriorized through lower quadrant counterincisions. In the absence of pelvic surgery, a small sump drain is placed into the pelvis for evacuation of urine in the event of a temporary leakage. If pelvic surgery has been performed the pelvis is drained according to individual preference. A soft, medium caliber, rubber catheter is placed through the new bladder so that there is constant evacuation of urine. Colonic mucus may occasionally impede the flow of urine through the catheter. Irrigation of the catheter with small amounts of sterile saline solution takes care of this problem. The management of these patients is otherwise similar to that of any others who have had major surgery. The patients are taught to catheterize themselves just as they are taught to irrigate their colostomy. The patients soon determine the necessary frequency of catheterization.

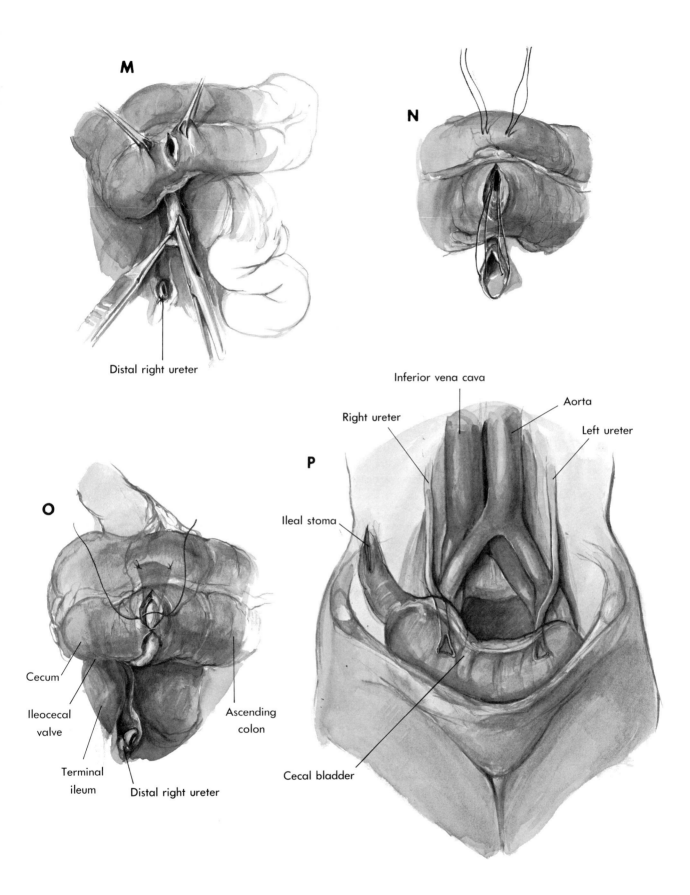

M

N

Distal right ureter

O

Cecum

Ileocecal
valve

Terminal
ileum

Distal right ureter

Ascending
colon

P

Inferior vena cava

Right ureter

Aorta

Left ureter

Ileal stoma

Cecal bladder

AORTIC ANEURYSM

The development of vascular surgery has been lengthy and delayed because of the highly critical nature of the diseases and techniques for treating them. The pioneer experimental work of Carrel anticipated most of the developments of modern vascular surgery. The ligation of the patent ductus arteriosus and the first uses of a graft for coarctation of the aorta by Gross in 1939 and 1948 were major steps in initiating modern vascular surgery. The studies of De Bakey and his colleagues in developing synthetic vascular grafts and exploring their use in all varieties of vascular disease have been notable contributions.

Among the most dramatic moments in surgery is the correction of an aortic aneurysm. The surgery of the aorta is highly specialized in its techniques. Although modern advances have made this surgery safer, dangerous emergencies are always potentially present.

Most aortic aneurysms are abdominal in location and arteriosclerotic in etiology. The commonest location in the abdomen is just below the renal arteries. This aneurysm may involve the common iliac arteries also. Occasionally, the abdominal aortic aneurysm involves one or both renal arteries. In this case, the technical repair is more complicated because of the possible ischemic damage to the kidney. Rather infrequently an abdominal aneurysm will be high and will involve the celiac axis, the superior mesenteric artery and the renal arteries. This is a more formidable technical challenge because of the multiple branch reconstruction required.

The thoracic aortic aneurysms may involve the aortic arch, the descending aorta or, rarely, both. Saccular aneurysms are more commonly caused by syphilis, whereas the much commoner atherosclerotic variety is usually fusiform. The traumatic aneurysm of the aorta usually occurs just distal to the left subclavian artery and may present as a vascular mediastinal mass or may present a picture simulating coarctation of the aorta.

The so-called dissecting aneurysm presents a different pathologic picture. In this type of aneurysm a break in the intima occurs and two vascular channels develop, one the true lumen which is occluded to a varying degree, and the second a false subintimal channel which may or may not rebreak the intima and re-enter distally. The act of re-entering tends to alleviate the situation. A widened aortic shadow, associated usually with severe pain and an inequality of pulses, should suggest the aneurysm. Hypertension is usually present proximally, at least at the outset. The intimal break usually occurs distal to the level of the left subclavian artery. From here it may progress distally to the iliacs or beyond. The dissection may go proximally as far as the aortic valve and produce aortic regurgitation. Sometimes the clinical picture may present a combination of dissection in both directions. The risk of surgery in an acutely dissecting aneurysm has been so high that the present tendency is to treat the patient with rest, hypotensive agents and general support, unless the aortic valve is being damaged or the aorta is rupturing. In the latter instances the formidable risk of surgery must be accepted in view of the catastrophic nature of the disease.

The inherent risk in all aneurysms is that they may rupture. There may be embolism produced from the blood clot which usually is present in the aneurysmal sac. The patient with an aneurysm who develops pain has a suspect rupturing aneurysm until proved otherwise. A free rupture of an aortic aneurysm will usually result in death before anything can be done. More commonly the aortic aneurysm ruptures into the mediastinum or retroperitoneally, and the hemorrhage is limited for a time. If prompt surgical treatment is carried out, some of these patients can be saved.

The abdominal aortic aneurysms should ordinarily be repaired when diagnosed. Large abdominal aortic aneurysms should always be repaired in a patient who is a good surgical risk. A small abdominal aortic aneurysm in the poor risk surgical patient is currently not operated by some surgeons. Hypertension, coronary artery disease and previous myocardial infarctions all increase the risk of repair. The correct decision for treatment of the relatively large aneurysm in the relatively poor risk patient requires experience and judgment. Most large aneurysms will rupture in less than two years. The abdominal aortic aneurysm that has ruptured requires immediate surgery. It has been estimated that 10 per cent of acute abdominal emergencies in patients over the age of 60 years are vascular in nature. For this reason all surgeons should be well trained in the principles of vascular surgery.

The usual history, physical examination and laboratory tests should be done. An abdominal mass may be felt which may or may not be pulsatile. All peripheral pulses should be palpated, and the blood pressure should be measured in the four extremities. The peripheral arteries as well as the chest and abdomen should be auscultated for bruits. Plain roentgen views of the abdomen may show calcification in an expanded abdominal aorta. This, if present, is pathognomonic. If it is thought that an unusual abdominal aneurysm is present, an aortogram can be done.

At the time of surgery a large incision is made. The abdominal viscera are retracted to the right and the abdominal aorta exposed. Proximal and distal control is obtained by careful dissection and passing tapes proximal and distal to the aneurysm. Usually the lesion is below the renal arteries. The inferior mesenteric artery must be divided. This causes no difficulty unless there is disease in the celiac axis and superior mesenteric arteries. A dilated inferior mesenteric artery with dilatation of the collateral artery of Drummond along the colon should warn the surgeon.

An important part of all abdominal explorations is palpation of all the important arterial pulses. This is too frequently neglected. Before repair of an aortic aneurysm a complete abdominal exploration is carried out. Incidental carcinomas in older patients are not infrequent. Infection of a vascular graft is a calamitous event, so careful asepsis is indicated, as is extreme caution when a bowel resection or feces could contaminate a vascular prosthesis. In elective aneurysmectomy, 50 mg. of heparin is given at this time. This can be given systemically, injected distally into the iliac vessels or injected directly into the aneurysm immediately before the proximal and distal clamps are applied. The anterior surface of the aneurysm is then opened. Bleeding from the branches of this segment of the aorta is controlled by sutures placed from within the aneurysm if the lumbar branches have not been ligated outside the aorta. The aneurysm may be intimately adherent to the inferior vena cava. The sac of the aneurysm should be left in place. The sac serves to cover and to protect the prosthetic graft and it is safer to leave it in than to try to remove it from the vital adjacent structures.

The proximal aorta about 2 to 3 cm. distal to the occlusive clamp is cut, and the appropriate location in the iliacs 1 cm. proximal to the occlusive clamps then is cut. An appropriate Dacron bifurcation graft is selected. Over-and-over sutures are placed posteriorly first and then anteriorly. The proximal anastomosis is completed first. Since the "normal" aorta proximal to the aneurysm is diseased, good secure bites of tissue should be taken. The distal anastomoses should be done last and the graft placed under modest tension, otherwise it may buckle when circulation is re-established.

The technique used most commonly is to complete one distal anastomosis, then unclamp that distal artery to permit retrograde flushing of that limb of the graft. The unanastomosed graft limb is then clamped at its origin. The proximal aorta clamp is removed and circulation is restored through the anastomosis distally. The second distal anastomosis is begun. Just before completion of the anastomosis, the second distal artery is unclamped for retrograde flushing and the anastomosis completed. The circulation is then restored through the second distal vessel by unclamping the second limb of the graft. Before removing the proximal aortic clamp, it is wise to be certain that the blood volume is replaced. The ischemia of the hindquarters has permitted distal vasodilatation plus accumulation of acid metabolites.

Page 371

Sudden removal of the proximal clamp, especially in a hypovolemic patient, may permit loss of blood into the distal vascular bed and the return of acid metabolites to the body; severe hypotension may result. Whole blood and bicarbonate buffering with the slow removal of the proximal clamp is helpful. The sac of the aneurysm should be closed over the prosthesis. The sac should cover especially the proximal anastomosis, since a bare anastomosis occasionally erodes into adjacent bowel.

In the instance of a ruptured abdominal aortic aneurysm speed is essential. A clamp must be placed on the aorta immediately, usually just below the diaphragm. Resuscitative measures are simultaneously carried out. Venous cannulae should be in the arms. After exposure the aorta clamp is changed to below the renal arteries. Repair of a ruptured aortic aneurysm by inexpert hands will have almost 100 per cent mortality. In expert hands this mortality will decrease to less than 50 per cent with survival depending upon the patient. In contrast, an unruptured abdominal aortic aneurysm in a reasonable risk patient should be repaired with less than 5 per cent risk.

If the abdominal aortic aneurysm involved one or more renal arteries, the situation becomes more complicated. The normothermic kidney is tolerant of only 30 or so minutes of ischemia. Two hours of normothermic ischemia destroys the kidney. Hypothermia to 80° F. doubles the period for safe ischemia. If a graft can be placed in an hour, local hypothermia of the kidney may permit the operation to progress. An alternative is to place the proximal end of the graft to the side of the aorta above the renal arteries and the distal end of the graft end-to-end as described before. After this graft is established, a side graft is placed end-to-side on the proximal main graft. This side graft is placed end-to-end or end-to-side into the renal artery. A second side graft can be used for the second kidney if necessary. After the kidney (kidneys) is (are) perfused and the grafts are patent, the proximal aorta distal to the graft is cut and sutured. The aneurysmal sac is handled as before.

If the celiac axis, superior mesenteric and renal arteries are involved, the situation is much more formidable. The best results have been when a by-pass graft was attached end-to-side above and below the aneurysm. This permits continued perfusion of all vessels. Then one by one branch grafts can be sutured from the side of the major graft end-to-end to the major arterial branches, renal first. In this fashion the graft can be "walked" into position and the aneurysm ultimately replaced. This technique avoids the use of anticoagulation drugs, which would be needed if a shunt were placed from the left atrium via a pump to the distal normal vessels in the groin. With the pump by-pass technique the graft can be started end-to-end in the distal thoracic aorta and "walked" down to the abdominal aorta.

The problem is complicated in aneurysms of the descending thoracic aorta. One cannot cross-clamp the descending thoracic aorta for prolonged periods of time because of left ventricular strain due to increased peripheral resistance. In addition there is the risk of ischemia to the vital organs distally, namely the abdominal viscera and the spinal cord with hindquarter paralysis. Less than 30 minutes of thoracic aorta occlusion is safe in normothermia, and less than 60 minutes is safe with hypothermia. The only exception is in coarctation of the aorta when there is well developed collateral circulation. Lesions of the descending thoracic aorta can be handled either with anticoagulation and by-pass from left atrium to groin, or a side of aorta to end of graft anastomosis proximally can be followed with an end of the graft to the side of the descending aorta distally, and the intervening diseased aneurysm cut free.

The most difficult situation of all is when the aortic arch is involved because the brachiocephalic arteries are involved. Here one is limited by the fact that the carotid artery can be occluded for only three or four minutes of normothermia, and only six to eight minutes of hypothermia. The present technique is to use total cardiopulmonary by-pass including individual perfusion of both coronary and major cerebral arteries. Prior to this, the technique was an end of graft to side of the ascending aorta, and end of graft to side of descending aorta. Then individual by-pass grafts were placed from the side of the major graft to the side of the branch arteries. When the main shunt and all its branches were functional, the diseased arch was resected. Either the by-pass graft was left or a graft was then placed in the normal arch position and branches anastomosed end-to-end to the innominate, left carotid and left subclavian arteries. The shunt is then removed. This operation was prohibitively tedious and lengthy and not infrequently impossible because of involvement of the ascending aorta.

Aneurysms of the ascending aorta, with or without involvement of the aortic valve, can be resected and reconstructed using total cardiopulmonary by-pass and coronary perfusion. In the presence of significant aortic insufficiency secondary to the aneurysm, the valve is replaced with an appropriate synthetic valve.

In the surgery of the aorta the surgeon must be well trained in vascular surgery, must be familiar with heart-lung by-pass apparatus and must be used to working within the limitations of hypothermia. Major arterial surgery does not require postoperative anticoagulation. Evidence of emboli and of hemorrhage occasionally require prompt reoperation.

References

Carrel, A.: Results of the transplantation of blood vessels, organs, and limbs. J.A.M.A. *51*:1662, 1908.

De Bakey, M. E. (ed.): Vascular Surgery. Surg. Clin. North America *46*:823, 1966.

Dubost, C., and Oeconomós, N.: Les greffes vasculaire. Étude expérimentale. Application chez l'homme. Rev. chir. *71*:167, 1952.

Gross, R. E., Bill, A. H., Jr., and Peirce, E. C., II: Methods for preservation and transplantation of arterial grafts. Observation on arterial grafts in dogs. Report of transplantation of preserved arterial grafts in nine human cases. Surg., Gynec. & Obst. *88*:689, 1949.

Gross, R. E., and Hubbard, J. P.: Surgical ligation of a patent ductus arteriosus; report of first successful case. J.A.M.A. *112*:729, 1939.

Julian, O. C., Grove, W. J., Dye, W. S., Olwin, J. H., and Sadove, M. S.: Direct surgery of arteriosclerosis. Resection of abdominal aorta with homologous aortic graft replacement, Ann. Surg. *138*:387, 1953.

Ruptured Abdominal Aortic Aneurysm

A Most of the anatomic relationships of the abdominal aorta are demonstrated in this illustration, which shows it flanked by the diaphragmatic crura as it makes its appearance in the abdomen at the level of the 12th thoracic vertebra. Normally, as it continues downward it deviates slightly to the left and bifurcates at the level of the iliac crests. The aorta is intimately related to the vena cava at the level of their respective bifurcation and lies somewhat anterior to it. This relationship becomes less intimate more cephalad as the vena cava separates to enter the thoracic cavity separately and more anteriorly than the aorta. Much of this topography may be greatly distorted with an aneurysm, especially if it has ruptured. A rupture may occur at several places, the commonest being dorsally and to the left, resulting in a pulsating hemorrhagic mass in the left flank.

The aorta is crossed by the base of the mesentery of the small bowel, which has an oblique course between the duodenojejunal flexure and the right sacroiliac articulation.

The left renal vein, the transverse position of the duodenum and the splenic or beginning of the portal vein (not shown) come in direct contact with the aorta as they pass anteriorly to it. They will serve as valuable landmarks and, of course, should not be injured. The inferior mesenteric artery is singular for an appreciable length and ligation close to its origin poses minimal risk in destroying any collateral circulation to the sigmoid and descending colon.

B It is extremely important that the patient be anesthetized only after everything is gathered in readiness. A long and rapid midline incision is made from the xiphoid to the pubis. In this instance, a catheter of generous caliber has been advanced into the inferior vena cava through a cut-down over the saphenous vein in addition to the two large bore catheters in arm veins. When possible, leg vein cannulation is avoided because of the increased risk of phlebitis. Also, leg veins have occasionally to be shut off during operations. The mortality of massive transfusions can be drastically reduced by administering blood warmed to 100° F., by buffering the patient to pH 7.4 with sodium bicarbonate, and by giving one unit of fresh frozen plasma per three units of blood.

C Dark bloody fluid may be encountered in the abdomen. The posterior peritoneal surface and perhaps the small and large bowel mesentery will be deeply bloodstained. Frequently a blood pressure drop occurs at this point, and rapid transfusion is required. Following confirmation of the diagnosis of aortic rupture, proximal aortic control is obtained. This is best achieved by retracting the left lobe of the liver cephalad and to the right. The lesser omentum is entered near the level of the esophagogastric junction and the aorta is palpated through fibers of the diaphragm. A large slightly curved aneurysm forceps is maneuvered into position and the aorta occluded. The diaphragmatic fibers usually present can be ignored. It is unnecessary to dissect and encircle the aorta prior to clamping. An assistant should provide dorsal pressure on the clamp against the vertebral column to insure complete occlusion. Once this proximal control is achieved, transfusion is used to bring the blood pressure to normal.

D A large self-retaining retractor is inserted. The omentum and transverse colon are pulled cephalad and the small bowel and its mesentery retracted out of the abdomen in an upward and right lateral direction. The bloodstained parietal peritoneum overlying the aneurysm is incised up to the duodenojejunal ligament (Treitz) and down into the pelvis.

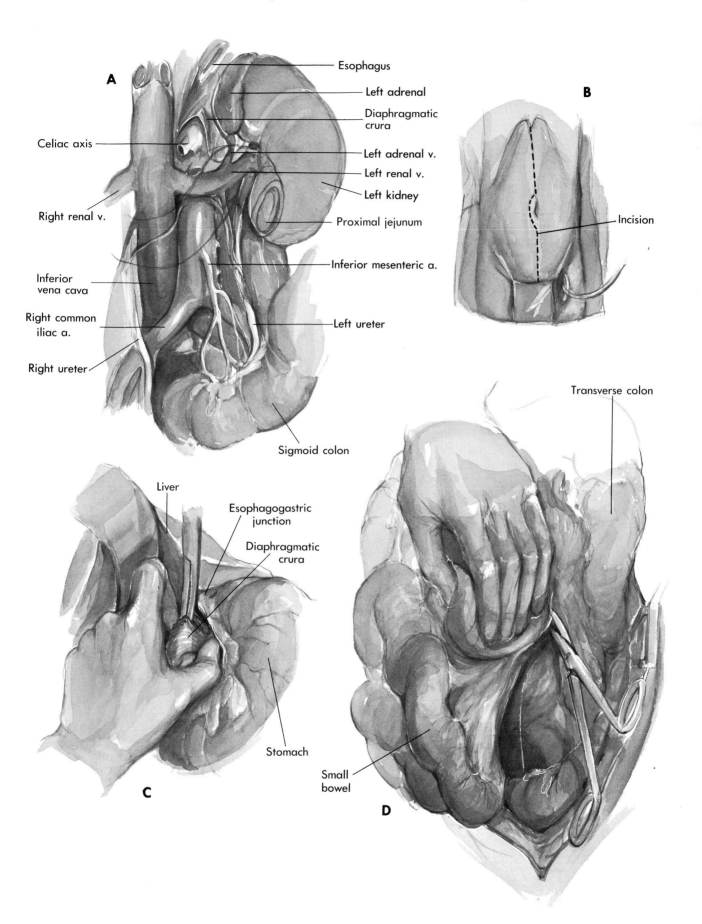

A

Esophagus

Left adrenal

Diaphragmatic crura

Celiac axis

Left adrenal v.

Left renal v.

Left kidney

Right renal v.

Proximal jejunum

Inferior mesenteric a.

Inferior vena cava

Right common iliac a.

Left ureter

Right ureter

Sigmoid colon

B

Incision

Liver

Esophagogastric junction

Diaphragmatic crura

Transverse colon

Stomach

Small bowel

C

D

E   The duodenojejunal ligament is divided and the distal duodenum reflected laterally to the right to expose the aneurysm over its anterior surface.

F   Distal iliac control is rapidly achieved. Frequently these vessels are isolated by digital dissection because of obliteration of tissue planes by infiltrating hematoma. Care should be taken to avoid injury to the iliac vein, which may be closely adherent to the arteriosclerotic arterial wall. This is best avoided by dissecting close to the arterial wall. So as to decrease even further the length of time the renal arteries are occluded, we have recently changed this sequence. The aorta just distal to the renal arteries is isolated and cross-clamped (Figures G to I) before isolation and cross-clamping of the iliac arteries. The back-bleeding from the unsecured iliac arteries results in only a modest increase in blood loss.

G   The aorta is dissected between the aneurysm and the renal arteries. Only rarely does the aneurysm involve a renal artery except for occasional accessory renal arteries which may originate from the aneurysmal area. This dissection is occasionally difficult because of a great amount of retroperitoneal blood. Avoid injury to the left renal vein, which may be flattened over the proximal end of the aneurysm.

H
I   It is possible to clamp the iliac vessels and open the aneurysm at this point (proximal aortic clamp still in place!). With the index finger of the left hand within the lumen of the aorta, the aorta is more easily dissected and encircled. At this point a clamp is placed distal to the renal artery.

J   With control of the aorta between the renal arteries and the aneurysm, the proximal aortic clamp is removed. This should be done slowly and with rapid transfusion, as the splanchnic bed and kidneys may be fairly empty of blood. The left lateral surface of the aneurysm is more completely freed of overlying tissue, care being taken not to interrupt the collateral arterial supply to the descending and sigmoid colon as it descends in the arcade from the middle colic artery. The inferior mesenteric vein is an important landmark and is located approximately where indicated by the asterisk (*).

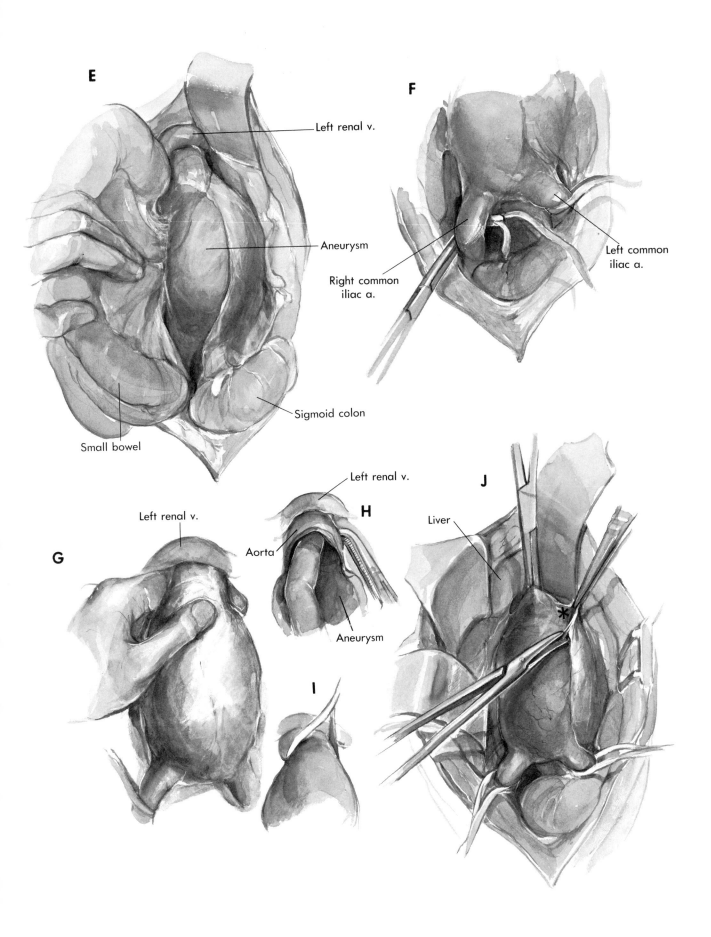

K   The inferior mesenteric artery is divided as close to an unruptured aneurysm as possible. It is frequently already occluded because of deposition of laminated clot within the aneurysm. Should retroperitoneal clot preclude accurate identification of the origin of the inferior mesenteric artery, it can be controlled easily after opening the aneurysm and identifying the origin of the inferior mesenteric artery from within. In a ruptured aneurysm this artery will be handled as seems best.

L   Twenty to 30 ml. of blood are withdrawn from the aneurysm and used to preclot the graft. The patient is then given 40 to 50 mg. of heparin intravenously, or directly into the aneurysm, and it is allowed to flush distally. With the aorta and both iliac vessels clamped, the aneurysm is opened longitudinally and aspirated.

M   The inner laminated clot and atherosclerotic material are removed, frequently by a sweep of the finger. Only adventitia and some media remain.

N   Often even in an elective aortic aneurysmectomy it is not convenient or reasonable to ligate the lumbar vessels involved in an aneurysm. It is certainly not necessary to do so with a ruptured aneurysm; it would, in fact, be very hazardous. Back-bleeding from lumbar and sacral artery orifices is controlled with mattress sutures of heavy silk placed from within the opened aneurysm.

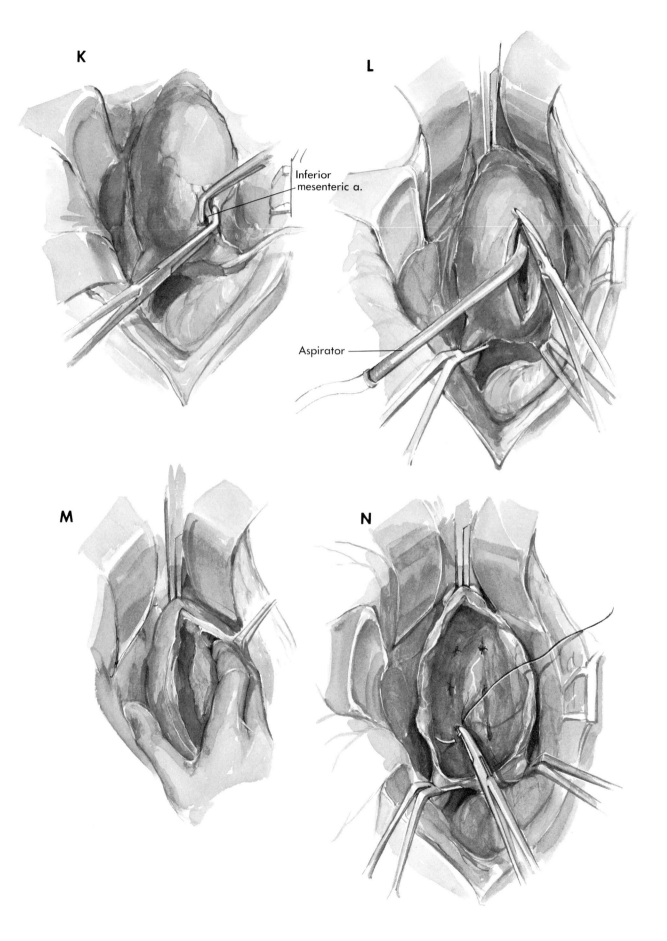

K

Inferior
mesenteric a.

L

Aspirator

M

N

O   The aneurysm is cut transversely just distal to its beginning except for the posterior third of the circumference. There is no objection to complete transection unless the posterior aortic tissues are thin and friable, in which case it is helpful to have the retroaortic tissues (e.g., prevertebral fascia) to aid in holding the posterior suture line.

P
Q   In these subsequent drawings the proximal or. aorta portion of the graft is depicted somewhat shorter than is usually the case. More often the aorta portion of the graft is equal, under tension, to the length of the aortic aneurysm. The iliac limbs of the graft are left long and appropriately trimmed just before each is anastomosed.

    Suturing the graft to the aorta is accomplished by passing the suture first through the graft and then the aorta. Generously deep bites are taken through the aortic tissue to insure a strong, blood-tight anastomosis. Several suturing techniques may be used. In this instance two separate sutures are being started posteriorly with the intention of continuing each laterally and then anteriorly. In performing the posterior suture line, the graft is retracted cephalad. For the sake of clarity, only one suture is shown in Figure Q.

R
S   The graft is then returned to its normal position. The aortic suture line is continued with a simple over-and-over running stitch, usually of 3-0 material (Tevdek, Dacron or silk), on a fairly large, atraumatic needle. The graft should lie within the aortic lumen to allow better hemostasis and to prevent dissection beneath an atherosclerotic plaque at the suture line.

T   It was customary to gently test the aortic anastomosis by temporary loosening of the aorta clamp while the graft was digitally occluded. A more recent and preferred practice is to open the aorta clamp completely for one full heart beat. When a clamp is only partially opened, eddy currents may let some graft debris go proximal and enter a renal artery. This is the time to be certain that the posterior suture line is secure, since it would be difficult to expose this area later in the operation.

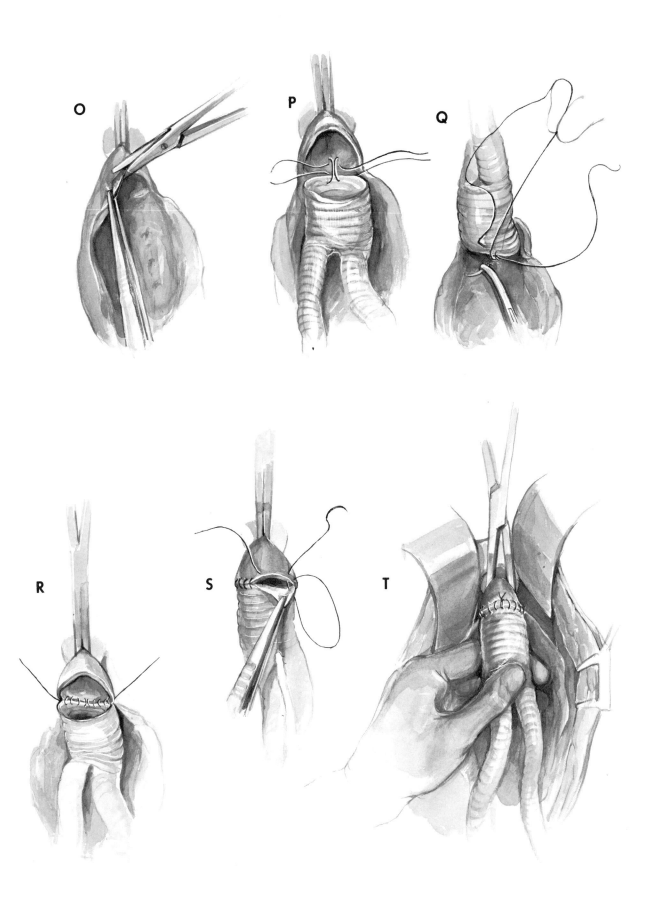

U   Liquid blood, clots and loose debris are aspirated from within the graft before proceeding with the iliac anastomosis.

V   An adequate length of iliac artery is freed from surrounding tissue and divided. Should the common iliac artery be aneurysmal or otherwise unsuitable for anastomosis, the external iliac or even femoral arteries may be selected for the distal anastomosis.

W   The distal artery is allowed to back-bleed, the patient, of course, having been heparinized. If, for any reason, dilute heparin is injected locally into the iliac vessels, it is usually to flush out debris. If a needle is used, care must be exercised not to injure the intima.

X   The appropriate distal limb of the graft is made long enough to allow for an anastomosis without tension, but not so long that buckling will occur.

Y
Z   The distal anastomoses are performed, again with continuous technique and using 4-0 or 5-0 suture material.

A_1
B_1
C_1 The order of clamp removal is considered important in prevention of air or embolic material from passing into the legs. The distal clamp is removed and the right iliac artery is allowed to back-bleed into the graft and out the unsutured opposite limb. A rubber-shod vascular clamp is placed on the proximal end of the sutured limb, and the aortic clamp loosened slightly for a few pulsations (B_1). The rubber-shod clamp is then transferred to the nonsutured limb (C_1). These maneuvers clear the graft of air and undetected clot or debris. The aorta is again clamped. Clamps placed on bifurcation grafts at the aortic-iliac junction should always be flush with the aorta. This avoids any tendency to clot formation in dead spaces. Preferably, these clamps should be slightly more proximal.

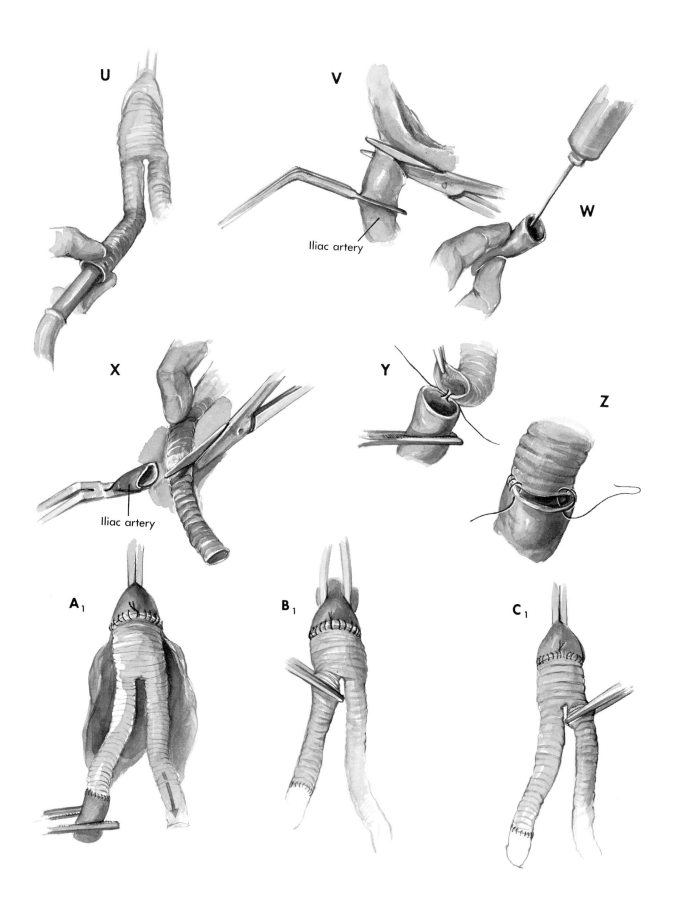

U

V

Iliac artery

W

X

Iliac artery

Y

Z

A₁

B₁

C₁

D₁   Digital compression is applied to the external iliac artery and the aortic clamp is loosened. After full flow has been established for a minute or so into the right internal iliac artery, the right external iliac artery is released. Rapid transfusion is necessary during these maneuvers, as the legs are usually empty of blood prior to release of the aortic clamp. Temporary occlusion of the external iliac artery allows any remaining debris to be swept into the pelvic area with its rich collateral circulation, rather than to embolize to the lower extremity.

E₁   The second or left iliac anastomosis is now performed, but just before its completion, the iliac artery is unclamped for retrograde flushing of clots and the anastomosis completed. With the second distal anastomosis completed and the operative field dry, the aneurysmal sac is trimmed and closed over the graft. The size and configuration of the residual aortic sac will determine the type of closure. A great effort is made to cover the proximal anastomosis. The graft is not otherwise attached to the aorta. The closure of the sac over the graft does not extend into the pelvis.

F₁   The posterior parietal peritoneum is then reconstituted. To lessen the risk of an aorto-duodenal fistula, an attempt is made to prevent the duodenum from lying directly in the aortic suture line. The anterior abdomen wall is closed in a routine way.

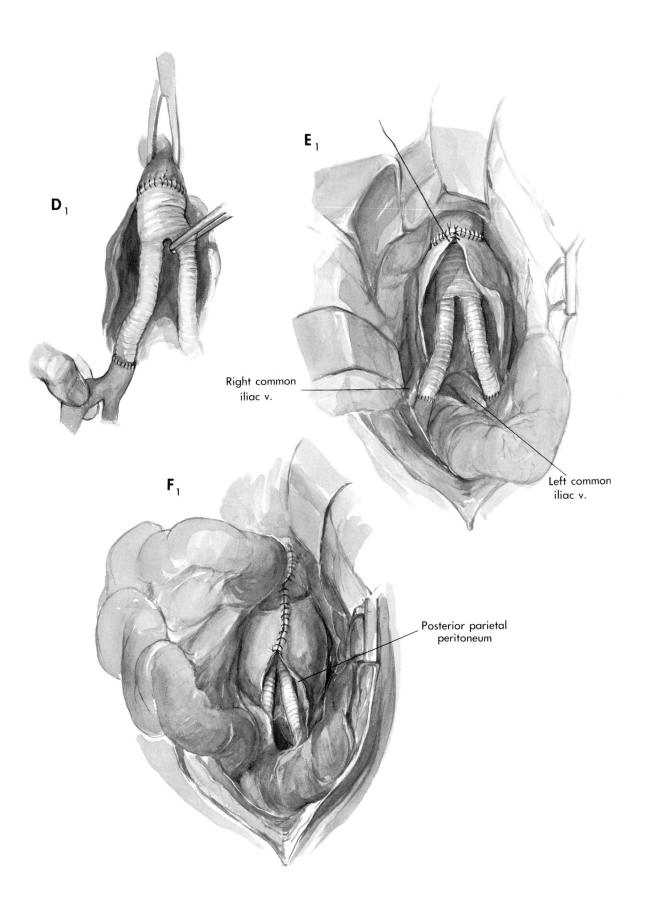

D₁

E₁

Right common
iliac v.

Left common
iliac v.

F₁

Posterior parietal
peritoneum

ILIOINGUINAL LYMPH NODE DISSECTION
(RADICAL GROIN DISSECTION)

Ilioinguinal lymph node (radical groin) dissection is a procedure whose objective is the en bloc removal of the lymph nodes and channels and associated adipose tissue of the inguinal and iliac areas. The indications for this operation are always for the resection of either proved or suspected cancerous lymph nodes. Under some circumstances it is performed as a prophylactic operation in a clinically negative inguinal area, primarily for the benefit derived from removing lymph nodes which are clinically nonpalpable or innocuous to palpation but which may contain microscopic foci of cancer cells.

The malignancies for which and the areas of the body in which this operation can be utilized include epidermoid carcinoma of the vulva, clitoris and lower vagina, the external male genitalia, the lower extremities, the anus and the skin of the perineum and gluteal area; it is also widely applied for the excision of malignant melanoma, primarily of the lower extremities, but also of sites mentioned above. If involved ilioinguinal lymph nodes are not excised, they will almost invariably lead to death of the patient within two years.

The operation may be performed with in continuity removal of the primary lesion. This plan of synchronous removal of the primary tumor, the intervening lymphatics and the regional lymph nodes en bloc is logical and feasible when the primary tumor is in reasonable proximity to the groin. This necessity of reasonable proximity between the primary tumor and the groin effectively excludes use of the combined operation for primary lesions situated below the knee, in the posterior thigh and the gluteal area.

At any specific time cancer cells may be in transit within the lymphatic channels between the primary cancer and the inguinal lymph nodes. One should not, therefore, excise the primary tumor and do a radical groin dissection at the same time but rather in a discontinuous manner. Theoretically, and in fact, the ablation of the inguinal lymph nodal area will result in stasis of lymph in the limb, with entrapment and cutaneous growth locally of any cancer cells which are in transit to the inguinal lymph nodes. Or it may result in metastases appearing at aberrant sites as a result of new paths sought by the regenerating lymphatics. Experience has shown that there is scant chance of curing such a patient. Occasionally, amputation, as for example in melanoma, will effect a cure.

Unfortunately, the sequence of tumor present between the primary site and regional lymph nodes occurs with the regional lymph nodes uninvolved. The explanation is that we do not understand all the relevant factors. For example, what are the factors which result in embolization of cancer cells? What conditions of the walls of the lymphatic channels predispose to cancer cell implantation and growth? What factors permit implantation in the lymph vessels but delay observable growth until a much later date? One immediate practical question is the time interval required for cancer cells to travel from a primary site to the filtering lymph nodes in the groin. Studies of the time it takes for dye to travel from the ankle to the groin have been inconclusive in that the dye will reach the groin in minutes in some patients and in others will not reach the groin for days, if at all. Even less is known of the possibility that cells may by-pass the groin. Additionally, how soon and with what frequency do cells which have metastasized to the groin metastasize further? There is no one correct time interval that should be allowed to elapse between excision of the primary cancer and the performance of the radical groin dissection. Arbitrarily, one to two weeks (with wide personal preference) is usually allowed before proceeding with the radical groin dissection.

There is some value to the performance of preoperative lymphangiography. It may demonstrate more extensive lymph node involvement than suspected on clinical examination or expected from the size of the primary. Sometimes lymphangiography may show the metastases to be beyond the reach of this operation. A roentgenogram done immediately after the operation and on the operating table and compared with the lymphangiogram done before surgery may reveal missed lymph nodes. If cerulean green is added to the preoperatively injected lymphangiographic dye, the vividly colored nodes will enable the surgeon to identify them more easily and remove them more surely. We do not yet know to what degree, if any, lymphangiography will make certain the cure of more patients.

Page 387

Radical groin dissection synchronously or metachronously is always indicated if the nodes are clinically involved with cancer. In such an instance it is often termed a therapeutic dissection. However, as was mentioned in the opening paragraph, prophylactic radical groin dissection is beneficial and therefore indicated for a variety of malignant tumors. This includes malignant melanoma, with the exception of those superficial lesions limited to the upper third of the corium. Inguinal node dissection is indicated in carcinoma of the leg, with the exception of those lesions which are superficial and less than 2 cm. in diameter or of the larger lesions if they arise in burn scars or osteomyelitic ulcers. Epidermoid cancers of the anus which are less than 2 cm. in diameter will almost never require a groin dissection at any time and it is therefore reasonable merely to keep these patients under close observation. As the size of the lesion in epidermoid cancer of the anus increases, so does the incidence of inguinal metastases. On this basis it appears beneficial in the total sense to perform prophylactic radical groin dissection when the primary lesion is greater than 2.5 cm. in diameter. Penile cancers warrant a prophylactic node dissection if they involve the middle or base of the shaft or are moderately to highly anaplastic. The final decision on whether to perform a radical groin dissection must be made by the surgeon, who will weigh the statistical chances of finding involved lymph nodes in a clinically negative groin, the consideration as to what benefits will accrue in excising cancer at this stage as against excising it when it becomes clinically obvious, and to what degree the admittedly increased morbidity and mortality of a prophylactic radical groin procedure cancel out its benefits.

There are several adjunctive procedures that are still clinically experimental in nature whose value to the standard radical groin dissection is not yet clear. One of them is the application of a proximal tourniquet to a toe or finger during biopsy of a presumed malignant melanoma. If the diagnosis on frozen section confirms the malignancy, the amputation is performed proximal to the tourniquet. There is here the assumption that cancer cells would break loose into the venous or lymphatic channels during the manipulation of the biopsy and that they would be contained by the tourniquet.

There is increasing use of perfusion of an extremity with anticancer agents for locally recurrent malignant melanoma which, for some reason, may not be resectable or may present as metastasis in transit. At present, this is largely a palliative procedure. The question naturally arises as to the value of perfusion as a prophylactic measure. The perfusion would be carried out immediately after a synchronous but discontinuous removal of the primary lesion and performance of the groin dissection or could be done immediately after a groin dissection performed metachronously. In either instance, the purpose of the perfusion would be to destroy any cells in transit between the primary lesion and the groin.

The preoperative preparation of patients for a radical groin dissection is similar to that for any major operation. Particular attention is paid to cleansing the inguinal areas, which are usually moist and bacteria-laden, especially in the elderly woman with vulvar

Page 388

cancer. To decrease the bacterial contamination of the skin and, expectantly, the incidence of postoperative wound infection, we ask the patients to wash with a bacteriostatic soap preoperatively. They are placed on a low residue diet for several days preoperatively, on clear liquids for the noon and evening meals on the day prior to surgery and have a cleansing enema administered on the morning of surgery. This reduces the likelihood of defecation too soon after surgery. A radical groin dissection alone should not require any transfusion of blood. If the groin dissection is done as part of a combined procedure, blood transfusion is often necessary and preparations for this should be made.

The practice of placing the wound on suction postoperatively has eliminated the necessity for pressure dressings, which tend to keep the operative site warm and humid, with a tendency to maceration. The patient is kept in bed for seven to ten days postoperatively, and the light dressings over the wound are changed as necessary. If there is ischemic skin flap necrosis, the necrotic tissue is debrided surgically as soon as there is a line of demarcation. Because such clean demarcation is often not the case, it is impossible to do a debridement early and adequately without also excising healthy tissue. Accordingly, the wound is soaked for several days with half-strength Dakin's solution. Under general anesthesia a thin split thickness skin graft with abundant "pie-crusting" (or "postage-stamp" grafts, if one wishes) is applied. The wound is managed postoperatively in an open manner, a practice prompted by a realization that once such necrosis has occurred, a bacterially "clean" wound is difficult to obtain. This involves placing a nonreactive, nonadhering one-eighth inch mesh over the graft and anchoring it in position with appropriate stitches. The nurse is instructed to place over this mesh every four hours gauze that is moistened with physiologic saline solution. The capillary action of the moist gauze in contact with the graft helps to keep it clean, or if "postage-stamp" grafts are in place, the intervening granulation tissue sticks to the constantly replaced gauze, resulting in a microdebridement. The interposed nonadhering mesh prevents the moist gauze from dislodging the skin graft but will not stick to either gauze or skin graft. Primary skin grafts are frequently handled in the same manner.

References

Hovnanian, A. P.: Radical ilio-inguinal lymphatic excision. Ann. Surg. *135*:520, 1952.
Pack, G. T., and Rekers, P.: The management of malignant tumors in the groin. Am. J. Surg. *56*:545, 1942.
Southwick, H. W., Slaughter, D. P., Hinkamp, J. F., and Johnson, F. E.: The role of regional node dissection in the treatment of malignant melanoma. Arch. Surg. *85*:79, 1962.
Stehlin, J. S., Clark, R. L., Vickers, W. E., and Monges, A.: Perfusion for malignant melanoma of the extremities. Am. J. Surg. *105*:607, 1963.

A   The anatomic considerations in the performance of a radical groin dissection are pictured. The lymph node bearing tissue to be excised extends from the bifurcation of the common iliac vessels to the apex of the femoral (Scarpa's) triangle. The femoral triangle is bounded by the inguinal ligament superiorly, the sartorius muscle laterally and the adductor longus muscle medially. The floor of the femoral triangle is formed by the fascia over the iliopsoas, adductor longus, and pectineus muscles and the roof is formed by the fascia lata. Actually, most of the lymph node bearing tissue is to be found in the fatty areolar tissue superficial to the roof of the triangle. The important arteries are the common iliac artery, which bifurcates into the hypogastric artery which, in turn, ramifies into the pelvis and the external iliac; this lies on the iliopsoas as it runs laterally and downwardly toward the groin. Just before the external iliac artery passes under the inguinal ligament to become the common femoral artery it gives off the deep circumflex iliac artery and the inferior epigastric artery. The corresponding vein leading up to the inferior vena cava lies medial and posterior to the artery. The common femoral artery gives off three superficial and two deep branches; only the former will be encountered and require interruption: the superficial external pudendal artery, the circumflex iliac artery and the inferior epigastric artery. The common femoral artery bifurcates into the deep femoral and superficial femoral arteries, the latter leaving the operative field just lateral to the apex of the femoral triangle. The femoral vein, as with the artery and nerve, lies deep to the fascia lata. It can be seen to lie more dorsal to the artery at the apex of the femoral triangle but at the inguinal ligaments it is directly medial to it.

The femoral nerve appears in the pelvis lateral to the iliopsoas muscle. As it proceeds distally it is flanked laterally by the iliacus muscle. After the femoral nerve exits from under the inguinal ligament it gives off its multiple branches and proceeds to disappear under the sartorius muscle. The genitofemoral nerve lies lateral to the femoral nerve in the pelvis and is under the fascia of the iliacus muscle. It is the lateral boundary of the iliac dissection and need not be disturbed.

The lymph nodes to be excised are the inguinal and the iliac, the former being more numerous. The inguinal lymph nodes are divided into the superficial group, which is more numerous, and the deep group, which lies deep to the fascia lata. The superficial group is arbitrarily divided further into five groups by perpendicular and horizontal lines crossing at the saphenofemoral junction, with the central area as the fifth group. Cancers in certain locations metastasize more readily to certain quadratic groups. However, there are sufficient exceptions that a routine excision of all these nodes should eliminate this concern. In instances of clitoral or penile cancer, however, the prepubic nodes, not otherwise routinely excised, should receive special attention. Most of the deep femoral nodes are medial to the femoral vein, the most cephalad being the node of Cloquet. The iliac nodes can be classified as to location but this has no meaning to the surgeon whose task is to remove all of them. The nodes over the obturator foramen and in surgically troublesome relationship to the obturator vessels and nerves must also be removed in this dissection.

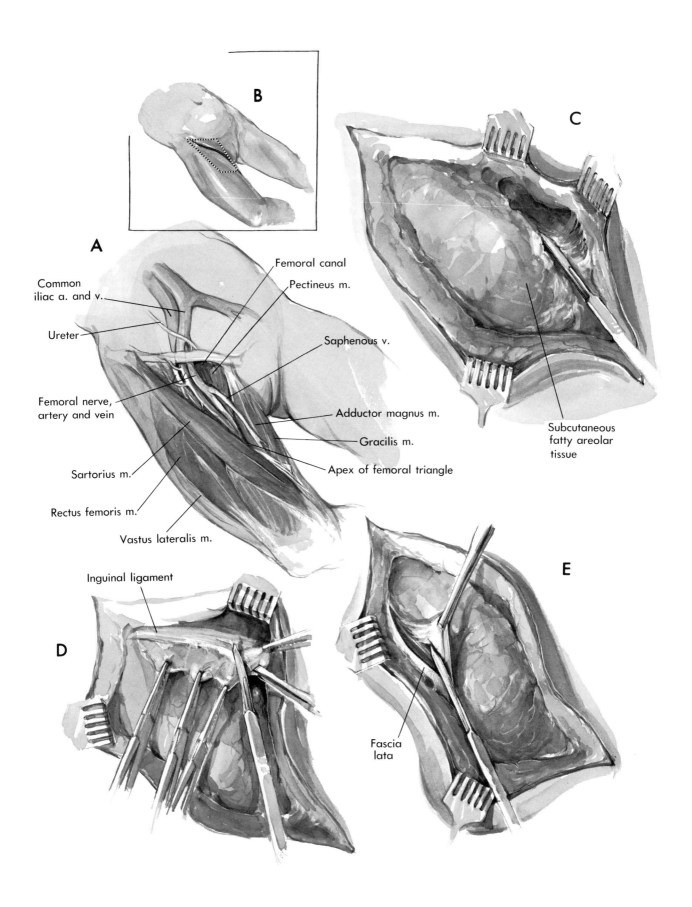

A

Common
iliac a. and v.

Ureter

Femoral nerve,
artery and vein

Sartorius m.

Rectus femoris m.

Vastus lateralis m.

Femoral canal

Pectineus m.

Saphenous v.

Adductor magnus m.

Gracilis m.

Apex of femoral triangle

B

C

Subcutaneous
fatty areolar
tissue

Inguinal ligament

D

E

Fascia
lata

B   The area to be shaved routinely, regardless of the location of the primary tumor, includes the lower abdomen, the perineum and genitalia and the thigh on the operative side. The gluteal area or the opposite groin and thigh are shaved when necessary. If only a radical ilioinguinal dissection is planned, the patient is placed in a supine position with the leg on the operative side abducted, flexed slightly and externally rotated. It is supported in this position by a sandbag under the calf. The scrotum and penis are secured to the opposite groin. If there is to be concomitant perineal surgery, then both legs must be abducted while extended; this is done most conveniently on an orthopedic table.

   We prefer an oblique incision beginning several centimeters cephalad and medial to the anterosuperior iliac spine, progressing down to 1 or 2 cm. below and then parallel to the inguinal ligament and, while over the vessels, curving gently to point to the apex of the femoral triangle. Special circumstances may dictate other incisions which extract the price of more frequent necrosis of the skin flap. We distinctly do not recommend a straight vertical incision centered over the vessels. This drawing also indicates the extent of the roughly quadrilateral area that is to be dissected in the inguinal portion of the operation.

C   The depth of the skin incision is about 3 to 4 mm. and the skin flaps are mobilized at this thickness for at least 5 cm. from the center portion of the incision. The skin flaps are then tapered so that peripherally they almost blend with the full thickness of the surrounding fat.

D   The subcutaneous fatty areolar tissue over the abdominal area is dissected first. The dissection is carried down to the aponeurosis of the external oblique muscle. The surgeon will find that in the inguinal crease he has to carry this dissection slightly caudal and under the inguinal ligament to where Scarpa's fascia is attached.

E   The infrainguinal dissection is commenced next as the fascia lata is incised along the lateral border of the sartorius muscle. The lateral femoral cutaneous nerve should be watched for in the upper aspect of the incision.

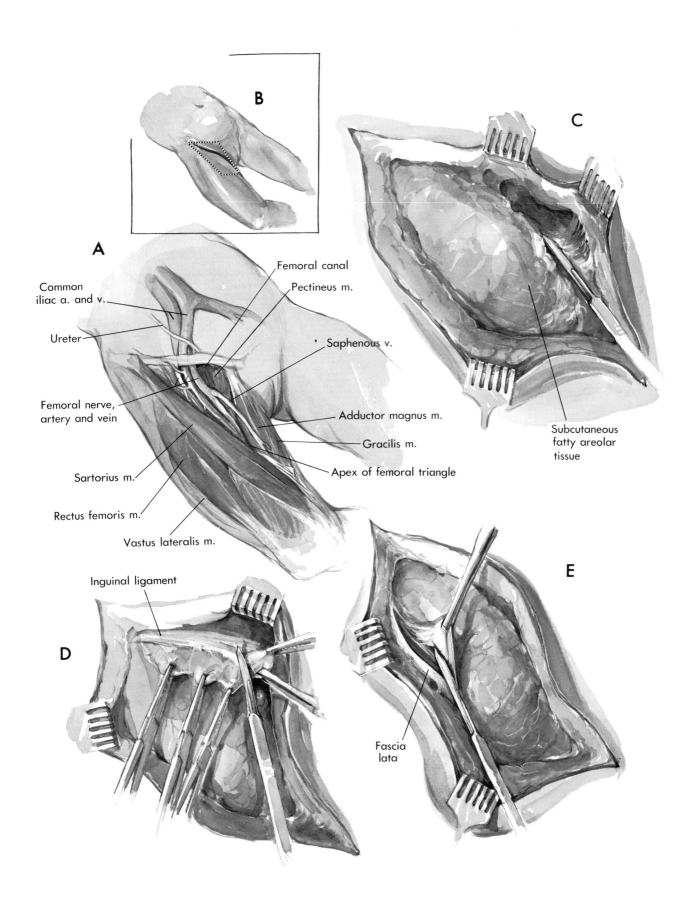

B

A

Common
iliac a. and v.

Ureter

Femoral canal

Pectineus m.

Saphenous v.

Femoral nerve,
artery and vein

Adductor magnus m.

Gracilis m.

Sartorius m.

Apex of femoral triangle

Rectus femoris m.

Vastus lateralis m.

C

Subcutaneous
fatty areolar
tissue

Inguinal ligament

D

E

Fascia
lata

F   The tough fascia lata is caught along its free edge and, with the overlying lymph node bearing fatty areolar tissue, is retracted medially as it is freed from the underlying sartorius muscle. As the dissecting knife dips slightly at the medial border of the proximal sartorius muscle, care should be taken not to damage the branches of the femoral nerve that are to be seen disappearing under this muscle.

G   The superficial surface of the femoral nerve has been dissected free. The femoral sheath will have to be entered here. This sheath is a continuation of the iliac and transversalis fascia and surrounds both the artery and vein as they pass under the inguinal ligament to the medial space of the femoral arch.

H   The three superficial branches (two lateral and one medial) of the common femoral artery will be encountered at this point. If they are inadvertently sectioned, it will be at a point so close to their origin that it is likely that it will be necessary to work on the femoral artery itself in order to secure the branch. Awareness of the anatomic relationships is again one of the better ways to avoid this time-consuming complication. The reader will notice the dissection being performed with a scalpel; it is a matter of preference and scissors will do as well.

I
J   As the dissection continues medially the fascia lata is disengaged from the undersurface of the inguinal ligament. The saphenous vein is divided at the saphenofemoral junction and the saphenous vein stump is doubly ligated, with the outer one secured with a transfixion ligature of 3-0 silk. The femoral vein can then be dissected cleanly along its entire medial aspect, which contains no branches, thus exposing the pectineus muscle.

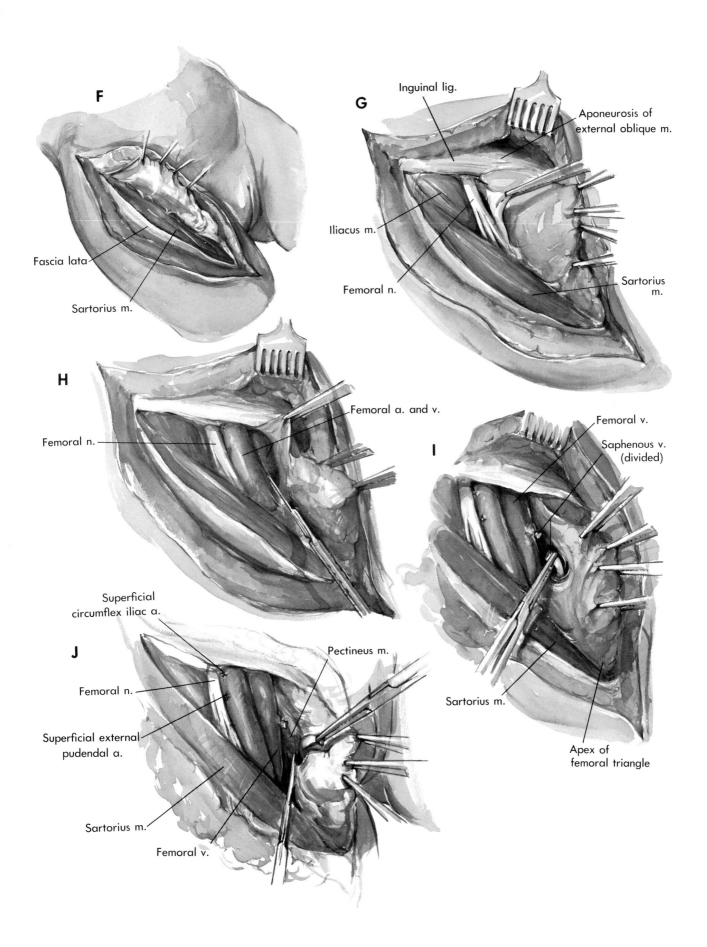

F

Fascia lata

Sartorius m.

G

Inguinal lig.

Aponeurosis of external oblique m.

Iliacus m.

Femoral n.

Sartorius m.

H

Femoral n.

Femoral a. and v.

I

Femoral v.

Saphenous v. (divided)

Sartorius m.

Apex of femoral triangle

J

Superficial circumflex iliac a.

Pectineus m.

Femoral n.

Superficial external pudendal a.

Sartorius m.

Femoral v.

K The previous step will have led to the apex of the femoral triangle, which is the point at which the saphenous vein has to be ligated and divided a second time. This is the area richest in lymphatic channels and, when divided, results in a lymphorrhea. In order to reduce the incidence and rate of accumulation of serous fluid under the skin flaps postoperatively, this fatty areolar tissue should be ligated as it is being divided even though the vascular channels are not apparent. This, in turn, is associated with less wound infection, an important cause of lymphedema of the extremity on the operated side. The sequence of these last three steps can be reversed so that the saphenous vein is ligated first at the apex of the femoral triangle and lastly at the saphenofemoral junction. Early proximal venous ligation is always desirable when feasible and, in this instance, there is negligible venous pooling in the interval before the vein is ligated the second time at the apex of the femoral triangle.

L Rarely are there lymph nodes over the gracilis muscle. The dissection, therefore, proceeds toward the femoral canal with the medial border of the adductor longus muscle comprising the medial border at the plane of dissection.

M Now all the inguinal tissue to be excised has been dissected free except that leading directly into the femoral canal. If the ilioinguinal dissection is to be done en bloc, and this should certainly be the choice with clinically positive nodes, then some method must be used to open the femoral canal.

N One method is to detach the inguinal ligament from its insertion at the pubic tubercle. Although the simplest way is to divide the inguinal ligament over the femoral canal, it is difficult to reconstruct this ligament later and it is liable to disruption. In thin patients or in those in whom dissected iliac tissue has been scant, lymph node bearing tissue from the iliac vessels can be retrieved downwardly through the intact femoral canal. An excellent method is that depicted in Plate 5, which shows a portion of the anterior iliac spine and the associated lateral inguinal ligament reflected medially. In this instance we chose to separate the iliac and femoral masses of tissue in the specimen to be excised. This is done by using electrocautery to divide between ligatures. Theoretically, this step may increase the chances of spillage of tumor cell bearing lymph with subsequent "seeding" of the wound with cancer cells. The absence of clinically involved lymph nodes reduces such a risk to a minimum. The aponeurosis of the external oblique is divided along its fibers 1 cm. above and parallel to the inguinal ligament. The medial extent is the external inguinal ring. In males the fatty areolar tissue over the cord is included in the specimen, but the cord is displaced medially and safeguarded.

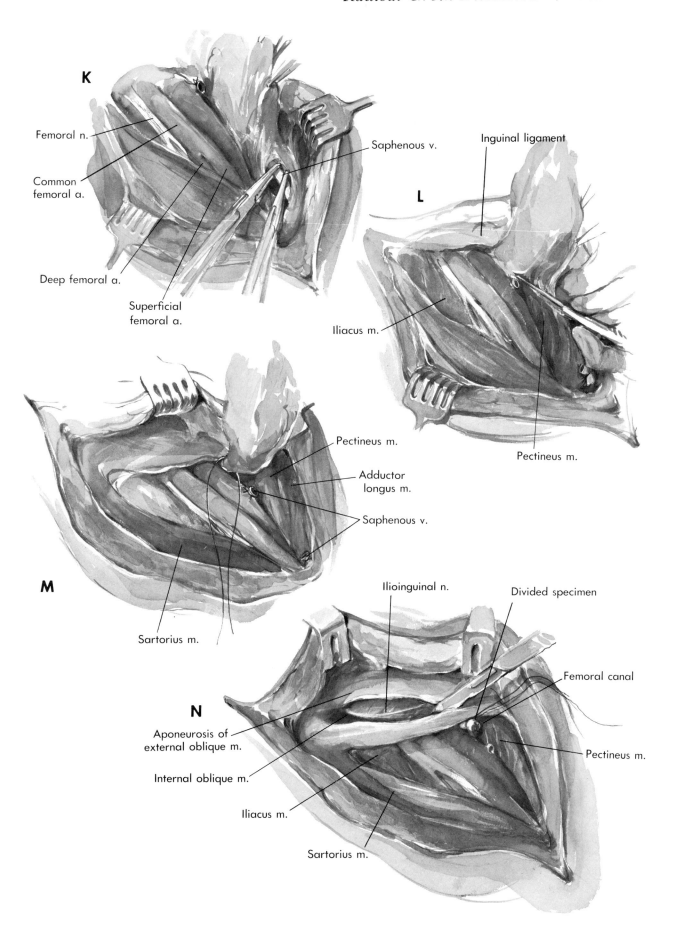

K

Femoral n.

Common femoral a.

Deep femoral a.

Superficial femoral a.

Saphenous v.

L

Inguinal ligament

Iliacus m.

Pectineus m.

M

Pectineus m.

Adductor longus m.

Saphenous v.

Sartorius m.

N

Ilioinguinal n.

Divided specimen

Femoral canal

Aponeurosis of external oblique m.

Internal oblique m.

Iliacus m.

Pectineus m.

Sartorius m.

O   The aponeurosis of the external oblique muscle has been divided, exposing the ilioinguinal and iliohypogastric nerves, which, of course, are preserved and are subsequently displaced medially as the iliac vessels are exposed. One can see how the inguinal ligament over the femoral canal can be pulled downwardly and medially with relocation of the severed specimen to the point indicated by the asterisk(*).

P   The internal oblique muscle is divided just above the inguinal ligament and the division carried to the anterosuperior spine laterally. This division can be extended if necessary for better exposure of the retroperitoneal area. The index finger establishes the plane of dissection and bidigital pressure provides the control necessary for exact hemostatic clamping.

Q   At the lateral aspect of Hesselbach's triangle and, therefore, over the inferior epigastric vessels, the thickened extension of the transversalis fascia is attached to the inguinal ligament as the interfoveolar ligament. This thin but definite tissue is incised to expose the inferior epigastric artery and vein. When they are divided the operator can easily separate the remaining transversalis fascia and expose the iliac artery by displacing the peritoneum and urinary bladder medially. Invariably the ureter will remain attached to the peritoneum and so also travel medially. A small retractor is shown medially so that the anatomic structure would not be obscured. In reality in this and in Figures R and S one must use a broad Deaver retractor to obtain the necessary exposure. Considerable traction may be necessary since one actually is displacing abdominal contents. Additionally, care should be exercised that the displaced tissue is padded and that the end of the Deaver retractor does not injure the ureter.

R   The ligature on the proximal side of the divided inguinal tissue has been shifted above the inguinal ligament so that the iliac dissection may begin. Often it is necessary to ligate the inferior epigastric artery and vein a second time flush with the femoral vessels, with the tissue between the two ties to be included in the iliac dissection. A scissors is necessary for the dissection from now on. In thin individuals the tissue to be removed may be so scant that it is difficult to maintain as one piece.

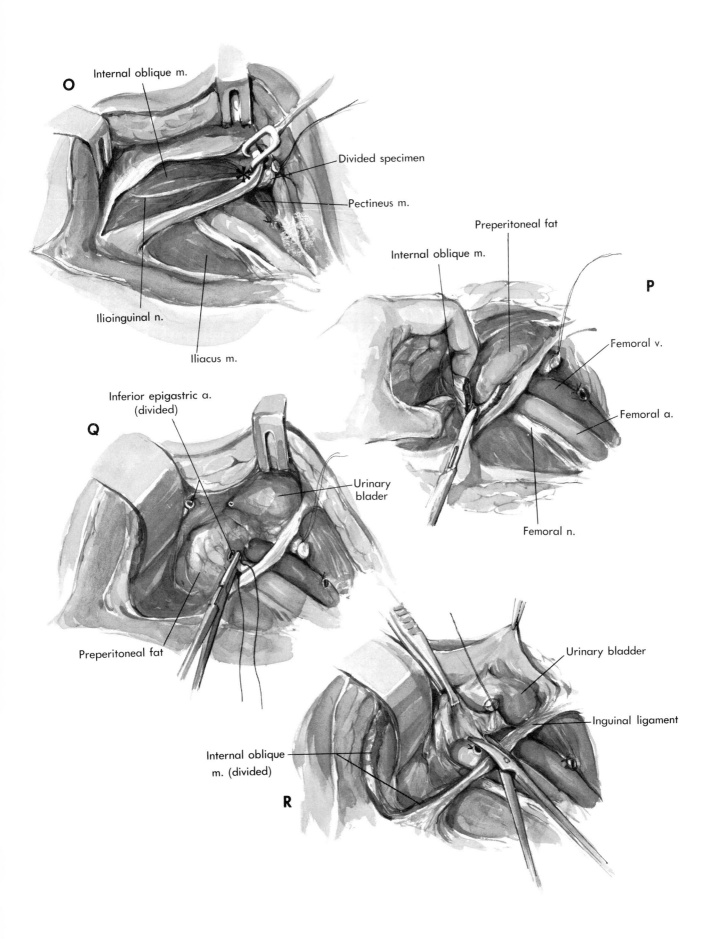

O

Internal oblique m.

Divided specimen

Pectineus m.

Ilioinguinal n.

Iliacus m.

Preperitoneal fat

Internal oblique m.

P

Femoral v.

Femoral a.

Femoral n.

Inferior epigastric a.
(divided)

Q

Urinary
blader

Preperitoneal fat

Internal oblique
m. (divided)

R

Urinary bladder

Inguinal ligament

S   The genitofemoral nerve is covered by the endopelvic fascia and is the lateral boundary of this dissection. This fascia is incised from just medial to this nerve and from the inguinal ligament to the bifurcation of the common iliac vessels. The dissection continues by retracting the tissue in a cephalad and medial direction.

T   This view is from a more medial vantage point and is meant to demonstrate the anatomy over the obturator foramen. At the time of operation the ureter would be displaced more medially. The lymph nodes along the medial aspect of the iliac vessels are most important because they are more numerous and more often involved and represent a direct extension of the deep inguinal nodes. In order to remove them properly it is necessary that the fatty areolar lymph node bearing tissue in the obturator fascia be removed. The problems here can be those of exposure in general; in particular they include patients with protuberant abdomens, excessive adipose tissue over the foramen, adhesions from previous pelvic irradiation, and fragility and inconstancy of location and number of the vessels in the area of the obturator foramen. The external iliac vein is retracted laterally to permit exposure and dissection of the obturator foramen cleanly, save for the nerve. Unilateral injury to the obturator nerve is not serious but bilateral injury will make walking difficult because of the abductor paralysis.

U   When there is skin flap necrosis it characteristically occurs at the middle portion of the wound, which is usually over the femoral vessels. To eliminate the risk of exposed vessels we cover them with the sartorius muscle. This muscle is detached at its origin and turned medially as a flap but remains hinged on its neurovascular supply. Anticipation of this maneuver influences the beginning of the inguinal incision at the lateral aspect of the sartorius (Figure E) and promotes care to prevent injury to the neurovascular supply of this muscle as the dissection dips along its medial edge (Figure F). The severed proximal edge is sutured to the inguinal ligament with interrupted stitches of 3-0 silk. It is held in its new rotated position by suturing the now medial edge to the underlying musculature with interrupted 3-0 chromic catgut.

    Often with gross inguinal lymph node involvement it is advisable to excise the ellipse of skin over the inguinal nodes with anticipation of placing a skin graft over the defect. In such a circumstance the rotated sartorius muscle performs the double function of protecting the underlying vessels while serving as an excellent bed for the overlying graft.

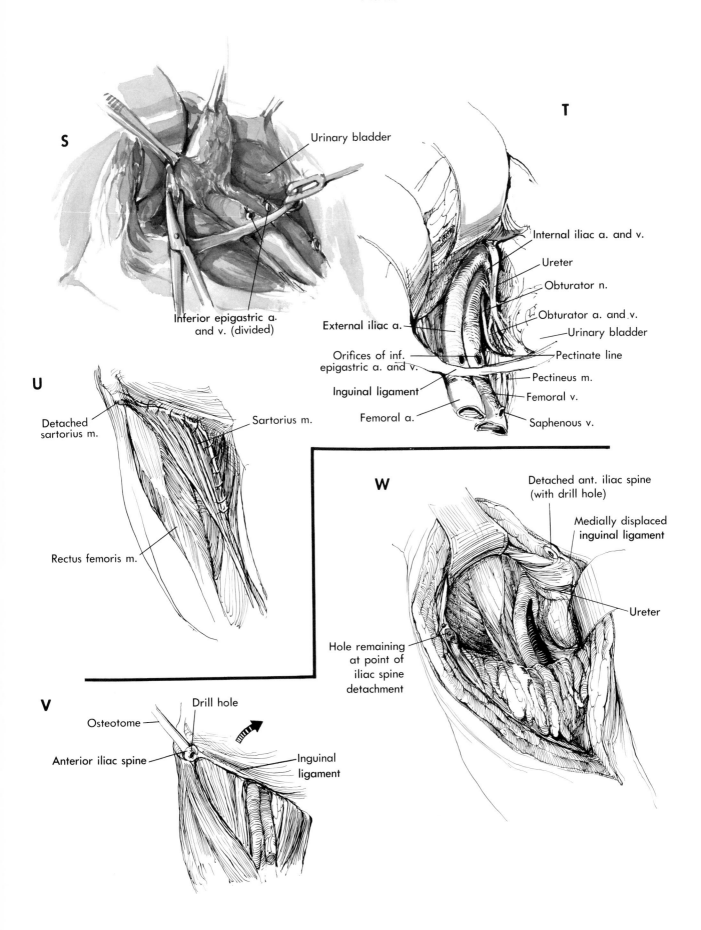

S

Urinary bladder

Inferior epigastric a.
and v. (divided)

T

Internal iliac a. and v.

Ureter

Obturator n.

Obturator a. and v.

Urinary bladder

External iliac a.

Pectinate line

Orifices of inf.
epigastric a. and v.

Pectineus m.

Inguinal ligament

Femoral v.

Femoral a.

Saphenous v.

U

Detached
sartorius m.

Sartorius m.

Rectus femoris m.

W

Detached ant. iliac spine
(with drill hole)

Medially displaced
inguinal ligament

Ureter

Hole remaining
at point of
iliac spine
detachment

V

Drill hole

Osteotome

Anterior iliac spine

Inguinal
ligament

These two figures depict an excellent method of unroofing the femoral canal without having to divide the inguinal ligament at the time the superficial and deep inguinal dissection are completed (Figure M). A small hole is drilled in the anterior superior projection of the ilium with the drill directed so that it exits several centimeters away at the crest of the ilium. This hole will be used to realign the bone later, but it is easier to make it now. The anterior iliac spine and the attached inguinal ligament are separated cleanly with an osteotome on a plane perpendicular to the drill hole. This results in a drill hole in the separated and retained segments of bone.

With the attached iliac spine, the inguinal ligament is separated inferiorly from the fascia lata for its entire length. During this separation the femoral canal is unroofed and, since the crura of the inguinal rings are not cut, the external inguinal ring and its contained spermatic cord or round ligament remain securely within it. The underlying interfoveolar ligament is incised along the inguinal crease, permitting exposure of the retroperitoneal space as heretofore described. In order to gain more mobility for medial displacement of tissue it may be necessary to divide some of the anterior fibers of the external and internal oblique muscles as they come off the anterior iliac crest.

Closure of the inguinal area following the latter method of exposure involves re-attaching the caudal edge of the inguinal ligament to the fascia lata as medially as the femoral nerve, artery and vein; medial to this it is sutured to the fascia over the pectineus muscle. The iliac spine is reattached to the iliac crest with a wire ligature passed through the hole that had been drilled at the beginning of this exposure. With the method of exposure described in the main body of this section, the inguinal ligament (if divided) is approximated with 2-0 silk. The aponeurosis of the external oblique is repaired with similar material and the femoral canal is obliterated by suturing the inguinal ligament to the pectineus muscle. We prefer to drain these wounds by suction because this offers the important advantage of maintaining coaptation of the flaps to the underlying structure with less pressure dressing, or more surely than with the usual spica dressing. The retroperitoneal area obliterates itself adequately and any drainage from it finds its way to the inguinal wound, so that the catheters are brought just to the inguinal crease, one on either side of the vessels, and then exteriorized through snug counterincisions. If the wound is closed primarily or if the skin graft is applied to a non-infected area, a spica dressing is applied to include the entire leg. If the inguinal area contained a fungating or otherwise infected mass, the leg is wrapped in elastic bandages but the inguinal area is handled in an open fashion. A sheet of Marlex mesh the same size as the graft is placed directly in contact with the heavily "pie-crusted" graft and anchored in position lightly with interrupted stitches of 4-0 nylon. This nonwettable nonreactive, relatively coarse mesh does not adhere to the skin graft or to the gauze moistened with saline at room temperature and placed over it every four hours postoperatively; yet it permits continued microdebridement and cleansing of the grafted field of infected exudate without the risk of dislodging the skin graft. In two or three days the moistened gauze is applied intermittently, and as the viability of the graft becomes obvious and is no longer endangered by minimal infection, the regimen is discontinued and the mesh removed. The patients remain in bed for one week in all instances, but if serum has collected under the flap they are kept inactive until this development is corrected.

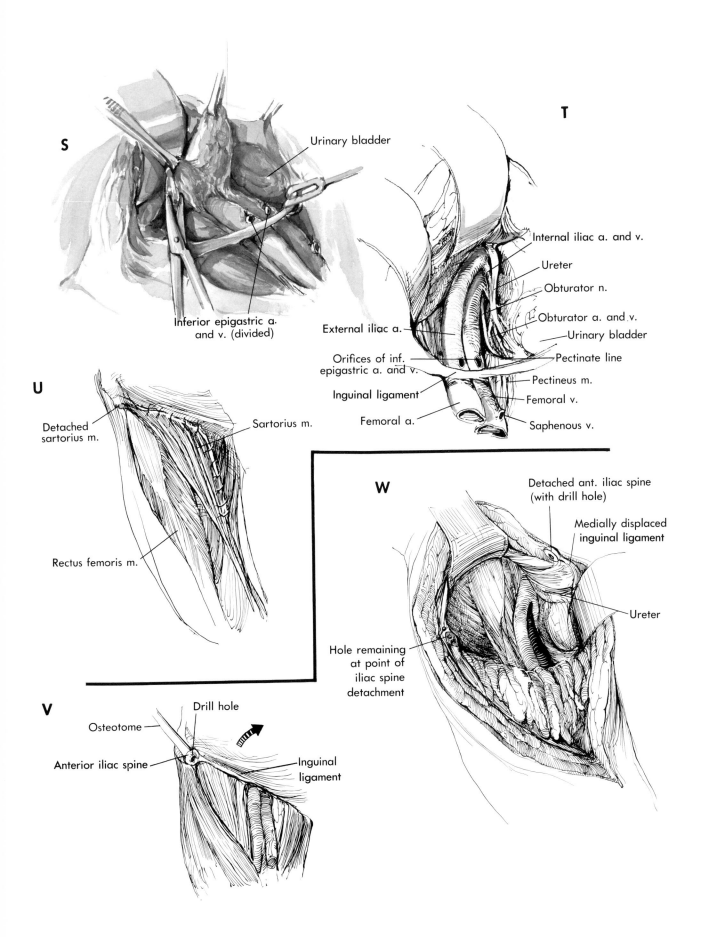

S

Urinary bladder

T

Inferior epigastric a.
and v. (divided)

Internal iliac a. and v.

Ureter

Obturator n.

Obturator a. and v.

Urinary bladder

External iliac a.

Pectinate line

Orifices of inf.
epigastric a. and v.

Pectineus m.

Inguinal ligament

Femoral v.

Femoral a.

Saphenous v.

U

Detached
sartorius m.

Sartorius m.

Rectus femoris m.

W

Detached ant. iliac spine
(with drill hole)

Medially displaced
inguinal ligament

Ureter

Hole remaining
at point of
iliac spine
detachment

V

Drill hole

Osteotome

Anterior iliac spine

Inguinal
ligament

HINDQUARTER AMPUTATION

Many names are used for this operation whose purpose is the removal of the lower limb and the ipsilateral half of the bony pelvis, except for the sacrum and the associated muscles. It is more traumatic and somewhat more difficult to perform than a forequarter amputation, rehabilitation is more difficult and the deficiency therefrom is more disabling. Although for many years patients have consented to amputation of a hind limb, inclusion of half of the pelvis as well has caused it to be resisted by the patient because of repugnancy, and to be resisted by the physician because of the seeming excessive mutilation and the low cure rate. As the operative mortality has been reduced to a figure consistently below 5 per cent, as gratifying cure rates have been realized by applying this operation earlier in the course of disease and as rehabilitation has improved, hindquarter amputation has become more acceptable when its alternative is inevitable death. It is even a proper operation to perform for palliation in a few carefully selected, but otherwise categorically incurable, patients, such as those with distant metastases but with huge fungating foul-smelling hindlimbs containing the primary tumor.

A past error has been to substitute the less disfiguring but also less effective hindlimb disarticulation when in essence its only physical advantage is retainment of the tuber ischium, which makes sitting easier. Otherwise, disarticulation is technically as difficult, or more so, to perform and problems in rehabilitation with a prosthesis are nearly the same. A serious disadvantage is the lack of resection of muscles and fascial planes in their entirety, an essential requisite in treating soft tissue sarcomas of the thigh.

Although this operation has always been used sparingly, it is interesting to realize the relative frequency with which, in the preantibiotic era, it was used in the treatment of tuberculous involvement of the hemipelvis or for nontuberculous osteomyelitis. At present, hindquarter amputation is used almost exclusively for treating malignant tumors, these being mostly chondrosarcomas, usually of a pelvic bone, or osteogenic sarcomas, usually of the femur. The cure rate is sufficiently gratifying with the chondrosarcomas that these tumors will probably remain the main indication for the operation. Osteogenic sarcomas are sufficiently incurable (15 to 20 per cent) that application of this operation to their treatment would be bound to decrease in favor if any other treatment were successful. Other tumors less frequently treated include neurofibrosarcomas, periosteal fibrosarcoma and Kaposi's sarcoma.

The operation should never be done without microscopic confirmation of the presence of a malignant tumor. The experienced clinician is aware that certain clinical diagnosis or x-ray findings can, on occasion, be misleading. An unnecessary hindquarter amputation because of such an error is truly a catastrophe.

Provision must be made to excise the biopsy incision or needle track whether the biopsy is performed as a separate procedure or at the same operation. The risk of implanting cancer cells in the wound if the biopsy is performed through the operative incision is so great that this approach should be resisted assiduously. The magnitude of the operation demands attention to the usual details if the operative mortality is to be kept low. The need most commonly misjudged is the intra- and postoperative requirement for blood. For this reason, it is mandatory that a large bore plastic catheter be inserted intravenously before the operation and that blood replacement keep pace with blood loss. A central venous catheter can be of considerable assistance in gauging the rate and amount of transfusions during the intra- and postoperative period.

The patient must be psychologically prepared for this major procedure, the true extent of which is not grasped by even the most understanding patients. Even then, they will invariably be alarmed at the enormity of the physical loss. Reassurance throughout their confinement by the surgeon, the physical therapist who will be responsible for the rehabilitation and the hospital social worker is an important adjunct to therapy.

The patient is placed on a low residue diet for three days preoperatively and on clear liquids the day before surgery. A cathartic and enemas are used to empty the bowel before surgery and to lessen the number of bowel movements in the early postoperative period. In order to be more certain than usual that pulmonary metastases are not present, we ask for a laminagram of the lungs for the greater area it can scan and the smaller nodules it can detect. The appropriate tests to detect liver metastases are performed and if there is a question of metastases the liver is scanned after the administration of radioactive rose bengal. If the surgeon is still unable to exclude metastases, a celiotomy should precede the amputation so that the peritoneal cavity can be explored thoroughly. The patient has the routine electrocardiograms and, since it may be necessary to transfuse a large amount of blood quickly, the cardiac status is assessed with particular care.

References

Gordon-Taylor, G., and Monro, R.: The technique and management of the "hindquarter" amputation. Brit. J. Surg. 39:536, 1952.

Higinbotham, N. L., Marcove, R. C., and Carson, P.: Hemipelvectomy: A clinical study of 100 cases with five-year follow-up on 60 patients. Surgery 59:5 and 706, 1966.

Pack, G. T., and Ehrlich, H. E.: Exarticulation of the lower extremities for malignant tumors: Hip joint disarticulation (with and without deep iliac dissection) and sacro-iliac disarticulation (hemipelvectomy). Ann. Surg. 124:1, 1946.

A Despite the magnitude of this operation the psoas is the only major muscle divided across its center. This is in keeping with the principle of excising entire muscle groups and associated fascial planes if at all possible in the treatment of mesothelial tumors — the commonest soft tissue type treated by such an operation. It is clear from this illustration that excellent exposure can be obtained for the accurate and deliberate dissection that is necessary if one is to keep to a minimum the operative morbidity of this procedure. The femoral nerve is shown after it has appeared lateral to the psoas muscle, but it will be divided while it is still dorsal to this muscle. The obturator artery is seen as the first ventral branch of the internal iliac; the large superior gluteal artery usually appears directly dorsal to this. The ureter and ovarian vessels will be displaced medially to gain access to the iliac bifurcation.

B General anesthesia is used and is administered endotracheally. A Foley catheter is inserted into the urinary bladder. In the male it is placed across the opposite leg, which keeps the genitalia effectively out of the operative field. At least one large caliber catheter is placed in an arm vein and six units of whole cross-matched blood are kept available. A central venous catheter is helpful to the anesthesiologist who may have to transfuse the patient massively intraoperatively or in the recovery room. The patient is placed in the supine position, but sandbags are placed under the lumbar area and shoulder so that the affected hip is clearly off the table. The anus is sealed with a purse-string suture of 2-0 silk. In females the vagina is cleansed with soap and water and then painted with whatever germicide is used on the skin.

The method of skin preparation is influenced somewhat by the status of the tumor; a fungating one can only be painted. Most frequently it appears reasonable to scrub the operative field gently with soap and to rinse it abundantly with water. The skin is then painted with Betadine, tincture of Zephiran, or skin germicide. The left lower quadrant of the abdomen is left exposed anteriorly and posteriorly when draping.

The extremity is so draped that it can be moved freely. An adhesive transparent plastic drape applied over the perineum and to include the towels draping this area minimizes the shifting of drapes as the leg and then the hindquarter are manipulated. The extremity is prepared in a sterile fashion to permit manipulation during the operation.

A variety of incisions can be used, and the choice will depend on the clinical circumstances. The one depicted is the most widely applicable and the least likely to result in skin necrosis. Those shown in Figures B_1 and B_2 can be used when the base of the flap must be in a different location.

C The first portion of the incision is started at the iliac crest at the midaxillary line and extended along the inguinal crease. The inguinal ligament and the insertion of the ipsilateral rectus abdominis muscle are detached from the pubic bone. Laterally, the fibers of the external and internal oblique muscles are disengaged from the iliac crest, as are the fibers of the latissimus dorsi muscle at the most posterior extent. The interfoveolar ligament, which is a thickened extension of the transversalis fascia, is incised to expose the inferior epigastric artery and vein which are then divided and ligated with 3-0 silk. Throughout this operation the skin flaps are kept full thickness unless there are compelling reasons to do otherwise.

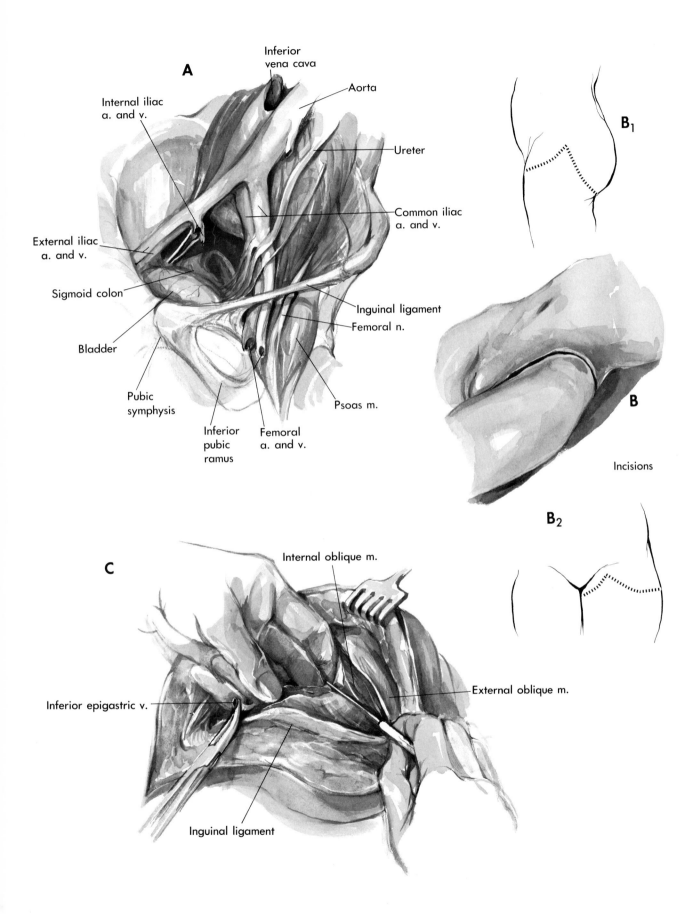

A

Inferior
vena cava

Aorta

Internal iliac
a. and v.

Ureter

Common iliac
a. and v.

External iliac
a. and v.

Sigmoid colon

Bladder

Inguinal ligament

Femoral n.

Pubic
symphysis

Inferior
pubic
ramus

Femoral
a. and v.

Psoas m.

B₁

B

Incisions

B₂

C

Internal oblique m.

External oblique m.

Inferior epigastric v.

Inguinal ligament

D   Completion of the previous steps permits entry into the retroperitoneal space. This fatty areolar tissue is dissected by blunt technique and displaced medially, thus exposing the iliac area most adequately. The ureter remains attached to the peritoneum (but one must check to make certain of this) and is also displaced medially. Here the ureter is left exposed for illustrative purposes; otherwise, one or two laparotomy pads are used to cover the upper wound surfaces so that the tissues are protected from possible injury by the Deaver retractors.

Much has been made of the necessity of sparing the superior and inferior gluteal vessels if the gluteal flap is to have the best chance of survival. This is questionable and certainly not proved. The most important determining factors should be the height at which one wishes to divide the vessels in order to encompass the tumor. The bleeding during the posterior dissection seems to be the same regardless of how the gluteal vessels are handled. Nonetheless, in this instance the external iliac has been ligated immediately beyond its origin; for whatever reduction in bleeding there accrues during the gluteal and perineal dissection, another ligature has been applied distal to where the gluteal artery branches from the internal iliac artery. If the division is to be at the level of the common iliac vessels, we prefer not to ligate the artery but to divide it with an artery clamp placed proximally and then to oversew the vessel with 5-0 arterial silk.

E   The psoas muscle is divided next. This should be done at the highest possible point if there is bone tumor adjacent. Sometimes it is convenient to do this while lifting the muscle with a finger. There is no need to attempt to taper the cut to accommodate the closure.

F   The femoral nerve is encountered posterior to the psoas muscle and may be ligated prior to division as shown here, or it may be divided sharply with a scalpel and without previous ligation. In either case it should be divided sufficiently short that the proximal stump retracts under the belly of the psoas muscle. The genitofemoral nerve is also divided.

G   The pubic symphysis is clearly visualized but not denuded on the opposite side of the midline. It can be divided swiftly and accurately with a scalpel, but an osteotome may be used instead. Least desirable is the use of the Gigli saw. Considerable bleeding may occur from the underlying ischiocavernosus muscle but can be controlled with a gauze pack. This largely completes the major aspects of the anterior dissection.

The posterior portion of the dissection will be performed now. The patient was so positioned and supported initially that the buttock is well off the table on this side. The hip is flexed at least halfway and the leg is adducted severely, usually by an assistant simply leaning on it.

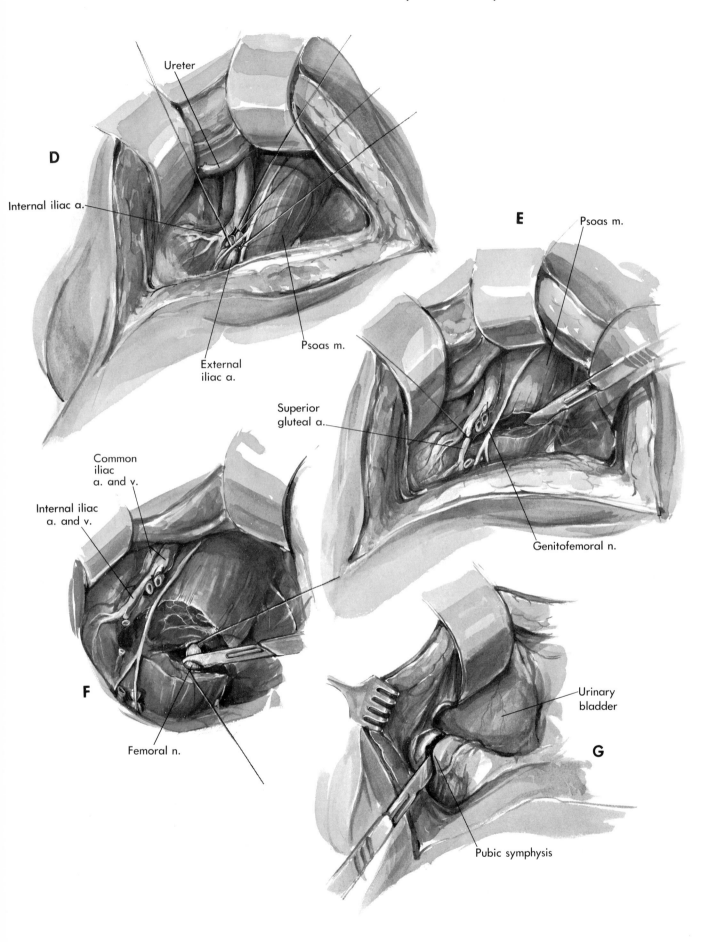

D

Ureter

Internal iliac a.

Psoas m.

External
iliac a.

E

Psoas m.

Superior
gluteal a.

Genitofemoral n.

Common
iliac
a. and v.

Internal iliac
a. and v.

F

Femoral n.

Urinary
bladder

G

Pubic symphysis

H   This phantom drawing shows some of the structures that will be sectioned during the remaining dissection. The areas of origin from which the gluteus maximus muscle will have to be separated are the posterior surface of the lower part of the sacrum and the side of the coccyx. The other areas of the origin are within the ilium, as are those of the gluteus medius and gluteus minimus muscles.

The piriformis muscle which arises mostly from the front of the sacrum also has to be divided as it passes to the outside through the greater sciatic foramen. Notice that the superior and inferior gluteal arteries proceed to their destination from either side of this muscle. The sciatic nerve, which also comes through the greater sciatic foramen, can be seen to pass deep to the piriformis muscle. That portion of the quadratus lumborum muscle which arises from the posterior portion of the iliac crest is divided. Those lateral fibers of the sacrospinalis muscle that are attached to the posterior iliac crest also need division.

I   This drawing shows the sacroiliac joint and the several ligaments that will have to be divided in the remaining course of the operation. Those that will require deliberate sectioning are the sacrotuberous and sacrosciatic ligaments. If cut across near the sacrum they will be almost as one. Those across the sacroiliac joint will be severed by the Gigli saw, with the exception of the iliolumbar ligament which needs to be cut if one is to seat this saw properly inside the posterior iliac spine. The heavy dashed line indicates the anticipated skin incision.

J   The posterior incision is made according to plan. Usually it passes over the greater trochanter of the femur. One is often concerned about not making the flap large enough, but in fact the error is usually in making it too large, necessitating that it be trimmed at the conclusion of the operation. The gluteal flap is kept at full thickness. The fibers of the quadratus lumborum muscle are separated from the iliac crest. Most medially on the ilium, some of the fibers of the latissimus dorsi muscle and the sacrospinalis muscle are to be cut.

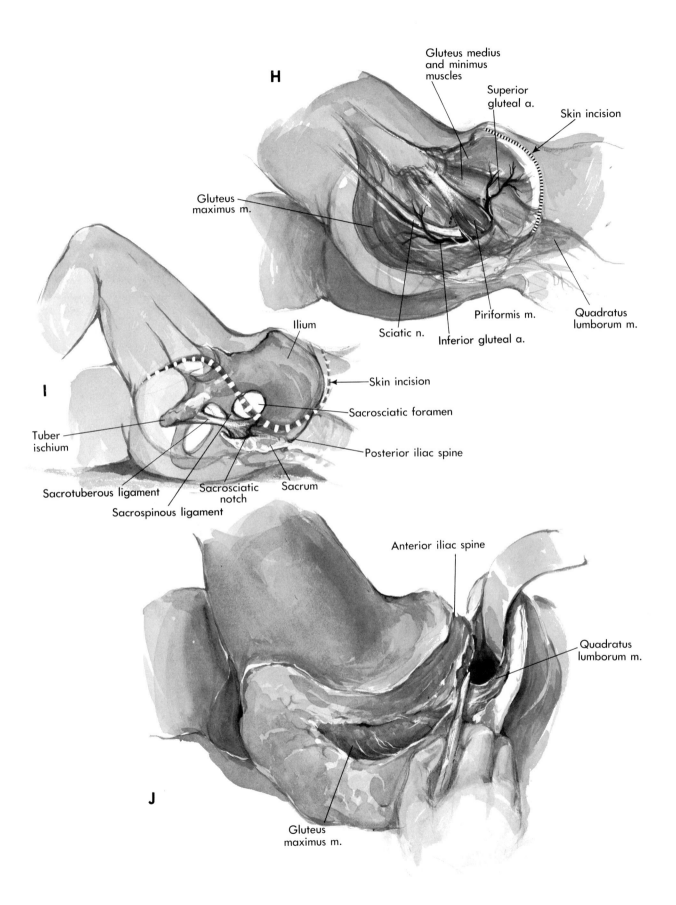

H

Gluteus medius and minimus muscles

Superior gluteal a.

Skin incision

Gluteus maximus m.

Sciatic n.

Inferior gluteal a.

Piriformis m.

Quadratus lumborum m.

Ilium

Skin incision

Sacrosciatic foramen

Posterior iliac spine

Sacrum

I

Tuber ischium

Sacrotuberous ligament

Sacrospinous ligament

Sacrosciatic notch

Anterior iliac spine

Quadratus lumborum m.

J

Gluteus maximus m.

K   The gluteal flap is mobilized to just short of the midline in the back. The fibers of the gluteus maximus muscle are separated from the sacrum, but a few fibers are left on this bone rather than denuding it completely. That part of the gluteus maximus originating from the ilium is, of course, not disturbed. The gluteus medius and minimus muscles are not encountered. As the gluteal muscle mass retracts forward, the piriformis muscle is exposed. A finger is looped around it to define it before it is cut. The superior and inferior gluteal vessels emerge from the upper and lower aspects, respectively, of the piriformis muscle and they must be specifically sought for and ligated. As mentioned previously, even ligation of the common or internal iliac arteries will not eliminate the risk of brisk hemorrhage from the cut gluteal vessels.

L   The piriformis muscle has been divided and the gluteal vessels secured. Immediately deep to the divided muscle is the sciatic nerve, which is ligated with silk and transected. The tough sacrotuberous and sacrosciatic ligaments are divided close to the sacrum where they practically fuse.

      The sacroiliac division is next. Superiorly the iliolumbar ligament must be cut so that the Gigli saw may be seated posterior to the posterior iliac spine. Inferiorly the saw is seated in the sacrosciatic notch and no attempt is made to slant the cut. Although this cut will almost certainly not go exactly through the sacroiliac synchrondosis, this is a minor matter. Any ilium remaining on the sacrum (this is usually the case rather than the removal of excess sacrum) can be pried off separately or not at all as one wishes. One can use an osteotome for the sacroiliac division but it is more difficult. Attempting to "crack open" the sacroiliac synchrondosis and to separate the two bones accurately by this maneuver has no merit.

M   With the last firm restraints divided, the leg and hemipelvis fall away further, creating an even more generous exposure. Bleeding from the cut bone can be stopped with beeswax. The obturator vessels and nerve will also need ligation or division at this time. The levator ani muscles are divided in line with the skin incision, which proceeds toward the perineum. With this the rectum is brought into view.

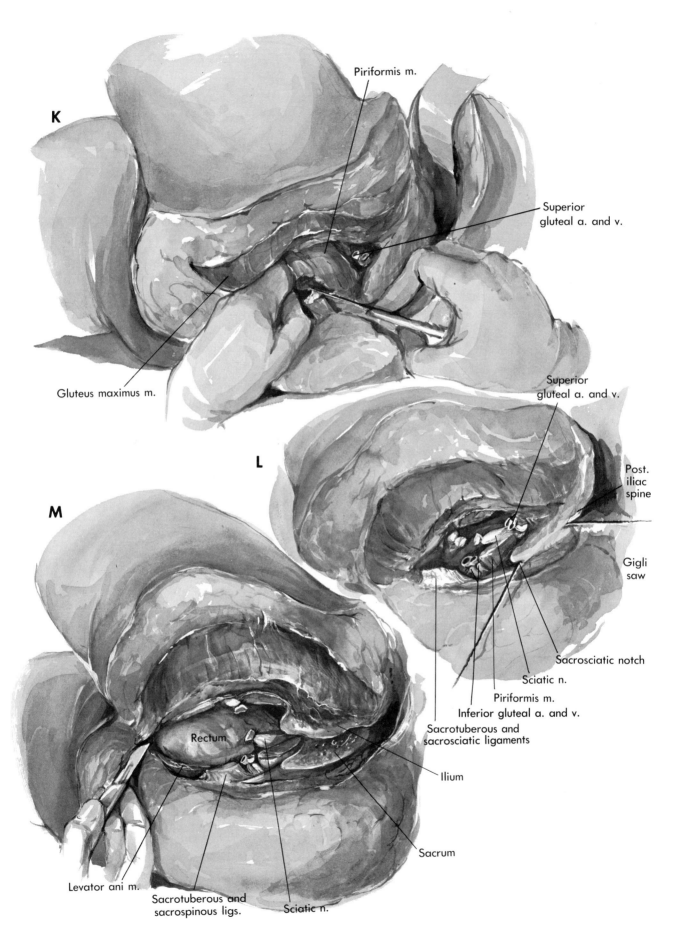

K

Piriformis m.

Superior
gluteal a. and v.

Gluteus maximus m.

L

Superior
gluteal a. and v.

Post.
iliac
spine

M

Gigli
saw

Sacrosciatic notch

Sciatic n.

Piriformis m.

Inferior gluteal a. and v.

Sacrotuberous and
sacrosciatic ligaments

Rectum

Ilium

Sacrum

Levator ani m.

Sacrotuberous and
sacrospinous ligs.

Sciatic n.

N   The leg must now be abducted while maintaining some degree of flexion. The skin incision is completed circumferentially, remaining in the crease between the perineum and thigh. The solid line indicates the dorsal incision and the broken line the ventral portion of the skin incision.

O
P   The perineal musculature involved in this dissection is shown. Although the skin incision will generally run the course indicated in Figure N, the muscles are usually divided more medially. The ischiocavernosus muscle is divided near its medial border. It is very vascular and should be ligated before being divided. The bulbocavernosus is removed in part, or entirely if some of the vagina is to be taken. The deep and superficial transverse perinei muscles are taken in their entirety, but a considerable amount of the levator ani muscle is left attached to the rectum. The gluteus maximus muscle is excised in its entirety. The specimen is now free.

Q   The field is wide open for inspection for bleeding points. Bleeding from remnants of the ischiocavernosus muscle can be controlled best with transfixion stitches of 4-0 chromic catgut. If the stump of the sciatic nerve appears too long and threatens to lie within the healing wound, the nerve can be shortened at this time. The closure is begun by approximating the inguinal ligament to the periosteum at the anterior cut edge of the sacrum. This important step utilizes a layer of muscle (the internal and external oblique muscles) to support this weak area which otherwise would have only peritoneum just under skin.

    The gluteal flap is now trimmed if it seems excessive since nothing is gained by too loose a closure and, in fact, this might permit the easier accumulation of serum in the wound. Two No. 18 catheters with at least six openings are exteriorized through snug counterincisions from the inferior aspect of the field and are placed on suction. The subcutaneous tissue is approximated with 3-0 chromic catgut and the skin with narrowly placed vertical mattress stitches of 3-0 silk. In contrast to other wounds in which suction keeps the skin flaps adequately coapted against a bony surface, this area is too flabby and must also be supported and the potential "dead space" obliterated with a firm dressing.

    The patients are gotten up within two or three days unless there is an intervening complication. This is in keeping with our practice of early ambulation and it also keeps the patient occuppied in learning how to manage in getting about.

    During the course of the operation the stomach is intubated; otherwise, the ileus secondary to the retroperitoneal dissection will lead to troublesome abdominal distention postoperatively. The tube can be removed in two or three days, or sooner if the patient has resumption of peristalsis and passes flatus. The magnitude of the operation, the patient's frequent debility before surgery and the loss of appreciable serum and lymph during healing make it necessary that the red blood cell count be determined frequently, the plasma volume assessed, and any deficit replaced.

    The urinary catheter that was inserted before the operation is retained because it easily, and relatively harmlessly, eliminates an uncomfortable task, especially in the female. Paresis of the bladder is not a concern. Defecation may not be spontaneous because of local trauma and the severance of the levator muscles. An enema is given if necessary and before the first change of dressings. Phantom pain of variable severity almost always occurs but is significant or serious in only a minority of patients. In the absence of wound or distant complications most patients can be discharged from the hospital by the end of the second week.

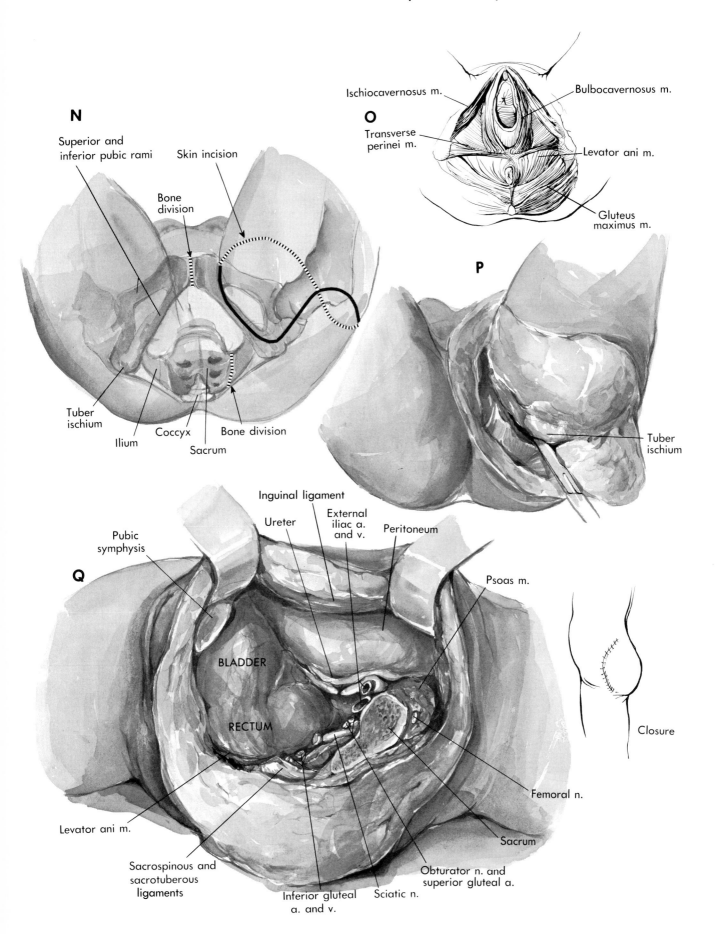

N

Superior and inferior pubic rami

Skin incision

Bone division

Tuber ischium

Ilium

Coccyx

Sacrum

Bone division

O

Ischiocavernosus m.

Bulbocavernosus m.

Transverse perinei m.

Levator ani m.

Gluteus maximus m.

P

Tuber ischium

Q

Inguinal ligament

Ureter

External iliac a. and v.

Peritoneum

Psoas m.

Pubic symphysis

BLADDER

RECTUM

Femoral n.

Levator ani m.

Sacrum

Sacrospinous and sacrotuberous ligaments

Inferior gluteal a. and v.

Sciatic n.

Obturator n. and superior gluteal a.

Closure

INDEX